Transportation in Iowa

A Historical Summary

William H. Thompson

Printed and bound in the United States of America

Library of Congress Cataloging-in-Publication Data

Thompson, William H., 1909-
Transportation in Iowa: a historical summary/William H. Thompson.
p. cm.
Includes index.
1. Transportation—Iowa—History. I. Title.
HE213.I8T48 1989
388'.09777—dc20 89-15269
ISBN 0-9623167-0-9 CIP

This book is dedicated to the
memory of Evelyn C. Thompson,
devoted wife and research associate
of the author

and to

the administrative officials of the
Iowa Department of Transportation
and members of the
Iowa Transportation Commission
who rescued the author from a dull
and boring retirement.

We wish to express our appreciation for the many hours of effort numerous individuals have contributed to make this history of Iowa transportation possible. Without these people, the original manuscript could not have become the book you now have in your hands. Those people include:

Elaine Allen
Deke Barrett
Butch Bowers
Nola Mortenson Brown
William Carl Burns
Mary Clark
Ralph Cook
Jerry Dickinson
Joyce Emery
Gregory Fay
Patricia Hutchinson
Sam Koehler
Diane Lange
Diane McCauley
Richard Michaelis
Skip Nelson
Michael Slyby
Julie Taylor
Ruth Vander Schaaf
Richard Vincent
Robert Whitman

We would also like to thank others who, while not named, have also played a role in the completion of this project.

The contributions of the following to the publication of the book are gratefully acknowledged.

Association of American Railroads .... Washington, D.C.

Cedar Rapids & Iowa City Railway Co. .... Cedar Rapids, Iowa
Central Electric Railfans Association .... Chicago, Illinois

Des Moines International Airport .... Des Moines, Iowa
Dome Pipeline Corporation .... Iowa City, Iowa
Dubuque Chamber of Commerce .... Dubuque, Iowa

Hydrocarbon Transportation Co. .... Omaha, Nebraska

Edward D. Meyers Collection .... Boone, Iowa

Inland Waterways Journal .... St. Louis, Missouri
Ione Alleman Sieben Collection .... Ames, Iowa
Iowa - Illinois Gas & Electric Co. .... Davenport, Iowa
Iowa State Aeronautics Commission .... Des Moines, Iowa
Iowa State Commerce Commission .... Des Moines, Iowa
Iowa State Department of Economic Development .... Des Moines, Iowa
Iowa Department of Transportation .... Ames, Iowa
Iowa State Highway Patrol .... Des Moines, Iowa
Iowa State Historical Society .... Des Moines, Iowa
Iowa State Historical Society .... Iowa City, Iowa
Iowa State Railroad Commission .... Des Moines, Iowa
Iowa State University Press .... Ames, Iowa
Iowa State University Special Collections .... Ames, Iowa

R.E.G. Davies Collection, National Air & Space Museum .... Washington, D.C.
Ruth Jackson Collection .... Ames, Iowa

Santa Fe Pipelines System .... Tulsa, Oklahoma
Sioux City Public Museum .... Sioux City, Iowa

U.S. Army Corps of Engineers .... Rock Island, Illinois
U.S. Army Corps of Engineers .... Omaha, Nebraska
University of California Press .... Berkely, California
University of Chicago Press .... Chicago, Illinois
University of Nebraska Library .... Lincoln, Nebraska
University of Pennsylvania Press .... Philadelphia, Pennsylvania

Williams Pipeline Company .... Tulsa, Oklahoma
Wood River Pipeline Company .... Wichita, Kansas

Contents

Prologue

Regardless of the accuracy of Santayana's statement that "those who cannot remember the past are bound to repeat it," there probably is acceptance that the past offers insight into problems of the present and partial guidelines to the future. Sidney Harris, columnist, has said: "The ancient ages remained immature because they looked backward toward a mythical golden age and refused to face the future. The modern age remains immature because it looks forward and refuses to benefit from learning only what the sad lessons of history can teach us." Perhaps history cannot precisely forecast the future, but it is doubtful that the present can be understood or the future anticipated without some knowledge of the past.

In some respects, the history of transportation in Iowa reflects the history of the state. In his *Principles of Economics,* published in 1920, Alfred Marshall noted: "Probably more than three-quarters of the whole benefit (England) derived from the progress of manufacturing during the 19th century has been brought about through the indirect influence of lowering the cost of transportation of men and goods, of water, light and electricity and news; for the dominant fact of our age is the development not of manufacturing but of the transportation industries. It is they that have done the most toward increasing England's wealth."

By annihilating distance, transportation made possible a more efficient distribution of goods in a highly mobile and productive society, created new markets, expanded old ones, transformed the organization and location of industry, encouraged settlement, created great cities, united the nation politically and strengthened national defense. Without its development, there would have been little progress in agriculture, manufacturing, or the lifestyles of the people. Its causal and residual forces in the march of civilization make the industry a complex, fascinating, yet sometimes frustrating subject for study as it mirrors the ever-changing tides and currents of economic, social and political trends in our history.

This book traces the development of transportation in Iowa from territorial days to the 1980s. It shows the evolution of the transportation systems; how they originated, progressed and functioned; their structural organizations; effectiveness in overcoming obstacles, under the guidance of state and federal legislation; and their impact upon the development of the state. With some exceptions where the continuity of the discussion would be interrupted, the work has been organized on a decade-to-decade approach—to my knowledge, the first such experiment undertaken by any state in the nation.

To keep the length within reasonable bounds, it was necessary at many points to limit the presentation, with full realization that anyone who writes history will be criticized for what has been included as well as for what has been omitted. However, as the title suggests, this is a historical summary and nothing more, written to bring together in one volume the widely scattered works of many authors. The research covered hundreds of books, journal articles, government and university research reports, annual reports of state and federal regulatory commissions and departments of transportation, masters' theses and Ph.D. dissertations. Conferences and personal interviews were scheduled wherever appropriate to the research effort. From the seemingly inexhaustible list of materials available, only those examined have been included in the notes and references at the end of each chapter, by which the reader may be compensated for omissions of details on particular subjects.

The project was endorsed by Iowa Department of Transportation Directors Raymond L. Kassel and Warren B. Dunham and recommended by Ian MacGillivray, Director of the Planning and Research Division, to the Iowa Transportation Commission for approval and funding. Research was conducted in four libraries in Washington, D.C., at the three state universities, the State Department of Transportation, state historical facilities in Des Moines and Iowa City and at the Ames Public Library.

Guidance in the collection of source materials and suggestions for their use came from many individuals whose interest and assistance is gratefully acknowledged. In particular, I wish to express appreciation to Robert J. Anderson, Director of the Office of Economic Analysis, Department of Transportation, who acted as coordinator of the project. The following persons reviewed all or parts of the manuscript: From the Transportation Department, Harvey Sims, Railroad and River Division; Conrad Amend, retired, Transportation Regulatory Authority; George Norris, Information Services; Donald McClean and Robert Given, retired former Directors of the Highway Division; and G.W. Anderson, Deputy Director, Highway Division. Lester Paff, former General Counsel, assisted in clarifying court decisions and interpretation of Iowa laws. Alice Bear typed the first draft.

Iowa State University personnel involved in the reviews were: Keith Huntress, Distinguished Professor Emeritus of English; Professors Benjamin J. Allen and R. D. Voorhees, Transportation and Logistics Department; Professors Robert L. Carstens and Stanley Ring, Department of Transportation Engineering.

Singled out for special recognition are the efforts of Joseph H. Zaletel Jr., at the Department of Transportation, for his assistance in obtaining research materials and his interest in the project. Also to Ann Holtgren Pellegreno, leading authority on Iowa aviation history, my sincere appreciation for her contributions to the sections on air transportation.

Compiling the bibliography, researching and writing the manuscript was a pleasant experience—the fulfillment of an idea which began to stir during my final years as an active member of the Iowa State University faculty. It offered me a selfish opportunity to learn more about the evolution of transportation in the state and its impact on the state's development and to hopefully make a contribution to the state's historical literature. The effort will have been worthwhile if students of transportation find the book an informative reference source for future research projects and readers enjoy the narrative describing the growth and development of the transportation systems which currently serve the people and industries of Iowa.

Ames, Iowa

September 1, 1986

William H. Thompson

W. H. Thompson

Transportation in Iowa

A Historical Summary

Chapter One
Early Transportation in Iowa Before Railroads

Introduction

Iowa, formed as a state in 1846, encompassed an area of over 55,000 square miles and had a population of 100,000, concentrated in the eastern counties. Cheap land and fertile soil attracted many settlers who followed agricultural pursuits, whereas others were engaged in retailing, lumber and lead mining. Pioneers tended to settle along the rivers, which offered the best available means of transportation. Over crude roads or tracks into the interior, stagecoaches carried mail and hardy travelers. Steamboats ran the major rivers and tributaries, offering a somewhat regular service for passengers and freight, and played an important role in the development of river towns and cities. The Des Moines River Improvement Project was a serious but unsuccessful attempt to make an interior river a meaningful artery for trade and commerce.

Development, Geography, and Land

Iowa officially became the 29th state in the Union on December 26, 1846, when President Polk signed the enabling bill passed by the Congress. Previously, it had been a "District" of the Territory of Wisconsin, established on April 20, 1836. The territorial census showed 6,257 residents of "Desmoines County" and 4,273 settlers in Dubuque County. Population was concentrated in the Black Hawk Purchase within a strip of 40 to 50 miles bordering the Mississippi River. In 1838 the Territory of Iowa was created to include the District of Iowa, all of future Iowa, most of future Minnesota and parts of the Dakotas. During the next eight years, political debates settled the final boundaries between the extremes of approximately 40°, 22′ to 43°, 30′ North, and 90°, 08′ to 96°, 90′ West, encompassing an area of 55,475 square miles.

Geographically, the state was described by Wall as closely resembling the physical form of the nation. "If drawn to a scale of 1 to 10, Iowa, like the United States, is three units east-west to two units north-south and is bordered on both east and west by water. In Lee County, projecting below Missouri, Iowa even has its own shorter and more pointed Floridian peninsula."[1] The geographic location proved to be both an advantage and disadvantage in transportation economics.

The land consisted of timber and prairie grasses, slowly rising in gentle swells from the lowest elevation at Keokuk (480 feet above sea level) to the highest elevation in Osceola County (1,675 feet), except in areas where there are bluffs along the rivers. The land was first opened for settlement in 1833, and census figures from 1836 to 1846 showed an increase from 10,531 to 96,088 in population. By 1850 almost 200,000 people had settled in the state.

Many had migrated to Iowa attracted by cheap land and the rich and fertile soils, which consisted of black vegetable mould mixed with a sandy loam, clay and gravel, averaging 18 to 24 inches in depth on the uplands to 30 to 48 inches on the bottom lands. The soil was sufficiently compacted to retain water, and good water was found 20 to 30 feet below the surface. It has often been stated that 25 percent of the prime agricultural land of the nation lay in Iowa.[2] In addition to agricultural pursuits, settlers were engaged in lumber extraction and milling, retail businesses and employed in the lead mines in the vicinity of Dubuque.

Settlement

By 1840, the date of the first federal census, 43,000 people resided in the state. Six of the organized counties lay north of parallel 42 north latitude, and of the territorial population, 16 percent were in the north half of Dubuque County. Northern Iowa drew half of its population from the southern areas as people moved upstream, and the proportion did not change between 1840 and 1850. In 1849 the population reached 192,214, divided into roughly the same percentage north and south of the 42nd parallel in 18 of the 33 counties established by 1846. The people tended to avoid the prairies because of the absence of timber and fuel until these were brought by the railroads. During the next decade, the population of the northern section of the state increased by over 30 percent.

[1] Joseph F. Wall, *Iowa: A Bicentennial History*, New York: W. W. Norton & Co., 1978, p. 45.

[2] For a description of soils, geology and agricultural areas, see John B. Newhall, *A Glimpse of Iowa in 1846*, Iowa City: State Historical Society, 1957.

The tendency to settle near rivers and streams is well documented in the history of the state. In 1840 the population of the southeastern quarter was concentrated along the Des Moines River. Only a short distance away were the Skunk and Maquoketa which, although relatively small, drained fertile districts. Combined with the Iowa and Red Cedar Rivers, the land had a magnetic appeal to the pioneers. Above parallel 42 North, the streams were small and shallow, the Wapsipinicon and Turkey being two which showed settlement progress. It would be another 20 years before the fertile prairie to the west would be opened and settlement spread gradually across the state, creeping up the tributaries of the Missouri River. By 1860 counties had organized governments and started the procedures toward permanent geographic settlement—movements which have held with few exceptions to the present time.

Roads and Highways

No roads existed when Iowa County was opened for settlement in 1833. An Indian path on the banks of the Iowa River was the first "road" in the county. Where these trails could not be used, men "blazed" new roads by marking trees or plowing furrows from village to village. In 1836 the Assembly of the Territory of Wisconsin appointed six commissioners to "mark and lay out a territorial road west of the Mississippi River, commencing at Farmington on the Des Moines River, thence to Moffits Mill, thence to the nearest and best route to Burlington in Des Moines County, thence to Wapello, thence to the nearest and best route to Dubuque and thence...to the ferry opposite Prairie Du Chien."[3]

When the Territorial Assembly convened in Burlington in 1838-1839, one of the first items of business was the enactment of road laws. Section 1 of the First Act directed three commissioners to locate and make a territorial road from Keokuk to Iowa City. In March 1839 Congress appropriated $20,000 for a military road to begin at Dubuque and run "to such a point on the northern boundary of the state of Missouri as may best be suited for its future extension by that state to the cities of Jefferson and St. Louis." The road ultimately extended beyond Iowa City and offered access to the new Capitol (Fig. 1-1).[4]

The river towns were the commercial centers of pioneer Iowa. Dubuque, Bloomington (Muscatine), Burlington, Fort Madison, and Keokuk were the towns where immigrants settled or passed through on their journeys to the west. The demand for roads came from the scattered interior settlements and also from river towns, which needed transportation routes for their trade and commerce. The early roads connected the river cities and spread in random

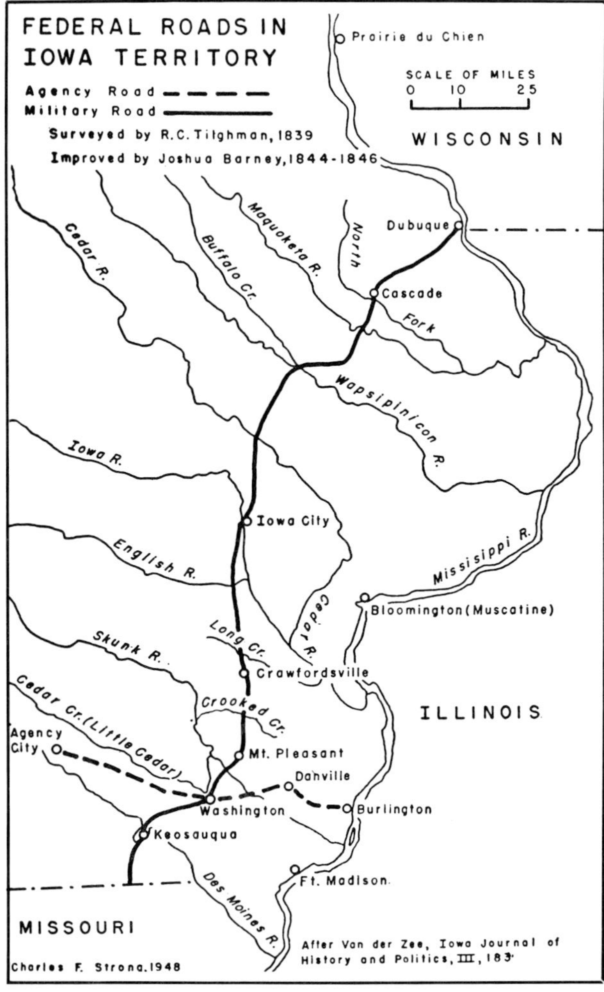

Figure 1-1
(Courtesy: State Historical Society of Iowa)

[3] Jacob Vanderzee, "Roads and Highways in Territorial Iowa," *Iowa Journal of History and Politics 3,* (April 1905): pp. 175-226; P.T. Christensen, *The Hawkeye State,* Cedar Rapids, Iowa: The Laurence Press, 1956, pp. 57-59.

[4] Stanley Ring, "History of Highways/Legislative Influences," *The Iowa State Highway Commission Annual Conference,* (January 25-26, 1973), p. 2; John C. Parish, "The Old Military Road," *Palimpsest* 51 (June 1970): pp. 249-280.

fashion into the interior. In laying out the first roads, builders chose ridges or highlands to avoid the swamps, marshes and floods which came in the spring and fall. The term "ridge roads" is an inheritance of early days, and some of the present highways follow the twisting and turning patterns of roads constructed to avoid these obstacles, especially in northeastern Iowa, where travelers get spectacular views of distant villages, farmsteads and picturesque valleys. (Fig. 1-2).

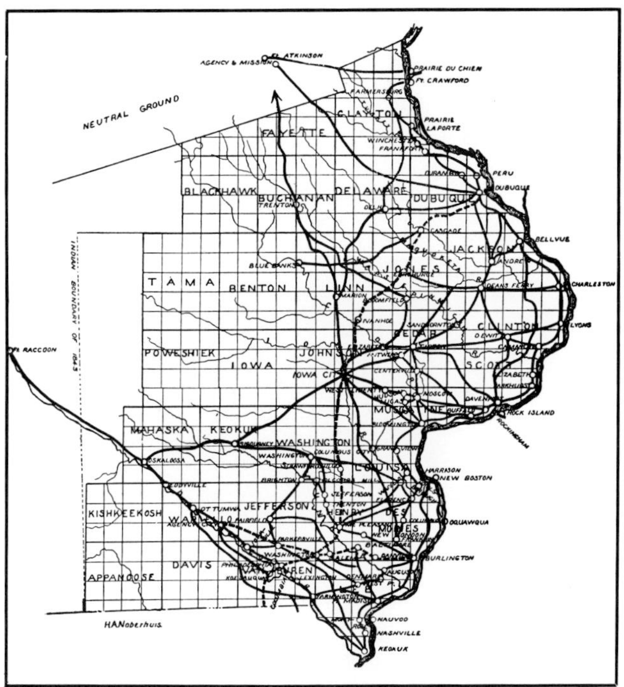

Figure 1-2
The More Important Roads of Territorial Iowa. The Broken Lines Indicate U.S. Military Roads
(Courtesy: State Historical Society of Iowa)

Until the Territory of Iowa was organized, little attention was paid to roads, except for the actions described above. Afterward, over 200 acts were passed, authorizing not only establishment of roads but also legislating the organization of townships and township roads. These defined the duties of supervisors, determined the labor that each male between the ages of 21 and 50 was to give to road work, the fines for refusal to work, and the taxes assessed for construction and maintenance. The only turnpike recorded was that of the Burlington and Iowa River Turnpike Company, chartered in 1839 to build a graded road from Burlington to a point on the east bank of the Iowa River opposite the town of Black Hawk in Louisa County. The interest in roads continued after statehood, when 37 of the 125 Chapters of the Acts of the First Assembly and 17 of the 135 Chapters of the Second Assembly dealt with highways. By that time the settled areas were covered with a network of roads running in every direction and connecting the principal cities and towns.

Of the first historic trails, perhaps the most famous was made by the Mormon trek across the state. The exodus from the "Camp of Israel" on Sugar Creek in Lee County began in 1846 and followed the Des Moines River through Farmington, Bonaparte, and Keosauqua to the center of Davis County near Bloomington. By the time the Mormons had reached the vicinity of Centerville, they had traveled approximately 94 miles in 21 days, averaging over three miles per day. At Shoal Creek the route took a northwesterly direction, with camps established at Garden Grove, thence through Union County and along a route, currently Highway 92, between Greenfield and Council Bluffs. It had taken five months to make the 300 mile journey, and it continued through Nebraska and Wyoming until the valley of the Great Salt was reached in 1847. In 1846, 15,000 Mormons were camped or moving slowly across Iowa in caravans of 3,000 wagons, 30,000 head of cattle, horses and mules and vast numbers of sheep. These pioneer trail blazers marked the first great route between the Mississippi and Missouri Rivers
(Fig. 1-3).

In 1801 U.S. Secretary of the Treasury Albert Gallatin suggested that 1/10 of the net proceeds from the sale of public lands be used for road building if agreed to by the states through which the roads might pass. The Ohio Enabling Act of 1802 incorporated the suggestion except that only five percent of the land sales was to be used for roads. This was modified by Ohio's Constitutional Convention to the effect that 3/5 of the funds were to be spent on roads within the state and under control of the legislature, and was accepted by Congress in 1803. A three percent grant was given to six states, upon their admission to statehood, for roads, canals, levees, river improvements and schools. Congress later granted an additional two percent to these states, except Indiana and Illinois which, with Ohio, had already received the equivalent in expenditures for the National Road. The additional two percent was used for railroads. The remaining 24 states admitted between 1820 and

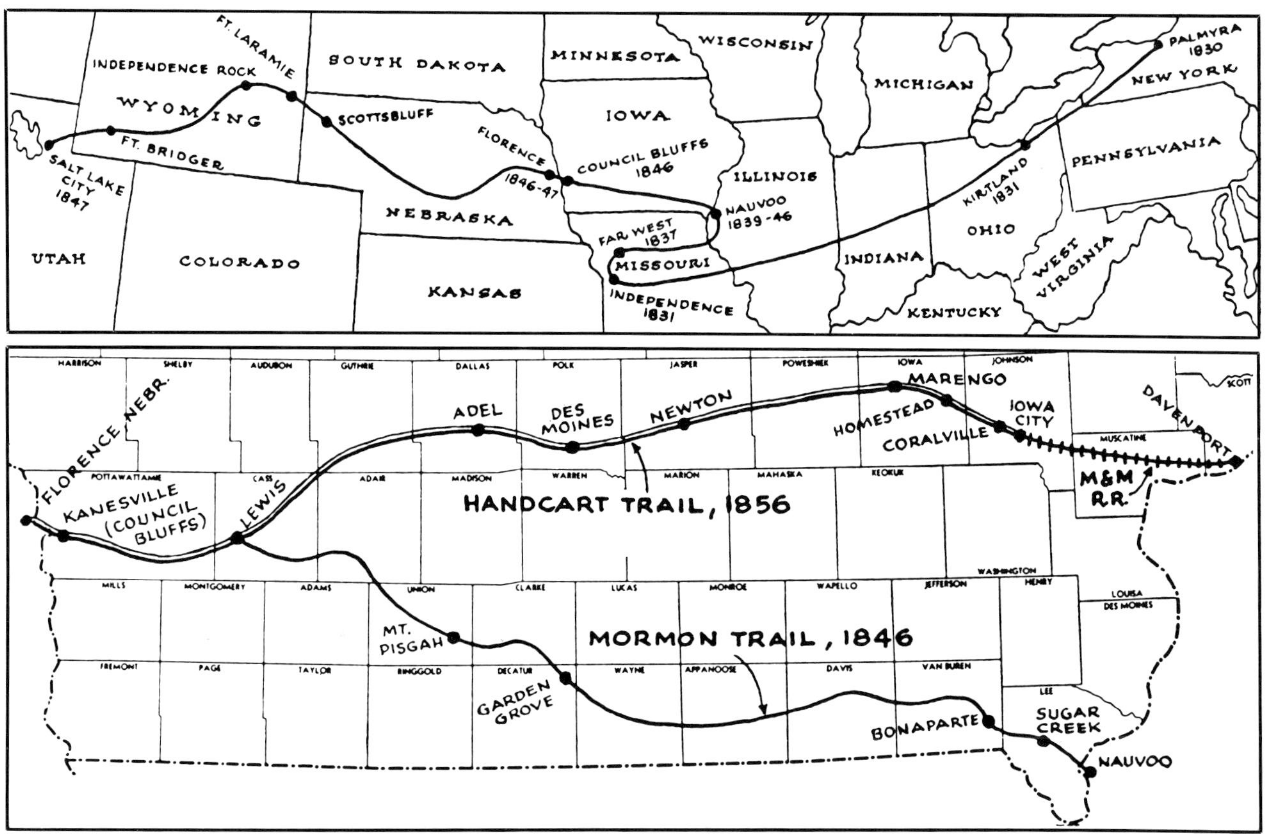

Figure 1-3
Mormon Trails
(Courtesy: State Historical Society of Iowa)

1910 received five percent grants, except for West Virginia and Texas, in which the federal government had no lands. Of the 22 states receiving grants, nine were authorized to use them for public roads, canals and internal improvements, and 13 for schools. The 1846 Iowa Constitution contained a requirement that five percent of land sales be set aside for road and canal construction. However, the citizens had another priority and had the Constitution amended to allocate the funds to educational facilities.[10]

The road problems were different in the "public land" states, formed out of the public domain from those previously settled in the East. These lands had been subdivided into rectangular townships and sections; the right-of-way was one chain or 66 feet wide with each property owner donating 33 feet on his side of the section line, the road to be maintained by statute labor. The tendency in the Great Plains states was to fix local roads on section lines and was strengthened by Congressional action in 1866 which granted free right-of-way access for public roads over unreserved public lands. A number of counties took advantage by declaring all section lines to be public roads, thus reserving the right-of-way before public lands became private property.[5]

[5] U.S. Department of Transportation (US DOT), Federal Highway Administration (FHWA), *America's Highways 1776-1976,* Washington, D.C.; 1976, pp. 36-37.

The Land Grant Act of 1785 and North West Ordinance of 1787, which divided the subject land into states, have been referred to as the last great decisions based upon the pace of human walking. Townships were made six miles square in anticipation of the location of a town in the center—thus, at three miles per hour, it would require one hour to walk to or from the edge. Counties were laid out later based upon horse walking. These decisions set the pattern of land organization for westward expansion and are the reason why Iowa is divided into one-mile squares. Iowa is approximately 300 miles east-west by 200 miles north-south, resulting in approximately 56,000 square miles. A road built around each square would total 112,000 miles. (Information furnished by G.W. Anderson, Iowa DOT.)

Generally, road administration was the responsibility of township and county government, and in Iowa the township was to become the more important unit. State roads continued to be authorized by special acts of the General Assembly, with the only new feature the granting of authority to private corporations to build graded and plank roads, charging tolls fixed by county commissioners.

The Plank Road Era

The plank road, developed in Russia and Canada, experienced only a brief life span in Iowa. The first built in the nation was between Syracuse and Oneida Lake in New York state, a distance of 14 miles. Others had been constructed in Indiana and Illinois. By an Act of the Second General Assembly in 1849, a grant was made to James Weed and Associates to construct "a graded toll road from Bloomington (Muscatine) in Muscatine County, by way of Tipton in Cedar County to the county seat of Benton County (later described as Vinton)...not less than eight feet wide. At the expiration of the grant (20 years), the road was to be deemed a public highway under control of the county commissioners."[6] Burlington was the center of the plank road fever and enthusiasm brought liberal amounts of capital for construction. Financial returns, however, proved to be disappointing and individuals and the city lost most of their investments.

The method of plank road construction consisted of laying stringers of black walnut six inches square on the graded road surface. These were embedded in the earth road base and across them were placed oak, pine or hemlock planks two to three inches thick and eight feet long with no uniformity in width. The lumber, cut from nearby forests, was unseasoned. Ordinarily, the planks were fastened to the stringers with iron spikes or handwrought wooden pegs. Earth was then packed around the stringers and between the planks for a firm base and to prevent deterioration. The devastating incursion on the stands of hard woods used for what proved to be temporary hard-surfaced roads was a wasteful exercise of resources, especially when considered in terms of the later scarcity and value. During the years 1847 to 1853, 14 different organizations were granted authority to build graded and planked roads, totaling almost 600 miles. Probably no more than 50 miles were built. These roads and dates of approval by the General Assembly are found in Table 1-1.

Table 1-1
Plank Road Construction Authorized in Iowa

Description	Authorized	Miles
1. Bloomington (Muscatine) to Tipton	Jan. 8, 1849	94
2. Montrose to Keokuk	Jan. 16, 1849	10
3. Burlington to Mt. Pleasant via New London	Jan. 15, 1849	28
4. Burlington to Mt. Pleasant	Dec. 18, 1850	28
5. Muscatine to Oskaloosa via Washington	Jan. 18, 1851	104
6. Burlington to Toolsborough	Jan. 21, 1851	28
7. Keokuk to Birmingham via Charleston	Feb. 4, 1851	69
8. Burlington into Louisa County	Feb. 4, 1851	25
9. Muscatine to Iowa City	Feb. 4, 1851	40
10. Mt. Pleasant to Trenton via Deedsville	Feb. 5, 1851	33
11. Fort Madison to West Point to Salem	Feb. 5, 1851	25
12. Port Louisa to Virginia Grove	Feb. 5, 1851	25
13. Ottumwa to Libertyville	Feb. 5, 1851	24
14. Mt. Pleasant to Fairfield	Feb 18, 1851	25

(Source: Remley J. Glass, "Early Transportation and the Plank Road," *Annals of Iowa* 21 (January 1939): pp. 502-534.)

[6] *Acts of the Second General Assembly of the State of Iowa, 1849*: Chapt. 33.

The Burlington-Mt.Pleasant road was to be graded 30 feet wide with a right-of-way of 60 feet and was to follow the existing road as nearly as possible. From Burlington to Louisa County, the project was partially completed before it failed financially. The Montrose to Keokuk road paralleled the Des Moines Rapids of the Mississippi River, over which ran a high volume of traffic. In low water, boats had to be unloaded and passengers and freight transferred to land transportation. Approximately 15 miles were built, complete with toll houses and gates. It failed also and was taken over by Lee County. The grant for the Montrose-Keokuk road was the only one in which tolls were set by legislative action. All others allowed county commissioners to set the charges. Tolls to be paid for the use of all roads are listed in Table 1-2.

The graded and planked road idea mushroomed rapidly as a means of building hard-surfaced roads and died almost as fast through competition of the railroads, either planned or built. The expense of grading and planking roads with the expectation that railroads would be built paralleling them proved a serious deterrent. By 1860 the era of the plank road in Iowa had ended.

Stagecoaching

The period of stagecoaching lasted about 30 years but flourished for only 18 years between its introduction into the territory and the beginning of the railroad movement in 1855. The most important means of transportation was the waterways, but the need for mail delivery, a function of the federal government, made land transportation necessary. Stagecoaches came to deliver mail, not necessarily to satisfy public transit, although the scattered settlements received benefits through ancillary passenger service.

Routes developed gradually because most of the habitation was on or near the Mississippi River. The pattern of mail delivery was first to designate a post road, then to dispatch by horseback, and finally by stage, with seats available for passengers as coaches became more adaptable to their demand. Mail rates were based upon a single sheet which could be folded, at the following rates: on all mail delivered within a radius of 30 miles, six cents; between 30 and 80 miles, 10 cents; between 80 and 100 miles, 12½ cents; and between 150 and 400 miles, 18½ cents. All mail sent over 400 miles was charged 25 cents. Since most of the people of Iowa had left homes in far distant places, it was only rarely that the fee was less than 25 cents. These rates held until the postal laws of 1845.

The first regular stagecoach line, the first of four granted federal mail contracts, operated in 1838. Stages ran twice weekly from Burlington through Fort Madison and Montrose to St. Francesville, Missouri, an 18 hour trip over 45 miles. During the

Table 1-2
Toll Charges for Travel on Plank Roads

Description	Toll
1. For each carriage, wagon, cart or sled drawn by two horses, oxen or mules	2½ cents per mile
2. Each additional animal	1 cent per mile
3. Vehicle drawn by one horse, ox or mule	2 cents per mile
4. Each horse and rider	1 cent per mile
5. Each head of horses, oxen, mules or cattle led or driven	1 cent per mile
6. Each sheep, goat or hog	½ cent per mile
7. Merchandise (not including furniture of immigrants)	2 cents per ton mile

(Source: Glass: p. 524.)

same year, three additional routes were established, all originating in Burlington. One of the most popular was the Burlington-Davenport line with a schedule of 27 hours for 80 miles. Another was the route between Burlington and McComb, Illinois, for connections with other stage lines. A third was an inland route to Mt. Pleasant, covering 30 miles in 16 hours. Other principal lines developed after 1838 were between Dubuque and Cedar Falls, Dubuque and Iowa City, Clinton and Cedar Rapids and Davenport to Council Bluffs through Oskaloosa and Des Moines. Stages also ran from Cedar Falls to Cedar Rapids, Iowa City to Keokuk and Dubuque to Keokuk.

Before a system of stage lines could be established, improvements had to be made in the miserable existing roads and a satisfactory type of vehicle had to be constructed. Bad roads were not the exception in Iowa vis-a-vis other midwestern states, but they had a reputation for consistently muddy and sticky qualities. Colton quotes a traveler describing his journey in Iowa in 1857. "I had heard a great deal about Iowa mud and now saw it to my hearts content. It was as thick as dough and greasy at the same time. The horses would slip up and the wheels slide fearfully at every inclination of the road and whenever we got out to walk, it seemed as though we lifted a common size farm at every step."[7]

Vehicles ranged from farmers' wagons to the Concord Coach, the Rolls-Royce of the American horse-drawn carriage. The use of wagons, some lacking springs, inspired the *Muscatine Democratic Enquirer* to complain "that owing to the lumber wagons, mud wagons or carts plying between Muscatine and Iowa City, one passenger had all the pegs and tacks shaken out of his boots by vibration of the vehicle." Another editor wrote that "the coaches were the best medicine for indigestion...the horses had one peculiarity . . . their bodies offered no impediment to the sunshine and offer travelers a good opportunity to study the osseous structure of the animal."[8]

By 1845 the initial period of stagecoaching ended. Changes in the postal laws no longer required bidding for mail contracts nor standards set for the type of vehicle for mail transportation. More competition resulted and operators were hard pressed to maintain their routes much less consider expansion. In the mid-1850s, the legislature acted to provide state roads, and coach service spread to the central and western counties.

Among the early Iowa operators awarded mail contracts were William Wilson of Fort Madison, A.C. Donaldson and George Kerrick of Dubuque, Richard Lund and Morton McCarver of Burlington, and Samuel Head of Lee County. In 1846 John Frink, from Illinois, and Robert Stewart, a livery stable proprietor in Burlington, started large scale operations from Burlington to Keokuk, Fairfield and Iowa City. In three years, the network spread to Des Moines and later to Council Bluffs. In 1854 the Western Stage Company purchased the Frink interests and became the largest stage line in the state. One of their original coaches is on the ground floor of the State Historical Building in Des Moines (Fig. 1-4).

Iowa's mud roads and hostile Indians, winter blizzards, prairie fires and robberies were major obstacles to stage travel. Muddy roads resulted in slow travel and long distances between stops made for passenger discomfort and hunger. Fares varied from station to station, usually five cents per mile, were higher in bad weather and varied also with the size and weight of the passenger. The fare from Des Moines to Keokuk was $10, from Muscatine to Iowa City, three dollars, with half fare for children. Legislators traveling to or from Iowa City rode free, a practice later adopted by the railroads. Male passengers worked their way in addition to the charges. As late as 1870 on the Haskell & Company's Northwestern line, the fare was 10 cents a mile and a fence rail, the latter to assist in getting the coach out of the mud.

Stagecoach companies such as Frink and Western Stages were important to the public and economy of Iowa prior to 1870. The Western Stage Company employed 1,500 men, used over 3,000 horses and 600 coaches and invested $1.5 million in the business. It operated in Iowa, Wisconsin, Missouri and Nebraska, as far west as Fort Kearney, some 300 miles beyond the Missouri River. But good service did not necessarily follow. In 1858 the *Council Bluffs Eagle* declared, "The Western Stage Company deserves the greatest credit for their untiring energy and

[7] Kenneth E. Colton, "The Stagecoach Comes to Iowa," *Annals of Iowa* 35 (Winter 1960): pp. 161-186. Stagecoach routes are described in Inez E. Kirkpatrick, *Stagecoach Trails in Iowa,* Crete, Nebraska: J-B Pub. Co., 1975.

[8] Ruth S. Beitz, "Iowa's Stagecoach Era," *Iowan 9* (April-May 1961): pp. 22-27, 43.

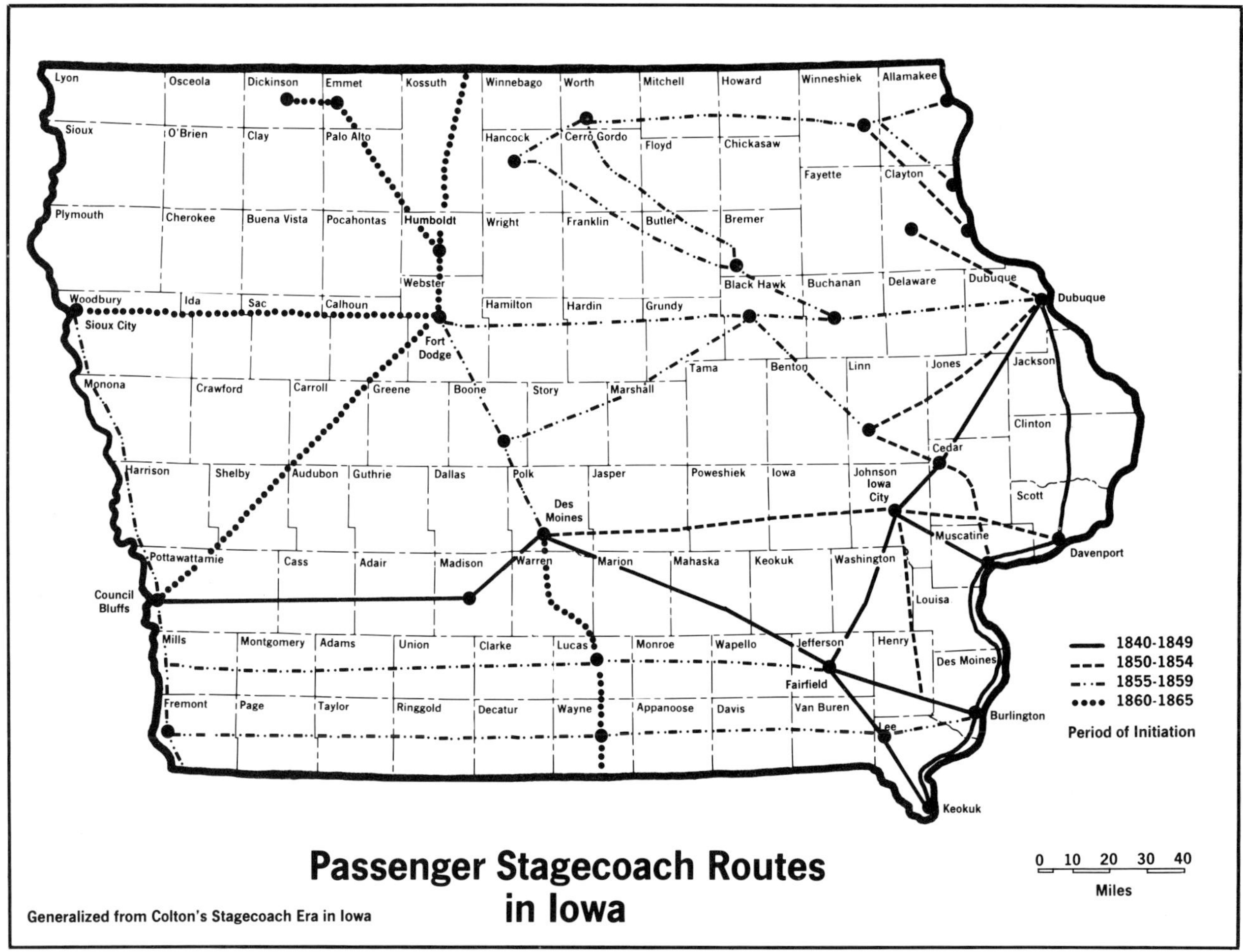

Figure 1-4
(Courtesy: Clare C. Cooper, "The Role of the Railroads in the Settlement of Iowa," M.A. thesis, University of Nebraska, Lincoln, 1958.)

perseverance in bringing mail to this city...in a wet and pulp-like state, perfectly saturated with water and wholly unreadible...We are sickened at the sight of every mail that arrives...When agents are asked why this repeated occurence, they offer the same silly and stereotyped reply that the stage upset in the creek. The Western Stage Company have proved an intolerable nuisance..."[9]

Even though the stages during the latter part of their era often connected with main line railroad stations, they ceased as a means of transportation when the railroad network spread to smaller communities. The first coach entered Des Moines on July 1, 1847, and the last left on July 1, 1870. In 1870 the Western Stage Company sold coaches which had cost $1,000 for as low as $10.

[9] Compiled from the Newspaper Clipping File, State Historical Library, Des Moines, Iowa.

Steamboating on the Eastern Rivers

The Dubuque-Galena area furnished the most important commodity (lead) moved on the Mississippi before 1850. In fact, in 1847 lead traffic was worth five times the entire St. Louis fur trade.[10] Surplus corn and pork went downstream and up the river came the steamboats, stopping at the river ports to discharge immigrants with their household goods, to deliver tobacco and molasses from the South, and farm implements and retail merchandise from the East.

The first steamboat to pass along the eastern border was the *Virginia,* a 109-foot stern-wheeler which reached Fort Snelling in Minnesota in 1823. The 664 mile trip from St. Louis required 20 days. The boat grounded frequently on sandbars and took five days to get over the Des Moines and Rock Island Rapids. Wood was burned for fuel, and stops had to be made while fresh supplies were cut from the forests along the shore. Approximately 30 steamboats ran the Des Moines River to Raccoon Forks prior to 1860, and one, the *Charles Craft,* reached the present site of Fort Dodge. Low water, which was common during the use of steamboats in the Civil War, and the construction of the railroads to Des Moines, Boone and Fort Dodge diverted the river traffic to land transportation.

Navigation of the Iowa and Cedar Rivers was possible only in high water. Eight different boats navigated the Iowa River, the first being the *Ripple.* The *Iowa City* was actually launched from that city in 1866. The *Black Hawk* became famous on the Cedar River, running between Cedar Rapids and Waterloo, and in 1858 made scheduled trips from Cedar Rapids to St. Louis. Attempts to navigate smaller streams proved to be impractical. Settlers on the Turkey, Maquoketa and Wapsipinicon built flatboats, keelboats and barges to float their products downstream to markets. "No better evidence of the prosperity of the territory can be given," declared the *Burlington Hawkeye* in 1840, "than is seen in the numerous covered flatboats that are going downstream, laden with all kinds of produce, animal and vegetable. Upwards of 100 boats of this description have already passed Burlington."

The length of the navigation season depended upon the weather as the winter months iced and closed the Mississippi River from St. Paul to Keokuk and occasionally to St. Louis. Between Dubuque and Keokuk the river was ice-locked for an average of 75 to 105 days, and St. Paul was locked in for almost five months each year. The opening of the river in the spring was a celebrated event in the life of river towns, and prizes, including free wharfage during the year, were given for the first boat to deliver its cargo. These awards were sufficient encouragement for captains to fight for this distinction and the popularity which accompanied it. Another problem was related to the winter storage of the boats. It was necessary to keep them off the river when the ice broke or jammed and caused flooding, so they were usually quartered in sheltered areas, lagoons or sloughs in the small tributaries, guarded by workmen who overhauled and repaired them during the winter months.

The Missouri River Steamboat Era

Petersen observed that "steamboating on the Missouri is one of the most colorful and dynamic stories in the development of the Trans-Mississippi West. So great was the contribution of the steamboat to the Missouri Valley that it deserves equal rank with the covered wagon as a symbol of the westward movement." Four years before the *Virginia* ran the Mississippi, the *Western-Engineer* reached Omaha, the only one of five boats that attempted to navigate the Missouri in 1819. The voyage opened a period of development for Council Bluffs and Sioux City. Even before western Iowa was settled, the fur trade was responsible for river traffic, and it continued for two decades between the 1850s and 1870s. However, the tonnage was insignificant compared with the demand for transportation during the migration which started from assembly points at Missouri River towns. Both Iowa cities became busy river ports, and by 1867 at least a half dozen packets were working the Sioux City trade (Fig. 1-7).

There were 46 boats operating on the Missouri in 1857, but the Civil War virtually stopped commerce until 1866, when trade expanded on the upper Missouri. Thirty-one steamboats arrived at Fort Benton, 50 percent more than recorded in the seven previous years. Construction of the Union Pacific provided an additional boom to postwar traffic. Between 1865 and 1867, materials and men to build pontoon bridges were transported by river steamers.

[10] William J. Petersen, "Steamboating on the Missouri River," *Iowa Journal* 53 (April 1955): pp. 97-120.

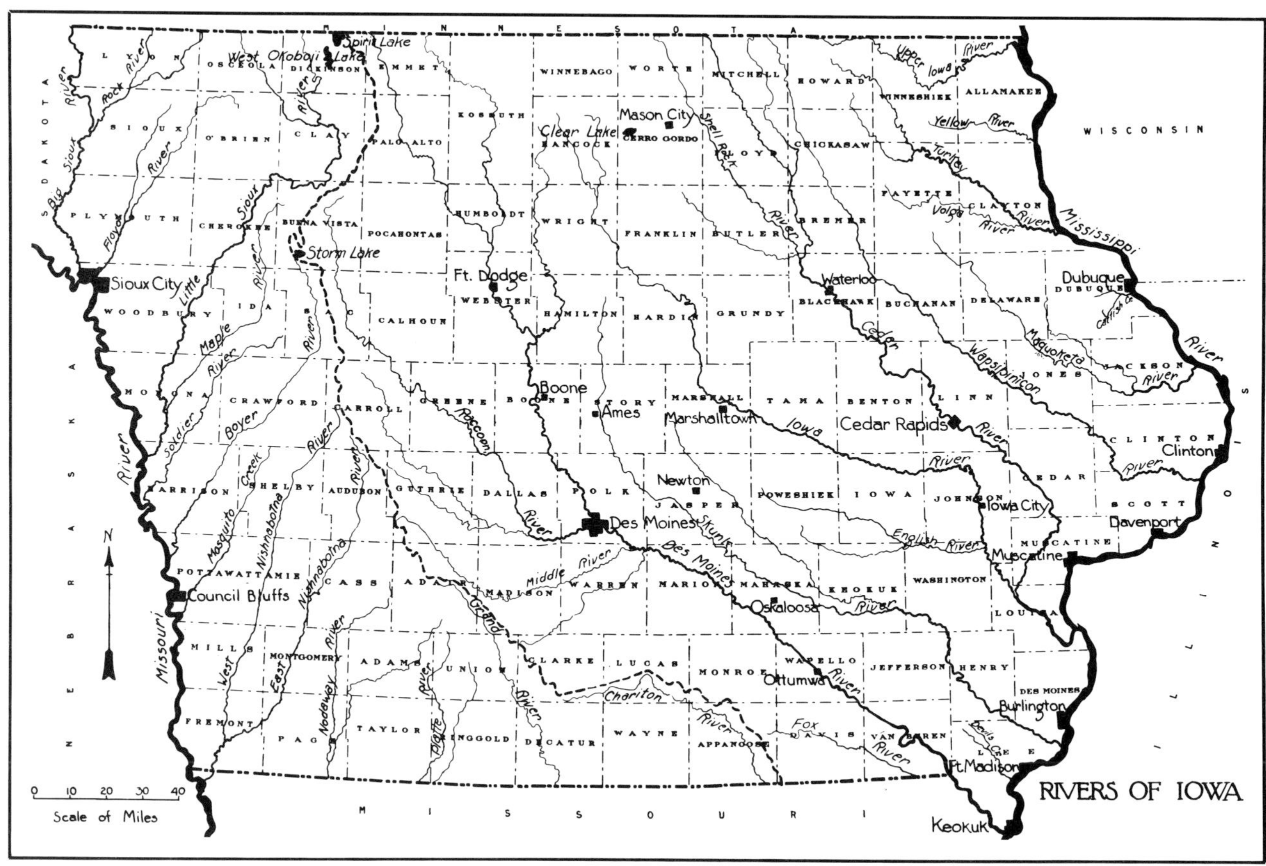

Figure 1-5
(Courtesy: State Historical Society of Iowa)

Although slowed by the arrival of the Chicago & North Western R.R. at Council Bluffs in 1867, the boats continued to carry supplies until the completion of the transcontinental railroad in 1869.

The *Omaha* and *Florence* were among the most popular steamboats on the Missouri River, both furnishing frequent passenger and freight service. Merchandise and equipment were carried upstream; potatoes and corn came downstream on the return trip. The *Florence* ran a regular military supply service to Fort Randall and Fort Stewart and broke speed records from St. Louis. The Missouri steamboat era contributed to the rapid growth of the Missouri Valley, particularly in northwest Iowa, and hastened the statehood of Nebraska. When the railroads reached the river, the early steamboat period ended; just as it had when they crossed the Mississippi, to be revived at a later date in history.

Canals

Sage discusses the potential of canals as a means of inland transportation had the railroads not been developed. These were proposed as feeders and connecting links to the river system. One was to run from New Boston, Illinois, at the mouth of the Iowa River, to Columbus Junction, thence to Cedar Rapids, Waterloo and Austin, Minnesota; another from Columbus Junction to Marshalltown; yet another from Peterson to the Missouri River; and one from Ortonville, Minnesota to Fort Dodge, Des Moines and on to the Missouri. These were ambitious projects and while noteworthy in their conception, could not have filled the requirements for future transportation facilities needed by the state.

Actually, four small canals were built. One ran seven miles through the Amana Colonies. Another served a grist mill on the Iowa River near Wapello, abandoned

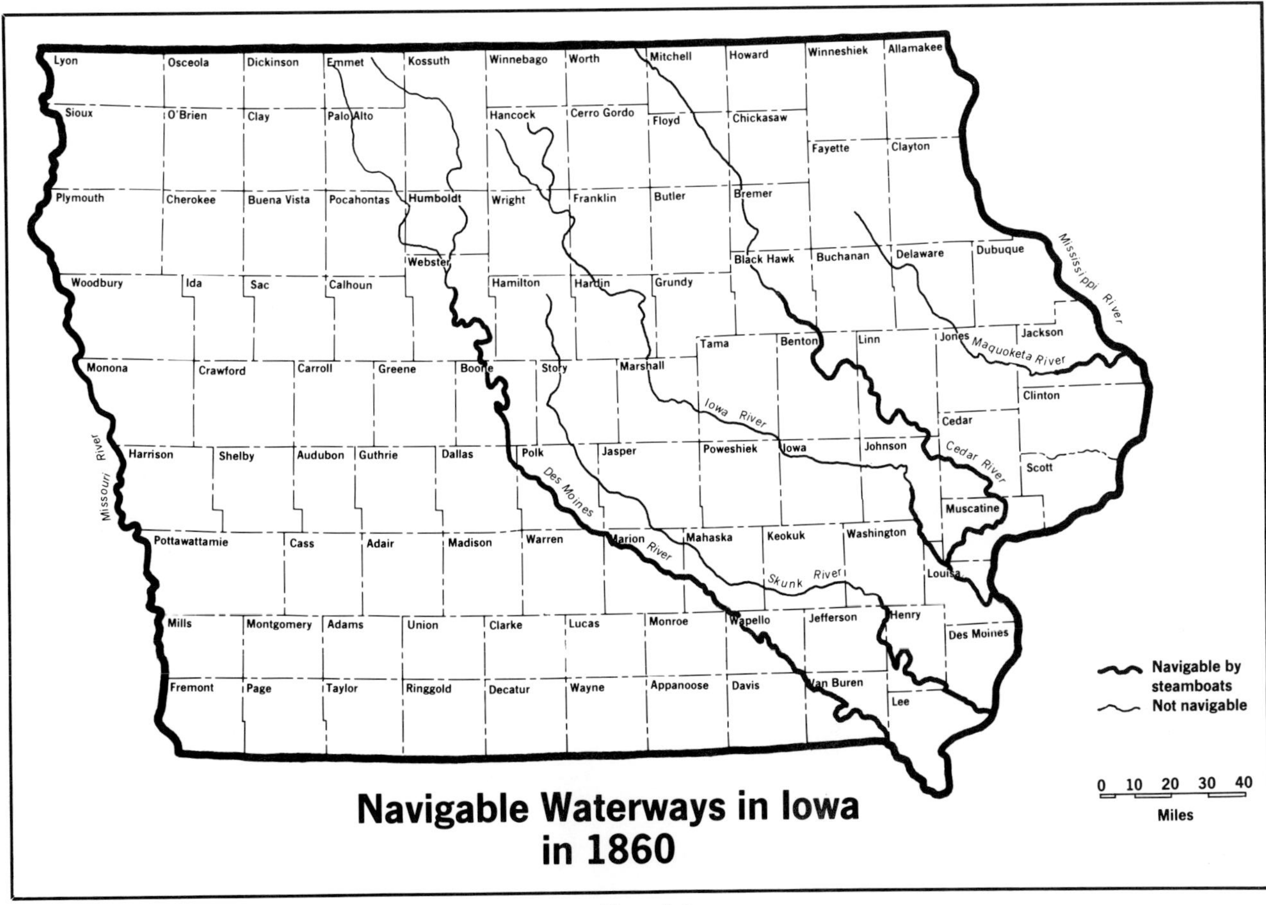

Figure 1-6
(Courtesy: Clare C. Cooper, "The Role of the Railroads in the Settlement of Iowa," M.A. thesis, University of Nebraska, Lincoln, 1958.)

in 1900, and two were built around the rapids on the Mississippi River. According to Amana residents, the canal was built in 1880 and provided some of the power used by the woolen mill. Probably the most important canal was the lateral built around the Des Moines rapids, north of Keokuk, in a section of the river which dropped 27 feet in 12 miles. Boats traversed the canal through three locks which measured 350 x 75 feet. When the dam at Keokuk was built in 1913, the canal ceased to operate and all traces disappeared. A second lateral canal was in use at LeClaire and was bypassed when Lock and Dam No. 14 was built in the 1930s, although it is still used for small pleasure craft.

The Des Moines River Project

Purpose and Plan

The Des Moines River enters Iowa from Minnesota somewhat west of the center of the boundary and flows in a southeasterly direction to its junction with the Mississippi River. Nearly half way across the state, the Des Moines is joined by the Raccoon flowing from the west, at what was known as Raccoon Forks, the site of the city of Des Moines. Since Congress had been granting lands to states for public improvements, the importance of river transportation suggested that assistance to aid navigation would accelerate agricultural and industrial trade in the areas through which the river flowed. Steamboats had run the Des Moines River since 1830, and it was believed that through a system of locks and dams an important channel of trade could be opened. Accordingly, in 1846, the state was granted alternate sections of land (640 acres) within five miles of the river which had not otherwise been appropriated or disposed of for other purposes. Although the grant was made to improve navigation, it did not offer any guarantees of success.

The grant stated that the area to be improved was that portion of the river between its mouth and Raccoon Forks, but nothing expressly defined the northern point to which it applied. So the question immediately arose as to whether the grant was specifically for the area to be improved or extended to the entire length of the river. If it applied only as far as Raccoon Forks, 300,000 acres would be involved; if to the Minnesota border, the grant would cover over 1,000,000 acres. Iowa was admitted to the Union four months after the territorial grant, and in early 1847 it was accepted by the General Assembly under the assumption that the grant embraced the lands south of Raccoon Forks. But, in his address to the Assembly, Governor Clark pointed out that at least two-thirds of the area granted was claimed by settlers, who expected to purchase the lands for $1.25 per acre.

To supervise the sale of land and oversee expenditures for the river improvements, a Board of Public Works was created. The plan called for construction of 28 dams, nine locks, and several canals over a distance of 240 miles from the mouth to Racoon Forks. Seven dams and locks were built: at St. Francesville, Missouri; Cowper's Mill near Belfast; Tom's Mill near Croton; Farmington; Bonaparte; Bentonsport; and Keosauqua (Fig. 1-8).

In 1848, under pressure from the Iowa Congressional delegation, Richard D. Young, Commissioner of the General Land Office, declared that the grant applied to the entire river within the state. Yet, a few months later, portions of the lands above Raccoon Forks (25,000 acres) were sold by the Land Office to individuals, complicating the problems of land disposal by the Board and rendering uncertain the intent of the 1846 grant. More confusion occurred in 1849, when the Secretary of the Treasury affirmed the

Figure 1-7
Steamboat *Ida Rees #2* on Missouri River, 1877.
(Courtesy: U.S. Army Corps of Engineers, Omaha District)

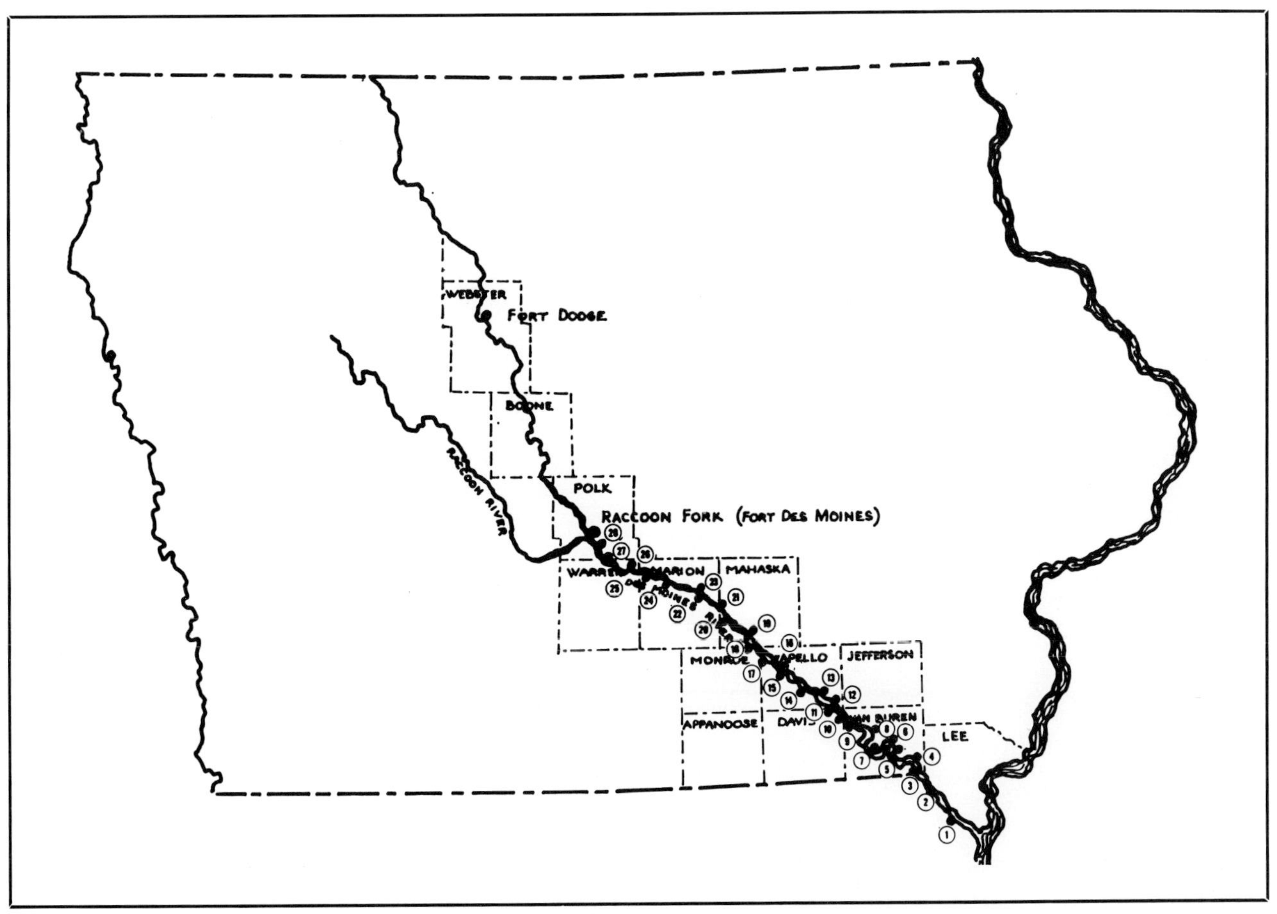

Figure 1-8

KEY TO MAP OF PROPOSED DAMS ON DES MOINES RIVER—(1) St. Francisville, Mo., (2) Cowper's Mill, near Belfast, (3) Tom's Mill, near Croton, (4) Farmington, (5) Bonaparte, (6) Bentonsport, (7) Keosauqua, (8) Phildelphis, near Kilbourn, (9) Portland, (1) Jordan, near Iowaville, (11) Kalesback, near Eldon, (12) Rowlands, near Cliffland, (13) Sugar Creek, near Agency (14) Above Ottumwa, (15) Near Chilicothe, (16) Near Chilicothe, (17) Below Eddyville, (18) Above Eddyville, (19) Rocky Ripple, near Givin, (20) Tally's Ford, (21) English Creek, (22) Amsterdam, southwest of Pella, (23) South of Whitebreast Creek, (24) Cordova, just below Red Rock, (25) Bennington, near Swan, (26) Lafayette, (27) Southwest of Adelphi, (28) Levey.

(Courtesy: State Historical Society of Iowa)

decision of the Land Commissioner. This decision was reversed by the Secretary of the Interior but again reaffirmed by the Attorney General during the same year. However, in 1856 the Secretary of the Interior refused to certify the additional lands, stating that the grant applied only to Raccoon Forks.

The sale of the lands did not bring the necessary funds, and in 1853 Henry O'Reilly, a New York contractor, organized the Des Moines Navigation and Railroad Company and agreed to complete the project within four years from July 1, 1854. He was to be compensated by funds from the unsold lands, future tolls on the waterway, water rents and other profits over a period of 40 years. At the expiration, the improvement was to become the property of the state. After a direct expenditure of nearly $800,000 in the four years, little progress had been made and a settlement was negotiated and reported to the General Assembly in 1860. On the same day the resolution for settlement passed, the Assembly adopted a measure which provided that the lands remaining be given to the Keokuk, Fort Des Moines, and Minnesota Railroad. By transfer, the work of improving navigation on the river ended.

Amana Canals (Photos by author)

Impact of the River Project

The river improvement plan was not only of historic interest but set off legal and political controversies within the state, between it and the federal government and with settlers who claimed title to the lands. In 1856 Congress granted lands to the states consisting of alternate sections of six miles along the proposed right-of-way construction of four railroads being built east to west, but not to include any lands previously reserved for other public improvements. The grants crossed the Des Moines River grant two miles north of Racoon Forks. If the 1846 grant included the area above, as well as below, this point, the railroads could not get these lands. So, with the coming of the railroads, the attitude of the people changed. Before, they desired the river grant to be extended to the Minnesota border; afterward, citizens supported the railroad interests, who were content to have the grant stopped at Raccoon Forks. The crossing of the river grant by the railroads, the question of where the grant applied, and the lands claimed by settlers resulted in long and extensive litigation in the courts. Land claim cases went to the U.S. Supreme Court at least eight times in 40 years before finally settled. Two comments on this project are worth noting. One, by Weaver, termed the river project as "possibly the most dramatic chapter in the history of settlement in Iowa." The other, by Cole, stated that "the state had spent 10 years and a million dollars to learn that politicians are not transformed into businessmen by being elected to offices with big names." [11]

[11] James B. Weaver, "The Story of the Des Moines River Lands," *Annals of Iowa 18* (October 1932): pp. 420-433. Cyrenus Cole, *A History of the People of Iowa,* Cedar Rapids, Iowa: The Torch Press, 1921, p. 219.

Remnants of the Dam and Lock at Bonaparte. (Photos by author)

Summary

The stagecoach and steamboat of pioneer days could not provide the transportation necessary for rapid development of the state. The first was handicapped by natural and human obstacles which made for slow, tedious, frustrating and uncomfortable travel and had little or no capacity for handling freight. The second was limited to the north-south pattern of movement, as determined by the flow and boundaries of the rivers. Both served well their primary purpose during the period of the yearly life cycles. One disappeared in time, and the other shifted in importance as the economic and social evolution of the state and nation dictated its future. Water transportation eventually evolved into a major instrument of commerce in Iowa, but in those days the migration of people was from east to west, and the commerce and industry that followed were the result of a new form of land transportation. Railroads made Chicago a commercial challenger to St. Louis and the lower Mississippi River ports, and it was only a matter of time before their tracks would be laid to and through Iowa enroute to the West. The failure of the Des Moines river project emphasized the difficulty of making interior rivers navigable, brought with it conflicting claims over land ownership and, in the end, proved to be a boon for railroad development.

The author interviewed residents of the river towns of Bonaparte, Bentonsport and Keosauqua and photographed remnants of the locks and dams built at these sites. Little remains as evidence except at Bonaparte, where a lock and rock line across the river is clearly visible. The dams were rather crudely built and were washed away frequently by ice and floods.

Selected References

Briggs, John Ely. *Iowa Old and New.* New York: University Publishing Co., 1939.

Brindley, John E. *History of Road Legislation in Iowa.* Iowa City: State Historical Society, 1912.

Brown, D. Clayton. *Western Tributaries of the Mississippi.* National Waterways Study (Navigation History NWS-83-7), Washington, D.C., 1983.

Chittenden, Hiram M. *History of Early Steamboat Navigation on the Missouri River.* New York: Frances P. Harper, 1903.

Colton, Kenneth E. "Bringing the Stagecoach to Iowa." *Annals of Iowa 22* (July 1939): pp. 8-9.

Davis, C.F. "Voyage of the First Steamboat from Keokuk to Fort Dodge." *Annals of Iowa 7* (July 1905): pp. 140-142.

Glass, Remley J. "Early Transportation and the Plank Road." *Annals of Iowa 21* (January 1939): pp. 502-534.

Grahame, Orville F. "Stagecoach Days." *Palimpsest 5* (May 1924): p. 176.

Grahame, Russell C. "Voyage of the Black Hawk." *Palimpsest 9* (May 1928): pp. 157-159.

Gue, Benjamin. *History of Iowa.* New York: Century Historical Co., 1903.

Harlan, Edgar R. *A Narrative History of the People of Iowa.* Chicago Historical Society, Inc., 1931.

Hoolette, William. *Iowa, the Pioneer Heritage.* Des Moines, Iowa: Wallace-Homestead Book Co., 1970.

Hussey, Tacitus. "History of Steamboating on the Des Moines River from 1837 to 1862." *Annals of Iowa 4* (April 1900): pp. 323-382.

Larson, Gustav E. "Notes on the Navigation of Iowa Rivers." *Iowa Journal of History and Politics 39* (October 1941): pp. 404-411.

Lathrop, H. W. "Early Steamboating on the Iowa River." *Iowa Historical Record 12, 14, 15* (January 1897): pp. 44-46.

McCoy, Hugh. "Steamboat Era River Towns." *Iowan 10* (Spring 1962): pp. 10-28.

Meyer, B. H., et. al. *History of Transportation in the United States before 1860.* Washington, D.C.: Carnegie Institution, 1917.

Parish, John C. "The Ripple." *Palimpsest 2* (April 1921): pp. 113-122.

Parker, George E. *Iowa Pioneer Foundation.* Iowa City: State Historical Society, 1940.

Parker, N. H. *Iowa As It Is In 1855.* Chicago: Keen & Lee, 1855.

Petersen, William J. "A Century of River Traffic." *Palimpsest 27* (October 1946): pp. 289,293.

______. *The Story of Iowa.* New York: Lewis Historical Co., 1952.

———. "The Mormon Trail of 1846." *Palimpsest 4* (September 1966): pp. 353-367.

Pratt, Leroy G. "Ten Cents a Mile and a Fence Post." *Annals of Iowa 39* (Spring 1969): pp. 597-604.

———. *The Counties and Court Houses of Iowa.* Mason City, Iowa: Klepte Printing Co., 1977.

Sage, Leland L. *A History of Iowa.* Ames: Iowa State University Press, 1974.

Swanson, Leslie L. *Canals in Mid America.* Moline, Ill.: By the author, 1984.

Tuttle, Charles R., and Daniel S. Durrie. *Illustrated History of the State of Iowa.* Chicago: Richard S. Peale & Co., 1876.

Vestal, Stanley. *The Missouri.* New York: Farrar & Rinehart, 1946.

Wilson, Ben Hur. "The Genesis of Planking." "The Boom in Planking." "Planked in Places." *Palimpsest 15* (September 1934): pp. 289-320.

———. "Burlington Westward." "Planked from Burlington." *Palimpsest 16* (October 1935): pp. 360-380.

———. "Notes on Planked Roads in Northeastern Iowa." *Annals of Iowa 22* (July 1939): pp. 77-81.

Chapter Two
Railroad Construction and Influence in Iowa

Introduction

The linking of the Eastern cities to Chicago made inevitable the westward move of railroads to the Mississippi River, thence through Iowa to the Pacific Coast. Efforts to improve transportation on rivers and roads did not aid in rapid development of Iowa, which in the early decades was still in the pioneer stages of growth. So while the interior settlers plowed the tough prairie sod, eastern settlements began to plan for the railroad era, influenced by developments in the states east of her borders. Iowa's railroad history, therefore, was tied directly to the construction of railroads from Chicago, since the great trunk lines built across the state were extensions of the roads to the Mississippi River.

The railroad era in Iowa is replete with railroads chartered but not built; those built but often leaving a trail of bankruptcies, insolvencies, and reorganizations; of roads named and renamed. From this atmosphere of change and confusion, the major railroads emerged, forming the systems so well known. They influenced the development of settlements, expanded the agricultural and industrial base, and were supported and controlled by political attitudes which prevailed during the period. The story of railroad construction and its impact on Iowa is one of the most interesting chapters in the history of the state.

Building to the Mississippi River

In the middle of the 19th Century, the Mississippi Valley was engaged in a struggle which pitted forces advocating north-south transportation against those advocating the east-west movement. Parish suggests that "it was a contest between the old lines of migration and the new; the South and the East; between the slow and cheap transportation by water and the rapid but more expensive transportation by rail and it arrayed St. Louis and Chicago against each other in intensive rivalry." [1] Joseph Sheffield and Henry Farnam built the Michigan Central (MC) into Chicago in 1852 and wanted a line to the Mississippi. The Chicago & Rock Island (CRI), previously known as the Rock Island & La Salle, was incorporated in 1851, with John B. Jervis as president, later replaced by Farnam. Among those involved were Peter Anthony Dey and his assistant, Grenville M. Dodge, engineers and surveyors, who were to become famous in Iowa railroad construction and regulation. By October 1852, the road had been built as far west as La Salle and reached Rock Island in February 1854, the first to build to the river (Fig. 2-1). So great was the traffic that the rolling stock stipulated in the contract was inadequate to meet the demand.

Three men, James Frederick Joy, John Murray Forbes and John W. Brooks, brought the Burlington (CB&Q) to Iowa. Forbes, the financier, was convinced that not only were there economic, political and military advantages to be gained by a transcontinental railroad, but also the rich prairies of Illinois and Iowa would yield investors substantial rewards. The CRI was already under construction and the Illinois Central (IC) and Galena & Chicago Union (G&CU) were building through northwestern Illinois. So Joy turned to the southwest to find an outlet by combining four lines which "sprawled aimlessly" in a westward direction. Three, the Aurora Branch, the Northern Cross (Quincy & Chicago) and Peoria and Oquawka (P&Q), had been incorporated in 1849 by local interests. The fourth, the Central Military Tract (CMT), was chartered by Galesburg citizens in 1851.

The nucleus of the CB&Q was the Aurora Branch, built to Mendota in 1852 and extended by the CMT to Galesburg in 1854. Through the P&Q, it reached East Burlington in 1855. The Chicago & Aurora was incorporated as the CB&Q in 1855, absorbed the CMT in 1856, and purchased the Northern Cross in 1864. That portion of the P&Q built between Peoria and East Burlington was acquired in the consolidation of 1864 (Fig. 2-2).

[1] John C. Parish, "The First Mississippi Bridge," *Palimpsest 3* (May 1922): p. 153.

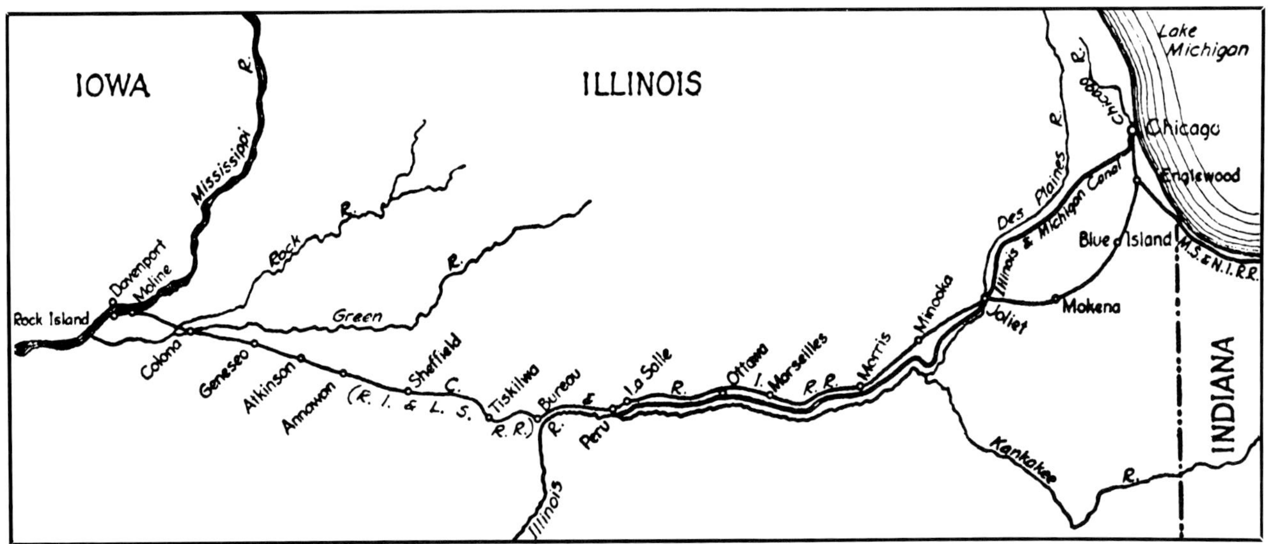

Figure 2-1
The Route of the Chicago and Rock Island Railroad
(Courtesy: State Historical Society of Iowa)

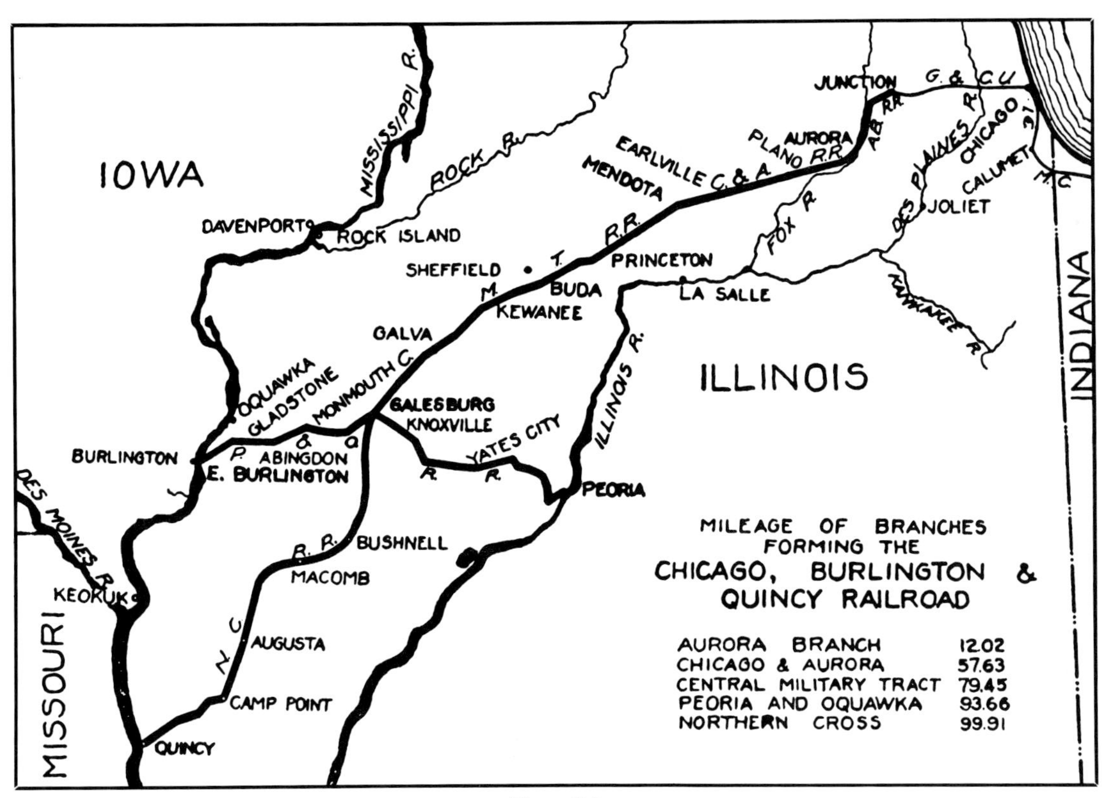

Figure 2-2
(Courtesy: State Historical Society of Iowa)

The Chicago & North Western (CNW) began with the incorporation of the G&CU in 1836. An economic depression in the 1830s delayed construction until 1848. William B. Ogden was president and built 121 miles from Chicago to Freeport in 1853, where the westward extension ended. From there to Galena, there were two possible routes for the G&CU and IC to build to the River: one northwest through Warren and Scales Mound and the other southwest to Savanna. But it was feared that the area would not support two competing parallel railroads, so the two roads agreed to jointly construct one line. The IC completed the Freeport-Galena route in 1854. Although opposed by Galena residents who hoped their city would be the terminus, the track continued to Dunleith opposite Dubuque in 1855. The IC built and owned the road but the G&CU operated its equipment over the line during the construction period.

As a result of failure to gain the northwestern route, a line was planned through consolidations and mergers from Junction, 30 miles west of Chicago, to continue through DeKalb, Dixon, Sterling, and Morrison to Fulton on the river, arriving there in December 1855. Connections were made with the IC from Dixon to Freeport and with the CRI from Dixon to Rockford. By use of the tracks of the IC to Dunleith, the G&CU had two contacts with the river, an accomplishment not duplicated by any other railroad. The pioneer name of the G&CU was eventually discontinued and the CNW emerged as the result of purchases and mergers with other roads, the name considered sufficiently comprehensive to indicate the territory served (Fig. 2-3).

The IC was organized in 1851, five weeks after receiving its charter. Robert Schuyler was elected president and guided it through its formative years. Federal land grants were obtained after seven years of congressional debates. Under the terms of the land grant, the first to be given any railroad, approximately two and one-half million of the 11 million acres in the public domain were transferred to the state for railroad construction. The grants called for a right-of-way through public lands with alternate sections (640 acres) in a strip six miles wide on each side of the railroad. It was stipulated that the lands would revert to the federal government if construction had not begun within two years and finished within 10 years from passage of the legislation, signed into law by President Fillmore in 1850. The Illinois land grant marked the beginning of a national policy which disposed of public lands for railroad development and was of particular significance in construction of Iowa's railroads. When finally built, the railroad covered 705 miles and was considered the best built road in the West at that time (Fig. 2-4).

The Milwaukee was the last of the major railroads to reach the Mississippi River. Chartered in 1847 under the name of the Milwaukee and Mississippi (Mil&M) Railroad, it reached Madison in 1854. From there, it took three years to get to Prairie du Chien, opposite McGregor. The road was in constant financial difficulty, for no state or federal aid was forthcoming, and it was necessary to call upon cities, towns,

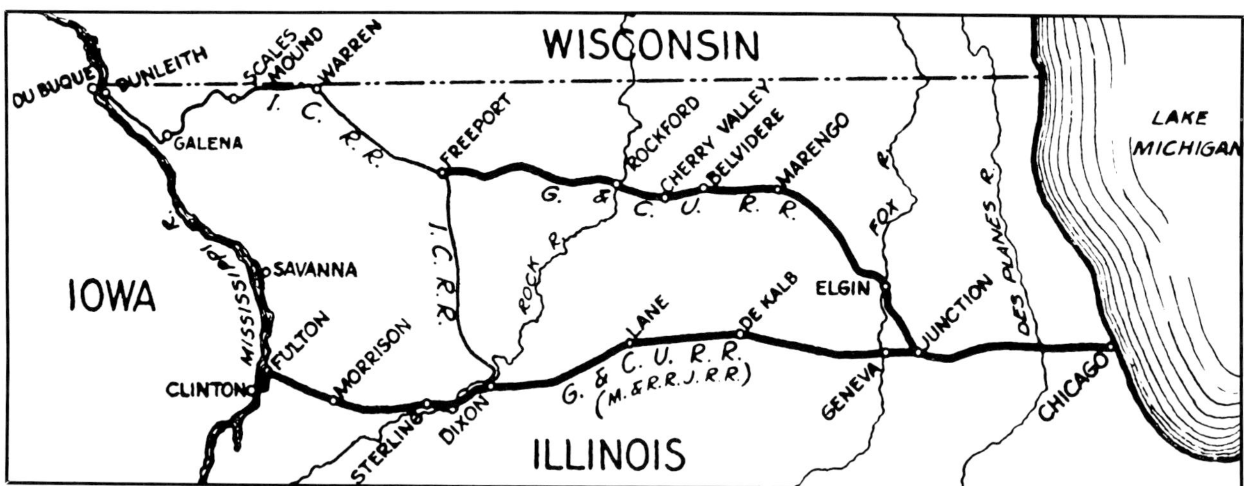

Figure 2-3
The Galena & Chicago Union Railroad, forerunner of the Chicago & North Western
(Courtesy: State Historical Society of Iowa)

farmers and merchants to finance the project. This was the only road built across Wisconsin and became an important route for the northern tier of Iowa counties. It tapped valuable areas of mineral and agricultural wealth in Wisconsin and attracted a large share of the business of Dubuque and northeastern Iowa (Fig. 2-5).

Thus, by 1857, of the 10 railroads linking the Atlantic seaboard with the Mississippi River prior to the Civil War, five reached the river opposite Iowa: the CRI in 1854, CB&Q in March, IC in June, G&CU in December 1855, and the Milwaukee in April 1857. There, construction slowed in their extensions to the West by the necessity of building permanent structures across the river.

Crossing the Mississippi River—Ferries

Ferries and canoes provided the only means of crossing the river before railroads, meeting the needs of early explorers, travelers, and the occasional homesteader. But when migration reached the wagon-train era, regular ferries developed. The first ferries were licensed by Illinois, the first recipient being James White of Hancock County in 1833, to operate to Fort Madison. In that same year, 19 licenses were issued, 10 of which were for ferries crossing into Iowa. Half of these were granted to operators in the Dubuque mining area, and by the close of 1833, 15 ferries operated into Iowa, of which at least eight served Dubuque and Davenport.

Public ferries progressed from the flatboats and skiffs, with power provided by men manning sweeps, oars and poles. Clark's Ferry at Buffalo marked the opening of flatboat crossings in Iowa in 1833, and in 1836 Antoine LeClaire began operations at Davenport. Horse ferries followed in 1841, but the most important step was the introduction of steam power, shortening the crossing from several hours to regular trips of five to 15 minutes. The first steam ferry was operated by John Wilson in 1852 at Davenport.

On the Iowa side, jurisdiction over ferrying was first exercised directly through charters by the General Assembly. Boards of county commissioners were empowered to grant licenses for river points not provided by charter. Ferries, however, were not to be established within two miles of each other, and rates were fixed by county courts. Most were privately owned and operated. The demand was so brisk at the onset of territorial history that ferries were running

The Antoine LeClaire, a pioneer Rock Island locomotive, is said to be the first railroad engine ferried across the Mississippi into Iowa. Since the Rock Island was the first railroad to reach the Mississippi (1854), it was natural that the first bridge across the Father of Waters should bracket Davenport and Rock Island in 1856.

(Courtesy: Iowa State Printer)

from and to all major cities and towns along the river.[2] When the bridges were built, the once prosperous ferry business practically disappeared.

Bridging the Mississippi River

The topic of steam transportation was frequently discussed in eastern villages and towns as the railroads slowly crept across Illinois and Wisconsin. The interests of the people were crystallized through the laws of Iowa in 1850, "granting rights-of-way to a number of companies for construction." Many of the proposals proved to be dreams, as was John Plumbe's

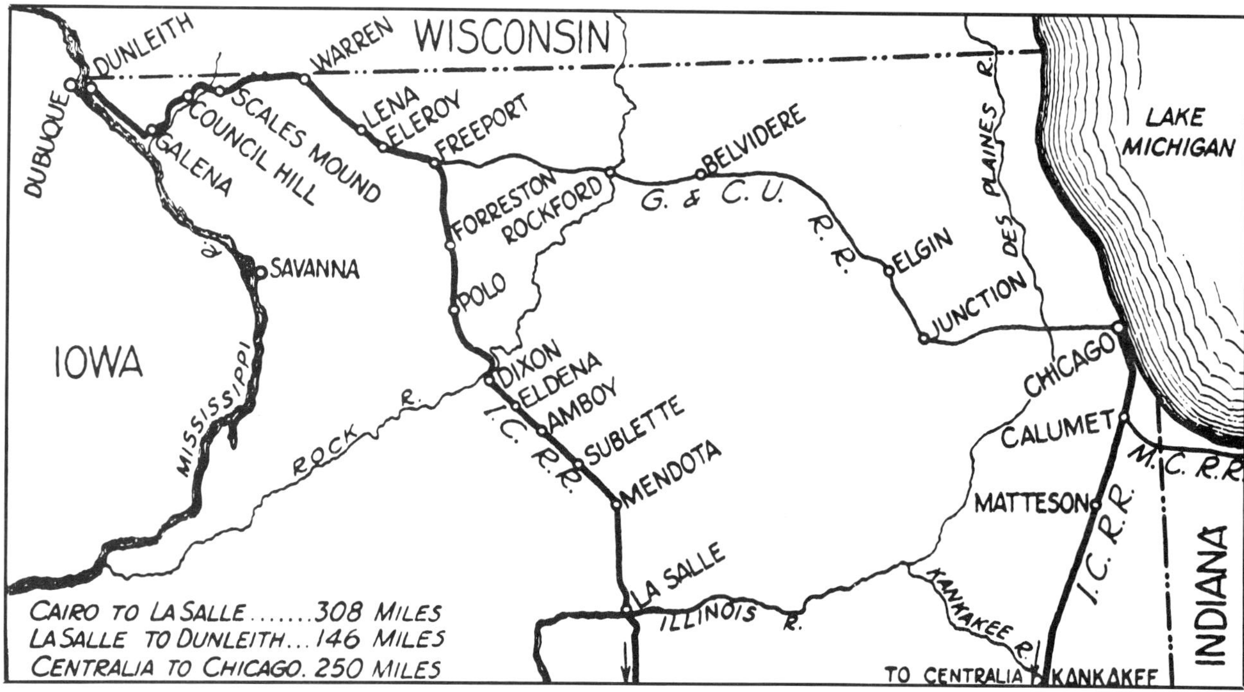

Figure 2-4
The Route of the Illinois Central
(Courtesy: State Historical Society of Iowa)

Figure 2-5
The Route of the Milwaukee & Mississippi
(Courtesy: State Historical Society of Iowa)

[2] William S. Johnson, "Crossing the Mississippi," *Palimpsest 1* (December 1920): pp. 173, 175-176.

transcontinental railroad, first proposed in 1833.[3] Sharp suggests that "they merited the description of the Philadelphia, Fort Wayne and Platte Valley Air Line Road; it was an airline—hot air. It so exhausted the corporation to write the whole name, no energy nor breath was left to build the road."[4] However, the determination to have railroads resulted in the incorporation of the Mississippi and Missouri Railroad (M&M) in 1853, one year before the CRI reached the river. The M&M was eventually an extension of the CRI and numbered among its organizers, Jervis, Sheffield and Farnam, of the MC and CRI roads.

To unite the two lines it was necessary to bridge the river, and the Railroad Bridge Company was incorporated in Illinois in 1853. It was authorized to build, maintain and use a railroad bridge over the Mississippi River across that portion of the river lying in the state at or near Rock Island. Farnam was president and chief engineer of construction. Bonds to finance the project were guaranteed by both railroads. The Iowa section was to be built under authority of the laws of Iowa. Antoine LeClaire deeded the land on the west side of the river, and the right-of-way was cleared on the Iowa side to the middle of the channel. Construction involved three segments: a span across the narrow part of the river from the east bank to the island; tracks across the island; and a long bridge with a draw span from the island to the Iowa shore. The middle of the channel running west of the island was the boundary between the two states.

Complications arose immediately. The federal government owned the island and steamboat interests brought pressures to prevent construction on federal land, arguing also that bridges hampered navigation which violated bridge authority. The case of the *United States v. Railroad Bridge Company et al* came before Judge John McClean in the U.S. Circuit Court in July 1855. An injunction against the bridge company sought by the Secretary of War was denied and the rights of the company upheld.[5] The bridge was completed in April 1856. A second complication arose in May of that year when the steamboat *Effie Afton* was wrecked against the piers. The boat caught fire and was destroyed, also destroying part of the bridge and putting it out of commission for four months. The owners sued the Bridge Company, hoping to recover damages by proving that the bridge was a menace to navigation. The case of *Heard et al v. Railroad Bridge Company* again came before Judge McLean in September 1857. Abraham Lincoln was a member of the defense team, and after a bitter trial, the Bridge Company gained a temporary victory through a hung jury.

The verdict was recognized by both sides as an uneasy truce. The struggle reached Congress, where a House committee concluded that the courts should make the final decision. Judge John M. Love of the U. S. Circuit Court of Southern Iowa ruled on a petition of James Ward, a St. Louis steamboat operator, that the bridge was "a common and public nuisance" and, further, that the piers and structure on the Iowa side should be removed. The Company appealed to the U.S. Supreme Court, which in 1862 reversed the lower court and allowed the bridge to remain.[6] The CRI not only built the first bridge across the river and won the right to keep it but also opened the way for other railroads to cross the river with legal approval. From this time and for many years afterward, steamboats played a subordinate role to the railroads.

Railroads in Iowa

The Initial Phase

The development of Chicago as a center of inland commerce practically guaranteed that Iowa would be on the rail routes to the Pacific, so attention centered on potential routes across the state. The two that seemed to offer the most promise were the M&M and Lyons and Central railroads. The first General Assembly had provided for incorporation of "railroads and other works of internal improvement" in 1846. An extra session in the following year

[3] Jack T. Johnson, "Plumbe's Railroad to the Moon," *Palimpsest 58* (March 1938): pp. 89-97; John King, "John Plumbe, Originator of the Pacific Railroad," *Annals of Iowa 6* (January 1904): pp. 289-296.

[4] Mildred J. Sharp, "The M&M Railroad," *Palimpsest 3* (January 1922): pp. 1-2.

[5] United States v. Railroad Bridge Company, Fed. Case No. 16114 (6 McClean) 517 (1855).

[6] The Mississippi and Missouri Railroad Co. v. Ward, 67 U.S. (2 Black) 485 (1862). For a complete discussion of the case, see John W. Starr Jr., *Lincoln and the Railroads,* New York: Dodd, Meads & Co., 1927, pp. 90-117. The Court supported the arguments of Lincoln who stated: "But there is travel from east to west whose demands are not less important than the river... This current of travel has its rights as well as that of north and south... the statement of its business is in evidence from September 8, 1856 to August 8, 1857; 12,586 freight cars and 74,179 passengers passed over the bridge... This shows that the bridge must be treated with respect in this Court and is not to be kicked around with contempt." Of interest was the position of the two leaders of the warring states in the Civil War, involved in this controversy. Jefferson Davis was Secretary of War at the time of the initial protest of the steamboat owners, and Abraham Lincoln was one of the lawyers defending the railroad.

requested of Congress "a grant of land to aid in the construction of a Rail Road from Davenport by way of Iowa City, Monroe City, Raccoon Forks to some point near Council Bluffs on the Missouri River in this state."[7] However, this request as well as others went unheeded for eight years.

The M&M planned to build in three directions across Iowa. The main line would run west from Davenport through Iowa City to Fort Des Moines and continue to Council Bluffs, a distance of 311 miles at an estimated cost of $9 million. A second line would run from Wilton Junction through Muscatine, thence southwest through Oskaloosa to the Missouri state line or Missouri River or both. A third was to be built from Muscatine to Cedar Rapids and north to the Minnesota border. Peter Dey and Grenville Dodge had surveyed the projected main line in 1853 and 1854. Antoine LeClaire turned the first shovelful of dirt at Davenport in September 1853, but actual work did not begin until July 1855. The road entered Iowa City on December 31, 1856, encouraged by a bonus of $50,000 and stock subscriptions if they reached the city by that date.

Meanwhile, other railroads were being organized and planned. The Iowa Central Air Line (ICAL), also known as the Lyons and Iowa Central, organized in 1853, was to run from Lyons, near Clinton, to Tipton, Iowa City and on to Council Bluffs. However, the road was never built beyond the grading stage because of misappropriation of funds by H.P. Adams, principal backer and a director, and later found to be a fugitive from justice. The financial collapse in 1854 left families of construction workers stranded in Lyons, paid off in groceries, dry goods and miscellaneous articles instead of money. Thereafter, the road was known as the "Calico Road." Backed by eastern capitalists, among whom was Oakes Ames, the Chicago, Iowa and Nebraska (CI&N) was organized and began construction at Clinton in 1856. It reached Cedar Rapids in 1859, the farthest west of any railroads built to that time.

To the north, the germ planted by John Plumbe in 1833 culminated in the 1850s, the decade of Dubuque's "railroad fever." George W. Jones and Augustus C. Dodge, Iowa's first senators, were instrumental in getting the IC extension from Galena to Dunleith (East Dubuque) in 1851. Once that line was assured, Jones, Platt Smith, General C.H. Booth, Jessie Farley, Edward Slossan and Judge John J. Dyer formed the Dubuque and Pacific (D&P) in 1853. At the time of organization, not one mile of railroad had been built in Iowa, and in the 29 counties eventually traversed by the IC, there were fewer than 5,000 families, concentrated primarily in Dubuque and Linn Counties.

Financial problems delayed construction until October 1855, and it was not until May 1857, that trains ran to Dyersville, making the trip of 79 miles in three hours. The road was extended to Earlville, eight miles west, where construction halted because of poor credit, unfavorable economic conditions and the lack of a western terminus. Building was resumed in the summer of 1859 under John Edgar Thompson, builder of the Pennsylvania Railroad, and reached Independence in December. By March 1860, the line moved to the western border of Buchanan County where a station was named Jesup, after Morris K. Jesup, a financial backer and later president of the road. He held many of the bonds which were in default, forced the railroad into receivership, and reorganized it as the Dubuque and Sioux City (D&SC) in 1860.

Forty-six men—lawyers, businessmen and public officials—organized the Burlington and Missouri River Railroad (B&MR) in January 1851, some three years before the CB&Q arrived at the Mississippi. William Coolbaugh, a merchant, was elected president, and James W. Grimes, banker and soon to be Governor of Iowa, worked for a land grant. Capital was raised through bond issues voted by the people of Des Moines, Jefferson and Wapello counties, where 85 percent of the population was concentrated. But the bond issues did not provide the necessary funds, so the founders turned to the "Boston Group" led by John M. Forbes, who had been involved in the financing of the MC and CB&Q in Illinois.

In August 1856, the track came into Mt. Pleasant via Danville and New London, two years after it began. Another year passed before the five miles were built to Rome on the Skunk River, where construction stalled. In 1857, Edward Baker of Massachusetts was elected president, indicating the growing eastern control. Forbes also placed Charles Russell Lowell, a 23-year-old nephew of James Russell Lowell, as assistant treasurer to protect his interests.

[7] 1847 Laws of Iowa, Chapter 81; 1848 Laws of Iowa, Extra Session, Joint Resolution 5.

Early Wood Burning Locomotive
(Courtesy: State Historical Society of Iowa)

Capital was relatively scarce during these early years. Iowa granted rights for incorporation and of eminent domain, but the Constitution prohibited giving or lending state credits to individuals, associations or corporations, and that prohibition was continued in 1857. Borrowing through bond issues for construction was allowed but the interest rate was not to exceed 10 percent. European and eastern financiers provided funds which, together with local aid, formed the financial base. Municipalities, counties and individuals made loans, purchased and guaranteed railroad bonds, and made outright contributions of cash, land, materials and labor. Some local governments also exempted railroads from taxes. Locklin states that "it is impossible to determine what proportion of such aid consisted of donations by county and municipal governments and what proportions consisted of donations by private individuals, corporations or associations."[8] But the result was creation of public and private debt, since the necessary finances were essentially borrowed and the load of indebtedness sometimes exceeded the assessed value of all taxable property in the political subdivision. Financial distress was a principal reason for pressures on Congress for land grants to complete the railroad systems.

The Land Grants

The land grant to the IC was typical of those made later, with some variations. Whereas the Illinois railroad received a right-of-way 200 feet wide and six sections of land for each mile of road, others received 10 to 40 sections per mile and a right-of-way of 400 feet. In 1856, congressmen Augustus Hall of Iowa and Henry Bennett of New York introduced bills requesting grants for the railroads, approved on May 15, and Iowa received grants for construction of four railroads: the M&M, ICAL, D&P and B&MR. On July 14, 1856, the General Assembly accepted the grants with the following terms, conditions and restrictions as contained in the act:

[8] Phillip Locklin, *Economics of Transportation,* 7th ed., Homewood, Ill.:Richard D. Irwin Inc., p. 127. See also Hobert C. Carr, *Early History of Iowa Railroads,* New York: Arno Press, 1981, pp. 65-82.

1. The railroads were required to build and equip 75 miles within three years and 30 miles in addition for each year thereafter for a period of five years. If the railroad failed in any particular, the state could resume the lands unearned and regrant them to another company.
2. The gauge was fixed at four feet, eight and one-half inches.[9]
3. The rights of any claimant or occupant of any of the lands granted were protected and the company was required under certain conditions to deed the land to claimants.
4. Companies were required to file written acceptance of the act and were subject to such rules and regulations as may from time to time be enacted by the General Assembly of Iowa, and to make annual reports to the Secretary of State.

The federal grants were made to states, which could grant, revoke, resume or transfer the lands. Railroads could use the lands not necessary for construction as a source of funds by either selling or mortgaging them. Over three and one-half million acres were disposed of, and when sold averaged approximately seven to eight dollars per acre. It was claimed that through the grants the entire cost of construction might be recovered, that proceeds would eventually pay for bonds issued and make stockholders owners of unencumbered properties. The Civil War temporarily suspended the activity, but it was vigorously pursued at its conclusion. The press, public and politicians in both state and federal legislatures promoted the grants as their patriotic duty. Grants were expected to provide increased economic opportunities for settlers who migrated to the new regions to obtain farms, for others who aimed at becoming founders of new towns, and also for profits to investors. Sales of land by the "Iowa Roads" were over $6.6 million of federal granted lands and $26.2 million of state granted lands by 1880. Generally, the sales did not cover the total or, in some instances, the interest on the cost of construction. But acceptance of the grants by railroads carried certain obligations. For example, the federal government required land grant railroads to carry mail, troops and government property at reduced rates. Mail was moved at 80 percent and troops and property at approximately 50 percent of published tariffs.

It was estimated that the the value of the 131 million acres of federal lands granted from 1851 to 1871 was approximately $130 million, based upon prices received from the sale of federal public lands during the period. Additionally, it was estimated that railroads received 48.8 million acres from the states. The total of all land grant deductions, including voluntary equalization of rates by competing railroads from 1851 to 1943, was estimated at $580 million. Iowa received 3.7 million acres, roughly 13.1 percent of the state's area, although some history texts indicated that about 90 percent of the state's lands had been given away (Table 2-1).

The War and Postwar Period

By 1860, there were 655 miles of railroads built in Iowa (Fig. 2-6). Westward movement was slowed by the Panic of 1857 and political issues between North and South. In 1862, the Pacific Railroad Act was signed by President Lincoln, chartering the Union Pacific (UP) and setting the conditions for building the transcontinental line between Omaha and Sacramento. The railroad which reached Omaha would reap rich rewards offered by the connection with the UP, and as soon as conditions permitted, the race across the state was accelerated. The strategic location of Iowa as a bridge state was solidified in railroad construction to either coast and was equally important in later years in the evolution of the national highway programs.

[9] The standard gauge was determined by British locomotives imported into the United States. The wheel span corresponded to the width of the early English road cart, measured from inside to inside rim. In 1860, there were seven widths of gauge in the nation, ranging from four feet, eight inches to six feet. However, because of agitation for cheaper and more economical roads, 14 narrow gauge railroads were built in Iowa, independent of the major systems and of relatively short distances. The first line to be abandoned was the 12-mile wooden track narrow gauge line built from Loscomb through Conrad to Beaman. Descriptions of narrow gauge railroads and those built in Iowa are found in Ben Hur Wilson, "The Matter of Gauge," and "Iowa and the Narrow Gauge," *Palimpsest 13* (April 1932): pp. 133-165.

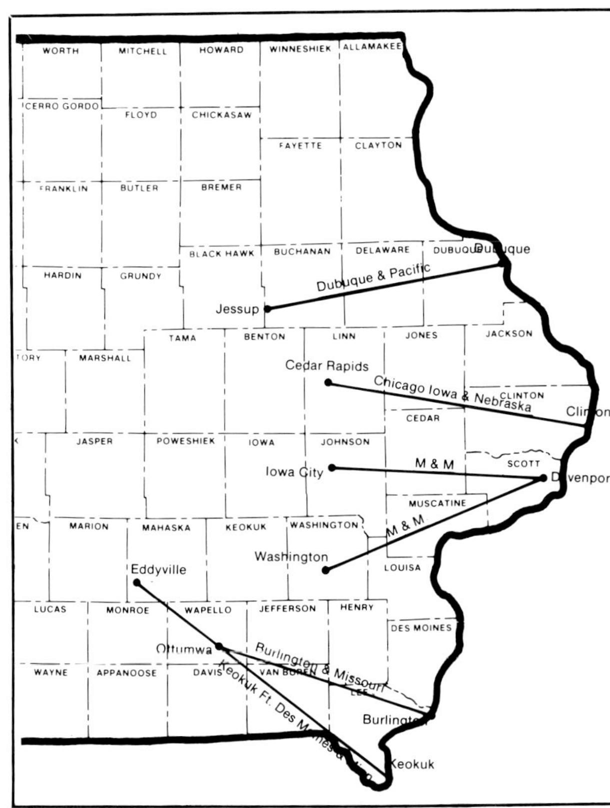

Figure 2-6
Iowa Railroads 1860
(Map by author)

The Chicago and North Western

A new road, the Cedar Rapids and Missouri River (CR&MR), was incorporated in 1859 and given the land grant of the defunct ICAL. Improved economic conditions and the infusion of eastern capital plus local backers such as John F. Ely and John Weare of Cedar Rapids and G. M. Woodberg of Marshalltown furnished the impetus for further construction. It was at this time that John I. Blair of New Jersey became interested in the possibilities of a prosperous railroad west of Cedar Rapids. Donovan describes him as one who "built railroads faster and more extensively in the state than anyone else—before or since," and further "as a human dynamo let loose in railway-mad Iowa."[10]

After Blair became involved in the management in 1861, the railroad began to move. By 1866, it reached Denison, built through Marshalltown (1863), Nevada (1864) and Boone (1865). From Denison the line ran down the valley of the Boyer River and into Council Bluffs in January 1867. Within the period required to complete the Cedar Rapids-Marshalltown segment, both the CI&N and CR&MR railroads were leased to the G&CU, later incorporated into the CNW system.

Table 2-1
Acres Granted and Values of Lands Realized by Iowa Railroads

Railroad	Acres	Values
Milwaukee	372,656[1]	$ 1,601,730[1]
Rock Island	550,193	4,984,341
Burlington	385,424	3,870,890
Des Moines & Fort Dodge	42,636	117,972
Iowa Falls & Sioux City	640,256	3,676,902
Sioux City & St. Paul	320,002	742,148
Cedar Rapids & Missouri River	956,597	6,017,259
Dubuque & Sioux City	444,161	No Report
Sioux City & Pacific	39,876	299,000
Total	3,751,801	$21,310,232

Summarized from the Reports of the Iowa Railroad Commission, 1874, 1878, and Reports of Land Commissioners of Iowa Railway Land Company, et al, 1874. Values estimated on average prices received for the land. Figures were revised in 1901 to 4,802,878 acres and $26,373,518 for values received.

[1] Fractions and cents omitted.

[10] Frank P. Donovan, "The North Western in Iowa," *Palimpsest 43* (December 1962): pp. 549-551.

The Rock Island

While Blair was building across Iowa, his competitors were not idle. The M&M built to Marengo in 1862 and was in Kellogg by 1864. The road was heavily in debt with foreclosure a probability, and to protect its land grant, a new company, the Chicago, Rock Island & Pacific (CRI&P), was formed in Iowa and purchased the M&M in July 1866. It was authorized to build from Kellogg to Des Moines, arriving there in 1867. With clear title, including land grants, the Illinois and Iowa lines were consolidated. The charter called for construction between Des Moines and Council Bluffs, completed on May 11, 1869, the day after the UP-Central Pacific tracks were joined at Promontory Point, Utah. The CNW had a monopoly into Council Bluffs for two and one-half years before the CRI&P arrived and had been hauling much of the material used for building the UP.

The original plan of the M&M had been to build in three directions in the state. While the Council Bluffs line was being constructed, the southwest segment was extended beyond Muscatine to Washington in 1858. It continued southwesterly to Lineville through Fairfield, crossing the Missouri border, thence to Stallings Junction opposite Leavenworth, a military post, with operations commencing in 1871. In the enthusiasm to build west and southwest, the third division to Cedar Rapids was ignored. But other interests were planning a north-south route through the city. Between 1865 and 1867 two railroads, the Cedar Rapids and St. Paul (CR&STP) and the Cedar Rapids and Minnesota (CR&M), were organized and merged into the Burlington, Cedar Rapids and Minnesota (BCR&M) in 1868. Known as "Judge Greene's Railroad," it was unique in that it was organized by Iowans and headquartered in the state. Judge George Greene of Cedar Rapids was president; Charles Mason of Burlington, vice-president; and J. D. Cameron of Burlington, chief engineer. The road was built south to cross the main line of the CRI&P at West Liberty and the Muscatine line at Columbus Junction. To the north, it ran through Cedar Falls to Plymouth Junction, connecting with the Milwaukee to St. Paul, with segments to Independence, Oelwein and Postville. A feeder line was built from Vinton to Traer by 1873. With funds raised in the East, the railroad had built 368 miles by 1874.

The BCR&M suffered financial reverses after the Panic of 1873, and the Blair interests reorganized it as the Burlington, Cedar Rapids and Northern (BCR&N). Affiliated with the BCR&N was the Cedar Falls, Iowa Falls and Northwestern, incorporated in 1880, which built the bulk of new construction in the 1880s. It was absorbed by the parent company in 1902, which was purchased by the CRI&P in 1903. The main line ran from Burlington through Cedar Rapids and Waterloo into Albert Lea, Minnesota, and another line ran through Emmetsburg and Sibley to Watertown, South Dakota. In 1903, the CRI&P had 1,310 miles of track in operation in three states.

The CRI&P was not the first railroad to enter Des Moines. That honor or glory belonged to the Des Moines Valley, Keokuk and Des Moines Railroad. It was first organized as the Keokuk, Fort Des Moines and Minnesota Railroad in 1853, routed through Bentonsport, Ottumwa and Eddyville, where construction halted because of the war. In 1864 the name was changed to the Des Moines Valley Railroad, reaching that city in 1866.[11] Considered a secondary road, it was important to the development of Des Moines, to which considerable traffic moved from Keokuk by land and water. Des Moines had a growing population and wanted the state capital moved from Iowa City. Polk and Lee counties made an agreement whereby financial support would be given the railroad in exchange for votes for adoption of the Constitution of 1857 which transferred the capital to Des Moines. Lee county voters swung the election. Keokuk saw the railroad started and Des Moines became the capital.

With finances apparently exhausted, construction north of Des Moines stopped, to the disappointment of Fort Dodge, whose residents promised land and tax assistance. When the line was finally built, instead of taking the direct route up the Des Moines River Valley, it ran circuitously through Perry, Grand Junction, Gowrie and Tura, reaching Fort Dodge in 1870. In 1873 the road was declared bankrupt. The northern section was sold to Colonel C. H. Perry and was known as the Fort Dodge and Des Moines Railway. The southern section was purchased by John E. Henry of New York and became the Keokuk and Des Moines Railroad, serving as a direct line to Keokuk with connections to St. Louis. It was integrated into the CRI&P system in 1878.

[11] This was the railroad that received the land grants of the Des Moines River Navigation Company.

The Burlington

The CB&Q was in Ottumwa by 1859, in time to meet the requirements of the land grant. Charles Elliot Perkins, 18 years of age, was hired to assist Lowell, whose duties of managing the treasury and land department had become too heavy for one person. Twenty-two years later, he would be president and continue his close association with the "Boston Group" to whom he turned for capital from time to time. The two lines to the north—the CRI&P and CNW—had built their bridges across the Mississippi River, but the CB&Q still relied on ferries. Their bridge, built in 1868, enabled the road to redouble its efforts to reach the Missouri River.

The energy and enthusiasm of James Joy and Charles Perkins, spurred on by new capital, pushed the road to Chariton and Woodburn by the end of 1867. Trains ran into Osceola in January 1868 and by November the tracks had reached Red Oak. Crews started east from East Plattsburg and met the westbound track at Hastings in November 1869, without formal ceremony. To compete for the business of the Omaha gateway, regular service was started over the St. Joseph and Council Bluffs (StJ&CB) Railway from Pacific Junction in January 1870. The CB&Q was the third railroad to reach Council Bluffs and was the only federal land grant road that never filed for bankruptcy during construction. It was also one of the very few railroads that had never been in receivership.

The Illinois Central

Sioux City was the objective of the D&SC Railroad, which meant building 250 miles west of Jesup. Sioux City was expected to rival St. Joseph, Missouri and Omaha as gateways to the west—a possibility that excited and stimulated other interests. Within a short time at least six railroads were chartered to build to that city.[12] Construction from Jesup reached Cedar Falls in 1861, and with exception of a feeder line to Waverly, the war stopped further building. Five years later, the main line was at Iowa Falls, with regular service by June 1866. Both the western and northern lines out of Cedar Falls were moving into virgin territory and trains from Dubuque brought settlers from eastern and midwestern states and from Scandinavia, Ireland, Scotland and England. These settlers purchased land at prices from $2.50 to $10 per acre.

Illinois Central Locomotive - 4-4-0
Design in 1860s
(Courtesy: State Historical Society of Iowa)

[12] Poor's *Manual of Railroads, 1871-1872.* The six were the Iowa Falls & Sioux City, St. Paul & Sioux City, Sioux City & Columbus, Sioux City & Pacific, Sioux City & St. Paul, and the McGregor & Sioux City Railroads.

It was at this point that the IC purchased the properties, fearful that rival companies would move in and deprive the company of its western connection and eliminate it from northwest Iowa. Platt Smith, vice president of the D&P, was a leader in the leasing arrangements. He organized a subsidiary, the Iowa Falls and Sioux City Railroad, in 1867, to build the 167 miles between the two cities. Blair, who had built the CNW, was named to head the new company which acquired the franchise, rights-of-way and land grants to Sioux City. The line moved westward to Fort Dodge in 1869. While continuing westward, another crew moved the rails east and met at the "Sag" (milepost 431.5), some three miles west of Storm Lake in January 1870. Blair and his men had built more miles in two years than had any one else in the history of east-west railroad construction in Iowa.[13] During the extension of the main line, tracks on the Waverly branch were built to Charles City in 1868, to St. Ansgar in 1869, and the gap to the Minnesota border was closed by 1870. The final link joining Sioux City with the UP was built by the Sioux City and Pacific Railroad along the east bank of the Missouri River to Missouri Valley Junction on the CNW, which eventually incorporated the road into its system. By the close of 1870, the IC operated 1,107 miles of railroad: 705 in Illinois and 402 in Iowa.

The Milwaukee

The Milwaukee was the fifth main line built across the state. Its history began with the completion of the MIL&M into Prairie du Chien in 1857. McGregor, on the opposite side of the river, like other towns, was filled with excitement for railroads and planned them in all directions, including a horse-powered line to Fort Atkinson. Actually, the Milwaukee built two lines across Iowa. At the close of the war, the McGregor Western (MCGW), incorporated in 1863, reached Monona. The railroad was promoted by William B. Ogden of the CNW, Judge Greene of Cedar Rapids, and William Larrabee of Clermont, later Governor and a leading proponent of regulation. In 1866 it was completed to Cresco and the following year into Owatonna, Minnesota, thence to the Twin Cities, already connected by the Milwaukee and St. Paul to the city of Milwaukee. The MCGW and MIL&M were purchased by the Milwaukee and St. Paul which in turn became the Chicago, Milwaukee and St. Paul (CM&StP) Railway in 1874, the same year that John Lawler completed the pontoon bridge across the Mississippi River.

The McGregor and Sioux City Railroad was incorporated in 1868 to resume construction across northern Iowa and to get the land grant. By 1869 it had built the 64 miles from Calmar to Nora Springs. Renamed the McGregor and Missouri River Railway, it reached Algona in 1870, the point to which the land grant applied, but progress was halted by the Panic of 1873. The grant expired in 1875 since the railroad had not met the mileage requirements. The CM&StP, which had absorbed the McGregor and Missouri, got the grant transferred, and by 1878 the segment from Algona to Hull, through Sheldon, was in operation.

The second line across the state was started by the Sabula Valley and Dakota Railroad, organized in 1870. The road was built with assistance of the Western Union Railroad (no relation to the telegraph company), controlled by the CM&StP which had reached Savanna, Illinois, opposite Sabula. Twenty miles were built in 1870 and in less than two years, the rails were laid to Marion. The Sabula was purchased by the CM&StP, enabling through service from Cedar Rapids to Milwaukee. But the usual financial problems halted westward movement for the next decade. When building resumed, the 260 mile line through Tama, Perry, and Coon Rapids to Council Bluffs was built in one year.

The remaining link in the system in Iowa was known as the River Road from Clinton through Dubuque to the Minnesota border. Platt Smith was a leading promoter of the Dubuque and McGregor Railroad, organized in 1868. The name was changed to the Dubuque and Minnesota in 1869 and to the Chicago, Dubuque and Minnesota in 1871. Crews started

[13] Blair was not only well known for his promotional and managerial ability but also for naming towns along the lines he built. Among those were Aurelia and Marcus in Cherokee County, named for his daughter and son. Ames was named for Oakes Ames, friend and backer. Belle Plaine was named for his granddaughter, Ogden for the first president of the CNW. Remsen, in Plymouth County was named for a friend in Sioux City. LeMars in the same county was named during an excursion party when the ladies were given an opportunity to name a new settlement. By using the first initials of their Christian names, the result was "Selmar or LeMars," the latter chosen by majority vote. Towns were also named on the two roads on which Blair built the highest mileage. They are Blairsburg on the IC in Hamilton County, and Blairstown on the CNW in Benton County. Towns named for railroad officials, directors, employees, relatives or persons who donated land number 119 of the 835 listed by Harold, Ann, and Linda Joe Dilts in *From Ackley to Zwingle,* Ames: Carter Press, 1975. See also Donovan, "The North Western in Iowa," *Palimpsest 43* (December 1962): p. 579, and "The Illinois Central in Iowa," *Palimpsest 43* (June 1962): pp. 282-283.

construction north from Dubuque and an affiliate, the Dubuque, Bellevue and Mississippi Railway built south, reaching Sabula Junction in 1871. From there, using the tracks of the CNW and other roads, it operated into Clinton (Fig. 2-7). Dubuque served as headquarters of the two roads, was the location of the repair shops, and later became the operating center of the "Dubuque Division" of the CM&StP. The Panic of 1873 put the River Road into receivership, and the roads were combined in 1878. The CM&StP took title in 1880.

The North-South Lines

East-west construction did not dim the enthusiasm of Iowans for railroads to connect major cities to the north and south of the state. Josiah B. Grinnell headed a company in pre-Civil War days to initiate such a project, but it was dropped because of economic conditions and the war. In 1865 the Iowa Central was organized with headquarters at Oskaloosa, to be built from the terminus of the North Missouri (NM) road on the southern border and connect at Cedar Falls with the Cedar Falls and Minnesota Railroad (Fig. 2-8). Two of the early promoters were David Morgan of New Sharon, first president, and Peter Melandy of Cedar Rapids.

Local and regional interests supported the railroad. Oskaloosa and Montezuma had been bypassed by the east-west trunk lines and wanted railroad service. Others urged construction as a means of competing with these roads since the line would cross each one and hopefully provide additional gateways for traffic. But perhaps more important was the fact that the road would be an integral part of "the grandest

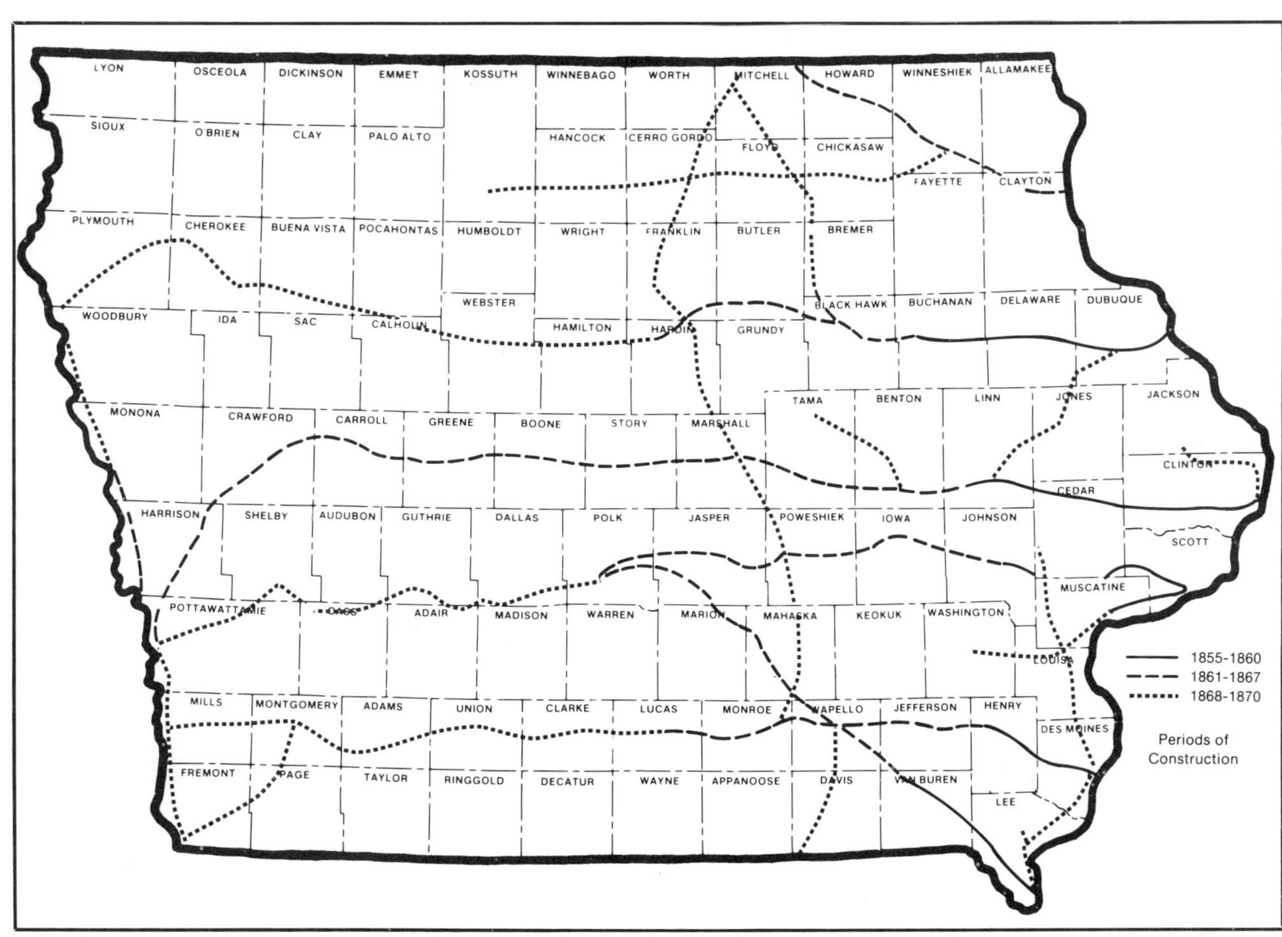

Figure 2-7
Railroad Construction in Iowa to 1870
(Reprinted by permission of William Whitehill from *The Ups and Downs of Iowa's Railroads.*)

railroad project of the age"—an interregional railroad which would connect St. Louis with St. Paul.[14] St. Louis was especially interested because of loss of river traffic and saw the Iowa Central as an answer to recapturing some of the business.

After grading between Albia and Oskaloosa, between Cedar Falls and Toledo, and in the vicinity of Tama, the "grandest project" was terminated when finances became exhausted. The dream of a north-south line seemed to be doomed, but such was not to be the case, for the main line of the Minnesota and St.Louis (M&StL) was built through the middle of the state. The railroad traced its ancestry in Iowa to the Eldora Railroad and Coal Company, formed after discovery of coal at Eldora. It was organized in 1866 to build 16 miles north to Ackley where it would connect with the main line of the IC. The company was taken over by the Iowa River Railway in 1868 to build the 28 miles south of Eldora to connect with the main line of the CNW at Marshalltown. In turn, the Iowa River became the Central Railroad of Iowa before the completion of the Marshalltown line in 1869, the same year that witnessed the death warrant of the Iowa Central.

The route between Mason City and Albia was completed in 1872, but for the next 30 years the road was plagued with financial problems, reorganizations and name changes. During the reorganization of the mid-1870s, the road emerged as the Central Iowa Railway in 1879. It built the road across the state as part of the line linking St.Louis and St. Paul and was merged with the M&StL in 1912, which also purchased the Fort Dodge and Des Moines in 1915.

The NM planned to build to Ottumwa and Cedar Rapids to connect with the lines serving these cities. For this purpose, the St. Louis and Cedar Rapids Railroad was organized in 1865 to extend the line from Coatsville, Missouri, to Cedar Rapids. J. P. Farley of Dubuque County and George Gillespie, Wapello County, were principal backers. H. C. Angel of Cedar Rapids was president, succeeded by H. H. Trimble of Bloomfield. By December 1866 the road reached Appanoose County, where the town of Moulton was established, and by 1870 the tracks were in Ottumwa. The new line was leased by the NM and both roads were soon in financial trouble. The Iowa road was reorganized as the St. Louis, Ottumwa and Cedar Rapids in 1875 and the NM became the St. Louis, Kansas City and Northern Railway (StLKC&N) which continued to lease the Iowa road.

But their interests shifted to Des Moines, abandoning the plan to build to Cedar Rapids.

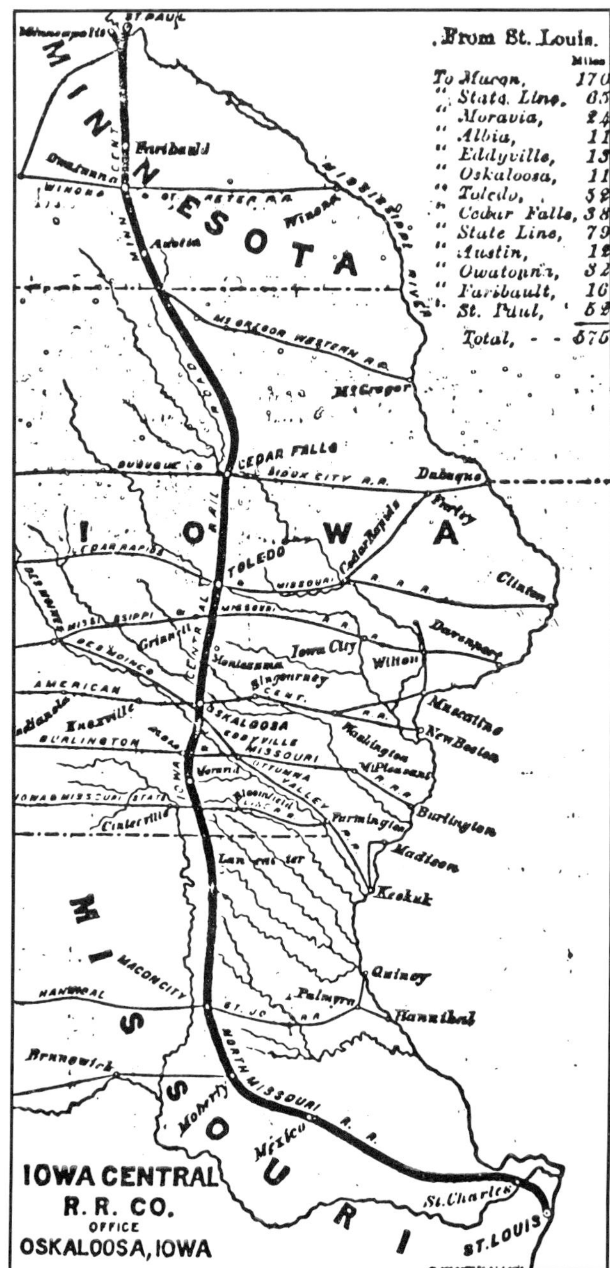

Figure 2-8
The proposed route of the Iowa Central Railroad.
(Courtesy: State Historical Society of Iowa)

[14] Donald L. Hofsommer, "The Grandest Railroad Project of the Age," *Annals of Iowa 44* (fall 1977): p. 120.

At this stage, Jay Gould, the notorious financier, entered the picture. He controlled the StLKC&N and united it with other roads to form the Wabash, St. Louis and Pacific (Wabash) Railway.[15] Gould wanted Des Moines in his system and Des Moines responded by incorporating the Des Moines and St. Louis Railroad in 1881 to build to Albia, 68 miles away. In 1882 the first passenger train arrived in Des Moines from St. Louis. The Des Moines Company was headed by James Clarkson, former editor of the *Iowa State Register* and then postmaster; John S. Runnels, vice president; Frederick M. Hubbell, secretary; and Jefferson S. Polk, treasurer. Both Hubbell and Polk were active in promoting narrow-gauge lines radiating from the city. The railroad, from the time of completion, was leased to Gould. The outlet from Des Moines was built over a patchwork of short lines connected to the Wabash properties.

The Wabash in Des Moines also included the Des Moines Union Railway, a terminal facility with 42 miles of industrial and terminal tracks, jointly administered by it and the CM&StP. The Union was incorporated in 1864, promoted by Hubbell, Polk and Grenville Dodge. It was part of a small "railroad empire" created by Hubbell which included the narrow-gauge lines from Des Moines to Boone and Panora. Hubbel also assisted in building the three-foot gauge line to Ames and Jewell, later the Des Moines branch of the CNW. In 1902 Hubbell organized the Des Moines Terminal Company, consisting of 10 miles of track and operated by the Union. Charges for cars interchanged with the Union resulted in a long period of litigation which was decided by the Iowa Supreme Court in 1932.

Gould wanted to get to Omaha for a share of the transcontinental traffic. The competition of the lines built across the state was not conducive to the construction of another direct road, so the alternative was to gain control of secondary lines and extend them to meet his goals. Before 1869 a road had connected St. Louis to Kansas City, later incorporated into the Wabash system, but it was not until he gained control of the Council Bluffs and St. Louis Railway that the route was cleared to Omaha. It had been built from Council Bluffs to the Missouri border and Gould operated the 143 mile road as the "Omaha Division" of the Wabash. He controlled the UP through heavy investments and was in an excellent position to bargain for traffic through the advantage of having a road to cities east of Chicago.

Following the same patterns, Gould picked up the 142 mile Missouri, Iowa and Nebraska Railway, serving Keokuk, Centerville, Corydon, Humeston and Van Wert. From Shenandoah, it was only 95 miles to Council Bluffs, and by extending the road, he would have a shorter line into Chicago. But Gould's plans were upset by the CB&Q which considered southern Iowa as its exclusive territory. When he attempted to build the line, he was threatened by the CB&Q with possible construction into Wabash territory. The outcome was a joint ownership of the Humeston and Shenandoah Railroad, completed in 1882. The Wabash went into receivership in 1884, and the narrow-gauge lines leased or owned around Des Moines were later purchased by the CM&StP.

Other Railroads

The Chicago Great Western (CGW) Railroad was known as "Stickney's Road." He founded, built and headed the 1,500-mile railroad in Iowa, Minnesota, Illinois, Missouri and to a limited extent, in Kansas and Nebraska. Acquiring the charter of the Minnesota and North Western (M&NW), he built from St. Paul to Manly Junction in Worth County in 1885. In 1886 a stem was built from Mayfield, Minnesota to Dubuque and construction continued across Illinois to Chicago. To avoid possible confusion with the name M&NW, the Chicago, St.Paul and Kansas City (CStP&KC) was incorporated in Iowa in 1886, and purchased the Wisconsin, Iowa and Nebraska Railway which had built from Waterloo to Des Moines with a branch from Cedar Falls Junction to Cedar Falls. The CStP&KC purchased all of the properties of the M&NW in 1887.

The Stickney road then moved toward Kansas City, closed the gap between Waterloo and Oelwein in 1887, and built from Des Moines to St. Joseph, Missouri, by the end of 1888. Through leases and trackage rights over other roads, it ran into Kansas City, thus serving all of the cities in its name. Over half of the mileage was in Iowa. Its history can be traced to the Iowa Pacific in 1870 which had graded

[15] Jay Gould, together with Jim Fisk and Daniel Drew fought Commodore Vanderbilt in the Erie-New York Central War in the late 1860s. He bought into the UP during the Panic of 1873 and by 1874 was made a director and virtually controlled the railroad. Stewart H. Holbrook, *The Age of the Moguls,* New York: Doubleday & Co., 1954, pp. 30-43, 97-100.

from Fayette Junction in Fayette County west through Sumner, Waverly and Hampton to Belmond in Wright County. Another section went from Belmond to Fort Dodge. Tracks were laid from Sumner to Hampton in the late 1880s. A line had been built from Mason City to Fort Dodge by the railroad of the same name, controlled by Stickney, in 1886. Building the 133 miles from Fort Dodge to Council Bluffs was completed in 1901, including a bridge over the Des Moines River at Fort Dodge. The 2,588-foot structure was considered to be the second largest bridge in Iowa. From Council Bluffs the CGW had trackage rights into Omaha. To complete the "Maple Leaf" system, the Hampton-Clarion gap was closed in 1902 and the Waverly-Oelwein segment in 1904. At the turn of the century, the repair shops, later supervised by Walter P. Chrysler, were moved from South Park, Minnesota to Oelwein, which was to be the key strategic location on the system. When the CStP&KC became insolvent, it was reorganized in 1892 as the CGW (Fig. 2-9).

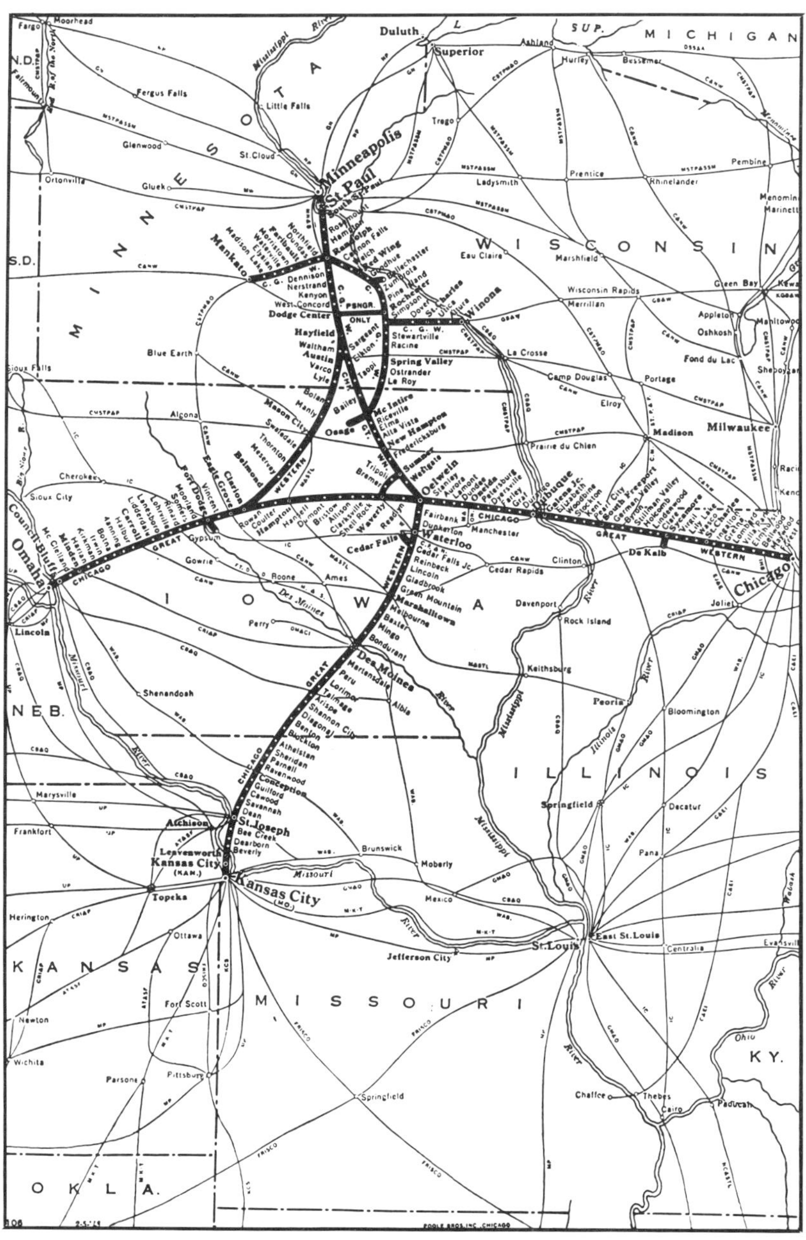

Figure 2-9
Route of the Chicago, Great Western
(Courtesy: State Historical Society of Iowa)

Although Sioux City in the 1880s was well supplied with railroads that ran in all directions, commercial interests and meat packers wanted an independent railroad built to the north to connect with the transcontinental lines serving the Pacific Northwest. Such a line, it was envisioned, would allow a direct route to Duluth for export, bypassing Chicago, and would provide for expanded shipments of grain and livestock. This was the incentive for organizing the Sioux City and Northern (SC&N) in 1887, projected east to Duluth and north to Minot, North Dakota. Actually, the most feasible connection for the 96-mile line was at Garretson, South Dakota, on the Wilmar and Sioux Falls (W&SF) Railway, a James Hill road, and was opened in 1890. A 30-year contract was signed with the W&SF road, an arrangement which proved profitable for both railroads. But the prosperity was interrupted by the Panic of 1893 which depressed the economic structure of the city. When the SC&N went bankrupt, it was integrated into the W&SF, purchased by the Great Northern (GN) in 1907. The Sioux City line became the southernmost leg of the GN system.

When President Lincoln signed the Pacific Railroad Act of 1862, the eastern terminus was not clearly specified, other than the road was to be built westward from the Missouri River. After consultation with Grenville Dodge and others, Executive Orders were issued in 1863 and 1864 which established the eastern terminus at the "western boundary of the state of Iowa, east of and opposite to the east line of section 10, in township 15 north, of range 13, east of the sixth principal meridian in the territory of Nebraska."[16] The Missouri River was bridged as a single structure in 1869, rebuilt for double track in 1887 and later in 1916. It was the first to cross the Missouri and the only one between Council Bluffs and Omaha. The UP, with only 2.08 miles of track across the bridge, is the shortest railroad line into Iowa. The major trackage of 84 miles in the area consists of spurs and yard tracks in the terminal at Council Bluffs, covering 725 acres. It became a vital exchange point for eastern and western transcontinental trains. Only in passenger service (before termination) did Omaha supercede Council Bluffs as a major terminal.

The Santa Fe (AT&SF) concluded that its interests dictated the control of an independent line from Kansas City into Chicago. The extension of the lines from Chicago beyond the Missouri River could bring new competition to their 6,500 mile system from Kansas City to the West Coast and jeopardize further growth. There were three possibilities to gain entrance into Chicago. One was to buy the Chicago and Alton, or the financially ailing Chicago and St. Louis, or to build its own line. It chose the second alternative— use 100 miles of the Chicago and St. Louis and build the remainder. If a ruler were laid on a map tracing the route from Kansas City to Chicago, it would cut across the southeast corner of Iowa, and while the railroad was not constructed "as the crow flies," there was little deviation from the ruler's straight line.

Originally, the AT&SF considered Keokuk for the river crossing,but when citizens of Fort Madison learned of the proposal, they agreed to a grant of 80 acres of land for construction and to pay one-fourth of the expense of the right-of-way through Lee County. These inducements and other factors were sufficient to change the route from Keokuk to Fort Madison. The Chicago, Santa Fe and California Railroad was incorporated in Illinois in 1886, with a separate charter in Iowa and Missouri for construction. The entire line from Kansas City to Chicago, including the Mississippi River and Toll Bridge, was completed in 1887, although service was not begun until the following year. The bridge was designed for both railroad and highway traffic, and at the time it was built, its 525-foot draw span near the Iowa shore was considered the longest in the world. The Bridge Company and railroad were absorbed into the AT&SF system in 1900.

Although the railroad had only 19 miles of track in Iowa, it has had an important place in the state's railroad history. Fort Madison was the Illinois Division headquarters between 1901 and 1903 and again from 1956 to at least 1965. Shopton, two miles west, was the site of shop facilities, an employee hospital, blacksmith shop and roundhouse. The shops and hospital were closed in 1951, and the hospital building together with five acres of land were given to Fort Madison to be administered by a trust fund. Shopton remained as a yard facility.

[16] Frank P. Donovan, "The Union Pacific in Iowa," *Palimpsest 46* (April 1965): pp. 193-194.

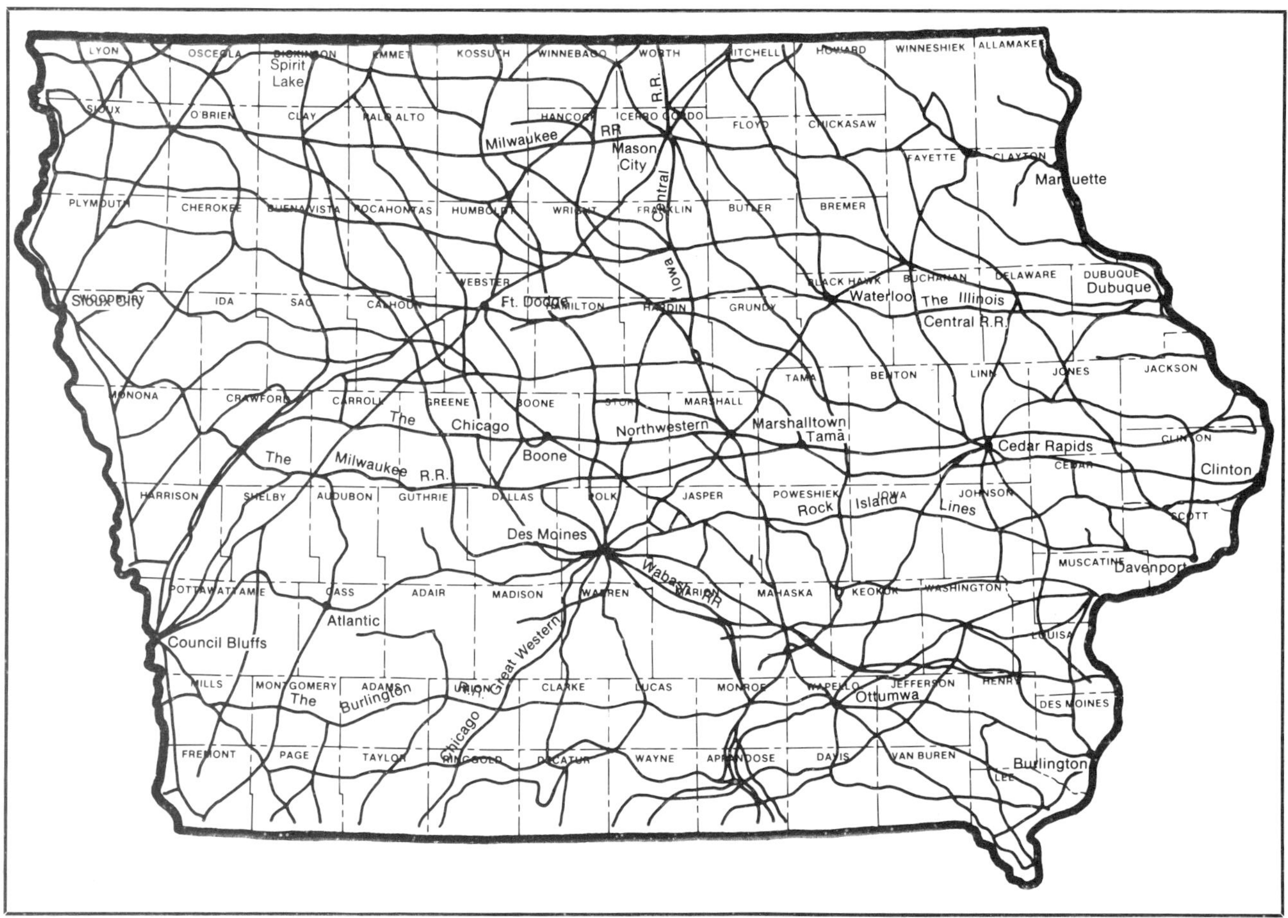

Figure 2-10
Iowa's Steam Railways in 1900
(Reprinted by permission of William N. Whitehill from *The Ups and Downs of Iowa's Railroads.*)

Narrow Gauge Railroads

The narrow gauge movement began in Colorado in 1870 when the Denver and Rio Grande Railroad was organized to build through the mountains south and west of Denver into the Rio Grande valley. During the next decade, railroads with track width of three to three feet, six inches, sprang up over the nation, and by 1880, there were at least 154 of these roads in operation. The movement reached its peak in the early 1880s. The principal reasons for this type of construction were economy in building and maintenance and also the equipment was less expensive than that used on standard gauge roads. On level terrain without bridging, laid with 25-35 pound rail, the roads could be built for as little as $5,000 per mile, exclusive of right-of-way, as compared with about $25,000 for standard width railroads.

Their greatest disadvantage was the interchange of traffic without reloading and the lower volume hauled when contrasted to standard gauge roads. The level of wages paid was the same on both types and the narrow gauge paid, if not fully, the taxes per mile. These and other factors gradually led to conversion of narrow gauge to standard gauge, but nearly every major railroad system originally included narrow gauge lines. Narrow gauge lines are shown below with names, dates of organization, mileage and final disposition:

1. Farmers Union Railroad, 1875. Liscomb through Conrad Grove (Conrad) to Beaman, 12 miles. Abandoned.
2. Crooked Creek Railway and Coal Company, 1876. Judd to Lehigh on the Des Moines River, eight miles. Ft. Dodge, Des Moines & Southern.

3. Waukon and Mississippi Railroad Company, 1877. Waukon to the Mississippi River, 23 miles. Milwaukee.
4. Iowa Eastern Railroad Company, Elkader to Beulah, 19 miles. Milwaukee.
5. Cedar Rapids and Marion Street Railway, five miles. Street Railway Company of Cedar Rapids.
6. Fort Madison and Northwestern Narrow Gauge Railway Company, 1879, 12 miles. Reorganized into the Fort Madison and Northwestern Railroad Company which extended the line to Birmingham and McKee in 1883, 33 miles. Burlington.
7. Chicago, Bellevue and Western Railroad Company, 1880. Bellevue to Cascade, 36 miles. Milwaukee.
8. Iowa and Minnesota Railroad Company, 1874. Des Moines to Ames and Calanan (near Jewell), 57 miles. Chicago & Northwestern.
9. Des Moines, Adel and Western, 1878. Waukee to Adel, seven miles. St. Louis, Des Moines and Northern completed the line from Waukee to Des Moines in 1881. Wabash.
10. Wabash, St. Louis and Pacific Railroad, 1880. Adel to Jefferson and Fonda, 114 miles. Clive to Boone, 1882, 35 miles. Milwaukee.
11. Des Moines, Osceola and Southern, 1880. Osceola to Des Moines. Osceola through Leon to Cainsville, Missouri, 111 miles. Burlington.
12. Burlington and Northwestern Railroad, 1875. Washington to Burlington, 38 miles. Burlington.
13. Burlington and Western Railroad, 1881. Winfield to Oskaloosa, 71 miles. Burlington (Fig. 2-11)[17].

Branch Lines

Intense competition existed among communities for service along the trans-Iowa routes. Satisfaction was achieved when the main line was routed through them. Others who had been by-passed could either build their own independently chartered and often locally financed roads to connect with major routes, request the main line to build them, or cease to exist. In most instances, the railroads were sought through "feeders" or "branches," lured by monetary or physical rewards. Hofsommer lists approximately 40 railroads, including the five major east-west lines,

Narrow gauge line, 10 miles North of Ames in 1879
(Courtesy: State Historical Society of Iowa)

[17] Ben Hur Wilson, "Iowa and the Narrow Gauge," *Palimpsest 13* (April 1932): pp. 141-153.

which were built in Iowa.[18] Many of these were probably known as "branch lines" which the major railroads operated and later consolidated into their systems. Others were the "short lines" built to connect new settlements. Until World War I, with few exceptions, these relatively short lines were considered a source of strength for any railroad. They made easier and shorter the haul by horse and wagon to the towns and grain elevators, and generally, the railroad that blanketed its territory got most of the traffic. The major railroads owned most of the branches, often spun off as laterals north and south of the main tracks. Expansion of branch line construction underscores the increase in railroad mileage between 1870 and 1880. By the latter year, 4,366 miles had been built, up from the 655 at the close of the 1850s and the 2,683 miles built by 1870.

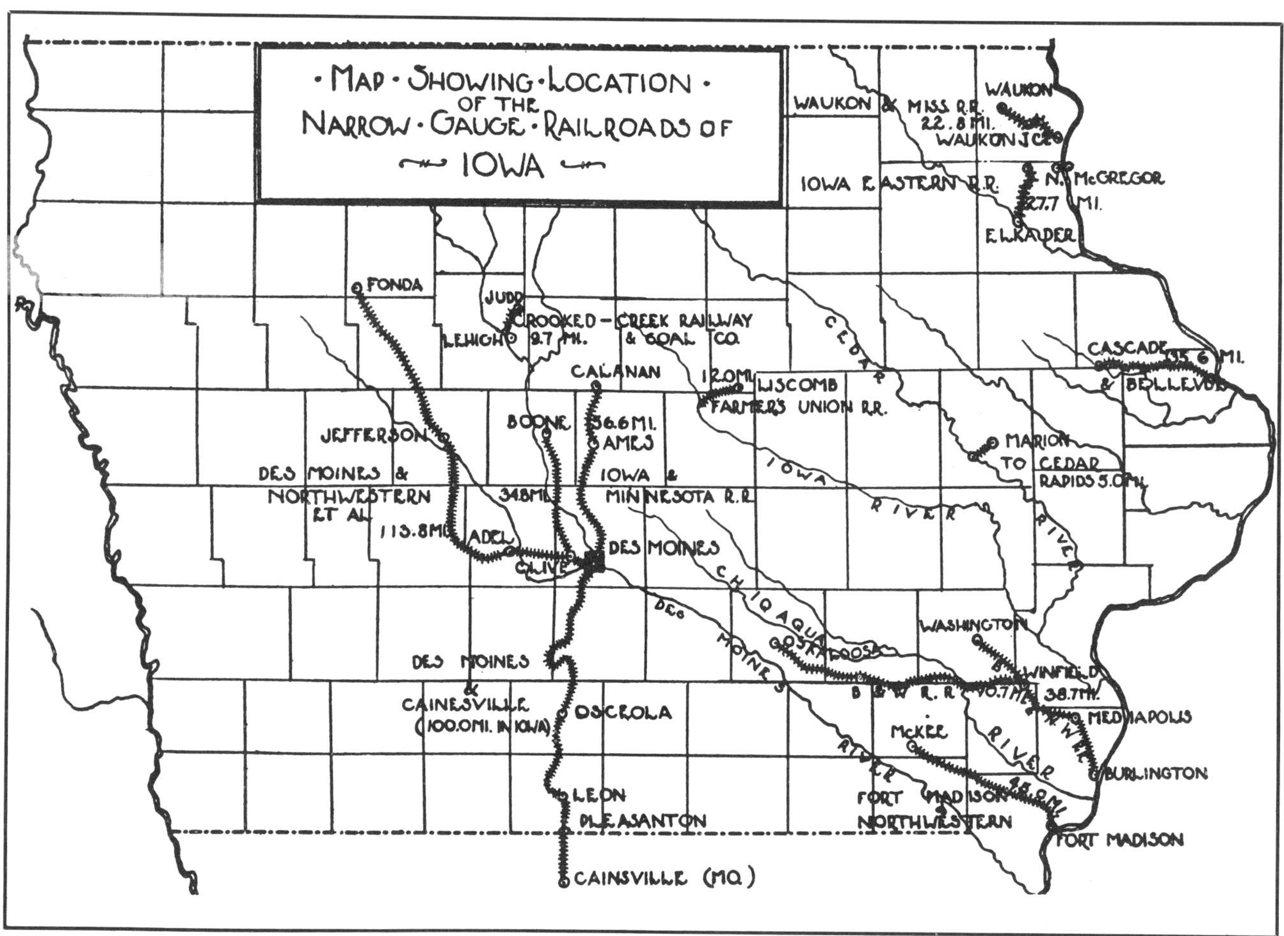

Figure 2-11
(Courtesy: State Historical Society of Iowa)

[18] Donald L. Hofsommer, *Railroad Development in Iowa,* (mimeograph) Cedar Falls, 1965. The author counted almost 60 railroads built or partially built, including main lines, short or branch lines and interurbans.

Evolution of the Passenger Train

"Traveling on the cars" was an adventure not always pleasant in the early days when passenger trains, labeled by Henry as "Houses on Wheels," were nothing more than renovated stagecoaches mounted on flanged wheels. These were soon replaced by vehicles with an appearance of boxcars with windows. Throne describes the first passenger train in Iowa as "consisting of two coaches and five flat cars decked with chairs and settees, protected by a temporary railing."[19] The hardy pioneers sat on two-passenger wooden benches in cars hot and dirty in summer and cold and drafty in winter. Lighting was provided first by candles and then oil lamps; heat, by stoves, which were a dangerous hazard at any time but particularly when wrecks occurred.

The earliest significant improvement was the invention of an axle moving with the wheel, rather than the wheel revolving around the axle. The wheels were then combined into four-wheel trucks. Cars were linked together by three feet of chain. The engineer in charge of the train signaled the start of a trip by a blast on the locomotive whistle, and passengers braced themselves against the shocks as the slack in the chains was taken up. Gradually, passenger cars became larger and more comfortable, and by 1887, travelers were enjoying steam heat, electricity and plumbing. The air brake replaced the hand brake, and the link and pin coupler, which replaced the connecting chains, gave way to a more safe and dependable automatic coupler. In the same year, open platforms between cars were enclosed, and the first all-vestibule train was placed in service on the Pennsylvania Railroad.

Introduction of Pullman Cars

In the early 1850s, George M. Pullman could not sleep on the hard, springless bunk of a "sleeping car." The wind whistled through cracks in the window, candles flickered and the coarse woolen blanket offered little comfort. Determined "to do something about this deplorable condition," in 1857, he converted a coach on the Chicago and Alton Railroad into a sleeping car with berths and bedding but without sheets, because male passengers refused to take off their boots. The second experiment, the *Pioneer,* built in 1864, became the car that made the Pullman name famous, especially when it was used on the last leg of President Lincoln's funeral train.[20] Pullman's original contribution was the upper berth which could be closed during daytime. Dining and

In 1860, this coach was the last word in travel comfort. Enclosed vestibules and other improvements were unheard of. (Courtesy: American Association of Railroads)

[19] Mildred Throne, "Iowa's Streamliners," *Palimpsest 32* (June 1951): p. 229.

[20] Robert S. Henry, *This Fascinating Railroad Business,* New York: Bobbs-Merrill Co., 1946, p. 262.

hotel car construction followed shortly thereafter and were in operation by the 1870s.

In 1894, steel replaced wood in construction of freight cars and between 1908 and 1910, the Pullman Standard Company began manufacturing all-steel passenger and sleeping cars. The sectioned sleeping cars reached their peak of popularity in the 1920s and will evoke memories for the older generation of what Lyons calls "the nights of the green curtains" and characterized by Robert Young as "rolling tenements." Lyons described these cars as "ugly, uncomfortable dormitories as lacking in privacy as a jail house. Each passenger swayed longitudinally in a berth cloaked by a swaying curtain of heavy green fabric that might have been better used as upholstery for funiture in the lobbies of commercial hotels. At one end of the car was the men's room—one toilet, one pseudo-leather couch and a meager triad of commercial wash basins inadequately equipped with mirrors . . . At the other end was the womens' room—similarly fitted but littered with someone else's face powder and hair combings rather than cigar butts."[21] The observation may seem somewhat harsh but was fairly accurate. During later years, single occupant "roomettes" and multi-person "bedrooms" replaced many of the sectioned pullmans.

The Influence of Railroads on Iowa's Development

Through colonization efforts, an activity little known and less understood, railroads made significant contributions toward development of permanent communities. Not all land granted was used for construction. The excess was available for sale by land departments organized for this purpose. Encouraging people to settle near the right-of-way or within terrritorial claims offered the prospect of good business in the future. Not only were special fares given to homesteaders by the railroads, but they also depended upon their skills, talents and industry to provide the traffic.

Population Trends

Before railroads, the 192,214 Iowa residents in 1850 were primarily settled along the Mississippi River and its tributaries, except for some concentration in Pottawattamie County and a scattering in southwestern counties. Between 1850 and 1860, the population increased by 251 percent to 674,913. Fourteen counties experienced the greatest growth during the decade before railroads, all except Grundy, Ringgold, and Webster in the eastern block, but within 10-20 years after construction, the greatest growth occurred in 27 counties. The four largest were Des Moines, Polk, Woodbury and Pottawattamie, with increases primarily in the major cities. Similar trends were noted in the rural population growth. Rural growth was less dependent upon the arrival of railroads and more so on the establishment and growth of towns. The population grew rapidly from 1860 to 1870, reaching a total of 1.2 million and advancing Iowa from 20th to 11th among the states (Fig. 2-12, 2-13). In the east and south central sections, railroads had little apparent effect on total or rural settlement, but the west, north central, central and southwest were settled after railroad construction. These areas witnessed the building of railroads in advance of demand, and settlement followed slowly due to the lack of lumber, poor drainage of land, and the lure of cheaper land in Nebraska and the Dakotas. The major growth in rural population did not occur until some years after railroads (Fig. 2-14, 2-15).

An example of rapid growth may be seen during the decade of the 1850s when the D&P was building westward. Dubuque County tripled its population, Delaware County increased sixfold, and the population of Buchanan County multiplied 14 times. Black Hawk County, with 135 residents in 1850, had 8,244 in 1860. Webster County had no settlers in 1850 and 2,414 in 1860. When it was learned that Iowa City would be the western terminus of the M&M, property values increased for several years.

As settlers moved west, towns were built 8 to 10 miles apart. They existed as markets for farmers and competed with each other in offering financial and other assistance for railroads to build to or through them. If bypassed, the merchants stood to lose their captive markets, since farmers would take their grain and livestock to the nearest railroad terminal and while there conduct business with stores built around the railroad complex. Wall commented that "it was far more important to get a railroad station than it was to have a courthouse. One reason why J. B. Grinnell founded his town on open prairie. . . was that he had advance information that the M&M Railroad would pass that point and be interested in building a station there."[22]

[21] Peter Lyon, *To Hell in a Day Coach,* Philadelphia: J. P. Lippencott Co., 1968, p. 225.

[22] Joseph F. Wall, *Iowa—A Bicentennial History,* New York: W. W. Norton & Co., 1978, p. 141.

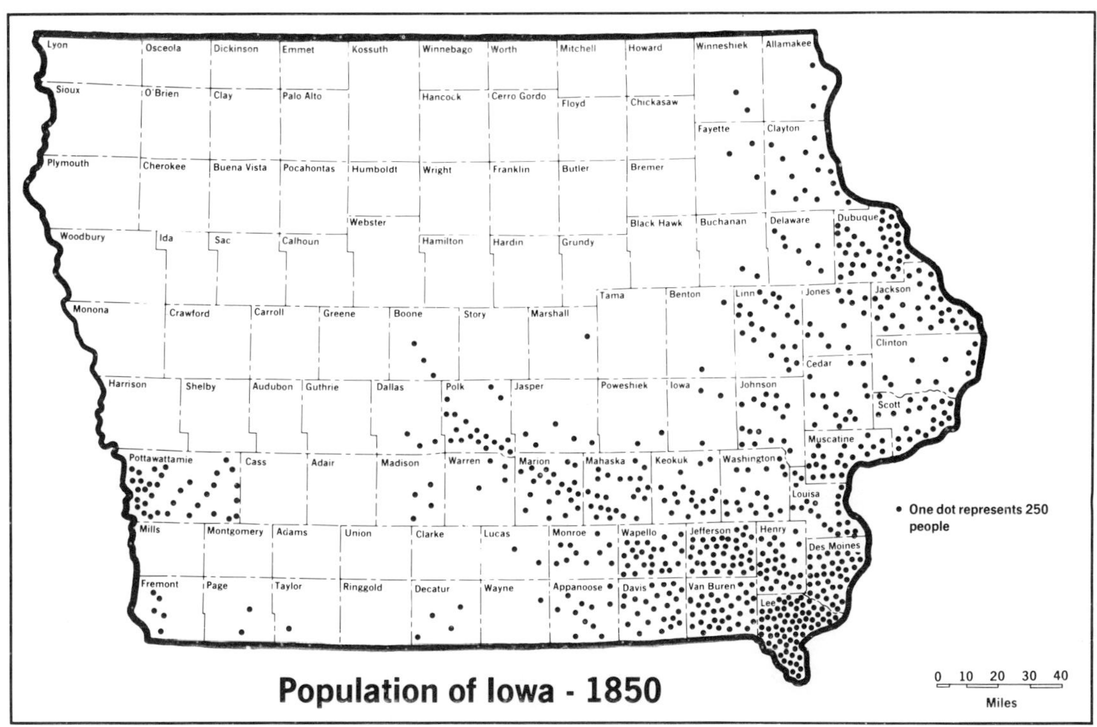

Figure 2-12
Population of Iowa - 1850
(Courtesy: Clare C. Cooper, "The Role of the Railroads in the Settlement of Iowa", M.A. thesis, University of Nebraska, Lincoln, 1958.)

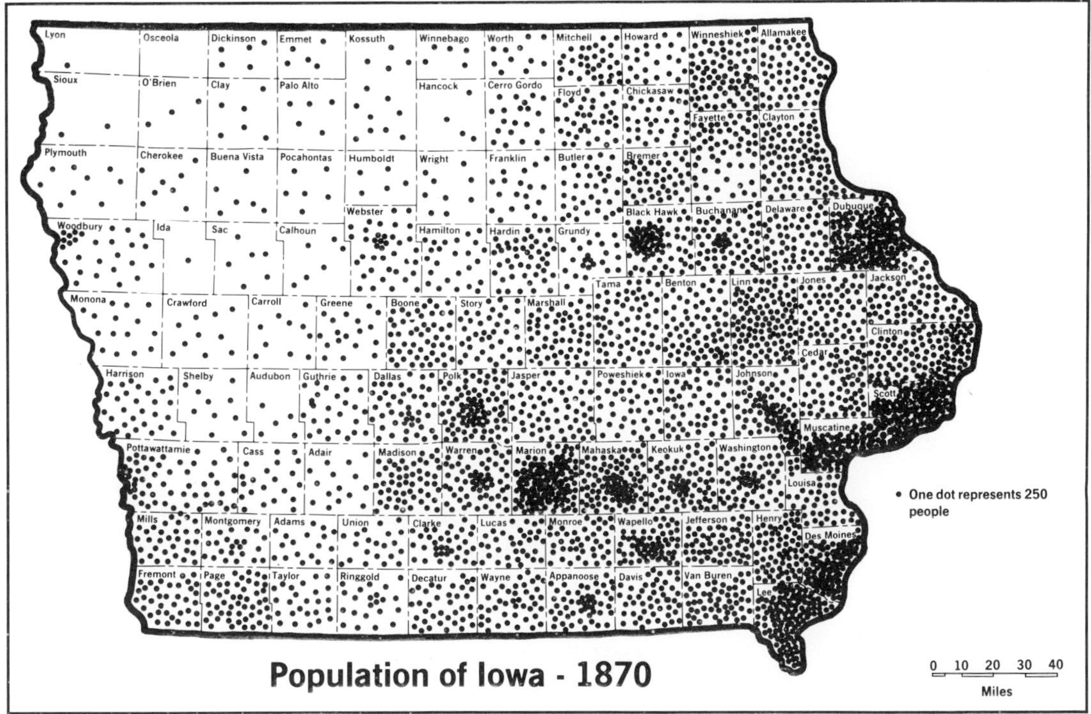

Figure 2-13
Population of Iowa - 1870
(Courtesy: Clare C. Cooper, "The Role of the Railroads in the Settlement of Iowa", M.A. thesis, University of Nebraska, Lincoln, 1958.)

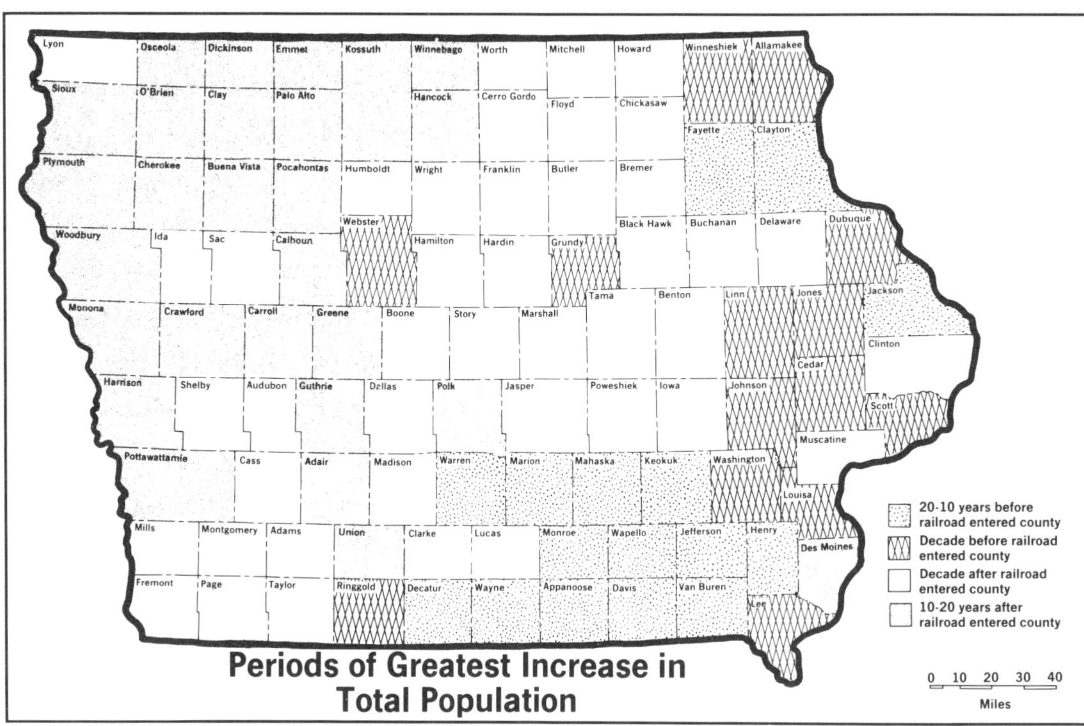

Figure 2-14
Periods of Greatest Increase In Total Population
(Courtesy: Clare C. Cooper, "The Role of the Railroads in the Settlement of Iowa", M.A. thesis, University of Nebraska, Lincoln, 1958.)

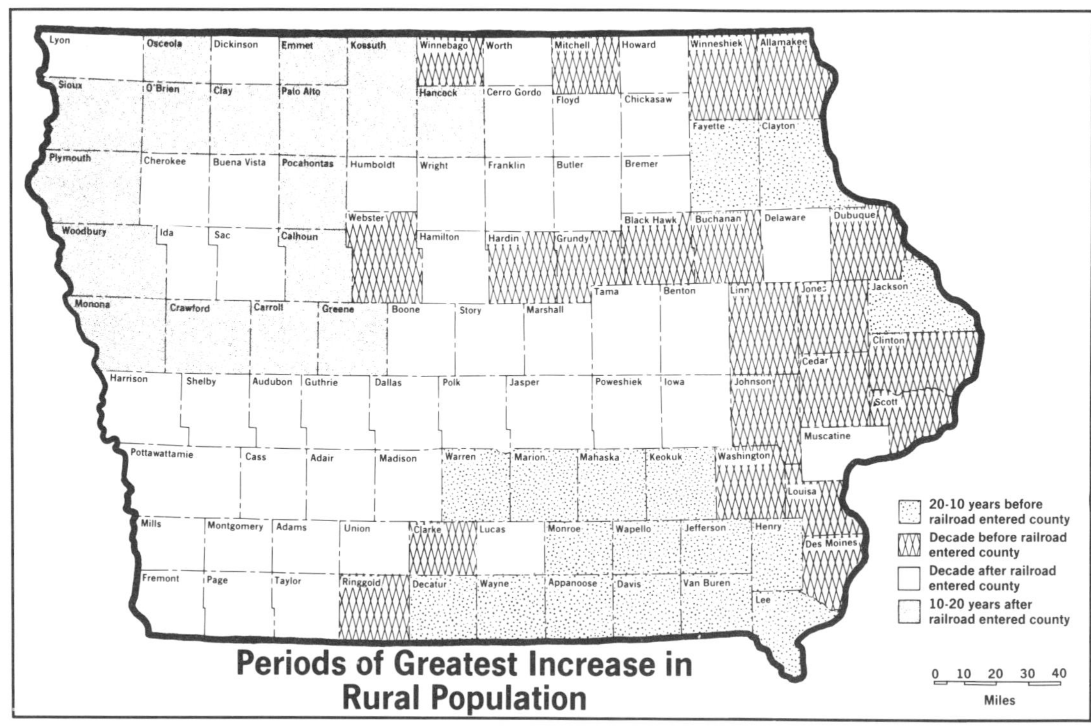

Figure 2-15
Periods of Greatest Increase In Rural Population
(Courtesy: Clare C. Cooper, "The Role of the Railroads in the Settlement of Iowa", M.A. thesis, University of Nebraska, Lincoln, 1958.)

Agriculture and Industry

Henry Varnam Poor, a railroad analyst, in a speech in 1854, stated: "The pioneer, as he moves forward over the prairies of the West, carries with him the railway, as necessary to his life as are the axe and the plough. This railway keeps pace with the frontier of settlement so that the crop of the year on a frontier farm in the great march of civilization has only to be held to the next; to be sent whizzing to the Eastern markets at a speed of 30 miles to the hour."[23] There were 14,805 farms in the state in 1850 and 61,136 by 1860. Much of the land was undeveloped, with only 28 percent of the state's area in farms, valued at $12 per acre. By 1900 land in farms had risen to 96 percent of the land area, and value per acre had risen to $42. William G. Murray observed that "a substantial part of the farm value increase . . . represented farm improvements," but it seems reasonable to conclude that the presence of railroads had an important bearing on the "farm improvements."[24] Only six counties experienced their greatest increase in improved land acreage before railroads—the remaining 93 after railroad construction (Fig. 2-16). In 1850 the state ranked 18th in the nation in total grain production; by 1860 it was in 10th position. Corn led the list of grains, followed by wheat, oats, buckwheat, barley and rye. Potatoes were also an important crop. Hogs were raised where transportation facilities were available. Cattle were easier to drive and were raised where populations were sparse and transportation not fully developed. Cheap pasture, high wool prices, and easier transportation made the raising of sheep important in the 1860s but by the end of the decade it was on the decline.

Farmers quickly took advantage of the railroads once they were built. In a two-week period ending June 11, 1861, traffic to Chicago originating on the CI&N Railway alone included 38,445 bushels of wheat, 350 barrels of flour, 940 pounds of pork, 2,286 pounds of hides, 3,399 head of hogs and six cars of cattle. Freight was increasing so rapidly that special trains had to be run daily to accommodate the demand. Trading habits changed almost overnight. The *Marshall County Times* stated that "tide of trade had changed from the previous movement of wagons to Marengo to the railroad facilities at Otto Creek in Marshall County."[25] No longer was it necessary to deliver products long distances to river towns. Dozens of markets developed along railroad property and distances of hauling were reduced. The Mississippi River towns lost some of their advantage when the bridges were built but gained otherwise as railroad centers. Chicago and the large Eastern cities were primary markets for Iowa products, and England, Scotland and Ireland were important foreign outlets.

The banking industry developed almost simultaneously with the railroads as a service organization which not only invested in but also handled finances for equipment and construction and arranged for sales of securities. Industry no longer had to concentrate along the rivers and began to scatter throughout the state. In 1860 the six leading manufacturing counties had production valued between $500,000 and $1.5 million. All six were served by short line railroads built into the interior and were also associated with river movements. By 1870, 14 counties had manufacturing facilities with values between $1 and $3 million. Agricultural processing and farm implement firms ranked first, followed by lumber, carriages, boots and shoes, saddles and harnesses, clothing and blacksmithing.[26]

The growth of the lumber industry was a natural result of the demand for homes, farm facilities and industrial structures. Iowa's hardwoods were not the most suitable for building purposes, so the white pine from Minnesota and Wisconsin was cut and floated down the Mississippi to saw mills in the river towns. Railroads hauled the finished lumber to the interior and were also customers for buildings and ties. In 1869 Clinton had five lumber companies and was considered the leading producer of milled lumber in the world, boasting 17 millionaires in lumbering and allied businesses. By 1870 these firms had established lumber yards at various points along the CNW Railroad. Sage

[23] Alfred D. Chandler Jr., ed., *The Railroads—The Nations's First Business: Sources and Readings,* New York: Harcourt Brace & World Co., 1965, p. 22.

[24] William G. Murray, "Iowa Land Values," *Palimpsest 48 (October 1967): pp. 457-458.*

[25] Klazie Mae Smith, *"The Economic and Social Development of Iowa from 1860 to 1870,"* Masters thesis, Iowa State College, Ames, 1942, pp. 62-63.

[26] *Census of 1860,* volume on manufactures, pp. 146-161; *Census of 1870.* The six counties were Muscatine, Scott, Des Moines, Dubuque, Lee and Linn. They were joined later by Clinton, Polk, Wapello, Henry, Jackson, Clayton, Fremont, and Black Hawk.

comments that "it is safe to say that . . . for a comparable number of years, roughly the 50 years from 1859 to 1900, no single business in Iowa's economic history accounted for a greater concentration of wealth than the Mississippi River lumber business in its heyday."[27]

Aside from its fertile soils, Iowa's greatest natural resource was coal fields, underlying 21 counties in the south central section. Without railroads, production and marketing would have been non-existent. Oskaloosa in Mahaska County was the first center of extensive operations, later developed in Polk, Jasper, Monroe, Appanoose and Wayne counties. New communities were organized, the most interesting that of Buxton in Monroe County, established in 1900 by the CNW which had title to over 30,000 acres of coal fields. Unable to hire labor at prevailing wages, they imported hundreds of blacks from Kentucky and Alabama to work the mines. In one year the town grew to 6,000 people, 5,500 of whom were black.

While railroads were only one factor in the location of industry in the early years, it could well have been the most important. A history of Iowa industries by Cheever shows the locational advantages provided by access to railroads.

Nor were recreational possibilities overlooked for the people. The vacation potential of the Spirit Lake country was promoted vigorously by several railroads. The initial route was developed by the BCF&N in 1882, followed by the CM&StP in 1883. Advertising campaigns were joined by other railroads that connected with them at various cities. The BCF&N's efforts were directed toward Spirit Lake and the famous Hotel Orleans, whereas the CM&StP stressed the advantages of visiting West Okoboji, and its stations as might be expected were near that lake. The railroads eventually terminated passenger services and dismantled their tracks. The area, however, continued to prosper with most visitors of the auto/air age probably unaware of the role of the railroads in the development of the Iowa Great Lakes Region.

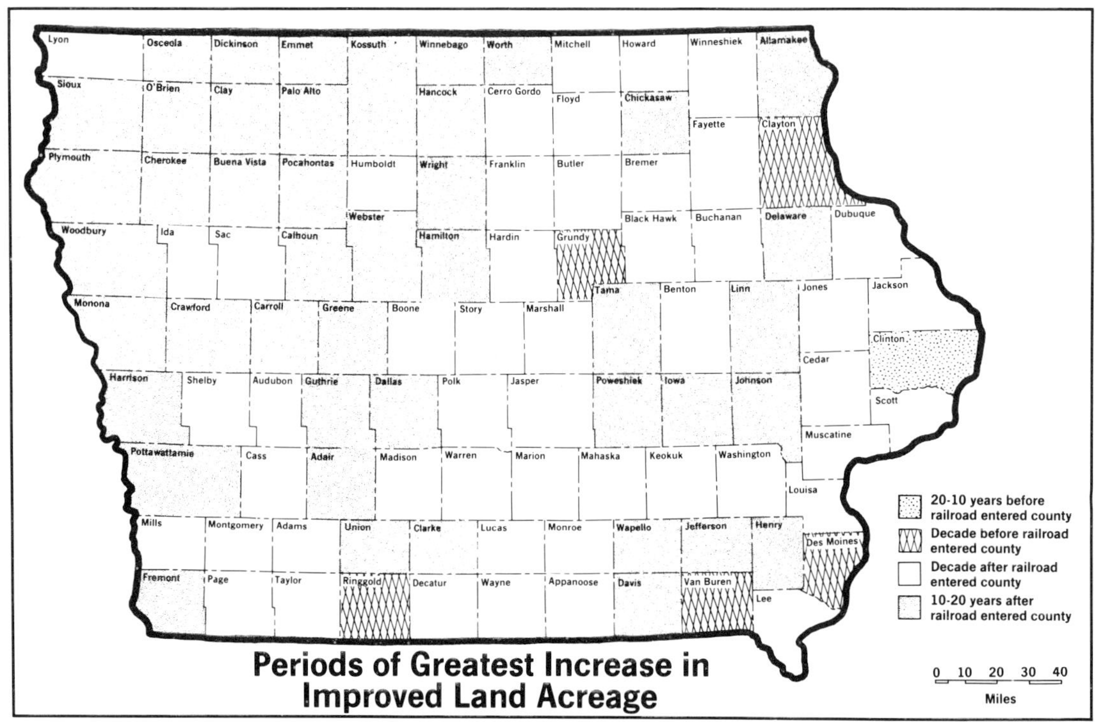

Figure 2-16
Periods of Greatest Increase In Improved Land Acreage
(Courtesy: Clare C. Cooper, "The Role of the Railroads in the Settlement of Iowa", M.A. thesis, University of Nebraska, Lincoln, 1958.)

[27] Leland Sage, *A History of Iowa,* Ames: Iowa State University Press, 1974, pp. 98-99; George W. Sieber, "Railroads and the Lumber Industry, 1858-1878," *Annals of Iowa 39* (summer 1967): pp. 33-46.

Railroads and the Legislature

Railroad circumstances and conditions in the Eastern states were considerably different than those faced by Western legislatures. Eastern states had been founded and developed without railroads, which were introduced into an economic and social structure well advanced and capable of handling new problems as they arose. Railroad construction in the West largely preceded economic development and was in part responsible for it. There had been some legislative experiments concerning canals, roads and rivers, but generally, railroad legislation was first discussed by Western states.

By the early 1870s, railroads had considerably altered the economic structure of Iowa. Service had been established in all the major cities by one or more roads. Businessmen found new opportunities and new competition. One area after another emerged from subsistence farming, produced a surplus to be sold outside the home markets, developed industries and hoped to achieve economic prosperity. Populations had increased dramatically, and virtually every person was affected in one way or another by railroad progress. Initially, state support and assistance was practically unanimous. Railroads received the power of eminent domain; right-of-way privileges; were allowed to finance through bonding, mortgages or special classes of stocks; could make connections within and outside the state with other railroads; received permission to build bridges; and acquired generous grants of land. But the rapid expansion of railroads and their growing influence raised many questions, and the people turned to their government for answers. Government was essentially the legislature, dominating the political scene not only from their constitutional powers but also because governors were reluctant or unable to exercise their powers.

The newly formed Republican Party controlled the legislature during the era of railroad construction, starting with the election of Governor James W. Grimes, and solidified its position in the national elections of 1856. Among the issues endorsed, one emphasized support of the promoters and builders of railroads—a wise political move at that time. Sparks refers to Iowa as "a perfect illustration of the special place railroad builders and promoters usually achieved in frontier communities."[28] Democrats and Whigs had long recognized the attitudes of the people toward encouragement for railroads, but the opposition of their national leadership to the northern railroads gave the Republicans the opportunity to champion railroad progress. The Republican successes of the late 1850s seemed to come partly from their exploitation of railroad enthusiasm.

Two of the early problems faced by the legislature related to land grants and railroad taxes. A corollary was that of rates, rate control and railroad liability. On these questions there were conflicting opinions between the eastern and western sections of the state, since the pattern of building had resulted in an uneven development between the two areas. The settled eastern counties had urged the state to bring the railroads to Iowa, to aid in their further development and led the movement for action on railroad matters. Geographic rather than political or economic factors were the predominant influences in settling the controversies between the older and newer settled sections. Compromise was necessary and formed the beginning of a legal framework within which the people and railroads could live and prosper.

Title to the land grants was given the states, and decisions had to be made as to how the maximum results could be obtained from the railroads so favored. These decisions, in turn, were complicated by disagreements relative to the responsibilities of the state. Could the legislature hold the railroads to strict compliance for maximum construction, or should they accept substantial compliance to encourage construction? Should the railroads be forced to settle conflicting claims of land holders? Could routes be controlled and roads forced to build on the lands granted? Then there was the question of taxation—how to balance the eastern demand for "fair share" payments against the western desire to encourage building. What basis would be used for tax assessment—income or property? Who would make the assessment, the state or local communities? Concurrent were questions of railroad liability for livestock injured or killed along the right-of-way and for the safety of employees, persons and property. Rate control became a dominant and violent issue as a result of discriminatory practices. The response of the state to these questions involved different

[28] David S. Sparks, "Iowa Republicans and the Railroads," *Iowa Journal 53* (July 1955): p. 275.

attitudes, interests and concerns. One centered on the sectional conflicts; another on the position of the governors, many of whom were sympathetic to the railroads. A third was the influence of railroad lobbyists on the legislature; and finally there were the courts which formulated the legal structure of railroad operations by reviewing legislation and initiating support or constraints.

In the years following the original act, Congress increased land grants to Iowa several times. These had different conditions than those of previous years in that they specified that 10 miles instead of 20 would be the unit of construction for certification, and required that only 20 miles be built annually for 10 years. After 10 years, the unclaimed land would revert to the state, which then had five years to convince another railroad to complete the line. Ralston observed that "one must eventually conclude that the state earned the maximum results from the land grants. Although the companies received all the leeway needed in difficult circumstances, they had to build as required. The state gained well-built, busy and prosperous railroads; no streaks of rust across the prairies resulted from the land grants. The state government deserves no small credit for the management of the grants."[29]

The Ninth General Assembly in 1862 imposed a tax on railroads of "one percentum on gross receipts," while real and personal property were to be taxed locally. One-half was to be apportioned among counties through which the roads ran, in proportion to the miles of main track in each county. In 1868, the system was revised to enable townships, incorporated towns and cities to aid construction by levying a tax, collected by the state treasurer—not to exceed five percent of the assessed value of property when sanctioned by popular vote. The amount had to be expended in the township or one contiguous to it after an equal amount was matched by the railroads. The roads had to report not only their gross receipts but also the mileage in each county, and the one percent of gross receipts was retained. Again, in 1879, the system was changed to one percent of receipts of $3,000 per mile, two percent on receipts of $3,000 to $6,000 per mile, and three percent on receipts over $6,000. Instead of one-half, the new law provided that four-fifths of the tax should be apportioned among the counties. Taxation of real and personal property was left to local authorities.

Geography again determined positions pro and con on these tax measures. The fight to tax and regulate freight rates further illustrates the conflict between Eastern businesses and interior rural communities. The river towns vigorously supported bills to regulate rates and just as vigorously opposed revision of the tax system. Under existing laws, towns on the river with large concentrations of railroad property could tax through local assessments. Opponents favoring tax revision sought to convince rural areas that by having the state control the assessment, the tax burdens would be equalized. Farmers, they charged, were paying the heavy taxes levied by cities through higher freight rates.

Under a bill passed by the 14th General Assembly in 1872, the Census Board, consisting of the Governor, State Treasurer, State Auditor and Secretary of State would assess railroad property. Exempted were lots, lands and other real estate not used in operations. The board required reports on the number of miles operated, amount of property in each county, numbers of rolling stock and gross earnings in the state. The data would be the base for assessment and prorating per mile of track. Taxes would then be collected from the railroads on the number of miles within the county.

Criticism of the new law was not long in coming and centered on the low level of taxes which resulted. Both Governor Merrill, in his last message to the legislature, and Governor Carpenter, in his inaugural address, agreed that the railroads should pay higher taxes but disagreed on the proper method of assessment. Carpenter stated that the railroads should not be assessed on the same basis as private property. While the State Constitution called for equal taxation, he argued that if railroads were equally assessed, a few townships in each county would receive all local taxes, and a few towns in the state, all taxes on rolling stock and other property. He further pointed out that the "value of a railroad was not in its right-of-way, embankments, masonry, bridges, ties, iron and machinery, locomotives, cars, buildings, etc., but in the essential franchise which was based upon dividends," and it was "very nearly impractical" to use the same assessment for railroads as for other

[29] Leonard F. Ralston, "Railroads and the Government of Iowa, 1850-1872," Ph.D. diss., University of Iowa, 1960, p. 249.

property. Merrill had stated that a great disparity existed between the taxes paid by railroads and those by the people, with the latter paying five times more. Despite criticism that Carpenter's position was in opposition to the Republican Party's platform which called for equal taxation and taxes based upon income, he signed the 1872 bill without comment, and a new basis was established for railroad taxation.

The legislation in 1868 which granted additional lands incorporated the following clause: "Provided said railroad company, accepting the provisions of the act shall at all times be subject to such rules, regulations and rates of tariff for the transportation of freight and passengers as may from time to time be enacted and provided for by the General Assembly of the State of Iowa, and further subject to the conditions, limitations, restrictions and provisions contained in the Act, and the Act of Congress granting such lands to the State of Iowa."[30] Actually, such reservations were in every bill distributing or redistributing such lands. Strictly interpreted, the railroad's acceptance of land grants could have the effect of establishing the principle of regulation through contract between the company and the state. The question, therefore, was whether or not the railroads would lose protection against regulation under provisions of the decision in the *Dartmouth College* case in 1819, which stated that charters were contracts between the state and corporation and could not be amended without consent of both parties.[31] However, the railroads apparently viewed the immediate value of the lands to be much greater than any disadvantages that might occur from possible future regulation.

Other legislation required that each company report under oath to the legislature the amount expended in construction, equipment, depots and other buildings, the length of road, average width of grade and number of ties laid per mile. In September of each year, they were to post passenger fares and freight rates at their stations. Proper safeguards were to be provided for cattle crossing from fenced lands when the railroad passed through such properties, and safe crossings were mandatory at road and highway intersections. If a railroad failed to fence both sides against livestock running at large, they were liable to the owners for injury or death. To recover damages, the owners needed only to prove the injury or death, and if the railroad refused or neglected to pay within 30 days, it became liable for double the value of the property destroyed. Equally, the railroads were responsible for damages sustained by any person or employee.

Injury and death among employees was a matter of deep concern. Men switching or coupling cars by the link and pin technique often lost fingers, arms or their lives, crushed between cars or while twisting the hand brakes. George Westinghouse had patented the air brake in 1869, and Eli Hamilton Janney, the automatic coupler in 1868, but the railroads were slow to adopt the devices. Lorenzo Coffin, a chaplain during the war, who operated the Willow Eye Farm near Fort Dodge, attempted through the press to persuade the railroads to stop "the needless slaughter of workmen" which in 1881 numbered 30,000 employees killed or maimed in coupling or hand brake accidents. His was a lonely crusade, writing thousands of letters to groups for assistance in his campaign and visiting conventions of railroad officials and equipment manufacturers where he accused the roads of murder. The Master Car Builders finally tested the devices in the late 1880s. Coffin, at the age of 60, was one of the first Iowa railroad commissioners and drafted the first safety appliance law written, requiring all trains operating in the state to be equipped with automatic couplers and air brakes. The railroads promptly disregarded the law. However, his efforts prevailed through a congressional act signed by President Harrison in 1893.

Growing Anti-Railroad Sentiment

It seemed inevitable that the railroads would be regulated as time passed. Through the period from 1850 to 1870, the public assumed that building numerous railroads would assure competition to guarantee fair and equal treatment and reasonable rates. Therefore, attention was centered primarily upon their construction rather than on any form of regulation, but by the early 1870s, the evils of unregulated competition began to appear. The belief that a state could control its corporations antedated Iowa's statehood. The principle was incorporated into the Constitutions of 1844 and 1846 and, although modified to satisfy Whig principles, retained the

[30] Benjamin Gue, *History of Iowa,* Vol. III, New York: Century History Co., 1903, p. 25.

[31] Williams v. Peyton's, 14 U.S. (4 Wheat.) 219 (1819).

theory of state supremacy over corporations that the state had created. A specific statement to this effect was contained in the Constitution of 1857 and in the Articles of Incorporation. Proponents of regulation, therefore, had a basis for their arguments when economic conditions in the post-Civil War years brought growing sentiment for railroad control, including the central issue of rates and rate relationships between commodities and communities.

All attempts to regulate were fought by the railroads who insisted that unlike other industries, they required huge injections of capital and control legislation would frighten investors and endanger the enterprise. Further, they argued that railroads had great value to the state, which no one disputed; that the "only reasonable explanation for restriction would be the hostility, malice, ignorance, cupidity or downright stupidity of legislators."[32]

Governors, though limited in power by the Constitution, were frequently embraced as allies by railroad interests. The only absolute power held by them was in certification of lands following completion of construction, and this power was later made subject to legislative approval. Governor Ralph Lowe, answering a request of Platt Smith of the D&P, was the only one to actively support state aid for the railroads despite the Constitutional prohibition, but opposition of the Republican Party killed the idea and was said to be partly responsible for his defeat for a second term.

It was to the General Assembly that the railroads turned in times of financial difficulties, made suggestions on taxation issues, and used the body as a primary target in attempts to hold off the increasing hostile positions which appeared to be growing in direct proportion to the rising pressures for regulatory action. Ralston commented that "those who concerned themselves with the legislature frequently expressed themselves on the subject, rarely in complimentary terms." A sample of correspondence he reviewed in his study of railroad interests in Iowa revealed Grenville Dodge's claim that the 1856 House had "not one smart man in it." David W. Kilbourne and Hugh Reid of the Des Moines Valley characterized the 1864 Legislature as "one with too many ministers and lawyers who wasted their time in oratory," and the 1866 body as very radical, introducing "all kinds of abominable anti-railroad bills." Charles Perkins was quoted as thinking that too many dishonest men were elected; too many "who understood very little about what real prosperity their constituents depend upon." Henry Farnham criticized as hostile legislation the act which required railroads to build fences along their rights-of-way and award damages to owners of livestock killed or injured.[33]

The necessity to control the legislature resulted in the organization of the railroad lobby, and their representatives worked diligently to influence legislation as anti-railroad sentiment mounted. They played the western areas without railroads against the eastern railroad-developed counties, approached the "proper persons" to campaign for election, and distributed passes to members of both Houses and other prominent supporters, a practice quite common by 1868. Despite their persuasive efforts, however, railroad interests were never able to halt the growing demand for regulation, and the legislature, never captured, eventually responded.

Hardly had the agitation over the taxation bill subsided when a new bill concerning freight rates was introduced and revived the river town-rural interior conflict. River interests supported it and rural areas without transportation were in opposition. Maximum rate legislation passed both Houses after lengthy debates, but the Senate added an amendment providing for a Railroad Commission. Conference committees could not agree on the amendment and the bill failed, to the delight of the railroads and disappointment of eastern businesses.

There have been two interpretations by students of early railroad history as to the sources and support for control of freight rates. One suggests that it stemmed from the agricultural depression after the War, when prices fell and rates held steady. Others supported the thesis that controlling rates originated with the Eastern business groups who wished to eliminate the preference given to markets outside the state. The interstate rates they could not control, so to retain their competitive positions, they proposed schedules of maximum rates within the state. Some authorities agreed that regulation should set an upper limit on rates but disagreed as to the purpose, arguing in one case that railroads would be forced to equalize

[32] Leonard F. Ralston, "Railroad Interests in Early Iowa," *Annals of Iowa 41* (winter 1973): p. 1136.

[33] Ralston, p. 1139.

rates and thus prevent discrimination against the river towns; another that such a move would lower rates to the benefit of all interests. But the positions of the river businesses and those of the agricultural communities, which numbered the largest percentage of the state's population in the early 1870s, did not necessarily coincide, and until rate control measures could serve the state without favoring one side or the other, they had little chance of legislative support.

Summary

Iowa's exuberance and eagerness for easily accessible transportation formed a broad stage for the dramatic era of railroad construction. In the 1850s and 1860s, of the factors influencing the state's growth, railroads were the most prominent. Assisted by local, state, federal and foreign sources of capital, they fed the economic base with huge expenditures on materials and manpower and through taxes on gross receipts and property, encouraged the migration of settlers, and had a direct bearing on the organization and location of cities and towns and an important impact upon land values. They brought quick, dependable transportation and offered the prospect of relatively prosperous conditions to pioneers, farmers and industrialists by expanding markets and moving freight and passengers at relatively low costs.

Within the state, new and different trade routes were established. Traffic was diverted from water-oriented patterns to more direct and economical land transportation, and the railroad network placed communities a few miles from their stations. Beyond its borders, railroads linked commercial centers on east-west transcontinental routes and served cities north and south of the state, thereby thrusting Iowa into a key strategic position in the railroad structure. Equally important in the construction era were the attitudes of the political parties, governors, the public and legislature, as well as railroad reactions to issues debated on the proper courses of action needed to establish some semblance of order in the mad rush of building, and conflicting opinions regarding their operations and control.

Selected References

Agnew, Dwight L. "The Rock Island Railroad in Iowa." *Iowa Journal 52* (July 1954): pp. 203-212.

American Association of Railroads. *American Railroads: Their Growth and Development.* Washington, D.C., 1956.

Beard, Earl S. "The Background of State Regulation in Iowa." *Iowa Journal 50* (January 1953): pp. 1-37.

Board of Investigation and Research. *Land Grants to the Railroads and Rates.* Washington, D.C., 1944.

Buck, Solon J. *The Granger Movement.* Cambridge: Harvard University Press, 1913.

Casey, Robert J., and W.H.S. Douglas. *Pioneer Railroad.* New York: McGraw Hill Book Co., 1948.

Cheever, L.O. "Industries of Iowa." Foreword by W. J. Peterson. *Palimpsest 47* (March 1967): pp. 89-144.

Chicago and North Western Railway Company. Compiled by W. H. Stennett. *Yesterday and Today.* Chicago: Press of Rand McNally, 1905.

Coffin, L.S. "Safety Appliances on the Railroads." *Annals of Iowa 5* (January 1903): pp. 561-562.

Cooper, Clare C. "The Role of the Railroads in the Settlement of Iowa: A Study in Historical Geography." M.A. thesis, University of Nebraska, 1958.

Corliss, Carlton J. *Main Line of Mid America.* New York: Creative Age Press, 1950.

Derleth, August. *The Milwaukee Road.* New York: Creative Age Press, 1948.

Dey, Peter A. "Railroad Legislation in Iowa." *Iowa Historical Record 9* No.4 (October 1893): pp. 540-561.

Dixon, Frank A. *State Railroad Control.* Boston: Thomas Y. Crowell & Co., 1903.

Donovan, Frank Pierce. *Mileposts on the Prairie.* New York: Simmons-Boardman, 1950.

Donovan, Frank P., Jr. "The Great Western Railway." *Palimpsest 24* (June 1953): pp. 257-284.

______. "The Minneapolis and St. Louis Railway." *Palimpsest 32* (July 1951): pp. 249-284.

______. "The Illinois Central in Iowa." *Palimpsest 43* (June 1962): pp. 265-272.

———. "The North Western in Iowa." *Palimpsest 43* (December 1962): p. 546.

———. "The Rock Island in Iowa." *Palimpsest 44* (September 1963): p. 384-431.

———. "Bridging the Mississippi." *Palimpsest 44* (September 1963): pp. 387-392.

———. "The Milwaukee in Iowa." *Palimpsest 45* (May 1964): pp. 179-209.

———. "The Wabash in Iowa." *Palimpsest 45* (October 1964): pp. 369-374.

———. "The Great Northern in Iowa." *Palimpsest 46* (April 1965): pp. 193-194.

———. "The Santa Fe in Iowa." *Palimpsest 46* (April 1965): pp. 219-223.

———. "The Burlington in Iowa." *Palimpsest 50* (September 1969): pp. 481-488.

Federal Coordinator of Transportation. *Public Aids to Transportation II.* Washington, D.C., 1938.

Gates, Paul W. *The Illinois Central and Its Colonization Work.* Cambridge: Harvard University Press, 1934.

Grant, H. Roger. *The Corn Belt Route.* DeKalb: Northern Illinois University Press, 1984.

Hayes, William E. *Iron Road to Empire.* New York: H. Wolff Book Manufacturing Co., 1953.

Henry, Robert S. "The Railroad Land Grant Legend in American History Tests." *Mississippi Valley Historical Review 32* (September 1945): pp. 171-194.

Hofsommer, Donald L. "Railroad Promotion of the Iowa Great Lakes Area." *Annals of Iowa 42* (Spring 1975): pp. 630-638.

Hoover, John T. *American Railroads.* Chicago: University of Chicago Press, 1961.

Johnson, Arthur M., and Barry Supple. *Boston Capitalists and the Western Railroads.* Cambridge: Harvard University Press, 1967.

Johnson, Jack T. *Peter Anthony Dey: Integrity in Public Service.* Iowa City: State Historical Society, 1939.

Landman, Anita. "The Pontoon Bridge at Marquette." *Annals of Iowa 37* (Spring 1955): pp. 179-197.

Manitor, Edward L. "Historical Influences Upon Iowa of Railroad Building from 1850 to 1860." M.A. thesis, University of Iowa, 1925.

Miller, George H. "Origins of the Iowa Granger Laws." *Mississippi Valley Historical Review 40* (March 1954): pp. 657-680.

Overton, Richard. *Burlington Route.* New York: Alfred H. Knoff, 1965.

———. *Burlington West.* New York: Russell & Russell, 1941, reissued 1967.

Petersen, William J. "The Rock Island Comes." *Palimpsest 14* (August 1933): pp. 285-300.

———. "The North Western Comes." *Palimpsest 14* (September 1933): p. 26.

———. "The Illinois Central Comes." *Palimpsest 14* (October 1933): pp. 363-378.

———. "The Burlington Comes." *Palimpsest 14* (November 1933): pp. 381-395.

———. "The Milwaukee Comes." *Palimpsest 14* (December 1933) pp. 413-429.

———. *The Story of Iowa I.* New York: Lewis Historical Publishing Co., 1952.

Preston, Ruth Irish. "The Lyons and Central Railroad." *Annals of Iowa 9* (October 1909): pp. 284-296.

Quigley, Ira B. "Horse Railways." *Palimpsest 12* (January 1931): pp. 34-37.

Ralston, Leonard F. "Governor Ralph Love and State Aid to Railroads—Iowa Politics in 1859." *Iowa Journal 56* (July 1960): p. 207.

Rosenberg, Martin M. *Iowa on the Eve of the Civil War.* Norman: University of Oklahoma Press, 1972.

———. "The People of Iowa on the Eve of the Civil War." *Annals of Iowa 39* (fall 1967): pp. 105-131.

Sage, Leland. *A History of Iowa.* Ames: Iowa State University Press, 1974.

Schwieder, Dorothy. *Black Diamonds—Life and Work in Iowa's Coal Mining Communities 1895-1925.* Ames: Iowa State University Press, 1983.

Starr, John W., Jr. *Lincoln and the Railroads.* New York: Dodd, Meads & Co., 1927.

Stover, John F. *American Railroads.* Chicago: University of Chicago Press, 1971.

Throne, Mildred. "The Burlington and Missouri River Railroad." *Palimpsest 33* (January 1952): pp. 1-26.

______. "The Fort Dodge and Des Moines Railroad." *Iowa Journal 54* (July 1956): pp. 263-283.

______. *Cyrus Clay Carpenter and Iowa Politics, 1854-1898.* Iowa City: State Historical Society, 1974.

Traffic World. April 7, 1980: p. 105.

Waters, L.L. *Steel Rails to Santa Fe.* Lawrence: University of Kansas Press, 1950.

Whitehill, William N. *The Ups and Downs of Iowa Railroads.* Marshalltown, Iowa:Marshall Print Co., 1977.

Chapter Three
Railroads and Public Opinion

Introduction

The mood of the public toward railroads changed by 1870. In order to overcome the isolation of the West and relieve the pressing need for transportation to the East, railroads and more railroads were needed and could not be purchased at too high a price. Financed by an apparently inexhaustible supply of local, eastern and European capital between 1865 and 1870, the roads were built, competing aggressively against each other in the larger cities and sometimes "built from places where no one lived to points where no one wanted to go."[1] Between 1867 and 1873, approximately $500 million was invested in construction in the so-called "Granger States," resulting in an increase from 6,972 to 17,646 miles of track. The "Granger States" were Illinois, Wisconsin, Minnesota, Kansas, Nebraska, and Iowa. In Iowa, the increase was from 1,288 to 3,160 miles.

These states had the use of railroads, yet they did not own them and were obliged to pay a portion of the indebtedness for their construction. Those who owned the roads did not live in the states but held the securities and expected dividends and interest to be paid, and the men who managed the roads knew their responsibilities. When discontent arose between the railroads and the public, the managers gave priority to the stock and bond holders—the absentee owners. Those who lived in the states had grievances which were ignored, but which were serious enough to stir the communities into retaliatory action. Two reasons are generally considered as the basis for the conflicts, and to one or the other, or both, can be traced the hostility and public discontent which led to the popularity of movements for regulation. These were competition and poor public relations.

Railroad construction was undertaken with an implicit reliance upon competition to regulate operations: railroads would be subject to the same laws of supply and demand generally found in agricultural and manufacturing industries. However, at that time there was no land-based modal competitor, and to have competition, so visualized, would require that every locality be served by two or more independent competing lines, a physical impossibility in the majority of communities. Secondly, where competition did exist, the tendency became one of combination or absorption of weaker by stronger roads. It was not until the systems were built that the public realized that competition did not produce the desired result. Whereas competition generally reduced and equalized rates, it also resulted in local discrimination and arbitrarily raised and reduced prices. The railroads had been built too rapidly and local business could not support them, but the railroad managers were under intense pressure to earn money, and they did, wherever, whenever and however they could.

Competition was vigorous and furious in the larger cities where several lines converged, but at points some miles away and served by only one road, every shipper would pay the highest rate that could be extracted without driving business away. Large firms negotiated their rates and services; small firms were held to strict tariff schedules. Farmers and firms with advantageous locations prospered; others not so fortunate faced ruin. These conditions were not helped by the corruption resulting from financial manipulation of construction companies in transferring assets to the pockets of promoters as evidenced by the Credit Mobilier of the UP and the Contract and Finance Company of the Central Pacific Railroads.

The aggressive attitudes of the railroads led to the second cause of hostility—poor public relations— which although not documented as clearly as the other, nevertheless added fuel to the fires of discontent. Complaints against discriminatory practices were dismissed, passengers treated discourteously, and attempts to control by legislative actions ignored. The issuance of free passes to favored individuals was another unpopular factor. Key issues in the revolt of the people, however, were the monopolistic attitudes and practices and absentee ownership of the roads.

The Iowa Pool

Early in their history, railroads found that competition could be destructive, and in order to sustain earnings, it was necessary that it be restricted. "All profit," stated James F. Joy, "was lost by competition which looked more like insanity than the

[1] Elliot Jones and Homer B. Vanderblue, *Railroads, Cases and Selections,* New York: The MacMillan Co., 1905, p. 797.

result of any wise consideration of the circumstances."[2] Various techniques were used to control competition. One was the territorial agreement whereby each railroad would agree to restrict extension of its lines into the other's territory. Another was the rate agreement requiring maintenance of specific rate schedules. But rate agreements did not eliminate or control competition, for the earnings of a carrier depended upon its traffic, and secret rebates and special rates were a consequence. Railroads had excess capacity, costs were constant, and if lower rates could attract business, profits would increase. Rate agreements were also subject to the ever-present threat of one carrier breaking away from the compact, and they were of questionable legality. Locklin states that "there was some difference of opinion as to whether the agreements were so unreasonable to be unlawful or whether they were legal, thus lawful."[3]

By 1870, competition among Iowa railroads for local and through traffic was intense. The completion of the UP's transcontinental route initiated the struggle for shares of eastbound business, with only the CNW in a position to benefit through interchange at Omaha-Council Bluffs. However, during 1869, the CRI&P and CB&Q entered the Missouri Valley, and a fight for the traffic through rate wars seemed a certainty. All three lines were substantially similar in mileage and service quality. The rate wars never occurred; instead the railroads turned to pooling agreements in which the traffic between Omaha and Chicago was divided.

The Iowa Pool, sometimes referred to as the "Omaha Pool," was organized in 1870 by the three railroads and was one of the first and most famous of pooling agreements (Fig. 3-1). With only a verbal agreement

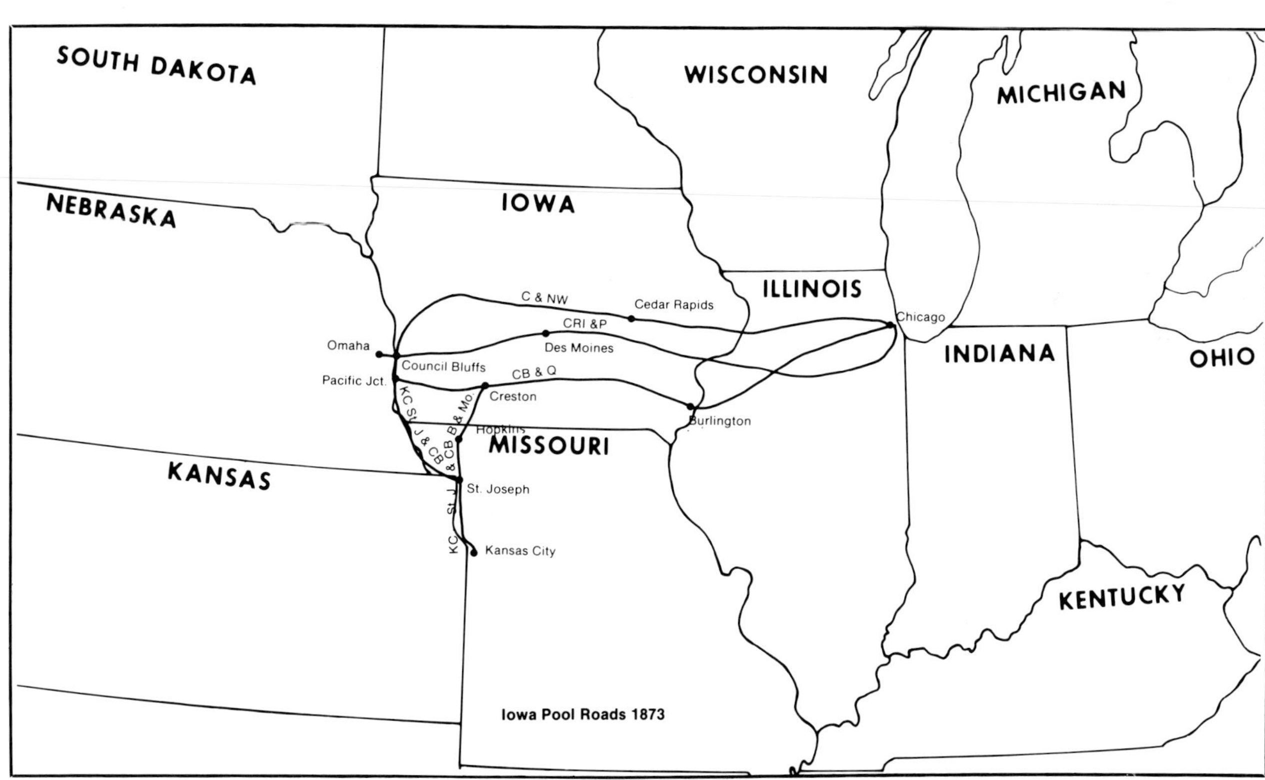

Figure 3-1
(Courtesy: The University of Chicago Press, from Julius Grodinsky "The Iowa Pool")

[2] Julius Grodinsky, *The Iowa Pool,* Chicago: University of Chicago Press, 1950, p. 13. For a detailed description of the origins of the Pool and its weaknesses, see chapters 2, 3, and 9.

[3] D. Phillip Locklin, *Economics of Transportation,* 7th edition, Homewood, Ill.:Richard D. Irwin, Inc., 1972, p. 314.

and no enforcement provisions, the arrangement depended upon the good faith of its participants for its success. Forty-five percent of passenger revenues and 50 per cent of freight revenues were to be retained by each carrier to cover operating expenses and the balance divided equally among the roads. All traffic from eastern connections was given to one road for one week and then in subsequent weeks to the others in turn. The plan led to a rate maintenance program and equalization of traffic instead of balancing accounts as originally agreed, and it proved moderately successful. The original agreement was modified in 1874 through a division of total westbound passenger traffic.

The harmony which apparently prevailed in the pooling arrangement was seriously disrupted when Gould purchased the controlling interest in the UP and was made a director in 1874. Through control of the Wabash, which reached Omaha in 1879 and extended its lines to Chicago in 1880, he was able to compete for the traffic through a circuitous combination of various roads. Gould dictated the policies of the UP and naturally tended to divert some of the traffic that fed the Pool to his Wabash system. In an attempt to circumvent his competitive influence, the Wabash was admitted to the Pool in 1881, with a result that each of the four railroads received 25 percent of the revenues (Table 3-1).

Generally, territorial agreements were maintained during the early years. The CNW's consolidation and expansion was to the north and west of the areas of her partners. The CRI&P expanded within its territorial limits, primarily in eastern Iowa. But the aggressive CB&Q pushed its expansion into the heart of the regions served by the Pool lines, partly to meet the growing competition of Gould. By expanding into Nebraska and eventually to Denver, the CB&Q competed with the UP but insisted that the latter road

Table 3-1
Individual And Corporate Railroad Control Of The Iowa Pool Roads, Affecting Their Relationships, As Members Of The Pool, 1870-1884

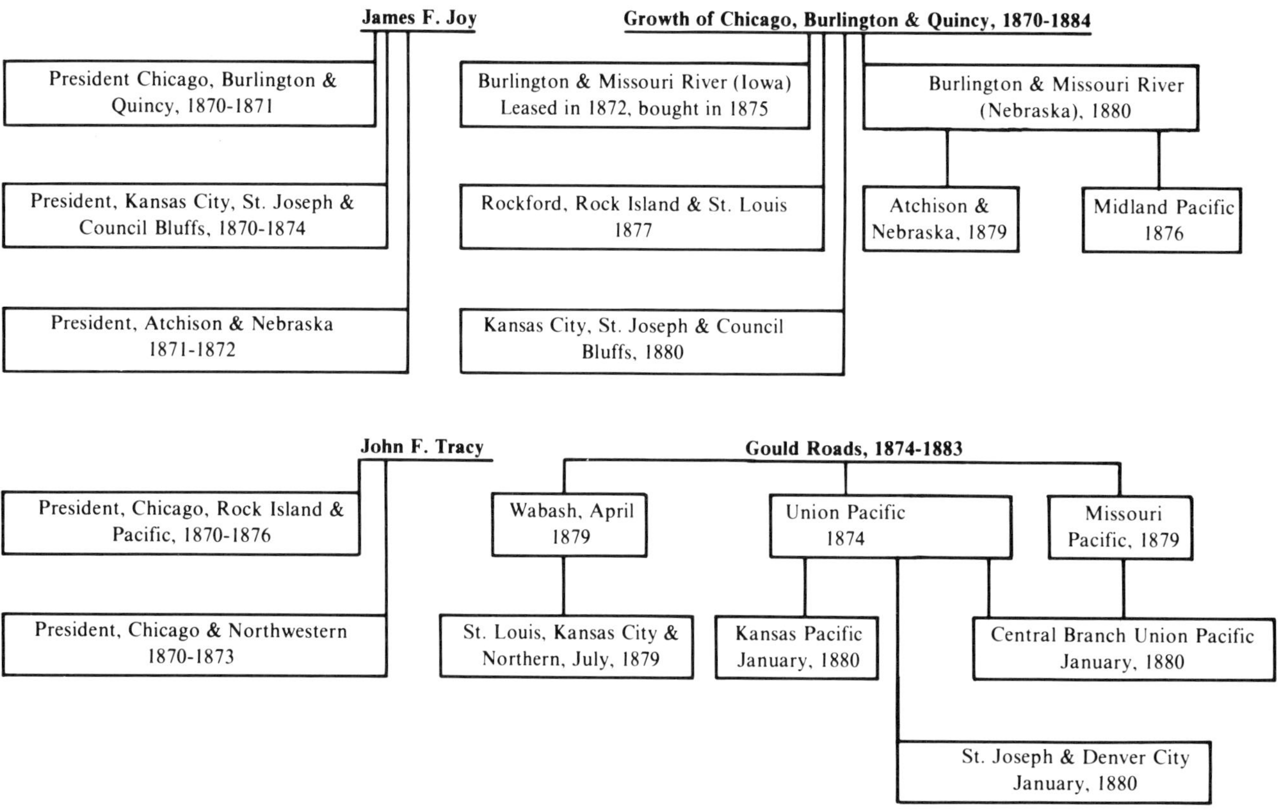

(Courtesy: The University of Pennsylvania Press from Julius Grodinsky *Transcontinental Railway Strategy 1869-1893.)*

prorate the Nebraska traffic. The request was refused, and there was some fear that the CB&Q would withdraw from the Pool in retaliation, a fear not realized.

Four railroads now constituted membership in the Pool with the prospect that a fifth, the CM&StP, would be admitted in the future. Rate and territorial issues continued to complicate the arrangements. More Missouri River points were being opened to traffic, and rate relationships had to be equalized among them and Omaha on through traffic to Chicago and the East. Local rates in Iowa were also a serious competitive problem. Rate wars were not uncommon, especially on livestock and grain movements. In 1882, the Pool was reorganized under the name of the "Iowa Trunk Lines Association" with written terms of agreement covering freight only, to be enforced by C. H. Daniel, appointed Commissioner.

The CM&StP completed its route to Council Bluffs in that year and was admitted under an arrangement which allowed each railroad 20 percent of the revenues. The Missouri Pacific (MP) had also reached the Omaha gateway, and while it would enter Chicago through a combination of roads, it had a strong hold on the traffic to St. Louis. In cooperation with the Wabash, it participated in secret rate reductions, further disrupting the rate tariffs of the Pool, but was admitted through a rearrangement of the divisions. The Kansas City, St. Joseph and Council Bluffs Railway, a key connecting road, and the IC also became members, further complicating the divisions of traffic and revenues.

Forces were operating which eventually destroyed the effectiveness of the Pool. The CM&StP, CRI&P and Wabash had no lines or preferential connections west of the Missouri River. The Wabash benefited by traffic diverted from the UP through the Gould influence. The UP, the principal source of traffic to the Pool, competed with one of its members, the CB&Q. Both the CNW and UP were considering expansion throughout Nebraska, and the CM&StP and the CRI&P complained that the CB&Q was giving them less traffic eastbound than they gave on westbound movements. Despite all of the agreements, competition was the key element in granting special privileges to shippers through rate and service concessions. While moderately successful in stabilizing rates, the weaknesses of the pooling arrangements not only resulted from carriers starting rate wars because of dissatisfaction with their traffic allotments, but also because the courts generally held them to be in restraint of trade and refused to enforce their conditions of agreement.

The Granger Movement

The Panic of 1873 resulted in currency deflation and depressed agricultural prices. Railroad rates fluctuated but did not fall proportionately to the price level. Farmers, equipment manufacturers and farm suppliers who had enthusiastically supported railroads and were dependent upon them for livelihoods now turned against them as a leading cause of their trouble. They realized how great was their dependence upon Eastern markets, upon the carriers for transportation and Eastern capitalists for their land. Railroads were an easy and prominent target for attacks, warranted by their practices. "Corruption of political units, wastefulness and mismanagement, pooling, construction companies, fast freight lines, fluctuations and discrimination in rates . . . all these things and more were rife."[4]

In 1870, Iowa had been settled and farmed for only 37 years, but it had become an important commercial farming state whose economy was based upon grain and livestock production. The Iowa farmer produced for the market and was subject to its wide swings. Although the railroads were maligned, the price index was a basic cause of economic difficulties. Corn fell from an average of 70 cents in 1864 to 24 cents per bushel in 1872; hogs sold for $7.75 in 1869 and $3.44 per 100 pounds in 1873. Wheat was $1.57 in 1867 and 68 cents per bushel in 1870, rose to $1.05 in 1872 and fell to 77 cents in 1876. Cattle sold for $4.55 in 1868 and $3.44 in 1872. In 1872, the secretary of the State Agricultural Society stated that it was costing the farmer about three bushels of corn to ship one to market, and in 1873, farmers complained that it cost "one-third of a bushel of wheat to ship it to Chicago." The state's leading horticulturist reported a charge of $84.00 to ship a carload of apples 90 miles.[5] Regardless of market fluctuations, rate discriminations practiced by the railroads bore the brunt of the farmer's anger.

[4] Lewis Henry Haney, *A Congressional History of Railways in the United States,* Madison: University of Wisconsin Press, 1910, p. 24.

[5] Mildred Throne, "The Grange in Iowa, 1868-1875," *Iowa Journal 47* (October 1949): p. 292.

The Grange, which had been organized as the National Grange of the Patrons of Husbandry in 1867, originally proposed to advance agriculture through education rather than politics. However, it grew rapidly as economic conditions worsened. It found fertile soil in Iowa where the farm surplus was increasing rapidly. In 1868, Iowa claimed the oldest Grange west of the Mississippi River, at Buena Vista, some four miles from Newton, and by 1872, over half of the Granges in the nation were in Iowa. The organization promoted weekly and monthly meetings to broaden the farmer's social outlook. It arranged education programs, encouraged reading, and established libraries. Emphasis was also given to the education of children, and on higher schools such as agricultural colleges and experiment stations. They established systems of cooperative buying and selling, considering the "middleman" in the same monopoly category as the railroads, and began manufacturing farm machinery. The social and educational activities were subservient to transportation and politics, however, although the order was supposedly non-political in character.

During the summer of 1873, the demand for railroad regulation and agricultural cooperation resulted in the organization of the Anti-Monopoly Party which requested the legislature to set maximum freight rates. In the fall, one-half of the legislators elected to the General Assembly were members of the Anti-Monopoly Party, and 70 of the 100-member body were members of the Grange. The Grange had formed a coalition with the Anti-Monopoly and Democratic Parties to elect candidates who favored their cause. It was reported that "the only reason why the Republicans were not defeated was that Governor Clay Carpenter was a Patron and stood for railroad legislation."[6]

Aside from the railroad question, the desired legislation included: the support and enactment of prohibition laws; a state income tax; military training in the colleges to be optional; abolition of county assessors; and the popular election of county school superintendents. These were but a few of the items on the Granger legislative agenda, but they illustrate the wide scope of their interests. However, it was the attempt to regulate railroads that received historical attention, and at their annual convention in Des Moines in December 1874, delegates from 2,000 Granges passed a resolution declaring "that the state had a right to establish passenger fares and freight rates."[7]

Meanwhile, other interests were also working for regulatory action. The 1870 Legislature debated a maximum rate bill designed to prevent diversion of trade from the Mississippi River cities to Chicago. Senator B.B. Richards of Dubuque, supporting a bill submitted by William Mills, also of Dubuque, cited examples of discrimination against river towns. They stated that flour mills along the river were being forced to close; farmers in the interior were losing markets on the waterways; grain buyers had to move to Chicago to survive; river towns were losing their advantage as lumber markets; all because of unequal freight rates. The railroads countered by stating that low through rates were made for the convenience of farmers, enabling them to compete in Eastern markets. Discriminations in rates were distinctions necessary and just, based upon variations in traffic volumes and operating costs. They argued that any proposals to regulate would necessitate the abandonment of through freight service. The bill failed passage, as did others proposed in 1872.

Granger Legislation

State interference with railroad management was not new. Land grant legislation in 1856 declared that railroads accepting the grants would be subject to rules and regulations . . . enacted and provided by the General Assembly. Regulatory legislation attempted in 1866 was nullified by the attorney general who held that the legislature had no power to prescribe railroad rates. Any restrictive laws that were passed proved to be of little account and were seldom enforced. But in the seventies, the state was shaken by anti-railroad rumblings from agrarian and commercial groups faced with better organized railroad opposition. The time had come to take action which came with the introduction of a bill by Senator William Larabee in February, 1874, "to protect the people against the

[6] Solon J. Buck, *The Granger Movement*, Cambridge: Harvard University Studies, 1913, pp. 89-91.

[7] J. Brooke Workman, "Governor William Larrabee and Railroad Reform," *Iowa Journal 22* (July 1959): p. 239. The delegates also recommended a government-built double-tracked all-freight railroad to the Eastern Seaboard: termination of land grants and regulation of intrastate rates. See also George H. Miller, *Railroads and the Granger Laws*, Madison: University of Wisconsin Press, 1971, pp. 108-112.

abuses of unjust discrimination of railroads, express and telegraph companies." His proposal was eventually incorporated into an omnibus bill, approved in March, under the title: An Act to Establish Reasonable Maximum Rates or Charges for the Transportation of Freight and Passengers on Different Railroads of the State. This Act became known as the "Granger Law."

The law divided the railroads into three classes on the basis of their annual gross earnings. Class A roads were those earning $4,000 or more per mile of track; Class B, between $3,000 and $4,000; and Class C, less than $3,000. Progressive freight rates were fixed per hundred pounds for distances up to 376 miles. Carload rates on four general classes of commodities were specified and separate rates listed for such traffic as flour, cement, grains, lumber, mules, cattle and hogs. Different rates for different classifications were to be posted and the railroads were to report annual earnings to the Governor. Class A roads were entitled to 90 percent of the schedule of maximum rates, Class B to 105 percent, and Class C to 120 percent. The law reduced rates as much as 50 percent, but since the through rates also declined, the river interests did not enjoy the immediate relief they sought.

Different rates were thus established for railroads according to their classifications, and all commodities were placed into one of the four classes, except for those in the special list. The rates became effective on July 4, 1874. Penalties for violations ranged from fines of $20 to $100 and five to 30 days imprisonment, to repayments for overcharges of five times the amount charged firms or individuals and $500 to be paid to the state for each offense. Enforcement of the law was given to the attorney general. The law was approved by the governor on March 23, 1874.

The concept of the legislation as the "Granger Law" was challenged by Throne who took issue with the description and stated that the title was inaccurate. "The very fact that the Iowa Grange did not recommend that type of law . . . should have indicated to observers that a 'cast iron tariff bill' was passed in spite of, not because of, the Grange. In Iowa, the struggle was one of farmers and small businessmen against the large corporations . . . Economics and geography determined the passage of the law, not the existence of a farmers' social group."[8]

The 1876 Legislature received strong protests from the railroads, claiming that the law was ruining their revenues despite the fact that revenues had increased in 1874 by $1 million over those of 1873. They stressed that higher through rates would be detrimental to farmers and shippers and that further investment in railroads would be difficult to obtain. These arguments were supported by many of the newspapers who wanted modification or repeal since they argued that any business should be free to operate without state interference or control.

From the industrial sector, the first complaint came from Clinton lumbermen who had received special rates on lumber shipped into western Iowa. These were prohibited under the new law, and higher rates resulted in lower traffic volumes. Cedar Rapids, Denison and Fort Dodge complained of increased through rates. In southern Iowa, the CB&Q ignored the law as it applied to both passenger and freight rates. Several suits were instituted against the roads who preferred to test the law in federal rather than state courts. They requested an injunction against prosecution by the Attorney General on grounds that it was contrary to the Constitutions of the United States and Iowa. The case was heard in the U. S. Circuit Court for the District of Iowa, and on May 12, 1875, Judges Dillon and Miller gave the verdict to the state on the principle that railroads were public highways and therefore subject to state regulation. The railroads appealed to the U. S. Supreme Court in 1876, which upheld the decision of the Circuit Court. Failing in the courts, the railroads next turned to the public for support of repeal, but efforts to influence public opinion were not successful until 1878.

Railroad Legislation in Midwestern States

The laws of Iowa and Wisconsin (Potter Law) prescribed schedules of maximum rates, difficult to fix by statute. Legislatures, with constantly changing personnel, inexperienced in railroad matters and, without precise information as to what constituted reasonableness of rates, faced a formidable if not impossible task. Statutory rates tended to become rigid and inflexible, and changing economic conditions required rate changes without political debates to delay the necessary adjustments.

[8] Mildred Throne, *Cyrus Clay Carpenter and Iowa Politics, 1854-1898,* Iowa City: State Historical Society, 1974, p. 179.

Uniformity of rates and classifications of roads were difficult to achieve because of main and branch line differences in operating and traffic conditions. Finally, political considerations played an important role in fixing rates especially under the circumstances in 1874, when sectional interests were pressuring for economic advantages.

The laws of Illinois in 1873 and Minnesota in 1874 established commissions to which the legislatures gave the power to fix maximum rates and administer the laws, an improvement over the practice of direct legislative intervention. Prorata clauses provided that rates should not be higher for the shorter than the longer haul; combinations of lines to restrain competition were forbidden in an attempt to slow the trend toward monopolies. The laws also prohibited free passes to public officials, given initially to curry favors from those in positions of power. These soon proved to be a form of bribery and raised questions of conflicts of interest when the concerns of the railroads and the public did not coincide.

The Granger Cases

The state laws resulted in the "Granger Cases," six in all, decided by the U. S. Supreme Court in 1877.[9] The most famous and often quoted was that of *Munn v. Illinois* which actually involved the regulation of grain warehouses, not railroads, as did the other five. The railroads argued that rate regulation directed by legislatures or commissions deprived investors of property without due process of law, thus violating the 14th Amendment of the Constitution. By limiting rates which could affect net earnings, railroad properties would fall in value since values were dependent upon earnings. This, the Court conceded, applied to ordinary businesses, but railroads were in that special class of business "affected with a public interest." They pointed out that certain types of business activity had been regulated under common-law principles of England and maximum charges fixed for ferries, common carriers, innkeepers, etc., as early as 1681.

Other arguments involved state interference with charters vesting the right to fix rates by management; that state legislatures could not assume the authority without violating constitutional provisions which forbade states to pass laws impairing the obligation of those contracts. Railroads also raised the question of whether or not determination of reasonable rates was a judicial rather than a legislative function. They claimed that states had no rights in regulation of interstate commerce, an authority granted only to Congress through the Constitution which empowered them to regulate commerce among the several states. To all of these arguments, the Court decided, although not unanimously, for the "public interest." The states had the right to regulate; they did not deprive the railroads of their property without due process of law; they did not violate the contractual obligations unless the charters expressly gave the railroads rate powers. Legislatures could fix rates, and until Congress acted, states could regulate rates even though interstate commerce was indirectly affected. The Court later reversed itself on some of these points.

The railroads were now faced with legal decisions which apparently placed them at the mercy of state legislatures. They had two possible courses of action. One was to take the political road which they did quite successfully; the other to continue their fight in the courts which they did unsuccessfully until 1886, when in *Wabash v. Illinois,* the Supreme Court handed down a decision which seriously impaired the legality of state regulation. The case concerned long and short haul rates on grains from origins in Illinois to New York City, and the Court held that states could not control rates on interstate commerce even in the absence of federal regulation.[10]

Impact of the "Granger Cases" on the State

The decisions in the "Granger Cases" had given the state the right to regulate intrastate rates, and the railroads proceeded to charge the maximum rates prescribed in the 1874 law. Often these were higher than rates which had been in effect in prior years. Some of the roads chose to ignore the law and some obeyed. The CB&Q stated that it would "experiment" with the new tariff schedules but would adjust its

[9] These were: Munn v. Illinois, 94 U.S. 113 (1877); Chicago Burlington and Quincy Railroad v. Iowa, 94 U.S. 155 (1877); Chicago Milwaukee & St. Paul Railroad Company v. Ackley, 94 U.S. 179 (1877); Piek v. Chicago and Northwestern Railway Company, 94, U.S. 164 (1877); Stone v. Wisconsin, 94 U.S. 181 (1877).

[10] Wabash, St. Louis and Pacific Railway Company v. Illinois, 118 U.S. 557 (1886).

interstate rates, a loophole through which the railroads eventually forced repeal. The rate adjustments on both intra- and interstate shipments brought numerous complaints of discrimination by both agrarian and industrial organizations.

Railroad mileage increased from 2,683 in 1870 to 4,157 miles in 1878. Iowa was devoting its attention almost entirely to agricultural pursuits and had to import its manufactured goods from the East. The geographical location of the state required low rates for the long haul to agricultural markets and the return movement from commercial origins. Railroad expansion brought with it manufacturing, wholesale and jobber firms as economic opportunities opened—firms which wanted to be able to compete with commercial centers in the Midwest and East. The rate adjustments did not favor this objective.

Between 1875 and 1878, political and propaganda campaigns by railroads, coupled with a change in public attitudes, contributed to the defeat of the "Granger Law." The Granger movement was declining; farmers had recovered from the depression of 1873 and were anxious to continue their quest for additional transportation. The press generally favored repeal and were joined by businessmen and the railroad lobby to stir up support. The greatest criticism of the law was its rigidity and lack of proper enforcement machinery for effective control. Yet, it had rendered indirect benefits to the public. Adams, writing on the "Granger Movement," stated that "the corporations have been made to realize that the roads were built for the West and that to be operated successfully, they must be in sympathy with the people of the West. The whole system of discriminations and local extortions had received a much needed investigation, the results of which cannot but mitigate or wholly remove the more abominable features . . . great principles of justice and equality heretofore ignored have been drawn by the sheer force of discussion, backed by rising public opinion into the very essence of railroad policy."[11] It also seemed that it was poor policy for the state, still needing more railroad mileage, to antagonize the builders.

The Repeal of the "Granger Law"

The law was repealed on March 23, 1878, eliminating all of the 1874 legislation except for the sections establishing railroad classifications, passenger charges and annual reports of revenues. The legislature created a three-man Advisory Commission, modeled after the Massachusetts Commission Law of 1869. The commission was given supervision over intrastate railroads, was to examine and inquire into any neglect or violation of state laws, examine books and documents of the railroads, investigate complaints, require annual reports, and provide the governor with annual reports on the railroad situation. Commission members represented eastern, western and central sections of the state and could have no financial interests in the railroads. Their expenses, including salaries, were pro-rated among railway companies. Discrimination between shippers under similar circumstances and conditions was prohibited. Special rates were to be available to all parties and unreasonable rates were considered illegal, although unreasonableness was not defined. Failure to comply with provisions of the law could result in fines up to three times the damages or overcharges plus court costs, and continued violations after warnings could lead to a report to the legislature, the only enforcement agent of the state. The railroad lobby saw that such enforcement was practically non-existent.

Federal Regulation of Railroads

Railroad regulation had been debated in Congress as early as 1867, when Granger discontent resulted in the election of candidates from the West. The issues centered on the railroad movement of grains to the eastern seaboard, alleging discriminations against the agricultural areas so as to consume in charges for transit more than one-third of their entire value, while manufacturing interests in the East are protected by a tariff. Congressman Wilkensen of Minnesota called attention to the price of the wheat crop of 1869 as being sold at various railroad origins for about 50 cents per bushel, yet purchased in New York for $1.20 to $1.25. "Railway rates were at least one-third too high and the people are being plundered by chartered monopolies—monopolies which had been aided by land grants or otherwise."[12]

[11] C. F. Adams, "The Granger Movement," *North American Review, 120* (April 1875): p. 423.

[12] Lewis Henry Haney, *A Congressional History,* p. 245.

Two Senate committees examined the possibility of securing cheap transportation from the western states to the East. The first, known as the Windom Committee, reported in 1872 and reflected the common and popular view that competition should be the regulator of rates, but that competition invariably ended in combination and did not offer the necessary protection to shippers and the public. Only through state or national ownership of one or more railroads could effective competition be expected and maintained, and the Committee recommended building railroads to the seaboard and further development of the inland waterways. The report created little attention. In 1874 and 1875, the House passed bills providing for regulation, and in 1884 and 1885, bills were introduced in both Houses of Congress only to become deadlocked over different provisions.

The impasse resulted in the appointment of the second, the Cullum Committee, to investigate the railroad problem. It made its report in 1886, emphasizing more the evils of discrimination than the levels of rates stressed in the Windom Committee report.[13] Senator Cullum earlier had reported that there existed 18 evils or railroad abuses, ranging from unreasonably high local rates versus through rates, pooling arrangements, secret rates, drawbacks and concessions to favored shippers, overcharges, free passes, etc., to railroad involvement in businesses other than transportation. Three major classes of discrimination were described: (1) those which affected certain individuals, the most objectionable and used for discounts; (2) those which affected certain localities and had as their origin the natural desire of competing roads to increase business at the expense of their rivals, and were used at competitive common points versus non-competitive points; and (3) discrimination between products, the most common of the unjust practices. Livestock versus dressed beef was an example. The cost of transportation from Chicago to New York for dressed beef was 6¼ cents per pound more than that of live animals but the rate was 75 percent higher. The Cullum report, with compromises between the two congressional bodies and possibly aided by the *Wabash* decision, hastened the enactment of the Act to Regulate Commerce in 1887.

The Act to Regulate Commerce

The legislation applied to all common carriers in interstate or foreign commerce and included water carriers when they and the railroads were used "under common management, control or arrangement for a continous carriage and shipment." The language was broad and indefinite and caused controversy over many years, requiring commission and court interpretations, in turn resulting in many amendments. The act required that all rates be just and reasonable, a statutory endorsement of the common-law principle; no personal discrimination was to be allowed, with certain exceptions; no undue preference nor prejudice between persons, kinds of traffic or places; prohibited were long and short haul discriminations and pooling agreements; and all rates were to be published with strict adherence by the railroads. Created was the Interstate Commerce Commission (ICC) of five members, appointed by the President, with powers and duties to hear complaints of violations, to investigate and assess damages, to inquire into the operations of the carriers, require annual reports, and prescribe a uniform system of accounts. The commission was to make annual reports to Congress for evaluation of the regulatory process and make recommendations for further legislation, if necessary. The act was amended many times as economic conditions changed, new modal competition appeared, and court and commission decisions clarified or confused carriers, shippers and the public with their interpretations.

Iowa Railroad Classifications

The first annual report of the Iowa Commission showed 29 railroads operating in the state, subject to the classifications invoked in the 1874 law. These are listed under the "A", "B," and "C" classifications in Table 3-2.

[13] *Report-of-the-Senate Select Committee on Interstate Commerce,* 49th Congress 1st Sess. Senate Report.

Table 3-2
Railroad Classifications

Class "A" Railroads

Chicago, Burlington & Quincy Railroad.
Chicago & North Western Railway.
Chicago, Rock Island & Pacific Railroad.
Kansas City, St.Joseph & Council Bluffs Railroad.

Class "B" Railroads

Burlington, Cedar Rapids & Northern Railway.
Central Railroad of Iowa.
Chicago, Milwaukee & St. Paul Railway.
Illinois Central Railroad.
Iowa Railway, Coal & Manufacturing Company.
Keokuk & Des Moines Railway.

Class "C" Railroads

Burlington & Northwestern Railway.
Burlington & Southwestern Railway.
Chicago, Clinton & Western Railroad.
Chicago, Clinton, Dubuque & Minnesota Railroad.
Crooked Creek Railway.
Davenport & Northwestern Railway.
Des Moines & Fort Dodge Railroad.
Des Moines & Minneapolis Railroad.
Dubuque & Southwestern Railroad.
Iowa Eastern Railroad.
Missouri, Iowa & Nebraska Railway.
Newton & Monroe Railroad.
Sabula, Ackley & Dakota Railroad.
St. Louis, Kansas City & Northern Railway.
St. Louis, Keokuk & Northwestern Railway.
Sioux City & Pacific Railroad.
Sioux City & Pembina Railway.
Sioux City & St. Paul Railroad.
Toledo & Northwestern Railway.

(Source: Iowa Railroad Commission, Annual Report, 1878)

The Railroad Commission's Interpretation of the New Law

From the beginning, the commission struggled with the concept of reasonable rates and questions concerning discrimination. Shippers preferred rates based on the cost of service plus a fair profit over fixed expenses. Railroads preferred the value of service principle, "charging what the traffic would bear." Any rate, in the judgment of the commission, that would not deter shipments was fair no matter how great the profit. Ripley commented on the basis of reasonable rates as follows: "Both principles are of equal importance and both must continually be invoked as a check upon each other. The tendency to the elevation of cost of service to the position of priority, rather characteristic of the relative bodies and legislatures, is no less erroneous than the marked disposition of railway managers to insist upon the universal applicability of the principle of what the traffic will bear. Neither will stand the test of reasonableness alone. Whether one or the other should take precedence can only be determined by a careful study of the circumstances and conditions in each case, and in practice the instances where either principle becomes of binding effect to the exclusion of the other are extemely rare."[14] With only the legal requirement that rates should be "just and reasonable" or only "reasonable," state and federal commissions faced difficult decisions, for there were no precedents in statutory or common law to guide them, and the issue of "reasonable rates" became a continuing problem for regulators.

The law prohibited unjust discrimination but permitted discrimination that was "just." Early the commission took the position that just discrimination should be allowed, and such was incorporated into the freight classifications of the railroads. Examples of "just" discrimination were higher rates on high-valued commodities than those classified lower, not because the cost of transportation was greater, although there was some acceptance of risk involved, but because the traffic would move on higher rates. Also, rate discrimination could be applied at competing points (unjust from the view of non-competing points), because if this was the only way railroads could gain traffic and make profits, the non-competing points would eventually benefit through lowered rates. Further, they argued that competition must exist and there must be absolute equality of rates. Discrimination, which was unjust, and undue preferences should be prohibited, and advantage given one place over another should be regarded as violations of the "just" principle of discrimination.

[14] William Z. Ripley, *Railroad Rates and Regulation,* New York: Longmans-Green & Co., 1912, p. 101.

Dixon suggested that the commission's position on discrimination was open to serious question. "The practice of granting special rates at competitive points seemed wrong in principle, for it was doubtful that the growth of cities and concentration at a few points was necessary to the prosperity of a state. In other words, was a policy which leads to the enrichment and advancement of a few places at the expense of many, productive of benefit to the people as a whole? While building up business at competitive points and increasing their net earnings, railroads were, in many cases, destroying business at non-competitive points. The effect upon the public at large must be taken into account in determining the reasonableness and justice."[15]

Using the same logic, the commission abandoned the theory that the state should prohibit higher rates for shorter than for longer distances. This, they stated, would compel the loss of through traffic and emphasize operations entirely on local traffic, with increased local rates to cover the losses sustained on the abandoned through movements. It was claimed by opponents of the long and short haul principle that if the roads were required to charge as much for the long haul as for the short one, they would raise the long haul rates rather than lower those on the shorter hauls. Cases which came before the commission included favored shippers, prorata rates ignoring distance, long and short hauls, distribution of cars and carload versus less-than-carload rates. Other questions were raised about adequate service, car shortages, handling of cars from connecting roads, maintenance of way, unsafe bridges, road and highway crossings, construction of viaducts, proper safeguards for cattle and fencing of track. Overcharge complaints were the most frequent, almost non-existent in the 1870's, but now commonplace. Damage claims were also frequent, and for these the commission acted as an arbitrator. The law prohibited pooling in state commerce but had no effect on the pooling arrangements in Iowa since these agreements covered interstate traffic. The Pool did not concern itself with local traffic, leaving that entirely to the discretion of individual companies.

A Potential Problem Emerges

Between 1880 and 1884, annual reports of the commission seemed to indicate a general satisfaction with the new law but also began to outline a pattern that could spell trouble for the future. Railroads were still expanding at a high rate, growing from 4,157 miles in 1878 to 7,249 in 1884. In 1884, of the 25,900 stockholders in Iowa railroads, only 740 were residents of the state. Only one Iowan was among the 11 directors of the CB&Q and none were on Boards of Directors of the CNW and CRI&P. The commission commented: "This great interest is thus practically without representation in the General Assembly, while in the boards of directors, as the majority runs the other way, it is but fair to suppose that the real interests of Iowa shippers are not fairly represented. We have here a form of absenteeism which can only result in clashing interests and conflicting methods . . . It would not be strange that the members of the General Assembly should hear and think about the calls and demands of the living, present, constituent shippers and producers, than of the absent, non-represented stockholders who are neither voters nor constituents. On the other hand, it would not be strange if the directors, meeting abroad and representing funds invested demanding remunerative returns, should think and act for the present aggresive, vigilant stockholders than for the absent unknown shippers and producers."[16] Absentee ownership had been a point of agitation during the Granger period and was surfacing again.

The Industrial Structure—1880 to 1890

From 1880 to 1890, urban population increased from 247,000 to 406,000 and manufacturing industries enjoyed a somewhat parallel growth. In 1880, industrial firms employed 28,372 people and had a production value over $71 million. Agriculture furnished raw materials and provided markets for such industries as agricultural implements, wagons and carriages, flour mills, breweries, saddles and harnesses and meat packing. Corn, the state's staple crop, could not be shipped in large quantities because railroad rates were too high a percentage of its value, so it was processed into commercial products as well

[15] Frank Dixon, *State Railroad Control,* Boston: Thomas Y. Crowell & Co., 1898, pp. 51-52.

[16] *First Annual Report of the Board of Railroad Commissioners for the Year Ending June 30, 1878,* State of Iowa, Des Moines: State Printing Office, 1878, pp. 155, 192, 223. See also the *Third Annual Report* for 1880, p. 4 and the *Seventh Annual Report* for 1884, pp. 5-6, 117.

as fed to cattle and hogs, where the rates would bear a lower proportion to value. Dairying became important for the processing of cheese and butter. The leading manufacturing counties closely reflected the concentration of population in the state (Table 3-3).

By the 1890s, 59,174 people were employed in industry which produced commodities valued over $125 million. Of the four industries with a production value of $1 million or over, three were dependent upon agriculture: meat packing, flour milling and dairy products. The fourth was lumber and mill products. The leading industrial counties, primarily on the Mississippi River, showed little change in rankings by 1890. Woodbury County, which included Sioux City, led the group, but six of the 10 most important in terms of production value were those on the river. Other cities developing industries were Marshalltown, Waterloo, Council Bluffs, Iowa City and Waukon. Wholesale growth, as reported by 22 towns, showed 399 wholesale houses with total sales of $68 million in 1884 (Table 3-4).

Table-3-3
Iowa's Ten Leading Manufacturing Counties, 1880

County	Major City	Est.[1]	Capital	Ave. No. Workers	Production
Dubuque	Dubuque	459	$3,749,761	3,187	$6,885,289
Linn	C. Rapids	207	1,564,150	1,320	5,205,859
Scott	Davenport	241	2,983,157	1,801	4,667,511
Polk	Des Moines	202	1,564,790	1,575	4,530,428
Clinton	Clinton	172	2,752,492	1,698	4,080,647
Wapello	Ottumwa	154	1,094,495	1,067	3,506,379
Lee	Keokuk	285	2,146,534	1,874	3,192,058
Des Moines	Burlington	134	1,420,373	1,426	2,838,053
Pottawattamie	C. Bluffs	120	546,541	719	2,448,842
Muscatine	Muscatine	195	1,056,985	1,010	1,913,149

(*Source: Census of Iowa, 1880.* The value of production was for the year ending May 31, 1880.)

[1]Number of industrial or manufacturing establishments.

Table 3-4
Iowa's Ten Leading Manufacturing Counties, 1890

County	Major City	Est.[1]	Capital	Ave. No. Workers	Production
Woodbury	Sioux City	242	$ 5,455,766	3,167	$14,343,545
Scott	Davenport	504	8,910,293	5,280	10,685,316
Dubuque	Dubuque	343	7,335,110	4,876	10,316,491
Linn	C. Rapids	221	2,983,026	2,776	9,485,824
Polk	Des Moines	346	3,906,240	3,974	7,979,300
Lee	Keokuk	328	5,143,569	4,145	7,977,198
Clinton	Clinton	510	10,598,890	5,312	7,088,262
Des Moines	Burlington	239	4,494,426	3,986	6,599,046
Wapello	Ottumwa	136	1,526,674	2,513	5,141,645
Muscatine	Muscatine	189	4,213,416	2,501	4,248,621

(*Source: Census of the United States, 1890.* Part I, IX.)

[1]Number of industrial or manufacturing establishments.

Thus, throughout the 1880s, the railroad question had materially changed. The emphasis upon agriculture alone as the leading and only economically viable industry shifted at least partially to processing and manufacturing. Industrialists and wholesalers had been able to compete with large metropolitan centers through rebates on rates but were helpless when rebating was prohibited by federal statutes. For Iowa merchants and jobbers, their trade was placed in jeopardy by discriminations which resulted from the fluctuating rates, and while Chicago grew—at the expense of many of the smaller cities and towns in Iowa—the public and press concluded that it was the result of railroad favoritism. Local rates were clearly higher than through rates.

The Iowa jobber had two rates to pay in his business. One was the rate from Chicago or other eastern cities to his location; the other, the local rate to his customers. The out-of-state competitor had only one rate direct to destinations, based upon lower interstate tariffs. Examples of rate problems faced by Iowa merchants are described by Murphy: "If a Cedar Rapids jobber wished to ship 100 pounds of first class commodities to Jefferson, he would pay a total charge of $1.81. From New York to Chicago, the rate was $.75; Chicago to Cedar Rapids, $.60; and from Cedar Rapids to Jefferson, $.46. The Chicago merchant paid $1.53 to the same city, or $.28 less. The difference was borne by the Iowa jobber who had to sell his goods at Chicago prices."

Discrimination also existed between the interior towns and Mississippi River cities as a result of lower interstate rates from Chicago and eastern origins. "On first class freight, the rate from New York to Davenport (1,000 miles) was $.96½; the rate from Davenport to Tama City (140 miles) was $.45, for a total of $1.41½. The rate from New York to Cedar Rapids (1,065 miles) was $1.25; the rate from Cedar Rapids to Tama City (54 miles) was $.27, for a total of $1.52, or a disadvantage of $.10½."[17]

Sunday Trains

An interesting sidelight in recommendations of the commission to the legislature was one concerning the abandonment of Sunday trains. Moving trains on the Sabbath was demoralizing, they observed. "The laboring man had a right to the seventh day of rest, and out of place in the quiet of a Sunday morning was the thunder and roar of long freight trains as they went rattling by vestibules of a church. Again, where trains come and go on a Sunday, there was always more or less gathering of people at the station, especially the boys of the town. Among these are sure to be some of the worst elements in the neighborhood and their influence is anything but good on these boys gathered there and who would not be there but for the expected train. In short, Sunday trains are demoralizing from any point of view . . . They disturb worshiping assemblies; they demoralize the young by bringing them into contact with the low and vicious; and they gradually undermine the reverence and regard that the Sabbath day should cultivate."[18] After several recommendations, the subject was dropped through lack of interest.

The Movement for Regulatory Reform

Governor Larabee and Regulatory Reform

William Larrabee was elected governor in 1885, and during his first year in office there was little railroad legislation. The press and some of the legislators raised questions concerning the continued policy of issuing free passes, and bills advocating an elective commission were introduced without passage. On December 6, 1866, the governor became involved in a complaint against the CB&Q on coal rates from Cleveland in Lucas County to Glenwood. He alleged that the railroad charged $1.80 per ton in carload lots on the Glenwood route, but only charged $1.25 per ton for shipments from the same origin to Council Bluffs, some 30 miles farther. Charles Perkins, president of the CB&Q, replied that the Glenwood charges were fair and produced little profit, and that competition at Council Bluffs required a lower rate. Larrabee challenged Perkin's position, stating that the CRI&P hauled coal from Colfax in Jasper County, practically equidistant, to Council Bluffs for $1.25 per ton, rebated $.25 and made a profit. The Railroad Commission supported the governor and recommended that the CB&Q revise its coal rates.

[17] Ronald S. Murphy, *Railroad Regulation in Iowa:* The Modification of the Advisory Commission, M.A. thesis, University of Iowa, 1965, pp. 11, 87-88.

[18] *Sixth Annual Report of the Board of Railroad Commissioners for the Year Ending June 30, 1883,* State of Iowa, Des Moines: State Printing Office, 1883, pp. 81-82.

Instead the railroad raised the Council Bluffs rate to $1.98 per ton, an action later regarded as a policy mistake. On March 17, 1887, the governor sent the commission a list of freight overcharges at Glenwood totaling $3,326.40, and demanded a hearing on the case.

The governor not only complained of the rates but vented his wrath against the commission who, in his opinion, had not made a complete study of rate issues and rate violations under the 1878 law. He was also irritated over the lack of funds which prevented the commission from performing their duties and coping with the powerful railroads. However, the commission was without power to enforce its findings even after examination of complaints, and Larabee's anger was somewhat like a "tempest in a teapot." Workman, quoting A. B. Frank, a close personal friend of Larabee, suggested that this incident had a great influence on his attitude toward regulatory reform. Following it, he became more adamant on reform philosophy, to the delight of the press, merchants, farmers and the public; to the dismay of the railroads.

The new federal legislation did not bring the expected relief from railroad abuses. Railroads lowered their through rates and raised rates on local traffic, as explained earlier. The governor expressed himself quite clearly on the subject: "Success greatly emboldened the railway companies. Discriminations seemed to increase in number and gravity. At many points in the western part of the state, freight rates to Chicago were from 50 to 75 percent higher than those from Kansas and Nebraska. A car of wheat hauled only across the state paid twice as much freight as another hauled twice the distance from its origin to Chicago. Minnesota flour was hauled a distance of 300 miles for a less rate than Iowa flour carried 100 miles."[19]

By 1887, farmers were once more in financial difficulty. Increased competition from states west of Iowa had dropped prices drastically. In 1881, corn sold for 44 cents per bushel; in 1889, for 19 cents. Wheat slipped from $1.06 to 83 cents, and cattle prices fell 39 percent from 1885 to 1890. Interest was eight percent on mortgages totaling $440 million in 1889, and there was confusion over land ownership and land titles between the settlers and the railroads. Despite the agrarian problems, railroads expanded and prospered. By the close of the fiscal year 1889, there were 8,298 miles built in the state, about double that of 1870, and gross earnings of the five major trunk lines rose from $26.5 million in 1870 to $72.9 million in 1887. By 1889, the assessed value was $43.3 million and the income over $13 million, equal to one-third of the value of the corn crop, $3 million over the value of the wheat crop, and one-sixth of the cattle sales. Yet, the railroads were paying less than one-tenth of the total tax assessments while two-thirds were paid by farmers.

Governor Larrabee was reelected in 1887, with agricultural, industrial and public support and was in an excellent position to push for regulatory reform. He made three recommendations in his biennial message to the General Assembly regarding railroad control: first, prohibit the issuance of free passes; second, establish passenger fares at two cents per mile; and third, establish reasonable rates and authorize the commission to reduce them when considered too high. He further attacked the anti-regulatory positions of the railroads in his inaugural address.

Railroad Legislation of 1888

Leaders of the reform movement in the House of Representatives were A. B. Cummins and James Beryhill; in the Senate, J. H. Sweeney and G. L. Finn. After much debate, a new law was passed without a dissenting vote in either chamber dealing with freight rates and strengthening the powers of the commission. It had the following exotic title: "An Act to Regulate Railroad Corporations and other Common Carriers in this State and to Increase the Powers and further Define the Duties of the Board of Commissioners, in relation to the same, and to Prevent and Punish Extortion and unjust Discrimination in Rates charged for the Transportation of Passengers and Freights on Railroads in this State and Prescribe a Mode of Procedure and Rules of Evidence in relation thereto and to Repeal Section 11 of Chapter 77 of the Act of the Seventeenth General Assembly in relation to the Board of Railroad Commissioners and all Laws in force in direct Conflict with the Provisions of this Act."[20]

[19] William Larrabee, *The Railroad Question,* Chicago: F. J. Schulte & Co., 1906, p. 337.

[20] *1888 Laws of Iowa,* Chapter 28.

The new law generally followed the provisions of the federal act. All charges were to be just and reasonable, and no special rates, rebates, or refunds were allowed. No preference would be given any person, corporation, firm or locality. Equal interchange facilities were to be available for all railroads. Included was the long and short haul clause and prohibited were all pooling arrangements. Rate schedules would be posted, copies of which, together with joint agreements with other railroads, were required by the commission, and 10 days notice was necessary for rate increases. The commission was empowered to make and review rates, such to be *prima facie* evidence in courts that the rates were reasonable. They could investigate violations, hold hearings and prosecute. Another act changed the manner of choosing commissioners, from appointment by the governor to election by the public, and they were to be paid by the state rather than the railroads. On the matters of discrimination, the new law differed from the original one which prohibited unjust discrimination but recognized that discriminations could be "just." Now, absolute equality was required.

With the new law in place, the problem was to get acceptance from railroads and shippers. Maximum rates were effective on July 5, 1888, and met immediate opposition from the railroads. On June 28, 1888, the CNW, CM&StP and CB&Q sought an injunction against the commission, and Judge David J. Brewer of the U. S. District Court granted it, stating that the new rates could adversely affect the rate of return on investment, but that the commission had the power to establish rate schedules as long as the rates resulted in compensation, whatever the level. The commission argued that their schedules were reasonably compensatory and that in some instances, the rates were higher than those established voluntarily by the railroads. There was also some evidence of further discrimination since the new law became effective. Charges were filed in August, 1888, by Davenport shippers against five railroads who they alleged had increased rates by eight to 25 percent.

Because of the growing number of shipper complaints, the CM&StP and CB&Q again applied for a court injunction against the commission's rate schedules. But on February 2, 1889, Judge Brewer reversed his previous stand and refused their requests. He stated: "The officers of the railroad companies declare that the rates fixed by the commission will so reduce income that it will not suffice to pay the running expenses of the road and the interest on their bonded debts, leaving nothing for the stockholders. The commissioners insist that their schedule was framed to produce eight percent income on the value of the roads after paying the cost of maintenance and running expenses. Which view is the correct one, is impossible to decide from the evidence submitted. There is one way, however, a conclusive way, and it seems to me it is the only way by which the controversy can be settled, and that is by experiment."[21] The essence of the decision was that rates must be tested to judge their compensatory nature and at the same time not violate other provisions of the law. The CB&Q accepted the decision almost immediately by adopting the new rates, and other railroads followed. But, as the press pointed out, the railroads could still refuse to cooperate, running the risk of heavy fines, or could adopt the rates and attempt to prove them unreasonable.

Results of the 1888 Legislation

Both railroads and the state benefited by the new law. Fiscal year 1891 showed a net increase of 1,369 million tons of freight carried over 8,440 miles of road compared with the tonnage of 1890. Gross earnings were $5 million higher, and net earnings increased almost $3 million between 1889 and 1891. The state benefited through development of home industry. Lower rates stimulated the opening of new mills and mines, and more industrial and agricultural products were traded within the state than ever before. Opponents of the law claimed that the decline in railroad construction was the result of the rate structure. However, by the late 19th century, demand for further railway construction was falling. Iowa had 8,500 miles of roads, with no community more than 15 miles from service. This would readily account for only 65 miles built in 1893, as it would for the fact that Illinois, with a higher rate level, built only 62 miles during the same year.

[21] *Twelfth Annual Report of the Board of Railroad Commissioners for the Year Ending June 30, 1889,* State of Iowa, Des Moines: State Printing Office, 1889, p. 31.

By 1890, the commission and governor were pleased with the results of the 1888 law. Railroad tonnage and earnings were impressive, and the governor stated that: "No further vindication of the law is necessary. These figures show plainly that the lowering and equalizing of the rates not only increased the roads' business and income but also their net earnings. It must be remembered that the reports . . . were made by railroad companies and were certainly not made with any intention of prejudicing the cause of the rail manager."[22] Two comments by the commission supported the governor. "The farmers gets his supplies cheaper, his lumber, coal, salt, and other heavy commodities at fair rates. He finds a market for a portion of his surplus corn, oats, hay, wood timber, etc., at home and saves transportation. He markets many of his hogs at Iowa packing houses and saves freight charges. Wood and logs that lay in the timber rotting, the Iowa rates are making a market for, and new mills are sawing the latter up for use in excelsior, fencing, pickets, handles, boxes and other industries unknown before. The railway policy of the long haul has in measure been supplanted by the new system, and the exchange of products between different parts of the state is one of commendable results. Hay and corn from northern Iowa are now sold at better prices in the dairy counties of eastern and southern Iowa in larger quantities, a thing hitherto unknown. These formerly paid tribute to Chicago."

A second comment had to do with stability of rates. "There have been no rate wars and consequent disturbance of business in Iowa the past two years. The stable character of Iowa rates which have been in force, with only such slight changes as have been made in classifications from time to time, are approved on every hand. . . The evil effects of rate wars on business are unknown here, and instead we have steady rates and uniform charges shared alike by all."[23]

In 1926, a speech by Clyde B. Aitchison, long-time member of the ICC, could aptly have described the railroad situation in Iowa during the last three decades of the 19th century. "The useless construction of competing lines, construction for wildcat financial purposes or to obtain subsidies, cutthroat competiton in rates—these were manifestly wasteful practices but they were part of a great economic system of trial and error which has evolved a transportation machine so efficient that we view what we have endured in the past with incredibility and inability to visualize. There was much that was selfish and much that was dishonest; but all that was selfish and dishonest played some useful part in the end. . . The Nation has developed primarily because adequate and growing means of transportation have facilitated the entrance of the settler and interchange of commodities produced, manufactured, used or consumed. Every error and waste has aided if only by showing what was unsound and should be avoided. But with all the misconceptions and losses, it would be ungenerous not to pay ungrudging tribute to the inventive genius and mechanical skill, to the daring of the financier, the constructor and operator who took risks which were often desperate and who hazarded their reputations and fortunes."[24]

Summary

Individualism, the mark of the pioneer, was transformed into corporate philosophy between 1850 and 1870, and the railroad was the instrument of its application to economic and political control. Throughout the period, the public assumed that competition would safely guarantee fair and reasonable treatment provided that sufficient numbers of railroads were built. Competition was given the opportunity to meet these expectations, but by 1870, the evils of unregulated competition were beginning to appear. Railroad pools were organized and public suspicion developed as competing systems formed combinations to restrain competition. Further aggravation resulted when, in their desire to increase traffic, railroads adopted policies of discrimination between persons, commodities and places.

When the public recognized the power of corporations to control transportation and arbitrarily build or destroy the business of a person or community, they turned to their government for protection. Iowa first attempted to control railroad abuses through an Advisory Commission. It failed because of lack of enforcement authority. A stronger commission, given the power to regulate and enforce

[22] William Larrabee, *The Railroad Question*, pp. 132-155, 266.

[23] *Fourteenth Annual Report of the Board of Railroad Commissioners for the Year Ending June 30, 1891*, State of Iowa, Des Moines: State Printing Office, 1891, pp. 9-10, 16.

[24] P. Harvey Middleton, *Railroads and Public Opinion, Eleven Decades*, Chicago: Railway Business Association, 1941, pp. 98-99.

its decisions, brought some order to rate and discriminatory practices. States throughout the nation had tried either the weak or strong commission approach, but Iowa was one of the few that tried both types.

The controversy between the public and railroads was based upon the insistence by the roads that their property was private and they had the right to determine rates and contracts—rights supported by the State and Federal Constitutions. This view was not endorsed by the courts. The "Granger Legislation" established the principle that the public had an interest in railroad operations and that legislators directly or indirectly could take steps to guard that interest. Resistance of the railroads made judicial interpretation and sanction necessary and settled for all time the question of whether or not the states could regulate industries of "public interest."

Expansion of interstate traffic and continued railroad discriminations limited and modified the state's jurisdiction, making imperative the Federal Act to Regulate Commerce in 1887. Further changes in the Iowa laws followed in 1888, and by 1890, the state and railroads appeared to benefit from the reforms.

Selected References

Beard, Earl. "The Background of State Railroad Legislation in Iowa." *Iowa Journal 51* (January 1953): pp. 33-34.

Beinhauer, Myrtle. "Development of the Grange in Iowa, 1868-1930." *Annals of Iowa 34* (April 1959): p. 610.

Bigham, Truman. *Transportation Principles and Problems.* New York: McGraw-Hill Book Co., 1946.

Buck, Solon J. *The Granger Movement.* Cambridge: Harvard University Studies, 1913.

Dey, Peter A. "Railroad Legislation in Iowa." *Iowa Historical Record 9* (October 1893): pp. 540-561.

Dixon, Frank. *State Railroad Control.* Boston: Thomas Y. Crowell & Co., 1898.

Grodinsky, Julius. *Transcontinental Railroad Strategy, 1869-1893.* Philadelphia: University of Pennsylvania Press, 1962.

Gue, Benjamin. *History of Iowa.* New York: Century Historical Co., 1903.

Holbrook, Stewart H. *The Age of the Moguls.* Garden City, New Jersey: Doubleday & Co., 1954.

Jones, Elliot, and Homer B. Vanderblue. *Railroads, Cases and Selections.* New York: The MacMillan Co., 1905.

1874 Laws of Iowa, Chapter 68.

Middleton, Harvey. *Railroads and Public Opinion, Eleven Decades.* Chicago: Railway Business Association, 1941.

Miller, George H. "Chicago, Burlington & Quincy Railroad Company v. Iowa." *Iowa Journal 54* (July 1956): pp. 289-312.

Nixon, Herman Clarence. "The Populist Movement in Iowa." *Iowa Journal 24* (January 1926): pp. 10-13.

Ralston, Leonard F. *Railroads and the Government of Iowa, 1850-1872.* Ph.D. diss., University of Iowa, 1960.

Riegal, Robert E. "Thc Iowa Pool." *Iowa Journal 22* (October 1924): p. 570.

Shambaugh, Benjamin F., ed. *The Messages and Proclamations of the Governors of Iowa.* Iowa City: State Historical Society of Iowa, 1903-1905.

Strand, Norman V. "Prices of Farm Products in Iowa, 1851-1940." *Agriculture and Home Economics Experiment Station, Bulletin No. 303.* Ames: Iowa State College, May 1942.

Throne, Mildred. "The Repeal of the Iowa Granger Law." *Iowa Journal 51* (April 1953): pp. 97-130.

Transportation Routes to the Seaboard, 43rd Congress 1st Session, Senate Report 307, Part I, 1874.

Chapter Four
The Movement For Good Roads

Introduction

The emphasis on railroad construction in Iowa effectively suppressed any comprehensive movement for road improvements beyond the era of plank roads and some local activity. So many railroads had been planned and built that it was thought that state or national road systems would not be necessary. Roads might be needed for local traffic, but this responsibility could be left to local authorities. Bridge building took priority over road construction and money was spent on roads only after bridges were built. It was assumed that horse, oxen and mule-powered wagons could navigate under any road conditions but could not ford the streams without danger. Improvements were confined to filling the low spots on the earth road to keep it above water in rainy seasons. There was little or no grading, no plans, no cost estimates or engineering except for surveying, little or no dirt moving machinery or men knowledgeable to operate such if available. The labor force functioned under the medieval practice of working out the road or poll tax, and competent foremen to supervise road work were extemely rare.

The Good Roads Movement

The near completion of the railway network and its influence on urban development marked wide differences in the level of improvements in rail as contrasted to highway transportation. Railroad service was being expanded and perfected technically, whereas highway services had seen little advancement for almost 50 years. Rural areas suffered from 18th century mobility while urban centers received direct benefits from improved transportation, communication and industrialization. Road reform was the result of public pressures for new arrangements to enable rural areas to participate in the developing economic and social structure of the state. Agriculture was undergoing a transition from a purely self-sufficient status to a capitalistic organization producing surplus crops, and all-weather roads were vital to farmers for transportation of products to urban markets. Wagons moved farm commodities to local markets or the nearest rail terminal—the cost often proportional to road conditions. The demand for better roads was oriented to the farm-to-market segment of the highway function.

As late as 1880, the sole responsibility for providing rural roads rested with local governments. Townships and road districts served as administrative units; management was on an amateur rather than a professional level. Townships gradually gave way to counties in local road administration. State governments entered the field, first by offering aid to local agencies and finally by assuming responsibility over primary roads, and the federal government slowly expanded financial participation. During the late 19th and early 20th centuries, road reform movements were the popular methods of gaining support for improvements and changes in road administration.

Despite the organization of the "good roads" groups, the situation at the turn of the century had not changed much since that time in 1840, when Judge George C. Wright asked a stagecoach driver how long it would take to reach Iowa City, 12 miles away. "About four hours," replied the driver, "if we can find the bottom of the road." Until the 1920's, Illinois and Iowa residents jokingly boasted that their "roads were as deep as they were wide."[1] A wagonload of 3,000 pounds was a heavy load. A trip of 10 miles was a long journey, and to travel 20 miles was a full and hard day's work.

Dearing described the good roads movement as one "variously interpreted as an effort on the part of American bicyclists and manufacturers to obtain facilities for pleasure cycling; as a movement to saddle the farmer with the cost of roads to be used by automobiles; as a device for expanding the market for building machinery and materials." He further suggested that all descriptions suffered from the defects of over-simplification and historical inaccuracies—that the major thrust of the movement was based on the need to modernize the roads and their management with the objective of "bringing the standards of rural road transportation up to those achieved in urban areas through railroad development."[2] The activity received wide support

[1] Mississippi Valley Conference of State Highway Departments. *Historical Highlights: 1909-1974,* Ames: Iowa Department of Transportation, 1980, pp. 1-2.

[2] Charles L. Dearing, *American Highway Policy,* Washington, D.C.: The Brookings Institute, 1941, p. 46.

from organized civilian groups, political parties, state and local agencies and businessmen and included railroads who wanted improved roads as feeders for their traffic.

The Iowa Initiative

Aggravated probably by impassible roads during the winter of 1882-1883, Samuel D. Pryce of Iowa City, in a letter to the *Iowa State Register* on January 3, 1883, pointed to the inadequacies of Iowa's roads and made several recommendations for improvements. He stated that farmers were suffering great economic losses through bad roads; that the state ranked high in agriculture but had a poor reputation in roads; that the statutory labor requirement that pulled farmers out of their fields during the planting and harvesting seasons was most inefficient; that roads needed to be graded, tiled, drained and surfaced; and there was a huge waste resulting from paying taxes in labor. He advocated repeal of the labor provisions, a uniform property tax of five mills for road improvements to be paid into the county treasury, appointment by the governor of a highway commissioner for each county to build the roads or contract construction to responsible parties, with drains and grades supervised by a competent civil engineer.

The proposals received statewide newspaper publicity and were responsible for a convention held in Iowa City in March, 1883, where the Pryce recommendations were adopted and a "State Road Improvement Association" organized. Its objective was to awaken public interest and work for road legislation. It met once again in 1884, but apparently satisfied with the progress made, lost its momentum. Another "Iowa Road Improvement Association" was organized in Des Moines in August, 1892, founded by Edward H. Thayer, editor of the *Clinton Morning Age,* and among those active were Peter A. Dey and William Larrabee of railroad fame, Henry C. Wallace, John H. Gear and John Scott. The association survived but a short time. In April, 1903, called by Governor Cummins, the first Iowa Good Roads Association with semi-official status met in Des Moines, and some historians consider this meeting as the one which really started the good roads movement. Others were formed in 1910, 1923 and 1948, the latter organized at Marshalltown as a permanent group with Claude Coykendall, administrative engineer for the Highway Commission, as executive secretary. Since then, the organization has promoted "good roads," with such men as Gerald Bogan, R. M. Hileman, John Coverdale, Archie Nelson, H. W. Callison and C. W.(Chet) Sloan, active and involved over the intervening years.

The movement for good roads was based upon the removal of some degree of control from local township trustees in favor of regional and statewide highway development through which administrative and engineering expertise could be provided. Progress, however, was slow for many reasons. The traditional conservative system of road building was difficult to change; there were differences of opinion among members of the association as to the proper courses of action to take; engineers disagreed on technical questions regarding road and bridge construction; bitter arguments occurred between advocates of earth roads and those supporting surfacing and over the types of surfaces to be used; between those who supported or objected to more centralized control of highway policy and authority; and those who wanted roads funded as a pay-as-you-go project as contrasted with funding through bond issues. Then there was the question of distribution of road funds among counties and cities, and the fact that groups representing road materials, bridge and construction companies fought changes that might be objectionable to their interests. Although many were active in the good roads movement, farmers generally offered the strongest opposition to highway improvements. They feared that heavy taxes would be levied, and until 1920, at least part of their fears were justified. Prior to 1919, farmers paid four mills in property taxes to support county roads while residents of first class cities contributed only half a mill.

National Roads Associations

Nationally, a League for Good Roads was organized in 1892, and in 1893, a Good Roads Convention was held in Washington, D.C. Their efforts resulted in establishment of an Office of Road Inquiry in the Department of Agriculture in 1893, with an initial appropriation of $10,000, to be used mainly for educational purposes. Another result of these meetings was the creation of the Rural Free Delivery Service which by 1900 had a nationwide network and became a powerful force for road improvement. The automobile appeared in 1890 and added further impetus: "The motorist had an even stronger incentive than the bicyclist to get the country out of the mud; a

mired car was more of a problem than a stuck bicycle."[3] By 1910, there were literally scores of organizations in the nation promoting good roads. A few of these were strong, effective and national in scope. The American Automobile Association, founded by owners in 1902, and the American Road Makers brought together state engineers, road contractors and road machinery manufacturers. Many of the associations were primarily pressure groups whose purpose was to get improved roads through legislation. Many had no dues-paying members but depended upon commercial interests—railroads, materials producers and automobile manufacturers—for financial support.
The American Association for Highway Improvement was formed in 1910 and sponsored the first American Road Congress in 1911 at Richmond, Virginia. It recommended that Congress extend financial aid to the states to assist in road building; that no appropriation be made without proper supervision for maintenance; that states provide supervision of main highways through a state highway department; that work on construction and maintenance be under the direction of an experienced highway engineer; and that all states provide for the employment of prison labor to work on public highways. Other Road Congress meetings took place in 1913 and 1914.

Road Legislation, 1880 to 1920

State Road Laws

There was little or no administrative control over roads by state government in the early 1880's. Previous laws had given authority to county supervisors to locate new roads, change the course of old ones and levy taxes for bridges. Township trustees determined the level of property taxes and how much would be paid in cash or labor. In the fall, the township was divided into road districts, each with a supervisor who spent the funds and directed the road work performed by men working out their taxes. May observed that "there was some logic to this system in pioneer days when virtually the only use of the roads was local in character, but as the state's economy grew and traffic volumes steadily increased, doubts arose as to the wisdom of permitting thousands of separate road systems to exist with no unifying standards."[4]

The 1884 General Assembly incorporated some of the recommendations of the State Road Improvement Association into "an Act to Promote the Improvement of Highways." It provided for a regular county fund as contrasted to a township road fund, the money to be raised by a one mill per dollar tax on property. The county boards of supervisors had authority to determine how the fund was to be used. By local option, the township trustees might organize the township into one road district but could return to the old multiple district plan after two years of experimentation. Road supervision in the township system was changed to allow trustees to order that township highway taxes be paid in money to the county treasurer, and to direct expenditures by letting contracts to the lowest responsible bidder or appoint a superintendent of highways to supervise the road work. The statutory requirement of highway labor was retained.[5] Opposition to the property tax to be paid in money and appointment of a superintendent was so strong that the provisions were made optional.

Few changes in road administration occurred between 1884 and 1890, except that the one mill tax was made mandatory in all counties. Important reforms by the 1902 General Assembly recognized the inefficiencies of the old system. A new road law, known as the

[3] John B. Rae, *The Road and Car in American Life,* Cambridge, Mass.: M.I.T. Press, 1971, p. 34.

[4] George S. May, "The Good Roads Movement in Iowa," *Palimpsest 46* (February 1965): p. 82. For a discussion of road laws before 1884, see John Brindley's *History of Road Legislation in Iowa,* Iowa City: State Historical Society, 1912, Chapters 4-7. Summaries will also be found in *Iowa Hiway Hilites* (May 1963), pp. 17-39, published by the Iowa State Highway Commission, Ames.

[5] 1884 Laws of Iowa, Chapter 200. The law provided that "nine hours of faithful work was required as a day's work on the road but that except for extraordinary occasions, no person shall be required to go more than three miles from his place of residence...and for the purpose of this Act, the residence of a man shall be construed to be where his family resides; for a single man, it shall be at the place where he is at work." N. S. Shaler, writing on "Common Roads" in *Scribners Magazine* in 1889, said that "in the United States the common roads were built in a most ignorant and inefficient manner...Generally, road-making and so-called roadmending were performed not by tax money but by an impost of labor of the county. The voting part of the population is summoned each year to one or two days to working out their road tax. The busy people and those who are forehanded may pay out their assesment in money but most of the population find it convenient to attend the annual road-making picnic in person...under the supervision of a road master. More commonly, some elder is by common consent absolved from personal labor and made superintendent of the operation." (See Rae, pp. 26-27.)

"Anderson Law," after its most ardent supporter, abolished the office of district road supervisor and the district road system and consolidated each township into one road district. Other sections covered changes in levying and collecting road taxes and conferred rights and powers on interurban railways built along public highways. Road taxes were to be paid in money but the statutory labor requirement was still in effect.

The most important feature of the new law was the one which consolidated road districts based on civil townships and resulted in a fundamental change in road administration. The authority of the district road supervisor, established in 1853, had existed for almost 50 years with strictly local supervision of highways until 1902. The long-standing tradition of local control, self-government and personal participation in highway policy was overturned and met opposition. The law also became the basis for more centralized control through state and federal participation in highway programs.

In 1909, permanent road improvement districts were authorized and could be established by county supervisors. Improvements were financed half by a two mill county tax and half by special assessments on property within a county. Road dragging by contract at 50 cents per mile was made mandatory for township trustees. In 1911, the legislature required township trustees to divide the public roads into permanent road-dragging districts, "designate which districts shall be dragged, to include all mail routes and main travelled roads within the township," and appoint a superintendent of dragging at $2.50 per day, to serve one year unless removed sooner by the supervisors. An annual fee of $15 was assessed for the registration or re-registration of any electric or steam motor vehicle and 40 cents per horsepower charged for every horsepower over 20. Motor bicycles or motorcycles paid three dollars. No distinction was made between ordinary and commercial vehicles. Fifteen percent of the vehicle tax went to the State Treasury and the remainder was "apportioned among the several counties of the state in the same ratio as the number of townships in the several counties bear to the total number of townships in the state."[6] Iowa not only had its first highway use tax in 1911, but by statute could not divert the funds to other than specific designated highway purposes. Previously, a $1.00 registration fee had been levied in 1904, increased to $5.00 in 1907, as a simple regulatory and general revenue measure.

A law which marked the first definite move away from pioneer roads and toward state road administration was passed in 1913 by the 35th General Assembly. It created a separate State Highway Commission of three men, replacing the original commission established in 1904, and was given control over all county and township road officials. The office of chief engineer was created to discharge this responsibility. In 1915 and 1917, bills to abolish the commission were introduced into the legislature but failed to pass, for in order to qualify for federal funds, the state had to have a highway commission. The law continued the policy of allowing county supervisors and township trustees to be in charge of roads and funds but only under the supervisory control of the commission.

County supervisors were required to appoint a county engineer who, if found incompetent, could be discharged by the commission. Plans, specifications, advertisements for bids, and public lettings for bridge and road construction were required. Contracts were subject to approval by the commission and county engineers, and all construction was under standard state plans. Maps showing the selected systems were prepared and updated by commission personnel, and surveys made by the county engineer. The commission was given a maintenance fund of eight percent of the money paid into the State Treasury for motor vehicle registrations.

The progressive legislation brought a clash between advocates of a more centralized control and rural elements favoring local domination of road policy, and the elections of 1914 removed many of the legislators who had voted for the 1913 law. County supervisors and township trustees resented the imposition of county engineers and the commission controls in their domain. Many county supervisors made no effort to hire engineers; others did under protest. Even if they wanted to hire, it was difficult to find the number of engineers needed in 1913. Supervisors also did not appreciate the requirement that standard highway plans be used and bids for construction taken after public hearing.

[6] 1911 Laws of Iowa, Chapters 70 and 72.

The Federal Road Act of 1916

The interest of the federal government in highway development dated from 1803, when aid was given for construction of the National Pike from Cumberland, Maryland, to Wheeling, West Virginia. Federal engineers advised as to the desirability of surfaced roads throughout the nation by 1900, and in 1912 an appropriation of $500,000 was made to pay one-third of the costs of improving highways over which the mail was carried. The Office of Road Inquiry became the Bureau of Public Roads in 1918.

Federal-aid policy involving federal-state cooperation for highway construction was the basis of the Act of 1916. An appropriation of $75 million over a five-year period was authorized for improvements to rural roads carrying mail and was limited to towns under 2,500 population. The aid was not to exceed 50 percent of the cost of roads constructed, not to exceed $10,000 per mile, and was to be matched by the states. Three criteria were used in funding, all having equal weight: (1) the area of the state in relation to the total area of the United States; (2) population of the state relative to total United States population; and (3) mail route mileage of the state in relation to total mail road mileage of the nation. Assistance was to be given to those states with established highway departments.

The General Assembly in 1917 accepted the provisions of the 1916 federal act and pledged the necessary matching funds. To be designated was a road system of 2,000 to 6,000 miles, equitably distributed among the 99 counties, on which federal-aid projects could be located. Also provided was a primary road fund to finance construction and maintenance, and the duties and responsibilities of the commission were expanded, reflecting the growing influence of motor vehicle traffic.

In most states, the major highway system was known as "the State Road System," "State Trunk System," or other similar designations. A state road system of approximately 6,500 miles was established by the General Assembly in 1919, to initiate paving of principal highways. So great was the opposition to the word "state" and a state-controlled road system, that legislators, fearing for their political futures, named it the "Primary Road System." The word "pave" was also considered suicidal if used, so the legislation substituted "hard-surfaced" to define their intentions. Over the years, the need to avoid the word "state" has long abated, but the principal state highway system continued officially to be known as the "Primary Road System."

The Primary Road Fund was to include all automobile registration fees, federal-aid allotments and funds from special paving assessments, effective only where improvements called for pavement, and which were to total 25 percent of the cost of the pavement slab. Primary road expenditures were under the control of the supervisors, subject to approval of the commission. Voters in a county had to approve any proposed "hard-surfaced" improvement before construction. They could also vote authority to supervisors for issuance of bonds to fund construction if not satisfied with progress permitted by current revenues. However, the legislation specified that in both the surfacing and the bond issues, balloting must be separate on each proposal. Special assessments on adjacent property were permitted only on "hard-surfaced" projects and could cover an area extending one and one-fourth miles on each side of the road to be improved.

Road Legislation, 1920 to 1930

The Federal Aid Highway Act of 1921

The Act required a designation of state and interstate highways eligible to receive federal funds. Aid was limited to seven percent of the total mileage of rural roads, and designated highways were divided into primary or interstate, and secondary or intercounty roads. Funds had to be matched by the state, which was also responsible for maintenance of federal-aid roads. Seventy-five million dollars was appropriated for 1922, and in 1923, Congress modified the provisions to allow specific appropriations when needed. The average was about $100 million per year during the 1920s. The 1916 Act had a significant influence on Iowa. It provided about $15 million annually as the 50 percent share of the road-building costs. The funds were earmarked for rural roads, a pressing and persistent problem for the state, and the act, by requiring federal approval for projects selected, established the basis for further federal involvement.

The Iowa road laws did not comply with the requirements of the 1921 federal legislation. The state law was in conflict in two important particulars: (1) The federal law required that maintenance of federal roads be under the direct control of the state highway department, whereas the state law placed this responsibility with county supervisors. If any county failed to maintain a federal-aid road, the commission had no power to assume charge of the work unless the road had been paved. Since only five percent of the state's primary roads had been paved, the commission was powerless to cause 95 percent to be maintained, yet federal law required that as a condition precedent to aid, maintenance must be under direct control of the commission. (2) Federal law required that federal-aid highways should be surfaced in a manner suited to the traffic, and the commission should have the power to determine and select the type of surfacing. Under state law, the commission had no power to initiate such action. This power was in the hands of the supervisors, and even they had no power to start paving unless authorized by a vote of the people.

In grading and draining of any road, the federal government required the commission to agree that within a reasonable time after the road was graded, it would provide the suitable surface before any additions were made to the federal-aid system. Under state law, the commission could not fulfill such an agreement, yet the state law made it the specific duty of the commission to do whatever was necessary to secure federal funds. Further, the federal act provided that the state would have five years, or until November 9, 1926, in which to amend its laws so as to conform to the legislation. After that date, Iowa would get no federal aid if the primary road law had not been properly coordinated with the Federal-Aid Law.

State Primary Road Laws

In 1925, the General Assembly remedied these matters by enacting a new Primary Road Law which conformed to the federal act. It granted the commission absolute control over primary road development funds to be spent on its own initiative. Also passed was the first gasoline tax bill, providing for two cents per gallon in revenues and dividing the proceeds in three ways; one-third to the primary road fund, one-third to the counties for county roads, and one-third for township roads. In the Primary Road Act of 1927, powers and duties of county supervisors in primary road administration were transferred to the commission. Also, the legislation required that all roads in the state were to be divided into two systems. The Primary Road System would include "those main market roads (not including roads within towns and cities) which connect all county seat towns and cities and main market centers." The 43rd General Assembly defined secondary roads as all public highways except primary roads, state roads and highways within cities and towns. Primary roads upon which federal-aid funds were expended were to be marked as United States highways and all other primary roads were considered as state highways. The secondary roads were classified as county trunk roads and local county roads. The local roads were formerly township roads.

The 1927 law provided that "improvement shall be made (in the primary road system) and carried on in such a manner as to equalize the work in all sections of the state where improvements have been retarded, to an equality and on the same basis with the more advanced sections."[7] A third cent was also added to the gasoline tax for the primary road fund. This section, as well as the entire act, remains as the basic philosophy of improvement programs to the present time. That the 1927 Primary Road Law was a giant step forward in road improvements is supported by the fact that it still remains on the statutes of Iowa. A large percentage of the 6,000 miles of primary road pavement built previous to 1956 was built under this law without important substantive changes, and during 1930, three years after the act was passed, 1,030 miles of high-type concrete pavement were built on the state's primary roads without legal difficulty or delay. Only one other state has ever equaled or exceeded that mileage record in one year.

Bonding for Highways

In the 10 years, 1919 to 1929, there had been spasmodic voting of county bonds for paving of portions of the primary road system. The possibility of bonding for primary roads was raised in 1926, when a bill authorizing the issuance of $100 million in bonds was introduced in the General Assembly. Its constitutionality was questioned since it provided for payment of interest and principal from primary road revenues but in case of deficits, taxes would be levied and collected on all taxable property in the state to make up the difference in bond obligations and primary road funds available. The sources of funds for the primary road fund were motor vehicle registration fees and motor fuel taxes. The section of the State Constitution at issue was Section 5 of Article VII which contained the following statement: "Except the debts hereinbefore specified in this

[7] John E. Nimmo, *State Involvement in Iowa Road Development*, Report prepared for the Iowa Transportation Commission, 1975, p. 12.

Article, no debt shall be hereafter contracted by, or on behalf of this State, unless such debt shall be authorized by some law for some single work or object, to be distinctly specified therein; and such law shall impose and provide for a direct annual tax, sufficient to pay and discharge the principal of such debt, within 20 years from the time of the contracting thereof . . ." To be resolved then, was whether or not this provision precluded the use of primary road funds to pay the interest and principal of the proposed bonds.

After consulting with legal authorities throughout the state on the constitutionality of the bill and receiving unanimous affirmative response, the governor called the 42nd General Assembly into special session in March, 1928. The bonding bill was passed on a two-to-one vote in both Houses and was supported by popular vote in the 1928 general elections, only to be declared unconstitutional by the State Supreme Court in March, 1929.

The Secondary Road Law

The Secondary Road Act, known generally as the Bergman Secondary Road Law, was passed in 1929. Previous to its enactment, about 6.5 percent of the public highways of the state were included in the primary road system, under control and jurisdiction of the Highway Commission; 13.5 percent were included in the county road system under jurisdiction of county supervisors whereas the remaining 80 percent were classified as township roads under control of 1,640 township boards of trustees. These township roads were renamed "local county roads." When the new law became effective on January 1, 1930, township trustees were virtually eliminated from responsibilities for road building, reducing the number of secondary road supervisory units from about 5,500 to 400. Supervisors controlled a secondary system of 12,377 miles of county and 84,246 miles of township roads.

The legislature also acted to facilitate the voting of county bonds for primary road improvement and raised the limit of indebtedness from three to four and one-half percent of the assessed valuation of property in the county. Immediately, 18 counties voted primary road bonds aggregating $21 million, and 18 counties which had previously voted primary bond issues voted additional issues totaling $12 million. Eventually 98 of the 99 counties in the state voted $118 million for county primary roads.

The process of centralizing road administration begun in 1884 was practically completed by 1929. Responsibilities had been transferred from many independent civil units to the centralized structure of state government. Authority for road construction and maintenance was clearly defined between the state and the counties, with general supervision over all roads and direct control over the state's primary highways exercised by the highway commission.

Evolution of the County Engineer

Creation of the office of county engineer was probably the most important reform measure promoting expert supervision of roads on a county level. As early as 1883, Samuel D. Pryce observed that road work should be supervised by competent civil engineers. Further efforts to establish the position were made immediately afterward by a legislative committee of engineers, and in 1910, by Governor Carroll and the Good Roads Association. Delegates defeated the proposal, considering the idea that road work could be efficiently managed by trained experts as an affront to many local road officials. May quotes one delegate as calling it a plan for "giving places to a lot of boys from college without accomplishing anything," and another contending that "they did not have to go to college to get men capable of using a level."

A compromise was effected in 1911, whereby supervisors could, if they wished, "employ a competent person" to work out plans and specifications for county roads. The Act of 1913 finally created the office of county engineer but there was considerable opposition. In 1923, critics made the county engineer an optional position, yet few counties took advantage. However, the Bergman Act of 1929 not only repealed this provision but gave the county engineer greater responsibility over road work. It was recognized by this time that engineers could save counties thousands of dollars, and at least one county board chairman declared that if counties had to choose between the engineer and the supervisor, "it would do well to give up the latter because the engineer could do the work of the supervisors but the supervisors could not do the work of the engineer."[8]

[8] George S. May, "The Good Roads Movement in Iowa," *Palimpsest 46* (February 1965), pp. 86-87.

State Road Administration
The Highway Commission, 1904-1913

Establishment of the first highway commission was primarily the result of the efforts of two men, namely, Charles F. Curtiss, Dean of Agriculture, and Anson Marston, Dean of Engineering, Iowa State College. Questions concerning the creation of the commission and providing for an appropriation were debated in the Thirtieth General Assembly in 1904. It became apparent that a separate department funded by the state could not be established until the public had been educated to the value of highways and the need for an efficient administrative system. Therefore, the General Assembly directed the Iowa State College to "act as a Highway Commission for Iowa" and appropriated $7,000 for the next biennial period. In 1906, Iowa was at the bottom of the list of 17 states in road appropriations. The funds were included in the regular college budget for experimental purposes and were under control of the board of trustees.

The college had for a number of years taken an active interest in road problems of the state and had gathered considerable statistical data previous to 1904 through student research. The research consisted of tests on different road surfaces to determine the resistance to traffic, and to establish the relationship between market prices and road conditions. The board of trustees appointed Deans Curtiss and Marston as commissioners and engaged Thomas H. MacDonald as an assistant in charge of field operations. MacDonald, a 1904 Civil Engineering graduate, was appointed Assistant Professor at $600 per year on the college budget and paid an equal amount from the state funds for an annual salary of $1,200. The act provided that the college should serve as the state highway commission with the following powers and duties:

1. To devise and adopt plans and systems of highway construction and maintenance suited to the needs of the different counties of the state.
2. Conduct demonstrations on such highway construction at least once a year at some desirable place for instruction of county supervisors, township trustees, superintendents, students of the college, and others.
3. Disseminate information and instruction to county supervisors and other highway officers who make requests on questions of highway construction and maintenance.
4. Keep a record of all important operations of the highway commission and report same to the governor at the end of the year.

Although the $3,500 annual appropriation was increased later to $10,000, the lack of funds limited the work. Despite this handicap, Professor MacDonald, in addition to his other duties, published a bulletin titled *The Good Roads Problem in Iowa* in June, 1905, which reviewed the early work of the commission and outlined a constructive program of reform for road legislation and administration. Efforts were made to investigate road conditions in the different sections of the state and to prepare road maps for about 12 counties. Research included the amount of funds collected in the counties, the methods used, and the results of the expenditures. Investigation of road materials was made by Professor S. W. Beyer.

A manual for Iowa highway officers was published in 1905 and revised in 1906. It contained a general survey and data pertaining to public highways, topography of Iowa, history and development of road legislation, the organization of the work of the commission to that time, and road construction and maintenance in the state. In particular, the manual declared that the Anderson Law had been generally disregarded by township trustees. "Some townships have appointed several men to work on roads and called them road superintendents, but this is merely a modification of the old, many district system. It would be much better and would follow the requirements of the law to have one superintendent for the township and let him have, if necessary, a number of assistants. The more the work is concentrated under one man held responsible for the proper expenditure of the fund, the more economical will be the administration of the road funds provided that the proper man is selected in the first place."[9]

The first annual report summarized the work of the commission. It pointed out that the act creating it provided that "it should not only act as a bureau of information on road matters but should also make as thorough an investigation as possible of the general

[9] Iowa Highway Commission, *Manual for Iowa Highway Officers*, 1905, p. 35.

road problems of the state." The report covered four major sections: (1) Investigations, (2) Experiments, (3) Plans and Publications; and (4) The Road School.[10] Many of the investigations were conducted by Dean Marston and MacDonald. Both studied road construction at various points in the state, traveling by train, buggy and spring wagon. Marston reported "that their investigations revealed that local units had been getting about 10 cents worth of road work for every dollar expended, a situation that generally existed throughout the Midwest."[11]

During 1904 and 1905, MacDonald continued his campaign for good roads, riding "good road" trains which the CNW and CB&Q were running at that time. He lectured at every stop, and by 1906-1907, he and the commission members were giving lectures at good roads organizations throughout Iowa and Missouri. An annual road school was first held in Ames in June 1905, then throughout the state. It became an annual event and grew so large that it had to be discontinued in 1918. In the 1907-1908 annual report, the commission stated that Iowa was ready for permanent roads in certain districts and that some mileage had been built. Further, the idea that farmers would oppose permanent roads was to be questioned. Doubts, however, were expressed about the permanence of macadam roads under automobile traffic. "Petrolithic" paving, consisting of asphaltic oil, earth, gravel and broken stone, was mentioned as a promising surface. The commission concluded its 1908 annual report with statistics comparing Iowa with progress in road building in other states. It urged that its powers and duties be increased and recommended in this and other reports many of the changes eventually incorporated into the road laws.

At an early meeting of the commission, it was decided that an organization was required that operated through four departments: Office, Design, Field and Education. The organization was developed entirely on the basis of experience in Iowa, since there were no other road laws in any of the states formulated on the principle of state supervision or control of highways without state aid. All other state laws provided for state aid in some form. In July, 1911, the entire staff of the commission consisted of three full-time employees; a highway engineer (MacDonald), an assistant engineer (Conde B. McCullough), a stenographer (Annie Laurie Bowen), and two part-time employees. These people were employed by and received their salaries from the Iowa State College, not from the highway commission.

The State Highway Commission, 1913

In 1913, forces favoring more centralized control of highway administration succeeded in passing a law which established a new highway commission, increased its powers and duties, and separated it from the administration of the college although still officed on the campus. The new commission consisted of three members, one of which was Dean Marston, made an ex officio member, and the other two appointed by the governor from opposite political parties for a term of four years. Dean Marston received no salary; the others were paid $10 per day with a limit of 100 days for which salaries would be paid for a total compensation of $1,000. T. H. MacDonald was hired as highway engineer at an annual salary of $2,400 and J. E. Kirkham as part-time consulting bridge engineer at $300 per year. Commissioners were bonded for $5,000; department heads, $3,000; and $1,000 for district engineers.

J. W. Holden of Scranton was the Republican member and H.C. Beard from Mt. Ayr, the Democratic appointee. The employees under the old commission were transferred to form the nucleus of the organization, considered adequate to carry out the provisions of the new law. Personnel were as follows: T. H. MacDonald, highway engineer; J. E. Kirkham, consulting bridge engineer; C. B. McCullough, assistant engineer; F. R. White, assistant engineer; Annie Laurie Bowen, and Merle Crabtree, stenographers; and J. H. Paulson, draftsman. MacDonald continued in his position until he was appointed Director of the U. S. Bureau of Public Roads in 1919 and was succeeded by Fred R. White.

By December 1, 1918, there were 62 people on the commission payroll, exclusive of the commissioners. The expanded volume of work created by the Federal-Aid and State Primary Road Acts, together with the end of World War I, increased the number of

[10] *First Annual Report of the Iowa State Highway Commission Made To The Governor of Iowa For the Year Ending July 1, 1905.* Des Moines: State Printer, 1905, p. 9.

[11] Mississippi Valley Conference of State Highway Departments, pp. 1-2.

employees to 156 in 1919. J. W. Holden held the chairmanship of the commission and William Collison of Chariton and Dean Marston were the other members. In 1919, the commission was extensively reorganized. New departments were created and new department administrators appointed. These were:

Administrative	F. R. White, Chief Engineer
Accounting	M. E. Davis
Road Management	C. Coykendall
Road Surveys and Plans	W. E. Jones
Road Construction	F. H. Mann
Road Maintenance	W. R. Root
Bridge	J. H. Ames
Drainage	R. H Clyde
Materials and Tests	R. W. Crum
State Parks and Institutional Roads	R. McCormick
Women's Drafting	Alda Wilson

To supervise the increased volume of work, the number of district engineers was increased from six to nine. All work in each district, as well as the men employed on preliminary surveys and in superintending construction of federal-aid projects, was placed under the direct supervision of the district engineer.

Chapter 328 of the Acts of the 40th General Assembly directed the commission to construct an office building as funds became available. It authorized the location of the building on ground adjacent to the sheds used for storage of surplus equipment distributed by the federal government to the state in 1919. Promptly after enactment of the legislation, citizens of Ames, through popular subscription, raised \$16,500 for the purchase of five acres of land west of the equipment sheds.[12] The tract (with a frontage of 240 feet on Lincoln Way and depth of 900 feet) was presented to the state as the site for a new office building. The total cost of the building, which was 160 feet long by 60 feet wide and three stories high, was \$123,518. It would provide sufficient space for all of the commission's personnel located in Ames and release the space occupied in the engineering buildings at the college. The date above the old Lincoln Way entrance shows completion of the building in 1923, but it was not occupied until June 1, 1924.

Responsibilities of the commission were further expanded when the General Assembly rewrote the Primary Road Law and granted them absolute power over the primary road development fund. Previously, the commission had been forced to await decisions by boards of supervisors for initiation of projects, often resulting in delay and lack of continuity in road improvements When controlled by the commission, the \$4 million fund was available to close gaps in the primary road system. Under the Primary Road Act of 1927, the powers and duties of the county supervisors with respect to construction and maintenance of primary roads were transferred to the commission. This action represented the final step in placing complete jurisdiction of primary roads under control of the state. The act also provided for reorganization of the commission by increasing the membership from three to five persons, appointed by the governor with the approval of two-thirds of the Senate in executive session, for a term of four years. Although not compulsory or suggested by law, it was generally accepted that members would come from different sections of the state and have personal knowledge and a better understanding of road problems in their areas. Each was to receive \$4,000 per year plus the necessary expenses. Anson Marston, who had served on the commission since its inception, requested to be relieved of his duties.

The original Highway Commission building completed in 1923. (Courtesy: Iowa State Highway Commission)

[12] *Report of the State Highway Commission for the Year Ending December 1, 1922,* Des Moines: State of Iowa, 1922, p. 13. A tract of land in Ames was leased with the option to purchase 18 acres. It was favorably located near both highways and railroads. For storage purposes, eight hollow tile sheds, 52′ X 142′, were constructed at a cost of \$75,000. The lease was \$400 per year and was to expire in 1926. The option price was \$12,000.

Aerial view of Highway Commission's Ames complex in the 1950's.
(Courtesy: Iowa State Highway Commission)

The new commissioners were Clifford L. Niles, Anamosa; Carl C. Riepe, Burlington; H. E. Dean, Ocheyedan; H. A. Dartin, Glenwood; and T.E. O'Donnell from Dubuque. On December 1, 1929, there were 896 people on the payroll, exclusive of commissioners and temporary and part-time help. Of the total, 544 were engaged in field construction and 71 in maintenance work. As the powers and duties of the organization expanded, some old departments were eliminated, others changed in their responsibilites, or new ones were created. "The ability of the organization to develop and change to meet the ever increasing duties without complete reorganization, has been of untold value in the work of the commission. No administrative system is at any time perfectly adapted to its work, but is in continual process of becoming better adapted to it. As an example . . . in the beginning road design and bridge design were of such prime importance that each was established as a separate department, but later, when much of the work was finished, the two departments were combined into the Department of Design."[13] The commission in 1929 was organized into seven major departments, namely: Executive, Construction, Administration, Design, Maintenance, Materials and Tests, and Purchases and Accounts.

[13] S. C. E. Powers, "The Iowa State Highway Commission," *Iowa Journal of History and Politics 29* (January 1931): pp. 51-53.

The chief engineer, selected by the commission, was head of the entire organization. Until 1930 the commission had only two chief engineers, T. H. MacDonald and Fred R. White, so they seldom had to exercise their powers for this appointive position. The salary of the chief engineer was $10,000. His duties were primarily administrative, to build an organization whose expertise, initiative and imagination would carry out the policies of the commission. In addition, the chief engineer was in charge of all litigation in which the commission was involved, and he advised on modification of both primary and county road systems.

The state was divided into nine districts to bring the commission into more direct contact with road work and road problems. Heading each district was the district engineer, selected by the chief engineer. He had general supervision of all road work in his district, including direct charge of surveyors, control of material inspectors, and supervision of all maintenance work. One or two assistants could be provided, also appointed by the chief engineer. One was in charge of construction and the other had responsibility for maintenance.

Aerial view of Department of Transportation's Ames complex in 1986.
(Courtesy: Iowa Department of Transportation)

Cooperative Activities

The commission worked closely with the Federal Bureau of Public Roads and with the county supervisors. Since 1927, the General Assembly required close cooperation of the state with the federal government in arrangements and funding on federal-aid highway projects. These had to be approved and accepted by the Federal Bureau before the federal share of the cost could be paid. For all practical purposes, this cooperation made the Federal Bureau a part of the state organization.

The relationship with the county supervisors concerned the secondary roads and road improvement. The commission acted in an advisory capacity with communications handled through the district engineer, or if necessary directly from the counties with the chief engineer. The county engineer often became a resident engineer of the commission for construction on primary roads and during these periods was considered an employee. These activities were in addition to his regular duties as inspector on secondary road work.

The powers over secondary road programs were thought necessary for uniformity, efficiency and economy on road plans and construction. Standard specifications and plans for culverts, bridges, railroad crossings, etc., were furnished without charge to the counties and had to be followed, assuring that their completion would be of proper design and location. Likewise, plans for all interconnecting roads and improvements on county boundary roads had to be approved by the commission. As provided by the Secondary Road Law, supervisors were required to submit definite plans covering one to three year programs to the commission for approval before funds were expended.

Where questions arose on bridging or improvements on interstate roads, highway commissioners of the states involved and supervisors of the counties on the borders negotiated the problems. Within municipalities, the commission had powers, subject to approval by local authorities, to construct or improve streets or roads which were continuations of primary roads within the limits of towns or cities under 2,500 population, or within a city where houses were not less than 200 feet apart. The cost of paving would come from the primary road fund. Along the primary road extensions, the commission was obliged to furnish suitable signs indicating whether the area was designated as business, school, residence, etc., and the speed limit in each instance. The commission also had to approve city ordinances regulating traffic at primary road extensions or on heavily traveled streets. Cities could not erect traffic signals or close or obstruct any primary road extensions within the city except for fire or construction without commission consent. These provisions applied to all cities in the state having populations of 4,000 or over, except for their business districts.

The Major Commission Funds

Three funds were provided for the commission's work: the primary road fund, maintenance or support fund, and emergency fund. In addition, revenues from county bond sales was another source for primary road construction. The primary road fund received motor vehicle registration fees, fuel taxes, federal-aid monies and any surplus from the support fund. Approximatately 93 percent of registration fees and supplementary revenues, such as penalties and transfers on motor vehicles, was spent directly on primary road projects. The remaining seven percent was divided into 2½ percent for highway department administration, 3½ percent for the motor vehicle department, and the remainder for reimbursement for overcharges in registrations. Counties charged a 50-cent collection fee for each vehicle registration. One-third of the original gasoline tax of two cents and all of the revenues from the additional one cent levied in 1927 were allocated to the primary road fund. Before using it for construction, however, the commission was required to establish a fund for maintenance of these highways during the year. In addition to construction, expenditures were used for right-of-way purchases, grading, graveling or paving, drainage, bridge and culvert work, guard rails, machinery and equipment purchases, and engineering. The fund was also used to pay interest and principal on county bonds issued for primary road improvements.

The support fund was used for the necessary overhead expenses of the commission. Indirect revenues came from sales of surplus equipment, road maps and guides, and forms for road improvement proposals. The emergency fund, which amounted to $350,000, was taken from the primary road fund for the payment of claims, labor and freight. It was used to enable the commission to make prompt payments when delays in the normal reimbursement schedules might occur and result in serious inconveniences to those presenting bills or claims.

Summary

Many forces were working toward improvement of roads and highways in Iowa during the late 19th and early 20th centuries. The realization that railroads could not completely satisfy the needs of the public for efficient transportation, especially in the rural areas, brought pressures for better roads. These took the form of organized groups composed of different and varied interests in Iowa and throughout the nation in proposals for highway improvements. The "good roads organizations" made slow but steady progress in convincing legislators of their cause and their resolutions were endorsed by the General Assembly and Congress. Laws were passed which gradually transferred local administration of roads to a centralized state unit, provided for funding and made possible a more comprehensive system of road construction and management. Congress, recognizing the nationwide scope of the problem, assisted the states with federal funds, tied to certain rules and regulations, one of which was the requirement that the state receiving funds had to have a highway commission to administer them.

The history of road building in Iowa could be written as the history of the State Highway Commission. It was established partly through the efforts of Deans Curtiss and Marston and T. H. MacDonald of the Iowa State College, who acted as the commission for approximately 10 years, a rather unique arrangement in highway administration. Handicapped by lack of funds and conservative traditions, the commission first attempted to educate the public as to the value of good roads, then proceeded to build an organization with expertise necessary and sufficient to lay the foundations for construction of the highway network of the state. The effectiveness of the commission in meeting its obligations and performing its duties and responsibilities in the early 20th century will be discussed in the chapters that follow.

Selected References

Davis, Rodney O. "Iowa Farm Opinion and the Good Roads Movement, 1903-1904." *Annals of Iowa 37* (summer 1964): pp. 325-326.

Iowa State College Engineering Experiment Station. Bulletin No. 6 (June 1902).

Iowa State Highway Commission. Reports of the State Highway Commission for the years ending 1913-1914, 1919, 1922, 1923, 1924, 1929. Des Moines: State of Iowa.

______. *Service Bulletin* Vol. 7 Nos. 3-4 (March-April 1919): pp. 3-5.

1902 Laws of Iowa, Chapter 53; 1904 Laws of Iowa, Chapter 103; 1913 Laws of Iowa, Chapter 122; 1925 Laws of Iowa, Chapter 114; 1927 Laws of Iowa, Chapters 101, 102; 1929 Laws of Iowa, Chapters 20, 159, 161.

Taff, Charles A. *Commercial Motor Transportation.* 5th ed., Cambridge, Md.:Cornell Maritime Press, 1975.

U.S. Department of Transportation, Federal Highway Administration. *America's Highways 1776/1976.* Washington, D.C.: U.S. Government Printing Office, 1976.

Chapter Five
The Transportation Structure of Iowa: 1900-1920

Introduction

The ebb and flow of transportation developments between 1900 and 1920 preclude a decade-by-decade approach. Because continuity of the analysis would be interrupted and perhaps lost, these two decades are combined in this chapter. By 1900, the basic railroad network was largely in place, and the emphasis was on improvements to properties and equipment and on service. Although the railroad commission had considerable regulatory experience since its inception, further challenges lay ahead as the result of ICC rulings, court decisions and congressional legislation which had an impact on carrier operations, shipper arrangements and public considerations. Among the issues were rates, rate relationships, rate structures and safety measures.

Both the 1904 and the 1913 highway commissions faced unenviable tasks in meeting demands for improvements on more than 100,000 miles of Iowa's roads. Earth roads and stronger bridges needed to be built or rebuilt to form a base for future permanent road systems. Centralized agencies gradually brought order out of uncoordinated local highway projects, and progress was further enhanced through federal-state cooperation and funding. The Lincoln and Jefferson Highways made Iowa an important segment on their transcontinental routes and offered organized compacts among states, industries and organizations in identifying national highways. The railroad and highway commissions actively supervised and administered the development of land-based transportation facilities, each working independently but cooperating on common problems.

Commercial long-haul transportation on the Upper Mississippi River had ceased to function as a system by 1914, although there was considerable short-haul traffic in sand, gravel and low class bulk commodities. The lumber trade, formerly of great magnitude, had virtually disappeared, and an era of packet trade, passenger service and the logging business came to an end. World War I brought the federal government into waterway operations through the Federal Barge Service, eventually known as the Federal Barge Line. It was operated by the Railroad Administration and transferred to the War Department in 1920. The Missouri River was difficult to navigate, obstructed by many snags. Its banks were alluvial and constantly eroding, changing the channels except where protected by revetments and dikes or by natural bluffs.

Iowans were among the early pioneers in the design and construction of aeroplanes, flying them in exhibitions and demonstrations, initiating flying schools, and challenging speed, distance and altitude records. Their efforts contributed in a large measure to the future development of commercial and general aviation in the state. Normal progress in these transportation systems was interrupted by the outbreak and entrance of the nation into World War I.

Railroads

General Observations

The nation generally experienced prosperity during the first few years of the early 20th century. The economy was well established, export trade was expanding, and railroads benefited by the high level of economic activity. The Iowa Railroad Commission indicated satisfaction with their operations, especially on the main lines. The carriers were making substantial improvements to their properties by constructing better stations and yard facilities, adding to rolling stock, improving roadbed and substituting steel for iron rails. Trains were equipped with automatic couplers and continuous air brakes. Block signals for control of train movements were installed, larger locomotives and cars constructed, double track laid, and the gauge widened and standardized.

Some of the trunk lines were spending up to one-half of revenues earned in the state on these permanent improvements. However, the commission was not complimentary on operations of branch lines considered inadequate to meet service demands. They were concerned with dangerous highway and farm crossings; strains on roadbed, superstructures, bridges and equipment by increased tonnage hauled by heavier locomotives or "double headers;" and the constant rate adjustments on inter- and intrastate traffic. Also questioned were accommodations for passengers during heavy demand periods—excursions, conventions and holidays—which resulted in dangerous overcrowding of trains. On matters of state railroad control, there had been no litigation for years.

During the second decade, expansion of traffic and the requirement of published rates greatly increased the railroad commission's work. A new rate department was established with the Honorable John Henderson of Indianola as commerce counsel to handle prosecuting functions and represent the people of Iowa in cases before the ICC. The work of the commission was further expanded by authorization to grant franchises for transmission of electricity for light, heat and power.

Highway and Farm Crossings

For some years, the railroad commission had called for improvement or elimination of highway and farm railroad crossings. In 1900, their annual report discussed the changed conditions resulting from railroad efforts to strengthen or render more substantial their roadbed and trackage throughout the state. Where excavations occurred or obstructions were removed, improvements often interfered with views of approaching trains which were running with increased speed and frequency, making crossings hazardous. The commission encouraged construction of subways or overhead crossings where such were feasible and not unreasonably expensive. But the State Supreme Court had held in a number of cases that the legal crossing under state statutes was "an adequate crossing." In most instances, the commission was able to convince county supervisors to change the highways in order to ensure a safe crossing but had no jurisdiction to compel such action and therefore called for laws to cover these situations without the necessity of court procedure. "It should not be necessary for a railway company to appeal to the courts to protect it against county supervisors who were insisting upon a crossing at a dangerous location when with a slight change in the highway a safe and adequate crossing might be made."[1]

The highway commission had no jurisdiction in these cases until 1913, after which cooperative efforts with the railroad commission were effected to make the necessary changes in road design and location. The highway commission had made changes suggested on the primary road system but where disagreements occurred, the railroad commission was asked to determine the type of crossing and apportionment of the cost to railroads and highway authorities. The increase in motor vehicles on public highways and the deaths of 240 persons in grade crossing accidents between 1915 and 1920 emphasized the problem. Most of the accidents were at crossings where the view was unobstructed for hundreds of feet and appeared to have been caused by miscalculating the speed of oncoming trains. Recommendations were made for installation of gates, bells and warning signs on the highways, and the railroad commission ordered the railroads to remove all obstructions from their property.

Railroad Operations

In 1900 there were 38 steam railroads serving a population of slightly over 2.2 million people, operating over 9,170 miles of track (including trackage rights) and employing 37,696 workers. Ten years later, 24 railroads operated 9,781 miles of track, an increase of 610 miles on main and branch lines, and employed 57,715 people. If yards and sidings were included, there would be an additional 1,600 miles. In 1920, the number of roads had declined to 20 carriers, operating over 9,843 miles of track. Earnings and operating expenses at five-year intervals are shown in Table 5-1.

The slight drop in mileage after peaking in 1915 resulted through elimination of roundabout routes, line relocation and reduction in trackage rights. Gross earnings more than doubled between 1910 and 1920, but net earnings showed a drastic decline between 1917 and 1918 and a deficit in 1920, even after rate increases during federal control in World War I. Inflationary trends carried over to 1920, indicated by the large increase in operating expenses. Fourteen railroads had disappeared from commission records between 1900 and 1910, and four more by 1920. Absorption of smaller lines had a beneficial impact upon shippers by placing the consolidated roads into higher classifications and reducing maximum freight rates. Also, continuous or through rates could be applied rather than having to use two or more short distance or "local" rates which usually resulted in higher freight charges.

What little extension of lines was accomplished during the ten years, 1905-1915, was generally to close gaps and connect detached portions of the various railroad systems. Only 200 miles were built during

[1] *Thirty-Second Annual Report of the Board of Railroad Commissioners for the Year Ending December 7, 1909,* State of Iowa, Des Moines: State Printing Office, 1909, p. 12.

these years. Every county seat had railroads as did every town and village over 100 or more inhabitants, and a 15-minute automobile journey connected every farm home with a railroad station. Table 5-2 shows the distribution of railroads according to population size of cities and towns in the Iowa Census of 1915. Two observations can be made from the table: one, a high number of cities and towns in the 1,000 to 5,000 category were served by more than one railroad; indeed, a surprising number had three railroads (it was probable that the roads used small towns and cities as junction or interchange points); two, the importance placed on towns with populations between 10,000 and 50,000 and over as locations for routes of three railroads, indicative of the potential competitive nature of the traffic.

Table 5-1
Comparative Earnings and Operating Expenses, Mileages Operated and Earnings Per Mile for Railroads in Iowa

Year	Mileage[1]	Gross Earnings[2] (Millions)	Operating Expenses[2] (Millions)	Net Earnings[2] (Millions)	Net Earnings Per Mile
1900	9,171	$ 52.07	$ 35.40	$16.67	$1,815
1905	9,827	58.47	41.95	16.52	1,681
1910	9,781	74.89	59.08	14.81	1,616
1915	10,002	88.44	65.36	23.08	2,308
1920	9,843	156.54	167.32	-9.78	-940

(*Source:* Iowa Railroad Commission, *Annual Report, 1921*)
[1] Including trackage rights.
[2] Figures rounded to the nearest number.

Table 5-2
Number of Railroads Serving Cities and Towns in Iowa by Population Size

Population Cities and Towns	Number	One Railroad[1]	Two Railroads[1]	Three Railroads[1]
1,000- 5,000	144	59	70	15
5,000-10,000	17	7	6	4
10,000-20,000	6	--	1	5
20,000-30,000	5	--	--	5
30,000-40,000	3	--	--	3
40,000-50,000	2	--	--	2
50,000-Over	1	--	--	1

(*Source:* Earle J. Robinson & Co., *Illustrated Review of the Development of the State of Iowa.* Press of George F. Cram, Chicago, 1916.)
[1] Including Interurbans.

Agricultural Traffic

Sage refers to the period from 1897 to 1920 as the "Golden Age of Agriculture" which might have terminated in 1913 if not for World War I. In 1915, there were 199,175 farms in the state with a value of $3.5 billion ($4.0 billion including equipment). The state ranked first in the value of farm crops and cultivation of fruits and vegetables, and it was second only to Texas in the extent and valuation of livestock production. Price inflation raised farm income from $7.8 billion in 1913 to $9.5 billion in 1916, and exports rose from $1.3 billion to $3.8 billion during these years as against virtually no imports. Railroad revenue freight was a measure of the state's agricultural importance, with grains, fruits and vegetables, livestock, packing-house products and dressed meats as the dominant tonnage. Industrial products hauled related to the agricultural sector and included coal, sand, stone, brick, lumber, cement, petroleum and machinery.

The Corn Gospel Trains

Railroads had been utilized to spread information regarding road building and maintenance techniques throughout the state. They also cooperated in furthering agricultural education and extension activities. One of the most notable efforts was the development of the Corn Gospel Trains between 1904 and 1906. P. G. Holden, a corn breeding specialist, became a faculty member at Iowa State College in 1903. Holden had directed extension work for Fink Brothers Seed Corn Company in Illinois, spending much of his time on the road demonstrating the superiority of yellow dent corn to Midwestern farmers. Shortly after arriving in Ames, he organized experimental plots on demonstration farms to teach improved cultivation methods. His success moved him to a plan to bring the college to the people. Following meetings with railroad executives, grain dealers, friends and supporters, he initiated the "Seed Corn Gospel Trains" consisting of three coaches and a baggage car, complete with lecture charts, displays and a speaker's platform. Expenses were underwritten by the CRI&P, Wallace's Farmer, the Iowa Grain Dealers Association and the Central Iowa Grain Company.

For three years the train covered the state, logging 11,000 miles to reach farmers and grain dealers in 97 of the state's 99 counties. An estimated 145,700 people heard the lectures which included not only methods of finding and testing the best seed corn, germination techniques and specifications for testing equipment, but also crop rotation, manure handling and hog raising. He also organized short courses throughout the state before leaving Ames in 1912 to administer the extension program for the International Harvester Corporation.

Railroad Rate Regulatory Control

The Federal Level

From the beginning, the ICC was seriously handicapped in administering the 1887 Act in rate matters. Basic weaknesses appeared in the enforcement provisions, and court interpretations stripped the commission of authority to deal with rate grievances which had led to its passage. In prescribing reasonable rates, it was assumed that if a certain rate had been found unreasonable, maximum reasonable rates could be prescribed, a practice followed between 1887 and 1897. But in 1897, the U. S. Supreme Court decided that the ICC was without power to prescribe rates for the future and also overruled them on interpretations of the long and short haul clause. Legislation to correct these weaknesses was passed by Congress in 1903, 1906 and 1910.[2]

The General Rate Level Cases

Rate level cases are revenue cases and were proposed by the railroads to ensure an adequate rate of return on their investment. In 1898, the U. S. Supreme Court in *Smyth v. Ames* established a standard for determining reasonableness of the general level of rates. "We hold that the basis of all calculations as to the reasonableness of rates to be charged by a corporation maintaining a highway under legislative sanction must be the fair value of the property being used for the convenience of the public . . . . What a company is entitled to is a fair return of that which it

[2] ICC v. Cincinnati, New Orleans & Pacific Railway Co., 167 U. S. 479 (1897); ICC v. Alabama Midland Railway Co., 168 U. S. 144 (1897). The first case was known as the "Maximum Freight Rate Case." The second gave a new interpretation to decisions relating to the long and short haul clause. In addition, the Elkins Act, Statutes at Large 32, sec. 1, 847-849 (1903), was a railroad-sponsored measure relating to personal discrimination. The Hepburn Act, Statutes at Large 34, sec. 1, 539-557 (1910), further strengthened the commission's powers on rate matters and clarified the distance principle at issue in the long and short haul controversy.

Lecture aboard the Corn Gospel Train.
(Courtesy: Iowa State University Archives)

employs for the public convenience."[3] Thus, some authoritative determination of that value was necessary to satisfy the "fair return doctrine."

The first rate level cases came before the ICC in 1910, calling for an increase of 10 percent to meet rising operational costs. The ICC refused the request on the basis that the carriers had failed to show the reasonableness of the rate increases, citing their inability to substantiate the need for higher rates due to an acceptable valuation of the properties. It had become apparent that further proposals would require property evaluations, and the result was passage of the Valuation Act of 1913. The outbreak of World War I in Europe brought renewed pressures on the roads to meet increased traffic demands, and the inflationary price index of 1910 made further applications for rate increases necessary in 1913, 1915 and 1917. Rates were raised but not to the extent the railroads felt were necessary to meet the higher operating costs. But from the beginning of federal control in 1918, rate increases were inevitable, and they were made under General Order 28, allowing a 25 percent advance. For Iowa, with 90 percent of its traffic moving interstate on eastbound movements, the increases affected over 200 different commodities. Not only were interstate rate increases of concern, but usually the railroads petitioned state commissions for similar increases on intrastate traffic, again raising questions of competitive rate relationships between origins and destinations within the state.

[3] Smyth v. Ames, 169 U.S. 466 (1898).

The State Level

Making intrastate rates or determining changes was a difficult task for the Iowa Railroad Commission. Building a system of rates which would move the traffic without discriminations at levels providing for efficient service and acceptable prices for shippers, and yet return a "fair" amount of revenue to the railroads, was a complicated process. Complex rate structures were in force, including percentage, basing point, zoned and blanket systems. Key point rates from Chicago to New York were published, with locations between taking fixed percentages of the base rates. Large cities with industrial and processing facilities were used as basing points; in the Midwest, rates were made with special application to Minneapolis, St. Paul, Chicago and St. Louis. In the territory east of the Missouri River, origins were given "blanket" rates on traffic to the Pacific Coast. Rates were often equalized from Missouri and Mississippi River cities into Chicago. These rate structures had been built as a logical result of historical forces, transportation and industrial competition, proximity to the rivers and certain large distributing points; also because transcontinental lines had been obliged to rely largely on through business. Among other factors that tended to slow the development of Iowa manufacturing and processing, rate structures which placed the state at a disadvantage played a prominent role.

The position of the railroad commission was that every Iowa industry should be protected to the utmost limit of their rate-making powers, and that Iowa shippers should not be placed at a disadvantage vis-a-vis shippers outside the state who shipped into common markets. Iowa markets should be encouraged and protected to the end that raw materials produced in the state could be processed at home, giving employment to labor and allowing investment of Iowa capital. Packing houses should be encouraged by a low intrastate rate on livestock, particularly hogs: process the product in Iowa and ship to regional or national markets. To accomplish this objective required less interest in the interstate than intrastate rates. "It is much more important, in order to maintain packing houses in Iowa, that freight rates within the state for short distances be low ones than it is to have the interstate rate so low that it will result in taking the hogs raised in the state to Chicago and other distributing centers for packing purposes."[4] What was needed was more flexibility in the Iowa Distance Tariffs.

The Iowa Tariff had been developed by Peter A. Dey and included 10 different classes in the intrastate schedule of freight rates. First class was fixed at 100 percent and the remaining classes at varying percentages, ranging from 85 to 20 percent of first class. Brindley concluded that the Tariff was not a distance schedule except for the first 100 miles, and that beyond, chaos reigned in rate-making and rate relationships. "It would seem that freight rates have not been made but have grown like Topsy and the British Constitution," a conclusion he was not alone in making.[5]

Changes in the Railroad Route Structure

Closing the Gaps

New track was laid to complete direct railroad lines into common points. The CGW built 133 miles from Fort Dodge to Council Bluffs in 1903, featuring a 2,588 foot bridge over the Des Moines River, said to be the second-longest bridge in the state. The CRI&P needed a more direct line from the Twin Cities to Kansas City to eliminate the roundabout route in which they used the St. Louis line to southeast Iowa, thence to the southwest. Independent roads, later taken over by the CRI&P, were built 70 miles from Des Moines to Iowa Falls in 1903, completing the extension to Clear Lake in 1909. A southern section from Carlisle to Allerton was finished in 1913. The short cut through Des Moines eventually became part of the new north-south route cutting diagonally across the Midwest to link the Twin Cities with the Gulf of Mexico.

The CMStP&P was the last railroad to reach Des Moines, absorbing short, independent lines from Des Moines to Boone and Fonda. At Des Moines, it competed with the CRI&P, CNW, CB&Q, CGW and Wabash roads. But the CMStP&P could not compete successfully for Kansas City traffic until its last major construction in Iowa was completed—the Kansas City cutoff. Previously, trains ran from the north and east over the circuitous and hilly route between Marion and Ottumwa. By 1903, a new line was in operation from Muscatine to Rutledge, where it joined the main

[4] *Thirty-Second Annual Report of the Board of Railroad Commissioners*, p. 15.

[5] John E. Brindley, *A Study of Iowa Population as Related to Analytical Conditions*, Bulletin No. 27, Ames: Engineering Experiment Station, Iowa State College, 1912.

line running southwest. Between Muscatine, Davenport and Clinton, the route was further strengthened by reciprocal trackage agreements with the CRI&P and joint arrangements with the CB&Q. Through construction, purchase or lease of trackage rights, gaps on all lines were closed by 1914. Other construction occurred on branch lines carrying coal traffic, and for sidings.

The CNW had double-tracked its main line across Iowa by 1902, and its trains ran on the left-hand track as was customary in Great Britain. Contrary to popular assumption, this situation was more a matter of economy than the influence of British investment. Most CNW stations were built on the north side of the original single track, and it was less expensive to add another set of tracks to the south. Reversing the normal direction of trains meant that stations would not have to be relocated, and passengers would not have to cross tracks to board eastbound trains to Chicago. Those who remember riding the passenger trains from Chicago to Ames will recall the off-boarding on the south side and the walk through the subway to the station and parking lot.

Line arrangement on the CNW resulted in building the "longest, highest, double-tracked railroad bridge in the world," which opened in 1901 over the Des Moines River near Boone. It was 184 feet above the valley floor and 2,685 feet long, and when completed it eliminated the longer, hilly, single-line track through Moingona between Boone and Ogden. The structure became known as the "Kate Shelley Bridge," named for the 15-year-old legendary heroine of Iowa and American railroad history. Her fame in story, ballads, memorials and statues stemmed from her 1881 exploits in stopping the eastbound *Atlantic* (*Midnight Express*) from running over a damaged trestle during a heavy rainstorm, and assisting in the rescue of a brakeman and engineer on a "pusher"

Eastbound train speeding over embankment after crossing Kate Shelley Bridge, 1912.
(Courtesy: Edward S. Meyers Collection)

engine which had fallen into flooded Honey Creek. She was rewarded by being named station agent at Moingona by the railroad. When the CNW and UP railroads discontinued their joint operation of passenger trains in 1955, one of the substitute trains from Chicago to Boone was named the *Kate Shelley*.

Station Agent Kate Shelley at her Moingona Station. (Courtesy: Edward S. Meyers Collection)

Except for a spur near Sioux City, the last branch line in Iowa was built in 1915 by the CNW-controlled Iowa Southern Railway between Consol and Miami to handle coal traffic. Double-tracking the Omaha line of the CMStP&P started at Sabula in 1912 and was completed to Manilla in 1914. The 80-mile gap to Council Bluffs was never finished, and the expected traffic on the line never materialized.

Old main line through Moingona, south of Boone, 1900. (Courtesy: Edward S. Meyers Collection)

Improvements in Motive Power

Steel cars and longer trains required more power, and by the 20th century, steam locomotives had evolved through the Mogul (2-6-0), the Prairie (2-6-2), the Mikado (2-8-2), the Atlantic (4-4-2), the Pacific (4-6-2), the Hudson (4-6-4) and the Mountain (4-8-2), to the diesel electric, streamlined in the 1930s. The numbers after each name classified the locomotive according to wheel arrangements. A (4-6-2) engine meant a four-wheel leading truck, six driving wheels and two wheels behind the drivers. The diesel became the major power source because of its efficiency and low maintenance, getting approximately four times as much power from a pound of fuel as did the steamer.

Faster schedules were required to meet passenger and freight service and to enable carriers to bid for lucrative mail contracts. The CNW and CB&Q competed agressively for mail on the Chicago-Omaha route, both striving to cut the time in transit and often reaching 90 miles an hour. The fast mail trains were pulled by the most powerful locomotives, operated by the most highly skilled and experienced engineers and had clearance over all other traffic. The CNW was credited with operation of the first railroad post office unit and the CB&Q, the first railroad car used in sorting mail between stations. The glamour of a railway mail clerk, in the author's youth, was second only to being God or a city fireman.

Steam Passenger Trains

By the early 1900s, each of the major railroads in Iowa was running transcontinental trains to the West Coast. These were well advertised, popular and subject to numerous articles and books by travelers.

The Kate Shelley Bridge.
(Courtesy: Author)

The Kate Shelley Bridge.
(Courtesy: Author)

The CNW's *Overland Limited* ran continuously for 60 years from 1887; the CB&Q offered the *Overland-Express* and the CRI&P ran its luxurious *Golden State Limited,* scheduled to compete with the AT&SF's *California Limited.* The *Olympian* was the pioneer train of the CMStP&P, and the CGW provided sleepers from the Twin Cities. In addition, regional trains crisscrossed Iowa between Chicago, Omaha, Lincoln and Denver on the east-west routes and Minneapolis to Kansas City and St.Louis on the north-south lines. The CRI&P and CMStP&P promoted passenger service to the Iowa Great Lakes region, and the latter road—perhaps unwittingly—assisted in providing transportation for the first "hobo" convention at Britt in 1900.[6]

The Battles for Financial Control

Capital stock purchases and financial manipulation to secure control of railroads was common in the early years of the century. The CRI&P was a well-managed road which made dividend payments even through the Panic of 1893. However, broad distribution of the stock made possible speculation for quick profits. In 1901, four men—Daniel Reed, William B. Moore, who was leader of the group and had made a fortune organizing the National Biscuit and Diamond Match Companies, J. Robert Moore, his brother, and W. B. Leeds—took control of the railroad. Through holding companies which initiated new construction, mergers and purchases, the system expanded from 7,123 miles in 1903 to 14,270 miles in 1907. To make the railroad a transcontinental line, the St. Louis-San Francisco (Frisco), Chicago & Alton, and Chicago & Eastern roads were absorbed. Then, through an affiliated syndicate, they sought control of the eastern link, the Lehigh Valley and Lake Erie & Western. The over-expanded, overcapitalized system went into receivership in 1915, emerging two years later with its debt structure and ratio virtually intact. The Reed-Moore administration transformed a once profitable and highly respected operation into one which faced financial problems periodically throughout its existence.

James J. Hill controlled the Great Northern (GN) and Northern Pacific (NP) and wanted the CB&Q to round out his empire. E. H. Harriman of the UP had similar ideas. While Hill, in collaboration with the Morgan banking interests, secretly bought into the CB&Q, Harriman went after the NP to get partial control of the CB&Q. The bidding war between these two railroad giants caused the NP's stock to rise from $114 to $1,000 a share in three days, ending on May 9, 1901, resulting in a brief panic on Wall Street until called off by the parties. Hill got control but it was agreed that Harriman should have representation on the NP's board of directors. The Hill era were years of expansion although most of it occurred outside of Iowa. The CB&Q's historical tradition of developing its territory continued. In 1913, the road operated a Silo Train in Iowa, stopping at 42 stations where lectures were given on the proper storage of grains and silo construction. A Dairy Special followed in 1914, visiting 24 communities in the interest of improving dairying techniques.

Another contest for control took place on the IC when Harriman and Stuyvesant Fish, a long-time associate, became locked in battle. It culminated in 1906 with the ouster of Fish, president for nearly 20 years, and the election of James T. Harahan, second vice president and Harriman's choice as his successor. The internal fight had only modest impact on stock prices. Harriman, reputed to be the largest stockholder with 15,000 shares and a director since 1883, won the fight. Expansion of the road also was primarily outside of Iowa. Influenced by construction of the Panama Canal, it concentrated on sharing traffic originating in the southeastern United States and handling tonnage moving through the canal into the Midwest via the Southern ports as well as its own port at New Orleans.

A stock-purchasing coup was responsible for Edwin Hawley's M&StL taking control of the Iowa Central in 1900 and merging the two roads in 1912. These were relatively weak lines when operated as independents, but together they had both economic and strategic advantages. Through this merger, Iowa gained more than half of the total mileage of the

[6] Frank P. Donovan, Jr., "The Milwaukee in Iowa," *Palimpsest 45* (May 1964): pp. 225-226. The idea of a national convention of hobos came from T. A. Potter of Britt, who had heard of a similar assembly in Illinois. His efforts in organizing the meeting were assisted by E. N. Baily, editor of the *Britt Tribune.* Both men promised a carload of beer and sufficient food for 500 tramps. They noted that the Milwaukee ran on the main line through Britt and that north-south service was provided by the M & StL. Although the delegates rode the boxcars, the officers of the Association arrived in sleepers. An estimated 250 legitimate hobos attended the first convention and made Potter Britt's first member of the "Order of the Honorary Sons of Rest."

combined railroads. It was this unification which allowed Hawley and his associates to lay the foundation for expansion which, from its modest beginning in 1896, served four states with a fourfold increase in mileage by 1912.

Roads and Highways

The Highways of Iowa—1904-1908

When the highway commission was formed in 1904, less than two percent of the state's 102,000 miles were improved with gravel or broken stone.[7] Approximately 25 percent were recommended for classification as main travelled roads with no person situated more than two miles, or a large majority of the people less than one mile, from a main road running in each direction from centers of population. When hard-surfaced roads were built, it was predicted that a farmer would be able to reach town markets during any season, and communities could diffuse their business throughout the year. The remaining 75 percent were considered as second-class roads—cross roads in sparsely settled areas, to be kept passable but receive a lower priority on expenditures until a system of main roads was perfected. It was these roads that were giving Iowa the reputation of one of the worst "mud road states" in the nation, a condition noted by Dean Marston who stated: "It seems absurd that in a state so wealthy and prosperous, so advanced in education and intelligence, the entire agricultural economy and the basis for practically all business activity should be left to the mercy of bad weather on account of roads which would be a disgrace even to a barbarian."[8] In the first annual report of the 1913 commission, road mileage of approved county systems certified by county engineers totaled 104,082 miles, outside of incorporated towns.

Geology and Road Building

Although Iowa was considered a prairie state whose surface is a gentle undulating plain, road makers faced topographical and geological conditions which varied in different areas. Three principal incursions of ice, known technically as "drifts," were the origins of soils and glacial debris. These were the Iowan, Wisconsin and Kansan "drifts," each of which gave certain characteristics to their regions. The Kansan Drift, covering the entire southern and western sections, was the oldest formation, cut by streams causing deep valleys and affording good drainage. Gravel was not universally distributed throughout the area, although it was found in the valleys of the streams and at the margins of the other drift regions. Stone, as a road building material, was found principally in the eastern section.

The Iowan Drift covered the northeastern section within one or two counties bordering the Mississippi River. The terrain was level, and drainage required careful attention as streams did not have time to cut deep courses. Large deposits of gravel were available for road purposes, and limestone and large boulders suitable for road building were widely distributed. The Wisconsin Drift, youngest of the three, covered the north central area, was level and had little drainage development. An understanding of the features of the drift areas was necessary for the road builder because of soil conditions, drainage, hills and valleys, and the availability of building materials (Fig. 5-1, 5-2).

Early Road Building

Practically all of the public roads were laid out on section lines, and new roads opened were located without much deviation from this practice. As a result, the road system was developed without regard to engineering efficiency or economy. In the Iowan and Wisconsin Drift areas, this situation was not considered serious. However, the area covered by the Kansan Drift was cut by water and other natural forces into a series of ridges and valleys, and the exclusive system of section line road location caused impractical grades and heavy expenses for moving earth. The topography required that the road had to be curved in plan or profile. Section line location prohibited the first and made necessary the second, which was worse. The heaviest grade of any road will limit the size of loads hauled over it, and for economy the maximum grade should be kept as low as possible. Therefore, it was suggested by the commission that the cost of construction and

[7] Maurice O. Baldridge, *Public Road Mileage, Revenues and Expenditures in the United States in 1904,* Washington, D. C.: Office of Public Roads, Bulletin No. 32, 1904. In 1904, Iowa's 102,448 miles of roads placed the state third behind Texas and Missouri. Improved roads consisted of 1,408 miles graveled, 241 miles with macadam or stone surfaces, and 20 miles by other materials.

[8] *Iowa Hiway Hilites* (May 1963): p. 2. Published in Ames by the Iowa State Highway Commission.

maintenance would be considerably lower by building around rather than over the hills, and/or buying new right-of-way around a series of hills. Often, the total cost of entirely relocating a road would be less of a problem than making even a faint start on a good road on a section line.

The early commission gave technical specifications to road builders for construction of earth roads in the first-class category. The width was to be 18 feet for the traveled way, not too wide for easy maintenance, with ample space for ordinary traffic and with a rounding or parabolic contour. The most important consideration was efficient surface, side and sub-drainage. Next came elimination of steep grades and finally the surfacing with gravel, broken stone or some other wearing coat.[9] Advice was available for gravel and macadam construction, suggestions made as to the location of the materials, the necessary tests to be used and the costs. Information was distributed on the use of road machines, scrapers, graders, etc., and the training of men and teams in their usage. "Compared with the permanent roads many if not all of the other state's highway departments are building, the earth or clay road seemed simple and of doubtful value perhaps, but it must be remembered that practically all of the road building in Iowa in the early years is earth building; that men who can do this work are few and hard to find; that the earth road is fundamental and the basis for all road improvements."[10]

Sporadic Road Building

Experimental and permanent roads were planned and built during this early period. Scott County built five and one-half miles of broken stone base with gravel cover in 1907, at an average cost of $7,670 per mile. Des Moines County was building three miles of limestone-based roads at an estimated cost of $5,000 per mile. In and around Keokuk, broken stone roads had been built for many years and with a little maintenance would have lasted for a longer period. The City of Des Moines built two sections of pavement consisting of a mixture of asphaltic oil with earth, gravel or broken stone screenings which gave promise of good results as a new form of road construction in the state. These isolated developments again raised the question of state supervision over highways. "It is not to be expected that where cities or counties experiment with new forms of surface coverings that many of the other counties will profit by their experience unless the information is gathered and distributed by the state, and neither is it to be expected that all the experiments should be successful and the state is far better able to spend the money in experimenting and developing types of road construction than individual counties. Not only should experimental work be done, but as much as possible of the practical work in the counties of building roads should be under state supervision and state encouragement."[11]

The King Road Drag

Earth roads would not maintain themselves in good condition, and so the split log drag was introduced and used in every county by 1906. E. Ward King, a farmer living near Maitland, Missouri, developed the King Road Drag, probably constructed orginally from pump stock and an old fence post nailed together, 30 inches apart. King's success in smoothing his road attracted the attention and interest of Iowa road officials. During 1905, a special CNW train visited 15 northern counties from Onawa to DeWitt, stopping at various places to demonstrate the drag, and the state became familiar with this method of maintenance by additional lectures at the Road School in Ames, and before farm and business organizations. The interesting point about the drag

[9] *American Highways 27,* Washington, D. C.: American Association of State Highway Officials, 1980, 99.2-24. Four pioneers who laid the foundation for the science of modern roads building were Pierre Marie Tresagnet, Inspector General of Roads and Bridges in France in 1775. His fame rests largely upon the innovation of a relatively light road surface designed on the principle that the subsoil must support the load; John Metcalf (Blind Jack) was the first English road builder and a contemporary of Tresagnet. He built 180 miles of turnpikes consisting of a layer of gravel placed on a well-drained and dry subsoil, to be beaten by traffic into a solid road surface; Thomas Telford of Scotland who became a great bridge builder and road mender in the 18th century; and John McAdam, also from Scotland, who built roads in the same century and was best known for the design of "macadam" roads. Both Telford and McAdam used similar methods of building by raising the earth foundations high enough so that ground water would not soften the subsoil, crowning the earth subgrade to drain water into side ditches with a three-inch crown for an 18-foot width road. They used clean stone for surfacing without a mixture of clay, earth or organic material which would be affected by frost and built the highway to suit the traffic and not limit the loads to fit the road. They differed in the maximum thickness of the surface and size and uniformity of stone. McAdam's techniques were considered the less expensive.

[10] *Third Annual Report of the Iowa State Highway Commission For the Years 1907 and 1908,* Des Moines: State Printer, 1909, p. 10.

[11] *Third Annual Report,* p. 13.

was its ease of construction and cost, which varied from $1.50 to $3.00 (Fig. 5-3).

The theory behind the use of the "split" log drag was very simple. If the surface of an earth road was smoothed after each rain, ruts formed were filled and the road was in condition to shed water during the next rainy season. The drag was hauled at such an angle that a little earth was moved toward the center of the road each time, building up a crown by almost imperceptible degrees. If ordinary soil was subjected to continual wetting and mixing, it "puddled" and could be molded into shapes that would not hold water. This condition was observed on main traveled county roads where water stood in ruts and hollows. After the surface softened, the wheels of wagons and hoofs of horses mixed, molded and packed the earth into a series of cups which would hold water until it evaporated. Where the soil contained a mixture of sand or vegetable material, it would not puddle. In addition to preparing the surface for the next rainfall, the drag also distributed the puddled earth over the road in a thin layer which was beaten and packed into a very hard surface by heavy traffic. The gumbo soil held up for considerable periods even with water standing on either side of the traveled way.

Bridges

Bridges were built of wood, steel, masonry or a combination of these materials. The various forms of construction resulted in a heterogeneous array of structures designed and built by counties and townships without systematic planning for the vehicles they carried. Increased rural traffic made wood or pile bridges inadequate for heavy machinery, particularly the traction engines with large water tanks and coal supply. The cost of timber construction was rising, and timber deteriorated rapidly and was undermined and washed out in high water, making wooden bridges quite expensive and dangerous. The highway commission condemned the assorted collections of steel, cement, clay and iron culverts "whose best claim to recognition was the clear profit netted their sellers" and "the various forms of steel or concrete and steel bridges being built

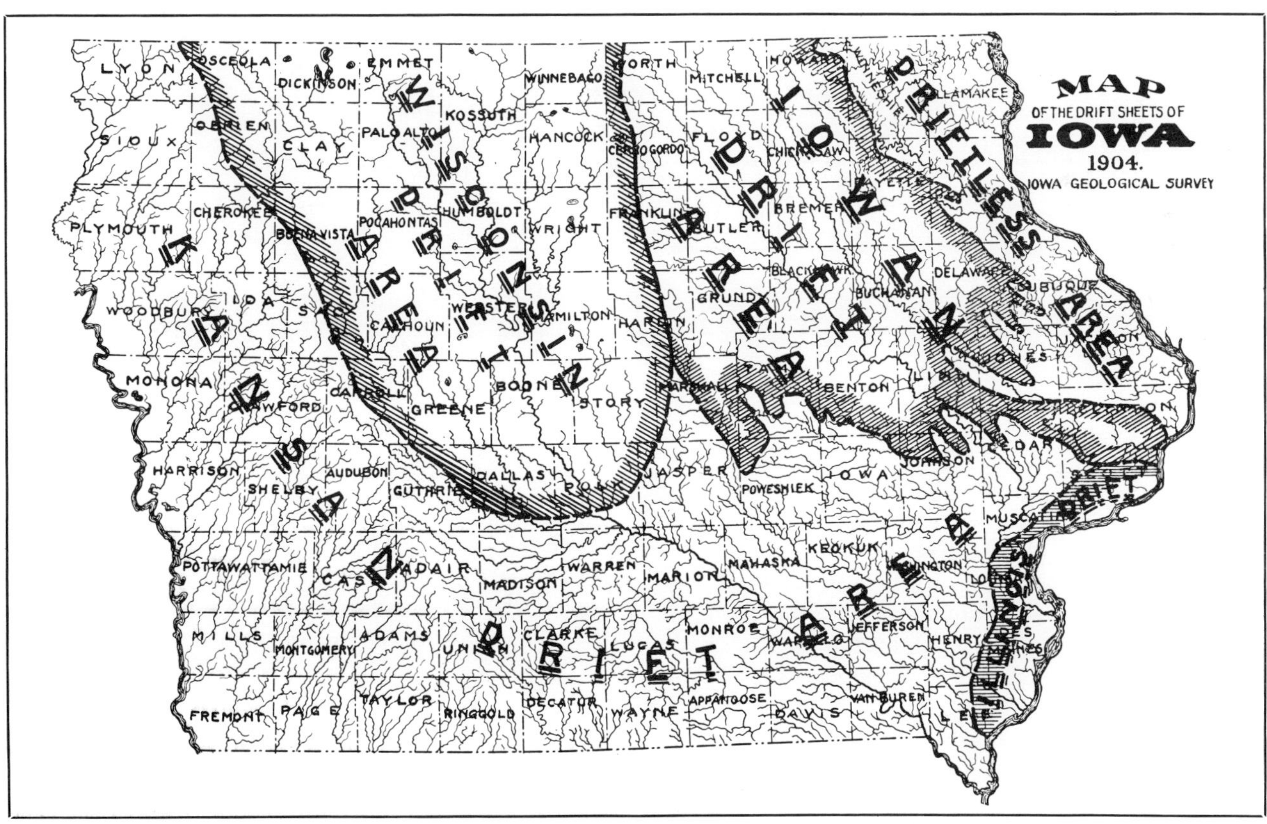

Figure 5-1
Areas of Iowa covered by the different glacial deposits.
(Courtesy: 1904 Iowa Geological Survey)

that have no claim as engineering designs."[12] After two years of study, the commission formulated standard loadings for which all bridges should be designed, and these were recommended for inclusion in state laws. Also recommended was appointment of a county engineer to supervise the road and bridge building programs.

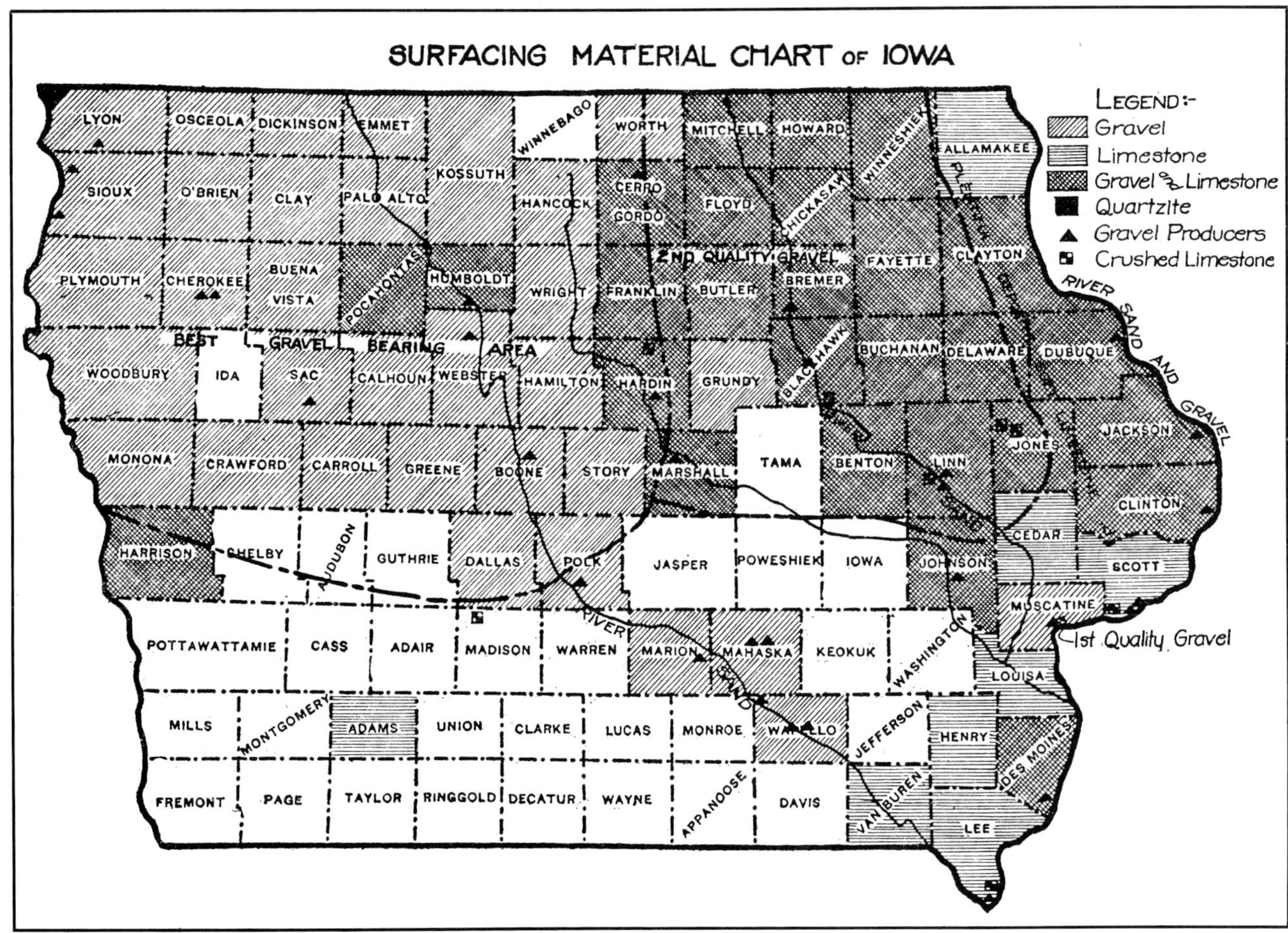

Figure 5-2
Availability of road building materials.
(Courtesy: Iowa State Highway Commission.)

Highway Funding and Traffic

The total income in 1904 for road construction, maintenance and bridges amounted to $4.5 million, not including revenue from poll taxes. Townships had revenues of $2.28 million, or an average of $22.83 per year for every mile of road. Although the counties had no jurisdiction or control over any road, supervisors built and maintained county bridges on all roads. For this work, each county assessed a bridge tax which amounted to approximately $1.63 million per year for the entire state. The county road tax resulted in annual revenues of $547,000 statewide. With this fund, counties could assist townships with road work or directly repair township roads. Since all parts of the township road system were consistently in bad condition, the supervisors had wide latitude as to

[12] *Second Annual Report of the Iowa State Highway Commission Made to the Governor of Iowa For the Year Ending July 1, 1906,* Des Moines: State Printer, p. 26.

where, how or when they spent the money. In some counties, the road fund became known unofficially as the "campaign" fund.

Based upon house-to-house canvasses in typical townships throughout the state in 1905, traffic counts indicated that heavy hauling over county roads totaled 55 million ton-miles, and that light hauling and general traffic totaled over 350 million miles per year. The mileages approximated would equal one string of teams traveling 30 miles per day reaching more than one and one-half times around the world. In monetary terms, if regular wages and expenses were charged for the actual time of men and teams, the amount would be between $30 and $40 million. A road census taken in one township in each county showed the following averages (Table 5-3):

Table 5-3
Average Highway Traffic of One Township in Each County

Component	Average
Average size of full loads hauled	2,090 pounds
Average distance to market	4.17 miles
Total ton-mile hauling	22,065 ton-miles
Average time per round trip	3.19 hours
Average time required per ton-mile	50 minutes
Total miles without considerable load to market	61,829 miles
Total miles traveled other than to market	92,818 miles
Total of all miles of light travel	162,923 miles

(*Source:* Iowa Highway Commission, *First Annual Report, 1904:* p. 23)

Since practically every business in Iowa depended upon agriculture, the condition of county roads as all-weather arteries of trade were of major concern. The commission studied records of agricultural price fluctuations relative to road conditions in all sections of the state. The relationship for one county (Woodbury) in 1902-1903 showed that the price of hogs reached the highest level at the same time or during the same period that the roads were impassable.

Highway Progress Under the New Commission

It became evident by 1913 that expenditures for bridges and culverts had to be placed on a more efficient basis, and that contracting practices had to be improved before any real progress on road construction could be made. As soon as the new highway commission began a study of these matters, it was subject to attacks by interests which would be affected by placing bridge work on open competitive bidding. Two situations were unearthed: (1) the state had been divided into districts by supplying companies, making competition impossible; (2) there were no standards or general knowledge among road officials as to the market value of bridge materials or labor, nor was there uniformity in quality or prices of the materials furnished.

Approximately half of the entire road taxes were spent on bridges and culverts, often to the neglect of necessary grading, drainage and dragging of roads. The influence of the suppliers was so great that it amounted to little less than blackmail schemes to control bridge and culvert funds. Not until supervisors were removed in Polk and Clinton counties and money refunded was the public aware of these circumstances. Similar conditions existed in other sections of the state, and these plus the demands for efficient and trained supervision of construction under responsible administrators resulted in the road law under which the new state highway department was organized and a new system of administration established.

The State Highway Department, 1913-1920

During the first year, personnel visited every county board of supervisors to explain provisions of the new road law, completed preliminary investigations, and approved 15,000 miles of county roads which eventually became a system of highways connecting every important market center. With county engineers, they surveyed county roads for the purpose of making maps, plans and specifications for permanent road building; assisted in designing and approving plans for more than 800 structures in 86 counties; and established a uniform system of records, accounts and reports for county road and bridge expenditures. Educational meetings were held throughout the state, and charts, maps, photographs and standard plans were exhibited at state and county fairs, conventions and county engineers' "short courses." To become fully informed of the work of various counties, the state was divided into five districts, each headed by a district engineer whose headquarters were located at convenient places in the district. The location was determined by grouping counties easily reached by railroad from one central point. The original five districts were reorganized into nine districts for administrative purposes in 1919.

By the close of 1913, the work of the highway department brought a change in the sentiment of the public, and criticism of the new road law gave way to a more fair consideration of the principles involved. Fayette, Clayton, Worth, Benton, Cerro Gordo, Story, Black Hawk and Woodbury counties, among others, built more miles of permanently graded earth roads and more permanent bridges and culverts than in any previous year. When the construction season of 1914 began, county after county started road building on a broad scale with the quality of workmanship and materials constantly improving. However, there were two major problems. One involved organization—the employment of men to do the work in an efficient manner—and the other concerned an adequate system of maintenance. The commission noted that the state had to depend upon earth roads for a long time and that good earth roads needed constant maintenance, "the greatest of problems to be faced in the future."

Special attention was given to dangerous railroad crossings. As of January 1, 1915, there were 8,676 crossings in the state, or one for every 12 miles of highway, exclusive of those within the limits of incorporated cities and towns, not a surprising number when the total mileage of all highways and railroads was considered. County road crossings totaled 1,533, and there were 7,143 on township roads. Nine hundred of these were classified as dangerous by county supervisors. Since the county road system carried the larger percentage of the

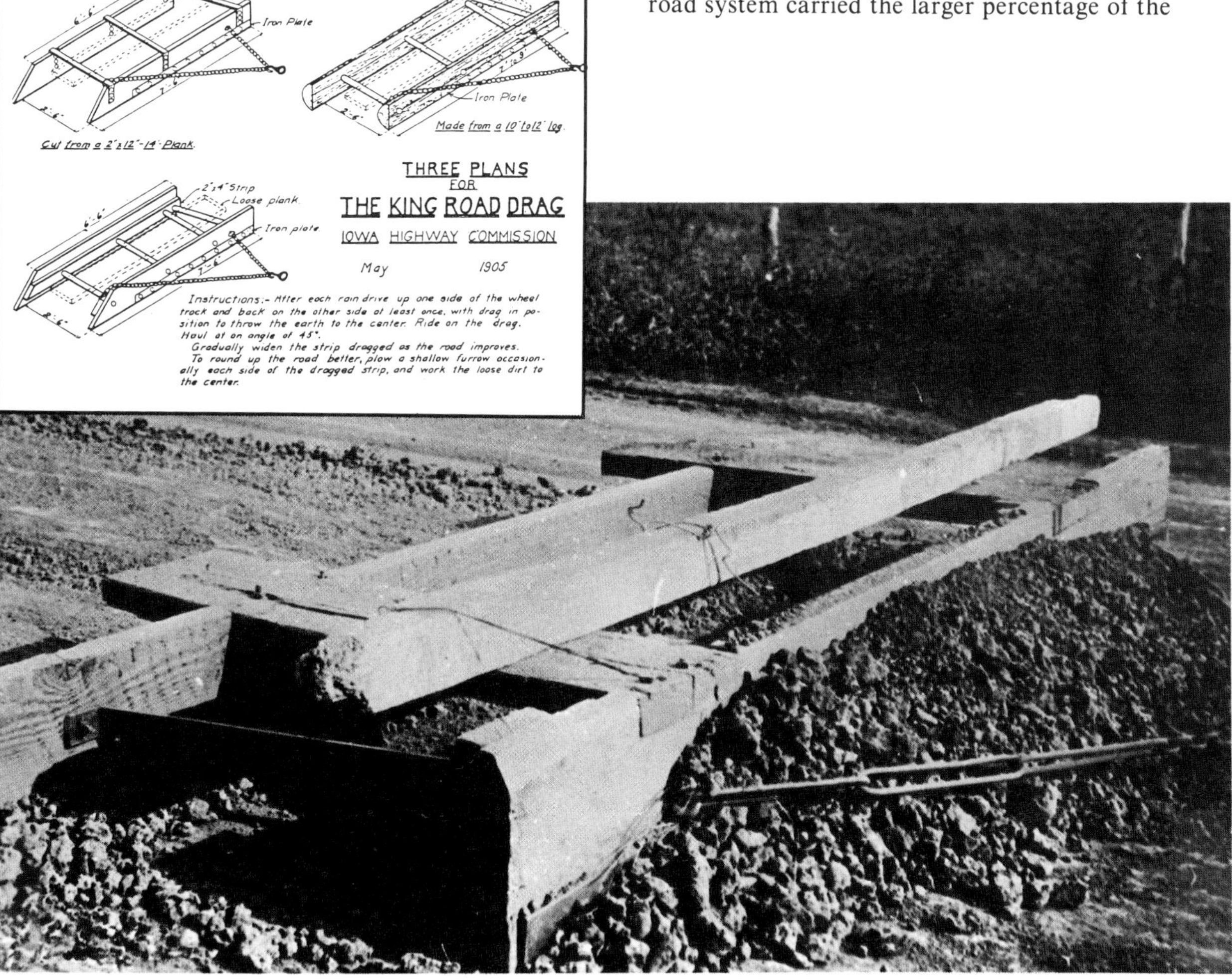

Figure 5-3
The King Road Drag, popularized in Iowa after 1905 by D. Ward King of Missouri. This is an "improved model." King preferred to use split logs, rather than the planks used in the drag shown above.
(Courtesy: Iowa Highway Commission)

traffic, the most dangerous county road crossings were given first priority for improvement or elimination. Distribution of crossings, with reference to railroads and road systems, are shown in Table 5-4.

Between November 1, 1914, and January 1, 1916, total expenditures from county road funds approximated $3.4 million. Townships were estimated to have spent about $3.5 million, but when divided into 88,300 miles they averaged only $40 per mile, little over half of the average cost of repairs and maintenance per mile of county roads. An appropriation of $30,000 was made by the U. S. Department of Agriculture for improvement of the Dubuque-Dyersville Post Road which when completed would be the most extensive single highway improvement undertaken to this time. The road was to be graveled for 19 miles and would cost $160,000, including the cost of viaducts and subways for railroad crossing elimination. A portion of this cost was shared by the IC railroad. Road and bridge expenditures by counties and townships did not change materially during 1916, but the average spent on township roads increased to $44 per mile, two-thirds of the average for county roads.

Funds available through the Federal Aid Act of 1916 provided $146,200 for road projects in 1916, increasing each year to $731,000 in 1920. The total over the five years of approximately $2.7 million was matched by state funds from automobile license fees. These were apportioned to counties on the basis of area. The 37th General Assembly, in accepting the provisions of the federal legislation, stated that the 2,000- to 6,000-mile program should include a part of the roads in each county, named subsequently the "Inter-County Road System." Counties could apply for funds and designate that portion of the inter-county system that they wished to improve, indicating also the character of the improvement. Dubuque county was the first to apply, followed by requests from 58 other counties.

Following the nation's entrance into World War I, prices of materials and supplies rose rapidly; for example, structural steel was 250 percent higher than in 1915. Transportation facilities were diverted to the movement of troops and war materials, labor was scarce, yet the amount of highway work was near normal levels. Counties and townships spent $15 million for road and bridge improvements with increased funding resulting from bond issues. Of the $11 million raised through bonds, over 80 percent was used for bridge work, the remainder on roads.

Table 5-4
Distribution of Crossings in Reference to Railroads and Road Systems

Railroad	County Road Crossings	Twp. Road Crossings	Total No. of Crossings
CRI & P	349	1,526	1,875
CMStP&P	251	1,227	1,478
CNW	208	1,183	1,391
CB & Q	272	915	1,187
CGW	123	633	756
M & StL	111	582	693
IC	95	442	537
Wabash	41	142	183
FtD, DM & S	15	93	108
Misc. Small Railways	68	400	468
Total	1,533	7,143	8,676

(Source: Iowa State Highway Commission, *Annual Report, 1913-1914:* p. 163.)

Automobile registrations rose from 799 in 1905 to 147,078 in 1915, and the increased usage brought renewed demands for hard surfaced roads. The early supporters of good roads considered macadam as an ideal surface, but it was difficult to obtain the necessary materials. The automobile quickly changed that idea. "Before the advent of the automobile, the stone dust that served as a binder for the stones in the macadam road was ground in by the steel tires of horse-drawn vehicles. The automobile . . . sucks out the binder and loosens the stones and . . . tears the road to pieces rather than bind it together."[13] It was fortunate that Iowa could not build macadam roads, for it would have been necessary to spend large sums to maintain them under the heavy pounding of motor traffic. Gravel was more plentiful in northern and eastern Iowa and had proved practical for surfacing less traveled roads, but heavy maintenance costs on main highways discouraged its use.

Hard-Surfaced Roads—The Problems

Although the state was making considerable progress in permanently grading earth roads, anticipating that they would serve communities under proper maintenance for years, generally they were not adequate for motorists. T. R. Agg pointed out that no one of the types proposed for hard-surfacing—gravel, broken stone, macadam, brick, concrete, etc.—would have universal application. Traffic, soil and financial conditions were the decisive factors in the selection of permanent surfacing, and the choice for one community would not necessarily satisfy the requirements of others. Even considering these elements, the category chosen would depend on maintenance or the lack thereof for its length of life. Agg further suggested that bonding for road improvements was a less objectional method of financing than direct property taxes, and by 1919, 26 counties had voted favorably for hard-surfaced road systems, thereby authorizing construction of 1,700 miles of pavement. The Primary Road Law provided that counties who wished to move faster on road improvements than possible through normal funding could use bonds after affirmative vote of the people in a special or general election.

The use of concrete as a road surface appeared to have started with a half block in LeMars in 1904. In 1909, Mason City and Davenport laid 6,000 square yards within their cities. In 1911, a quarter mile, 14 feet wide, was built near Eddyville, with materials, labor and cash supplied by businesses, farmers and the Mahaska County supervisors. By 1912, concrete, formerly relegated to a minor place in surfacing materials, began to achieve some prominence. A mile was built in 1913 west of Mason City, extended into that community in 1915, and in 1917-1918 the 11 miles between Mason City and Clear Lake were paved, marking the first interurban highway in Iowa. These "experimental" roads, together with the "seedling mile" in Linn County in 1918 on the Lincoln Highway, proved their ability to withstand heavy traffic and weather conditions and stimulated the demand for additional mileage. But while practical, construction expenses of $30,000 per mile in the 1920's were a deterrent. Yet, when the relative expenses for maintenance and motor vehicle operations on concrete roads were compared to those on gravel roads, such costs were cited by good roads advocates as evidence that concrete would be less expensive in all respects over long periods of time.

The Lincoln Highway

In 1912, a community of interest had developed between the automobile and highway users. Carl Fisher, manufacturer of the Pres-O-Lite automobile systems, conceived the idea of a transcontinental highway from the Atlantic to the Pacific coast, hard-surfaced and marked throughout its entire length. Because stone or rock were common surfacing materials, he called it "The Coast to Coast Rock Highway." An association with membership fees and annual dues was proposed to finance the estimated $10 million required to build the road. The title was changed to the "Lincoln Highway" through efforts of Fisher and Congressman Borland of Missouri, who suggested that the road plan would be more popular if some patriotic appeal was introduced into its title.

In addition to cash contributions, the cement industry agreed to furnish its product on the same basis as contributions of motor car manufacturers: one-third of one percent of the annual gross for three years, estimated to provide 2.3 million barrels of cement.

[13] George S. May, "Getting Iowa Out of the Mud," *Palimpsest 46* (February 1965): p. 96.

Western states joined the movement by improving roads and bridges along the proposed route, chartered originally by a series of automobile tours. The road was planned to start from New York City to Jersey City, N.J., thence to Philadelphia and Pittsburgh, Pa., Fort Wayne, Ind., around Chicago and westward through Geneva, Ill., to Clinton, Iowa. Continuing it would run through Omaha, Neb., and Cheyenne, Wy., to Salt Lake City. From there, it followed the old Pony Express Trail to Ely, Reno and Carson City, Nev., Sacramento and San Francisco. Entering Iowa at Clinton, it would pass through DeWitt, Cedar Rapids, Tama, Marshalltown, Ames, Jefferson, Denison and Logan to Council Bluffs, for a total of 358 miles across the state. Except for the "seedling mile" east of Cedar Rapids and short stretches of concrete west of Jefferson, the longest segment of 38 miles from Clinton to Lowden was not paved until 1924. Other sections of the route were surfaced with oiled dirt, graded earth and gravel. In dry weather, the trip on the highway could be comfortably made but rain made the earth roads a barrier to traffic. In this weather, "the tourist should stop if he wishes to save his car, his time, his tires and his temper"[14] (Fig. 5-4, 5-5).

The highway was marked four different times. The first was by use of red, white and blue bands painted on poles, rocks or other convenient objects. Later, the official insignia was adopted consisting of red, white and blue rectangles with the words "Lincoln Highway" in blue above and below the letter "L", painted on telephone poles and metal signs. More permanent enameled steel signs were next erected, and finally 3,000 concrete posts bearing the insignia and letter were placed along the route. Two of these may be seen on the south side of Lincoln Way in Ames, in front of the Department of Transportation building.

Lincoln Highway between Ames and Nevada, 1918.
(Courtesy: Iowa State Highway Commission)

[14] The Lincoln Highway Association, *The Lincoln Highway,* New York: Dodds-Mead & Co., 1935, pp. 210-226.

The joys of motoring, 1915-1920.
(Courtesy: Iowa State Highway Commission)

Difficulties on mud roads, 1915-1920.
(Courtesy: Iowa State Highway Commission)

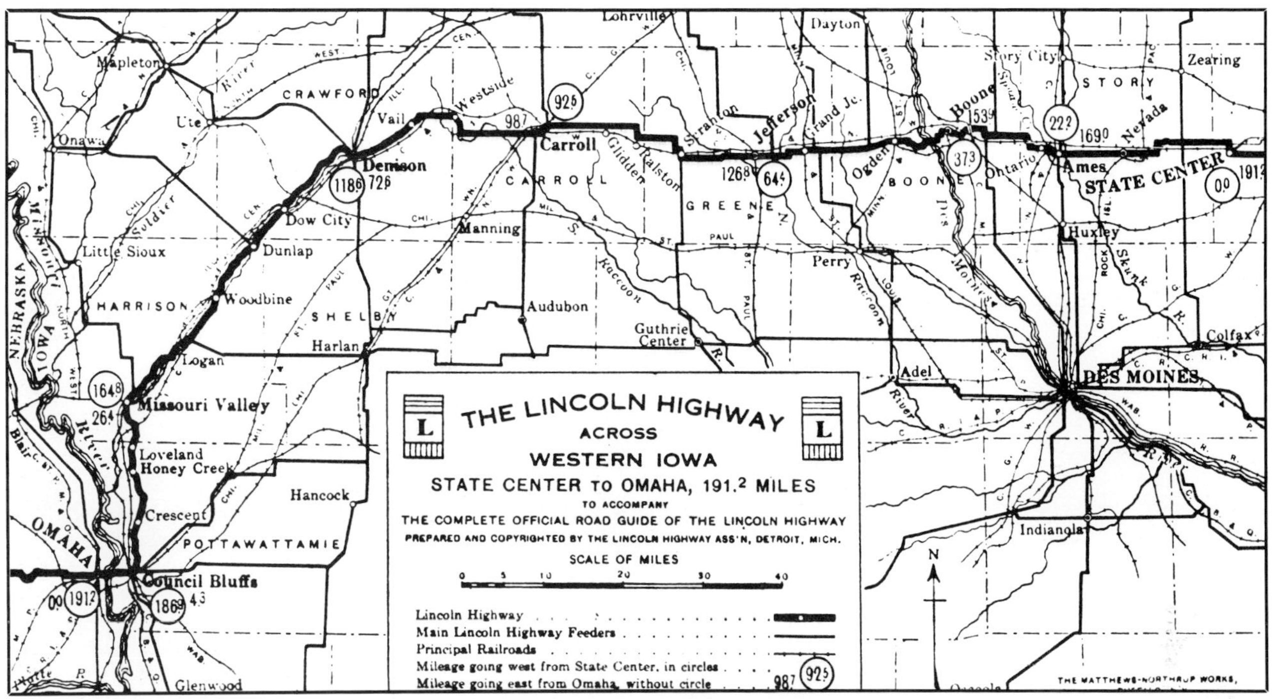

Figure 5-4
Lincoln Highway Across Western Iowa.
(Courtesy: Lincoln Highway Association, Detroit, Michigan)

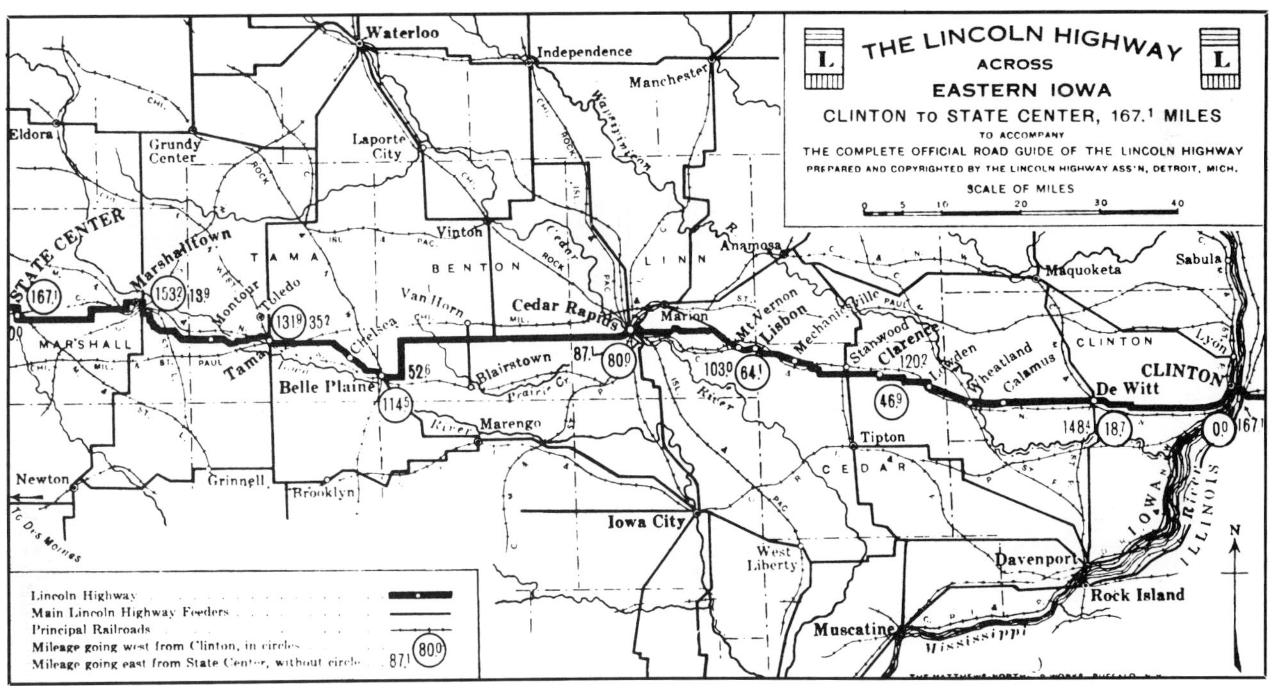

Figure 5-5
Lincoln Highway Across Eastern Iowa.
(Courtesy: Lincoln Highway Association, Detroit, Michigan)

The Lincoln Highway at Tama, 1920s.
(Courtesy: Iowa State Highway Commission)

Lincoln History Marker.
(Courtesy: Iowa State Highway Commission)

Bridge at Tama on old road, 1986.
(Courtesy: Author)

The Jefferson Highway

On March 14, 1911, the Des Moines-Kansas City-St. Joseph Interstate Trail was organized at Lamoni. In 1915, the original trail was extended to Mason City from Des Moines through Nevada and Iowa Falls and continued to St. Paul via Albert Lea, Faribault and Northfield, and the name changed to the St. Paul-Des Moines-St. Joseph-Kansas City Interstate Trail. It covered 503 miles, was well marked, and became part of the preferred road systems in Minnesota, Iowa and Missouri. With the exception of one county in Iowa, it connected all of the county seat towns and cities along its route.

The Jefferson Highway Association was organized in New Orleans in 1915 through the efforts of Walter Packer of the New Orleans Association of Commerce, the Honorable E. T. Meredith, later Secretary of Agriculture in the Wilson Administration, and Senator Lafayette Young, both of Des Moines. The Interstate Trail formed an important segment of the Jefferson Highway, and their organizational methods and marking system were followed largely by the Jefferson group. The major cities on the north-south route were Baton Rouge, Alexandria and Shreveport, La.; Muskogee, Okla.; Joplin, Kansas City and St. Joseph, Mo.; Des Moines, Iowa; St. Paul and Minneapolis, Minn.; and Winnipeg, Canada. The Mason City-Clear Lake paved road (Federal Project No. 1) was part of the projected road in Iowa. Paving across the state was expected to be completed by 1919. The insignia was similar to that of the Lincoln Highway with the letters "JH" in the middle band.

Highways or trails were not only organized on a national or regional basis but were quite common locally or statewide. The commission was authorized under Section 1527-S22, Supplement to the Code, 1913, to register highway routes promoted by voluntary organizations and to issue certificates for a fee of $5.00 to protect the names and markers used by the various associations. From 18 of these trails registered in 1914, the list grew to 64 by the close of 1925. A map showing these trails is included with this book.

Highway Accidents and Fatalities

Increased use of automobiles resulted in railway crossing accidents and caused injury and fatalities on Iowa highways. Speeding vehicles went over embankments, turned turtle, collided with each other and with bicycles and buggies, struck people, ran into trains and were hit by them. In 1916, there were 2,574 accidents which killed 199 people and injured 2,834. The headline in the Commission's Service Bulletin of January, 1918, read: "To be Safe, Go to War Until Careless Speeders are Banished from Iowa Highways."

As early as 1915, there were proposals to prohibit the sale of high speed automobiles in Iowa. "Limiting the speed of cars allowed in the state is the only effective way to cut the motor speed maniac and prevent the killing and maiming of people by reckless, inexperienced and incompetent drivers. Laws naming speed limits of so many miles per hour or, as Iowa puts it, 'reasonable speed,' with 25 miles per hour as evidence that a driver is exceeding that speed, are worthless. The high-powered car, advertised by manufacturers to hold the road at 50 miles an hour or accelerate from a standing start to 60 miles in 16 seconds, are a deadly menace to all users of the highways and sweep on their way unchecked. . . . The only effective way to curb the speed evil would be to forbid the sale of high speed cars, for there are reckless and careless drivers who will continue to have accidents as long as they are allowed to run cars on the highways."[15] Sixty-five years later, despite new laws, new regulations on driver qualifications, national speed limits, new enforcement procedures and much more improved and safe highways, the state still struggles to control the level of deaths and struggles carnage on the highways.

Convict Labor on State Institutional Roads

Under an Act passed by the 34th General Assembly and amended by the 35th General Assembly, the Board of Control was placed in charge of approximately 50 miles of roads through and adjacent to state lands at all of the state institutions. Except for county bridges, costs of improvements and maintenance came from the general funds of the state. The chief engineer of the commission was appointed to supervise the work and surveys, and planning was conducted by commission personnel. Labor was provided by convicts, 20 of whom were used to build

[15] "Can Appalling List of 1916 Highway Fatalities Shock Iowans Into Saner Driving in 1917?" *Iowa State Highway Commission Service Bulletin 5* No. 1-2-3, Ames: Iowa State Highway Commission, 1917, p. 3.

two miles of roadway at the Iowa State College in 1914, and in 1915, about 100 were engaged in building roads and culverts at other state institutions. They were housed in tent camps, wore any type of clothing and were paid 20 cents per hour. There were no visible restraints on the men as they went about their work, and the camps were virtually unattended. While the commission considered that convict labor had made a good showing in these isolated instances, they did not feel that the experience warranted its use in general road work as contrasted to contracting the projects to those with the necessary experience and equipment. "It is not practical to use men who must be placed under guards . . . and no economy would result to counties or townships in attempting to use prisoners in this way."[16]

Traffic Surveys

In 1917 and 1918, traffic counts were taken for a continuous period of seven days on the inter-county system, and for the two years, survey results were compiled for 87 stations in 36 counties. These locations were away from the immediate vicinity of larger cities, widely distributed, and considered as fairly representative of state patterns. They did not cover traffic on main roads leading to major cities. Briefly summarized, the survey showed that the average traffic was 300 vehicles carrying 800 people per day and that more than 80 percent were motor driven. Forty-six percent were local (town-to-town, town-to-farm and traffic originating in the towns); 47 percent were inter-urban or inter-county and the remaining 7 percent was interstate travel. An additional study made by T.R. Agg in 1919 showed the traffic situations as follows:

1. Tonnage was considerably higher than generally supposed, which emphasized the wisdom of constructing road surfaces of great durability. The system of earth roads had been carrying traffic considered moderately heavy for paved roads.
2. Passenger automobiles were predominant.
3. The present highways did not encourage the use of motor trucks because of the extreme variations in surface conditions.
4. Interstate traffic was insignificant, emphasizing that Iowa roads were constructed not for tourists but for Iowa people to be used for their pleasure and business.
5. About 90 percent of the traffic was motor driven, which indicated the equity of requiring a substantial contribution from motor vehicles for construction and maintenance on Iowa highways.[17]

The Highway Situation by 1920

By the close of 1920, considerable progress had been made on highway improvements despite the interruptions caused by World War I. Road builders looked forward to 1919 and 1920 in keen anticipation of a return to normal conditions. But labor was still scarce and remained so until mid-1920; rail transportation was uncertain and materials difficult to obtain. Highway officials had authority to build roads and could pay for them, but could not produce the product in a quantity desired. However 1919 should be remembered as a year of great achievement—a year in which the state embarked upon a program of modern highway construction. From 1913 to 1920, 3,216 miles of road had been built to permanent grade, 1,256 miles to temporary grade, 13,660 miles were tractor graded, 2,035 miles gravel surfaced, and 43 miles of the primary system paved.

River Transportation—The Doldrums

The Upper Mississippi River

The original project for improvement of the Upper Mississippi between the Missouri River and Minneapolis was adopted in 1879. Proposed was a channel or waterway by means of wing and closing dams so as to allow a depth of four and one-half feet at low water. The plan to secure a depth of six feet was adopted in 1907. During that year, President Theodore Roosevelt appointed the Inland Waterways Commission to prepare and report on a project to improve and control the waterways of the United States. Traffic had fallen on the Mississippi since Civil War days. Shallow depths, inefficient boats, irregular schedules, lack of terminals, and the seasonal nature of the traffic were among the reasons. On the other hand, railroads offered regular and efficient services.

[16] *Report of the State Highway Commission for the Year Ended December 1, 1916,* Des Moines: The State of Iowa, 1916, pp. 143-144, 149.

[17] T. R. Agg, *Traffic on Iowa Highways,* Bulletin No. 56, Ames: Engineering Experiment Station, Iowa State College, 1920.

The most important commerce on the river during the first decade of the 20th century was lumber products, although rapidly declining due to deforestation of the pine forests in Wisconsin and Minnesota. In 1882, 87 sawmills were operating along the river, keeping about 100 towboats busy. The largest milling centers in terms of board feet of lumber processed were Minneapolis, Winona, Dubuque, Clinton, Rock Island, Muscatine and Davenport. The impact of the lumber trade can be measured by the commerce through the Des Moines Rapids Canal in 1900, when 822 steamboats and 381 barges were counted. By 1914, the lumber traffic had almost disappeared.

During 1909, 22 packets, 36 towboats, 17 ferryboats, 147 pleasure boats and 26 government boats, totaling 16,103 gross tons, were in operation between Minneapolis and St. Louis. In addition, there were 300 unregistered barges of various sizes used for freight and construction materials. The principal steamboat lines were the Diamond Joe, the Eagle, the Carnival City and the Acme. Traffic, consisting mainly of lumber, rock, sand and gravel, reached a high of 4.53 million tons in 1904 and fell to a low of 761,522 tons in 1921. Passenger traffic between 1904 and 1920 averaged between two and three million annually.

A shortage of rail cars in the Mississippi Valley during World War I led to the formation in 1917 of a Committee on Inland Transporation to study the possibilities of the use of waterways to relieve congestion on the railroads. Their report concluded that rail freight could be handled on the waterways with adequate terminals and recommended that the federal government initiate such action. From the U.S. Shipping Board, $3.9 million was granted to the Emergency Fleet Corporation to build and operate towboats and barges between St. Paul and St. Louis, the first federal operation of equipment on the River. The Federal Control Act of 1918 commandeered all floating equipment on the Mississippi and Warrier Rivers, and appropriated $12 million for new construction. The Federal Barge Service emerged from these actions and eventually became known as the Federal Barge Line on the Upper Mississippi. It was operated by the Railroad Administration and transferred to the War Department in 1920.

The Missouri River

Steamboats had navigated the Missouri since 1819 when the first boat reached Council Bluffs; arrived at the mouth of the Yellowstone in 1832; and to the head of navigation, Fort Benton, Montana, in 1859. The length of the navigable river from Fort Benton to the Mouth is 2,285 miles. Originally, and into the 20th century, the condition of the river was one of alternate pools and bars. Water depth ranged from three feet in low water to nine feet in high water. The navigable depth did not increase as rapidly as the water height since the bars rose with the stage of the river. No projects for improvement throughout its length had been adopted by 1919.

Under a federal appropriation of $1 million in 1910, improvements were made from Kansas City to the Mouth with a view of securing a permanent six-foot channel. Previously, in other sections, work on the removal of snags, miscellaneous obstructions and trees had the effect of equalizing and reducing freight rates to approximately 60 percent of rail rates, a somewhat similar ratio as the 66 percent found on the Upper Mississippi. The maximum draft in 1910 at mean low water from Kansas City to the Mouth was four feet; from Kansas City to Sioux City, and on to Fort Benton was three feet. Traffic on the river never exceeded one million tons annually during the 1900-1920 period; the high of 843,863 tons was reached in 1907, thereafter falling steadily and especially during the war years. Generally, the character of upstream movements was merchandise and supplies; downstream, grains and livestock.

Early Aviation in Iowa

The Pioneers

Space permits only a brief discussion of individuals who contributed to aeronautical development in the state. For those interested in an inclusive description of general aviation history from 1845 to 1918, the most authoritative coverage is found in Ann Holtgren Pellegreno's *Iowa Takes to the Air.* A considerable portion of the presentation which follows has been drawn from this publication.

The fascination of flying in Iowa dates back to the gas-filled balloon era before the Civil War. An unmanned flight occurred in Burlington in 1845, and the first manned balloon was piloted by Professor Silas Brooks in the *Hercules,* also at Burlington in 1856. Following the war, when captive observation balloons were used by both armies, this form of aerial activity was taken seriously, and balloon ascensions and races were popular at state fairs and city and town celebrations. The Mississippi River cities, Des Moines and Sioux City, were among leading metropolitan areas for these events. Parachuting was an innovation of the Baldwin brothers, Sam and Thomas, who became world famous for their daring feats, one of which almost cost Sam his life during a jump at Muscatine in 1888, when he fell into the Mississippi River.

Toward the end of the 19th century, gliders were being designed and flown, and the experiments led to the development of the first flying machine. Flying gliders had been proven practical by German and American engineers and in 1898, Carl Bates, a 14-year-old from Clear Lake, built and flew the first man-carrying glider in Iowa. Bishop Wright, an official in the United Brethren Church, lived in Cedar Rapids from 1878 to 1881, later settling in Dayton, Ohio, where sons Orville and Wilbur began experiments which led to their manned engine-powered flights on December 17, 1903 at Kitty Hawk, North Carolina. The four flights that day averaged 31 miles per hour and initiated the age of powered airplanes. Rotary engines were designed by F. Oscar Farewell and built by the Adams Company of Dubuque, and a version rated at 55 horsepower was available by 1909.

As small internal combustion engines were developed, innovators began installing them on sausage-shaped dirigible balloons, giving the operators some directional control. Among aeronauts who flew these dirigibles were Thomas Baldwin, Roy Knabenshue and Charles Hamilton. It was Hamilton who flew Knabenshue's dirigible at the 1906 State Fair in Des Moines, landing at the Capitol and returning to the fairgrounds. However, despite the numerous balloon ascensions, parachute leaps and powered airship flights, no aeroplane had been flown over Iowa at the close of 1909.

This situation changed in 1910. Arthur J. Hartman built and operated a two-cylinder monoplane at Burlington in May. Eugene Ely of Williamsburg and James C. "Bud" Mars flew at Sioux City in June, and Thomas Baldwin at Iowa City in October. Ely, a member of the Glenn Curtiss exhibition team, worked with the U.S. Navy on plans for launching an aircraft from a ship and took off on November 10 from a slanted platform built over the forward deck on the cruiser *Birmingham,* steaming down Chesapeake Bay, for a two and one-half mile flight to shore. His next flight was from shore to ship and on January 11, 1911, at San Francisco, Ely flew to the cruiser *Pennsylvania,* landed on a platform built on the stern and returned safely to shore. These flights made Ely an international celebrity. On October 19, 1911, he was killed in exhibition flight at Macon, Georgia.

In his *Story of Iowa,* Peterson listed some 46 flights by 23 aviators over different cities and towns in Iowa during 1910-1911, although no identification was given. Over the next five to six years, the challenges of flying brought new developments on engine and plane design and construction and pushed pioneering efforts to greater heights with rather astounding success, given the extremely poor condition of landing fields. One of the most famous flyers of this period was William "Billy" Robinson of Grinnell, internationally recognized for piloting mail planes in Canada and well known in central Iowa.

Robinson organized the Grinnell Aeroplane Company with a view of establishing a factory and flying school, plans cut short by his premature death. His most successful flight was sponsored by the *Des Moines Capital* and *Chicago Tribune* in 1914. The trip started from Des Moines on October 17 for a non-stop mail flight to Chicago, authorized by the federal government. Weather conditions and a fuel shortage forced him down at Kentland, Indiana, about 80 miles southeast of Chicago. The distance covered was 300 miles, exceeding the American record by 125 miles, and took four hours and 30 minutes, averaging 80 miles per hour. Having established the non-stop record, Robinson then tried to break the altitude record which in 1916 was 17,000 feet, about 3,000 feet higher than he had ever flown. On March 11, 1916 he crashed and was killed in the attempt. The plane was completely wrecked but the engine is preserved in the museum at Grinnell College as a memento to his exploits.

Others active during the early years were Oscar and Mary Solbrig of Davenport—designers, builders, mechanics and pilots who invented an airplane which could be quickly taken apart, crated and reassembled. They flew exhibitions throughout Iowa and midwestern states until Oscar joined the U.S. Air Force in World War I. Ruth Law soloed in 1912, was the first woman to fly at night and held the women's altitude record. Katherine Stimson received her license also in 1912 at age 16, becoming the fourth woman to be enrolled in the Davenport School of Aviation. J. Herman Banning, also from Ames, was the first black aviator to receive his license. Glen Martin of Macksburg left Iowa at an early age, flew his first plane in 1909, and became a stunt pilot before starting an aeroplane factory on the west coast.

World Famous Aviators

Three internationally famous pilots linked to early Iowa aviation history made news in the 1920's. Clarence Chamberlin of Denison captured the long distance record by flying from New York to Berlin. He was the first to fly a passenger, his financial backer Charles Levine, across the Atlantic Ocean. Later, Chamberlin and Bert Acosta broke the endurance record in his Bellanca monoplane, *Columbia,* by staying in the air for more than 51 hours. Charles Lindberg, whose exploits need no detailed descriptions, flew at many points in Iowa and dedicated several airports. Amelia Earhart lived for a time in Des Moines, and in 1928 flew as the first woman passenger from Newfoundland to Wales in a tri-motored Fokker monoplane. Four years later, she made a solo Atlantic flight and subsequently made long distance flights across the United States. Her career ended in an unknown spot in the Pacific Ocean in 1937.

Steamboat *Andrew S. Bennett* on Missouri River, 1880s.
(Courtesy: Scott Sorenson, Sioux City Public Museum)

The War Years—1917-1918

Within five days following the declaration of war on Germany on April 6, 1917, representatives of all major railroads met in Washington and voluntarily merged the roads into an operational system of 254,000 miles under the direction and control of a Railroad War Board of five railroad executives. But the railroads under private operation could not meet the demands for service, and on December 28, 1917, President Wilson took possession for the war effort. William G. McAdoo, Secretary of the Treasury, was appointed Director General, followed later by Walker D. Hines. Despite an increase in rates in 1918, revenues did not keep pace with increased operating expenses. The result was that the ratio of expenses to revenues, commonly known as the "operating ratio", rose from 78.14 percent in 1917, the last year of private operation, to 102.5 percent in 1920. For the first time in railroad history, operating expenses exceeded operating revenues for the railroad system.

The net cost of federal control to taxpayers from 1917 to 1920 amounted to more than $1.6 billion, cited over and over as evidence of the evils of federal ownership and operation of the nation's railroads. The experience of federal control during wartime does not offer a sound argument for or against control in peacetime. The effect was to provide "as to the country's war needs and as to the interests of railroad security owners, a protection which had become impractical on the part of private control in view of the emergencies and limitations with which it was confronted. Any fairly balanced study of the situation as a whole must lead to the conclusion that in periods of extraordinary difficulty, the government's temporary operation of the railroads accomplished with credit the objects which made resort to it imperative."[18] What the experience demonstrated was that railroad regulations since 1887, despite numerous amendments, were so restrictive as to prevent a unified system from operating under private control during periods of extreme emergency. Historians have referred to this period as one of "negative regulation" which reached its climax during the war years and which necessitated serious consideration of a more positive legislative approach toward railroads in the 1920s.

Pilot sent to Iowa State Fair by the Wright brothers, 1911. A box of rocks is strapped to the passenger seat to balance the weight of the engine. (Courtesy: Des Moines International Airport)

[18] Walker D. Hines, *War History of the American Railroads,* New Haven: Yale University Press, 1928, p. 239.

Summary

The physical structure of the railroads was largely in place in Iowa by the turn of the century, in contrast to the archaic conditions of the roads over which journeys were often hazardous. Additional railroad mileage had been built between 1900 and 1920, primarily to close gaps in the systems, make more direct connections between major cities, for branch line service, and to expand yards, terminals and sidings. Private investment and state support provided a network of almost 10,000 miles connecting nearly all of the small towns and large cities within and outside the state.

With principal building programs behind them, railroads focused attention on operational techniques and improvements. Supervision and regulation of these operations in conformity with federal and state laws, and the solution of local problems, was the responsibility of the railroad commission. Safety of employees and the public was of paramount importance as passenger and freight schedules increased in speed and frequency. Rate and service changes raised issues of discrimination with which the commission struggled in order to protect Iowa's industries. The period was one of railroad stabilization, road and equipment improvements, of consolidation of weaker into stronger lines—all designed to provide more efficient service at lower costs.

Progress in developing statewide systems of highways and roads was slow and widely scattered until the state and federal governments realized the necessity for improvements for private travel and commercial trade. The first highway commission laid the foundation for organized effort in planning and managing road construction even though hampered by limited funds and personnel. The second commission was given broader powers and responsibilities to provide uniform programs for highway and bridge design, construction and maintenance.

Organization, planning, specifications, supervision, uniformity of standards, accurate record keeping and cooperation with local road officials, were key elements in the 1913 commission's program for road development. Original concerns centered on the type of highways needed, materials to be used and methods of financing, rather than the nature of the traffic. Yet, the expanding number of vehicles and their impact could not be ignored, especially in the accident and fatality records on railway crossings and elsewhere. The second decade, principally from 1913 to 1920, was characterized by fairly rapid progress, culminating in the organization of a Primary Road System and the use of county bonding for construction.

Navigation on the Upper Mississippi and Missouri rivers was difficult because of shallow water, snags and obstructions. Wing and closing dams were built on the Mississippi, and dikes and revetments were built on the Missouri to partially alleviate the problem and to maintain navigable channels. Lumber and construction materials furnished the heaviest traffic on the Mississippi, whereas on the Missouri, general merchandise and agricultural products were the major commercial movements.

Iowa aeronautical history started before the Civil War with balloon ascensions and progressed through gliders to engine-powered machines in which Iowa pilots challenged distance, altitude and endurance records. The pioneering efforts of builders and flyers, many of whom lost their lives, were instrumental in the future advances of aviation in the state.

Selected References

Agg, T. R. "The Hard Surfaced Problem in Iowa." *Iowa State Highway Commission Service Bulletin 3,* Ames: Iowa State Highway Commission, 1915.

Board of the Railroad Commission. Annual Reports for the years 1900, 1910, 1913, 1915, and 1920. Des Moines: State Printing Office.

Casey, Robert J., and W. H. S. Douglas. *Pioneer Railroad.* New York: McGraw Hill Book Co., 1948.

Corliss, Carlton J. *Main-Line of Mid America.* New York: Creative Age Press, 1950.

Daggett, Stuart. *Railroad Reorganization.* New York: Houghton-Mifflin, Inc., 1908.

Hayes, William E. *Iron Road to Empire.* New York: H. Wolff Book Manufacturing Co., 1953.

Iowa Highway Commission. *The Good Roads Problem in Iowa.* Bulletin No. 6. Ames: Engineering Experiment Station, Iowa State College, 1905.

Iowa Highway Commission. *Manual for Iowa Highway Officers.* 1906 Revision. Ames: Iowa Highway Commission, 1906.

Iowa State Highway Commission. Reports of the State Highway Commission for the years ending 1913 to 1920. Des Moines: State of Iowa.

Lincoln Highway Association. *The Complete Official Road Guide of the Lincoln Highway.* Detroit: Lincoln Highway Association, 1924.

Overton, Richard. *Burlington Route.* New York: Alfred H. Knoff, 1965.

Pellegreno, Ann Holtgren. *Iowa Takes to the Air.* Story City, Ia.: Aerodrome Press, 1980.

Ray, W. G. "Billy Robinson, Bird Man." *Palimpsest 11* (September 1930): pp. 369-375.

Ritland, Everett D. "The Educational Activities of P. G. Holden." Master's thesis, Iowa State College, 1941.

Sage, Leland. *A History of Iowa.* Ames: Iowa State University Press, 1974.

Shepard, Hugh S. "Jefferson Highway Association, An Address by Hugh S. Shepard of Mason City before the 16th Annual Convention of the U.S. Good Roads Association at Des Moines, May 20, 1928." *Annals of Iowa 6* No. 6 (October 1928): pp. 432-447.

Sizer, Rozane, and William Selig. "P. G. Holden and the Corn Gospel Trains." *Palimpsest 62* (May-June 1981): pp. 66-71.

Swisher, Jacob. "The Corn Gospel Trains." *Palimpsest 28* (November 1947): pp. 321-334.

Thompson, W. H. "The Economics of Ex Parte 162, General Rate Increase Case of 1945." Ph.D. diss., Iowa State College, 1948.

Throne, Mildred. "From Woodburners to Streamliners." *Palimpsest 32* (June 1951): pp. 226-229.

Tweet, Roald D. *History of Transportation on the Upper Mississippi & Illinois Rivers.* National Waterways Study. Navigation History NWS-83-6. Washington, D.C.: U.S. Government Printing Office, 1983.

Wagner, Dorothy. "Destination Unknown." *Palimpsest 11* (September 1930): pp. 376-397.

Chapter Six
Street Railways and Electric Interurbans to 1920

Street Railways

Introduction

Horse-drawn passenger vehicles appeared in the larger cities in the early 19th century. However, the poor condition of the streets meant a slow, bumpy ride or the prospect of becoming mired in the mud. Iron tracks were introduced to partially alleviate this problem, reducing the number of horses needed and permitting a somewhat smoother and faster ride. Speeds of four to six miles per hour were possible, hardly more than the pace of walking. A substantial part of the total costs was that of the horse, often priced at $100 or more, and because they were usually limited to four to six hours of work, several teams were necessary. Often, the cost of the horses was greater than the average cost of $750 for the car. It was estimated that 40 percent of the total investment was in the horses and stables.

Operating a horsecar cost about 20 cents per mile, including the wages of a two-man crew. As recently as 1908, public transportation was dependent upon animal power even though the average working life of a horse was only four years. Pollution was a problem as each horse generated ten pounds of waste on the streets each day. The invention of the steam engine brought experimentation with steam power, and electrification soon followed and spread rapidly. Fares through the first two decades of the 20th century were universally five cents and produced sufficient revenue until World War I. In 1920, fares were revised to distance schedules. Land values rose along the routes as transit companies developed commercial and residential housing, creating their own demand. By the end of the war, almost one-third of the companies nationwide were bankrupt as a result of over-capitalization, poor management and their inability to meet riders' needs. At the beginning of the 1920s, with automobile competition becoming important, the industry was in poor financial condition, unable to maintain its share of the growing urban transportation market.

Two-horse streetcar in Boonesboro, 1897.
(Courtesy: Edward S. Meyers Collection)

Horsecar in Sioux City, 1884.
(Courtesy: Scott Sorenson, Sioux City Public Museum)

The Iowa Experience

Streetcar service started in five of the largest cities in Iowa during the early post-Civil War years. Operations by horse- or mule-drawn cars began in 1868 in Des Moines and Dubuque, and in 1869 in Davenport, Clinton and Council Bluffs. A brief review of the evolution of streetcar service in these cities will show the patterns that were rather typical in the development in other communities.

Des Moines

The capital of Iowa had a population of about 10,000 people at the close of the Civil War. Dr. M. P. Turner, who had operated toll bridges over the Des Moines River until tolls were abolished by the city council, received the first franchise for a narrow-gauge horsecar line to run from the Polk County Courthouse to the foot of Capitol Hill. In 1878, rails were laid on Walnut Street and ten years later, a line was opened on Fourth Street. Electric power was introduced by the Broad Gauge Railway Company, organized by Messrs. Van Ginkel, Teachout and Weber in 1886, to operate on Locust Street and Grand Avenue. In 1889, Jefferson Polk, an associate of Turner, acquired control of the independent lines and consolidated them into the Des Moines Street Railway. A separate company, the Inter-Urban Railway, was incorporated in 1898 by the Des Moines Railway management to build an interurban three miles from Greenwood Park to Valley Junction (West Des Moines). Interurbans and street railways were often operated under common management with joint use of tracks, stations, repair shops and power facilities.

By 1890 the Polk interests operated 103 electric powered cars over nearly 50 miles of track in the city, and by 1911 they added 23 cars and 29 miles of trackage. In the early 1900s, the system came under control of the Harris Trust Company of Chicago and was petitioned into bankruptcy in 1911. Emil Schmidt, appointed receiver, became president of the newly organized company, later succeeded by Frank Chambers. Between 1911 and 1920, there was continuous labor-management strife over wages, conditions of work and the "two-man streetcar," climaxed by a four-month strike in 1921.

Dubuque

In 1867, when Dubuque citizens voted to allow streets to be used for public transportation, the city was the largest in Iowa. In 1868, J. K. Graves organized the Dubuque Street Railway and operated the first horsecar from the levee at the foot of Jones Street to Coulter Avenue and 24th Street. Extensions were later built to the Fairgrounds and Eagle Point. Rather interesting and novel was the use of horse-drawn sleighs during the winter months. Joseph A. Rhomberg acquired the system in 1876. Electric storage battery cars used in the 1880s were unsuccessful, as was the Graves Hill Street and West Dubuque Steam Railway, in negotiating the steep hills. In 1889, the Key City Electric Street Railway operated the first electric car on the Eighth Street hill and Rhomberg, faced with this competition, electrified the Dubuque Street Railway in 1890. The Union Electric Company, incorporated in 1900, acquired all of the street railways which passed into control of the Dubuque Electric Company in 1916. Expansion of the electric power industry resulted in acquisition of the street railways by the Interstate Power Company in 1924.

Electrified streetcar in Des Moines, 1890s.
(Courtesy: Iowa State Highway Commission)

Davenport

Five companies were involved in construction of street railways in and around Davenport. The first horsecar service by the Davenport City Railway began in 1869 on Third Street. In 1870, the Davenport Central Railway started operations on Brady Street and ran the first electric car in 1888. The Bridge, Second Street and Northwest Davenport Railway initiated service also in 1888 from the Mississippi River bridge on Second and Marquette to Eighth Street. In the same year, C. B. Holmes of Chicago acquired control of the various companies and incorporated the Davenport and Rock Island Railway to build a line on the bridge to Illinois. By 1890 electrification was completed, and in 1895 the company was reorganized into the Tri-City Railway and Light Company, controlled by the United Light and Railway Company of Grand Rapids, Michigan. The fifth line was organized in 1902 as the Davenport and Suburban Railway. The system was built on Fourth Street and started operations in 1904. This line was also acquired by the Tri-City Railway in 1907. Additional service was provided between Davenport and Rock Island by the "Bridge Line," a part of the system serving the area and the only Tri-City route that was double-tracked. During World War I, traffic was especially heavy to the Rock Island Arsenal, with ten cars permanently coupled in pairs and used during rush hours. Davenport cars were converted to one-man operations in 1921.

Clinton

The first narrow-gauge horsecar line in the Clinton area was operated between Lyons and the CNW depot in Clinton in 1869, franchised as the Lyons Horse Railway Company and later extended south into Clinton. In 1878 a Clinton lumber firm received permission to open a narrow-gauge horsecar line in the city. Both lines were consolidated into the Clinton and Lyons Horse Railway in 1889, and by 1891 it had 24 cars pulled by 60 horses and mules over 10 miles of track. In 1890, franchises were granted to the Baldwin Electric Company and its successor, the State Electric Company, to build and operate electric or cable cars. This was done to compete with the horsecar lines, later controlled by the utility and widened to standard gauge and electrified. By 1904, the street railways were reorganized into the Clinton Street Railway and the system, expanded somewhat within the city, remained intact until the mid-1920s.

Council Bluffs

Service began in 1869 by the Broad Street Railway, reorganized in 1872 into the Council Bluffs and Omaha Railway. Its initial project was a horsecar line from Tenth Avenue and Broadway to the Missouri River, a distance of three miles. In 1883 the UP gained control, but financial losses resulted in another reorganization through which the Council Bluffs Railway emerged. To purchase the UP interests, the Omaha and Council Bluffs Railway and Bridge Company was organized in 1887. Electrification followed, and a streetcar bridge over the Missouri was constructed and opened in the same year.

To Lake Manawa, formed during the spring flood of 1881 and subsquently developed into a resort area, service was subject to a bitter legal dispute between two rival railways. The Omaha, Council Bluffs and Suburban and the Manhattan Beach Railway, the latter chartered by the Omaha and Council Bluffs Railway and Bridge Company, sought to furnish transportation to the lake region. The former had purchased a steam locomotive to haul cars running from the UP station and had purchased the resort property in 1899, starting operations in 1900. But before the legal arguments reached a climax, the Omaha and Council Bluffs absorbed the Omaha, Council Bluffs and Suburban. Further solidification of the properties was arranged through lease of the Omaha and Council Bluffs Railway and Bridge Company and its wholly owned subsidiaries. The corporate management operated the street car service until it terminated in the 1940s.

Other City Street Railways

Coverage of the street railway development in other cities in Iowa is confined only to the dates on which service began since the patterns were essentially similar; horsecars to steam to electrification with control by utility companies and reorganizations interspersed throughout the expansion. Burlington, Marshalltown and Cedar Rapids-Marion began in the 1870s, followed in the next decade by service in Oskaloosa, Boone, Keokuk, Muscatine, Waterloo, Fort Madison, and the first of five independent lines in Sioux City. Red Oak, the smallest of Iowa towns with municipal transportation, began operations in 1881, but faced with paving assessments, discontinued service in 1901. Ames started with a steam dummy line between the city and the Iowa State College campus in 1890, joined in the same year by electrified

Electrified streetcar in Sioux City, 1890.
(Courtesy: Scott Sorenson, Sioux City Public Museum)

systems in Independence and Fort Dodge. Iowa City, whose central business district lay adjacent to the University of Iowa campus, saw no need for urban transportation until 1910.

Novel and Unique Projects

The Dubuque "Inclines": The Dubuque cable car system was built by J. K. Graves, banker, former mayor, state senator and a promotor and builder of street railways. His home was on a high bluff overlooking the central business district only three blocks away in a direct line but without adequate road or highway access. In 1882, Graves built a steam-operated cable car on an incline from Fourth and Bluff streets to the top of the hill, known after settlement as Fenelon Place. There was no charge for its use by residents for ten years until it was destroyed by fire. When Graves decided not to rebuild, his neighbors incorporated the Fenelon Place Elevator Company and purchased the cable car property. In the 1900s, C. B. Trevis, a resident of the bluff since 1893, became sole owner, and after his death in 1940, the family continued operations. Family members and the city realized the importance of the "Incline" not only as a facilty to transport commuters but also as a tourist attraction, and it has remained as such to the present time. Another cable car "incline" was built in 1887 at Eleventh Street, electrified in 1900 but abandoned in 1927.

The Sioux City Elevated: This experiment in urban transportation attracted national interest. It was oberved that: "Urban Mass Transit, the past pride and now future hope of many of the world's largest cities may very well owe a debt of gratitude to the founding fathers of Sioux City in northwestern Iowa. Indeed, the city of Chicago itself, might have been deprived of one of its more romantic transportation landmarks had it not been for this Missouri River town—home of Iowa's first and last elevated railway."[1]

In 1887, Sioux City was in the midst of the most frenzied economic boom in its history. New businesses were being established and packing houses flourished; served by the Missouri River and four railroads, farms and real estate were selling at fabulous prices. Geographically, the location of the city did not allow for easy real estate development. Steep hills rose to the north and west from the river, and the Floyd River Valley lay to the east with its profusion of packing plants, cattle pens, railroad lines and yards. Beyond was a grassy plain known as Morningside, potentially an attractive suburb but in need of a transportation link to downtown Sioux City.

Prior to 1887, Sioux City was served by only a few scattered surface lines with cars drawn by horses, cable, or powered by steam. None could overcome the problem of crossing the Floyd River bottoms which included 84 railroad crossings. To remedy these conditions, the Sioux City Rapid Transit Company was organized in 1885 to build a double-tracked elevated railway from Third and Jones streets in the business district to Leech Street, connecting with a single-tracked surface line to the east side of Morningside Avenue.[2] It was rumored that initial financing was obtained during a poker game when nine local investors, including James Booge, A.S. Garretson, E. C. Peters, and A. M. Jackson put $1,000 or more in the "pot" for seed money. Additional financing came from local, western Iowa and out-of-state interests. Peters was elected president and William Gordon, secretary of the company. At the time, only New York and Kansas City had elevated systems, and building the third in the nation would be Iowa's most famous and distinctive engineering feat. Upon completion, Chicago transit officials visited Sioux City to inspect the facility. Impressed with its engineering and apparent economy of operation, they used the model for construction of the Chicago elevated system. Visitors to the "Loop" would see the same type of construction that was once part of the Sioux City landscape.

The surface division was built first and opened for service in 1889. Original equipment consisted of a secondhand steam locomotive and two coaches scheduled for five trips per day. The elevated tracks were built some 25 feet above the central business district and on bridges which spanned the main railroad lines. The tracks dropped on a concrete and iron ramp to ground level at Fowler Street where the operation continued into Morningside. Four stations were built on the elevated at Third and Jones, Iowa, Steuban and Divison Streets, with wrought iron stairways for access to the platforms. Six other ground stations were built on the Morningside route.

In 1891, the Rapid Transit officially opened for business, using one anthracite-burning locomotive and two rather ornately painted and decorated cars. Later, another locomotive was added with enough cars to make two three-car trains. The total cost of the elevated was $500,000, exclusive of $84,000 spent on the connecting surface line. For five years, the railway was prosperous. Fares were five cents for the elevated ride and an additional five cents for the surface line, making a total of 10 cents for the five-mile trip.

Several incidents indicated that work on the elevated was anything but dull. On one occasion, a mule wandered onto the right-of-way, although no one seemed to know how or why. The animal was struck by a train, walked away unhurt, but put the train in the repair shops for three days. A 16-year-old substitute engineer experimented with higher than normal speeds and almost toppled the train over the railing. The same individual ran through the wall of the Morningside engine house a few weeks later, thus ending his glorious railroading career. Another incident occurred when an important political party caucus was scheduled and the train somehow neglected to stop to board members of the opposition party.

In 1892, increasing competition from expanding surface lines forced the elevated to become partially

[1] B. Paul Chicoine, "Rails Across the Sky," *Iowan 28* No. 3 (Spring 1980): pp. 28, 41-45, 53-54.

[2] Norman Carlson, ed., *Iowa Trolleys,* Bulletin 114, Chicago: Central Electric Railfans Association, 1974, p. 147; C. Addison Hickman, "The Sioux City Elevated," *Palimpsest 22* (April 1941): p. 122. There appears to be a difference of opinion as to the length of the elevated railway. *Iowa Trolleys,* the most authoritative and illustrated research source found on Iowa street railways and interurbans, suggests that its distance was one and one-eighth miles, whereas Hickman states that it was two miles long.

electrified. In May, it received widespread publicity when its platforms were the refuge of residents during the Floyd River flood, saving many lives. Later that year, the first signs of impending disaster were noticed. The Panic of 1893 was a devastating blow to the economy of Sioux City. Among the business organizations forced into bankruptcy was the Rapid Transit Company, eventually sold for $50,000, one-tenth of its original investment. Electric trolleys used the facility for the next seven years, but the new owners closed the stations and sold the equipment. Finally, in 1899, both elevated and surface companies were consolidated into the Sioux City Traction Company. The elevated was abandoned soon after, unable to compete with the electrified street railways. For a few years, control of the Traction Company was assumed by the Swift and Armour Packing Companies which continued to make surface improvements. In 1905, the Sioux City Electric Company, also controlled by Swift and Armour, succeeded the Traction Company and ran the cars through World War I.

Fenelon Place Elevator at Dubuque.
(Courtesy: Dubuque Chamber of Commerce)

The Sioux City Cable Railway: The Company was incorporated in 1897 to operate on Jackson Street, which had an 11 percent grade from the river valley. Operations were delayed until 1899 expecting the city would reduce the grade, which did not occur. Two extensions were added in 1890 and 1892. By 1893, the Sioux City Street Railway was providing electrified service as close as two blocks from the cable railway on more efficient schedules. The cable company lost much of its traffic and converted to electric operation in 1894. It was sold to the Central Traction Company in 1895 which was merged with the Sioux City Traction Company in 1899.

Electric Interurbans

Introduction

Electric interurbans evolved from street railways or trolleys which had provided the public transit in the cities of Iowa. The trolleys had influenced the growth of the central city and linked it with the suburban areas. The next step was to connect regional cities and towns to nearby rural communities with a fast, frequent service not otherwise available. This was the convincing argument for interurban existence, and between 1900 and 1920 a dozen or more of these companies were operating in the state. Some started as steam roads and were electrified later; some operated as independents; others were associated with or were a unit within electric light and power utilities. Although developed originally for passengers, they expanded into freight service, interchanging with major railroads which crossed their routes, and they became important carriers for local traffic. The route maps later in the chapter show that with few exceptions, most were built in a north-south direction, filling the void for relatively short distance movements which existed by construction of the east-west roads. Their mileage and earnings reported from 1903 to 1920 are shown in Table 6-l in five-year intervals.

The decline in net earnings and earnings per mile between 1915 and 1920 was the result of wartime inflation. Although gross earnings nearly doubled, operating expenses nearly tripled and the result was a drastic deterioration in net earnings and earnings per mile. The table does show, however, that from 1903 to 1915, the interurbans were in a rather favorable financial condition.

Table 6-1
Mileage and Earnings of Electric Interurbans in Iowa

Year	Mileage[1]	Gross Earnings[2] (thousands)	Operating Expenses[2] (thousands)	Net Earnings[2] (thousands)	Earnings Per Mile
1903	98	$ 228	$ 132	$ 96	$ 975
1905	151	497	316	181	1,194
1910	373	1,450	951	409	1,322
1915	472	2,923	1,805	1,118	2,173
1920	510	5,628	4,923	685	1,341

(*Source:* Railroad Commission, *Annual Report, 1921:* p. viii.)
1903 was the first year for interurban reporting.
[1]Single track only.
[2]Figures rounded to the nearest unit.

Sioux City Elevated. Western terminus and main depot.
(Courtesy: Scott Sorenson, Sioux City Public Museum)

Sioux City Elevated. Third over Division Street.
(Courtesy: Scott Sorenson, Sioux City Public Museum)

Major Electric Interurbans

The Fort Dodge, Des Moines & Southern Railway.

Operating over approximately 150 miles, Iowa's longest interurban was organized to serve the cities in its name—the word "Southern" added in the expectation that the road would be built south of Des Moines. It started in 1893 as a small carrier, known as the Boone Valley Coal and Railway Company, to move coal three miles from Frazer to Frazer Junction on the M&StL. The road was headed by Hamilton Browne, mine manager of the Clyde Coal Company. Among its directors was Norman D. Frazer, after whom the town was named. In 1895, a new company, the Marshalltown and Dakota Railroad, was organized by Browne and his associates and purchased the property. In 1901, the name was changed to the Boone, Rockwell City and Northwestern Railroad with Browne again serving as president. The Newton and Northwestern (N&N) emerged in 1896 as a Browne road and extended the line from Frazer to Newton on the east, and from Gowrie to Rockwell City on the west. The entire line from Newton to Rockwell City was completed in 1904.

Expansion to common carrier status came about when eastern capitalists gained control of the N&N and in 1905, Henry Loring of Boston replaced Browne as president. The 100-mile railroad connected two small communities and owned large coal deposits which provided the major source of revenue. But some of the mines soon became unprofitable and the road needed new capital, a new industrial base, and larger terminals for further expansion. With capital furnished by New England financiers, the Fort Dodge, Des Moines & Southern (FTD, DM&S) was incorporated in 1906, with Loring as president and Henry W. Poor, publisher of *Poor's Manual of Railroads,* as a director.

The new company stopped the east-west expansion of the N&N and focused attention on the gypsum areas of Fort Dodge and the expanding industries in Des Moines as sources of new business. Three segments were built, each connecting with the N&N. One ran 28 miles from Hope to Fort Dodge, another 20 miles south from Midvale to Des Moines, and a third from Ames to Kelley. A branch into Ames was built in 1907. In 1909 the N&N went into receivership and was purchased by Loring. He conveyed it to the FTD,

DM&S which also acquired control of the Fort Dodge Street Railway and the two-mile line between Ames and the Iowa State College campus.

The Dinkey at Ames College Station
(Courtesy: Ruth Jackson Collection)

Following the purchase of the N&N, the newly built lines were electrified with a 1,200 volt system furnished by a 6,000-kilowatt turbo generator at Frazer, fueled by company coal. Steam power was used for passenger service over the remainder of the road and freight service over the entire system until electrified in 1912. Electrification and the expenditure of $2.5 million for 58-foot passenger cars put the railway into bankruptcy in 1910. Loring and Parley Sheldon of Ames were appointed as receivers. They terminated the Goddard-Midvale service in 1911 and abandoned a branch line from Niles to Ogden. Receivership, however, did not end improvements, the most notable being the replacement of the high wooden trestle with a steel structure over a tributary of the Des Moines river near Frazer, opened to traffic in 1912. In 1913, the railway was reorganized and sold to the Old Colony Trust Company of Boston for $3.9 million. The new company was chartered in Maine, retained the old name and continued with Loring as president.

The Frazer generating plant had more capacity than needed to operate the electrified railroad and sold excess power to industrial users, especially in the Fort Dodge region. In 1915, the road acquired the Central Power and Light Company and became a commercial supplier of power on an area-wide basis. Freight trains were operated during nighttime hours when commercial demand was at its lowest level in order to balance the 24-hour power generation and distribution.

The railroad competed aggressively for freight traffic, operating 2,462 freight cars in 1918 as compared to 274 cars hauling freight on all other interurbans. For its size, it was said to have more freight cars than any other railroad in the nation. When the federal government took control of the railroads during World War I, the FTD, DM&S was included, together with the Waterloo, Cedar Falls and Northern (WCF&N). Passenger travel peaked in 1918. Over one million passengers were carried on hourly trains between Des Moines and Boone with connecting service to Ames. Between Boone and Fort Dodge, trains ran every two hours. Luxury service was provided in two parlor-observation cars at an additional fare of 25 cents between Des Moines and Fort Dodge. The road followed the operating rules of steam railroads, interchanging passengers and freight with the major east-west lines.

Expansion to serve additional industries resulted in the purchase of the Crooked Creek Railway in 1916 for access to coal traffic. The eight-mile narrow-gauge road began operating in 1876 from Judd on the IC to the mines at Lehigh. It was widened to standard gauge in the 1880s and operated in conjunction with the Webster City and Southwestern Railway, a 14-mile line between Border Plain and Webster City. In 1892, the Crooked Creek purchased the Webster City road and abandoned the Border Plain-Judd segment. In 1917, the FTD, DM&S built its own line from Fort Dodge to Border Plain and through track realignment had a direct connection between Fort Dodge and Webster City. At this time, the railroad was operating a system which would be in place for the next 45 years (Fig. 6-1).

Crandic-Cedar Rapids & Iowa City Railway.
(Courtesy: Iowa Electric Light & Power Company)

Fort Dodge, Des Moines & Southern Interurban, Ames to Ames College, 1906.
(Courtesy: Ruth Jackson Collection)

Crooked Creek Railway & Coal Company, Lehigh, Iowa.
(Courtesy: Oscar Bjork, Agent at Lehigh)

Fort Dodge, Des Moines & Southern car on the High Bridge. (Courtesy: Iowa State Highway Commission)

Figure 6-1
Route of the Fort Dodge, Des Moines & Southern Railway. (Courtesy: Central Electric Railfans Association, *Iowa Trolleys)*

The Cedar Valley Road and Crandic

The second longest interurban route between major cities was a combination of the Waterloo, Cedar Falls and Northern (WCR&N), commonly known as the "Cedar Valley Road," and the Cedar Rapids and Iowa City Railway, referred to as "Crandic" from the initials in its name. The two roads operated independently, interchanging passengers at a station built jointly on Fourth Street in Cedar Rapids, two blocks from the Union Station. The Valley Road started as a Waterloo horsecar line in 1885 and was considered one of the best built and managed interurbans in Iowa, receiving acclaim from the Westinghouse Electric Company. From Waterloo, it ran eight miles to Cedar Falls, 21 miles north to Waverly and 64 miles south to Cedar Rapids, soon earning the reputation of "a steam line with a trolley over it."

Three Cass brothers—Louis S., Claude D., and Joseph F.—promoted and built the railroad. Louis and Joseph organized the Waterloo and Cedar Falls Rapid Transit Company in 1895 to connect the two cities. Street railways in both were purchased in 1896 and 1897, giving access to downtown districts. In 1901, the road was extended 13 miles north to Denver and one year later to Denver Junction, where a connection was made with the CGW and trackage rights obtained to Sumner via Waverly for through service from Waterloo. In 1904, the name was changed to the Waterloo, Cedar Falls and Northern Railway. The arrangement allowed the Stickney road to use the interurban as a short cut for traffic from Waterloo to destinations on its Omaha line instead of using the longer route through Oelwein. There was also a personal relationship involved since both Louis and Joseph had served as vice presidents of the CGW. The coordinated system was terminated in 1909 when the CGW went into bankruptcy and the interurban built its own line into Waverly.

Construction on the Cedar Rapids line was started in 1912, reaching Urbana in 1913, and Center Point and Cedar Rapids in 1914. Connections were made with the Cedar Rapids and Marion Railway and the "Crandic" line to downtown. Reciprocal schedules with the CNW at Cedar Rapids allowed through transit on interline tickets for passengers from Waterloo to Chicago. In 1918, the road operated 69 passenger cars, three of which were parlor-observation types with buffet service offered to those of the 7.3 million passengers who desired it. Freight operations were handled by 146 cars. The railroad suffered from poor maintenance during the War and when returned to the owners in 1920, it was in precarious financial condition.

The southern section of the route was incorporated in 1903 by the Dows family who provided, with one exception, it presidents throughout its history. It was organized as the Cedar Rapids and Iowa City Railway and Light Company, planned originally to operate through Iowa City and Muscatine to Peoria. Service began in 1904 with 13 trains daily, making the trip in 75 minutes. In 1913 the line was extended to Mt. Vernon, 15 miles east of Cedar Rapids, and later to Lisbon, two miles farther east. An important source of revenue came from college students attending the University of Iowa at Iowa City, Coe College at Cedar Rapids and Cornell College at Mt. Vernon. Traffic was especially heavy at home football games when WCF&N cars were leased, and on special occasions such as homecoming, special trains ran from Waterloo. This practice continued until 1938 when the WCR&N discontinued operations.

From its inception, the road was designed as a high-speed electric line for passenger service. As described by John M. Murray, the ride was "one of true adventure . . . always good for laughs and a myriad of jokes." Swinging and swaying from the great speed, the line was labeled by riders as the "Vomit Comet" or "as a ship rolling with an occasional leak."[3] However, by 1907 freight traffic, including coal for the Cedar Rapids power plant, was carried through interchange with the CRI&P at Iowa City. Originally the road was a unit of the Iowa Railway and Light Company, but as operations expanded, the title was changed to eliminate the words "and Light Company." It continued to be operated as a subsidiary of the parent company which became known as the Iowa Electric Light and Power Company in 1932. In addition to the interurban, the power company operated streetcar service in Cedar Rapids, generally along the interurban routes, in Boone and Marshalltown, and also along the three and one-half mile Tama and Toledo Railroad built around the edge of Tama to the State Juvenile Home. The Lisbon branch never generated the expected volume of traffic and was scrapped in the late 1920s, but company equipment continued to run over Cedar Rapids streets until the 1930s (Fig. 6-2).

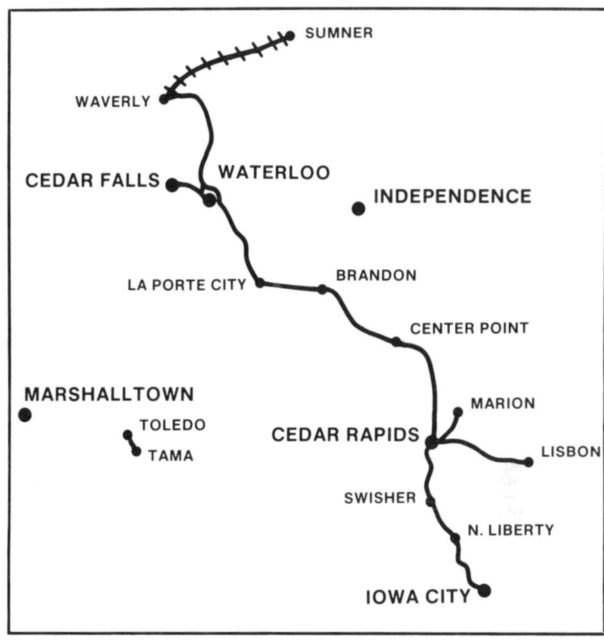

Figure 6-2
Routes of the Cedar Valley Road and Crandic Interurbans.
(Courtesy: Central Electric Railfans Association, *Iowa Trolleys)*

Crandic-Cedar Rapids & Iowa City Railway.
(Courtesy: Iowa Electric Light & Power Company)

[3] John M. Murray, *It Took All of Us: 100 Years of Iowa Electric Light and Power Company,* Cedar Rapids: Iowa Electric Light and Power, 1982, p. 28.

Train west of Boone, around 1900.
(Courtesy: Iowa Electric Light & Power Company)

The Des Moines and Central Iowa Railway

The interurban fanned out of Des Moines to the east and northwest. It was incorporated in 1899 as the Interurban Railway by H. H. Polk, G. B. Hippee and W. I. Haskit of Des Moines and A. W. Harris of Chicago, with operations tied into the Des Moines street railway system. The first construction was an electric passenger road to Colfax through Altoona in 1903, connecting with the Douglas street car line at a point called Klondike Junction. Freight, consisting primarily of coal, ran on a line built on the north side of Des Moines, later used also for passenger service. The interurban planned to build north to Eldora, south to Indianola, southwest to Winterset and northwest to Audubon, but the only road that materialized was the 34-mile "Beaver Valley Division" to Granger, Woodward and Perry, built in 1906. Riders labeled the line as the "Galloping Goose." The area served was rather sparsely settled and the frequent passenger service originally scheduled was never supported, although Colfax, then a popular health resort, accounted for relatively heavy business. Freight on both east and west lines was interchanged with the CGW at Des Moines, giving the railroad an entry into what was considered CRI&P territory. World War I brought a significant change in the passenger traffic. Camp Dodge on the Beaver Valley route was a training site for 40,000 to 50,000 military personnel, and dozens of trains running as frequently as the cars could be turned around made the trip from the interchange points on the major railroads to the Camp. In 1918, the interurban carried over two million passengers, second only to the total of the WCF&N, but by 1920 the volume had dropped to slightly over 500,000. The Perry to Colfax interurban was named the Des Moines and Central Iowa Railway in 1922.

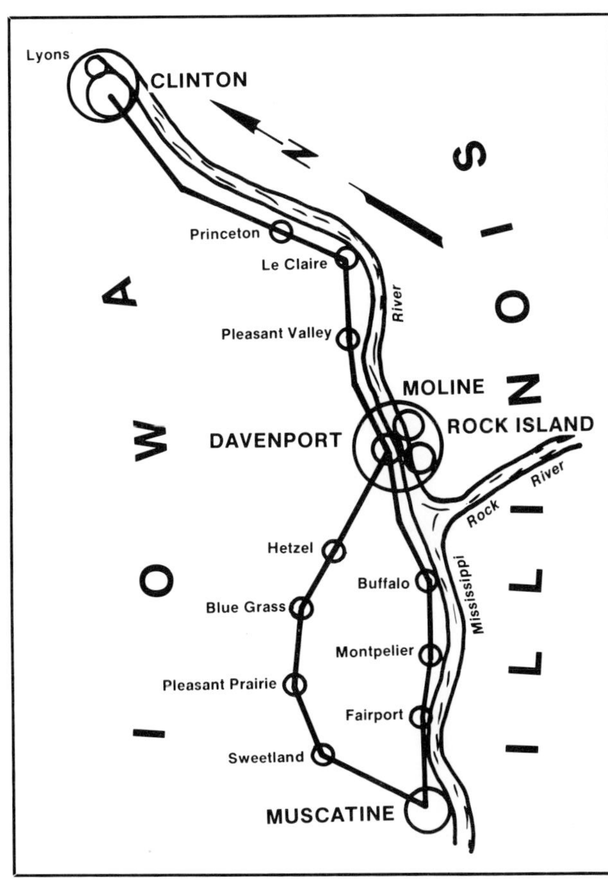

Figure 6-3
Route of the Clinton, Davenport, and Muscatine Railway.
(Courtesy: Wayne DeJohn, "The Interurban Years")

The Clinton, Davenport and Muscatine Railway

In terms of mileage operated, the fourth largest interurban was a combination of the Iowa and Illinois Railway, incorporated in 1901, and the Davenport and Muscatine Railway, incorporated in 1910. The Iowa and Illinois started operations in 1904 on a 33-mile route from Clinton to Davenport through Princeton, Le Claire and Pleasant Valley with seven daily schedules. The Davenport and Muscatine began in 1912 on a 25-mile right-of-way veering west from the river through Hetzel, Blue Grass, Pleasant Prairie and Sweetland and ran over five miles of streets in the terminal cities. An express route from Davenport went through Buffalo, Montpelier and Fairport. In 1916, the two roads were consolidated under the name of the Clinton, Davenport and Muscatine Railway, but through service was not possible because of the differences in the voltage systems used to power the equipment. As a result, the two roads were maintained as separate divisions with transfer at Davenport (Fig. 6-3).

During the peak of passenger travel in the war years, 15 daily trains were scheduled from Clinton to Davenport and 12 between Davenport and Muscatine. Passengers boarded the cars on city streets as they would on local trolleys. Rural travelers signaled the cars to stop by extending their arms horizontally above the tracks and at night would show and wave a light until acknowledged. By 1920, freight interchanged with the CNW at Clinton and the CRI&P at Davenport became more profitable than passenger traffic. Local freight carried included a variety of commodities ranging from perishable goods to sand, stone, gravel, coal, livestock, vegetables and agricultural supplies. Their passenger business was approximately the equivalent of the Crandic line—about 600,000 in 1918.

Short Line Interurbans

The Southern Iowa Railway traces its ancestry from the Albia Centerville interurban, believed to be the oldest in Iowa. It was incorporated as the Centerville, Moravia and Albia Railroad by Francis M. Drake, a former Iowa governor and founder of Drake University, and Russell Sage of New York. The road was built as a branch of the Missouri, Iowa and Northern of the Wabash system in 1880. The Wabash operated trains between St. Louis and Des Moines over the two roads to Centerville and Albia until 1885 when it went into receivership. In 1880, the railroad was reorganized as the Albia Centerville Railway, leased to the Iowa Central which was later controlled by the M&StL and operated from Oskaloosa via Albia to Centerville until 1910. That year, W. A. Boland of New York and J. L. Sawyers of Centerville, dissatisfied with the M&StL service, reorganized the road, changing the name to the Southern Traction Company.

Although the name implied electric-powered equipment, it ran by steam. In 1914, Frank S. Payne and D. D. Bradley of the Centerville Light and Traction Company purchased the road and changed the name to the Centerville, Albia and Southern Railway, electrifying it shortly thereafter. By utilizing the street car tracks in both towns, the 30-mile interurban reached the depots of the CB&Q at Albia and the CRI&P at Centerville. Freight revenues came from coal and package traffic, interchanged with the M&StL at Albia, the Wabash at Moravia and the CMStP at Trask. The inventory of 10 passenger cars included two with wooden box motors and two center entrance steel cars with separate compartments for women, especially appreciated since miners constituted the major passenger business and tended to become quite boisterous on pay days. In 1916, the Centerville Light and Traction Company changed its name to the Iowa Southern Utilities Company and the railroad was conveyed to the utility firm. In 1918, passenger volume totaled almost 400,000 riders.

The Mason City and Clear Lake Traction Company was organized by W. E. Brice of Mason City and L. H. Ong of Tama in 1896 as an integral part of their real estate development in the southwest section of Mason City. Brice, who had been associated with steam railroads and later became a vice president of the CNW, was president and Ong, with experience with several power companies and the Tama-Toledo Railway, was vice president, secretary and superintendent. The 10-mile route was laid out over what is now Highway 106. Opened for traffic in 1897, it eventually had the longest tenure of continuous electric interurban operation in the nation. Equipment was purchased to handle the summer traffic to the popular Clear Lake area, reaching a peak of over one million passengers in 1918. Through cars from connecting roads ran directly to Clear Lake, and railroad executives transferred their private cars to the line to enjoy the movement by electric power. Ice from the lake was hauled during the winter to destinations within and outside the state. Coal and milk were major sources of revenue from local traffic.

Shortly after 1900, the word "traction" was dropped from the company name and "railway" substituted. It was assumed that the change was made to secure tariff agreements with additional steam lines. In 1910, the company was controlled by the Peoples Gas and Electric Company of Mason City and reorganized as the Mason City and Clear Lake Railway. In 1913, the United Light and Railway Company acquired the stock as well as the utility, and Brice stepped down as president to become a director. He was succeeded by F. J. Hanlon, a member of the original administration. The new company also received franchises for street railways from both Mason City and Clear Lake.

Niles two-man car of the Davenport and Muscatine Railway.
(Courtesy: Iowa Illinois Gas & Electric Company)

Two-car train in downtown Davenport.
(Courtesy: Iowa Illinois Gas & Electric Company)

The Charles City Western Railway was chartered in 1910 by local interests and started operations on a 13-mile line between Charles City and Marble Rock. Originally, it ran as a gasoline and steam road. Passengers rode in a 55-foot "wind splitter" car with porthole windows and a center door entrance. The road was electrified in 1915 and an extension built to Colwell, eight miles northeast of Charles City. The cars ran within the city and interchanged with the CMSTP and IC at Charles City and the CRI&P at Marble Rock. The railway received considerable publicity during World War I when Marjorie Dodd, a college student and daughter of the mayor, became the first woman "motorman" on an electric interurban in Iowa. City service was discontinued during the early 1920s.

The four remaining railways in the interurban category were essentially passenger roads, no more than three miles long, connecting with larger interurbans or steam railroads. Except for the fact that they ran between closely situated cities or towns, they probably would have been classified as street railways. **The Tama and Toledo Electric Railway and Light Company** started service in 1894 to link Toledo, the county seat of Tama County, with Tama on the CNW and the St. Paul Railroads. The line used the streets of both cities as its right-of-way. When Leander College in Toledo merged with Coe College, the state took over the vacated buildings for a State Juvenile Home and insisted that railway service be provided for coal movements. The result was a relocation of the road in 1919 around the edge of Tama to the home in Toledo. Street trackage was abandoned when paving assessments were placed against the railway, which then routed its passenger cars over the belt line originally built for freight service.

The Cedar Rapids and Marion Railway was organized in 1891, and it immediately purchased the franchise for electric railways in Cedar Rapids. A 25-year franchise was granted for service from the terminal at Marion to the southwesterly city limits. By 1909, 12 miles of main line trackage was constructed within Cedar Rapids and 2.28 miles from the city limits at Kenwood to Marion. In 1912, the railway was acquired by the United Light and Power Company, a holding company with other roads in Iowa. The railway carried almost half a million passengers in 1918, probably the heaviest volume transported within the Cedar Rapids city limits.

The Oskaloosa to Buxton Railway began operations in 1906. It was owned and operated by the Oskaloosa Traction and Light Company, which planned ultimately to reach Albia but never built beyond Beacon, three miles distant. Expectations for passenger service to Buxton were never realized because the mines closed soon after World War I and the unincorporated town disappeared from the Iowa maps. In 1913, the city and interurban railways were taken over by the Illinois Traction System, and later by the Des Moines Electric Light Company (Iowa Power and Light Company). Rail operations were abandoned in the 1920s.

The Colfax Springs Railway started in 1908, some years after the discovery of a mineral spring near Colfax. A hotel was built on the bluff overlooking the town, and an inclined plane connected it with the CRI&P station at the foot of the bluff. The health spa, reported to be one of the finest west of the Mississippi River, attracted thousands of visitors during the 1890s, but business declined drastically in the early 1900s. Colonel James P. Donahue, whose wife had ostensibly been cured by the mineral waters, bought the hotel and built a one-mile electric railway from the hotel into Colfax. Service began in 1909 but patronage was somewhat less than anticipated. Scheduled rail service ended with the closing of the hotel in 1920.

Electric interurbans made a strong contribution to the growing transportation structure of the state in the early years. Especially notable was their expansion during the second decade. This is indicated by selected operational data in Tables 6-2 and 6-3, presented in two-year intervals.

Table 6-2
Operating Revenues and Expenses of Electric Interurbans 1910-1920

Year	Mileage[1]	Revenues[2] (Thousands)	Expenses[2] (Thousands)	Op. Ratio (Percentage)
1910	482	$1,450	$ 951	65.58
1912	427	1,783	1,272	71.34
1914	538	2,682	1,722	64.20
1916	619	3,120	1,967	63.04
1918	666	4,460	4,123	92.44
1920	658	5,628	4,923	87.82

(*Source:* Iowa Railroad Commission, *Annual Reports for the Selected Years.*)

[1] All trackage, including branches and sidings.

[2] Figures rounded to the nearest unit.

Table 6-3
Passengers, Revenues and Equipment of Electric Interurbans 1910-1920

Year	Passengers Carried[1]	Passenger Revenues[2] (Thousands)	Freight Revenues[2] (Thousands)	Passenger Cars	Freight Cars
1910	7,419	$ 968	$ 368	156	404
1912	10,076	1,180	508	151	604
1914	13,350	1,611	762	216	2,248
1916	12,905	1,762	1,029	204	2,785
1918	15,077	1,948	1,270	205	2,746
1920	13,523	2,570	1,934	225	2,795

(*Source:* Railroad Commission, *Annual Reports for the Selected Years.*)
[1] In Millions.
[2] Figures rounded to the nearest unit. Freight revenues do not include those from milk, mail and express traffic.

In every category listed in the tables, the interurbans showed a remarkable expansion in operations. The exception was in passengers carried, a movement which peaked in 1918. The operating ratio (relationship of operating expenses to revenues) has always been a key indicator of financial progress with 70 percent generally considered as an ideal level. In that regard, the interurbans were fairly successful until the war years when inflation dramatically increased operating expenses. For example, the 102.2 percent of the FTD,DM&S and 93.7 percent of the WCF&N greatly influenced the overall ratio for all railways. Not much change was noted for the year 1920, when inflationary forces were still evident. The large increase in freight cars between 1912 and 1914 resulted from capital investments by the above roads and additions to the fleet of the Iowa Railway and Light Company.

Summary

Street railways began operations in the largest Iowa cities during the early post-Civil War period and spread rapidly to other communities in the latter years of the 19th century. With few exceptions, the service started with horse- or mule-drawn cars and progressed through steam power to electrification as electric utilities were organized and their influence expanded in urban areas. These companies were instrumental in consolidating competing lines within the cities into more efficient systems. Novel experiments in public transit were introduced by cable car innovations and elevated railways in Dubuque and Sioux City. The Dubuque Incline remained as a permanent structure, whereas the Sioux City elevated system operated for only ten years before abandonment. During the 1920s, many of the urban systems faced economic distress through paving assessments against their properties and the competition of automobiles.

Electric interurbans played an important role in the transportation structure of the state. They provided fast and frequent service on short or medium distance routes not serviced by main or branch line railroads and influenced the development of cities and towns within their territorial boundaries. Their value was enhanced by interchange agreements with major steam railroads and coordination with street railways in the joint use of trackage, stations, repair shops and power facilities. Although often steam powered initially, interurbans were converted to electrification through ownership by electric utilities. Built primarily for passengers, they soon found freight, especially coal traffic, to be a profitable source of revenue. Freight traffic was a principal reason why two of the largest interurbans were brought under federal control during World War I. As measured by their operating ratios, their financial condition was quite satisfactory until 1918 but was seriously undermined by inflationary forces during and following the war years. Passenger traffic peaked in 1918, thereafter succumbing to the same trends which forced abandonment of street railways.

Selected References

Brewer, Luther A., and Barthlemus L. Welk. *History of Linn County.* Chicago: Pioneer Publishing Co., 1911.

DeJohn, Wayne. "The Interurban Years." *Palimpsest 62* (March-April 1981): pp. 34-44.

Donovan, Frank P., Jr. "Interurbans in Iowa." *Palimpsest 35* (May 1954): pp. 183-184.

Grant, Roger W. "Electric Traction Promotion in the South Iowa Corn Fields." *Palimpsest 58* (January-February 1977): pp.18-31.

McCormick, John, and Jon Jacobson. "Dubuque's Street Car Years." *Iowan 23* No. 1 (Fall 1974): pp. 46-50.

McGlothlin, W. F. "Des Moines Street Transit." *Annals of Iowa 31* (January 1952): pp. 223-227.

Rothburg, Morris, & Associates. *Public Transportation: An Element of the Urban Transportation System.* Washington, D. C.: U. S. Government Printing Office, 1980.

Chapter Seven

Transportation Policy and Operational Changes in the 1920s

Introduction

There were contrasting economic and transportation trends in the 1920s. Industrial prosperity was partially offset by a depressed agricultural economy resulting from wartime over-expansion. Non-regulated motor and air operations expanded at a rapid pace presenting challenges to the railroads for freight, passenger, mail and express business. On the horizon, but not yet a formidible competitor, were the oil and products pipelines. Federal and state legislation changed railroad policies and provided increased support for improved highways, aviation facilities and river development. National prosperity enabled the railroads to improve properties and equipment. Interurbans shifted to freight traffic and city street railways started on the slow decline toward obscurity. Increased motor vehicle ownership and operation renewed demands for hard-surfaced roads, from which emerged the twin problems of planning and financing highways, possibly the most important transportation issues debated in the state during this decade.

Rail-Highway Competition

Although maladjustments growing out of World War I had not been fully overcome, the nation was prosperous during the 1920s. Construction of public and private works was booming, exports expanding and business failures declining. Steam railroads in 1921 experienced a remarkable recovery from early postwar gloom, but their net operating revenues were only three percent on investment, not enough to cover fixed charges. The economic expansion was paced by the automobile industry which recorded substantial production, improved the vehicles and reduced prices. By introducing installment sales and strengthening the used-car market, the industry increased sales from 1.6 million units in 1921 to 5.3 million units in 1929, valued at $3.4 billion and produced by a work force of 471,000 employees.

Truck competition was used by some railroad executives as a reason for failure to make a better financial showing—competition they claimed was "subsidized" by relatively free use of highways paid for, in part, by railroad taxes. Their arguments were given some recognition in President Hardings' address to Congress in 1922, when he stated that motor haulage would be wasteful if assessed its proper share of highway costs. But realists in the railroad industry knew that improved highways and motor vehicles would become a permanent segment in the nation's transportation structure and railroads would have to accommodate them. Some suggested that low volume unprofitable branch lines could be replaced by motor trucks to assist in the local collection and delivery of long-haul carload freight.

American railroads had been accustomed to intense intra-industry competition, but now they faced inter-industry rivalry. One notable result was the dramatic decline in their passenger traffic. Before 1920, passenger miles had increased an average of five percent per year, but between 1921 and 1929 ridership fell by two percent annually. Freight tonnage increased in every year since 1890, but the rate of increase slowed through highway competition. Agricultural tonnage was particularly vulnerable to diversion, and losses occurred in less-than-carload, agricultural products and animals and products, three categories which represented 15 percent of total traffic and 30 percent of freight revenues. Inroads by trucks on railroad carriage of mine, forest and manufactured products had not yet developed.

For the electric interurbans and street railways, motor vehicles were a disastrous and eventually fatal competitor. Few states in the early 1920s regulated motor buses as common carriers so that bus companies sprang up by the hundreds and competed for passenger business. In the cities, unregulated "jitneys" operated alongside the street railways. These vehicles were in violation of traction company charters, however, and were outlawed after a relatively short period.

Agricultural Distress in the Postwar Years

The demands of World War I had enormously stimulated production of farm commodities. Loans were made by the federal government to allied nations for purchases of food and war supplies—part of the "war debts" about which there were endless political debates. The slogan "Food Will Win the War" was an incentive for farmers to produce to the limit, and bankers urged them to buy more land with borrowed money to meet this objective. It seemed that no one could lose by making the down payment, mortgaging the balance and discharging the debt in a few years. Wheat sold for $2.30 to $3.60 and corn from $2.00 to $3.00 per bushel. At the close of the war, President

Wilson ordered an immediate return to the free enterprise system although price supports and foreign loans continued through 1919. Despite warnings of possible disaster, farmers were surprised when both were discontinued in the spring of 1920.

Agricultural commodities were priced too high for foreign purchases when loans stopped. While exports continued at the same or higher levels, they did so at greatly reduced prices. Farm income dropped about 50 percent before 1920, and just when the farmer needed credit to carry him through this difficult period, the Federal Reserve Board raised the discount rate, resulting in tight money and reducing the possibility of renewing mortgages. Adding to their discomfort was the large increase in freight rates granted in 1920. As a result, farm bankruptcy rose on a national level from 5.5 percent of the farm community in 1914 to 14.4 percent in the early postwar years.

From 200 in September 1920, the farm price index fell to 120 in December and reached 90 by the end of the year. In terms of income from leading commodities, grain declined 53 percent; hogs, 39 percent; and cattle, 30 percent. The relatively high level of other prices intensified the distress. Henry C. Wallace summarized the imbalance confronting the farmer: "In the Corn Belt, the value of an acre of corn in 1921 was 20 percent under the prewar value, whereas monthly wages for farm labor were 14 percent higher; land values were 107 percent higher; implements, 66 percent higher and freight rates about 60 percent higher."[1] During the last half of the decade, farm prices recovered somewhat but in no way proportionate to the general price level. At the peak of the industrial boom in 1929, the index was 146 as contrasted to 220 in 1919, and purchasing power was still five points below prewar averages.

While agricultural distress was admittedly a major problem to Iowa's economy, some attention should be given to the remarkable growth in the industrial sector. In 1860, the ratio between the value of farm crops and that of manufacturing was two to one. By 1920, the ratio was one to one and three-tenths. In 1924, farm crops increased in value 19 times over that of 1860, but during the same period the increase in the value of manufactured products was 49 fold. Histories of the state dealt generously with politics, communications, and civic problems but maintained an almost complete silence with respect to industrial growth. State census reports gave industry slight emphasis as compared with population changes and farm statistics.

The Transportation Act of 1920

Efforts of individual states to develop and control transportation systems in most instances were subjected to policies initiated in the nation's capital. The early 1920s was a time to pause and reflect upon progress made in providing transportation services to the nation with the war experiences of the railroads a vivid memory. The railroads, still the dominant carrier, had come through a difficult period between 1917 to 1920. Were internal management deficiencies or regulatory inadequacies and defects or both the cause of the failure to adjust rapidly to wartime conditions? If in periods of emergency their private operational performance was in question, then their future effectiveness was a matter of public concern. Not only were their problems inherent to the industry, but government supported modes posed a serious threat to their position.

The Act of 1920 was a landmark piece of legislation. It represented an attempt to repair regulatory defects and brought about changes in the emphasis on national transportation policy. The railroads were transferred from federal control back to private operation, but only after serious public debate showed that under a different political climate, nationalization might have been made permanent. The act did more than refine previous legislation. It endeavored to restructure the railroads into a national system. Its provisions were variously described as "radically constructive" or "shifting from a negative to a positive regulatory philosophy" and were hailed as the solution to the railroad problem.[2] Rates,

[1] U.S. Department of Agriculture, *Yearbook*, 1921, pp. 5-7; *Congressional Joint Committee of Agricultural Inquiry, Greater Iowa*, Report 28 (December 1920): p. 2; Henry C. Wallace, *Our Debt and Duty to the Farmer*, New York: The Century Co., 1925, p. 65.

[2] 41 Statutes at Large, part 1, pp. 466-497 (1920). Senator Albert B. Cummins of Iowa, chairman of the Committee on Interstate Commerce, was joint author of the Act. Other Iowans prominently involved were Clifford Throne of Washington, an attorney for shippers, and Glen Plumb of Clay, who represented labor. Details of the Act are found in D. Phillip Locklin, *Economics of Transportation*, 7th edition, Homewood, Ill.: Richard D. Irwin, Inc., 1972, Chapter 11; Truman Bigham, *Transportation Principles and Problems*, New York: McGraw-Hill Book Co., 1946, pp. 173-181; Edgar J. Rich, "The Transportation Act of 1920," *American Economic Review* (September 1920): pp. 507-527.

consolidations, securities control, services, abandonments and labor disputes were dealt with in its most important sections.

"The Rule of Rate Making" (Section 20), was designed to allow the carriers a "fair return" on invested capital, assuming operations were conducted in an honest and efficient manner. The movement to protect earnings grew out of the impaired credit position facing the railroads after the war. The concept required determination of what constituted "fair return" and the amount to be used as a valuation base for rate-making purposes. Congress decided that a uniform "fair return" was to be fixed at five to five and one-half percent of valuation with no guarantee by the federal government. The valuation process had been underway since 1913 and was established at an aggregate figure of $18.9 billion, some $1.1 billion below book value estimates. To assure the carriers of this level of income, the ICC allowed rate increases of 25 percent in the South, 35 percent in the West and 40 percent in the East—the highest rate advances in history. The increases were to be applied as a whole or in rate groups, not on a specific railroad-to-railroad basis.

Impact on Shippers and the States

The first indication of discontent came from grain and livestock shippers. A petition for reduced rates was approved for hay and grain but denied on livestock traffic. However, the experiment of reducing rates on limited classes of products did not prove successful. As the price level of the nation declined, rates remained rigid, and it was the contention of shippers that the rate level was a barrier to business recovery and a return to normal traffic patterns. Their arguments convinced the ICC to allow reductions in 1922 amounting to 12.5 percent in the South, five percent in the West and 14 percent in the East.

Important to the states were provisions relating to intrastate rates. States, including Iowa, had rate structures on passenger and freight services that were attacked on grounds of discrimination against out-of-state points. The 1920 legislation amended Section 13 by preventing any state from setting the level of intrastate rates so low as to discriminate against interstate commerce. Further, it provided that the ICC might if necessary raise intrastate rates to the level of interstate rates. In essence, control over intrastate rates by state commissions was to be limited.

Other Provisions of the 1920 Railroad Legislation

To restructure the railroads into a viable, efficient system, Congress proposed massive railroad consolidations which were to result in a modified number of systems, 19 in all, to be organized voluntarily. Mergers could not be required but could be rejected if they did not conform to the overall plan. The proposal and final plan were doomed to failure since railroad managements would not suppress their competitive ambitions and cooperate intelligently to meet the highest standards of public welfare. Twenty years later, a Senate investigating committee pointed out that "the consolidation provisions of the Transportation Act (1920) presupposed a higher sense of public responsibility on the part of the railroads and railroad investors than was warranted by the experience."[3]

The ICC was given control over issuance of securities, hopefully to prevent further overcapitalization; authority to regulate the use of equipment covering car and terminal service and abandonment of facilities, all designed to promote a more effective use of rolling stock. The fact that controversies over wages and working conditions of employees were pending when federal control ended prompted Congress to include methods for settling these disputes. A Railroad Labor Board was established as a permanent board of arbitration without binding authority, provisions which were superceded by the Railway Labor Act of 1926. To the maximum rate power granted in 1906, Congress gave the ICC control over the minimum rate in order to prevent rate wars.

The Hoch-Smith Resolution

To relieve the agricultural depression through transportation legislation, the "Hoch-Smith" Resolution sponsored by the "farm bloc" was enacted by Congress in 1925. It required that in adjusting freight rates the ICC consider "the conditions which at any given time prevail over our several industries . . . insofar as it is legally possible to do so to the end that commodities may freely move." On products of agriculture, including livestock, the ICC was directed

[3] *Report of the Committee on Interstate Commerce,* 74th Congress, 1st session, part II, 1940, p. 524.

to establish "the lowest possible lawful rates comparable to the maintenance of adequate transportation service."[4] In 1930, the U. S. Supreme Court in *Ann Arbor Railroad v. U. S.* stated that "the requirement of the lowest possible lawful rates on products of agriculture is more in the nature of an object deemed desirable than a rule intended to control rate making." Although the decision was commonly considered to have nullified the effect of the resolution, it was still law and used in a number of cases to justify comparatively low rates on agricultural products.

Federal Highway and Air Legislation

The Federal Aid Highway Act of 1921 marked the beginning of a sustained highway program. By authorizing appropriations for several years in advance, state legislators, most of whom met biannually, were better able to plan matching funds and budgets. Uncertainty in federal-aid programs had existed in prior years and was now removed. Falling wage and price levels for road construction, combined with the development of higher managerial efficiency in highway departments and construction firms, spurred highway building to record mileages in 1922. This was some three and one-half times as much as had been accomplished since the start of the 1916 federal legislation. The record was made possible by building the roads in stages, first in low type work such as grading and draining earth, clay and gravel roads, and delaying expensive pavement until a later date, depending upon traffic volumes and finances. Building by stage construction was by project agreement or contract with the federal share paid upon completion of the first stage; the remainder deferred until the final stage was finished. Increasing traffic resulted in upgrading the initial construction with better surfaces, but the second-stage projects did not become an appreciable part of the total federal-aid program until about 1926.

Stage construction was viewed as an appropriate program for highway development, but it failed to consider the enormous increase in vehicular traffic during the 1920s or the rapid evolution in highway engineering. The years between the first and second stages witnessed changes in state standards resulting in the abandonment of some of the original construction but avoiding premature investment in high-type work which might later have proven inadequate. The stage construction policy accomplished its objective by giving the poorest sections of the federal-aid system a modest improvement as soon as possible. In his annual report of 1926, Thomas MacDonald stated: "An exact similar policy was followed by the builders of the railroads, whose first objective was to get the traffic through, leaving until a later date the perfecting processes of ballasting, banking of curves, etc. It is the only satisfactory method of dealing with conditions in many of the southern, midwestern and western states in which there are thousands of miles of road still entirely devoid of any improvement whatever."[5]

To the mid-twenties, federal and state legislation had emphasized surface transportation. However, pioneering in airship and aircraft technology and construction, the adventurous spirit and challenge of individuals to fly these machines had slowly advanced this new form of transportation, and aviation possibilities began to attract public attention. By 1918, the United States had built about 17,000 planes and trained approximately 10,000 men to fly them. These were the postwar aviators who barnstormed across the nation, flew the first flights across the seas, carried sightseeing passengers, took aerial photographs and gave instruction in flying. Surplus planes and pilots following World War I were useful in initiating air mail service, an experiment in 1918, established on transcontinental routes in 1919, and expanded into 24-hour schedules in 1924. In 1925, the Kelly Air Mail Act authorized the Post Office Department to contract with private companies for air mail transportation. The first contracts were made in 1926, and in 1927 the federal government ceased operation of air mail routes. Except for a three-month period in 1934, air mail has been carried by private companies ever since. In 1926, the Air Commerce Act was passed by Congress. It was primarily promotional in character, dealing only with safety regulations and changes in the rates of compensation for air mail carriage.

[4] 143 Statutes at Large, 801 (1925).

[5] Bureau of Public Roads, *Annual Report,* 1926, p. 2.

Railroad Operations

The Railroads Adjust to Postwar Conditions

Railroads experienced falling revenues and income during the federal control period. Adjustments in employee wages and working conditions and inflation in prices of materials and supplies greatly increased operating expenses without compensating rate increases. Following termination of federal control, the carriers filed claims against the U. S. Railroad Administration for under-maintenance, deficiencies in materials and supplies turned back to them as compared to inventories taken over, for value of properties retired during the control period, etc. Not all roads were as successful as the CNW which received a $15.5 million settlement in 1921, one of the few positive notes in their annual report for that year. Business increased in 1922 but was tempered by a strike of railroad shopmen on July 1. The coal industry was also having labor problems, affecting fuel supplies and prices.

Probably the situation was best expressed by Hale Holden, president of the CB&Q, when in 1923 he discussed the "recurring economic disturbances" that for three years had affected the entire industry. He pointed to the "sharp and shifting changes in the volumes of traffic, the general rate reductions of 1922, labor strikes and the continued high cost of materials, all of which contributed to a confused and variable set of conditions which make the problems of management perhaps more difficult than ever before in the history of the railroads."[6]

Overton observed that there were three strategies that the industry could follow in attempting to solve, or partially solve, the internal and external problems and return to normal service patterns. The first was improvement of the physical plant to overcome the under-maintenance of the war years and enable the industry to handle any future emergencies without further federal interference. A second was to coordinate freight car supply and demand to improve equipment utilization, freight service and reduction of car shortages. The third involved rationalization of plant and equipment through combinations-mergers, stock control or lease-to bring about economies of consolidation. All three received serious attention by the railroads.

Huge expenditures were made for plant and equipment. New stations, terminals, yards and bridges were built or remodeled; locomotive round-houses, grain elevators, shops, coal, gas and water treatment facilities and heavier rails were added to the properties. The IC alone planned a $250 million modernization program over the 1920s. Thirty-two additional tracks at the Proviso (Chicago) classification yard of the CNW made it one of the largest freight terminals in the world. The CM&StP introduced roller bearing cars, practically eliminating hot boxes at slow speeds. New and more powerful locomotives resulted in a spectacular rise in tractive power and more efficiency in passenger and freight service. To combat highway competition, gasoline or gasoline-electric equipment was operated on branch lines by the CB&Q, CGW and M&StL Railways. These innovations reduced operating costs by substituting three-man crews for the five-man crews of steam trains. Of the approximately 5,000 new or rebuilt freight cars of the CNW, 1,000 were automobile carriers. On the M&STL, the shifting emphasis from passenger to freight service changed the name designation from the Albert Lea route to the Peoria Gateway Line.

To meet truck competition in the less-than-carload category, somewhat significant in animals and products traffic, train schedules were shortened between major cities. But highway rivalry was only one of the problems. In 1927, the ICC required railroads to establish joint rates with the barge line operating between Dubuque and the Twin Cities and the opening of the municipal barge terminal at Burlington in 1928 indicated the rising importance of river transportation. Inevitably, rail-highway coordination had to be seriously considered, so the CB&Q moved into the highway field in 1929, incorporating the Burlington Transportation Company in Illinois. Substituting buses for unprofitable branch line passenger service began in Illinois and Nebraska. The operations were not profitable but the losses were estimated to be offset by savings in the reduction of rail services on the specific routes.

Railroad Passenger Services and Fares

George W. Hilton observed that railroads probably provided 95 percent of intercity travel during the mid-1880s. Electric interurbans and street railways, while not successful in the long run, slowed the rate of

[6] Chicago Burlington & Quincy Railroad, *Annual Report*, 1922, p. 7.

increase in steam railroad passenger volume. Railroad passenger traffic peaked in 1920, when 1.2 billion passengers generated 47.3 billion passenger-miles. By 1929, approximately 483 million passengers or 38.1 percent of the 1920 volume had been lost to the automobile and bus. Deficits began to appear in 1930 and in three years, passengers and passenger-miles fell to about one-third of the 1920 levels.

Section 2077 of the Supplemental Code of Iowa (1913), stated that Class I railroads would be restricted to two cents compensation per mile for passengers. In 1920, the railroad commission authorized increases in the intrastate freight rates to correspond to those ordered in the general rate increase case but dismissed the carriers' request for higher passenger fares and surcharges on sleeping and parlor car service for lack of authority under the Iowa statutes. The fare at that time was three cents per mile, ordered by the Director General during the federal control period. The railroads petitioned the ICC for permission to continue these fares and charges rather than revert to the two cent fare in the Iowa Code.

A decision was handed down in 1921. Intrastate passenger fares in Illinois, Wisconsin and Minnesota were three cents and were found lower than those established for interstate travel, thus unduly preferring intrastate and unjustly discriminating against interstate commerce. These were ordered increased. The advantage of the lower Iowa intrastate fares was obvious when the Council Bluffs-Burlington charge of $8.61 for 286 miles was compared to the Omaha-Burlington fare of $10.64 for 290 miles. The ICC ordered the fare to be three and six-tenths cents per mile with a surcharge of 50 percent on pullman and parlor car service.

Merger Proposals

Mergers or combinations had been common in the railroad industry, but these had the objective of completing the individual railroad complex. However, the 1920 legislation encouraged consolidation designed to combine large and powerful railroads into giant regional or national systems. It seemed timely therefore for Hale Holden to dust off a plan originally proposed by James J. Hill to merge the CB&Q with its proprietory companies, the NP and GN railroads, into a new company to be known as the Great Northern Pacific Railroad. After prolonged public debate and hearings throughout the decade, the ICC in 1930 approved the merger of the two Northerns on condition that the CB&Q be divorced from their control. The potential loss of this strategic railroad was not acceptable and the proposal was dropped.[7]

Empire building by mergers through stock control was also on the mind of Edward N. Brown of New York and his associates who controlled the Frisco, but his plan never proved practical. James Gannon, president of the CRI&P, had made considerable progress since 1920, aided by discovery of oil at El Dorado on the Arkansas lines and increased oil movements from Oklahoma and Texas. Charles Hayden was chairman of the executive and finance committees which set company policies geared to increasing net income to a level where dividends on common stock were possible. No matter that maintenance had to be deferred to meet this goal, it was, in the words of Hayes, "Dividends or Bust."[8]

Brown saw in the CRI&P the use of dividends to shore up his shaky financial position, so that in 1926, having purchased 183,000 shares of its stock, he claimed seats on the Board of Directors. Brown and Jerome Hinscham, a New York banker, were appointed to the executive committee and J. M. Kurn, president of the Frisco, was placed on the finance committee. The Brown group was in control and dreamed of merging the two roads. In 1927, the CRI&P common stock earned $12.10 per share and distributed a dividend of five percent; in 1928, the earnings were $12.81 and the dividend, six percent; and in 1929, a record-breaking year, earnings reached $14.04 with a dividend of seven percent, which held through 1930 although earnings dropped to $5.56 per share. The 1930 dividends were paid out of surplus.

[7] Piersall v. Great Northern Railway Company, 161 U.S. 646 (1896). An attempt was made during the 1890's to merge the Great Northern and Northern Pacific. It was blocked by the U.S. Supreme Court as contrary to the laws of Minnesota, stating that public regulation would be a "feeble protection against the monopoly thus created if a combination was effective." The merger of the Burlington, Great Northern and Northern Pacific was finally approved in 1970 under the corporate title of the Burlington Northern Railroad.

[8] William Edward Hayes, *Iron Road to Empire, The History of 100 Years of the Progress and Achievements of the Rock Island Lines*, New York: Simmons-Boardman, 1953, p. 211.

Thirty-two million dollars in 30-year bonds were issued for new equipment, extension of lines in Missouri, and realignment of track on the main line from Chicago to Kansas City. As a result, the total debt of the road in 1930 was a staggering $380 million, carrying an annual interest cost of $13.8 million. In the annual report for 1930, stockholders were assured that the properties were in excellent condition, adequate to handle the expected return to normal traffic, even though acknowledging that a reduction in gross revenue was possible. What the report did not mention was the acquisition of 25,000 shares of Frisco stock for $1.7 million, also paid out of surplus. Brown paid an average of $70 a share, and by the time the purchase was approved by the directors the price had dropped to $46 and was still falling. At the end of 1930, the dream of merger had vanished and both roads were in unstable financial positions.

Bankruptcies

Two railroads went into bankruptcy during the 1920's. Financial reverses during and after the war, the agricultural depression, and an unfavorable economy in their territory resulted in a petition for receivership by the M&StL in 1923. The CM&StP had completed its expansion in Iowa but extended its lines into other areas. Since the early years of the century, the road planned to build to the Pacific Coast. The route required construction of 1,400 miles over five mountain ranges, a bold step indeed at that time. By 1909, freight and local passenger service had been opened to Seattle and Tacoma and by 1911, through passenger trains were in operation. However, the heavy expenditures for construction and maintenance, the increased water competition when the Panama Canal was opened in 1914, and the depressed economic conditions in the Northwest forced the road into bankruptcy in 1925. In 1928, the railroad was reorganized under the name of Chicago, Milwaukee, St. Paul and Pacific (CMStP&P), the word "Pacific" added to the former corporate title.

Railroad Operations in Iowa

Following the transition to private ownership, Iowa railroads gradually returned to normal operations and showed continued growth during the decade. Three tables (Tables 7-1, 7-2, 7-3) using subjectively selected two-year intervals present a trend analysis. The first includes mileage operated and earnings; the second, revenue freight traffic in the major commodity classifications; and the third divides revenues into passenger and freight categories.

The decrease of 142 miles of road operated was the result of abandonment of 91 miles of branch lines on the CRI&P, M&STL and Muscatine, Burlington and Southern Railroads. The remaining 51 miles were due to line corrections and realignment of track. From a relatively low level in 1921, the first year of postwar private operation, net earnings and earnings per mile rose in each of the selected years. Operating ratios averaged 91 percent for 18 railroads reporting in 1921 and fell to 79 percent for 15 roads in 1929.

Table 7-1
Comparative Earnings and Operating Expenses of Railroads Operating in Iowa, 1921-1929, for Selected Years

Year	Mileage[1]	Gross Earnings[2] (Thousands)	Expenses[2] (Thousands)	Net Earnings[2] (Thousands)	Earnings Per Mile
1921	9,841	$148,509	$138,621	$ 9,888	$1,005
1923	9,827	153,216	131,621	21,627	2,201
1925	9,756	139,764	115,819	23,945	2,454
1927	9,744	141,779	116,617	25,162	2,582
1929	9,699	151,472	118,757	32,715	3,372

(*Source:* Iowa Railroad Commission, *Annual Report, 1930,* pp. 6-7.)
[1] Excluding trackage rights.
[2] Figures rounded to the nearest unit.

Table 7-2
Revenue Traffic of Railroads in Iowa in the Major Commodity Classifications for Selected Years, 1923-1929

Commodity Classifications	1923 Tons[1]	%	1925 Tons[1]	%	1927 Tons[1]	%	1929 Tons[1]	%
Products of Ag.	12,372	31	10,341	26	15,901	25	17,917	24
Animals & Prod.	4,376	11	4,286	11	5,775	09	6,496	09
Prod. of Mines	9,193	23	9,018	23	16,036	25	20,238	27
Prod. of Forests	2,561	06	2,474	06	3,655	06	3,826	05
Man. & Miscell.	9,346	24	11,069	29	19,422	31	23,136	31
Less-Carload	1,785	05	1,841	05	2,717	04	3,205	04
Totals	39,633	100	39,029	100	63,506	100	74,818	100

(*Source:* Iowa Railroad Commission, *Annual Reports* for Selected Years.)
[1] In thousands of tons of 2,000 pounds

Table 7-3
Passenger and Freight Revenues of Railroads Operating in Iowa for Selected Years, 1921-1929

Year	Passenger Revenues (thousands)	Freight Revenues (thousands)	Net Operating Revenues[1] (thousands)
1921	$31,742[2]	$105,103[2]	$ 9,888[2]
1923	27,796	112,883	21,627
1925	23,601	104,476	23,945
1927	21,009	108,389	25,346
1929	18,045	119,212	32,699

(*Source:* Iowa Railroad Commission, *Annual Reports* for Selected Years.)
[1] Gross operating revenues minus gross operating expenses.
[2] Figures rounded to the nearest unit.

There was no commodity data in the Annual Report for 1921. Between 1923 and 1929, revenue tonnage increased by 88 percent with all classifications showing some increase. As a percentage of total tonnage, however, two categories showed little or no change; agricultural products and animals and products declined, whereas, mine and manufactured products increased percentagewise. The traffic gains in the latter group were not surprising when value added to manufacturing was considered, rising from $18.7 million in 1921 to $32.8 million in 1929. Less-than-carload traffic was not seriously impaired by motor carriers at the end of the decade.

The table speaks for itself. Passenger revenues showed a declining trend throughout the decade, freight revenues fluctuated but rose significantly from 1921 to 1929, and net operating revenues provided a key to a relatively prosperous railroad situation.

Electric Interurbans

The interurbans reached their highest level of earnings in 1920, while operating 514 miles of single track. However, by the close of 1929, gross earnings had fallen by 30 percent and net earnings per mile by 70 percent with four fewer railways reporting to the commission. As contrasted to the 50 percent decline in passenger revenues, freight revenues rose by 40 percent. The operating ratio of 81 percent in 1921 increased to 90 percent in 1929. Both interurbans and street railways were affected by improvements in highways, paving of city streets and the increased use of motor vehicles. Throughout the twenties, line segments of the interurbans were abandoned as were routes on street railway systems. Motor buses were introduced, services curtailed and fares increased to meet the competition. No city was immune from the changing public response to the automobile age; they directed their efforts to preserve the street railway systems through reorganizations and operational techniques designed to reduce operating expenses.

The Motor Vehicle in Iowa

It was assumed that the number of motor vehicles had steadily increased year after year, but the extent of the increase was not generally known. In 1905 there were less than 1,000 vehicles in the state; a decade later the number reached 147,078. The percentage of increase declined but the numerical increase became larger. By 1920 there was one motor vehicle for every 5.5 persons and by 1925, one for every 3.6 persons, surpassed only by the state of California. The number of vehicles on farms was second only to Texas. Table 7-4 presents the total vehicle registrations between 1905 and 1927 together with the ratio between registrations and population.

Distance between towns in rural Iowa may have been a factor in the ratio of vehicles to population. In 1920, automobiles accounted for 90 percent of highway traffic and rose to 98.8 percent in 1926. In the latter year, 14.4 percent of travel was interstate, 29.6 percent was intercounty and 56 percent was on an intracounty basis. By 1927, automobiles were responsible for approximately 85 percent of total highway traffic in the state.

In addition to the expenditures for construction and maintenance, an important item in highway transportation costs is that of vehicular operation. With increased volume, savings in operation made possible by improved roads became an irrefutable argument for construction of all-weather roads. Table 7-5 shows how savings could accrue, using the Lincoln Highway as an example. Data was obtained by actual vehicle count. Fuel costs were estimated by tests conducted by the Engineering Experiment Station at Ames.

Table 7-4
Iowa Motor Vehicle Registrations

Year	Total Vehicles Registered	No. of Persons Per Motor Vehicle
1905	799	2,766
1910	10,422	215.4
1915	147,078	16.03
1920	437,378	5.50
1925	659,202	3.65
1926	718,013	3.37
1927	782,634	3.31

(*Source:* Charles H. Sandage, *The Motor Vehicle in Iowa,* Iowa City: Bureau of Business Research, February 1928, p. 4)
[1] Estimated

Estimates of economies resulting from motor vehicle operations on surfaced rather than earth roads did not consider cost of travel under unusual conditions over rough and slippery highways. Wear and tear on tires and chains, engine or car damage, loss of time or injuries to persons were not included. These items were under investigation to determine the life of automobiles on different types of roads. However, even with the data at hand, the thoughtful motorist needed little proof to convince him that bad roads had an appreciable impact upon the depreciation and maintenance of his vehicle.[9]

[9] Further studies were published by Robley Winfrey, *Automobile Operating Cost and Mileage Studies,* Bulletin 106, Ames: Engineering Experiment Station, July 1931; and Ralph Moyer and Robley Winfrey, *Cost of Operating Rural Carrier Motor Vehicles on Pavement, Gravel and Earth,* Bulletin 143, Ames: Engineering Experiment Station, July 1939.

Table 7-5
Fuel and Maintenance Costs Alone Would Pave Lincoln Highway in 15 Years (East of Ames)

Daily Average Traffic	904 vehicles
Daily Average Tonnage	1,232 tons
Savings per ton-mile on Concrete over Gravel	0.38 cents
Daily Average Fuel Saving per mile	$4.78
Savings per mile, per Year	$1,746
Cost per mile of Maintaining Gravel, Average	$803
Cost per mile of Maintaining Concrete, Average	$89
Fuel Savings plus Maintenance Saving per mile, per Year, nets	$2,460
Average Cost of Concrete in 1922	$26,400
Average Interest on Investment per mile for term of Years	$660
Fuel and Maintenance Saving less Interest Costs nets	$1,800
Net Savings would pay for Road in	15 Years

(*Source:* Iowa State Highway Commission, *Service Bulletin,* August-September, 1922, p. 13)

Supervision of Motor Buses and Trucks

The General Assembly gave the railroad commission supervision of motor buses and trucks in 1923, requiring the addition of a motor bus department, later changed to a motor carrier department. The law was difficult to interpret. There were no penalties for violations except revocation of certification, unless they were deemed a misdemeanor. Also, appropriations were inadequate for employment of supervisors and inspectors. In 1924, the commission noted that many persons were operating motor buses and trucks contrary to the law; that they had great difficulty in determining what "public convenience" signified, either in law or in fact, and whether evidence would show that the proposed service would actually promote the public welfare. The law was challenged by various organizations. Manufacturing firms objected to it. County supervisors protested that authority given to heavy vehicles would injure or deface their roads. Railroads fought the threat of short haul competition and the resultant loss of revenue. Civic bodies split on the issue, whereas, small communities generally indicated support.

In 1929 the law was clarified, and under its provisions the commission published rules and regulations covering operations of trucks, effective July 1. These covered applications for permits, annual fees ($5.00), liability insurance requirements, schedules of rates and charges, equipment certificates, marking of trucks (permit number and owner), freight receipts, accident reports, safety requirements, and the sale or lease of the permit. At the close of 1929, there were 12 Class I passenger carriers certified with annual gross operating revenues of $30,000 or above. Twenty-two passenger and 99 freight-hauling vehicles were operating in Class II—revenues under $30,000. The number of employees in the motor carrier department of the commission had risen from three in 1923 to 39 in 1930.

A Busy Railroad Commission

During the years 1920-1924, valuation of Iowa railroads was a concern to the commission. Provisions of the 1920 Act required an aggregate valuation to be made; also, that it be kept current and established to state lines. The work required permanent employment of a valuation department, established in 1921 with J. R. Rolls as valuation counsel and five land appraisers. Control over motor carriers and airport construction were responsibilities of the commission. In addition to the seemingly endless number of cases on grain elevator sites, their rental terms and contracts, the commission was responsible for: farm and public highway crossings, separation of grades, warning signals, applications for building stations, terminals, spurs and switch tracks, warehouses, electric transmission lines, etc. The variety and number of cases handled by the commission during the 1920s are found in Table 7-6.

Table 7-6
Cases Decided by the Railroad Commission During the Decade of the 1920s

Year	R.R.[1]	Express	Air-ports[2]	Elec. Trans.	Motor Carriers	Ware-houses	Signal Engineering[3]
1920	280	20	---	30	---	---	---
1921	208	11	---	26	---	---	---
1922	295	12	---	36	---	---	---
1923	147	3	---	42	18	---	---
1924	209	4	---	82	150	---	---
1925	143	5	---	174	391	2	---
1926	189	1	---	137	301	1	49
1927	227	1	---	167	183	---	86
1928	111	1	---	214	241	---	263
1929	126	2	4	388	588	2	375
Total	1,935	60	4	1,296	1,872	5	773

(*Source:* Iowa Railroad Commission, *Annual Reports*)

[1] Including condemnation cases.

[2] Applications for building permits.

[3] Interlocking, signal and safety devices at crossings but not regular inspections.

The State Highway Commission

Highway Progress

There were startling contrasts in highway conditions in 1920. In some instances, roads were so impassible that county engineers had to lay planks over mud holes. Just when Iowa had begun to feel proud of her excellently graded earth roads as a near foundation for paving, it was rather humiliating to have to return to pioneer days of plank roads to keep them passable. The driver of a motor vehicle on the famous Lincoln Highway between Ames and Nevada was not consoled that the road was surfaced with gravel when it did not drain properly. On the other hand, concrete surfacing was progressing slowly. One example was the Des Moines-Ankeny stretch of the heavily traveled Des Moines to Ames highway. No road in the state had been "cussed" or "discussed" as much as this section of one of the oldest roads leading to the state Capitol. It had passed through every stage of highway improvement, having been scraped, dragged, wheel-scraped, blade-graded and steam-rollered. It had been a prairie trail, earth road and an oiled dirt and graveled road. Finally, it was built into a 20-foot concrete highway with hopes that it would last for at least one generation.

Under federal law, the Secretary of War was authorized to distribute excess war materials to various state highway departments. In March, 1920, Iowa received 578 motor vehicles consisting of 512 trucks, 37 cars, and 29 ambulances. Also included were 16 tractors, two concrete mixers, and other miscellaneous equipment. Of the total, 288 trucks were distributed to counties and to seven state institutions which had control over their roads. To store and properly care for the equipment, the state had to provide facilities. A tract of land, west of the Des Moines branch of the CNW lying along the Lincoln Highway in the south edge of Ames, was leased for seven years with the privilege of purchase in two years. On this land four buildings were erected. They were 52 x 142 feet, constructed of hollow brick tile, with a rubberoid roof and cinder flooring, to be used as storage warehouses. Title and possession of the equipment remained with the highway commission, but could be assigned to the counties for highway work with the understanding that counties would maintain the equipment in good condition and pay all costs.

The year 1921 was the first since the primary road law

was enacted that it was possible to carry on road construction without delays for reasons beyond state control. There were three and one-half times as much graveling and paving and two and one-half times as much grading as had been accomplished in 1920. The construction also played an important part in relieving unemployment in communities where the work was in progress. Since primary road construction was not funded by property taxes, the work did not increase tax levies except in a few counties where bonds had been voted by the people.

Congress, in the Federal Act of 1921, authorized the Secretary of Agriculture to select and establish with cooperation of State Highway Departments, a system of national roads comprising not over seven percent of the total mileage of the nation. The Iowa primary road system included approximately six and one-half percent (6,422 miles) of total mileage and was laid out on a state rather than a county system. The network met all of the requirements of the federal program with minor adjustments along the Missouri border.

The interstate system would consist of important through east-west transcontinental as well as Gulf-to-Canada routes, which in Iowa would include portions of the Lincoln and Jefferson Highways, the River-to-River Road, plus such routes designated for long-distance interstate traffic. The balance of the Iowa primary system would comprise the federal intercounty system.

Planks covering mud holes on Grand Avenue, north of Ames, 1920.
(Courtesy: Iowa State Highway Commission)

Des Moines-Ankeny concrete road, 1920.
(Courtesy: Iowa State Highway Commission)

Numbering and Marking Highways

With the advent of the automobile in the early 1920s, signings and markings became prevalent on principal highways and in and around cities. Naming, numbering and marking roads began with motorist associations or clubs, Chambers of Commerce, and in some instances, the states. Numbering county roads in Iowa was proposed as early as 1915 and 1916 under a system whereby the state Capitol would be the central location and roads would bear such designations as North 1, 2, etc.; South 1, 2, etc.; East 1, 2, etc.; West 1, 2, etc. The idea was that a tourist who found himself at a corner marked North 67 and West 32 could locate himself instantly. Chapter 70 of the Acts of the 37th General Assembly described a system of numbering township roads for the purpose of designating road-dragging districts.

Marking primary roads began in 1920. Standard symbols were adopted with each main traveled road given a specific number, painted on telegraph or specially built poles at every intersection, turn or crossroad between transportation centers. For example, the Jefferson Highway became No. 1; the River-to-River Road, 7; the Red Ball Highway, 40; the Lincoln Highway, 6; and the Blue Grass Trail, No. 8. All numbers corresponded to those used on connecting interstate routes in adjoining states. Marking was important to provide directions for the rising tide of motorists who had depended upon local trail associations and automobile clubs for route guidance.

From the total of 1,068 cities, towns and villages in the state, 556 were on the primary road system, including all towns over 1,000 population, except for Hiteman, Buxton and Lockman, mining camp communities. Eighty-five percent of the state's population either lived on the system or in towns nearby. Every county seat was linked by the most direct route to every other county seat and with the state Capitol and other important centers. With such coverage, it was necessary that a uniform numbering system be developed. There was no interference with the special signs to indicate association trails.

Road associations smeared paint of various colors on telephone poles as high as painters could reach and when the colors gave out, the roads were marked with association names. The rivalry was intense between main road associations and private automobile owners to show off their roads and attract people to the communities served. An example of an automobile guide for motorists traveling between Mason City and Des Moines is found in Table 7-7. Note the precise directions, landmarks for identification and the total and intermediate mileages listed.

By 1924 there were at least 250 marked trails nationwide and about 64 in Iowa, sponsored by separate organizations, each with its own headquarters which issued maps and other materials and collected support funds. The situation finally became so confusing that the American Association of State Highway Officials (AASHO), acting upon recommendations of the Mississippi Valley Association of State Highway Departments, approved a resolution calling for a Board of Public Road Engineers to formulate a system of numbering and marking interstate highways. The chairman was Thomas MacDonald, and Fred White of the Iowa department played a prominant role. Initially, an interstate system of 75,884 miles was established, of which Iowa supplied approximately 3,000 miles. Within Iowa, five routes crossed from east to west and five north and south and were renumbered to conform to the federal plan. The Jefferson Highway, formerly State Highway No.1, became U.S. 65, and the Lincoln Highway was changed from State No. 6 to U.S. 30. A partial list of Iowa's portion of the new numbered interstate system is shown in Table 7-8. The new markers were placed on the roads in 1926 and the familiar black and white shields have guided American motorists ever since (Fig. 7-1, 7-2, 7-3).

Private trails were replaced by one or more of the U.S. numbered routes, and one by one the trail associations disappeared, their purposes accomplished in promoting road identification. Yet, for many years afterward and to the present, sections of highways in many states continued to be referred to as "the Lincoln Highway," "Prairie Trail," "Dixie Highway," and "Yellowstone Trail."

Placing monolithic brick pavement for the Des Moines to Camp Dodge road, 1917-1918. (Courtesy: Iowa State Highway Commission)

Rolling the Des Moines to Camp Dodge brick pavement with a 700 pound roller, 1917-1918
(Courtesy: Iowa State Highway Commission)

Numbering License Plates

In January, 1922, every Iowa county was given an individual prefix number for its license plate followed by a dash and the number assigned to the individual motor vehicle which could run as high as necessary. For automobiles, the five counties having more than 10,000 cars registered-Polk, Woodbury, Scott, Linn and Pottawattamie-were given the first five numbers in the order mentioned. The remainder of the counties, starting with Adair with six, were numbered in alphabetical order to 99. Black Hawk County was 12; Dubuque, 36; Johnson, 57; and Story, 86. In 1927, letters from A to N were assigned as prefixes for counties with 9,000 or more registrations. Black Hawk, Dubuque, Clinton, Webster, Cerro Gordo and Des Moines joined the previous five counties with the highest registrations. Now Adair took 1 and the others followed in alphabetical order. Johnson County carried 47 and Story 76. License plates showed black colors on a white background, a color scheme selected by Iowa and five other states.

The Primary Road System in the Early Twenties

Most of the improvements on the primary roads were mainly in the form of grading and graveling. Actually when dry and well-maintained, the earth roads were excellent highways, but no matter how well they handled traffic in dry weather, in rainy seasons they became quagmires. A famous incident in 1922 illustrates the point. Following a homecoming football victory on a rainy November 12 at Iowa City, hundreds of motorists were mired in the mud enroute to Cedar Rapids. Their plight provided a bonanza for farmers who used teams of horses to extracate the cars, charging as much as $50 for each vehicle in addition to a fee for overnight accommodations for those who sought them. The *Chicago Tribune's* headline the next day read: "Autos Stuck in Iowa Mud: Gold Harvest in Iowa."[10]

Iowa's economic advantages were hampered by poor roads. In 1923, the Greater Iowa Association spent large sums of money in Eastern newspapers advertising the potential economic wealth of the state,

[10] George S. May, "The Good Roads Movement in Iowa," *Palimpsest 46* (February 1965): p. 68.

Table 7-7

Automobile Guide for Motorists

Route 267 **Mason City Section**

Route 267—Mason City to Des Moines, Ia.—133.4 m.

Route map, page 184 **Reverse route, No. 205**

Via Iowa Falls, Story City and Ames. Good dirt roads most of the way.

The Blue Book car did not cover part of this route between Iowa Falls and Ames, the data having been compiled from accurate local information and no trouble should be encountered in following same.

MILEAGES Total	Intermed.	(For this and other exits, see **city map,** page 185.)
0.0	0.0	**MASON CITY,** Main & State Sts.—park on right. Go south on **Main St.** with trolley under RR. 0.7. Cross RR. 1.5.
9.8	9.8	End of road; turn left with telephone to next
10.2	0.4	Right-hand road—poor road ahead; turn right with poles, passing **Rockwell** to left 11.8, crossing RR. 12.9.
15.1	4.9	End of road; turn right with wires to next.
15.6	0.5	Left-hand road; turn left, still with poles. Avoid good road to right into **Sheffield,** crossing RR. 28.3 into western edge of
28.8	13.2	**Hampton,** large brick high school on left—business center a few blocks to right. Straight ahead, crossing RR. 29.3, continuing straight south through all intersections. Cross RR. 43.7.
43.9	15.1	4-corners; turn right. Cross RR. 46.1 and 46.4, running onto Rocksylvania Ave.
46.7	2.8	**Tremont St.;** turn left 2 blocks and then right on Washington Ave.
47.0	0.3	**Iowa Falls,** Washington Ave. & Main St. Keep ahead on Washington St. For diverging routes see **index map,** page 184.
47.1	0.1	4-corners; turn left between livery stable and blacksmith shop.
47.2	0.1	Fork; bear right across iron bridge, crossing RRs. 47.4 and 47.6. Jog right and left with road 48.7, 50.1 and 50.6.
56.6	9.4	4-corners; turn right.
57.1	0.5	Left-hand road; turn left past school on right 58.1.
62.2	5.1	4-corners, RR. just ahead; turn right, avoiding road to left leading into Hubbard 62.6.
65.1	2.9	End of road; jog left across RR. and immediately right along same. Cross another RR. 67.6, continuing straight ahead, following RR. through Radcliffe 69.6.
76.1	11.0	4-corners; turn left around school.
82.1	6.0	4-corners; turn right.
83.1	1.0	4-corners; turn left, shortly running onto winding road. Turn square right with road 84.6.
85.1	2.0	Left-hand road; turn left.
87.1	2.0	**Story City.** Turn right along RR., turning left across same 87.6. Pass school on left 89.0.
93.0	5.9	4-corners; turn right around school.
94.0	1.0	4-corners; turn left. Pass school on right 96.0, running onto winding road.
100.0	6.0	4-corners; turn left.

Table 7-7 (Cont.)

Mason City Section **Route 268**

100.4	0.4	Right-hand road; turn right.
101.3	0.9	**Ames.** Business center on right. **Ames Auto Co.** For diverging routes, see **index map,** page 184. Straight ahead on Duff St. across RR., keeping straight south across RR. 106.7. Meeting trolley from right just beyond, follow same for over a mile, where turn left with road 109.0.
109.5	8.2	End of road; turn right past **Huxley** to right 110.7, crossing RR. 110.8.
117.6	8.1	End of road, school on left; turn right to first.
118.1	0.5	Left-hand road at trolley crossing; turn left, following trolley straight south, jogging right and left across same 120.1. Take first right and first left with main travel to
122.4	4.3	**ANKENY.** Go east 1 block from center of town, where turn right.
122.6	0.2	4-corners immediately after crossing RR.; turn left along tracks curving right away from same 123.1. Straight ahead through all crossroads, passing County Poor Farm buildings 126.7, through old mining settlement of Marquesville 127.6, same thoroughfare becoming **14th St.,** which follow
130.8	8.2	**Washington Ave.,** brick school on right; turn right, leaving trolley to first paved cross-street.
131.1	0.3	**12th St.;** turn left crossing RR. 131.2, picking up trolley from left 131.8.
132.1	1.0	**Grand Ave.,** Historical building on right; turn right with trolley to far side of Capitol Bldg., where turn left 1 block, then right onto **Locust St.,** which follow straight ahead across long concrete bridge 132.9 to center of
133.4	1.3	**DES MOINES,** Locust & 5th Ave.

Wellington Hotel, 5th & Grand.
Iowa Auto & Supply Co., Fourth & Locust Sts.
For city map, see page 135. For diverging routes, see **index map,** page 137.
For diverging routes, see **index map,** page 210.
For through connections, see trunk-line chart and map in front of book.

(Source: Official Automobile Bluebook, 1913. Automobile Bluebook Publishing Company, Illinois, 1913: 104-105.)

hoping to attract industries and people. The Bridgeport, Connecticut *Evening Post,* perhaps smarting over Iowa's victory at Yale in 1922, replied editorially that Iowa's football fans faced the prospect of spending Saturday nights in their cars during rainy periods. The editorial further suggested that each Iowa farmer should add one hen to his flock so that money from the sale of additional eggs could be used to build permanent surfaced roads. "Who would live in this kind of state, for all its agricultural wealth?" the editor asked. Naturally, Iowa newspapers responded in the same spirit of friendliness and compassion.

Table 7-8

IOWA'S PORTION OF THE NEW U. S. INTERSTATE SYSTEM

Federal Number	Former Primary Road Number	Mileage	Route
U. S. No .18	No. 19	287	McGregor-Mason City to Primary Road No. 22
U. S. No. 20	No. 5	201	Dubuque to Fort Dodge
	No. 23	130	Fort Dodge to Sioux City
U. S. No. 30	No. 6	369	Clinton to Council Bluffs
U. S. No. 32	No. 7	181	Davenport to Des Moines
	No. 2	141	Des Moines to Council Bluffs
U. S. No. 34	No. 8	283	Burlington to Council Bluffs
U. S. No. 53 U. S. No. 61	No. 20	324	Minnesota State Line thru Dubuque to Missouri State Line
U. S. No. 63	No. 2	61	Des Moines to Oskaloosa
	No. 24	32	Oskaloosa to Ottumwa
	No. 13	36	Ottumwa to Missouri State Line
U. S. No. 65	No. 1	228	Minnesota State Line to Leon
	No. 3	14	Leon east 14 miles and south to Missouri Line at Lineville
	No. 14	22	Road No. 3 to Missouri State Line
U. S. No. 69	No. 1	20	Leon to Missouri State Line
U. S. No. 71	No. 4	86	Minnesota State Line to Early
	No. 23	10	Early to Sac City
	No. 18	154	Sac City to Missouri State Line
U. S. No. 75	No. 22	34	Minnesota State Line to Sioux City
	No. 12	77	Sioux City to Missouri Valley
U. S. No. 161	No. 28	72	Dubuque to Cedar Rapids
	No. 40	123	Cedar Rapids to Missouri State Line
U. S. No. 218	No. 40	139	Minnesota State Line to Primary Road No. 6 west of Cedar Rapids.

(Source: Iowa State Highway Commission Service Bulletin, 1923)

Figure 7-1
Primary road markers prior to 1926.

Figure 7-2
New primary road markers adopted in 1926.

Figure 7-3
New U.S. road markers adopted in 1926.

Take your choice to Omaha.
(Courtesy: Iowa State Highway Commission)

Example of a historic highway.
(Courtesy: Iowa State Highway Commission)

State Policy Requested on Future Highway Improvements

As long as the roads remained in a generally deplorable condition, economic and social progress was in jeopardy. The Iowa farmer was the heaviest loser since he used the roads most often; consolidated school movements were crippled and rural churches closed during the winter and early spring. These conditions were recognized in 1922 when Fred White challenged state officials and legislators to decide future policy relative to highway surfacing (Fig. 7-4). Traffic had outgrown the unsurfaced roads, and the rapid increase in vehicle numbers, size and weight was causing problems. Iowans owned 718,000 automobiles, increasing the daily average of cars on the roads from 20-30 to 500-600. Speeds had risen from 4-8 to 25-35 miles per hour, and loads increased from 2 to 10-14 tons. Some action was necessary, and quickly. Highways in 1921 carried more passengers than railroads and nearly as much freight at almost equivalent speeds. The question White raised was whether primary road improvements should end with graded earth roads or with hard surfaces.

He also indicated that road revenues averaged $552 per car registered in 1910 as contrasted with $50 per vehicle registered in 1921. Supporting his position were studies showing comparison of Iowa's license fees with averages in other states on different models of automobiles (Tables 7-8, 7-9). Additional support came from research by the highway commission and the Iowa State College which concluded that when traffic reached 320 tons per day on an earth road or 470 tons on a graveled road, it became economical to pave (Table 7-10). Paving could be financed through bonding. It was estimated that savings in vehicle operating expenses would retire bonds and pay interest charges over a 15-year period.

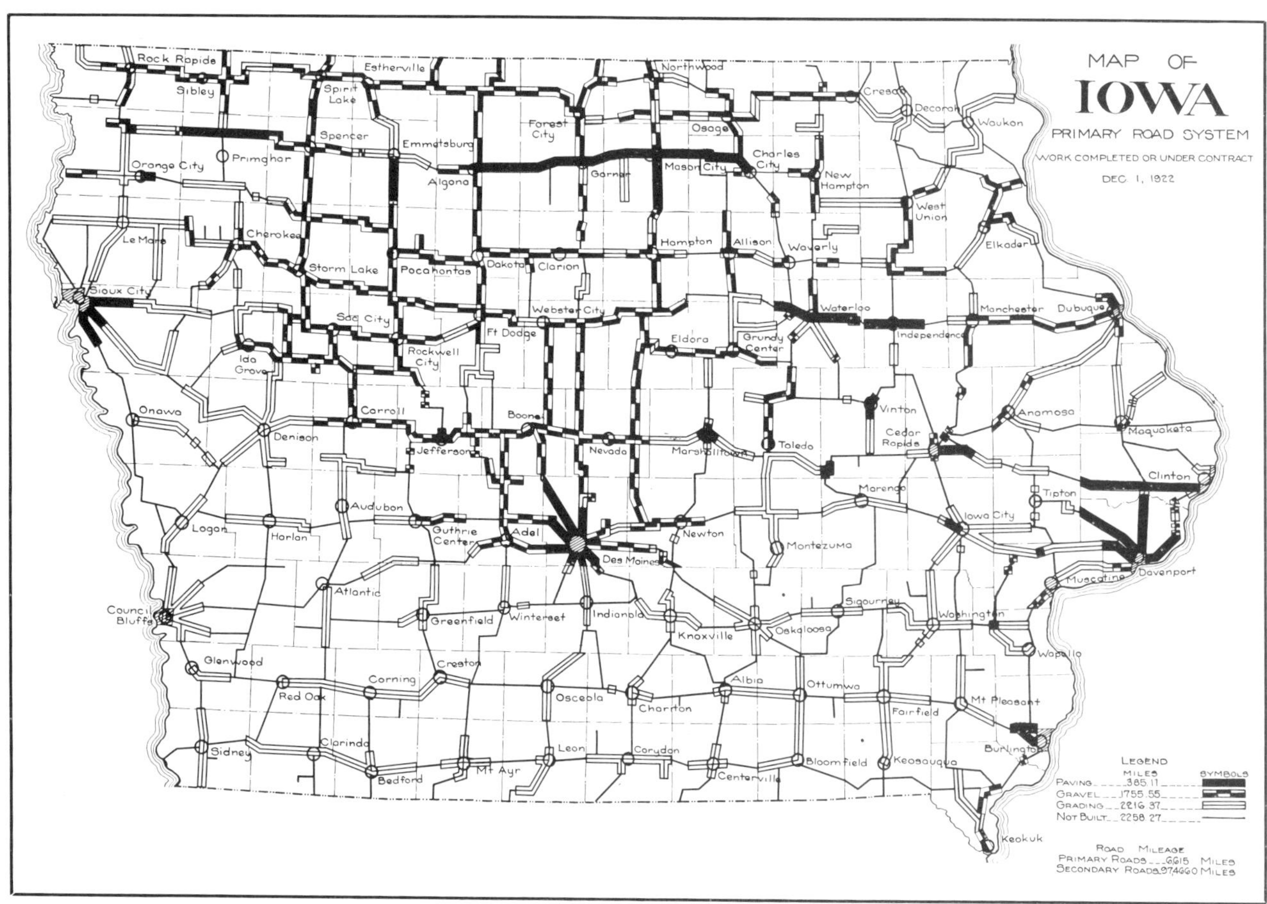

Figure 7-4
Primary Road System by surface type, 1922.
(Courtesy: *Iowa State Highway Commission Service Bulletin,* 1922)

Iowa Motor Vehicle Fees Lower Than Average for the United States

Table 7-8

COMPARISON OF AUTOMOBILE LICENSE FEES AND TAXES COLLECTED IN UNITED STATES

	Ford 5-Pass. Tour. 15 Mi. per gal.		Dodge 5-Pass. Tour. 13 Mi. per gal.		Buick 6-cyl. 5-Pass. Tour. 12 mi. per gal.		Cadillac 8-Cyl. 7-Pass. Tour. 8 mi. per gal.		Packard 12-Cyl. 7-Pass. Tour. 6 mi. per gal.	
	Country	City	Country	City	Country	City	Country	City	Country	City
Iowa	$11.40	$11.40	$19.40	$19.40	$26.00	$26.00	$48.40	$48.40	$67.00	$67.00
Average all states	14.54	19.58	19.32	29.69	24.33	38.42	41.35	75.37	53.67	99.08
Difference	3.14	8.18	.08	10.29	1.67	12.42	7.05	26.97	13.33	32.08

Basis of Computation—Registration Fee. Actual Amount.

Personal Property Tax—Assessed Valuation taken at 60% List Price. Levy taken at 60 mills in country and 170 mills in city.

Gasoline Tax—4,500 miles driven at rate of gasoline consumption given for each car above.

Table 7-9

ACTUAL TAXES AND FEES PAID ON MOTOR VEHICLES IN CERTAIN CITIES IN UNITED STATES

Place		Ford	Dodge	Buick	Cadillac	Packard
Jefferson City, Missouri	State tax + city tax of ½ the rate charged by State	$23.08	$35.94	$48.30	$ 91.11	$121.76
Pierre, South Dakota	Registration fee $6.00 flat	26.59	......	58.19	144.12	....
Little Rock, Arkansas	State tax + city tax of $5.00 + county tax of $2.645 per $100. 50% assessment	30.82	44.84	55.62	104.77	135.36
Lincoln, Nebraska	Registration fee + county tax 1% of list price + city tax ½% of list price	16.28	......	48.40	91.23	....
Raleigh, North Carolina	State tax + city tax of $1.00 + $2.50 per $100 on valuation of car	26.50	......	54.75	109.12	....
Madison, Wisconsin	State tax + city tax of 23 mills on 90% of true value of car	19.20	......	37.00	74.75	....
Any city, New Hampshire	State tax + city tax of 24 mills on list price	25.89	40.32	51.00	99.84	....
Any city, Rhode Island	State tax + city tax of $23.00 per $1,000 on 90% of list price	21.40	......	41.59	81.23	....
Any city in Iowa	Registration fee only	11.40	19.40	26.00	48.40	67.00

(*Source: Iowa State Highway Commission Service Bulletin,* 1923)

Table 7-10

Tests Show That It Pays to Surface Dirt Roads When Average Daily Traffic Reaches 320 Tons

Saving in Operation of Motor Vehicles Will Pay Interest and Retire Bonds in Maximum Period of Fifteen Years.

Gravel Economical Until Traffic Reaches Daily Average of 470 Tons.

F. R. White, Chief Engineer, as President of American Association of Highway Officials, Gives Information Based on Iowa Tests to Congressional Committee.

VEHICLE OPERATING COSTS ON VARIOUS TYPES OF ROADS

(Cost in cents per ton-mile)

Type of Surface	Solid tire trucks, 10 M. P. H.	Pneu. tire trucks, 15 M. P. H.	Automobiles, 25 to 35 M. P. H.	Motor busses cts. bus-mi. 25 M. P. H.
Best gravel, yearly average	7.75	7.70	9.3	22.50
Average P. C. concrete and asphalt filled brick	8.00	8.3	10.00	24.00
Best P. C. concrete and asphalt filled brick	7.75	7.70	9.3	22.50
Best gravel, yearly average	8.5	8.8	10.9	25.7
Ordinary gravel, yearly average	9.0	9.40	11.8	27.8
W. B. Macadam, well maintained	8.7	8.95	11.1	26.0
Bit. macadam, well maintained	8.5	8.80	10.6	25.7
Average sheet asphalt yearly average temperature	8.10	8.3	10.00	24.0
Average asphaltic conc. yearly average temperature	8.00	8.3	10.00	24.0
Best earth, well packed by traffic, yearly average	9.0	9.40	11.70	27.8
Ordinary earth with light traffic, yearly average	9.5	9.95	12.6	29.6

(Source: *Iowa State Highway Commission Service Bulletin*, 1924)

Proposed Improvement Plans

In 1923 and 1924, two six-year improvement plans were introduced. One by White called for hard-surfacing approximately 3,000 miles, or about half of the primary road system. Gravel would be used for the remainder, and grading and graveling was planned for the secondary road system. His proposal included 1,000 miles of grading, 500 miles of graveling and 500 miles of paving each year on the primary system and 1,000 miles of grading and 500 miles of graveling on the secondary system. A second plan was proposed by the Good Roads Association which involved 3,115 miles of pavement, 1,786 miles of gravel surface and 2,013 miles of grading on the primary system between 1927 and 1932. The total cost was estimated at $125 million. Funds expected to be available were estimated at $40 million, leaving a balance of $85 million to be borrowed.

Both plans were difficult to refute. For each of the six years following enactment of the Primary Road Law, an average of 700 miles of grading, 300 miles of graveling and 85 miles of paving had been completed. If this construction schedule was maintained at current levels, the necessary grading would be completed in three years, graveling in six years and paving in **36 years.** But the work could not be programmed at the same pace under present funding. On the basis of annual revenues entering the primary road fund, it would require 20 years to pay outstanding bonded indebtedness and complete the work—16 years if a third cent were added to the gasoline tax. The third cent was added in 1927. The association plan would require no increase in grading or graveling, but paving would advance to about 500 miles per year, similar to the White plan with very few additional employees needed.

Most of the progress in building the well-graded, drained and bridged road system had been possible through current revenues, but considerable indebtedness had occurred by county bonding, anticipation certificates and special assessments against abutting property which totaled $20.7 million against the primary road fund. Interest payments in the association plan would amount to $38.6 million and would represent the extra cost of building roads under "use while you pay" as compared with the cost under "pay as you go." The former would complete the road system in six years, the latter in 16 years. The emphasis once more was strongly on bonding to provide the funds.

While plans were being debated over funding, road construction continued. By January 1, 1928, 63 percent of the primary system had been surfaced. Of the 6,655 miles included, 14 percent were paved, 46 percent graveled, 22 percent permanently graded and 16 percent earth improved. It was possible to travel by direct route from Des Moines to 62 county seat towns and to 15 others by indirect routes (Fig. 7-5). This progress had been made despite the fact that 76 counties did not pay their way on the system in 1926 and only 56 of the 99 counties had voted county bonds for primary road improvements by mid-1927 (Fig. 7-6, 7-7).

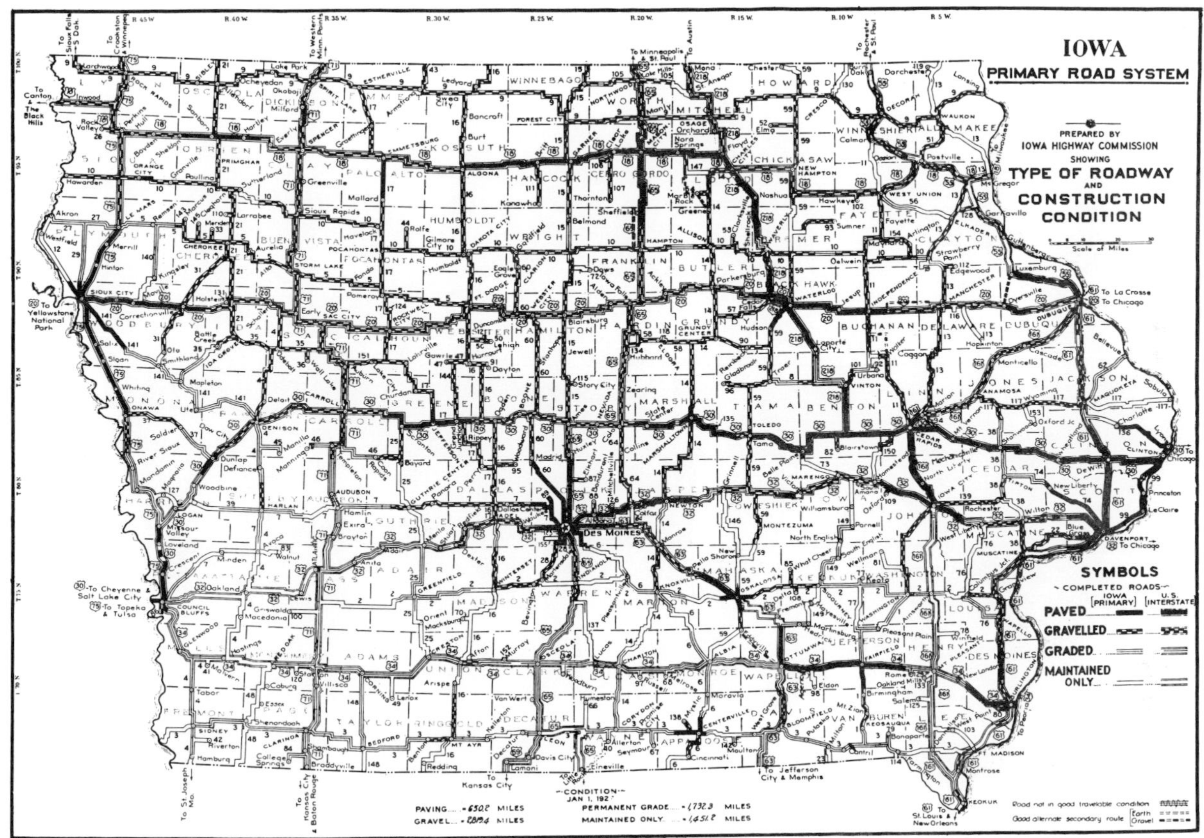

Sixty-Two County Seat Towns Can Be Reached from Des Moines by Direct Route on Surfaced Road—15 by Indirect Route

Figure 7-5
(Source: Iowa State Highway Commission Service Bulletin, 1928)

The State Highway Bonding Issue

Bonding for highways was discussed in Chapter Four. It was the six-year improvement plan that initiated the $100 million bonding proposal, endorsed by Governor Hammill as far preferable to the continued use of county bonds. His principal arguments were: (1) that $5 million in interest would be saved; (2) county bond issues, with only two-thirds of the counties participating, were producing disconnected sections of paved roads instead of a system of connecting routes; (3) under the county bond plan, the commission could not, in fairness to counties voting bonds, pave gaps in counties not participating; (4) the special election in November, 1928, if successful, would provide funds for construction in 1929 and 1930; and (5) state bonding would provide for a comprehensive state highway program (Fig. 7-8).

The state bond issue was declared unconstitutional by the Iowa Supreme Court at a time when the General

Assembly was in session. Legislators voted a resolution aimed at amending the constitution to provide for authorization and issuance of state bonds, also raised the legal limit of bonded indebtedness of counties for primary road improvements, and encouraged additional counties to vote bonds.

Although the county bond programs were not always supported unanimously, five major east-west highways were surfaced entirely across the state including the Lincoln Highway. Two had been completed north and south including the Jefferson Highway.

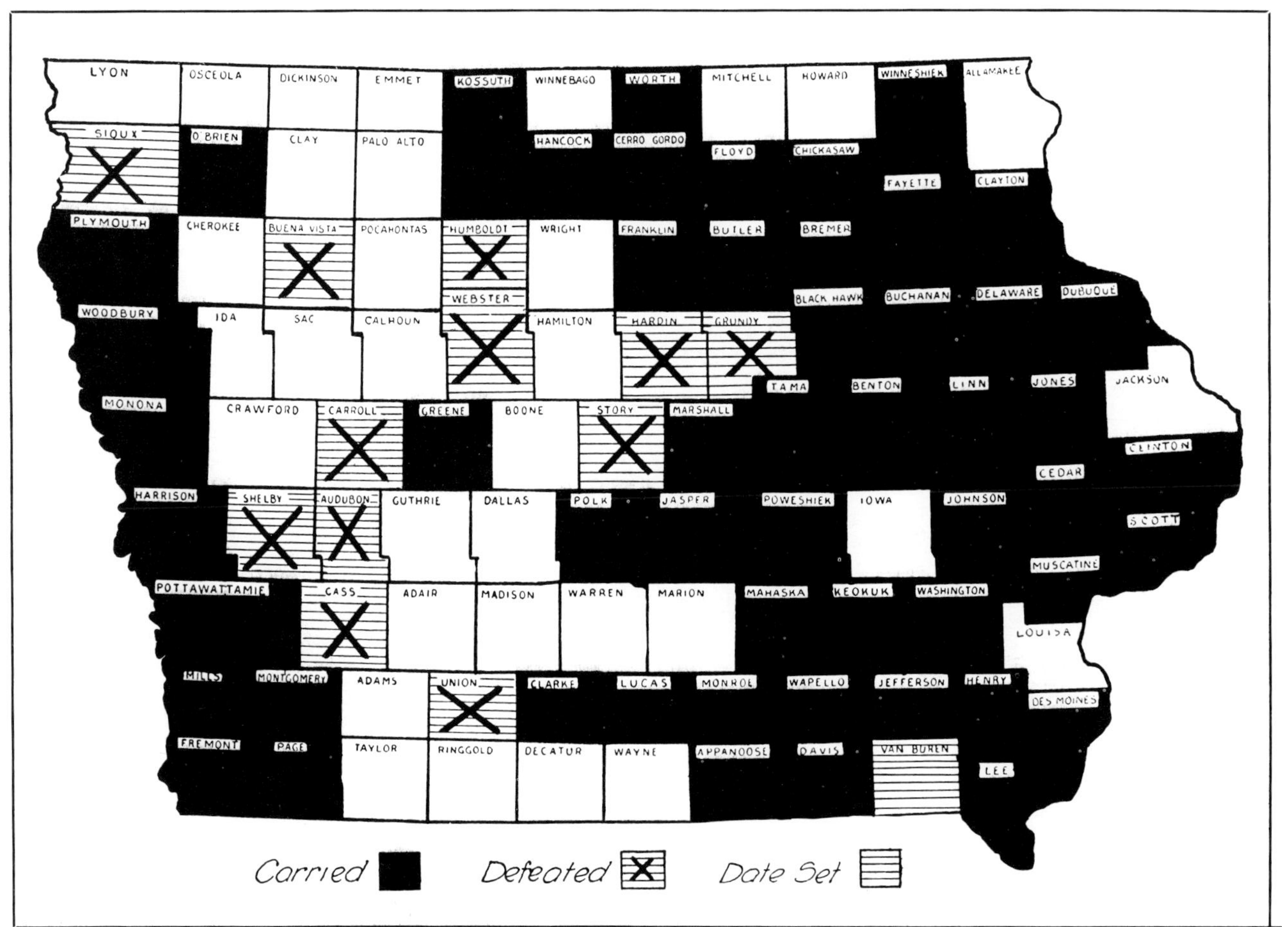

How Iowa Counties Have Voted on Question of Bond Issues for Hard Surfacing of Primary Roads

Figure 7-6
(Source: Iowa State Highway Commission Service Bulletin, 1927)

Highway Safety Measures

Whereas motor vehicle registrations and regulations were under the jurisdiction of the railroad commission, highway safety was the responsibility of the highway commission, and protection of the public was not neglected during the debates on construction and funding. In 1921, legislative and commission directives were issued relative to glaring headlights. No lenses could be legally sold unless tested by the commission and approved by the Attorney General. Plain lenses were banned. Homemade glare-preventing devices had been used for some years and if carefully made or adjusted proved satisfactory. Painting a portion of plain glass to obstruct offending rays of light was most common. Some motorists used froth from foaming beer, smearing it over the glass and allowing it to dry, with good results. Probably putting it there was better than putting it somewhere else. However, this method soon proved obsolete due to a failure in supply.

In 1924, billboards and advertising signs were banned where they interfered with safe views of highways. County supervisors and attorneys were charged with enforcement. From 1916 to 1923, railroad crossing elimination or reduction progressed faster in Iowa than in any other state. Maximum speed limits were set in 1925 at 35 miles per hour, up from the previous 25 mile limit, for vehicles whose weight and load were less than three tons and were equipped with pneumatic tires. The limits then ranged down through 25 miles if the vehicle load and weight was more than three tons, to 16 miles per hour if vehicle and trailer were equipped with two or more metal wheels. The increase to 35 miles per hour followed the general trend in other states, and as a means of speeding up traffic and reducing accidents, motor clubs advocated that highway departments be authorized to designate sections of highways where varying rates of speed were permissible. Experiments on paved versus graveled or earth roads were being conducted in other states on this possibility. In 1926, a black line was painted on every mile of primary road pavement as a reminder that vehicles should be on the right-hand side of the road. The cost of $6.50 per mile was thought to be well spent if the lined highway reduced head-on collisions when cars moved too close to the center of the road.

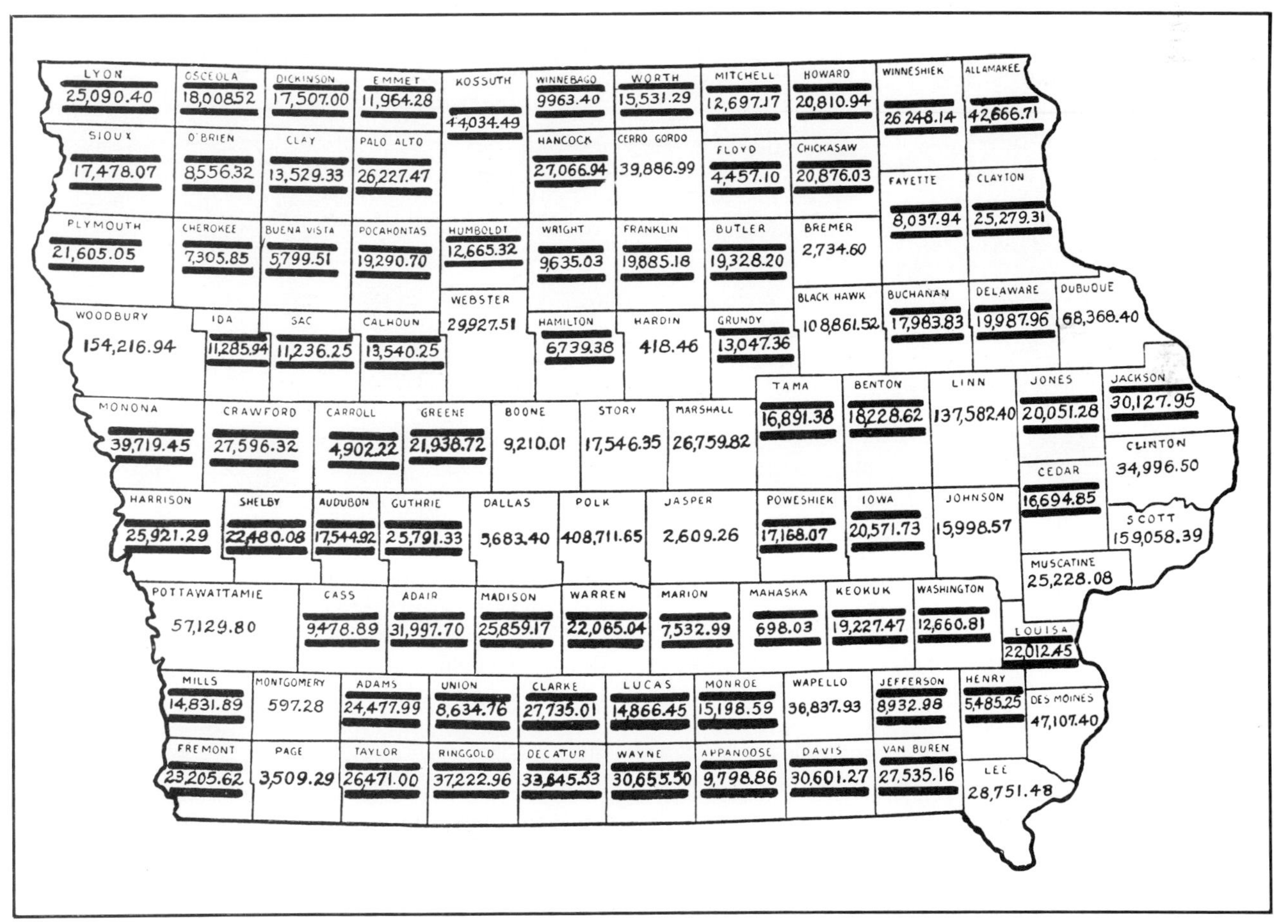

Figure 7-7
Seventy-six counties did not pay their own way on their own primary road system.
(Source: Iowa State Highway Commission Service Bulletin, 1927)

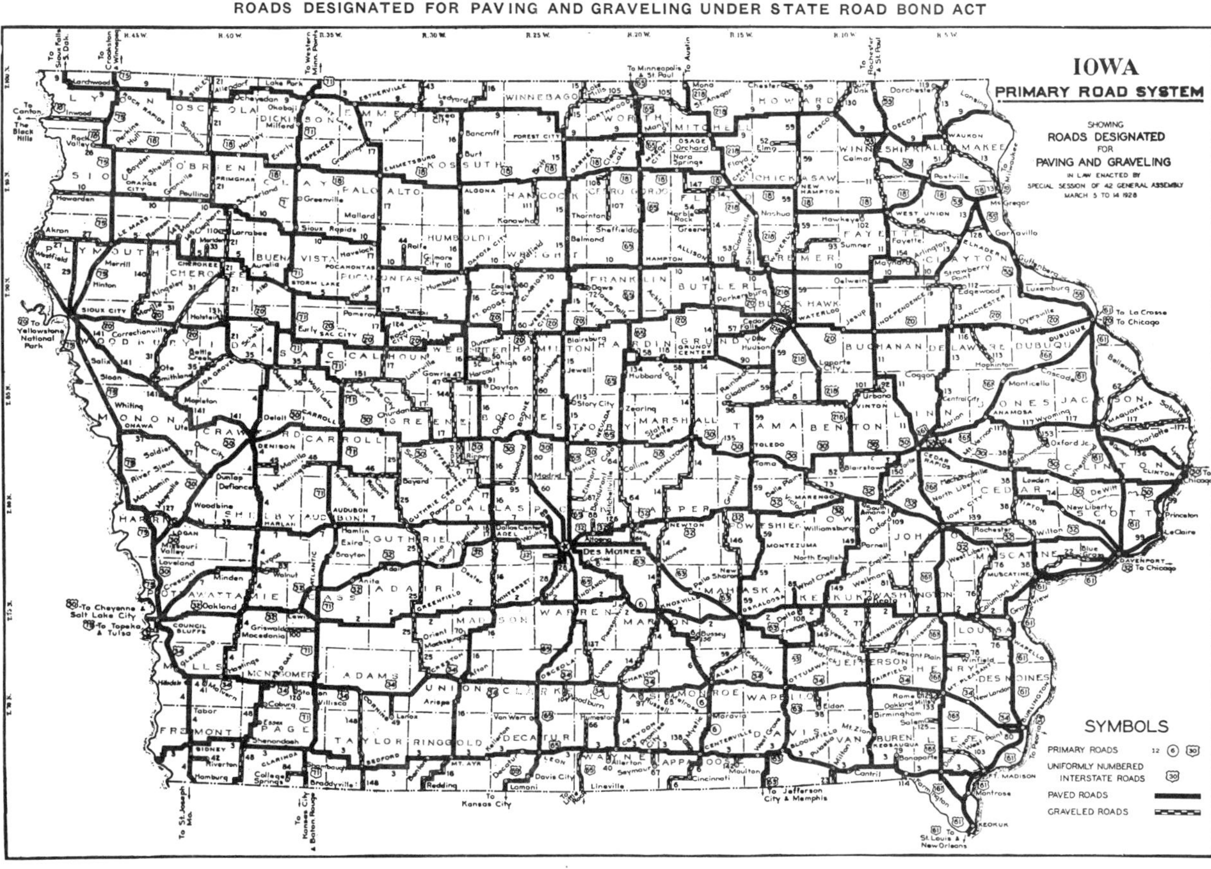

Figure 7-8
(Source: Iowa State Highway Commission Service Bulletin, 1928)

Commercial Air Service

The Iowa City airport was the first in the state to be used for the Chicago-Omaha mail route, initiated in 1920. The first official consignment on January 8 included 400 pounds of mail for Omaha and meat for a banquet in honor of General John Pershing. On the return trip, the plane carried a hog for the Congress Hotel in Chicago, part of the cargo dispatched on the eastern leg of the flight. It was not until May that the first official consignment of airmail reached Iowa City—a motion picture destined for Maquoketa. Iowa City residents hoped that their airport would be chosen as the permanent intermediate point on this route, but Washington authorities instead chose Des Moines. However, construction of a hangar, lighting beacons and the first airport radio station in Iowa made the facility an important landing site on later transcontinental routes. Because of the loss of a federal lease which had been in effect since 1922, it was transformed into a municipal airport in 1929. In 1930, a contract was signed with the Boeing Company, giving them free use of the field in return for financial aid.

Airport Construction

When the first transcontinental airmail flight was scheduled in 1921, Des Moines needed an airport. The impending arrival of planes stirred city officials to select a field at Southwest 30th Street and Vandalia Road. The field was the embryo of the present airport. In the early twenties, there was no legislation covering the funding of airports by cities. However, there was authority to fund "parks" outside city limits. So the field was named the "Des Moines Aviation Park," a romantic title with political overtones. On July 1, 1925, Des Moines was listed as a scheduled stop for the first transcontinental mail plane which landed at the Vandalia field, where The Post Office Band welcomed the flight with the "Iowa Corn Song." But fog and flooding on the original site required location of a new field, and a 160-acre tract near Altoona was leased on the James Hanna farm, eight miles northeast of the city. The field was dedicated in 1927, with Charles Lindberg as the honored guest. A citizens' organization raised $35,000 for a hangar, lighting, grading, drainage and sanitation.

In 1929, the General Assembly acted to allow cities to levy assessments and provide for bond sales to fund municipal airports. Also authorized were the licensing of aircraft and pilots and establishment of air traffic rules. A bond issue was proposed in Des Moines in the 1930 general election and passed by a margin of 1,000 votes, resulting in a sum of $200,000 becoming available for the purchase of land and construction of an airport. After studying some 80 possible locations, the site selected was the 160 acres owned by Truman Jones at southwest 21st Street (now Fleur Drive) and Army Post Road. It was chosen because of its location on a hilltop affording natural drainage and reducing fog to a minimum. It offered a clear approach from all directions, with plenty of space for expansion. A two-lane highway extending four and one-half miles from downtown Des Moines allowed easy accessibility. Actual construction began in 1931 and continued throughout the 1930's.

Postwar enthusiasm for aviation stimulated other Iowa communities to build airports, in part motivated by the Boeing system. By 1931 there were 229 licensed pilots flying 112 airplanes, and 47 airports were registered with the U. S. Department of Commerce. Twenty-two of these were equipped with lighting facilities for night flying, and some of the larger fields had crushed rock runways. The Centerville Airport, opened in 1928, was unique. Its first runway was made from coal shale, mined in the area. It was the only airport in the state, perhaps in the Midwest, which had an orchard and grape arbor and on which cows, sheep and hogs were raised while planes landed and departed (Fig. 7-9) (Table 7-11, 7-12).

Adair, intermediate, lighted
Adel, intermediate, lighted
Algona, auxilliary
Ames, commercial
Atlantic, intermediate, lighted
Battle Creek, commercial
Bedford, municipal
Belle Plaine, commercial
Bloomfield, intermediate, lighted
Boone, commercial
Burlington, municipal
Carroll, commercial
Cedar Rapids, municipal, lighted
Centerville, municipal
Clarinda, commercial
Clinton, commercial, lighted
Cluncil Bluffs, municipal, lighted
Davenport, commercial, lighted
Decorah, auxiliary
Denison, commercial
Des Moines, municipal, lighted
DeWitt, commercial, lighted
Dubuque, municipal
Estherville, municipal
Fort Dodge, commercial
Grand Mound, intermediate, lighted
Grinnell, intermediate, lighted
Ida Grove, municipal
Iowa City, municipal, lighted, surfaced runway
Libertyville, intermediate
Marengo, intermediate, lighted
Mason City, American Legion, municipal
Milford, commercial
Muscatine, municipal, lighted
New Albin, intermediate, lighted
Newton, intermediate, lighted
Oakland, intermediate, lighted
Ottumwa, American Legion, commercial
Rockwell City, municipal
Scranton, auxiliary
Shenandoah, auxiliary
Sidney, intermediate, lighted
Sioux City (Steven's So. Dak.)
Tipton, intermediate, lighted
Waterloo, commercial, lighted
Wesley, commercial
Winfield, intermediate, lighted

* As reported by the U. S. Dept. of Commerce, February 7, 1931.

Figure 7-9
Iowa Airports, February 7, 1931.
Iowa airports registered with the Aeronautics Division of the United States Department of Commerce, with type of airport and equipment.

Airline Service and Routes

Commercial airline service began when a single-engine Boeing mail and passenger biplane carried one person —Jane Eads, a 20-year-old reporter for the Chicago Herald—who flew from Maywood, Illinois to Iowa City in 1927. Boeing was the predecessor of United Air Lines and had been awarded the Chicago-San Francisco air mail route. The passenger was to fly the entire distance. Des Moines was a scheduled stop but was not able to handle night flights, thus the landing at Iowa City. The plane, piloted by Ira A. Biffle of Lincoln, Nebraska, Lindberg's first instructor, flew from Iowa City to Omaha where pilot and plane were changed, and with additional intermediate stops, Miss Eads and the mail arrived in San Francisco about 24 hours later (Fig. 7-10).

Table 7-11

Distances, times and fares from Davenport to selected cities served by the United Air Lines.*

From / To	Davenport-Moline		
	Distance, miles	Time Hours and minutes	Passenger fare
Chicago	152	1:15	$10.00
Kansas City	275	2:35	17.00
Tulsa	492	4:55	29.50
Oklahoma City	601	6:00	36.50
Dallas	813	8:23	46.00

* Data from special report by United Air Lines, July 15, 1931.

The principal lighted route was a section of the Transcontinental Airway from New York to San Francisco. It entered Iowa near Clinton, proceeded southwest and west through Iowa City and Des Moines and left the state near Council Bluffs. Three daily scheduled planes each way were operated by Boeing with regular stops at Iowa City and Des Moines. National Air Transport, a subsidiary of United, flew the lighted airway route from Chicago to Dallas through the Davenport-Moline-Rock Island Airport to St. Joseph and Kansas City. Other subsidiaries of United which began operations in 1926 were Varney Air Lines, Pacific Air Transport and Boeing Air Transport, consolidated in 1928. A third lighted airway from Omaha to Kansas City and St. Louis, flown by American Airways, passed along the east side of the Missouri River near Glenwood and Sidney.

Early Operations

Boeing operated 25 planes, each costing $25,000. The A, B and C models cruised at 105 miles per hour powered by one nine-cylinder, 425-horsepowered Pratt Wasp engine. The company received $1.25 per pound for flying mail the first 1,000 miles, and 15 cents for each additional 100 miles. The first transcontinental flights required about 23 hours and initially carried two passengers and 1,600 pounds of mail. The passenger seats were often reserved for mechanics, but public response made necessary the addition of two more seats which were always sold. In 1930, Boeing began using the 80 and 80A planes from

Table 7-12

Distances, times and fares from Iowa City and Des Moines to selected cities served by the United Air Lines.*

From / To	Iowa City			Des Moines		
	Distance, miles	Time Hours and minutes	Passenger fare	Distance, miles	Time Hours and minutes	Passenger fare
San Francisco	1,828	19:10	$151.50	1,727	18:10	$142.50
Salt Lake City	1,136	12:10	94.00	1,035	11:10	85.00
Omaha	231	2:11	19.50	130	1:11	11.00
Chicago	202	2:15	17.00	303	3:15	25.50
Cleveland	520	7:25	36.75	621	8:25	45.25
New York	938	9:10	76.50	1,039	10:10	85.00

* Davenport is served by the United Air Lines through an airport located at Moline.

the Des Moines airport, the latter type a tri-motored plane with capacity for 18 passengers. The 80A was also the first to use stewardesses who were registered nurses, following the suggestion of Ellen Church, a native of Cresco, who was hired as Chief Stewardess. The women were paid $125 per month. Church resigned after 18 months and resumed her nursing career. During the 1930s a number of Iowa women from Iowa and Des Moines were employed as stewardesses on major airlines.

In 1928, the Des Moines Register and Tribune purchased a five-place Fairchild cabin monoplane, one of eleven used over a 30-year period, and became the first newspaper to own and operate a commercial airplane. It began active service under the name "Good News," selected through a statewide contest in which thousands of people participated. In the first two years of flying, the monoplane became quite familiar in Iowa and neighboring states. It landed at 45 Iowa cities, seven in Missouri, two in Nebraska and one each in Illinois, Minnesota and Wisconsin: 1,114 flights with only four forced landings. The plane was used primarily for news gathering but also promoted interest in and development of aviation whenever possible. The pilot was Charles Gatschet, a veteran flyer who flew the first seven aircraft. George Yates was the photographer and flew in all eleven planes.

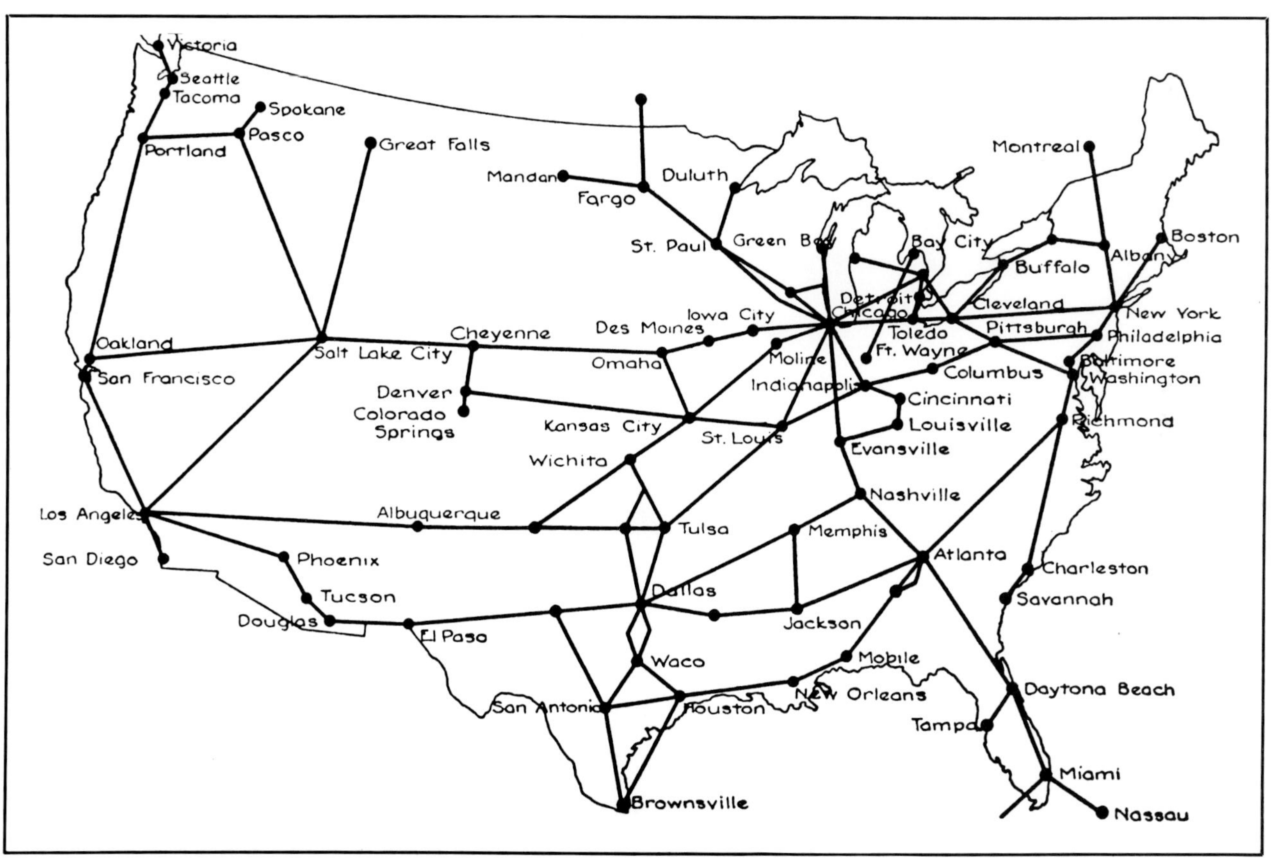

Figure 7-10
Air transportation lines in the United States, mid 1920s.

Boeing Clipper (Model 80A).
(Courtesy: Des Moines International Airport)

Des Moines Register & Tribune "Good News I".
(Courtesy: Des Moines International Airport)

Karen Keen aircraft at Leeds Airport in Sioux City, 1920.
(Courtesy: Sioux City Public Museum)

Revival of River Transportation

The need for a renaissance in inland waterway programs was clearly outlined in the Transportation Act of 1920: "It is hereby declared to be the policy of Congress to promote, encourage and develop water transportation service and facilities in connection with the commerce of the United States and to foster and preserve in full vigor both rail and water transportation."[11]

The Inland Waterways Corporation

In 1924, the Inland Waterways Corporation was created, federally owned, organized and capitalized similar to the railroad companies. It would operate the Federal Barge Service and would attempt to demonstrate to commercial shippers the economic feasibility of river transportation, develop suitable techniques, routes and equipment, and encourage private enterprise to enter water transportation. Despite an expenditure of $175 million on various Mississippi River improvements, by 1924 not one common carrier barge line was operating on the river. Capitalization of the corporation was increased to $15 million and responsibilities expanded by the Denison Act of 1928. The act practically forced the railroads to establish through routes and joint rates with barge lines on the Mississippi and its tributaries. It was repealed by the Transportation Act of 1940, but not before it had developed the rail-barge routes and

[11] 41 Statutes at Large, part 1, section 500 (1920).

rates. The corporation was to continue operations until an adequate navigation channel had been achieved, terminals built and private companies were willing to provide service. Then, the Secretary of War could lease or sell the equipment. The Barge Line was transferred to the Department of Commerce in 1939 and sold to a private corporation in 1953—the Federal Barge Line, Incorporated.

The Federal Barge Line operated only south of St. Louis until 1926 due to shallow water depths and lack of terminals on the Upper Mississippi. This changed, however, when a Minneapolis-St.Paul group formed the Upper Mississippi Barge Line Company and requested service. In 1927, an agreement was reached whereby the private group would build a fleet of towboats and barges to be leased to the corporation and operate north of St. Louis. Three of the towboats were built by the Dubuque Boat and Boiler Works and one, the *S. S. Thorpe,* took three 500-ton barges of sugar to Minneapolis in August, 1927.

The semi-weekly service above St. Louis was unable to handle the demand for cargo space, especially in the grain trade. Traffic rose from 14,061 tons in 1927 to 119,648 tons in 1928. Northbound cargoes consisted of coal, coke, sisal, sugar, coffee, iron products, agricultural implements and bagging and burlap. Southbound, corn, wheat, barley, rye and other agricultural products were the important freight commodities. In 1928, the corporation purchased the leased boats from the Upper Mississippi Barge Line.

Terminals, Towboats and Barges

In addition to navigable channels, proper terminal facilities and suitable floating equipment had to be provided. New terminals were opened at Dubuque and Burlington in 1928. The Dubuque terminal was turned over to the Federal Barge Line, whereas, the Burlington facility was a municipal terminal which could handle most of the commodities shipped on the river. Other Iowa cities had no terminals or limited facilities for handling specialized freight. The third and largest terminal on the eastern border of Iowa was built at Rock Island in 1931, after approval of a bond issue for $300,000. The city had been selected to represent the Quad Cities area by the corporation and was expected to make the region a great industrial center.

By 1928, barges with a 500-ton capacity were redesigned to carry 1,000 tons on the six-foot channel of the Upper Mississippi and 2,000 tons on the nine-foot channel of the lower river. The use of a standard design meant less expensive construction and avoided transshipment at St. Louis. In 1929, three new towboats were built for different sections of the river; 1,000-horsepower boats for the six-foot channel between St.Louis and Minneapolis, more powerful ones for the eight-foot channel between St. Louis and Memphis and larger ones for the lower river to New Orleans. Such towboat names as the *Mark Twain,* the *Huck Finn,* the *James W. Good* and *Patrick J. Hurley* were well known in river movements.

The corporation made meaningful advances in towboat engineering technology, replacing paddle wheels with propellers and steam with diesel engines. Propellers required deeper drafts than were available on the Upper Mississippi so a tunnel stern design was adopted in which the propeller was located inside a spoon-shaped recess on the bottom of the boat, with part actually above the water surface. With the propeller operating, vacuum action filled this tunnel. Another propeller was added for maneuverability in shallow water. These innovations made water transportation more competitive and were quickly adopted by private commercial carriers when they entered river transportation. A 6,000-horsepowered boat could move tows of 40,000 to 50,000 tons as compared to a 6,000-horsepowered locomotive hauling 150 cars of 50 tons for a total of 6,000 tons. In the 1920s and 1930s, the corporation was the only source of technological innovations in water transportation.

Missouri River Developments

Progress toward development of a navigable channel on the Missouri was slow despite the fact that by the 1920s, water transportation was generally considered economically viable for commercial traffic. In 1927, Congress ordered a study of a possible nine-foot channel from St. Louis to Kansas City. Congress also directed that a comprehensive examination of river use, including flood control and navigation, be undertaken in the late 1920s. From 1900 to 1927, five severe floods had occurred on the Missouri and more would occur in later years. The result of the study was the start of construction of the Fort Peck Dam in 1933, located about 175 miles north of Bismark, North Dakota.

Summary

Railroads, aided by federal legislation in 1920 which returned them to private ownership and resulted in changes in regulatory policy, recovered fairly rapidly from their wartime experience. During the decade, mileages operated in Iowa remained relatively constant, freight revenues and earnings showed steady growth, but passenger traffic fell as the result of highway competition. The depressed agricultural sector, further impaired by large increases in freight rates, detracted from the general prosperity of the state and was responsible for congressional action for relief through rate adjustments. The challenge to the railroads was not confined exclusively to highway rivalry but also to air and water transportation development sponsored and supported by federal legislation.

While these circumstances and conditions were important to Iowa, they were not the overriding issues facing the state. "Getting out of the mud" was the principal problem to be addressed and was the focus of highway interests and legislators. Despite the fact that Iowa lagged behind other Midwestern states in permanent highway improvements, Iowans bought automobiles in record numbers, and motor buses and trucks appeared by the hundreds. To alleviate confusion, commercial vehicles were controlled and supervised by the railroad commission and for motorist convenience, primary roads were marked by state and federal standardized symbols and numbers. The basic policy question centered upon planning and financing decisions to speed construction of hard-surfaced highways. Voiding of a state bonding plan by the Iowa Supreme Court spurred counties to greater efforts for primary road funding and improvements.

Commercial air service began with airmail and passenger traffic at the Iowa City and Des Moines airports, both of which were on transcontinental routes. River transportation on the Mississippi was revived by creation of the Inland Waterways Corporation which operated the Federal Barge Service. On the Missouri, studies concerning channel depths as well as river use for flood control and navigation were underway and would provide the basis for further river control.

Selected References

"An Industrial Message to Congress." *Engineering News Record* (December 14, 1922):p. 106.

Bird, Jeffrey L. "History of the Des Moines Municipal Airport, January 20, 1977" Manuscript [photocopy]. Des Moines International Airport Aviation Department, Des Moines.

Board of the Railroad Commission. *Annual Reports* for the years 1921, 1926, 1927, 1929, 1930. Des Moines: State Printing Office.

Brown, D. Clayton. *Western Tributaries of the Mississippi.* National Waterways Study, Navigation History, NWS-83-7. Washington,D.C.: U.S. Government Printing Office, 1983.

Bryan, Leslie H. *Principles of Water Transportation.* New York: The Ronald Press, 1939.

Class Rate Investigation. 262 ICC 447 (1949).

Daggett, Stuart. *Principles of Inland Transportation.* 4th ed. New York: Harper & Bros., 1955.

Fitzpatrick, John. *Wings Over Iowa.* Sgt. Bluff, Ia.: Wings Over Tomorrow, 1979.

Hoadley, Ruth E. *Industrial Growth in Iowa.* Iowa City: Bureau of Business Research, July, 1930.

Increased Rates. 58 ICC 220 (1920).

Iowa State Highway Commission. *Report of the State Highway Commission for the Year Ending December 1, 1929.* Des Moines: State of Iowa, 1929.

Iowa State Highway Commission Service Bulletin 6 (1915): p. 7; See also *Bulletins* for the years 1920-1927.

1923 Laws of Iowa, Chapter 27.

1929 Laws of Iowa, Chapter 129.

LemMon, Jean, ed. *50th Anniversary of the Des Moines Municipal Airport.* Des Moines: City of Des Moines and the Greater Des Moines Chamber of Commerce Federation, 1980.

Leonard, William R. "Effects of Highway Competition on Railroads." Ph.D. diss., Cornell University, Ithaca, New York, 1934.

McFall, Albert J. "The Farm Income Situation." *Annals of the American Academy of Political and Social Science 117* (1925): pp. 20-21.

National Livestock Shippers League v. A.T. & SFR. R. Co. 63 ICC 107 (1921).

Petersen, William J. "The Iowa City Airport." *Palimpsest 11* (September 1930): pp. 405-415.

______. *The Story of Iowa.* New York: Lewis Historical Publishing Co., 1952.

"Railroad Revival." *Engineering News Record* (January 5, 1921): p. 4.

Rates on Grain, Grain Products and Hay. 61 ICC 85 (1921).

Ross, Earle D. *Iowa Agriculture: An Historical Survey. Iowa City: State Historical Society, 1951.*

Sharfman, I. L. *The Interstate Commerce Commission.* New York: Commonwealth Fund, 1931.

State of Iowa 1931-32 Official Register, Thirty-Fourth Number. Des Moines: The State of Iowa, 1932.

Tweet, Roald D. *History of Transportation on the Upper Mississippi & Illinois Rivers.* National Waterways Study, Navigation History NWS-83-6. Washington, D.C.: U.S. Government Printing Office, 1983.

U.S. Department of Transportation, Federal Highway Administration. *America's Highways 1776/1976.* Washington, D.C.: U.S. Government Printing Office, 1976.

Waymack, W. W."Good News." *Palimpsest 11* (September 1930): pp. 398-403.

Chapter Eight
The 1930s—Depression and its Aftermath

Introduction

By 1930, population distribution in Iowa was more rural than urban, but the state had moved to a fairly even balance between the values of agricultural and manufacturing production. However, the depression hit hard on farming communities which had never really recovered from the distress of post World War I years. Depressed economic conditions and intense highway competition combined to force many of the railroads into receivership and subsequent reorganization. Federal emergency aid for both agriculture and the railroads was moderately successful and also instrumental in supporting the states in their continuing programs for highway development. Permanent federal legislation brought a portion of the motor and air carrier industries under regulation and eased some of the previous regulations on railroads. Pipelines made their appearance in Iowa in the early thirties, and inland water transportation was stimulated by the building of locks and dams on the Mississippi River for the purpose of standardizing channel depths and promoting a rebirth in waterborne commerce. Private, business and commercial aviation expanded, substantial increases in pilots were recorded and Iowa-based airlines began operations. There were pressures for new municipal airports, expansion of existing ones and construction of airport facilities.

National Economic Indicators and A Profile of Iowa in 1930

Evidence of a slowing of economic activity throughout the nation occurred in the construction industry during the late twenties, and by the summer of 1929, related industries such as steel, cement and lumber were reducing output. Even though ominous signs were beginning to appear, the automobile industry which had paced the prosperity of the 1920s produced 5.33 million cars in 1929. By 1932, output dropped to 1.33 million, idling thousands of workers. Nationally, unemployment increased from 1.5 million in 1929 to over 12 million or 25 percent of the work force in 1933. The gross national product fell from its 1929 high of $103.4 billion to $55.8 billion in 1933.

The population of Iowa was 2,470,939 people, approximately 67,000 more than in 1920, distributed as 60 percent rural and 40 percent urban. The state had 213,993 farms averaging 160 acres each. Nineteen cities had 10,000 or more residents; between 5,000 and 10,000 people inhabited 16 cities; and 31 cities had populations ranging from 3,000 to 5,000. Steam and electric interurban railways operated 10,175 miles of track, and motor vehicles ran over 101,801 miles of roads and highways. The Iowa Bureau of Labor in 1928 listed 4,578 manufacturing plants located in 645 cities and towns. The number was greater than was found in the 1930 Census, which included only firms with an output of $5,000 or more, while the Iowa Directory covered all plants fabricating products on a factory basis. The Iowa Census of 1925 gave total farm income of 10 major products as $659.3 million; for manufacturers, $757 million. However, at least five of the leading manufacturing industries were agriculturally related. There was a fairly even geographical distribution of cities and towns in the state, served by excellent railroad facilities and an increasing number of hard-surfaced roads and highways.

The Crisis in Agriculture

Agricultural shipments comprised a considerable amount of revenue traffic for the railroads and to a degree, for the fledgling trucking industry. Thus the economic conditions in the farming communities were more than a passing interest, especially to the "Granger Railroads" in the state. The devastation of financial catastrophe suffered through the excesses of World War I production and the deflated price levels of the 1920s showed clearly in the 1930s. Between 1926 and 1931, one farmer in every seven lost his land. In addition, 58 percent of the 111,333 farms operated by private owners were mortgaged. In 1930, each farmer paid an average of $1.31 per acre in real estate taxes and carried a debt of $9,626.

The index of farm prices dropped from 200 in 1920 to 55 in 1932 and reached an all-time low of 40 in January, 1933. Cash farm income fell from $660 million in 1929 to $277 million in 1932. During the period, interest and principal payments on mortgages remained constant; taxes were slightly lower while machinery costs and freight rates were relatively high. Drought accentuated financial problems in 1930, 1934, and 1936. Land values tended to stabilize by 1930 at 25 to 30 percent over prewar averages but in 1933 fell to 75 to 80 percent of previous levels. By 1932, 600 banks had suspended operations, 200 of the failures occurring in 1931. Corn, the largest money crop, dropped from $1.51 per bushel in 1919 to $.70 in 1925 and $.32 in 1931 and was still falling. The continuing depression with no immediate relief from the mounting burdens of debts and taxes "precipitated an agrarian uprising of a degree and persistence never before experienced in this state of conservative enterprise."[1] A "Cow War" resulted from a misunderstading of tuberculin testing of cattle in southeastern counties. The "Milk War" in northwestern Iowa and a "Farm Holiday Movement" with demonstrations against the insensitivities of local and national authorities followed. There were buying, selling and taxpaying strikes, and picketing against farm foreclosures.

The national elections of 1932 turned around historical political traditions of the state with agricultural problems a major issue. For the first time since Iowa began to vote Republican in 1856, state and national Democratic candidates were swept into office. Six of nine Democratic congressmen were elected, one of the most notable being Guy M. Gillette of Cherokee, later elected to the Senate. Louis Murphy from Dubuque captured the Senate seat, and Republican Governor Dan Turner was replaced by Clyde Herring.

The farm emergency was recognized and dealt with rather promptly and with some effectiveness. Henry A. Wallace was appointed Secretary of Agriculture, and programs were introduced for crop control, preservation of bank deposits, extension of credit and delay in farm foreclosures. The Agricultural Adjustment Act was passed in 1933 with the avowed aim of raising purchasing power to that of the 1909-1913 period, the climax of the "golden years of agriculture." The legislation offered voluntary compliance by farmers to reduce acreage planted and litters of pigs farrowed. In return, they would receive payments for land idled and a flat rate per head for hog reduction. The act was declared unconstitional by the U. S. Supreme Court in 1936 on grounds that it involved regulation and control of production that belonged exclusively to the states, and a tax on processing was considered an illegal use of taxing powers. New legislation in 1936 and 1938 brought together other programs for soil conservation, balanced output, crop loans, marketing agreements, crop insurance and rural security.

Depression Hits the Railroads

During their history, railroads had faced and weathered severe economic depressions or "panics," particularly in 1873, 1903 and 1907. The industry had always been able to recover rather quickly because it was the only transportation mode available when national production revived. The 1930's were different. This time, railroads faced tough and resourceful competition, ready to move traffic quickly and cheaply. The 1921 truck of one-ton capacity offered little challenge to the freight car moving almost 40 tons. But freight rate increases in the twenties, federal and state expenditures on highway development, and advanced technology in manufacturing brought thousands of trucks with higher tonnage capabilities into the nation's transportation arena.

The first four years of the 1930s were a financial disaster for American railroads. Net income fell from $809 million to a deficit of $16.8 million between 1926 and 1934. Weekly carloadings, which had ranged from 800,000 to almost one million in 1930, fell to about 550,000 in 1932, a year when railroads representing 72 percent of the national mileage failed to earn their fixed charges. Such a record would have ordinarily required receivership pending revision of capital structures, but for most railroads this was avoided through loans from the Reconstruction Finance (RFC) and Railroad Credit Corporations. The first was a federal agency formed to extend credit to banks and industries; the second, a railroad corporation organized to grant loans to distressed carriers from funds generated by the emergency freight rate increases of 1931. Despite these efforts, by 1933, 38 of 147 Class I roads had petitioned for receivership or bankruptcy, representing 31 percent of the mileage and 24 percent of the industry's capital investment.

Economic Problems of Iowa Railroads

By 1931, it was obvious that Iowa railroads were going to bear their share of the national depression. Between 1930 and 1939, mileage operated by steam railroads declined by 650 miles, net earnings by approximately $10 million, and earnings per mile by over $900. Revenue freight of agricultural products fell by 21 percent; animals and products, 27 percent;

[1] Earle D. Ross, *Iowa Agriculture, An Historical Survey*, Iowa City: State Historical Society of Iowa, 1951, p. 164.

products of mines, 47 percent; forest products increased .07 percent; manufactures and miscellaneous traffic declined by 14 percent and less-than-carloadings were off 57 percent. Operational trends of railroads system-wide and in Iowa are shown in Table 8-1.

Operating ratios were rather respectable throughout the decade as serious attempts were made to reduce operating expenses when revenues declined. However, deterioration in passenger service by 1939 resulted in operating ratios ranging from a high of 183 percent for the M&StL to a low of 118 percent for the IC. Wages and salaries amounted to a substantial part of operating expenses, normally constituting over 50 percent. About $95 million was saved by system-wide furloughing of approximately 80,000 workers between 1930 and 1939, and those employed, voluntarily took a temporary cut of 10 percent in wages between 1932 and 1934.

Depression probably speeded abandonments although economic conditions were not the only reason. Others included disappearance of the traffic for which the lines were originally built, or relocation of economic activity. For example, 81 miles were abandoned through exhaustion of coal mining, and the Tabor and Northern ceased operations when Tabor College closed. Far more important was the competition of motor vehicles. In 80 percent of the abandonments between 1920 and 1940, and for about one-third of the mileage abandoned between 1930 and 1940, this type of competition was cited as the sole cause of the lines' unprofitability. The highest percentage of mileage abandoned was in the eastern and central counties and averaged about 15 miles on branch lines.

The primary cause of the railroads' difficulties lay in the heavy load of fixed charges, consisting of interest on funded debt, taxes, rentals of equipment and leasing of lines. System-wide, unfunded debt was approximately $2.8 billion in the 1930s, a substantial amount which was incurred in the road and equipment improvements of the 1920s. From 1936 to 1939, the CMStP&P, CNW, CRI&P, M&StL and Wabash showed deficits in income after payments of fixed charges. The CGW joined the group in 1938 and 1939.

Table 8-1
Comparison of System and Iowa Railroad Operating and Financial Conditions for Selected Years in the 1930s

	1930		1933		1939	
Account	**System**	**Iowa**	**System**	**Iowa**	**System**	**Iowa**
Mileage[1]	61,193	9,668	61,013	9,531	71,239	9,078
Op. Rev.[2]	$1,176.1	$132.4	$671.6	$77.2	$967.3	$93.5
Op. Exp.[2]	$ 863.6	$104.8	$496.0	$61.6	$744.4	$76.0
Net. Rev.[2]	$ 312.5	$ 27.6	$175.6	$16.6	$234.9	$17.5
Op. Ratio %	73.4	79.2	73.9	79.3	75.8	81.3
Frt. Rev.[2,3]	$ 925.6	$107.4	$549.5	$66.3	$792.5	$78.8
Pass. Rev.[2,3]	$ 139.8	$ 13.6	$ 60.1	$ 5.2	$ 89.5	$ 7.7
Employees	321.369	N/A	201,445	N/A	240,925	N/A
Payroll[2]	$ 544.6	N/A	$303.7	N/A	$459.7	N/A

(*Source:* Iowa Railroad Commission, *Annual Reports,* 1931, 1934. Iowa Commerce Commission, *Annual Report,* 1940.)

[1] Miles of road owned, single track.

[2] In millions of dollars, rounded to nearest unit.

[3] Passenger and Freight revenues will not add to total Operating Revenues. Omitted from the Table are the "Other Revenue Accounts."

Bankruptcies and Reorganizations

On June 28, 1935, CNW president Fred Sargent filed a petition for bankruptcy after defaulting on the payment of interest and principal on bonds maturing that year. The reorganization took nine years before being approved by the U. S. Supreme Court in 1944.[2] The dividend-happy CRI&P had a deficit after taxes and interest of over $386,000 in 1931, having suffered the lowest gross revenues since 1917. Despite borrowing from the RFC in 1932 and 1933, which took all available collateral, the outlook was dismal. In 1934, the road faced maturities of more than $144 million and with borrowing power ended, the CRI&P filed for reorganization on June 7. For the second time in 31 years, a cycle that began with the Reid-Moore syndicate completed the devastation and the "sprawling Rock Island was desperately ailing in weeds, dust and cinders."[3]

Here was a prime example of a situation that should have been crystal clear to the ICC and railroad managements—namely, that no railroad could survive Eastern investment strategy when management had little or no interest in operations except for the dividends and interest that could be obtained from their securities. The CMStP&P staved off bankruptcy until 1935 but then succumbed and requested reorganization for the second time in 10 years. The CGW went into bankruptcy in 1935 and was reorganized in 1941. Reorganization of the Wabash occurred in 1942.

Two of the railroads operating in Iowa managed to weather the economic storm, although it was touch and go for both in the early thirties. In 1931, when no one dared speculate on the immediate future of the railroads, Ralph Budd, born on a farm near Waterloo, was elected president of the CB&Q. Graduated from Highland Park College in Des Moines in 1899 with a degree in Civil Engineering, he worked through engineering and administrative positions on the CGW, CRI&P, Panama, and Spokane, Portland and Seattle roads to the presidency of the GN before taking over as chief admistrative officer of the CB&Q. Budd was opposed to borrowing from the RFC. He concluded that wages, then 64 percent of operating expenses, were the important factor to be considered in recovery of earning power. The agreement with labor over the 10 percent reduction in wages was to expire in one year, but negotiations extended it to 1933, with stipulations that further changes in wage scales might be made. Through the compromise, wages were stabilized for a period sufficiently long enough to enable further study toward solutions to the deepening crisis. Budd was also convinced that further expansion of freight service would prove difficult in view of truck competition. The only other source of revenue was through passenger service to which he turned in spite of the declining trend since the mid-1920s. Stating that the demand curve would be elastic if passenger trains offered fast, clean and cheap service, he experimented with stainless steel gas-electric powered cars and lightweight trains which were the prototypes of the famed Burlington Zephrs.

During the fall of 1932, revenues on the CB&Q would not cover fixed charges, but by mid-1933, earnings were more than $300,000 over these expenses. The interim period was marked by a partial recovery of freight traffic, increased passenger movements, and a further extension of the labor agreement to 1934. Overton states that: "In retrospect, then, the six weeks between late March and early May, 1933, marked the turning point in the company's fortunes . . . Not until business became stimulated by the threat of World War II did the revenues approach the 1931 level, and in the meantime some of the proposed remedies for the depression proved worse than the disease."[4] Except for 1935, net income from 1933 to 1940 ranged between $3.6 and $5.5 million, a far more impressive record than that of the CB&Q's competitors. The railroad stayed in the "black" but with little to spare.

The relatively stable and satisfactory financial condition of the IC during the 1920s, when earnings allowed a seven percent dividend on common and six percent on preferred stock, came to an abrupt end in 1931. Drastic economies were instituted, maintenance of road and equipment deferred, train operations curtailed, including discontinuance of the pride of the passenger fleet—the *Panama Limited*—and payrolls reduced. Net income dropped from $9.3 million to a

[2] Reorganization proposals are found in *Traffic World,* November 16, 1935, September 16, 1936, and May 29, 1937. A merger proposal between the CNW and the CMSTP&P is discussed in *Railway Age,* August 21, 1938.

[3] William Edward Hayes, *Iron Road to Empire, The History of 100 Years of the Progress and Achievements of the Rock Island Lines,* New York: Simmons-Boardman, 1953, p. 221.

[4] Richard C. Overton, *Burlington Route, A History of the Burlington Lines,* New York: Alfred H. Knopf, 1965, p. 382.

$3.6 million deficit in 1931, and for the first time since 1859, management passed the common stock dividend. By 1933, total operating revenues had fallen 51 percent below the 1929 level, employment was cut by 50 percent, and indebtedness represented the heaviest burden in the railroad's history. The deficits brought the road to the brink of bankruptcy, so close that legal papers were ready for filing at an hour's notice. However, a strong and alert board of directors, efficient administrative officers and the cooperation of employees and stockholders pulled the railroad through the emergency.

The Chicago World's Fair of 1933-1934 was scheduled at an opportune time, materially increasing passenger revenues for all railroads serving the city. As in 1893, the IC provided the principal service, operating over 19,000 extra suburban trains which carried almost four million fairbound passengers over the two-year period. Loans obtained from the RFC and the Public Works Administration were paid in full by 1943. A resourceful management, headed by a new president, John L. Bevin, had prepared the railroad for the sharp upturn in traffic which came by 1939.

Economic Problems for the Electric Interurbans

The experiences of the interurbans paralleled those of the steam railroads, except that they were more vulnerable to commercial motor carrier and automobile competition on relatively short line operations. Table 8-2 shows the trends:

Table 8-2
Operational Conditions of the Electric Interurbans During Selected Years in the 1930s

Account	1930	1933	1939
Mileage[1]	647	618	564
Op. Rev.[2]	$3.93	$ 2.04	$3.46
Op. Exp.[2]	$3.42	$ 2.22	$2.85
Net Rev.[2]	$0.51	$-0.18	$0.39
Op. Ratio %	87.0	108.6	82.3
Frt. Rev.[2]	$2.92	$ 1.60	$2.80
Pass. Rev.[3]	$ 709	$ 262	$ 394
Funded Debt Unpaid	$1.70	$ 2.30	$8.90

(*Source:* Iowa Railroad Commission, *Annual Reports,* 1931, 1934. Iowa Commerce Commission, *Annual Report,* 1940.)

[1] Mileage includes all tracks.

[2] In millions of dollars, rounded to the nearest unit.

[3] In thousands of dollars, rounded to the nearest unit.

There was a slight decline in mileage operated during the decade through abandonments. In the critical period, 1930-1933, operating revenues dropped by 48 percent, passenger revenues by 63 percent, and freight revenues by 45 percent. However, the decline in operating expenses did not equal that of revenues, resulting in an operating ratio of 108 percent in 1933. Except for the Crandic lines and the Tama and Toledo, every interurban suffered a deficit in income. Even with a modest recovery from 1933 to 1940, passenger revenues never returned to their previous levels, ending the decade approximately 45 percent below the 1930 figures. Freight revenues, however, showed a remarkable increase over the low of 1933, and by 1939 were only slightly below the volume in 1930. Net income from all operations fell into a deficit position in 1940. The key to financial distress, similar to that of steam railroads, was the amount of unfunded debt unpaid, increasing from $1.7 million in 1930 to $8.9 million in 1940.

Bus service on the FtD,DM&S was substituted for trains on branch lines as early as 1926 and through a subsidiary in 1927 which ran from Des Moines via Ames to Fort Dodge. The bus company was sold to Interstate Transit Lines, a subsidiary of CNW, in 1931. The interurban went into receivership and was operated under a trustee until 1943, when it was returned to private control and incorporated as an Iowa corporation, using the same company title. During the receivership period several operational changes were made. Parlor car service ended in the winter of 1931-1932. By 1935, only two daily round trips were scheduled between Des Moines and Fort Dodge, and operations over street trackage ended in Des Moines in 1938 and in Fort Dodge in 1940. In the World War II years, service expanded to four daily round trips but returned to former schedules by 1950.

On June 20, 1932, the Crandic road merged with the new Iowa Electric Light and Power Company. The service remained popular in the thirties with eight daily round trips between Cedar Rapids and Iowa City. In 1938, the railway moved 16,800 cars, representing a traffic density of 616 cars per mile, surpassing the record of many steam railroads. The bus and automobile slowed passenger traffic, which was to have a last reprieve during World War II. The well-managed road had the second lowest operating ratio (62 percent) of any of the interurbans in 1939.

The trend toward substitution of motor buses, reduction of passenger trains and abandonment of service was common in the operation of other interurbans. A few examples will suffice. The Cedar Valley line had reduced service by 1936 to three round trips daily from Waterloo to Cedar Rapids, a substantial change from the dozen round trips when the line opened. The Clinton, Davenport and Muscatine, primarily a freight carrier in its last days, abandoned passenger and freight service on the Muscatine Division in 1938 and on the Clinton Division in 1940. The Des Moines and Central Iowa cut service on the Colfax Division to three daily round trips, but the road received a new lease on life when Camp Dodge was reactivated in the war years. Some trackage on the Mason City and Clear Lake was abandoned in 1931, and street railway franchises in both cities expired in 1935.

Pre- and Postwar Streamlined Passenger Trains.

Probably the most glamorous period of railroad passenger service in Iowa began in the 1930s and 1940s with the introduction of the dieselized lightweight streamlined passenger trains. It ended in the 1960s. Aluminum and its alloys replaced steel, reducing weight without sacrificing strength in car construction. By rounding at the end and at roof lines, the trains were given the appearance of sleek speed attractive to the public. Bright and distinctive colors were used in contrast to the dull and drab green of older cars. Air-conditioning, reclining seats and adjustable footrests in coaches, luxurious appointments and private accommodations in sleepers, vista domes, buffet, lounge and parlor cars, and improved dining arrangements made long distance travel a comfortable experience.[5]

The Burlington Zephyrs

In 1934 the CB&Q tested a three-car articulated streamlined train on a non-stop trial run from Denver to Chicago, covering roughly 1,000 miles in 14 hours. The regular steam schedule was 26 hours, and no locomotive had run non-stop for more than 775 miles up to this time. By averaging 2.77 miles per gallon of fuel priced at four cents, the fuel cost for the trip was $14.64. Maximum speeds ranged up to 112 miles per hour. This pioneer train went into regular service to Kansas City, Omaha and Lincoln shortly thereafter and was followed by other *Zephyrs* on regional routes. The *Zephyr Rocket* was the first north-south streamliner between St. Louis and the Twin Cities, jointly operated by the CB&Q and CRI&P. But the most famous and popular streamliner was the *California Zephyr,* a $2 million, 12-car vista-domed train which started in 1949 on a daily schedule from Chicago to Oakland (San Francisco) over a scenic route through the Rocky Mountains and down the Feather River Canyon in California. The train was later selected to operate on the AMTRAK route across southern Iowa.

The Northwestern's Cities

Under joint arrangement with the UP, the CNW was the first to offer coach-pullman streamlined transcontinental service when on June 8, 1935, the *City of Portland* made its maiden trip from Chicago. It stopped at six stations in Iowa, covering the 347 miles across the state in five hours and 45 minutes as compared with the 13-hour schedule of local trains. The 13-car train was painted a brilliant yellow with red stripes and cost $1.6 million to build. In 1937 three additional trains, the *San Francisco, Los Angeles,* and *Denver,* began operating on an every third day basis, expanding to daily schedules in the early 1940's. Into the mid-1950's one could stand at the CNW's mainline stations and watch the parade of giant diesels pulling the yellow cars, knowing that if one train were missed, another would be along in a relatively short time. There were seven of them, beginning with the *Denver* and ending with the steam-operated *Gold Coast.* By 1951, 14 CNW streamliners served Iowa.

The Rock Island Rockets

The CRI&P was the third road to initiate streamlined passenger trains in Iowa. The "Rockets," named after the first locomotive, started operations in 1937 from Chicago to Peoria and to Des Moines and were followed by the *Kansas City, Twin Cities,* and *Rocky Mountain* Rockets in 1939. The *Twin Star* and *Corn Belt* made their initial runs in 1946 and 1947. The former operated between Minnesota and Texas, which became known as the longest north-south route in the nation. East-west schedules were run by the *Golden State, Imperial,* and *Columbian,* allowing

[5] In 1923, Sam Felton of the CGW streamlined a Pacific-type locomotive which pulled the four-car *Red Bird* from the Twin Cities to Rochester, Minnesota. Six years later, the gasoline-electric *Blue Bird* was put into service with a rounded-end observation and club car. Frank P. Donovan, Jr., "The Chicago Great Western Railway," *Palimpsest 34* No. 6 (June 1953): pp. 276-277.

passengers a wide selection of departure times and different accommodations. The *Columbian* was unique in that it furnished stewardess-nurses and featured "economy meals," at 25 cents for breakfast, 30 cents for lunch and 35 cents for dinner. The CRI&P was the only Iowa railroad which had both north-south and east-west transcontinental service.

Donovan described the CRI&P as celebrated in "story, song, motion picture and drama until it became an institution in Iowa." James Norman Hall of Colfax, co-author of *Mutiny on the Bounty,* loved railroads and recounted his experiences on the main line in his autobiography, *My Island Home,* and in *Under a Thatched Roof.* "The Rock Island Line" was a popular song among work gangs. *Rock Island Trails,* a Republic motion picture in 1950, recorded the history of the lines' westward movement. Still popular to stage and screen audiences is Meredith Willson's, *The Music Man,* who came to River City (Mason City) on a CRI&P train to organize the town band. Excursion and special trains were scheduled for racing enthusiasts to watch the trotters and pacers at Rush Park in Independence. Football extras carried record crowds to Iowa City on Saturdays, a tradition that stretched over three generations of University of Iowa graduates and fans.

Burlington's *California Zephyr* coach.
(Courtesy: Iowa State Historical Society)

CNW observation car of the *City of San Francisco.*
(Courtesy: Iowa State Historical Society)

The Milwaukee Hiawathas and Other Streamliners

The *Midwest Hiawatha* started in 1940 between Chicago and Omaha. At Manilla, in Crawford County, the train was divided into two sections, one moving northwest to Sioux City and Sioux Falls and the other to Omaha. Seven years later, the *Olympian* began regular service to Seattle and Tacoma, making the trip in 45 hours. The former transcontinental *Olympian* continued service under the name *Columbian.*

The *Land of Corn* on the IC was inaugurated in 1947 from Chicago to Waterloo. It was one of eight diesel-powered streamliners operated by the railroad; the others running on north-south routes. The AT&SF furnished streamlined service throughout the southwestern United States to Iowa residents via *Chief* and *Super-Chief* which entered the state northwest of Keokuk, angled northeast to Fort Madison and continued to Chicago (Fig. 8-1).

Rock Island Rocket.
(Courtesy: Iowa State Historical Society)

Streamliners and Passenger Revenues

How much difference did these trains make in passenger revenues? On the CNW, by 1937-1938 they produced an increase of 22 percent over revenues of 1935. From an all-time low of $6.7 million in 1933, some 60 percent of the 1931 revenues, the CB&Q recorded an 18 percent increase in 1936 and in 1937, and revenues represented the highest earned in a decade. The "Rockets" returned $46 million, or 734 percent of the $6.6 million invested. The best paying train was the *Des Moines Rocket* which had expenses of $.51 and net revenues of $1.39 per mile in 1939. There seemed to be little question that the streamliners of the 1930s were a financial success.

Congress Acts to Meet the Railroad Emergency

In 1933, new procedures for financial reorganization of the carriers were enacted through addition of Section 77 to the Bankruptcy Act of 1898, amended further in 1935. Its objective was to reduce delays in reorganization, provide for a more sound and realistic capital structure and to overcome objections to previous reorganization plans. The new Federal Administration had pledged to reduce enforcement of competition between railroads and support consolidations, somewhat reversing historic regulatory policy. This proposal was not new, having been incorporated into the Act of 1920, but the economic circumstances were significantly different by 1933, and certain conditions written into the 1920 legislation suggesting consolidation were apparently to be eased.

A Transportation Commission created in the previous administration reported in February, 1933, that "parallel lines and systems" are wasteful and unnecessary; that regional consolidation should be hastened. Also, that railroads themselves should cooperate to reduce competitive expenses and that the rule of rate-making which established a "fair return" percentage in 1920 should be reversed. These recommendations and the influence of the work of earlier congressional committees formed the background of the Emergency Transportation Act of 1933, consisting of two parts. Title I included temporary provisions designed to assist the railroads in meeting depression conditions. Title II added permanent measures to the Interstate Commerce Act. The temporary provisions were not successful in bringing about the anticipated economies and expired in 1935. The permanent provisions related to changes in the laws regarding mergers and liberalized the rule of rate-making.

The Office of Federal Coordinator of Transportation was established in 1933 for the purpose of studying methods of avoiding useless duplication of service, eliminating losses, promoting financial reorganization and improving transportation conditions in general. Numerous proposals for relief were considered, ranging from consolidation of the roads into a single national system, to the "Prince Plan" which would merge the roads into seven systems—two in the East, two in the South and three in the West—estimated to save about $743 million on the basis of 1932 traffic. The estimates were challenged by opponents who pointed to the disastrous effects of eliminating competition. They countered by suggesting the joint use of terminals and pooling of equipment as a means of reducing expenses, objected to by both management and labor.

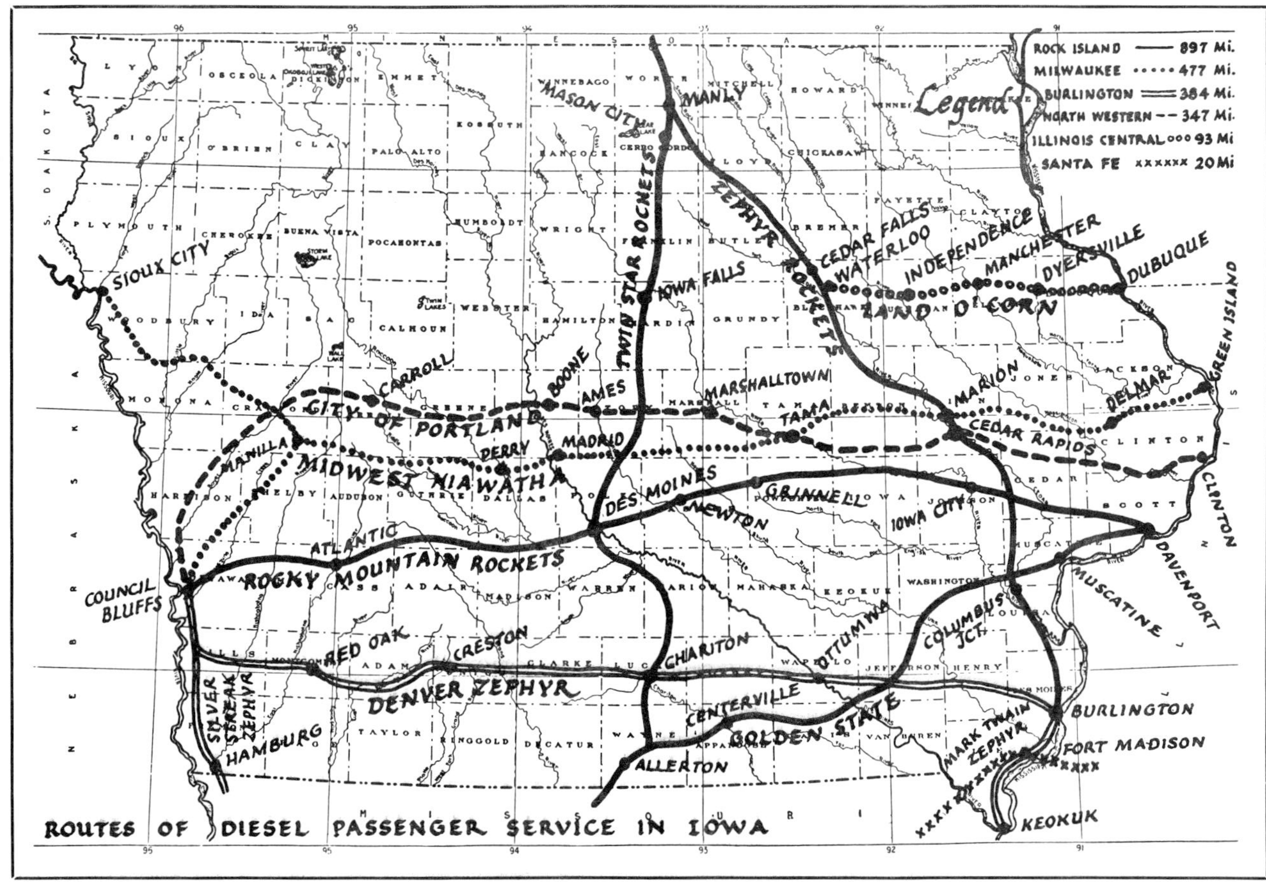

Figure 8-1
Routes of diesel passenger service in Iowa
(Courtesy: Iowa State Historical Society)

Federal Regulation of Other Modes

Interstate Motor Carriers

As early as the mid-twenties, it was recognized that motor carriers were going to offer more than token competition to railroads. Actually, until 1925, states had exercised some regulation over interstate as well as intrastate truck movements, for it had become a well-established fact that interstate carriers had to have state authority for intrastate operations. Authority for state control rested on the doctrine of *Gibbons v. Ogden* which stated that in the absence of federal legislation, states might prescribe reasonable provisions to meet local needs for those aspects of interstate commerce not demanding general or uniform regulation. In 1925, the U. S. Supreme Court declared that states could regulate interstate commerce where highway safety or conservation was the objective or where the indirect burden on interstate commerce was reasonable but could not where prevention of competition was at issue—a violation of the commerce clause of the Constitution. By 1920, 42 states had placed restrictions on vehicle width, 29 on height, 30 on length and 45 on gross weights. The diversity in weight and size limitations among states was controversial even in the 1930s and became subject to more heated arguments over the next 50 years.[6]

Following the Supreme Court cases, Senator Cummins of Iowa filed one of the first bills to regulate interstate motor carriers. Others followed in 1928, 1930, and 1932, without enactment. In addition to the legislative interest, extensive investigations of the industry were underway by the ICC. After a decade of discussion and debate, Congress finally passed the Motor Carrier Act of 1935, as Part II of the Interstate Commerce Act. It was the intense competition between railroads and motor carriers more than any other factor that was responsible. Expansion of the trucking industry in the early 1930s resulted in rate wars and evasion of state regulations, and it generated a feeling of unequal and unfair national regulatory policies.

The act produced sharp differences in regulatory philosophy between railroads and motor carriers, accentuated by differences in the structures of each industry. With few exceptions, railroads had been legally considered in the broad category of "common carriers." Contrarywise, motor carriers were placed into four general classifications: "common," "contract," "exempt" and "private." The distinctions, particularly in the "exempt" category, were a constant irritation to railroads as motor traffic expanded, and in many instances the ICC and courts were required to define the carrier operating authority and status within each one.[7]

Commercial Motor Carrier Passenger and Freight Traffic

In Iowa, approximately 1.8 million passengers rode the buses in 1931, increasing to over five million in 1939. Ten Class I carriers, including five affilitated with steam and interurban railways, had annual net operating revenues of $30,000 or over. There were 17 Class II passenger carriers with revenues under $30,000, and both classifications operated at a deficit in 1931 but showed profit positions by 1939. Of the 149 freight carriers reporting to the railroad commission in 1931, 107 had annual revenues of less than $5,000, indicating the relatively small operations of individuals or firms in the industry. By 1939, 40 freight "unclassified" motor trucking firms were in favorable financial condition.

Commercial Airlines

Many of the provisions of previous legislation (Air Commerce Act of 1926 and Air Mail Act of 1934) were incorporated into the Civil Aeronautics Act of 1938. A five-member Civil Aeronautics Authority (CAA) was created as an independent body comparable to the ICC. Within the CAA, an administrator was responsible for promotional and

[6] Interstate Commerce Commission, *Federal Regulation of the Size and Weights of Motor Vehicles,* House Doc. 354, 77th Cong., 1st sess., 1941. Difficulties encountered by truck operators are discussed in hearings before the Committee on Interstate and Foreign Commerce, *Regulation of Interstate-Motor Busses and Trucks on Public Highways,* 1934, H.R. 6836, pp. 404-407.

[7] To control entry, common carriers were required to operate under a certificate of public convenience and necessity; contract carriers under a permit to serve specific shippers. Private carriers were considered as an adjunct mode to extend the commercial activity of the firm owning them and were not on a for-hire basis. Exempt carriers were not subject to economic regulation, depending upon the commodity hauled or particular services offered. The most publicized and discussed were the motor carrier agricultural exemptions. Descriptions of the exemptions are found in Sections 203 (b) 4, 5, and 6 of the Motor Carrier Act. In Iowa, entry restrictions are found in Section 3257, and route restrictions in Section 3256, 327.1 and 327.6 of the Code of Iowa.

developmental functions and an Air Safety Board was to investigate accidents and make recommendations concerning preventative measures. Two Presidential Executive Orders in 1940 changed the CAA to the Civil Aeronautics Board (CAB), abolished the Air Safety Board and transferred their responsibilities to the CAB, which together with the administrator were placed in the Department of Commerce.

Title IV of the act pertained to economic regulation. It covered only common carriers and carriers of airmail as contrasted to safety regulations which extended to all aircraft. Entry into the industry required certificates of public convenience and necessity; rates and fares were to be published and all tariffs opened to public inspection. Abandonments, mergers and consolidations had to be approved but the carriers could be exempt from economic regulation under certain conditions. The principle of state regulation of intrastate carriers was recognized and upheld, not legalized away as was done in the Motor Carrier Act where the ICC had no control over abandonments or intrastate rates, even to prevent discrimination against interstate transportation. The state, therefore, could regulate intrastate airline rates and fares and issue certificates provided that the intrastate operations did not interfere with the Federal Act.

The first Iowa laws regulating aviation, aircraft licensing, and establishing air traffic rules and provisions were enacted by the 43rd General Assembly in 1929. In June, 1934, a special session passed an Act creating a Commission on Aeronautics to act under the advice and assistance of the State Adjutant General. It was "to regulate all flying activities in Iowa and to assist and advise in the promotion of aeronautics." No licensing powers were granted. The part-time members were Charles Gatschet of Des Moines, Ralph Cram of Davenport, and W. B. Swaney of Fort Dodge. Brigadier General Charles H. Grahl was Secretary. Their initial actions involved educating pilots, aircraft owners, airport managers and enforcement agencies concerning the air laws of the state and campaigning against "imprudent" flying which resulted in accidents. Formal rules and regulations were adopted in 1934, including establishment of minimum safe altitudes over open and congested spaces.

The Demise of the Railroad Commission

The Iowa Board of Railroad Commissioners was created in 1878 for the purpose of regulating railroads, the only major transportation system in Iowa at that time. But actions of the General Assembly over the years expanded their jurisdiction and control into other industries such as passenger and freight motor carriers, truck operators, pipelines, transmission lines, airports and bonded warehouses. The title was a misnomer—covering a conglomerate of activities relating to transportation, communication, storage, engineering, etc., for the protection of carriers, shippers and the traveling public. To better recognize the widening scope of assigned responsibilities, the name was changed to the "Iowa State Commerce Commission," on May 1, 1937. At the time of transition there were seven major departments. The largest in terms of employees (53 of 72) was the Motor Carrier Division. The chairman of the new commission was George A. Hoffman. Commissioners were Harry P. Dunlop and Mike P. Conway, and the executive secretary was J. J. Lynch.

Federal Aid for Highway Construction

The National Level

During the 1920s, road building capability of the states reached a point where they could obligate $100 million of federal aid each year. The amount exceeded congressional authorizations but was made possible through surplus funds built up in the program during earlier years. By 1928, the surplus had been expended and states reduced their highway programs to fit the $75 million yearly authorization. In fiscal year 1929, federal-aid mileage built fell to 9,386 miles, from 10,194 miles in 1928, and further reductions were carried over into 1930. To assist the sagging economy, President Hoover requested appropriations for public works, including highways, and Congress authorized an increase of $50 million in the federal-aid program for 1930, making a total of $125 million to be distributed also in 1932 and 1933. The new funds were apportioned to the states immediately by the Secretary of Agriculture, who also made the 1932 appropriations available in September, 1930. This decision raised the total available to $175 million, more than many of the states could match since their legislatures were not in session.

Highway construction problems were also eased by an additional appropriation of $80 million, divided among the states in the same manner as federal-aid funds, to be used for matching purposes. The appropriations were considered as loans rather than grants and were to be repaid through deductions from the regular federal-aid apportionments over a period of five years. The emergency funds were to be obligated by September 1, 1931. The loans stimulated road building, completing the inital and stage construction of 11,033 miles in 1931, and 15,997 miles in 1932. Employment on these projects expanded from 30,944 in January to 155,466 in July of 1931, bringing the total of federal and state employment during that month to 385,345 workers. However, the increases were short-lived and dropped considerably during the next few years. Total disbursements of state highway departments, together with the ratio of federal-aid payments from 1928 to 1939, are shown in Figure 8-2.

Continued decline in the national economy brought another stimulus in the form of the Emergency Relief and Construction Act of 1932. Funds totaling $120 million were authorized as temporary advances to the states for work to be performed before July 1, 1933, specifically to promote employment. The grants were to be repaid by deductions from federal aid over a ten-year period. Further emergency allocations were included in the Hayden-Cartwright Act of 1934 which appropriated $200 million of unmatched grants and made grants of the loans previously disbursed. Twenty-five percent was to be applied to secondary or feeder roads, including farm-to-market, rural free delivery roads and school bus routes. One and one-half percent could also be used for economic research.

The shortfall of revenues from income and property taxes caused state legislatures to look seriously at motor vehicle revenues, remarkably stable in the depression years, for support of other than highway functions. However, Congress limited federal extension of emergency grants only to states that used at least the amounts derived from motor vehicle taxes for highway construction, improvement and

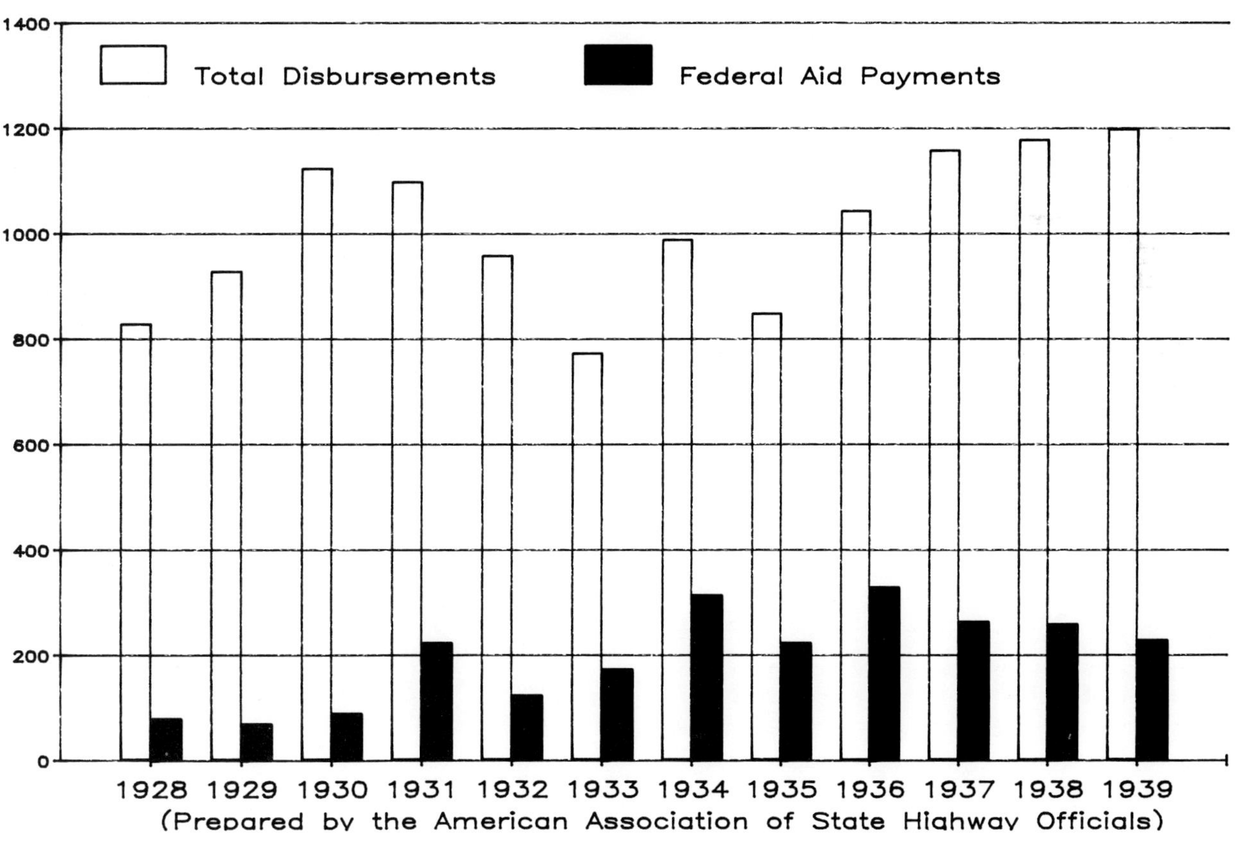

Figure 8-2
Disbursements by state highway departments showing ratio of federal-aid payments.
(Courtesy: American Association of State Highway Officials)

administration. In 1932, 16 states diverted over $87.8 million of road user revenues to non-highway purposes, over half of this amount by New York State alone. In 1933, the total increased to $143 million and to $164 million in 1934.

Granting federal aid to secondary roads became a permanent feature of national policy when the Federal Aid Act of 1938 established a federal-aid system of secondary roads to be designated by the states and to include not more than 10 percent of rural road mileage. In 1939, the General Assembly passed the first comprehensive farm-to-market road law in order to receive and match the annual allotment of $660,000 from the federal government. The matching funds were to be taken from the primary road fund, a move opposed by the highway commission without success. In addition, the law required that all funds in excess of $16 million in the primary road fund be transferred to the farm-to-market fund on or before June 30, 1941, exclusive of amounts received from primary road bond sales. In 1941, the ceiling of the primary road fund was raised to $17 million and remained at that level until 1949.

Highway Construction—The State Level

The increased funds from county bond sales accelerated primary road paving in the late 1920s. During 1930, the peak year of construction, 1,029 miles were paved at an expenditure of $42.6 million. This brought the total paved to 3,272 miles, whereas 2,863 miles were graveled, 513 miles built to grade but not surfaced and 593 miles not built. Added to the primary system were 429 miles, primarily stub roads to towns with populations of 400 or more, based on the 1930 Census. In three years, the number of completely surfaced roads spanning the state had increased to nine; seven east-west and two on north-south routes, and by the close of 1931, four more north-south roads were added. The 1931 road map proudly proclaimed in large, bold letters: "Motorist, Get This Once And For All, Iowa Is No Longer A Mud Road State."

Exhaustion of county bond funds and the effects of the depression sharply reduced primary road building after 1931, but by 1934, the state was within 600 miles of the goal set in the defunct state bond proposal. An additional 324 miles had been blacktopped, a method of surfacing introduced in 1932 that is inexpensive to put in place but expensive to maintain. Although construction costs dropped by 26 percent, highway revenues fell twice as fast in 1932 compared to 1931. For the first time, license fees and gasoline taxes declined after increasing every year prior to 1932. The depression played havoc with commission employment, wages and salaries. Between August 1, 1931, and March 1, 1932, 688 persons had been cut from the commission payroll, and for those remaining employed, salary reductions averaged 7.5 percent. The low point was reached in 1933, when the staff consisted of 531 people, and although the numbers increased later, employment during the thirties never reached the 1930 level.

Bank closings in 1933 tied up about $4.6 million of primary road funds, making payments difficult on interest and principal of the bonds. Had it not been for $10 million allotted by the federal government, there would have been few contracts awarded for primary road building in 1931. Bond payments continued to be a major problem, and refinancing was authorized effective January, 1934, to reduce interest and readjust maturity dates. The average interest rate on old bonds was reduced from 4.77 to 3.61 percent; on new bonds to 1.19 percent in 1939. Between 1934 and 1937, $72 million in bonds had been refinanced, premiums amounted to $657,000, and interest savings were $1.5 million.

Formation of the Highway Patrol

Vehicle accidents, highway injuries and deaths were a serious problem in the early 1930s, and efforts were made by the legislature to establish a highway safety patrol. Bills were defeated in 1933 through opposition of farmers and labor. Farmers were blockading highways to prevent trucks from reaching markets in an attempt to raise prices for their products, and labor feared that a patrol would be used as a strike-breaking force. But Mrs. Alex Miller, a popular Secretary of State, decided to do what she had no authority to do—create a highway patrol. In 1934 she converted 15 motor vehicle inspectors on her payroll into an organization needed to combat the "Four Horsemen of the Highways;" namely, "Road Hogs, Drunken Drivers, Excessive Speeders and Unsafe Cars." Since there were no funds available, officers furnished their own uniforms.[8]

[8] George Mills, "The Patrol's 50th Anniversary," *Des Moines Register,* July 31, 1984. Motor vehicle inspectors were used for enforcement of laws pertaining to highway safety requirements among other duties.

Highway Safety Patrol, officer and early automobile.
(Courtesy: Iowa State Patrol)

Mrs. Alex Miller, Secretary of State
(Courtesy: Iowa State Patrol)

John Hattery, first patrol chief.
(Courtesy: Iowa State Patrol)

Armed with data showing the influence of the patrol on motorists and knowing that the makeshift group was inadequate to cover highways in 99 counties, Mrs. Miller requested the legislature to consider approval of a larger and legal organization. Deaths had dropped 21 percent during the last five months of 1934 compared to a similar period in 1933, and there were 2,000 fewer injuries for the full year. The record could not be ignored and the legislature responded by creating a force of 50 men and three officers in 1935. Salaries were fixed at $100 per month for the initial appointment and could rise to $125 after five years. The work week was 72 hours. John Hattery of Nevada, the first patrol chief, was paid $200 per month and his assistants E. A. Conley of Marshalltown and Harry Nestle of Carroll each received $165. Despite the relatively low pay scales and long hours, 3,000 applicants sought the positions. A majority selected held college degrees, some had attended college and none were chosen without high school diplomas. Forty-nine vehicles were purchased by the state for the work, consisting of 37 automobiles and 12 motorcycles. The latter were soon abandoned because of operational difficulties in the harsh winters.

One of the first controversies raged over the jurisdiction of the patrol, especially in the field of criminal enforcement. Critics did not want a state police force which would usurp responsibilities of county sheriffs and local police. However, in 1939 the legislature transferred the patrol from the control of the Secretary of State to a new Public Safety Department, gave it full legal police power and appropriated funds for an expansion to 125 officers. Since then, the highway patrol has been involved in criminal apprehension, has organized tactical teams for riot control and public disorders, and has been engaged in educational programs concerning highway safety—these in addition to the regular patrol responsibilities.

By 1984, the patrol had a compliment of 410 troopers and officers, 80 of whom operated 15 district offices with the remainder assigned to highway and law enforcement work. The 330 troopers on the road were nearly seven times greater than the 50 in 1935. However, the reduced work week (from 72 to 43½ hours) and the heavy increase in traffic meant that the patrol was nearly as thin proportionately as it was in 1935. Seven airplanes have been added to their vehicle inventory, to be used by air-ground teams to spot speeding motorists on primary highways. Coverage totaled 11 million miles in 1983, somewhat higher than the two million miles in 1935. Over the 50 years of its existence, the patrol has gained widespread recognition, respect and commendations for high standards of performance and the professional approach to its responsibilities and duties.

Table 8-3
State Highway Receipts and Distribution of Funds, 1930-1939

Year	No. of Autos[1]	No. of Trucks[1]	Receipts[2]	Distribution to Primary	Distribution to Secondary
1930	711,927	73,417	$22.3	$17.1	$5.2
1931	673,360	81,936	22.8	17.3	5.5
1932	611,003	76,936	20.1	15.5	4.6
1933	562,802	69,490	18.9	14.4	4.5
1934	592,350	75,536	19.4	14.7	4.7
1935	619,658	83,836	20.8	15.4	5.4
1936	645,759	87,535	22.1	16.4	5.7
1937	659,004	91,991	23.6	17.6	6.0
1938	651,843	94,234	24.1	17.8	6.3
1939	673,136	99,931	21.5	13.9	7.6

(Source: Office of Economic Analysis, Iowa Department of Transportation. All data are on a calendar year basis.)

[1] Automobiles and trucks registered.

[2] Includes motor fuel taxes, registration fees and miscellaneous receipts. Figures are in millions of dollars rounded to the nearest unit.

Table 8-4
Iowa's Primary Road System, 1920-1940

Year	Total Miles	Paved	Bituminous	Gravel	Dirt Graded	Dirt Ungraded
1920	6,619	67	---	792	1,021	4,739
1921	6,616	236	---	1,157	1,448	3,776
1922	6,615	334	---	1,558	1,761	2,962
1923	6,641	419	---	1,889	2,001	2,338
1924	6,660	502	---	2,164	1,934	2,059
1925	6,674	569	---	2,461	1,796	1,849
1926	6,654	650	---	2,818	1,732	1,452
1927	6,665	940	---	3,226	1,417	1,083
1928	6,761	1,625	---	3,221	1,114	801
1929	6,770	2,317	---	3,137	715	602
1930	7,274	3,272	---	2,863	513	594
1931	7,789	3,804	---	3,070	281	635
1932	7,845	4,086	137	3,067	117	438
1933	7,834	4,202	139	3,083	52	358
1934	7,909	4,313	324	2,933	175	165
1935	8,278	4,374	323	3,297	92	192
1936	8,318	4,546	469	3,030	63	109
1937	8,433	4,818	569	2,890	50	106
1938	8,498	5,090	587	2,690	52	78
1939	8,541	5,135	614	2,661	51	80
1940	8,559	5,208	671	2,592	22	62

(Source: Iowa State Highway Commission, *Annual Reports.)*
Fractions of miles have been reduced to the nearest whole number.

Highway Concerns at the Close of the Decade

There were 400,000 motor vehicles in Iowa when primary road improvements began about 1920. The legal speed limit was 30 miles per hour and no buses or freight-hauling trucks were on the roads. By 1930 the number of vehicles and average mileages had doubled, speeds had increased, and bus and truck traffic made up a considerable portion of highway usage. The concern of the commission lay in the fact that improvement of primary roads started far behind vehicle needs and never really caught up with the demand. They also emphasized the abandonment trends on railroad branch lines, rendering small towns wholly dependent upon highway transportation.

In 1940, the commission recommended that every town should be provided with a dependable year-round road and every primary highway with a dustless surface. Narrow bridges should be widened to not less than 24 feet. Continued attention should be given to elimination or protection of highway/railroad crossings. The cost of these proposals was estimated at $116 million at 1940 prices, and at the level of current revenues would require 16 years to complete. Even at this estimate, it was suggested that the program would not meet traffic demands, expected to double again during the period. Concerns notwithstanding, the record of highway construction throughout the depression years showed steady progress as indicated in Tables 8-3 and 8-4. The first table covers the number of motor vehicles registered in the state, receipts from taxes, and distribution of funds to primary and secondary roads from 1930 to 1939. The second table shows the progress in surfacing the primary road system between 1920 and 1940.

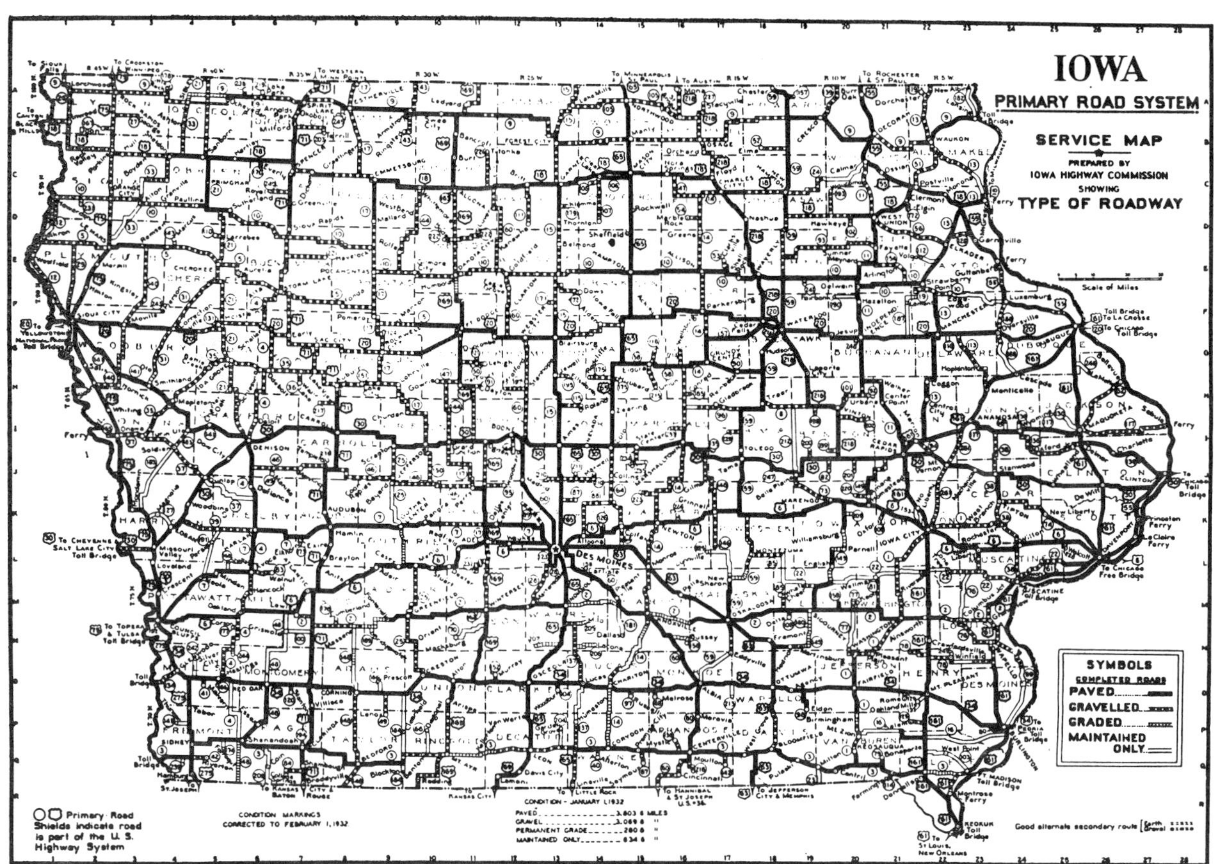

Figure 8-3
Iowa primary road system service map.
(Courtesy: Iowa State Highway Commission)

Pipelines Come to Iowa

Pipelines, often referred to as the "hidden industry," constitute a specialized transportation system used for moving crude oil, gasoline and other petroleum products, liquid propane, anhydrous ammonia and natural gas. Bulk commodities such as coal slurry have also been proven suitable for pipeline movement. Maps showing pipelines in Iowa during the 1930's and 1940's include both liquid lines and natural gas, but the subject of this discussion is the development of the liquid lines. Natural gas pipelines are considered as a part of the energy industries of the nation whereas liquid lines have been viewed as one of the five major transportation modes. Once the initial investment is made, the advantage of the pipeline lies in the operating cost. An ICC study in 1942 reported that the cost of transporting crude oil by pipeline was 1.98 mills per ton-mile as contrasted to 10.62 mills by railroad and 0.63 mills by tank vessels. Refined petroleum products cost 4.39 mills by pipeline, 11.19 mills by rail and 0.6 mills by tank vessels.

A Brief History

The first oil well in the nation was "brought in" by Colonel Drake in western Pennsylvania in 1859, and the oil was transported on streams tributary to the Alleghany River, thence to Pittsburgh. But as the oil fields developed away from the rivers, horse and wagon teams were used to haul the oil to shipping points. The charges varied with distance, road conditions and the season of the year, usually averaging $1.50 per barrel. Both teamster and water transportation were expensive and often hazardous, creating the need for a new alternative. After experimenting, the first successful crude oil pipeline was built in 1865, consisting of two-inch pipe with a capacity of 81 barrels per hour for a distance of five miles.

The success of the line led to construction of connections to railroad terminals and/or refineries. Railroads favored pipeline development to feed their tank cars for movement to refineries on the East Coast. By 1880, over 1,200 miles of pipelines served these regional fields; in 1900, 18,000 miles were in operation in the United States and shortly thereafter, pipelines were built from mid-continent locations and joined the eastern systems. Since the early days of the 20th century, extensions to new fields, "looping" of lines along existing routes for increased capacity, and the addition of gasoline and petroleum products resulted in systems of 120,000 miles by 1940.[9]

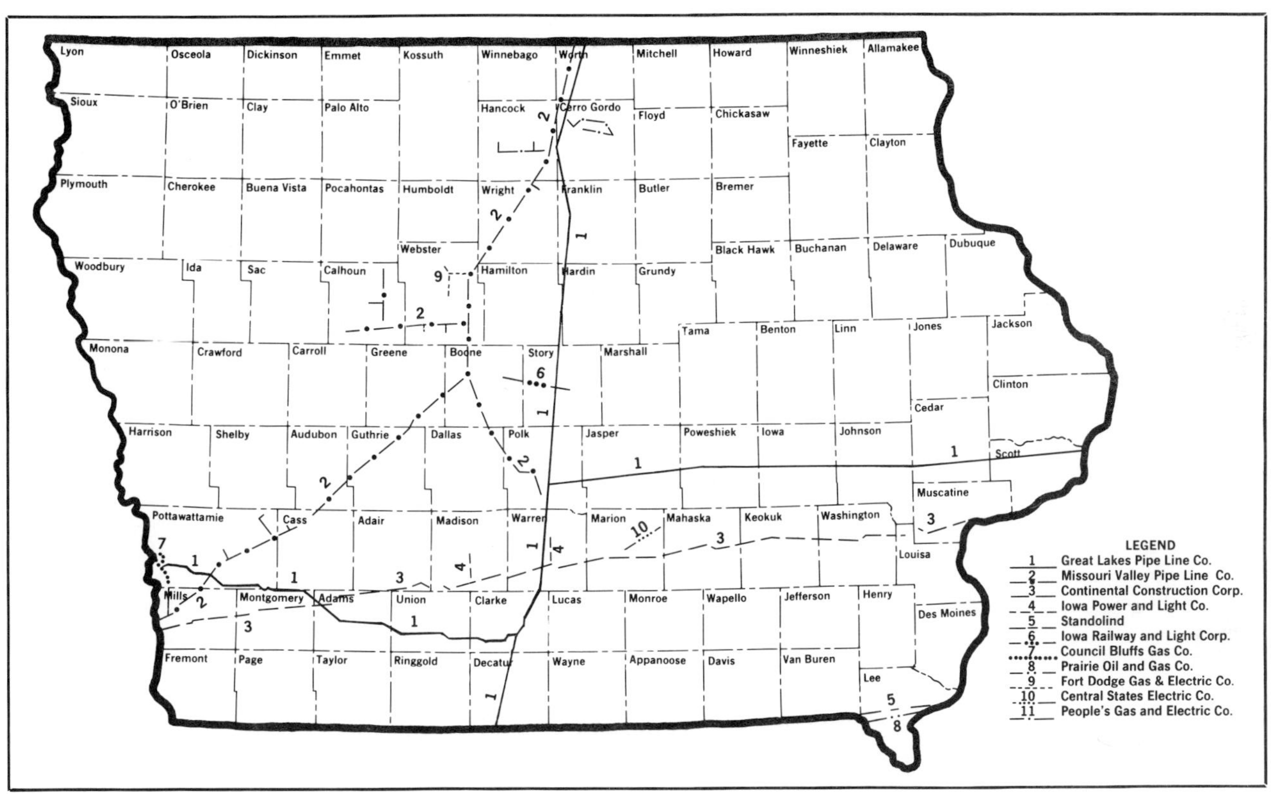

Figure 8-4
Natural gas, manufactured gas, and gasoline pipelines in Iowa, 1931.
(Courtesy: Iowa Development Commission)

[9] H. J. Struth, ed., *The Petroleum Data Book: Official Source Book of Information for the World's Oil and Gas Industry*, Dallas, Tex.: Petroleum Engineer Pub. Co., 1947. Pipelines are generally divided into three categories: gathering lines, crude trunk lines and gasoline or products lines. Gathering lines are usually two to four inches in diameter and "gather" the oil from leased tanks which have received the oil from producing wells through "lead" lines. Trunk lines are the main lines of the system, normally ranging from six to 16 inches in diameter. During World War II, a crude line of 24 inches was built from Longview, Texas to Phoenixville, Pennsylvania, and a products line of 20 inches from Beaumont, Texas to Linden, New Jersey. Pipe of 42 inches was used in the 1960's, and 48-inch pipe was proposed for the Trans-Alaska pipeline.

The ICC was given regulatory control over interstate pipeline transportation of property other than gas or water in the Hepburn Act of 1906. In Iowa, the General Assembly conferred on the railroad commission jurisdiction over pipeline companies in order that they may be of "safe and proper construction, operation and maintenance in the state" but gave no control over rates.[10] The Great Lakes Pipeline System (now the Williams Pipe Line Company) was the first "products" line approved for construction in 1931, with terminals at Des Moines, Omaha and later at Coralville. From Barnsdall, Oklahoma and Kansas City, eight-inch lines were built to Des Moines and six-inch lines from Des Moines to Minneapolis and Chicago. At Mason City, the first terminal to serve trucks rather than rail cars was opened in 1944. Other lines were built in the state in the 1930's and 1940's (Fig. 8-4, 8-5).

River Developments Affecting Iowa

Locks, Dams, and the Nine Foot Channel on the Mississippi

Despite the fact that river transportation had been declining for many years, the inland waterways were considered to have tremendous potential as an inexpensive facility if channel depths could be standardized and maintained. The champion of this idea was Herbert Hoover, who as Secretary of

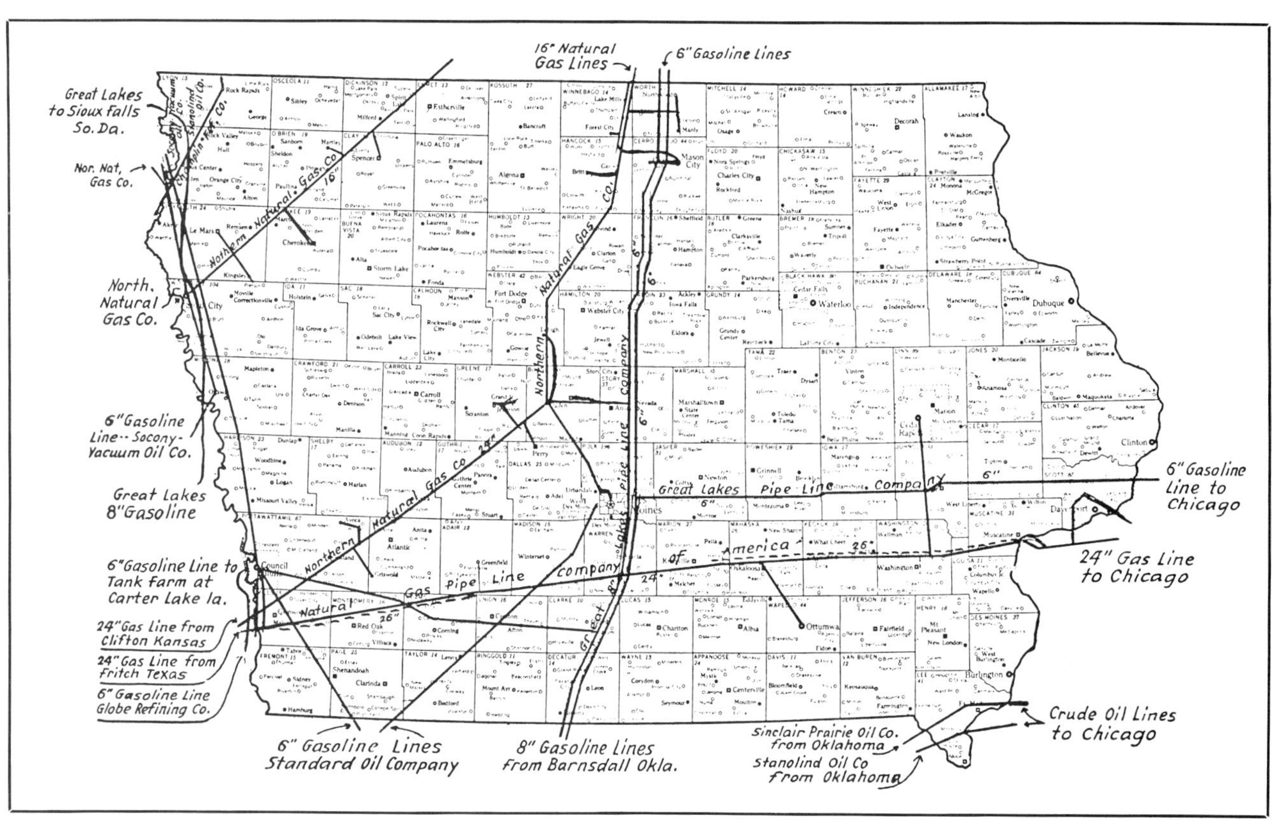

Figure 8-5
Natural gas and gasoline pipelines.
(Courtesy: Iowa Development Commission)

[10] 1931 Laws of Iowa, Chapter 383. Declared unconstitutional by the Iowa Supreme Court in State of Iowa Ex. Rel. Board of Railroad Commissioners of the State of Iowa v. Stanoland Pipeline Company, 249 N.W. 366 (1933). Another law, Chapter 10, Acts of the 45th General Assembly, became effective March 24, 1934.

Commerce visualized an inter-connected river system of 9,000 miles. It would consist of a north-south trunk line of 1,900 miles from New Orleans to Chicago, there to link with the Great Lakes; an east-west trunk line of 1,000 miles from Pittsburgh through Cairo, Illinois to Kansas City, and feeder lines on the Upper and Lower Mississippi tributaries, the Ohio and Missouri Rivers. A nine-foot canalization of the Ohio River had been completed in 1929, but the deep draft barges and tows were unable to navigate the Upper Mississippi. As a result, commercial interests along the route, led by the Chambers of Commerce in Minneapolis and St. Paul and firms producing and marketing bulk commodities, brought pressures on Congress to create a standard channel depth throughout the entire Mississippi River system.

There were two sections of the Upper Mississippi that could not be improved by construction of wing dams. One was a stretch of shallow water between St. Paul and St. Anthony Falls where a lock and dam were opened for traffic in 1907, replaced by a high dam in 1917 for both navigation and power to the Twin Cities industries. Another section was at Rock Island where the rapids were still obstructing traffic up river. A lock and dam was completed in 1907 which allowed the Moline farm equipment industry better access to water transportation and was used extensively for a few years. A second lock and dam was built by the Keokuk and Hamilton Water Power Company and opened in 1913. It replaced three locks in the Des Moines River Canal, deepened the river channel for 50 miles upstream and created a pool which covered the entire rapids.

On July 3, 1930, Congress authorized the U. S. Army Corps of Engineers to make the Upper Mississippi a commercial waterway, a development which was to have a profound impact upon Iowa. A nine-foot channel was planned without surveys or recommendations of the Engineers or one based upon economic feasibility studies. The legislation called for construction of 26 new locks and dams from Minneapolis to St. Louis, one of the largest public works projects up to that time and unprecedented in water resource development. The dams at

Locking through on the Mississippi.
(Courtesy: Author)

Minneapolis (No. 1) and at Keokuk (No. 19) were already in place, and the lock and dam at Hastings (No. 2) was opened in 1930. All locks in the Rock Island District were a uniform 110 x 600 feet except for Lock 19 at Keokuk which was 110 x 358 feet until replaced with a new lock in 1957. The dams were to be spaced at intervals of 9.6 to 43.3 miles, equipped with gates to provide for series of lakes (slack pools) to insure adequate depths for navigation in low water. The channel was to be maintained to minimum widths of 300 feet up to Hastings, 200 feet to St. Anthony Falls and 100 feet for the remainder of the waterway.

Opposition to deepening the channel came from environmental, recreation and sportsmen's groups who claimed that "a succession of stagnant or sluggish pools fed by sewage disposal plants would cause oxidation and diminish fish and wildlife populations."[11] But the Engineers worked closely with these organizations to ensure the continued maintenance and further development of recreational areas. Roller and Tainter gates were installed to permit migration of fish, to allow passage of silt and sewage, to help aerate the water for adequate oxegen levels and to stabilize water levels in the pools. In addition to the gates, dikes and spillways were provided wherever necessary. Because shorelines changed most above the dams and least below them, the dams were located above river towns to control changes in water fronts. The cooperation of the Engineers brought support from organizations who had originally opposed the nine-foot channel.[12]

Locking through on the Mississippi.
(Courtesy: Author)

[11] Raymond Merritt, "The Development of the Lock and Dam System on the Upper Mississippi River." Paper given at the National Waterways Round Table, Norfolk, Virginia, April 22-24, 1980, p. 15.

[12] Roald D. Tweet, *A History of the Rock Island District U.S. Army Corps of Engineers, 1866-1983,* Rock Island, Ill.: U.S. Army District, Rock Island, 1984, pp. 263-265. Roller gates developed in Germany were still under patent when the dams were built; and Tainter gates of French design could be moved vertically to control the level of water passing underneath. Tainter gates were used wherever possible as they were cheaper to construct and did not require royalty payments.

Within ten years, 1930-1940, 24 low-level dams were built and the nine-foot channel was completed. Construction was planned in the order of the seriousness of problems with the first at No. 15, located at the foot of the Rock Island Rapids where navigation was still impeded in 1930, completed in 1934. No. 14 at Le Claire was among the last. Of the others, one had been built in 1930, two in 1935, three in 1936, six in 1937, six in 1938, four in 1939 and one in 1940. Those along the Iowa and Illinois shores were at or near Guttenberg (No. 10), Dubuque (No. 11), Bellevue (No. 12), Clinton (No. 13), Le Claire (No. 14), Rock Island (No. 15) Muscatine (No. 16), New Boston (No. 17), Burlington (No. 18), and Keokuk (No. 19) (Fig. 8-6, 8-7).

Construction costs for the lock and dam system and nine-foot channel were funded through regular River and Harbor appropriations. Additional funds came from the National Industrial Recovery Act and the Federal Emergency Administration of Public Works. In 1935, the River and Harbor bill of August 20, authorized appropriation of sufficient funds to complete the project, and by 1940, more than $170 million had been spent (Fig. 8-8, Table 8-5). Even before the new channel was completed, traffic on the Upper Mississippi began to increase. In 1935, commercial movements between Minneapolis and the mouth of the Missouri were 804,490 tons up river and 739,505 tons down river. Comparable tonnage in 1940 was 2.23 million tons up river and 1.27 million tons down river.

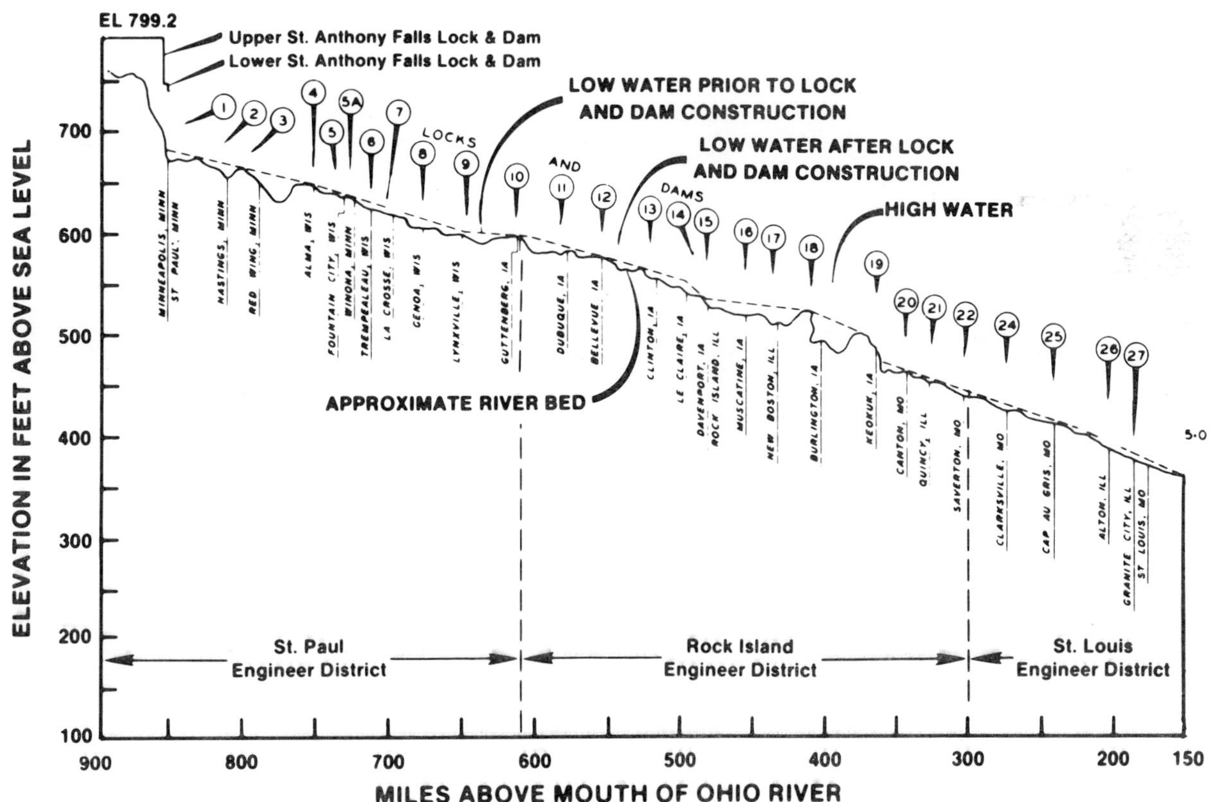

Figure 8-8
Mississippi stairway of water.
(Courtesy: U.S. Army Corps of Engineers, Rock Island District)

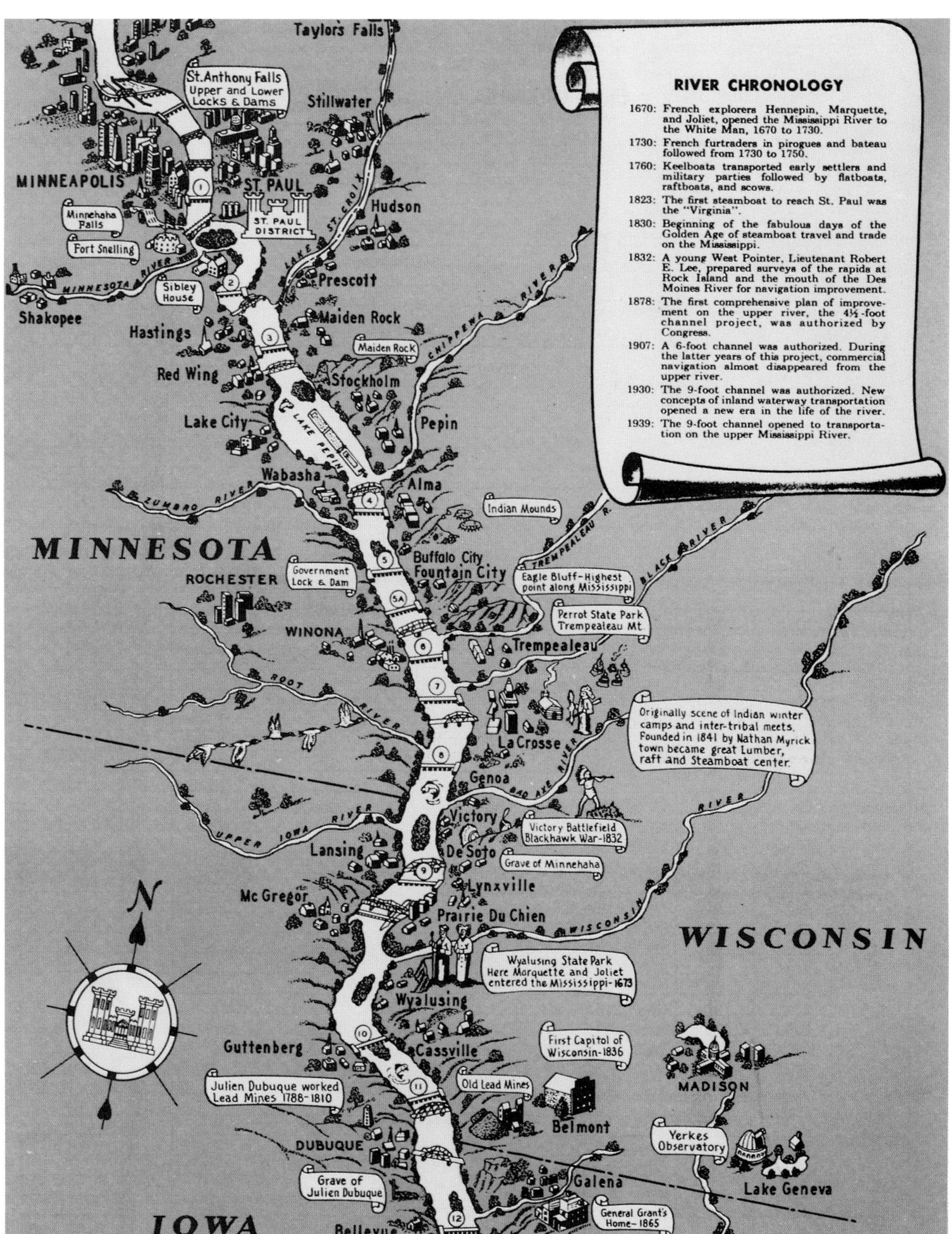

Figure 8-6
River chronology.
(Courtesy: U.S. Army Corps of Engineers as published in Quimby's Harbor Guide, 1984.)

Figure 8-7
River chronology.
(Courtesy: U.S. Army Corps of Engineers as published in Quimby's Harbor Guide, 1984.)

LOCKS AND DAMS - UPPER MISSISSIPPI RIVER

Lock and Dam	Miles Above Ohio River	Miles from Nearest Town	Lock Dimensions: Width of Chamber (feet)	Length of Chamber (feet)	Lift (feet)	Upper (feet)	Lower (feet)	Year Opened to Navigation	Estimated Cost(Millions) of Each Lock and Dam Including Work in Pool	1977 Tonnage (millions)
USAF	853.9	In city of Minneapolis, Minn.	56	400	49.2	15.7	13.7	1963	18.2	2.1
LSAF	853.3	In city of Minneapolis, Minn.	56	400	26.9	13.7	10.3	1963	12.4	2.8
No. 1	847.6	Minneapolis-St. Paul	56 56	400 400	35.9 35.9	13.5 12.5	10.1 7.6	1917	2.4	2.9
No. 2	815.2	1.3 above Hastings, Minn.	110 110	500 600	12.2 12.2	16.0 22.2	15.1 13.0	1930 1948	6.5	11.0
No. 3	796.9	6.1 above Red Wing, Minn.	110	600	8.0	17.0	14.0	1938	7.5	10.5
No. 4	752.8	Alma, Wis.	110	600	7.0	17.0	13.0	1935	4.9	11.0
No. 5	738.1	Minneiska, Minn.	110	600	9.0	18.0	12.0	1935	5.1	11.0
No. 5A	728.5	3 above Winona, Minn.	110	600	5.5	18.0	12.5	1936	7.0	11.0
No. 6	714.3	Trempealcau, Wis.	110	600	6.5	17.0	12.5	1936	4.9	11.6
No. 7	702.5	Dresbach, Minn.	110	600	8.0	18.0	12.0	1937	5.6	11.6
No. 8	679.2	Genoa, Wis.	110	600	11.0	22.0	14.0	1937	6.1	11.9
No. 9	647.9	3.3 below Lynxville, Wis.	110	600	9.0	16.0	13.0	1938	6.5	13.0
No. 10	615.1	Guttenberg, Iowa	110	600	8.0	15.0	12.0	1937	4.8	13.7
No. 11	583.0	3.7 above Dubuque, Iowa	110	600	11.0	18.5	12.5	1937	7.4	14.7
No. 12	556.7	Bellevue, Iowa	110	600	9.0	17.0	13.0	1938	5.6	15.1
No. 13	522.5	4.3 above Clinton, Iowa	110	600	11.0	19.0	13.0	1939	7.5	15.2
No. 14	493.3	3.7 below Le Claire, Iowa	110	600	11.0	20.5	13.5	1939	6.3	17.4
Le Claire lock(Canal)	493.1	3.9 below Le Claire, Iowa	80	320	11.0	17.6	10.9	1922		
No. 15	482.9	Foot of Arsenal Island, Rock Island, Ill.	110 110	600 360	16.0 16.0	24.0 17.0	11.0 11.0	1934 1934	10.5	18.0
No. 16	457.2	1.8 above Muscatine, Iowa	110	600	9.0	17.0	12.0	1937	9.8	19.8
No. 17	437.1	4.2 above New Boston, Ill.	110	600	8.0	16.0	13.0	1939	5.8	20.2
No. 18	410.5	6.5 above Burlington, Iowa	110	600	9.8	16.5	13.7	1937	10.3	20.8
No. 19	364.2	Keokuk, Iowa	110 110	358 1,200	38.2 38.2	14.0 15.0	9.2 13.0	1913 1957	14.8	21.0
No. 20	343.2	0.9 above Canton, Mo.	110	600	10.0	15.0	12.0	1936	6.3	23.0
No. 21	324.9	2.1 below Qunicy, Ill.	110	600	10.5	16.5	12.0	1938	8.1	23.9
No. 22	301.2	1.5 below Saverton, Mo.	110	600	10.2	18.0	13.8	1938	5.3	24.3
No. 24	273.4	Clarksville, Mo.	110	600	15.0	19.0	12.0	1940	8.3	25.1
No. 25 No. 25	241.4	Cap Au Gris, Mo.	110	600	15.0	19.0	12.0	1939	10.9	25.1
No. 26	202.9	Alton, Ill.	110 110	600 360	24.0 24.0	19.0 16.0	10.0 10.0	1938 1038	12.8	58.4
No. 27	185.4	Granite City Ill.	110 110	1,200 600	10.5 10.5	15.0 15.0	16.0 16.0	1953 1953	63.9	64.3

*Inoperable

Source: U.S. Army Corps of Engineers

Table 8-5

Mississippi River Lock & Dam No. 15. Naval Reserves boat and Str. J.S. locking through, 1933.
(Courtesy: U.S. Army Corps of Engineers, Rock Island District)

Mississippi River Lock No. 15. *John W. Weeks* with tow above, 1936.
(Courtesy: U.S. Army Corps of Engineers, Rock Island District)

Mississippi River Lock No. 15. Federal Barge Line steamer *Mark Twain* with tow entering main lock, 1936.
(Courtesy: U.S. Army Corps of Engineers, Rock Island District)

Mississippi River Lock No. 15. Looking downstream at tow of freight leaving Lock No. 15, 1937.
(Courtesy: U.S. Army Corps of Engineers, Rock Island District)

Multi-Purpose River Planning—The Missouri

For many years, debates raged over river basin resource management. River development was considered broadly associated with water resource issues such as flood control, water supply, irrigation, recreation, land reclamation and hydro-electric power generation in addition to navigation. To be determined were policies relating to the full development of the rivers for possible regional or national advantage as against proposals to limit development for a primary and specific use. The major purpose of the lock and dam improvement on the Upper Mississippi was to further the economic welfare of shippers and urban communities. "The vision of the supporters was improvement of navigation and restoration of the golden years of waterborne commerce that historically had made the cities and towns along the River the cultural and economic crossroads of the Mississippi Valley Basin. The means was controlled by political power, not technological knowledge or environmental priorities."[13] However, in the case of the Missouri River, there were major concerns over reserving the water for upstream irrigation, downstream navigation, and flood control over considerable lengths of the river.

Towboat *Hustler,* 1934.
(Courtesy: U.S. Army Corps of Engineers, Omaha District)

[13] Merritt, p. 21. Tweet quoted Merritt who suggested that success in obtaining the nine-foot channel on the Upper Mississippi was a victory "in which glory was shared by President Hoover, his Secretary of War, the Mississippi Valley Association, the Minneapolis Improvement Commission and Congressional representatives from Minnesota." Tweet, p. 82.

The Roosevelt Administration sought to promote widespread development of several river basins, including the Missouri. The Tennessee Valley Authority, created in 1933, became the best known national example of multi-purpose river planning. In 1936, under provisions of the Flood Control Act, the primary but not sole responsibility for river development was given the Corps of Engineers and included the concept of river basin organization and management for the complete use of all water resources. The legislation promised relief from perennial problems in the Missouri River Basin, provided that comprehensive engineering plans were approved and appropriate construction programs authorized.

Economic conditions in the Missouri Valley prompted the federal government to move quickly with river development plans. Agricultural income had declined as had wages and employment in the industrial sector. Farmers left the land, causing a migration from the Basin. The eastern area with fertile soil, adequate rainfall and large cities was relatively stable, but the western area was subject to periodic droughts and the necessity to irrigate crops, and much of the soil was adequate only for pasture. Industrial production centered on oil, copper, coal and phosphates, but not to the extent that the unemployed workers could be absorbed. Levees built along the river's edge to control the continuous flooding proved inadequate, soil and crop losses mounted, and urban communities suffered in the middle and lower river valley. Reservoirs were thought to be more effective and had the additional potential to provide hydroelectric power and water for irrigation. The possibility of water resource use to reverse the worsening economic conditions led to the creation of the Mississippi Valley Committee in 1934. Morris L. Cooke, Chairman, was a strong advocate of multi-purpose planning, and his report recommended full development of the Mississippi and its tributaries for all phases of river use. Centralized planning and coordinated development were basic to his proposals which did not achieve immediate success. Not until severe floods occurred on the Missouri in 1943 were serious efforts made for river improvements in the Missouri Valley.

Dredge *Meriwether Lewis,* 1938.
(Courtesy: U.S. Army Corps of Engineers, Omaha District)

Aviation Activity

Organization of flying and glider clubs and schools, supported by the National Aeronautics Association (NAA), offered individuals an opportunity to pursue aeronautical interests. In the late twenties, there were nine chapters of the NAA in Iowa whose major objectives were promotion of aviation, sponsorship of air meets and furnishing speakers to civic groups. Notable among these were the clubs in Ames, Dubuque, Waterloo, Cedar Rapids, Hampton and Orient. Others were the Aero Club of Des Moines, the Iowa Chapter of Ninety-Niners, the Southwest Pilots Association and the Iowa Airport Managers Association. Aircraft used in private and corporate businesses became an important phase of air traffic in the 1930s. Among firms involved were the Des Moines Register, the Automatic Washing Machine Company of Newton, the Morrell Company of Ottumwa and radio station WMT at Waterloo.

Airports and Pilots

In 1934, the state had nine municipal, 16 commercial and 36 private airports or landing fields of which 18 were partly or fully lighted. Four years later, 18 municipal and 14 commercial airports gave Iowa a ranking of 24th in the nation. Airport expansion resulted in an increase in the number of pilots and from 191 registered in 1937, the total rose to 471 in 1939. In that year, Sheldon had more registered pilots per 1,000 population than any city in the nation. The numbers continued to climb in the early forties when 1,882 were registered in 1941, nine of which had limited commercial licenses and five had transport licenses. World War II virtually stopped civilian flying.

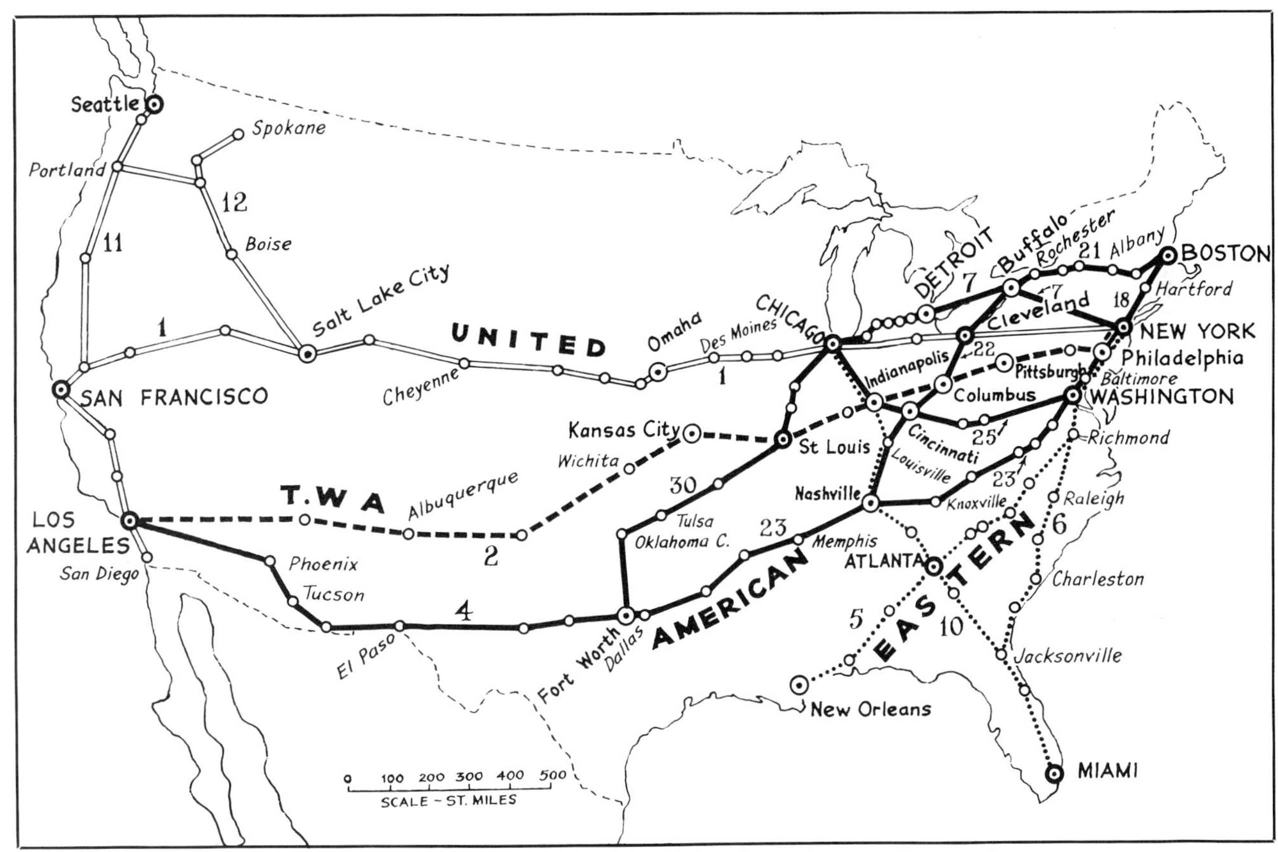

Figure 8-9
Trunk airline mail routes, 1934 (the Big Four).
(Courtesy: R. E. G. Davies Collection)

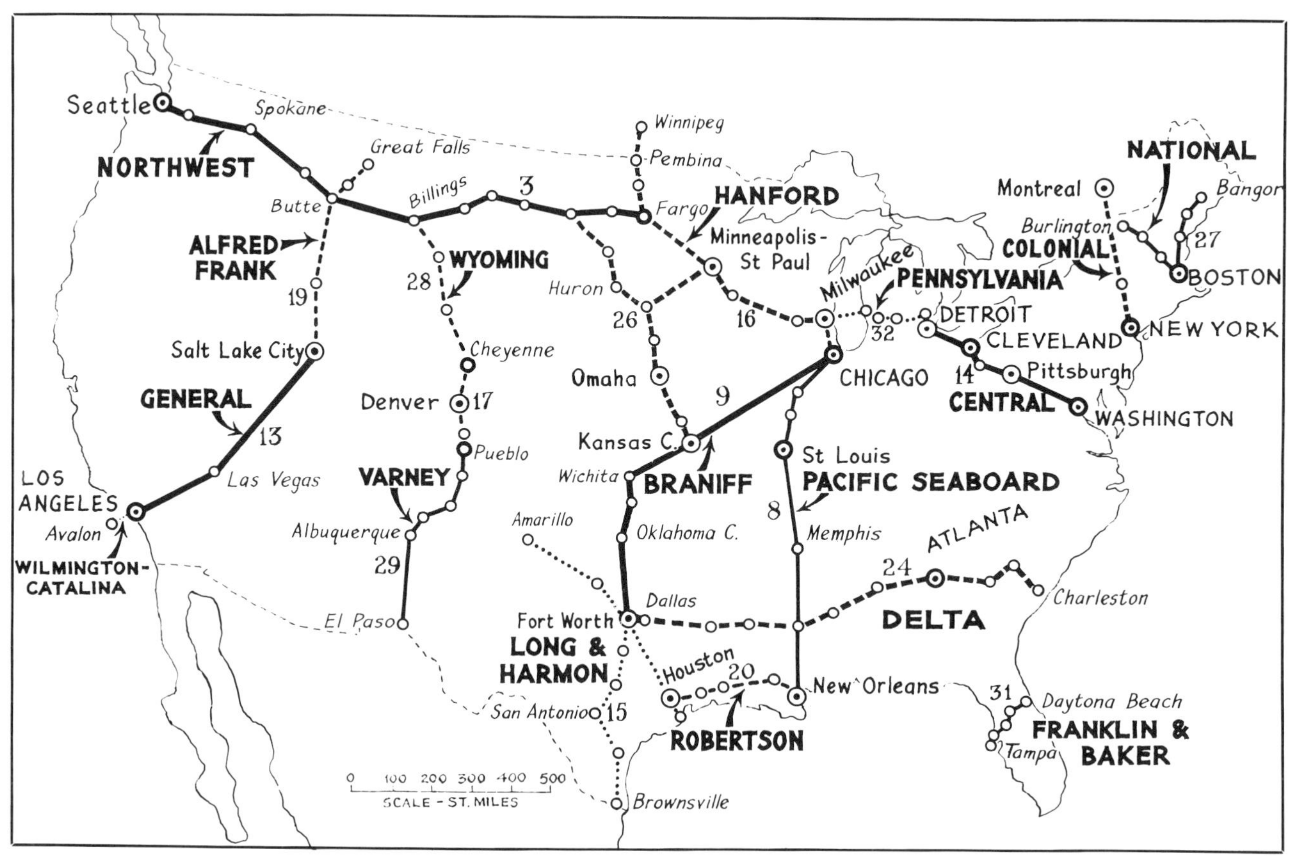

Figure 8-10
Trunk airline mail routes, 1934 (excluding the Big Four).
(Courtesy: R. E. G. Davies Collection)

Iowa-Based Airlines and Commercial Service

Except for one airline initiated by Iowans or serving Iowa cities, scheduled intrastate and regional service was not a successful venture. Mid West Airlines, owned by John Livingston, operated the first scheduled airline in Iowa, flying between Waterloo and Des Moines. The daily-except-Sunday service began in 1928, charging one-way fares of $10 and $18 for the round trip. Yellow Cab Airways, owned by Russell Reel of Des Moines, president of Yellow Cab Company and Aviation School, started scheduled flights between Kansas City, Des Moines and Minneapolis in May, 1929, and ceased operations in September. Eagle Airlines, based in Kansas City, operated through Des Moines to Minneapolis from August to November, 1930.

More successful was Tri-States Airline, owned by Arthur S. Hanford of Sioux City, who began charter service between Omaha, Sioux City, Bismark and St. Paul in 1928 and was certified for daily service between Sioux City and Omaha in 1933. Following a merger and reorganization, the airline emerged as Mid Continent in 1938, the name more appropriately describing the route structure, part of which had been purchased by Northwest Airlines in 1934. One year later, Braniff, Northwest and Mid Continent sought approval for the north-south route through Des Moines, awarded by the CAA to Mid Continent in 1940. Their schedule included regular service to Mason City, and at Des Moines one route went to Kansas City and another to St. Louis with an intermediate stop at Ottumwa. The airline flew Lockheed Lodestars which could carry 14 passengers in addition to mail and express. The airline was sold to Braniff in 1952 (Fig. 8-9, 8-10).

Airline passenger travel from Des Moines and Iowa

City increased substantially in the 1930s. In June, 1935, United Airlines had two daily eastbound planes stopping at Des Moines, and in 1936 the city was included on a new international route via United to the West Coast and Pan American to Hawaii and Manila, in the Philippines. Three daily eastbound and two daily westbound flights were initiated in 1940, using Douglas DC-3's. Requisitions for planes and pilots during the war and priorities for government and military personnel seriously restricted civilian accommodations.

The Douglas DC-1, ancestor of all Douglas airliners.
(Courtesy: R. E. G. Davies Collection)

United Airlines Twin Wasp powered Douglas DC-3.
(Courtesy: R. E. G. Davies Collection)

United Airlines Douglas DC-4E, 1939.
(Courtesy: R. E. G. Davies Collection)

Summary

Economic activity in Iowa at the onset of the depression was almost equally divided between agriculture and manufacturing. Railroads operated over 10,000 miles of track, and private and commercial motor carriers served communities located on over 100,000 miles of roads and highways. The agricultural crisis of the early 1930s, precipitated by the depression and lack of recovery from post-World War I years, influenced operations of both major carriers. Despite emergency legislation by the federal government, the majority of railroads operating in Iowa were forced into receivership, and the pace of highway construction was slowed materially. Intense intermodal competition brought motor carriers under federal regulation in 1935, followed by regulation of commercial airlines in 1938. Pipelines moving liquid products began service in the early 1930s, and inland waterway improvements in the form of lock and dam construction standardized channel depths of the Mississippi River and commercialized the Upper Mississippi section. Multi-purpose use of water resources was studied as a means of relieving critical economic conditions in the Missouri Valley. Aviation development consisted of increased civilian and business flying, expansion of airports and commercial airline schedules. The impact of the depression on transportation modes, as evidenced by federal, state and private concerns, appeared to indicate a growing awareness of the need for development of additional facilities, a more favorable balance in traffic potential and increased opportunities for public and private selection and use of the various transportation systems.

Selected References

Baker, George P. "The Possibilities of Economies by Railroad Consolidations and Coordination." *American Economic Review* Part 2 (March 1941): pp. 140-157.

Brown, D. Clayton. *Western Tributaries of the Mississippi.* National Waterways Study. Navigation History NWS-83-7. Washington, D.C.: U.S. Government Printing Office, 1983.

Buck v. Kuykendall, 267 U.S. 307 (1925).

Budd, Ralph. "Lightweight Diesel-Electric Trains." *Civil Engineering* (September 1938): pp. 592-595.

Bush & Sons v. Mallory, 207 U.S. 317 (1925).

Carlson, Norman, ed. *Iowa Trolleys.* Bulletin 114. Chicago: Central Electric Railfans Association, 1974.

Casey, Robert J., and W.H.S. Douglas. *Pioneer Railroad.* New York: McGraw Hill Book Co., 1948.

Coordination of Motor Transportation. 182 ICC 263 (1932).

Corliss, Carlton J. *Main Line of Mid America.* New York: Creative Age Press, 1950.

Daggett, Stuart. *Principles of Inland Transportation.* 4th ed. New York: Harper & Bros., 1955.

Davies, R.E.D. *Airlines of the United States Since 1914.* London: Putnam & Company, 1972.

Deliva, Frank H. "Iowa Farm Price Revolt." *Annals of Iowa 32* No. 3 (January 1954): pp. 171-202.

______. "Frantic Farmers Fight Law." *Annals of Iowa 32* No. 2 (October 1953): pp. 81-109.

______. "Attempt to Hang an Iowa Judge." *Annals of Iowa 32* No. 5 (July 1954): pp. 337-364.

Donovan, Frank P., Jr. "The North Western in Iowa." *Palimpsest 43* No. 12 (December 1962): pp. 545-597.

______. "The Rock Island in Iowa." *Palimpsest 44* (September 1963): pp. 384-438.

______. "The Milwaukee in Iowa." *Palimpsest 45* (May 1964): pp. 179-230.

______. "The Burlington in Iowa." *Palimpsest 50* (September 1969): pp. 481-533.

Fifteen Percent Case. 178 ICC 359 (1931).

Fox, Gertrude M. "Index Numbers of Iowa Farm Product Prices." *Agricultural Experiment Station Bulletin No. 336.* Ames: Iowa State College, 1935.

Healy, Kent T. *The Economics of Transportation in America.* New York: The Ronald Press, 1940.

Hudson, William J., and James Constantin. *Motor Transportation, Principles and Problems.* New York: The Ronald Press, 1958.

Interstate Commerce Commission. *Statistics of the Railways of the United States.* Washington, D.C.: U.S. Government Printing Office, 1938.

Interstate Commerce Commission Bureau of Transport Economics and Statistics. *War-Built Pipelines and the Post War Transportation of Petroleum.* Washington, D.C.: U.S. Government Printing Office, 1944.

Iowa Hiway Hilites. Ames: Iowa State Highway Commission, January 1960 to summer of 1974. (Published as *Hiway Hilites* from October 1974 to January 1975.)

Iowa State Highway Commission. Reports of the State Highway Commission for the years ending December 1930, 1931, 1934, 1937, 1939, and 1940. Des Moines: State of Iowa.

Locklin, D. Phillip. *Economics of Transportation,* 7th ed. Homewood, Ill.: Richard D. Irwin, Inc., 1972.

Lynch, Edward S. *Analysis of Accounting Practices in Railroad Abandonments in Iowa from 1920 to 1940.* Bulletin 149, Iowa Engineering Experiment Station. Ames: Iowa State College of Agriculture and Mechanic Arts, 1941.

Lyon, Peter. *To Hell in a Day Coach; An Exasperated Look at American Railroads.* Philadelphia: J. P. Lippincott Co., 1968.

Michigan Public Utilities Commission v. Duke, 226 U.S. 573 (1925).

Motor Bus and Motor Truck Operations. 140 ICC 685 (1928).

Murray, John J. *It Took All of Us: 100 Years of Iowa Electric Light and Power Company.* Cedar Rapids: Iowa Elecric Light and Power, 1982.

National Highway Users Conference. *Diversion An Analysis of Applying Motor Vehicle Impost Collections to Other than Highway Purposes.* Washington, D.C.: January 1936.

Nelson, Paul C. "Rise and Decline of the Rock Island Passenger Train in the 20th Century." Part I. *Annals of Iowa 41* No. 1 (summer 1971) pp. 655-665.

Petersen, William J. "The Federal Barge Line." *Palimpsest 53* No. 9 (September 1972): pp. 390-401.

Rivers and Harbor Act, Public Resolution No. 10. 72nd Cong. 1st Sess. (1930).

Sage, Leland L. *A History of Iowa.* Ames: Iowa State University Press, 1974.

Taff, Charles A. *Commercial Motor-Transportation.* Cambridge, Md.: Cornell Maritime Press, Inc., 1975.

Throne, Mildred. "Streamliners in Iowa." *Palimpsest 32* No. 6 (June 1951): pp. 233-235.

Tweet, Roald D. *History of Transportation on the Upper Mississippi & Illinois Rivers.* National Waterways Study. Navigation History NWS-83-6. Washington, D.C.: U.S. Government Printing Office, 1983.

U.S. v. Butler, et. al. Receivers for the Hoosic Mills Corporation. 297 U.S. 1 (1936).

U.S. Department of Agriculture. *Agricultural Statistics.* Washington, D.C.: U.S. Government Printing Office, 1940.

Wobert, George W., Jr. *American Pipe Lines.* Norman: University of Oklahoma Press, 1952.

Chapter Nine
World War II and Post-War 1940-1960

Introduction

Because of the war years, the decades of the forties and fifties are combined into one chapter. Domestic water carriers were brought under ICC jurisdiction in 1940 by legislation which also included a written declaration of national transportation policy. In the late 1940s and mid-1950s, previous regulations on railroads were eased or eliminated in recognition of the growing intensity of intermodal competition.

The entrance of America into World War II focused attention on logistical problems unprecedented in transportation history as the nation mobilized to fight on two fronts, thousands of miles from the mainland. Rationing of fuel and supplies curtailed domestic operations of motor, water and air carriers except for defense purposes while the burdens of supplying military and civilian requirements strained the capabilities of the railroads and also provided record earnings. However, even though granted a long series of rate increases, the railroads could not maintain wartime revenues in a peacetime economy as more normal traffic patterns returned.

Federal aid was expanded to improve and restructure the nation's highways which had deteriorated during the war years and were unable to meet the needs of postwar motor vehicle traffic. Multi-lane interstate and toll highways challenged planning and funding on both federal and state levels. Liquid pipelines spread to meet the demand for fuel for home heating and transportation facility usage. Expansion of waterway commerce resulted in rebvuilding and replacing locks and dams on the Mississippi and initiation of the Pick-Sloan project on the Missouri River. Air commerce legislation of he 1920s and 1930s was cancelled by the Federal Aviation Act of 1958, creating the Federal Aviation Agency. State aeronautical commissions were established and federal assistance became available for airport construction.

Federal Transportation Legislation

The Transportation Act of 1940

The Transportation Act of 1940 was a further attempt to aid the railroad industry and to reflect the changes in the nature and structure of transportation since 1920. Highway, water and pipeline traffic had intensified intermodal competition, and problems had emerged concerning relations between them as well as their respective places in the transportation system. The 1940 legislation put all domestic water carriers under regulation as Part III of the Interstate Commerce Act, with certain exemptions pertaining to bulk and liquid carriage. The effect was to eliminate about 90 percent of the carriers from economic regulation. Following enactment, all five major modes were under federal regulation, although by no means could it be said that the regulations fell with equal force on the carriers as to purpose, enforcement and assistance. Three of the modes operated under exemptions, a fact that the railroads never allowed Congress to forget. Pipelines in the early 1940s were under a consent decree which limited the percentage of dividends that they could pay to a parent company. In order to forestall a congressional investigation, the pipelines agreed to the decree.

In the 1940 Act, the first written declaration of a national transportation policy was expressed. Previously the federal government had relied upon a series of uncoordinated legislative actions that evolved from protecting the public against railroad abuses in 1887, to eventually encompassing other modes with somewhat different regulatory treatment or restraints. The declaration of policy left much to be desired in what it contained as well as omitted and was generally considered to be highly ambiguous. It was geared to the preservation of the "inherent advantages" of the several modes rather than promoting competition to protect the interests of shippers and travelers. As such, it became nothing more than support for the "status quo."

The railroad consolidation efforts of 1920 were dropped, but consolidations still had to have ICC approval. Land grant railroads were released from obligations to transport mail and government traffic at reduced rates, an obligation that dated back to the land grant era between 1850 and 1870. It is interesting to note that the military personnel obligation was not discontinued until October, 1945, following the war's end. Commenting on the legislation, the *Traffic World* stated: "Both motor and water transportation will now be under regulation by the same body as are the railroads with which they compete. That is as it should be. But the rails pay for their own right-of-way as do the motor vehicles, though there is some dispute as to whether the latter pay in full measure . . . But waterway operators . . . still are permitted to use free waterways deepened and maintained for them at public expense, even when, as the users are fond of saying, the waterways originally were provided by God. God does not, however, keep the channels deepened and clear, nor does He dig canals. Until this situation is taken care of, our transportation situation will still be lopsided in its regulatory aspects." On the land grant repeal, the publication further stated: "The saving to the railroads in actual money will be material not including the hire of clerks who figure these rates as well as the relief from wear and tear on their brains. Computing rates on government traffic is one of the most complicated and detested routine duties of railroading."[1]

Other Railroad-Related Legislation

The Reed-Bulwinkle Bill of 1948 legalized rate bureaus, exempting from anti-trust laws ICC approved agreements between or among two or more carriers relating to rates, fares, classifications, divisions, allowances or charges and procedures for joint consideration, etc. The Smathers-Harris Act, officially known as the Transportation Act of 1958, was designed to keep pace with changing economic and technical conditions. It authorized the ICC to guarantee up to $500 million in loans for maintenance or purchase of capital equipment, clarified the motor carrier agricultural exemption, and gave the commission greater authority over intrastate rates. It also repealed the three percent wartime tax on freight.

Wartime Transportation Arrangements—The Railroads

Unlike conditions existing during World War I when railroads were taken over and operated by the federal government, there was no attempt in 1941 to duplicate the procedure. Instead, the Office of Defense Transportation (ODT) was created. Its authority extended to all modes including private passenger cars and trucks, and its orders were not subject to judicial review. Under Section 1 of the act, the ICC already had broad powers over rail services during emergencies, and certain additional powers were granted over motor carriers in the Second War Powers Act of 1941.

The ICC and ODT sought cooperation between shippers and carriers to meet the war emergency. Attempts were made to promote pooling of railroad freight and passenger cars, interchange of locomotives, elimination of round-about routing of trains, substitution of trucks or buses on short distance routes, coordination of traffic toward ports to meet ship and convoy departures, higher minimum carloads, diversion of certain types of traffic to water carriers, discontinuance of lightly used trains and branch lines, discouragement of pleasure travel, improved maintenance of motor vehicles and reductions in their speeds. The efforts resulted in the movement of war and domestic traffic without serious congestion and to the general satisfaction of all interests involved—a sharp contrast to the experiences of 1917-1920.

Motor Carriers and Highways

The entry of the United States into the war brought German submarines to the Eastern seaboard and Gulf coastal waters, and by May 1942 they were sinking oil tankers at a rate high enough to result in fuel shortages in the East. ODT shifted railroad tank cars from inland points to the East Coast, assuming that the trucking industry would fill the gaps. But the plan ran into the historical obstacle of state size and weight laws, and the result was not only diversity but also chaos.[2] Manufacture of automobiles was prohibited as plants converted to production of tanks, aircraft engines and ordinance. New car production fell from 3.5 million units in 1941 to 610 in 1944. Tires were rationed and recapped to conserve the dwindling supply, and the states were requested to reduce highway speeds to 35 miles per hour to save rubber, fuel and engine wear.

By April 1942, severe shortages forced gasoline rationing in the East, and by November they extended

[1] *Traffic World,* Editorial, September 10, 1940.

[2] U.S. Department of Transportation, Federal Highway Administration, *America's Highways, 1776-1976,* Washington, D.C.: U.S. Government Printing Office, 1976, p. 145. In 1941, five states still limited wheel loads according to the width of a tire, a holdover from the days of solid rubber tires, long since disappeared from usage. Limits on payloads were as low as 7,000 pounds; limits on gross loads ranged from 18,000 to 36,000 pounds for four-wheeled vehicles. Permissible gross loads on one axle varied from 12,000 to 24,640 pounds. In January 1942, Congress gave the ICC the power to set uniform truck weights and sizes as a war measure. A provisional code was drawn up by the Public Roads Administration and AASHO, permitting axle loads of 18,000 pounds and gross loads of 30,000 pounds for four-wheeled vehicles and up to 40,000 pounds on vehicles with three or more axles. The code was effective in all states in May 1942.

to the entire nation. Four gallons per week were allowed for ordinary travel with exceptions for defense industry workers and farmers. To alleviate the hazards facing coastwise tankers, two crude oil pipelines were built by the federal government. The longest was the "Big Inch" from Longview, Texas to the New York-Philadelphia refining area. The line was 1,340 miles long, cost approximately $78 million and operated between 1943 and 1945. The "Little Big Inch" pipeline ran 154 miles from Corpus Christi to Houston, Texas and cost $6.1 million. The "Big Inch" was sold to the Texas Eastern Transmission Company in 1947 and converted into a natural gas pipeline.

Wartime mobilization emphasized the dependence of the nation on highways. Studies in Michigan indicated that 13 percent of the defense plants received all of their materials by truck, and in most of the remaining plants at least half of inbound and outbound traffic came by truck. In February 1942, Thomas MacDonald announced that only a fraction of the 10 million defense employees could be accommodated by rail and bus facilities; the remainder would have to depend upon private automobiles. Rationing not only reduced non-essential travel but highway revenues as well. The first to feel the pinch were the Eastern states, and in Iowa revenues dropped 33 percent in June 1942 compared to the same month in 1941. The Public Roads Administration reported that nationwide gasoline rationing resulted in a decline of 35-40 percent in highway traffic in 1942 below the corresponding levels in 1941. States that had laws preventing the diversion of highway funds handled the restrictions without serious difficulty; those which allowed diversion suffered severe problems. But there were bright spots midst the gloom of war, restrictions and shortages, for motor vehicle accidents dropped drastically in 1942, both in number and in the rate per 100 million miles of travel.[3]

Wartime Earnings for the Western Railroads

For the railroads operating in the Western District (west of the Mississippi River) between 1940 and 1944, operating revenues almost tripled, average revenue per mile increased two and one-half times, and the operating ratio fell from 73.70 to 63.07. Iowa railroads shared in the prosperity as the state harnessed its people and resources to meet demands for increased agricultural and industrial output. Mechanization of farm machinery and a new hybrid corn assisted in reaching record production levels of farm products. Cash value of crops used or sold amounted to $12.2 billion in 1945 compared with approximately $452 million in 1940. The number of industrial establishments, ranging from small town manufacturers to giant firms in the large cities, rose from 2,540 to 2,965 between 1939 and 1947, doubling the number of employees and increasing values added from $243 to $671 million during the period.

Operating over 8,900 miles of track, Iowa railroads increased net earnings from $21.2 million in 1940 to $63.3 million in 1944, and net earnings per mile of road rose from $2,274 to $7,357 in the years 1940-1943. Rising operating costs resulted in petitions for increases of 10 percent in passenger fares, six percent on freight and three percent on agricultural products and edible livestock and animal products, effective in March 1942. The requests were approved by the ICC until May 1943 when they were suspended as no longer necessary or justified—the suspension to remain until six months after legal termination of the war. Revenue traffic within the state showed substantial growth in all categories except for forest products, as indicated in Table 9-1. At the close of the 1940s, revenue traffic continued at relatively high levels except for animals and products, a classification more vulnerable to truck competition (Table 9-2).

The CMStP&P benefited from cancellation of commercial shipments through the Panama Canal. Heavy wartime traffic on the CNW offered optimism for the future, and indeed their operating revenues for 1947 were the highest in the history of the company. But operating revenues are not net profits. Rowland "Bud" Williams, who had become chief executive officer in 1939 and president in 1944, saw the war years as well as those following as an era of spiraling costs of materials, supplies and labor. Taxes also were siphoning large amounts of earnings into state and federal treasuries. Believing that any hope of a profitable future would lie in reduction of fixed and operating expenses, he began a "housecleaning program" by abandoning 266 miles of branch lines, 566 miles of side tracks and closing hundreds of stations and other buildings by 1943. Williams pointed out the differences in the operation of the railroads in two World Wars, stressing that federal

[3] National Safety Council, *Accident Facts 1973,* Chicago: National Safety Council, 1973, p. 59.

operations had cost the taxpayers $2 million per day in World War I, whereas the railroads paid more than $3 million per day in taxes during the second World War.

The CB&Q, following similar strategy, abandoned a system-wide total of 383 miles of branch lines during the war years. One was the lightly used 22-mile line from Mount Ayr to Grant City, Missouri in 1944, which led to what became known as the "Burlington Formula." Employees who found their positions worsened through abandonments were protected by a displacement allowance. If the employee lost his job, he was to receive compensation for the next four years. The formula was used by the ICC in comparable abandonment cases through the 1960s.

John D. Farrington headed the CRI&P since 1936 when the railroad was struggling through reorganization, but not until 1947, after 15 years and six months in the federal courts, was the road returned to its owners. In 12 years Farrington abandoned 650 miles of branch lines and, no longer content with a "Granger Road" label, induced 2,084 industries to locate on the system, producing $22.8 million annually in freight revenues. In the eight years from 1936 to 1944 the company spent $70 million on improvements, of which $19 million went into deferred maintenance and $51 million was charged to the capital account. Later, expenditures on road and equipment brought the total to $130 million. Estimated savings by 1944 were approximately $7 million per year, and in September 1944, Farrington proudly announced that the road had $100 million in cash and government securities. At the close of the 100th anniversary year (1952), the CRI&P reached a new all-time record for gross income—$213.9 million—and a net income of over $22.6 million. Common stock earned $13.57, and preferred, $32.43 per share. From the early 1930s, when the railroad had been frequently described as a case of total bankruptcy—financial, physical and managerial—the accomplishments of the Farrington regime were nothing short of miraculous, and in 1952 his railroad was rated as second to none in the United States.

Table 9-1
Revenue Freight Carried by Railroads Operating Within Iowa, 1940-1945

Classification	1940	1945	% Increase
	(Millions of tons)		
Products of Agricuture	13.44[1]	25.93[1]	92.9
Animals & Products	4.99	7.00	40.3
Products of Mines	11.14	16.93	51.9
Products of Forests	3.41	3.61	05.8
Man. & Miscellaneous	19.61	38.03	93.9
Less-Than-Carload	1.06	1.57	48.1
Totals	53.65	93.07	73.5

(*Source:* Iowa Commerce Commission, *Annual Reports,* 1941 and 1946.)
[1] Figures rounded to the nearest unit.

Table 9-2
Revenue Freight Carried by Railroads Operating Within Iowa, 1940-1949

Classification	1940	1949	% Increase
	(Millions of tons)		
Products of Agricuture	13.44[1]	19.80[1]	47.3
Animals & Products	4.99	5.43	08.8
Products of Mines	11.14	16.61	49.1
Products of Forests	3.41	5.79	69.9
Man. & Miscellaneous	19.61	32.84	67.4
Less-Than-Carload	1.06	1.72[2]	62.2
Totals	53.65	82.19	53.2

(*Source:* Iowa Commerce Commission, *Annual Reports,* 1941 and 1950.)
[1] Figures rounded to the nearest unit.
[2] Includes forwarder trafffic.

Highway Construction Curtailed, 1942-1945

Until 1941 approximately half of the funds available for primary road construction had been provided by the federal government. In November, President Roosevelt ordered that any funds used on highway work be confined to those projects essential to national defense. By April 1942 the War Production Board stopped all highway construction except that which had begun on or before that date, and no new projects in excess of $5,000 could be started unless certified as essential to the war effort. Highway facilities to provide access to war-related installations were funded by the Defense Highway Act of 1941 in the amount of $151 million to cover the full cost. Allotments to states were not based on fixed formulae but rather on the requirements of specific projects. In Iowa there were five installations that could qualify: the Iowa Ordnance Plant near Burlington, the Des Moines Ordnance Plant near Ankeny, the Sioux City Air Base, the Federal hospital near Clinton and the Naval Training Base near Ottumwa. By 1943 all projects had been approved or completed. From August 1941 to March 1945 the volume of traffic on the Iowa primary road system steadily declined, resulting in falling revenues in the fund from state sources (Tables 9-3 and 9-4).

It was in the latter years of the war that the trend toward "tandem axle" semi-trailers became apparent. These vehicles weighed between 51,000 and 56,000 pounds gross and carried a payload of up to 34,000 pounds. A few combinations used tandem axles under both tractor truck and trailer, raising the gross weight to about 59,000 pounds with a payload of 36,000 pounds. Tire and loading economies made the larger vehicles attractive to operators, but the state warned that the pounding of heavy vehicles would "definitely hasten the day when the cross-state pavements would have to be replaced."[4]

Throughout the war years, regular or ordinary highway work slowed perceptibly. About 298 miles were paved, 151 miles graveled, 277 miles graded and 81 miles bituminous surfaced, and on June 30, 1945, no uncompleted primary work was under contract. Construction expenditures paid from the primary road fund fell from $6.8 million in 1941 to $551 thousand in 1945, the lowest for any year since 1919. Secondary road expenditures declined from $105 thousand to $198 in 1945, and funds spent on urban streets dropped from $1.1 million to $18 thousand. Primary road maintenance varied between $4.0 and $4.9 million during the five-year period.

[4] Iowa State Highway Commission, *Report of the State Highway Commission for the Period July 1, 1944 to June 30, 1945,* Des Moines: State of Iowa, 1945, p. 19.

Table 9-3
Average Daily Traffic on Primary Roads, 1941-1945

Average Daily Traffic by Month

Month	1941	1942	1943	1944	1945
January	1,098	1,094	679	796	710
February	1,268	1,120	844	790	755
March	1,361	1,192	883	764	865
April	1,528	1,275	959	836	887
May	1,713	1,354	1,011	889	930
June	1,832	1,418	1,044	926	1,017
July	1,918	1,417	1,040	966	---
August	2,094	1,473	1,050	972	---
September	1,809	1,371	955	957	---
October	1,674	1,222	887	938	---
November	1,536	1,154	824	839	---
December	1,394	691	826	747	---
Average Annual Daily	1,598	1,232	917	868	

(*Source:* Iowa Highway Commission, *Annual Report,* 1945.)

Table 9-4
Primary Road Income, 1940-1945

For Year Ending June 30	Primary Road Fund—State Sources (In thousands)
1940	$19,298
1941	20,799
1942	21,311
1943	18,346
1944	17,517
1945	17,855

(*Source:* Iowa Highway Commission, *Annual Report,* 1945.)

The PostWar Years

Railroad Problems

As measured by freight ton-miles and passenger-miles, 1944 represented a peak in railroad movements. The 747 million ton-miles (68.6 percent of the total) were the highest reported until the 1970s, and the 98 million passenger-miles were double that of 1920. For four years passenger service was profitable, but by 1949 the deficit reached $650 million and continued at a somewhat lesser amount through 1970. Termination of European hostilities in April and the Pacific War in August 1945 resulted in a decline in every item of railroad performance in 1945, compared to 1944. Revenue ton-miles fell nearly 26 percent and the average length of haul over six percent. It took more than 85 cents of each revenue dollar to cover operating expenses for the first five months of 1946 as against slightly over 67 cents in 1945. For the 12 months ending in March 31, 1946, the rate of return on property investment averaged 2.56 percent, compared to 3.91 percent for a similar period in 1945. Fifty-nine Class I railroads failed to earn interest and rentals during the first quarter of 1946, of which 23 were in the Western District.

Alarmed by an inflated wage and price level and the prospect of replacing heavy retirements of worn out or obsolete equipment and motive power, the Class I Carriers on April 15, 1946, requested permission to raise freight rates by 25 percent, with exceptions, effective May 15, on one day's notice. On April 26, the ICC opened hearings on that part of the request concerning short notice and simultaneously reopened the 1942 case, then in a state of suspension.[5] Supplemental petitions for similar increases were filed at the same time by domestic water carriers and freight forwarders. Petitions for intervention, but not rate increases, were filed by motor carrier bureaus representing approximately 1,000 trucking firms operating throughout the Western District.

The suspended increases were restored on June 30, 1946, amounting to six percent on general traffic and three percent on agricultural products, animals and products and products of mines. The short notice petition in the new case was denied pending public hearings which were held throughout the nation during the next five months, and on December 6,

[5] *Increased Rates, Fares and Charges,* 264 ICC 695 (1946). The objective of the carriers was to secure rate increases which, if approved, would add approximately one billion dollars to their operating revenues, the largest single rate increase since 1920.

1946, rail and water common carriers were authorized an increase of 17.7 percent effective January 1, 1947. Further increases were granted in 1947 and 1948.

In June 1950 the United States, together with its allies in the United Nations, began efforts to repel the North Koreans from overrunning South Korea. Before the transition to a peacetime economy could be satisfactorily accomplished, additional burdens of rearmament were thrust upon the nation. The problems were not eased by widespread railroad labor disputes which resulted in federal possession, control and operation of Class I railroads under Presidential directive as of August 27; nor the replacement of equipment retired in the early postwar period. Freight car shortages developed due to the needs of the military and the higher levels of demand from agricultural, industrial and commercial transportation.

The inflationary trends resulting from the Korean War and the yet unfilled requirements of the economy translated into proposals by railroads and other common carriers for additional rate increases and curtailment or elimination of unprofitable services. Higher wages, materials costs, taxes, and diversion of traffic to motor and water carriers prompted requests which came almost annually during the 1950s. The ICC's Bureau of Economics and Statistics estimated that the cumulative increases authorized from 1946 to 1960, including the exemptions, averaged 115.2 percent. However, the higher rate levels did not forestall the declining trend in the rate of return on property investment, which dropped from 6.58 percent in 1942 to 2.86 in 1959 (Table 9-5).

Table 9-5
United States Railroad Rate of Return on Property Investment, 1940-1959

Year	Rate of Return (%)	Year	Rate of Return (%)
1940	3.02	1950	4.34
1941	4.41	1951	4.16
1942	6.58	1952	4.54
1943	6.03	1953	4.55
1944	4.87	1954	3.51
1945	3.90	1955	4.54
1946	2.82	1956	4.27
1947	3.53	1957	3.62
1948	4.36	1958	2.91
1949	2.91	1959	2.86

(*Source:* From 1940 to 1950, ICC *Transportation Statistics in the United States.* From 1950, ICC *Annual Reports.*)

Table 9-6
Revenue Carload Freight of Railroads Operating in Iowa, 1949-1959

Classification	1949 (Millions of Tons)	1959	Percentage Change
Products of Agriculture	19.80	18.50	-06.5
Animals & Products	5.43	4.30	-20.8
Products of Mines	16.61	16.67	---
Products of Forests	5.79	8.34	30.6
Man. & Miscellaneous	32.84	35.76	8.1
Less-Than-Carload	1.72[1]	1.51[1]	-12.2
Totals	82.19	85.08	3.4

(*Source:* Iowa Commerce Commission, *Annual Reports,* 1950 and 1960.)

[1] Includes forwarder traffic.

Operations in Iowa

In 1950, 12 Class I railroads operating in Iowa reported earnings of $51.7 million or $6,933 per mile of road; and in December 1955, net earnings averaged $53.6 million or $6,275 per mile. The Korean War armistice, declining traffic in farm products and the intensive competition of other modes, reduced earnings drastically during the second half of the decade. Net earnings averaged $25.1 million or $2,604 per mile of road, dropping by 1960 to $13.8 million and $1,655. On November 1, 1960, the M&StL was acquired by the CNW, reducing the number of Class I roads to 11. Trends in revenue freight showed an overall increase of less than four percent during the 1950s as losses occurred in products of agriculture, animals and products and less-than-carload freight. Virtually no changes were observed in the movement of mine products. Increases were recorded in manufactured and forest products (Table 9-6).

Meanwhile, motor freight operations within and throughout Iowa showed substantial gains over the 1940-1950 period. From three million tons carried in 1940, the volume rose to slightly under 10 million tons by 1959, and by the same year, an additional five million tons were handled by liquid motor carriers.

Trends in Railroad Passenger Service

The cyclical passenger decline in volume was reversed during the war years but fell back into prewar patterns afterward. Regulation hampered wholesale curtailment of service, normally a standard practice in unregulated industries when demand falls over long periods. Restrictions had been built into statutes regulating railroads, and state commissions ruled on abandonments with little or no consistency. The Transportation Act of 1958 gave the ICC authority over discontinuance of inter- and intrastate passenger service and could overrule states when national policy judgments indicated that the service should be terminated. The policy was supported by the railroads in the belief that more conformity in abandonment cases would result. In the same year (1958) commercial airlines introduced jet service, adding a new dimension of speed to their schedules, and another negative factor came in 1967 when first-class mail was shifted from railroad passenger trains to airlines. By 1970, 24 railroads operated 547 passenger trains, down from approximately 20,000 in 1920.

Realignment of the Service in Iowa

Although trends were unfavorable, relatively widespread service was available in Iowa in the 1950's but deteriorated in various stages soon thereafter. An Iowa State University research project analyzing the influence of small cities' intercity transportation on regional urban goals noted that of 54 study region counties, only Decatur County was not covered by a passenger route in 1950, and only eight study county seats were not directly served by scheduled routes. Nelson observed that "1960 appeared to be the turning point," and except for routes connecting major cities, almost all service vanished by that year. Ten years later, there was practically no passenger service available.[6]

By 1955 the CNW had reduced passenger service to five transcontinental trains in each direction. Disagreement between the road and the UP over service and division of revenues resulted in the October 30 decision to transfer the trains between Council Bluffs and Chicago to the CMStP&P, a bitter blow to residents using the former schedules. Henceforth, the familiar yellow streamliners would be routed through Manilla, Perry and Marion, to the delight of those cities. To counter the change, the CNW substituted three new trains in Illinois and Iowa. The *Corn King* was an overnight train with coaches, pullmans and a diner, and the daytime *Omahan* provided coach, parlor car and dining service. The third, appropriately named the *Kate Shelley,* ran from Chicago to Boone. But the bloom was off the CNW's passenger business for the trains were not profitable. Eventually, the *Kate Shelley* was cut back to Marshalltown, then to Clinton, and on May 15, 1960, passenger trains between Council Bluffs and Clinton made their final runs and passed into history. Not one train on the CNW's lines remained in service in Iowa, which meant that the state also lost some mail and express service over these routes.

[6] R. L. Carstens, Project Director, *Integrated Analysis of Small Cities Intercity-Transportation to Facilitate the Achievement of Regional Urban Goals,* U.S. Department of Transportation Report No. DOT-TST-75-13,Washington, D.C.:U. S. Government Printing Office, June 1974, p. 122; Paul C. Nelson, "Rise and Decline of the Rock Island Passenger Train in the 20th Century," *Annals of Iowa 41* No. 2 Part II (Fall 1971): p. 760.

By the sixties, the CB&Q's *Zephyrs* were running deficits. Gradually their streamliners in Iowa were terminated, and in 1968, the *Californa Zephyr* was recommended for abandonment but given an additional year of life by the ICC. Shuffled also were the transcontinental schedules of the CMStP&P, reducing the five crack streamliners to two daily and dropping the *Mid-West Hiawatha* which had begun operations in 1940. In June 1954 a Talgo-type lightweight streamliner named the *Jet Rocket* was ordered by the CRI&P and made its first appearance in Des Moines in 1956. It cost $788,000, consisted of 10 coaches, featured a low center of gravity and weighed about half as much as the conventional trains of the same length. Built by General Motors, the design allowed the train to take curves at high speed through the addition of wheels in the center of the cars. Initially it ran between Chicago and Peoria, but operational problems forced the train off the main line and into suburban service where it remained until 1965. By 1967 most of the CRI&P mainline trains had been discontinued except for those operating between Chicago, Peoria and Des Moines.

The Chicago, Rock Island & Pacific *Jet Rocket* in Des Moines. (Courtesy: Author)

The Chicago, Rock Island & Pacific *Jet Rocket* in Des Moines. (Courtesy: Author)

Electric Interurbans

There were eight electric interurbans operating in Iowa in 1950. One, the Tama and Toledo, was abandoned in 1953 and four, the Cedar Rapids and Iowa City; Des Moines and Central; Fort Dodge, Des Moines and Southern; and the Waterloo Railways, were reclassified as Class II railroads in 1954. These four operated 260 miles of tracks and had $186 thousand in net railroad operating income in 1950. The remaining three were the Charles City Western, Mason City and Clear Lake and Southern Iowa Railways, with only 60 miles of track and a net income of $24,543. The Waterloo Railway was formed by the CRI&P and IC in 1958 to acquire the Waterloo, Cedar Rapids and Northern and was integrated into the IC in 1970. The Des Moines Central and Fort Dodge, Des Moines and Southern became part of the CNW in 1968 (Fig. 9-1, p. 214).

Federal Aid to Highways

Huge wartime savings created an insatiable demand for consumer and industrial products including automobiles and trucks. Nationwide, registrations grew by 22 and 35 percent, whereas in Iowa, the growth was 36 and 55 percent. The end of rationing and emergency speed controls resulted in an increase in highway travel of approximately six percent nationally and was to continue at a high level for decades. But the highways were in poor condition to receive the accelerated traffic since wartime restrictions prevented maintenance, and structurally the roads were in worse shape after than before the war.

The Federal Aid Act of 1944 authorized $500 million annually for the first three postwar years, divided into $225 million for the federal-aid primary system (A system), $150 million for principal secondary and feeder roads (B system), and $125 million for improvement of urban extensions into and through cities with populations of 5,000 or more (C system). In the same act, Congress established a National System of Interstate Highways, requiring the states to select roads located so as to connect by direct routes the principal metropolitan areas. The total system was not to exceed 40,000 miles. By the legislation, state highway departments were brought actively into city and regional planning.

On June 29, 1956, President Eisenhower signed the Federal Highway Act of 1956. Twenty-four billion dollars were authorized for the Interstate System for 13 years, with the states' contribution to be about $2.5

billion. It was expected to provide for traffic needs anticipated in 1975. Subsequently, the system was formally designated as the "National System of Interstate and Defense Highways," and expanded to 42,500 miles. In 1978, the FHWA estimated that the system would cost 104.3 billion. It was 92 percent completed by January 1979. Prior to 1954, federal appropriations were made through the U. S. Treasury from funds collected on fuel and excise taxes on motor vehicles. Afterward, federal taxation and highway funding for interstate construction were linked together by a highway trust fund from which federal funds would be paid. The program was self-financed in that payments could not exceed the balance in the fund except through accumulation of surpluses. It was a pay-as-you-go system, or as some people complained, "pay-before-you-go."

Standards governing physical dimensions, control of access, and other design features had to be approved by the Secretary of Commerce (after 1967 by the Secretary of Transportation). Maximum weight and width limits were prescribed for motor trucks operating on the Interstate System. Funds could be denied any state permitting operation of vehicles heavier or wider than specified after July 1956, or those which on that date could be lawfully operated in the state, whichever was greater. Weights were "frozen" at 18,000 pounds on a single axle or 32,000 pounds on a tandem axle, gross weights at 73,280 pounds and width at 96 inches. About half of the states permitted weights greater than those specified at that time. The federal government appropriated 90 percent and the states 10 percent of the funding for Interstate construction, but the ABC program remained at a 50-50 percent matching basis until 1973 when the federal share was increased to 70 percent.[7]

In 1959 a number of changes were made in order to provide for increased funding. The federal motor fuel tax was raised from three to four cents per gallon for the period October 1, 1959 to June 10, 1961. After that date, the one-cent fuel increase was to be replaced by one-half of the 10 percent excise tax on new automobiles and five-eighths of the eight percent tax on motor vehicle parts and accessories, to be effective from 1961 to 1964. None of the revenues from the two excise taxes had been previously dedicated to the fund.

Highway Issues in Iowa

After 1945 it appeared that changes would have to be made in Iowa road financing. Matching funds from state sources for secondary roads were ample, but it was difficult to continue primary road improvements under limits placed on expenditures from the primary road fund. In 1947 the General Assembly created a Highway Investigation Committee to study highway problems and report to the next session. The committee was chaired by Senator J. T. Dykhouse of Rock Rapids and included three senators, four representatives and four private citizens. Clyde Coykendall of Ames was the Administrative Assistant. The report of November 1948 recommended a pay-as-you-go system covering 20 years, costing an estimated $943 million on the basis of 1948 prices. From this amount, $428 million would be required to pave 2,200 miles of graveled or unsurfaced primary roads and the remainder to "provide every reasonably located farmhouse a surfaced road outlet."[8]

To raise the additional $14.2 million annually to finance the program, it was recommended that motor vehicle registration fees would be increased, including a $10 fee on farm tractors driven on the highways. Use and sales taxes collected on new motor vehicles

[7] Charles A. Taff, "Commercial Motor Transportation," *Transport Topics* (January 9, 1978): p. 22. Since the Highway Act of 1916, apportionment of federal funds among the states for primary roads was based on a formula consisting of three criteria, each having equal weight: (1) the area of the state relative to the total area of the nation; (2) the population of the state relative to population of the nation; and (3) the rural road mileage relative to the total mail mileage of the nation. For secondary roads, the formula remained the same except that rural population was substituted for general population and for urban areas was based on the ratio of population in municipalities over 5,000 to populations in other urban centers in all states as shown in the Federal Census. For the Interstate program, the funds were divided by two-thirds in the population ratios, one-sixth by total areas and one-sixth by rural mail delivery and star routes.

[8] *Report of the Highway Investigation Committee Created by Chapter 351 Laws of the Fifty-second General Assembly, November 15, 1948.* Des Moines: State of Iowa, 1948. The committee found much to commend and little to criticize with respect to Iowa's highway progress. They stated that the road laws were fundamentally sound and that the highway program "had been kept reasonably free from graft or scandal." Tenure of highway engineers in both state and county organizations had been little influenced by changing political administrations. Essential features of the proposed program were summarized in the *Des Moines Register,* December 31, 1948; Iowa State Highway Commission, *Report of the State Highway Commission for the Period July 1, 1947 to June 30, 1948,* Des Moines: State of Iowa, 1948, p. 8.

and parts, tires and accessories but not used for highway purposes would be added to highway revenues. All road taxes would be placed into a single state fund and divided as follows: 48.5 percent for primary roads, 45 percent for secondary and farm-to-market roads and 6.5 percent for municipal roads and streets. No increases were proposed in the gasoline tax which had been raised to four cents per gallon in 1945. The program was supported by Governor Beardsley and the newly organized Good Roads Association and an amended version was adopted by the General Assembly in 1949.

The ceiling of $17 million in the primary road fund was removed, as was diversion of the excess amount above this limit to the farm-to-market fund. A Road Use Tax Fund was created, and distribution to the various systems was changed to allow 42 percent to primary roads, 50 percent to secondary roads and eight percent for city streets. The new formula increased the primary road fund to $27.4 million for the fiscal year ending June 30, 1950, or $10.5 million over the previous limit. An additional one cent gasoline tax was authorized in 1953 to be used exclusively for paving of graded primary roads.

There were few objections to the new road plan, and progress on secondary road work proceeded between 1948 and 1953 at a rate that would provide the all-weather surfaced highways to rural homesteads earlier than scheduled. Nearly three-fourths of the system was surfaced by 1954. Primary road construction, however, did not meet expectations. By 1954, $130 million had been spent with over $750 million still needed to complete the program. One of the major problems was heavy traffic, projected to increase 33 percent by 1960 but already up 38 percent from 1949 to 1954. Earl Hall, editor of the *Mason City Gazette,* commented early in 1955 "that the task of estimating future road needs calls for an imagination that just doesn't seem to be present in the human animal." Road problems like those found generally in transportation never end. Planning, whether for five, ten or twenty years, unfortunately at times implies that problems are solved when the programs are completed. Accurate forecasts are difficult when economic and social conditions change, weather cannot be controlled and heavy traffic wears out the pavements. Fred White clearly stated the frustration of road builders in 1920. "By the time we get the roads paved, the first of them will be worn out and we will be ready to start again. So let's go forward into it with our eyes wide open that we are starting something that we shall never finish."[9] The problems faced by highway officials in the intervening years certainly supported the wisdom of these words.

The legislature had provided for a farm-to-market road system of some 10,000 miles (not exceeding 10 percent of the highway mileage of the county), but federal-aid secondary funds matched with state funds were available for expenditure on a larger approved federal system, encompassing 33,000 miles. Upon recommendation of the highway commission, the General Assembly passed a Farm-to-Market Road Act in 1947 authorizing a farm-to-market system of not more than 35,000 miles of secondary roads and directing the commission to "equitably divide the mileage of the state among all of the counties."[10] The act also provided that a portion of the farm-to-market road fund should be allotted among counties in such a manner as to equalize, insofar as possible, the condition of construction or reconstruction in all sections of the state. This fund officially became known as the Farm-to-Market Equalization Fund.

From 1913 through 1949, highway research by the commission was conducted on an informal basis, specifically geared to individual projects with few publications summarizing the results. In 1950, a Highway Research Board was created whose members included the deans of engineering at the State University (University of Iowa) and the Iowa State College, six county engineers and three commissioners. Mark Morris, formerly the commission's traffic officer, was appointed director. In 1960 the position of director was abolished, and a Highway Research Department administered by a research engineer was established to coordinate programs with other departments and administrators.

Man-made and natural forces combined to make 1951 a difficult year for road building and maintenance. Steel and cement shortages resulted from the Korean War, and national rearmament prevented initiation of paving and bridge projects and completion of others. Nature caused more problems. Snowstorms in March exceeded any previously recorded during that month, and the spring breakup was the most destructive of

[9] George S. May, "Post War Road Problems," *Palimpsest 46* No. 2 (February 1965): pp. 116-128.

[10] *Laws of the General Assembly,* Chapter 162 (1947).

road surfaces since the advent of modern highway construction. Floods in the spring halted highway and bridge work, and crews were idled for weeks. The situation did not improve materially until 1953, the most productive year since the end of World War II. The black-painted centerline was discontinued in 1954 and replaced with a dash-reflectorized white centerline and yellow no-passing lines on all heavily traveled roads. During the fiscal year ending June 30, 1956, all paved roads were marked, and an additional 1,033 miles of bituminous surfaced highways were scheduled for painting before the spring of 1957. When completed, all primary roads except those surfaced with gravel or crushed rock would show the new lines.

Administrative Changes in the Fifties

Fred White, Chief Engineer for the highway commission for 33 years, retired in 1952 and was appointed Consulting Engineer until 1954. He was succeeded by Edward F. Koch who resigned after two years to enter private industry. His replacement was John G. Butter, Administrative Engineer since 1948, and a long time employee of the commission who served until 1960, when L. M. Clauson was appointed to the position. In the first 39 years of commission history, only two chief engineers had directed the highway programs; Thomas MacDonald from 1913-1919 and Fred White from 1919-1952. The record of their accomplishments on both state and national levels is well-documented in the highway progress made under their supervision.

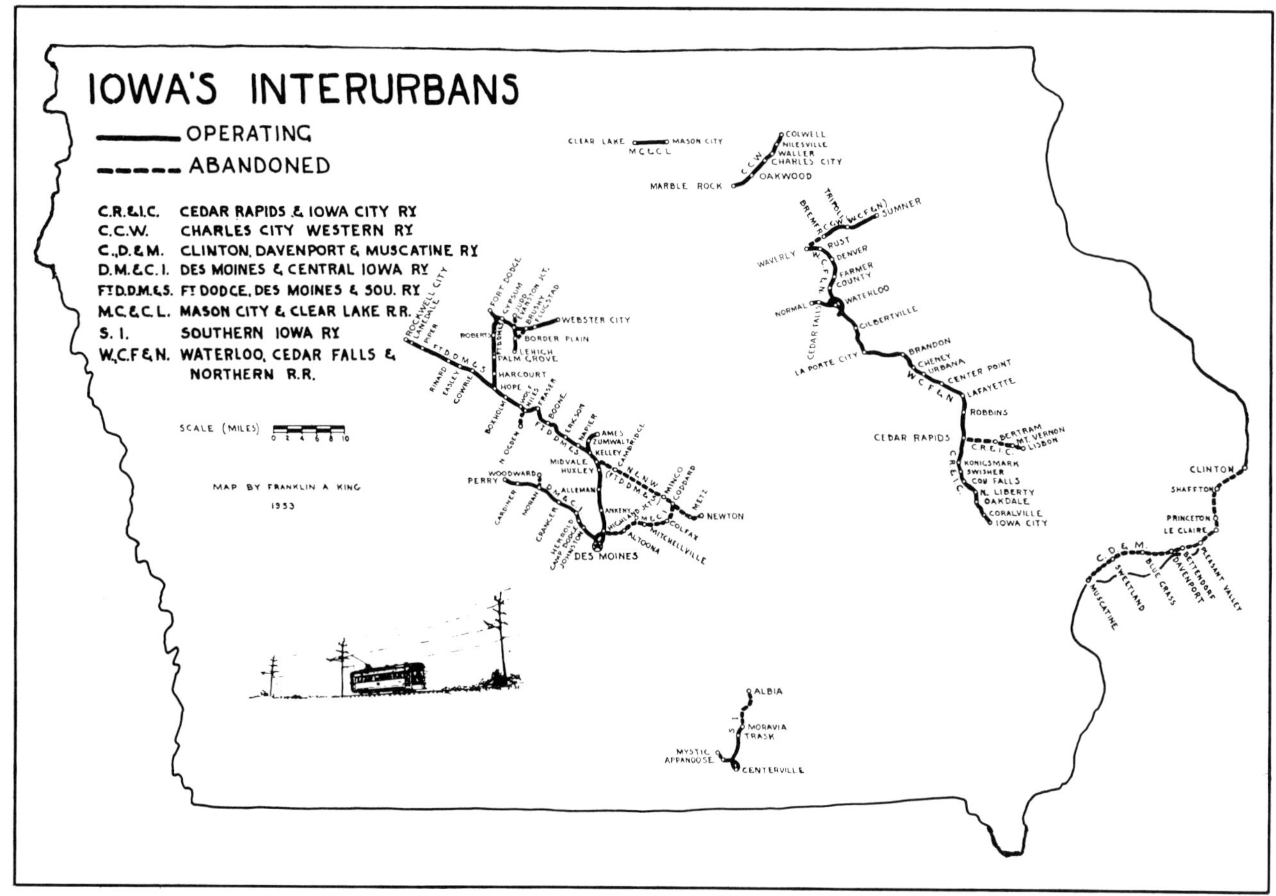

Figure 9-1
Map of Iowa's Interurbans by Franklin A. King - 1953.
(Courtesy: The Palimpsest Publication Vol. XXXV No. 5 - May 1954, Author: Frank P. Donovan, Jr.)

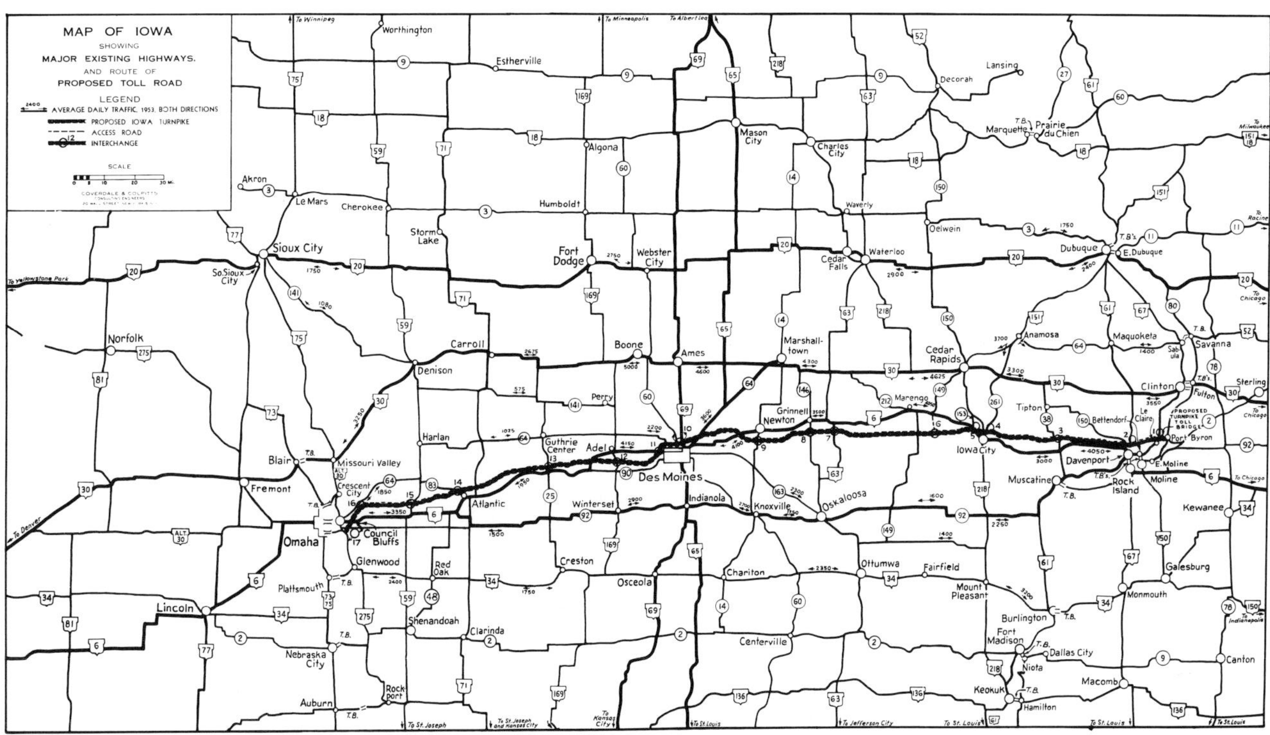

Figure 9-2

Proposed location of east-west Iowa toll road, 1954.

(Courtesy: The Initial Feasibility Report on The Proposed Iowa Turnpike - July 20, 1954, Coverdale & Colpitts, Consulting Engineers.)

The Toll Road Proposal

Historically, three general sources of funds have been used for highway improvements. Property taxes were an important revenue base prior to 1920 and continued to provide revenues for counties and municipalities. A second source consisted of vehicle registration and title fees, operator licenses, gasoline taxes, taxes on tires and accessories, use tax on the purchase of vehicles and special taxes on for-hire carriers or larger trucks. A third source was tolls collected directly from road users. In the early postwar years when highways were in poor condition through wartime neglect, toll roads became popular. They had the advantage of improving highway travel quickly without obligating state funds and were financed by the sale of revenue bonds to be repaid from the toll charges.

By the early 1950s the toll road bandwagon was rolling. Pennsylvania started the trend in the 1930s, building a four-lane superhighway between Pittsburgh and Harrisburg, and toll road authorities had been created in 15 states including Indiana, Illinois and Kansas. By 1954 there were 1,382 miles of toll roads under construction at costs estimated at $2.5 billion and plans made for an additional 3,314 miles estimated to cost $3.75 billion. If and when these highways were built in the states east of Iowa, it was visualized that a tremendous increase in traffic would be fed into Iowa's already overburdened roads. This prospect led the General Assembly to authorize the highway commission to study the feasibility of building and operating an east-west toll road to be a modern, four-lane, limited-access highway of approximately 300 miles.

A report was prepared for the commission on July 20, 1954 and delivered to Governor Beardsley on August 4. The principal conclusion was "that construction and operation of an east-west toll road across Iowa, including a new bridge over the Mississippi River from a new river crossing (Illinois State Road No. 20) near Davenport to a connection with Primary Road U.S. 275 near Council Bluffs by way of Iowa City,

Newton, Des Moines and Atlantic, appears to be economically feasible in 1959 if bonds can be issued and sold bearing an annual rate of 3.5 percent interest."[11] The road was estimated to cost $180 million, financed by bonds which could be retired in 21 years from receipt of tolls (Fig. 9-2).

In 1955, an Iowa Toll Road Authority was created entirely separate from the highway commission to construct and operate the road. The agency came into existence and was working with consulting engineers on road design at the same time that the national interstate program (which would not include toll roads) was being formulated by the federal government. Iowa's portion of the interstate plan was somewhat over 700 miles, running east to west in the general vicinity of the proposed toll road and north to south in two segments, one in the vicinity of U.S. 65 and 69 and the other along a road bordering the Missouri River between Hamburg and Sioux City. This program delayed work on the toll road, and in 1957 the Authority was abolished. Federal funds for the interstate system became available in 1957, and Iowa quickly took advantage, contracting for $13 million of construction in the same year (Fig. 9-3).

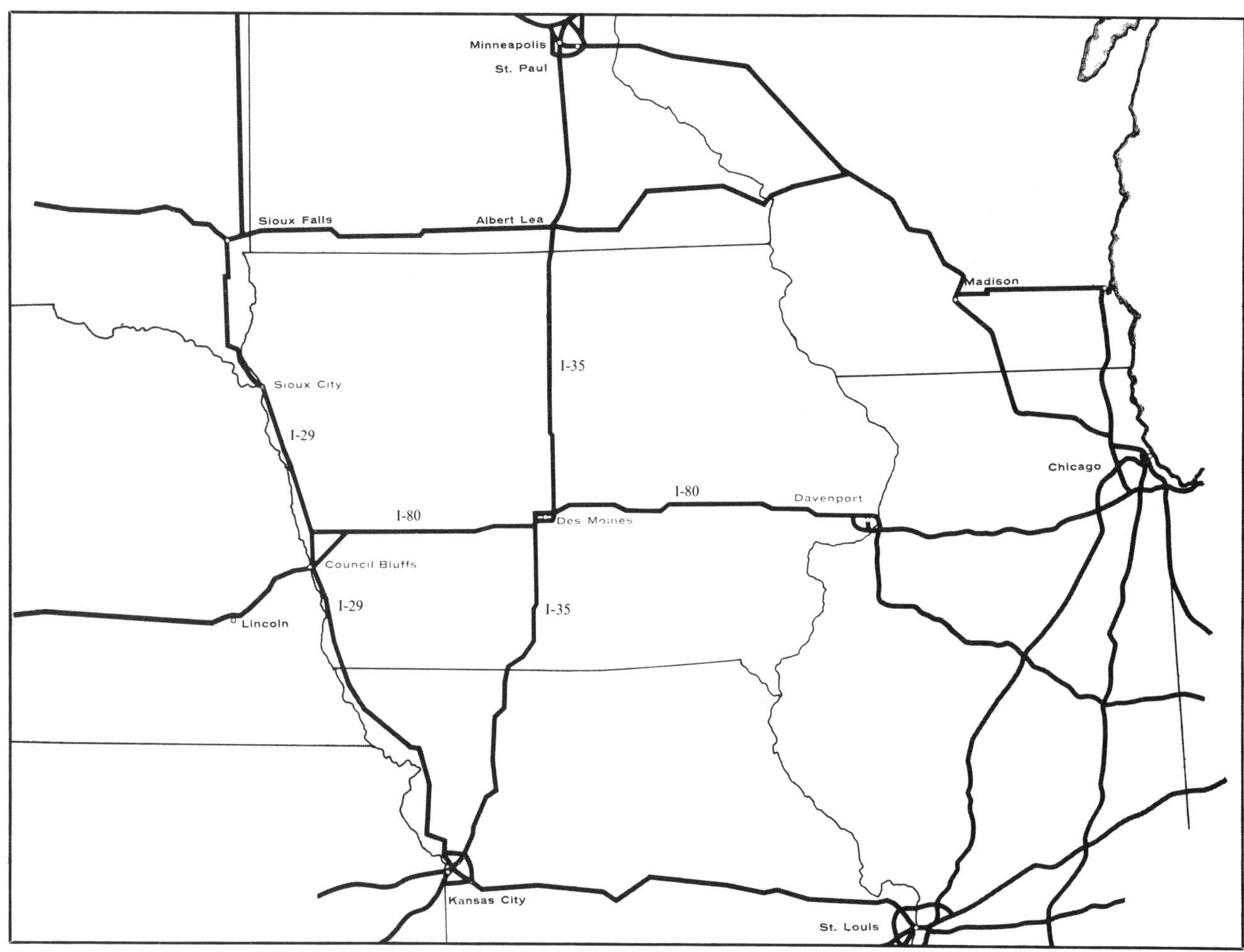

Figure 9-3
The Iowa portion of the original 41,000 mile National System of Interstate and Defense Highways totaled 711 miles.
(Courtesy: Iowa Highway Needs Study 1960-1980)

[11] Iowa State Highway Commission, *Report of the State Highway Commission for the Period July 1, 1954 to June 30, 1955.* Des Moines: State of Iowa, 1955, p. 6.

Inadequate roads and bridges typical of the state primary road system in the 1950s.
(Courtesy: Iowa Highway Needs Study 1960-1980)

Highway Improvements and a New Study Committee

At the close of fiscal 1955, over half of Iowa's paved roads were 25 years old or older, 3,272 miles having been built before December 1, 1931. Payment of principal and interest on county bonds, diversion of primary road funds, and the necessary construction of almost 5,000 miles of additional primary roads made impossible the modernization of 25-year-old, 18-foot pavements as fast as traffic warranted. There were three major critisims of Iowa's roads: (1) narrowness of pavements, (2) narrowness of bridges and (3) lip curbs. Pavement widening started in the fall of 1953 on U.S. 30 between Ames and Nevada where three feet of concrete were added to each side of the road and in 1954, U.S. 65 was widened between Mason City and Manley. A 22-foot pavement with four-foot shoulders for roads carrying fewer than 400 vehicles per day and special four-lane highways for daily traffic of 4,000 vehicles were the commission's standards for construction in 1954. At that time, approximately 3,300 miles of pavement were still in the 18-foot vintage of the 1920s and only 150 miles were wider than 22 feet. By 1959, 2,256 miles of 18-foot pavement on the primary system needed further attention.

The experiment of widening pavements met

immediate approval of the public. Governor Hoegh announced a program for widening 6,000 miles during 1955 and 1956 to be funded by an additional one cent gasoline tax. The tax was raised to six cents per gallon effective July 1, 1955. Bridges were modernizied and widened, using all of the substructure and as much of the superstructure as possible. This was a pioneering activity—a challenge to the bridge design department to make new bridges from old ones. By May, 1955, 11 bridges had been placed under contract for widening the roadway from 20 to 30 feet and by December 31, 60 bridge-widening contracts were in effect. Remodeling rather than rebuilding at the original sites saved the state over $214,000.

Motor vehicle registrations continued to climb rapidly. One hundred thousand additional automobiles and 23,000 trucks were registered between 1955 and 1960. Changing economic and demographic patterns put new strains on primary highways and urban streets, and secondary road problems remained to be solved in certain areas of the state. The number of farms had declined from 19,500 in 1955 to 18,400 in 1960, dropping the farm population from 772,000 to 755,000, but the average size of farms increased by 10 acres during the period. The impact resulted in consolidation of facilities in rural communities, including school reorganizations requiring expanded bus transportation; and the population movement to urban centers forced new programs for additional expenditures on highways and streets. The adjustments indicated a growing transition from a predominantly rural to a more urban society. Higher levels of traffic on major primary roads and mounting traffic control problems in the cities brought renewed demands for another study of the state's highway needs.

A Road Study Committee of 11 members was organized in 1958 with Senator D.C. Nolan of Iowa City as chairman. Commission engineers and specialists participated along with engineering advisory committees representing primary roads, county roads and city streets. Technical consultants included the Automotive Safety Foundation of Washington, D.C. for engineering and the Public Administrative Service of Chicago for fiscal studies. Following two years of work, the committee reported to the General Assembly in 1961.

Trends from 1960 to 1980 were projected, predicting a population gain of 400,000, all in cities, for a total of 3.1 million residents. Anticipated was a 40 percent rise in the number of motor vehicles to 1.8 million and a 70 percent increase in travel to reach 20 billion vehicle miles annually. About 61 percent of all traffic was found to be on rural and urban primary roads, 19 percent on other urban streets and 18 percent on secondary roads. Important provisions of the report were as follows:

1. The proposed State Primary Road System would be limited by legislation to 8,400 miles, rural and urban. Within the primary road system, the highway commission should establish a rural and urban freeway system not to exceed 2,000 miles, including the Interstate System (Fig. 9-4).
2. The commission should be given administrative and fiscal responsibility for all proposed primary roads inside municipalities similar to its responsibility in rural areas, thus changing the present permissive authority to mandatory responsibility.
3. The 1,900 miles of existing state primary roads that provide mainly local, not statewide, service should be transferred to counties and municipalities. If retained as a state responsibility, they should be treated like county roads or city streets and financed separately, with no other roads or streets added.
4. Reduce the existing 34,000 miles of the Farm-to-Market System to 32,000 miles by eliminating routes not included in the Federal-Aid Secondary System. Establish 12,000 miles of the more heavily traveled Farm-to-Market System as a County Trunk System; the remainder to be termed "county feeder roads."
5. Legislation should require that the 12,000 miles of municipal streets be classified into state primary, city arterial and access streets. The commission should select primary routes totaling about 860 miles and assist and approve municipal selection of arterial streets totaling about 2,300 miles. Combined primaries and arterials should be limited to 30 percent of the total street mileage of any municipality.
6. Local governments should establish with the commission approved minimum design standards for improvement of each class of roads and streets other than local secondary roads and access streets. Other recommended legislation included repeal of laws prohibiting diagonal roads; authority for the commission to

transfer to any other jurisdiction without arbitrary restrictions, any primary road whose function has been superceded by new locations; and clarification of responsibility for state park and institutional roads.[12]

The estimated average annual cost for the 20-year "catch up" program was $278 million; the total was about $5.6 billion at 1959 prices. This amount would cover the construction or reconstruction of 5,600 miles of two-lane rural primary roads and about 1,500 miles of multi-lane highways as well as the paving of all county trunk roads and arterial streets. It would also provide for a dustless surface on all but 500 miles of access streets. Maintenance over the period would range from 11 percent on the primary routes to 45 percent on county local roads. Acting on the recommendations, the General Assembly made permanent previous temporary gasoline taxes and placed the receipts in the road use tax fund rather than the primary road fund. After allocating $2.5 million as matching aid for the interstate system, $500,000 for operation of the Secondary and Urban Departments of the commission, and $125,000 for grade crossing work, the remainder of the funds were distributed as follows: 45 percent to the primary system, 30 percent to the secondary roads, 10 percent to the farm-to-market system and 11 percent to municipal streets.

A Brief Review of Commission Activities

The 69 percent increase in average daily traffic per mile of primary road between 1941 and 1959 was a concern to the state. Another concern related to safety and potential road damage from violations of laws on size and weight of trucks and for improper registration for loads carried. The commission had this responsibility since 1941, and in the 20-year period it had collected $3.7 million in fines at a cost of $2.5 million. Few of the summonses served by traffic officers were challenged by vehicle operators. Public demand for improvements was met by expenditures of $650 million between 1946 and 1960, which on an annual basis increased from $11 to $120 million. Improvements on the primary road system are found in Table 9-7.

Expansion of highway work required additional departments, boards and subdivisions in the commission's organizational structure. In addition to the Office of Chief Engineer, seven departments functioned with 623 full-time employees in 1940. By 1959 there were 13 departments employing 1,826 full-time workers. Added over the period were the Administrative, Bituminous, Right-of-Way, Secondary Road, Research and Urban Departments. A computing center was established in 1958 and a Reciprocity Board in 1959. The Board consisted of the Commissioner of Public Safety and representatives of the state highway and commerce commissions. Its purpose was to make agreements with other states or with trucking firms engaged in interstate transportation on reciprocity for motor vehicle registrations.

There was considerable progress on the elimination of dangerous railroad crossings during 1940-1960. In 1919 the primary road system of 6,400 miles had 1,063 grade crossings or an average of one for every six miles of road. In 1940 the system, including extensions within cities and towns, had 789 crossings or an average of one for each 12.1 miles, and 287 were protected by gates, watchmen or mechanical guards. A reduction of 69 occurred by 1959, leaving 720 crossings on 8,626 miles, 515 of them protected by automatic signals and reflectorized warning signs.

Table 9-7
The Primary Road System, 1940 and 1959

Type of Surface	1940 (Miles)	1959 (Miles)
Concrete and Asphalt Paving	5,208	6,258
Bituminous and Asphalt	671	1,647
Gravel and Crushed Rock	2,592	720
Built to Grade - Not Surfaced	22	---
Not Built to Grade	62	---
Totals	8,555	8,625

(*Source:* Iowa Highway Commission, *Annual Reports,* 1940 and 1959)

[12] Automotive Safety Foundation with cooperation of the Iowa State Highway Commission and Iowa Counties and Municipalities, *Iowa Highway Needs 1960-1980, A Plan to Pace Highway Development with Economic Growth,* A Report by the Automotive Safety Foundation to the Highway Study Committee, Washington, D.C.: Automotive Safety Foundation, November 1, 1960, pp. 6-8.

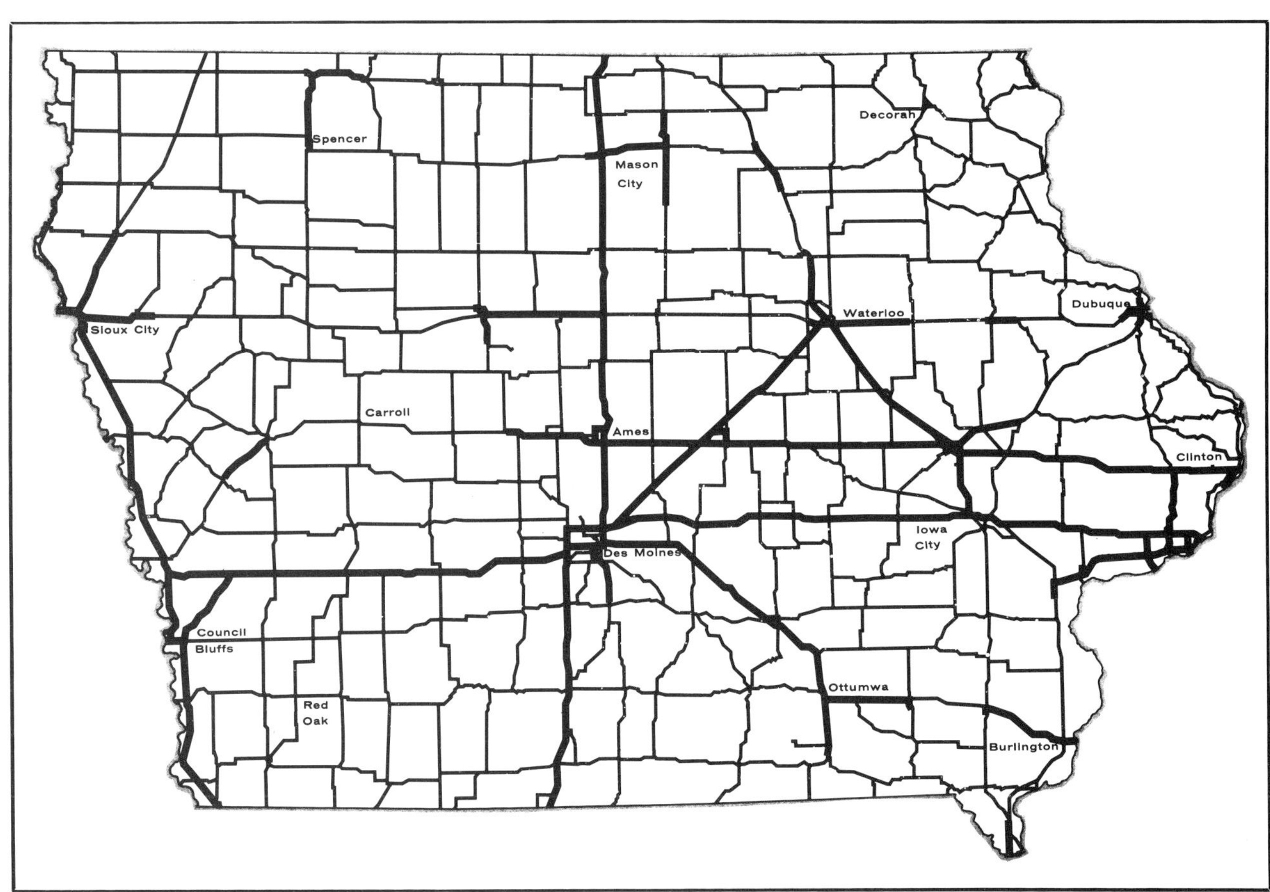

Figure 9-4
1,500 miles of multi-lane rural highways needed by 1980.
(Courtesy: Iowa Highway Needs Study 1960-1980)

The Liquid Pipeline Network

Crude oil and gasoline pipeline mileage more than doubled in the postwar years, increasing from 916 to 2,178 miles. The largest gains were in 12-inch pipes which expanded from 56 to 761 miles and eight-inch from 246 to 528 miles. Demand for the products resulted in additional lines built by the Great Lakes system. From 1946 to 1948, another line was constructed from Kansas City to Omaha and continued to new terminals at Sioux City, Sioux Falls and other northern points. Twelve-inch lines were built paralleling the original lines from Kansas City to Des Moines and Minneapolis in 1950 and in 1954. Twelve-inch and eight-inch lines were laid from Des Moines to the Mississippi River. A 12-inch line was built from Des Moines to Coralville in 1955 and extended to Middlebury, Illinois in 1959. New terminals were constructed at Bettendorf in 1957, and an eight-inch line was extended from Grinnell to Waterloo to serve a new terminal in 1960. Mobil Pipeline facilities in Iowa were originally built in 1941 and later purchased by Mobil Oil in 1959. The products line ran through Sioux, Plymouth and Woodbury counties with pump stations at Onawa and Hawarden. At Hawarden, the line connected with the Kanek Pipeline for delivery to other locations.

Fees to the state were collected on the basis of 50 cents per diameter inch of construction and at the rate of 25 cents per diameter mile, payable in advance as an inspection fee. During 1959, a number of pipelines were subject to renewal fees of 50 cents per inch regardless of size, plus an application fee of $25.00. The permits originally issued had been in effect for a period of 25 years, the maximum permitted under state law.

River Navigation

Mississippi River Improvements

Following World War II, river commerce reached levels sufficiently high enough to get the Inland Waterways Corporation out of the transportation business. North of St. Louis, traffic passed 10 million tons by 1950, 30 million tons in 1962, and 50 million tons by 1970. More powerful and sophisticated towboats with a range of 2,000 to 9,000 horsepower pushed specialized barges in tows which could carry cargoes equivalent to those in 25-35 railroad cars.

Dams were upgraded at Minneapolis and Hastings and the lock replaced at Keokuk. The Keokuk project for a 110 x 600 foot lock was planned in the 1930s but delayed by the war. Completion of the nine-foot channel had created a bottleneck at Lock No. 19, requiring double locking of tows after long hours of waiting. Also the drop in the river at Keokuk was 38.2 feet, the sharpest then in the channel, and for these reasons Congress authorized a 1,200 foot lock in 1945. Work was postponed by the Korean conflict and the lock was not opened until 1957. Between St. Louis and the mouth of the Missouri, a seven-mile stretch of ragged rock ledges known as Chain of Rocks impeded navigation in low water. A canal and locks were authorized for the area to be located one mile from the lower canal entrance. Because of difficulty maintaining the nine-foot channel depth below Lock No. 26 at Alton, a low-water, fixed-crest dam was built at Granite City, Illinois (No. 27), the first complete barrier across the Mississippi. The Chain of Rocks locks were opened in 1963. No further serious trouble was encountered until Lock and Dam No. 26 became a problem.

The *Lachland Macleay,* the most powerful towboat on the Upper Mississippi River, 1955. (Courtesy: U.S. Army Corps of Engineers, Rock Island District)

Towboat *Omaha* on Missouri River, 1954.
(Courtesy: U.S. Army Corps of Engineers, Omaha District)

The Pick-Sloan Plan on the Missouri

The flood control plan regarded as the most comprehensive made for the Missouri was proposed by Colonel Lewis A. Pick, Division Engineer. It called for a series of levees between Sioux City and the mouth, five multi-purpose dams on the main river and six on the tributaries. A study directed by William G. Sloan of the Bureau of Reclamation recommended 90 multi-purpose reservoirs and 16 hydroelectic plants. The Army Engineers filed a separate plan for a nine-foot channel from St. Louis to Sioux City. Pick's plan emphasized flood control, endorsed navigation programs and was supported by downstream interests. Upper Valley groups preferred the irrigation approach.

The conflicts in these plans were resolved through agreement by the Engineers and the Bureau in 1944 and were further supported by the President who suggested that the plans could be administered by a Missouri Valley Authority (MVA). The project was passed by Congress in the Flood Control Act of 1944 which omitted the nine-foot channel and the MVA, preferring instead that the Corps and Bureau develop the river on a piecemeal basis. But as the debate grew over creation of an MVA, Congress authorized the nine-foot navigation channel from Sioux City to the mouth of the Missouri in the Rivers and Harbors Act of 1945. However, there was a general concensus that some coordinating agency should be established to organize and coordinate the federal and state agencies involved in river development. The result was the Missouri River Interagency Committee whose members were drawn from federal agencies and representatives of the governors of five states.

With the death of the MVA, appropriations were made on a year-by-year schedule. By 1951, $125 million had been spent on flood control, the nine-foot channel between St. Louis and Kansas City and on irrigation facilities. Six main river dams and eight on the tributaries had been completed by 1967, but progress on the navigational channel was slow. Severe flooding in 1951 destroyed pilings and revetments, the worse occurring between Sioux City and Omaha. It was the navigation improvements that were expected to stimulate industrial development and transportation savings, but disagreements betweeen the Corps and Missouri Basin Survey Commission on estimates of increased traffic in 1952-1953 resulted in Congressional debates over further funding. Commercial traffic grew from 52,285 tons in 1952 to 287,000 tons in 1954. By 1962, the estimated tonnage was 2.25 million tons, most of which was on the river below Omaha since the channel above that city was only four feet deep. By 1976 an eight and one-half foot channel depth between Sioux City and the mouth increased traffic to over 3 million tons.

Benefits to Iowa from the Missouri River Basin project were expected to come from flood control, navigation, power development, improvement of municipal water supplies and sewage disposal, and incidental recreation benefits. These would apply only to the western section of the state. There were approximately 700,000 acres of bottom land in Iowa subject to flooding of which 247,000 acres were frequently flooded. The possible damage, assuming a $30 value per acre, would amount to about $6.5 million for each occurrence.

Improvement of navigation could affect an area along the river extending about 100 miles into Iowa, approximately one-third of the state. About 50 percent of the commercial corn and 68 percent of the commercial oats would be available for movement to markets during the navigation season. Power development would be expected to attract industries to the region, and a more even flow of water throughout the year could assist cities on the Missouri to eliminate some of their water supply and sewage disposal problems.

Iowa Officially Enters the Air Age

The third permanent regulatory agency—The Iowa Aeronautics Commission—was created in 1945. Five members were appointed, one from each of five districts into which the state was divided for the purpose of regional representation. The commissioners were Guy Richardson, chairman, from Jefferson; H. Lisk, Independence; F. C. Eighmey, Mason City; J. C. "Cy" Rapp, Shenandoah; and R. G. Starret, Spencer. Lester G. Olcutt was Director. They served without salary and were paid $9.00 per diem to a maximum of $450 per year. The legislature gave the commission the responsibility of promoting aviation in Iowa by making rules and regulations if necessary. To this end a seven-fold program was instituted to include: (1) registration of certificated air agencies and airmen in the state; (2) promotion and enforcement of safety regulations initiated by the CAA; (3) promotion of aviation and air safety education; (4) assistance for communities to establish, develop and operate airports; (5) sponsorship of an air marking program; (6) annual sponsorship of the Iowa Air Tour; and (7) in conjunction with the Iowa State College, sponsorship of the Aviation Clinic.

To perform these services and provide for additional functions, registration fees were assessed on airmen, planes and air schools. The annual fee for airmen was $1.00, for air schools $20 for the first registration and $10 for annual renewals, and for planes 1.5 percent of the list price on the first and second registration, following which fees were progressively reduced to the fifth where the fee was 25 percent of the original amount. Similar adjustments were made for used aircraft registered in Iowa for the first time. The fees represented the primary sources of income for the commission, except for a $50,000 appropriation in 1945, as a support fund for the biennium ending on June 30, 1947. However, in 1949 legislation was passed which provided that all unfunded gasoline taxes be transferred into an Aeronautics Trust Fund, an action recommended by the commission in 1945. The commission was headquarted in the poultry building at the fairgrounds in Des Moines until 1949, when they moved to 6003 Fleur Drive, across from the Municipal Airport.

As of July 1, 1945, there was little or no information available concerning the number, size, location and ownership of airports in the state. The data were gathered through personal contacts, letters of inquiry and various questionnaires, and in 90 days the commission had enough information to start registration of airports, air schools and airmen. An Airport Directory issued in October, 1946 listed 185 landing areas of which 47 were municipal airports. By 1947 there were about 200, mostly unpretentious. Sioux City's army-developed field was the largest, and other major airports were at Burlington, Cedar Rapids, Des Moines, Dubuque, Iowa City, Mason City, Ottumwa and Waterloo. Generally, the airports were located two to three miles from the community served, encompassed 150 acres and had an assortment of small buildings and hangars. Only seven had concrete runways, seven more some additional surfacing and for the remainder, pilots landed on turf. Seven CAA comunication stations made twice-hourly weather broadcasts; 17 other aircraft radio stations operated in the state[13] (Table 9-8).

The Federal Airport Act

Federal aid for airport construction became a reality in 1946, when Congress passed the Federal Airport Act. To communities willing to support airport projects, the federal government would pay half the cost with certain restrictions. No federal funds could be used for hangar construction or living quarters or to pay more than one-quarter of the purchase price of land. By the fall of 1947, 22 Iowa airports had been allocated $806,502 of federal funds to match $952,511 of local investment. Because local conditions varied, it was difficult to estimate the cost of a new airport which the CAA stated could range from a minimum Class 1 for $35,000 to a good Class 2 field for $400,000. If surfacing materials were nearby and the chosen site required a minimum of grading and draining, many Iowa cities were expected to invest less than these amounts.

Airplanes in Use

In 1947 there was an airplane for every 1,471 persons in Iowa as contrasted to a national average of one for nearly 1,600 people. Plane registrations totaled 1,760—691 in commercial service and over 1,000 used for personal and private business flying. There were 8,950 pilot's licenses held by Iowans and one in 2,500 had a private plane at his service. By contrast, in 1938 there were 384 pilots and 184 planes which landed on 35 airfields and airports in the state (Table 9-9).

Table 9-8
Iowa Airport Facilities, 1947

Service or Facility	Number of Airports
Concrete Runways	7
Other Surfaces	7
Turf	181
Hangar Space for Transient Aircraft	94
Minor Repair	77
Major or Minor Repair	45
Restaurant	19
Rest Rooms	49
Transportation to Town	156
80 Octane Gasoline	154
91 Octane Gasoline	13

(Source: John Isham Mattill, *Report From the Survey for the Development of Aviation in the State of Iowa.* M.A. Thesis (unpub.) State University of Iowa, Jan., 1948: Table IV, p. 38.)

[13] *Iowans Flying: A Survey for the Development of Aviation in the State of Iowa,* prepared under the direction of the Department of Mechanical Engineering, State University of Iowa, Iowa City, published by the Iowa Aeronautical Commission, Des Moines, 1948: pp. 17-19. The report was discussed as a project in "Technical Journalism" by John Isham Matill, M.A. thesis, State University of Iowa, January 1948.

Table 9-9
Pilots and Aircraft in Iowa, 1938-1946
(As of December 31 of each year)

Year	Number of Pilots	Number of Civil Aircraft	Pilots per Plane
1938	384	184	2.1
1939	598	245	2.4
1940	1,261	381	3.3
1941	2,299	549	4.2
1942	3,730	572	6.5
1943	3,870	644	6.0
1944	4,100	677	6.0
1945	6,640	802	8.2
1946	8,950	1,734	5.2

(*Source:* [1] Figures for 1938-1941 from *Aircraft Yearbook for 1942.* Aeronautical Chamber of Commerce, Inc., 1942: 666.
[2] Figures for 1942-1946 from Office of Aviation Information, Civil Aeronautics Administration.)

Fully one-third of the airplanes in use in 1956 were flown for business purposes. Two hundred Flying Farmers used planes for cattle buying, transportation of machinery and parts, or pleasure trips. Sixty-six fixed-base operators had about 250 planes for flight training, charter services, sales demonstrations, aerial photography, aircraft rental and other services. The 31 aerial spray firms used 50 planes for crop dusting, spraying, seeding and fertilizing and could cover 40 acres of cropland per hour. The state ranked ninth in the nation in the number of privately-owned business and personal airplanes and second in the number of Flying Farmers. In 1959, 78 airports had permanent runway lighting installations placing Iowa as one of the five leading states in this category.

Air Marking

Air marking was one of the earliest priorities of the commission. An air marker was the name of the town painted on top of the roof of a local building in ten-foot letters so that the name was clearly legible from an altitude of at least 3,000 feet. These air markers were highway signs in the sky and were a valuable aid to the private pilot. They contributed greatly to safety in planning flights since pilots could identify towns on routes without flying at low altitudes to read names on water towers or railroad stations. Each state, through its aeronautics department or commission, conducted a program of air marking to provide an uninterupted chain of "sky signposts" from state to state. At the close of 1959, 446 air markers had been placed in Iowa with an additional 151 contracted for painting.

Expansion at the Des Moines Airport

A new and complete lighting system installed in 1940 resulted in a Class 4 rating for the Des Moines Airport, the first in the nation and the highest ranking given by the federal government. During the war years, the first control tower was constructed: an observation deck with a light beam gun on top of the United Airlines hangar. Shortly after the war, with assistance of federal funds, a new northwest-southwest runway measuring 5,700 x 150 feet was built. A concrete landing ramp with a circular taxi strip was also built to serve the proposed terminal building completed in 1950. Previously, airlines and federal agencies operated out of five buildings; after, they were combined into one structure. Further improvements were made in 1950 when an addition was built and the open concourse enclosed to shelter passengers in inclement weather.

Airline Service

By 1960, four major and regional airlines provided service to 13 communities. United flew from Des Moines, Cedar Rapids, the Quad Cities and Omaha-Council Bluffs. Braniff Airways, which had acquired Mid-Continent and Midwest Airlines (a fixed-base operator) in 1952, served Des Moines, Waterloo and Sioux City. Ozark Airlines, organized in 1943, started service to Burlington in 1950 and expanded its routes to include Des Moines, Fort Dodge, Sioux City, Mason City, the Quad Cities, Ottumwa and Clinton. North Central was organized in 1946 and served Iowa through Sioux City. Parks Airline of St. Louis and Iowa Airplane Company of Des Moines were certified for feeder service in 1947. The former would serve eastern and central Iowa cities on two separate routes from Chicago terminating in Des Moines, and in northern Iowa on routes from Chicago terminating at Sioux City. The latter would serve western and central Iowa on routes from Council Bluffs to Minneapolis.

Ozark and North Central were also classified as "local service or feeder airlines," flying passengers into and out of "hub" airports served by the trunk carriers. An important difference between local service airlines and other commercial carriers was that most received federal subsidies for a portion of their operating costs considered necessary to pay for the service to small communities which did not generate large passenger volumes. The aircraft were primarily DC-3s, excellent for short haul traffic with stops 50 to 100 miles apart.

Later, these airlines flew larger equipment not suitable for short hops, broadened their markets and terminated with some success the service at smaller communities. Their managements convinced the CAB that the service had to be reconstructed and proposed that regional airports be constructed between existing major airports. They also requested longer routes into major city-pairs even though these routes competed with those of the trunk lines. These actions were being considered in the 1960s when trunk airlines were highly profitable and when longer hauls by the local service airlines might make possible a discontinuance of their subsidies. Charter flights had been made since the early days of aviation development. Initially, anyone with an airplane could fly it "for hire." However, in later years, federal regulations prescribed standards and operations for charter services. The objective was to make these flights as safe as those of scheduled airlines. Included also were regulations governing "light aircraft" (less than 12,500 pounds) which offered commuter services.

Aerial view of United Airlines hangar and municipal hangar, 1940.
(Courtesy: Des Moines Municipal Airport)

United Airlines hangar, Des Moines Municipal Airport, 1937-1950.
(Courtesy: Des Moines Municipal Airport)

Enclosed concourse, Des Moines Municipal Airport, 1959.
(Courtesy: Des Moines Municipal Airport)

The Des Moines Municipal Airport, 1947.
(Courtesy: Des Moines Municipal Airport)

The Federal Aviation Agency

In 1957 the Airways Modernization Act established the Airways Modernization Board (AMB). Although short-lived, the AMB started control of the nation's airspace by identifying separate zones for civil and military aircraft and created three 40-mile wide transcontinental airways at between 17,000 and 22,000 feet altitude. In 1958 the Federal Aviation Act went into effect, creating the Federal Aviation Agency (FAA) and cancelling the Air Commerce Act of 1926, the Civil Aeronautics Act of 1958 and the Airways Modernization Act of 1957 in one step. In January, 1959, the FAA absorbed the functions and personnel of the CAA and AMB and some of the duties of the CAB. The CAB, however, remained an independent agency responsible for the economic regulation of airlines as well as determining probable cause of aircraft accidents. The FAA was involved in matters of air safety, aircraft certification, pilot licensing, air navigation and air traffic control. Coincidental with the creation of the FAA was the entrance of the nation into the jet aircraft age, and with the guidance of the new chairman, General E. R. "Pete" Quesada, the airline industry stood poised for a new revolution "against which the transition from twin-engine to four engine aircraft seemed trivial by comparison."[14]

Summary

Railroads serving Iowa shared the wartime prosperity of the industry and generally maintained relatively high levels of traffic during the early postwar years. In the 1950s, however, the rate of increase in revenue traffic slowed considerably. Few electric interurbans survived as such. The majority were reclassified as Class II railways, integrated into Class I railroad systems or ceased operations. In contrast, motor carriers showed substantial gains in revenue traffic between 1940 and 1959 and began to take a prominent position in the movement of freight and liquid products. Work on the state's highways during the war period was virtually at a standstill with little construction and maintenance reduced to minimum levels.

The rising trends in motor vehicle operations, coupled with the inability of highways to handle increased traffic, led to the creation of two highway study

[14] R.E.G. Davies, *Airlines of the United States Since 1914,* London: Putnam, 1972, p. 357.

committees for evaluation and projection of the state's highway needs and necessary financing. Recommendations of both committees received widespread support of the public and the legislature who cooperated by raising gasoline taxes and making appropriations to match federal-aid funds. Toll road possibilities were examined but abandoned when the national system of interstate highways was formulated by the federal government. The increasing demand for petroleum products for highway and home heating usage more than doubled the liquid pipeline mileage, most of which was built by the Great Lakes Pipeline System.

Following the war, commercial traffic on the Mississippi and Missouri Rivers expanded rapidly through introduction of more powerful towboats and specialized barges. Dams at Minneapolis and Hastings were upgraded and a new lock built at Keokuk. The Pick-Sloan project on the Missouri resulted in deeper channels, irrigation facilities and flood control measures expected to benefit the western one-third of the state.

The "air age" officially arrived in Iowa with the formation of a full-time State Aeronautical Commission in 1945, charged by law to encourage, foster and assist in the general development of aviation. Widespread use of airplanes for private and business purposes, by Flying Farmers and fixed-base operators, placed the state high in national rankings. Four trunk and regional carriers served 13 cities and towns, three of which had flights into Des Moines, requiring expansion of its airport. Two additional feeder airlines were scheduled to begin service in the 1950s.

Selected References

American Association of Railroads. *Yearbook of Railroad Facts.* Washington, D.C.: Economics and Finance Department, Association of American Railroads, 1980.

Archie, Willard D. "An Iowa Toll Turnpike?" *The Iowan 1* (Oct-Nov-Dec 1952): pp. 5-7.

Automotive Safety Foundation. *Iowa's Highway Needs 1960-1980: A Plan to Pace Highway Development with Economic Growth.* A Report to the Iowa Highway Study Committee. Washington, D.C.: The Foundation, 1960.

Bigham, Truman C. *Transportation Principles and Problems.* New York: McGraw Hill Book Co., 1946.

Brown, D. Clayton. *Western Tributaries of the Mississippi.* National Waterways Study, Navigation History NWS-83-7. Washington, D.C.: U.S. Government Printing Office, 1983.

Bunke, Harvey C. "Toll Roads and Highway Policy." *Iowa Business Digest* (August 1954): pp. 1-3, 6-7.

Bureau of Public Roads. *Highway Statistics 1951.* Washington, D.C.: U.S. Government Printing Office, 1953.

Carlson, Norman, ed. *Iowa Trolleys.* Bulletin 114. Chicago: Central Electric Railfans Association, 1974.

Casey, Robert J., and W.H.S. Douglas. *Pioneer Railroad.* New York: McGraw Hill Book Co., 1948.

Coverdale and Culpritts, Consulting Engineers. "Initial Feasibility Report on the Proposed Iowa Turnpike, July 20, 1954. Manuscript.

Davies, R.E.G. *Airlines of the United States Since 1914.* London: Putnam, 1972.

Derleth, August. *The Milwaukee Road.* New York: Creative Age Press, 1948.

English, Emory H. "When Iowa Took to the Air." *Annals of Iowa 30* No. 2 (October 1949): pp. 81-104.

Harper, Donald V. *Transportation in America: Users, Carriers, Government.* 2nd ed. Englewood Cliffs, N.J.: Prentice-Hall, 1982.

Hayes, William E. *Iron Road to Empire, The History of 100 Years of the Progress and Achievements of the Rock Island Lines.* New York: Simmons-Boardman, 1953.

"Historical Summary of Willams Pipelines." Furnished by Keith E. Bailey, President, in letter of November 11, 1982. Letter from H. W. Walsh, Mobil Pipe Lines, of August 19, 1982.

Interstate Commerce Commission. *Statistics of the Railroads of the United States 1945.* Washington, D.C.: U. S. Government Printing Office, 1947.

———. *Statistics of the Railroads of the United States 1950.* Washington, D.C.: U. S. Government Printing Office, 1952.

Iowa Aeronautics Commission. *First Annual Report of the Iowa Aeronautics Commission.* Des Moines: State of Iowa, 1946.

———. *Twelfth Annual Report of the Iowa Aeronautics Commission Ending June 30, 1957.* Des Moines: State of Iowa, 1957.

———. *Fourteenth Annual Report of the Iowa Aeronautics Commission Ending June 30, 1959.* Des Moines: State of Iowa, 1959.

———. *Fifteenth Annual Report of the Iowa Aeronautics Commission Ending June 30, 1960.* Des Moines: State of Iowa, 1960.

Iowa Department of Transportation Office of Economic Analysis. *Receipts and Distribution of Road Use Tax Revenues Since Implementation of Iowa's First Motor Fuel Tax.* August 1, 1981.

Iowa State Commerce Commission. *Sixty-Third Annual Report of the Iowa State Commerce Commission for the Year Ending December 2, 1940.* Des Moines: State of Iowa.

———. *Sixty-Eighth Annual Report of the Iowa State Commerce Commission for the Year Ending December 1, 1945.* Des Moines: State of Iowa.

———. *Seventy-Third Annual Report of the Iowa State Commerce Commission for the Year Ending December 1, 1950.* Des Moines: State of Iowa.

———. *Eighty-Second Annual Report Iowa State Commerce Commission for the Year Ending December 3, 1959.* Des Moines: State of Iowa.

———. *Eighty-Third Annual Report Iowa State Commerce Commission for the Year Ending December 3, 1960.* Des Moines: State of Iowa.

Iowa State Highway Commission. Reports of the State Highway Commission for the Years Ending 1940, 1942, 1946, 1951-1953, 1955, and 1959. Des Moines: State of Iowa.

LemMon, Jean, ed. *50th Anniversary of the Des Moines Municipal Airport.* Des Moines: City of Des Moines and the Greater Des Moines Chamber of Commerce Federation, 1980.

May, George S. "Post War Road Problems." *Palimpsest 46* No. 2 (February 1965): pp. 116-128.

Mayer, Jonathan D. "Local and Commuter Airlines in the United States." *Traffic Quarterly* (April 1977): pp. 333-349.

Motor Vehicle Manufacturers Association. *1973/74 Automobile Facts and Figures.* Detroit: Motor Vehicle Manufacturers Association of the United States, Inc., 1974.

Presidential Executive Order 8959, December 18, 1941.

Progress and Feasibility of Toll Roads and their Relationship to the Federal Aid Program. H. Doc. 139, 84th Congress, 1955.

"Rock Island Revived." *Fortune 30* (December 1944): pp. 140-148, 218-224.

Schaffner, Leroy, Geoffrey Shepherd, and P.H. Elwood. *Economic Effects of the Missouri River Development Program with Special Reference to Iowa.* Bulletin 373. Ames: Agricultural Experiment Station, April 1950.

Thompson, W.H. "The Economics of Ex Parte 162, General Rate Increase Case of 1945." Ph.D. diss., Iowa State College, 1948.

"Transportation in War Period Dominates Atlantic States Highway Meeting." *Engineering News Record 128,* 10 (March 15, 1942): p. 368.

Tweet, Roald D. *History of Transportation on the Upper Mississippi & Illinois Rivers.* National Waterways Study, Navigation History NWS-83-6. Washington, D.C.: U.S. Government Printing Office, 1983.

Wood, Donald F., and James C. Johnson. *Contemporary Transportation.* 2nd ed. Tulsa, Okla.: PennWell Publishing Co., 1983.

Chapter Ten
The Transportation Industry in Transition —The 1960s

Introduction

Growth in the nation's Gross National Product (GNP), changes in economic trends and shifts in social attitudes resulted in a rearrangement of national transportation markets. Unable to adjust rapidly because of regulatory and structural restraints, railroads suffered percentage losses in their shares of passenger miles and revenue tonnage, relative to other modes, in an expanding national market. Failing to improve their financial condition through rate increases, they turned to mergers as a possible solution. Stimulated by construction of four-lane interstate highways and improved primary roads, motor carriers more than doubled their tonnage and became a dominant factor in agricultural movements. Increased grain exports and heavier bulk traffic supported inland water carriers. Pipelines evolved into the major carrier of energy-related traffic. Intermodalism, in the form of rail-truck combinations, provided a new coordinated system by combining the inherent advantages of each mode. Urban transport programs and airport expansion were assisted by federal programs involving comprehensive planning by states and municipalities for orderly development of private and commercial passenger systems. New transport programs were subjected to impact statements for all federal-aid projects affecting the quality of human environment. The changing nature of modal operations and relationships, under uneven regulatory rules and unbalanced public expenditures, raised serious policy questions as conflicts arose between economic and social goals and objectives for transportation development in the nation and the states.

Changes in the Transportation Markets, Gross National Product and the Modal Shares

The GNP almost doubled during the decade, rising from $503 billion in 1960 to $982 billion in 1970, and transportation outlays continued at 20 percent of the total. Measured by tonnage carried, the domestic intercity freight market grew by 63.4 percent between 1950 and 1970. The railroad share dropped from 46.7 percent to 31.3 percent whereas trucks, regulated and unregulated, and liquid pipelines showed the greatest percentage gain. Water carriers showed a rather consistent trend. Passenger-miles more than doubled. In the private sector, automobiles accounted for 86 to 90 percent of the total. In the public sector, commercial airlines increased their share from 1.8 percent in 1950 to 9.8 percent in 1969; bus travel declined, then remained constant during the 1960s. The railroad passenger share of 6.5 percent in 1950 was 1.1 percent in 1969. By 1970, railroads operated 547 intercity trains, down from approximately 20,000 in 1920. Part of the decline could be traced to the erosion of mail and express movements as the result of curtailment of passenger service; part to the shift of railway mail to highway and air carriers and the influence of jet aviation. From 64.1 million ton-miles reported by domestic air carriers in 1951, mail traffic increased to 670.5 million tons by 1970. The nation was becoming highway and airway oriented as automobiles and trucks dominated intercity and urban transportation, and scheduled airlines moved the bulk of the nation's mail and commercial passengers (Tables 10-1 and 10-2).

Railroads were unable to adjust rapidly to changing markets. The basic network had been built by the turn of the century and was attuned to patterns of economic activity at that time. Much of the freight market growth was in commodities suitable to carriage by other modes. Less-than-carload and medium to short distance traffic shifted to highway carriers, and increased transport of natural gas, oil and petroleum products was handled more cheaply by pipeline and water carriers. The rate of return on railroad average net investment fell from 4.22 percent in 1955 to 1.97 percent in 1961, representing the lowest level of earnings since mid-depression years. The return rose to 3.90 percent in 1966, then dropped again to 1.79 in 1969.

The long series of rate increases in the 1950s continued through 1960-1961, and additional proposals were approved between 1967 and 1972. But the rate advances did not materially improve finances and led to questions as to whether the industry could reverse the decline over the past 40 years. The deterioration and eventual disappearance of city street car systems and electric interurbans began simultaneously with the decline of railroads. This was brought about by the greater flexibility of motor carriers and freedom from the heavy fixed investment of the railroads. Another reason for pessimism concerning the railroads' future was the fact that their depressed condition was reached during periods of relatively uniform national prosperity. Suggestions of increasing reliance on market mechanisms as a means of slowing or reversing the railroad situation was partially met by regulatory reform measures in the federal legislation of the 1970s.

Table 10-1
Domestic Intercity Tonnage by Modes, 1950, 1960-1969
(In Percentages)

Year	Railroad Class I & II	Trucks[1]	Oil Pipelines	Water[2]	Air	Total Tons[3]
1950	46.7	26.1	9.3	17.9	.4	3,043
1960	36.1	32.7	13.0	18.2	.6	3,606
1961	34.0	35.7	13.1	17.2	.8	3,699
1962	33.4	36.6	12.9	17.1	.9	3,885
1963	32.4	36.2	12.5	18.9	1.0	4,164
1964	32.5	38.2	12.8	16.4	1.2	4,364
1965	33.3	37.0	13.3	16.4	1.4	4,435
1966	33.1	37.2	13.5	15.9	1.7	4,681
1967	32.3	37.3	14.2	16.5	1.9	4,792
1968	31.3	37.3	15.0	16.4	2.4	4,849
1969	31.2	36.5	15.3	16.9	2.6	4,973

(*Source:* Transportation Association of America, *Transportation Facts and Trends.* 14th Ed. Washington, D.C., July, 1978: 10.)

[1] Regulated and non-regulated trucks.

[2] Includes Rivers, Canals, Great Lakes and Deep Sea traffic.

[3] In millions of tons. Total percentages may be slightly higher than 100 percent because of rounding of figures.

Table 10-2
Intercity Travel by Modes, 1950, 1960-1970
(In Percentages)

	Private Carrier				Public Carrier				
Year	Auto	Air	Total Miles[1]	%	Air	Bus	Rail	Total Miles	%
1950	87.0	.2	439.1	87.2	1.8	4.5	6.5	64.5	12.8
1960	90.4	.3	708.4	90.7	4.1	2.5	2.8	72.6	9.3
1961	90.4	.3	715.9	90.7	4.1	2.6	2.6	73.1	9.3
1962	90.3	.3	738.6	90.6	4.3	2.7	2.2	76.8	9.4
1963	90.1	.4	769.3	90.5	4.6	2.6	2.2	80.5	9.5
1964	89.8	.4	805.5	90.2	5.1	2.6	2.1	87.2	9.8
1965	89.2	.5	822.1	89.6	5.9	2.6	1.9	95.1	10.4
1966	88.5	.6	862.1	89.1	6.6	2.5	1.8	105.6	10.9
1967	87.5	.7	896.8	88.2	7.9	2.4	1.5	120.4	11.8
1968	87.1	.8	944.6	87.8	8.6	2.3	1.2	130.8	12.2
1969	86.1	.8	985.8	86.9	9.8	2.2	1.1	148.3	13.1

(*Source:* Transportation Association of America, *Transportation Facts and Trends.* 14th Ed. Washington, D.C., July, 1978: 18.)

[1] Total miles are in billions of passenger-miles.

Determinants of the Total Freight Market

Five factors or trends were generally considered as major determinants of the national freight market. These were: (1) total population which had increased by 52 million between 1950-1970; (2) changing geographic distribution of population, shifting regionally and from rural to urban communities; (3) economic activity as measured by the GNP index, which had almost doubled; (4) location of economic activity, which changed as populations relocated; and (5) exhaustion of natural resources close to historical population centers and the necessary development at more distant domestic and foreign sources. The latter trend was particularly important with regard to petroleum, coal, iron ore and lumber.

The Iowa Transportation Market in the 1960s

Market Determinants

Iowa's transportation trends and changing market relationships followed the national pattern. Between 1960 and 1970 the population increased by 67,504 persons (2.4 percent), and a shift of five percent occurred in the rural-to-urban movement. Gross State Product (in current dollars) doubled from approximately $6.2 billion in 1962 to $12.4 billion in 1970, and per capita income rose from $1,983 to $3,751 during the same period.

Condition of the Railroads

In 1960, 10 Class I railroads (annual operating revenues of $3 million) operated 8,300 miles of road and reported net earnings of $13.8 million. At the close of 1968, nine railroads operated 7,864 miles of road, a decline of 436 miles. No comparable estimates can be given for net earnings since the Commerce Commission did not report operating expenses after 1964. Separation of operating revenues by categories of traffic showed "freight" and "other" with little or no change over the period, but substantial losses were noted in passenger, mail and express shipments (Table 10-3). Freight originations and terminations of Class I roads between 1950 and 1970 showed interesting trends. Tonnage originated increased by 73.4 percent, indicating a steady growth with yearly variations, whereas terminations were fairly constant, reaching a peak during 1966 and remaining at or near that level for the remainder of the 1960s (Table 10-4, Fig. 10-1). No analysis of traffic by commodity classifications was possible, as data on these movements was also discontinued after 1964. Revenue passengers carried on Class I railroads and interurbans declined from almost five million in 1950 to 156,000 in 1970.

Table 10-3
Railway Operating Revenues Within Iowa, 1960-1969
(In millions of dollars)

Year	Freight	Passenger	Mail	Express	Other	Total
1960	$183.0	$10.3	$ 9.1	$ 2.7	$ 2.7	$207.8
1961	180.6	10.0	9.6	2.9	2.5	205.6
1962	181.3	10.0	8.6	2.7	2.5	205.1
1963	183.0	9.2	9.9	2.4	2.6	207.1
1964	184.5	8.7	8.5	2.6	2.5	206.8
1965	156.2	5.6	7.6	1.9	2.2	173.5
1966	167.4	5.3	6.9	1.9	2.2	183.7
1967	161.1	3.9	4.4	1.7	2.2	173.3
1968	167.6	2.9	3.7	1.1	2.0	177.3
1969	180.8	2.5	3.4	0.8	2.4	189.9
% change (Base year = 1960)	-01.2	-75.7	-62.6	-70.3	-11.1	-08.6

(Source: Iowa Commerce Commission, *Annual Reports.)*

[1] Figures rounded to the nearest unit.

Table 10-4
Revenue Freight Originated and Terminated on Class I Railroads in Iowa, 1950, 1960-1970

Year Ending	Tons Originated (In millions)	Tons Terminated (In millions)
1950	15.8	21.4
1960	18.6	19.0
1961	19.2	18.8
1962	20.8	19.6
1963	21.6	20.3
1964	20.9	19.9
1965	22.4	20.6
1966	24.6	22.8
1967	23.0	22.1
1968	22.1	20.7
1969	24.3	22.5
1970	27.4	22.1

(Source: Iowa Commerce Commission, *Annual Reports.)*
[1] Figures rounded to the nearest unit.

Intermodal Relationships

Iowa followed national trends in modal relationships. Between 1960 and 1970, automobile registrations increased by 27 percent and trucks by 54 percent. Revenue freight carried by Class I motor freight operators (annual operating revenues exceeding $200,000) more than doubled when data of carriers operating within and through the state were combined with those operating only in the state. The number of Class I liquid motor carriers increased from 22 in 1960 to 82 in 1969, and tonnage hauled from 20.8 million to 135.9 million tons in 1967. In 1969 the Ruan Transport Company of Des Moines hauled almost 50 percent of the Iowa tonnage reported. The company was the fourth-ranking liquid carrier in the nation. Agricultural traffic was by far the primary market for trucks in Iowa. Research studies on the transportation of agricultural commodities from Iowa between 1962 and 1967 showed that trucks hauled almost 17 million tons and railroads 12.3 million tons of corn, soybeans, livestock, processed meats and poultry products from origins in the state to domestic destinations and export ports.

Commercial traffic in the Rock Island District of the Upper Mississippi River increased from about 11 million tons in 1960 to 22 million in 1970. The district data included movements through Locks 10 to 22 (Guttenburg, Iowa to Hannibal, Missouri) and was the combined total for the states served by the district. On the Missouri, commercial traffic between Sioux City and the mouth showed a gain of over one million tons. The principal products transported on both rivers were grains and grain products, coal, petroleum and petroleum products, and sand and gravel. Oil pipeline mileages were not available through commission reports, but an analysis of permits approved indicated a continuous expansion of oil and oil product lines. Additional mileages were built for anhydrous ammonia by Mapco, the Santa Fe Pipeline System and the Hydrocarbon Transportation Company.

Equipment Shortages

Historically, Iowa shippers have had difficulty in obtaining transportation equipment at harvest time. During the late 1960s the shortage changed from a seasonal to a chronic situation which reached serious proportions in 1969. Grain was piled on the ground because elevators were full, and emergency equipment such as open coal cars or boarded cattle cars were pressed into service. One major reason for the reduced availability was the rapid increase in commercial grain sales at the same time that the number of railroad-owned or leased box cars was

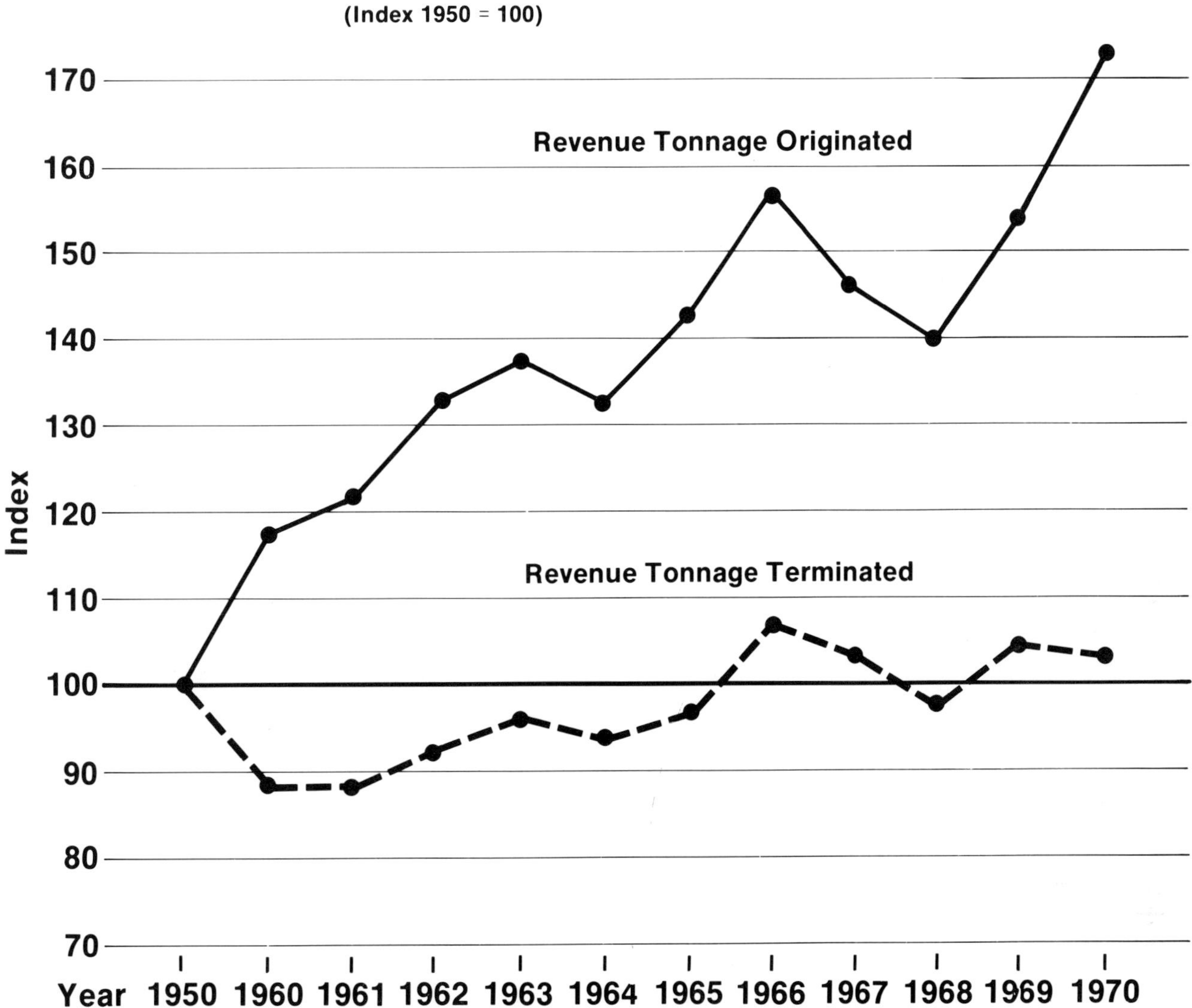

Figure 10-1
Graphic presentation of the revenue freight figures shown in Table 10-4.

declining. Although the number of owned and leased hopper cars doubled during the decade, the total carrying capacity of all equipment fell from 36.4 million tons in 1960 to 31.2 million tons in 1969. It was difficult to distribute fewer cars to individual elevators in response to the increased demand resulting from new harvest methods which shortened the harvest season. Also, the reduction in railroad grain rates during 1965-1969, after the "Big John" rates were established, made long-haul truck transportation less competitive and led to a decline in the supply of trucks.

Changes in equipment availability had serious implications for the grain industry. Sales contracts specified dollar penalties for delayed shipments, and grain inventories had to be financed for the additional time required to obtain equipment. Once elevators reached capacity, the choices were storage elsewhere, the use of substandard equipment, purchase of private trucks, or sale to itinerant truckers. It was estimated that in 1969, excluding lost business, total costs due to lack of equipment and substandard services were $3.6 million in Iowa.

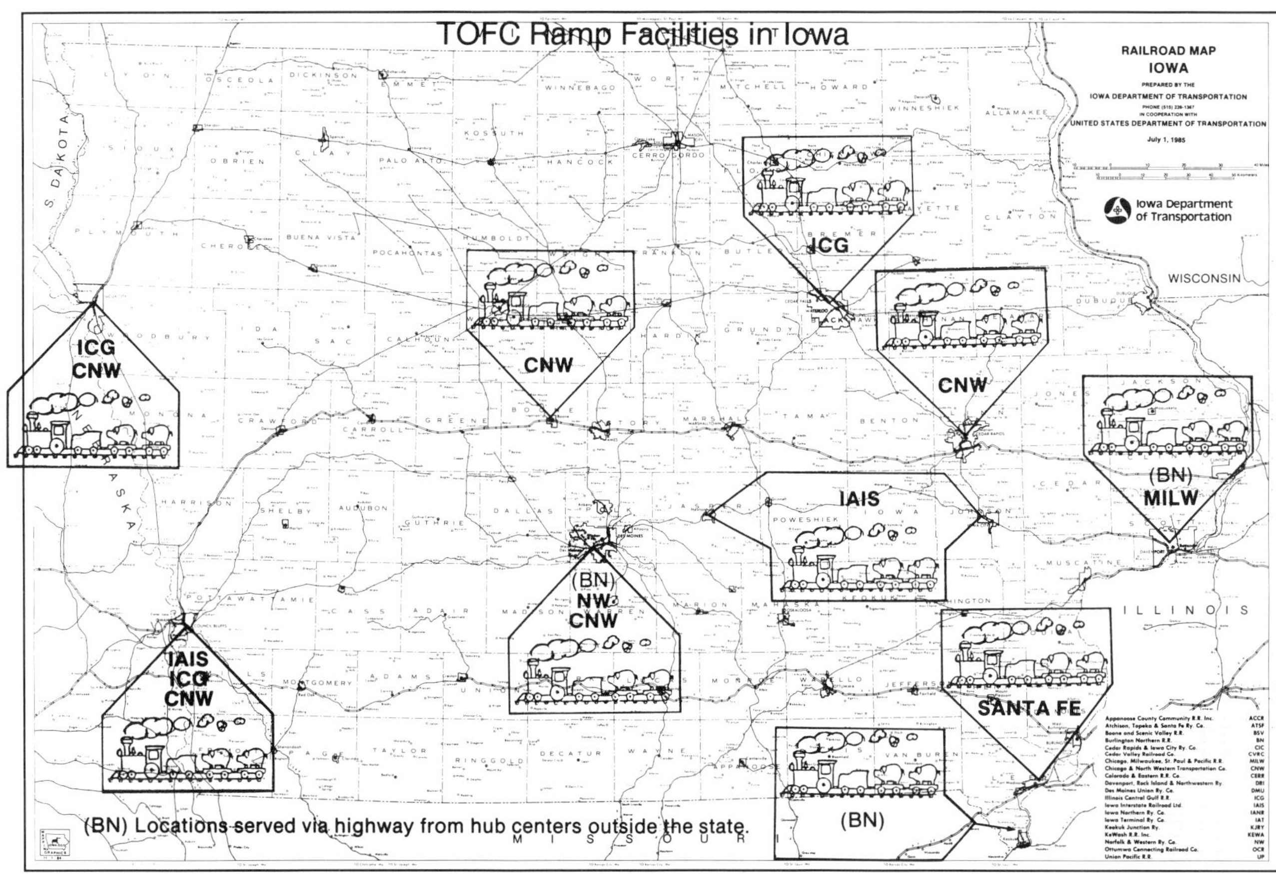

Figure 10-2
Trailer-on-Flatcar (TOFC) ramp facilities in Iowa.
(Courtesy: Iowa Department of Transportation)

Intermodal Coordination

Since no single mode of transportation is capable of moving all types of freight with equal efficiency, the various modes should be more complimentary than competitive. A system enabling each to perform the service for which it has the greatest advantage would contribute to a more efficient use of resources. Since the modal environment was highly institutionalized by the 1960s, the development of coordinated movements was in its infancy. The modal systems were aggressively competitive with each other, preferring to retain traffic and revenues for as long as possible.

All of the railroads serving Iowa offered rail-truck service known as Trailer-on-Flatcar (TOFC or Piggyback). The combinations were an experiment in the 1930s introduced by the Alton (1932), the CGW (1936), the CB&Q, Rio Grande and New Haven (1937), and the CRI&P (1938). The experiment did not survive, since gasoline and labor were inexpensive, highways were crowded, and railroads viewed truckers as interlopers who would eventually be restrained by taxes, weight and size laws, and user charges. Revival of the service followed the New Haven decision in 1954 when the ICC decided that railroads could haul trailers on flatcars under provisions of rail tariffs without motor carrier certification.[1] As a result, 32 Class I railroads offered

[1] *Trains,* Milwaukee, Wis.: Kalmbach Pub. Co., May 1960. Actually, the earliest recorded commercial movement was on the Nova Scotia Railway which began ferrying farmers' wagons in 1858. Circus wagons were moved in the United States in1856. The Long Island Railroad introduced the concept in the United States in 1885. *Movement of Highway Trailers by Rail,* 293 ICC 92 (1954). There were five original plans, later amended, to cover the service: Plan I. Rail movement, ramp-to-ramp of motor carrier trailers. Lading was on a truck waybill. Plan II. Door-to-door service on a railroad waybill in rail-owned trailer. Rates were similar to those of a motor common carrier. Plan III. Ramp-to-ramp railroad movement of shipper-owned trailers, based on a flat rate for two trailers per car. Plan IV. Ramp-to-ramp railroad movements of shipper-owned trailers and flat cars for which a flat rate was charged. Plan V. Joint rates between railroads and motor carriers for through movements for which each carrier could solicit traffic for the other.

TOFC service by January 1, 1955, originating 168,000 carloadings. Ten years later carloadings were up to one million (by 63 railroads) and reached the two million mark by 1978. In the annual reports of the Iowa Commerce Commission, TOFC and less-than-carload traffic were combined, preventing a trend analysis. TOFC ramp facilities in Iowa are found in Fig. 10-2.

Less visual forms of intermodal coordination in Iowa included combinations of truck, rail and water which developed in the 1970s. In 1979, over 10 million tons of Iowa waterborne commodities were distributed to or from the rivers by truck or rail. These combinations provided an opportunity to extend service and lower transportation charges by combining the flexibility and low cost pickup and delivery of the motor carrier with the low cost rail or barge haul.

Early Piggybacking.
Farm wagons carried into New York City in the late 1800s on flat cars belonging to the Long Island Railroad.
(*Source:* Ingersal-Rand "Compressed Air", July, 1957.)

The Movement Toward Railroad Mergers

The Issues

It was to mergers and/or acquisition of control that the carriers turned as a possible solution to their financial troubles. Mergers were not new in the railroad industry. Historically, they were end-to-end combinations to broaden the network, increase profits through economies of scale and acquire personal fortunes for the "Empire Builders." Between 1884 and 1888, some 425 consolidations occurred, and it was reported that 6,000 separate railroad companies were operating in the United States; reduced substantially to about 480 in the 1950s which accounted for 50 percent of the nation's mileage. The Burlington was said to have been a combination of 200 separate roads and the Pennsylvania System one of over 600 individual organizations.

The purpose of mergers was to reduce operating expenses and eliminate excess capacity, provide greater control of car supply and distribution, and under specialized management make possible economies in purchasing and credit arrangements. Achieving these objectives was expected to benefit the public by improved service and lower rates. The AAR reported that between 1955 and 1972 there were 55 mergers proposed of which 38 had been approved, nine were withdrawn or denied, and four were pending.

The greatest difficulties faced by the ICC in merger cases were the issues of competition and monopoly. Neither the commission nor Congress had developed criteria for determining the extent of competition, the types and numbers of systems to create, and whether the individual merger was in the public interest. It was the omission of these guidelines that led to the introduction of a bill in 1962 which would have declared a moratorium on railroad mergers until the end of 1963, and it would have made Section 7 of the Clayton Act applicable to future mergers. The bill never reached the floor of Congress for a vote. The initiative of a railroad in proposing unification meant that each case was decided on its own merits without positive guidance. This was a possible violation of the principle laid down in the Northern Securities case: "that the interests of private persons and corporations cannot be made paramount to the interests of the general public."[2] The merger movement was a readjustment in the organizational and operational structures of the railroads. "What is involved here is a major adjustment of an indispensible industry which is necessary because of the development of other modes of transportation . . . . Furthermore, it is an adjustment which the industry alone in all likelihood cannot accomplish soon enough to avoid penalizing the economy and the defense of the Nation."[3]

[2] 193 U.S. 197 (1904).

[3] United States Senate Committee on Commerce, Special Study Group on Transportation Policies in the United States, 86th Congress, *National Transportation Policy,* (Doyle Report), Washington, D.C.: U. S. Government Printing Office, 1961, pp. 266-267.

The issues were debated far and wide by carrier executives, ICC staff personnel, shippers, academicians and politicians. Professor Kent T. Healy contended that diseconomies were encountered when railroad size increased to more than 10,000 employees, rebutted by John Barriger, a railroad executive. The failure of the ICC to deal with consolidation proposals through determination of economic principles by which the mergers could be evaluated led the ICC's Bureau of Economics and Statistics to note that "no voice speaks before the Commission for the public as a whole in consolidation cases."[4] The question related to how much rail competition was necessary to protect the public interest. Should the ICC, in the exercise of policy leadership, decide on a single national system, balanced regional systems, regional rail monopolies or maintain competition with relatively numerous railroad systems? The consensus appeared to favor balanced regional systems.

While the debates continued, strong opposition came from those concerned with elimination of railroad competition, the future of competing lines and those interchanging roads not included, loss of service to communities affected and reduction in railroad employment. Decisions in the merger cases seemed to indicate that the ICC was not unduly concerned with intramodal competition but rather was intent upon developing regional systems to strengthen intermodal competition. This was supported by the report of the examiner in the CNW-CMStP&P proposal: "Our conclusions on this road must be that intramodal competition pales into insignificance. All the railroads do today is conditioned by intermodal competition. Railroads are not engaged in a struggle for primacy among each other; they have been engaged in a fight for survival with other modes of transportation, principally trucks and barges."[5]

In the opinion of Ben W. Heineman, chairman of the CNW, the merger proposals of the 1960s would have more widespread and lasting economic effects than any other business trends of the decade. Nationally, the two most important mergers approved were the Penn-Central in the East in 1968 and the Burlington-Northern in the West in 1970. The first proposed a route structure of 20,000 miles with anticipated annual operating revenues of $2 billion; the second, a structure of 27,000 miles and $1 billion in annual operating revenues. But merger proposals were not confined to railroads. The American Trucking Association (ATA) reported in 1968 that 115 mergers had occurred in the motor carrier industry between 1957 and 1967.

Merger Activity of Railroads Serving Iowa

All major railroads serving Iowa were involved in mergers or acquisition of control in one way or another, beginning with the proposal to consolidate the CB&Q with the NP and GN railroads in 1961. The Iowa Commerce Commission initially opposed but later approved it subject to certain protective traffic conditions suggested by the CNW and CRI&P. Endorsement was also given by firms, shipper associations, Chambers of Commerce and Governor Erbe. In 1963, the Norfolk and Western (NW) proposed merger with the Nickle Plate (New York, Chicago & St. Louis) and a lease of the Wabash lines which operated 192 miles of road in Iowa. In 1964, the CNW and CGW filed for merger, approved in 1968. That same year the UP filed for authority to acquire control of the CRI&P and its subsidiaries and to merge the properties and franchises into its firm. A Plan and Agreement had been drawn on June 27, 1963, contemplating this merger. On July 5, the CNW filed for authority to acquire the CRI&P through stock ownership as a first step in the complete unification of the two lines.

Now the situation really became complicated. In 1965 the AT&SF entered into an agreement with the CNW providing that upon approval of control of CRI&P, the lines south of Kansas City would be purchased except for those from Kansas City to Tucumcari, New Mexico, and trackage rights would be granted between Kansas City and St. Louis. Earlier that year the SP had applied for authority to purchase part of the CRI&P properties upon merger with the UP (Fig. 10-3). On June 19, 1966, the CNW and CMStP&P filed a joint application for authority to consolidate properties and franchises into the Chicago,

[4] Interstate Commerce Commission, Bureau of Economics and Statistics, *Railroad Consolidations and the Public Interest,* Washington, D.C.: U. S. Government Printing Office, March, 1962, p. 1.

[5] Finance Document No. 24182, Brief of Applicants North Western and Milwaukee to Examiner Henry C. Darmstadter, Washington, D.C.: April 26, 1968, p. 181.

Milwaukee and Northwestern Transportation Company, denied in 1970. Stock ratios agreed upon by the parties were considered inequitable by the ICC, and the merger was not approved.

The CNW and UP proposals for takeover of the CRI&P, as well as requests for purchase of certain of their properties, were consolidated into one docket and decided in 1974. Almost 11 years had passed since the case was filed, and it had become the lengthiest and most complex case ever considered by the ICC. Included were 16 separate proceedings affecting virtually every state and major railroad west of the Mississippi River, thousands of shippers, communities and public bodies. The administrative law judge who conducted the hearings concluded that the merger could be approved only if the entire railroad system in the western half of the nation would be restructured. The ICC's decision did not go that far, but it was necessary to impose numerous protective conditions for carriers who would be adversely affected. However, subsequent to the report and order of the commission, the CRI&P filed for reorganization under Section 77 of the Bankruptcy Act and the UP withdrew from the case. Other railroads continued to be interested in acquiring portions of the CRI&P properties.

Michael Conant viewed railroad consolidation as a movement in which the underlying issues were excess capacity and overinvestment. In his interesting discussion, he used six roughly parallel lines operating in the 1960s between Chicago and Omaha as an example of excess capacity on main railroad lines with parallel routes between major population centers (Table 10-5).

Des Moines was considered as the center of Iowa, and distances were measured north and south from the CRI&P, the most direct line across the state. Less than 100 scheduled freight and passenger trains were running on the Iowa segment of these lines. In a state so well supplied with paved highways, it seemed logical to conclude that investment in six mainline carriers represented substantial excess capacity. This was the thrust of CNW's parallel line merger proposals involving the CGW, CRI&P and CMStP&P railroads. If approved, the number of carriers would have been reduced from six to three, a number considered able to handle the east-west traffic of the larger cities and, with north-south connections, provide efficient services for the smaller communities.

Changing transportation technology and regulatory policies have been primary reasons for overinvestment in railroads. Parallel lines, even over short distances, were profitable before highway, water and air competition became intense. Disinvestment for reasons of rate competition and diversion of traffic were made partially through branch line abandonment, but rationalization of mainlines was difficult under economic and regulatory restraints. Technological developments, including dieselization of power, central traffic control and electronic yards tended to reduce operating expenses but also served to increase investment and excess capacity of the properties in the face of a stable or declining market.

Table 10-5
Parallel Railroad Lines Between Chicago and Omaha

Carrier	Length of Line Chicago to Omaha (miles)	Distance from Rock Island Line at Des Moines (miles)
CB&Q Railroad Company	496	42, south
CRI&P Railroad Company	493	----
CNW Railroad Company	488	23, north
CMStP&P Railroad Company	488	33, north
IC Railroad Company	515	67, north
CGW Railway Company	508	84, north

(*Source:* Michael Conant, *Railroad Mergers and Abandonments,* Table 5: 17.)

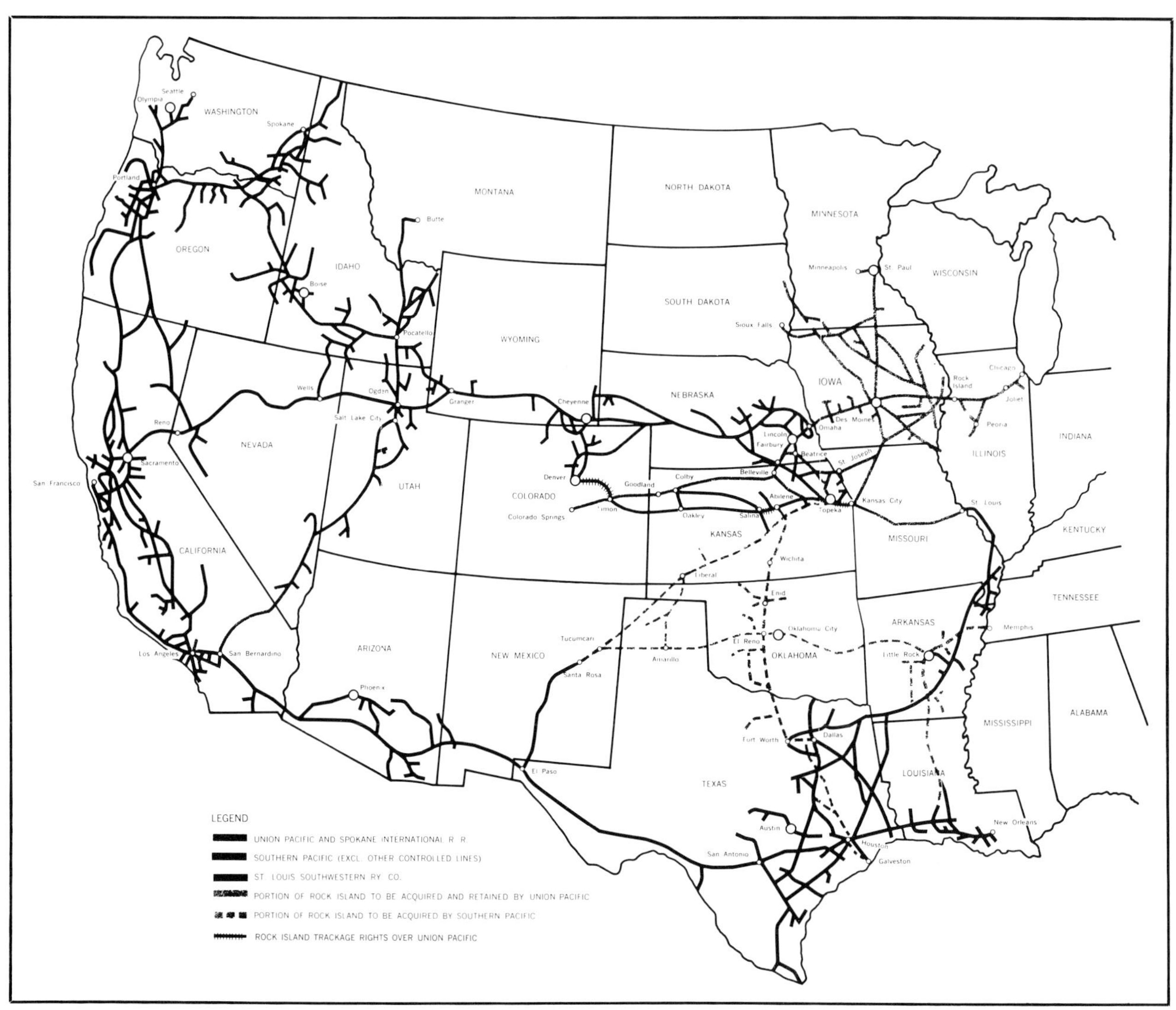

Figure 10-3
Railroads involved in the Union Pacific/Chicago, Rock Island & Pacific merger proposal.
(Courtesy: Chicago & North Western Railroad)

Public Transit

In 1968, legislation provided for federal matching grants for projects affecting capacity and safety for urban areas (TOPICS). Included in the funding were improvements in traffic control and fringe parking outside the central business district but adjacent to federal-aid highways and coordinated with planned transportation facilities. Also, 1,500 miles were added to the interstate system and the deadline for completion extended to 1974, later to 1977. The increase in statewide planning in the immediate postwar years included planning for urban areas, and the rate of road construction greatly accelerated after the 1956 federal legislation. From 1960 to 1970, municipal highway mileage had increased by 28 percent, marking a significant development in urban transportation. Despite the trend of people moving to the suburbs, the central cities of large metropolitan areas were still considered the focal point of the local transportation network, consisting of privately owned and operated transit systems and automobiles. But motor and trolley buses, railway commuter trains and rapid transit lines could not keep pace with the heavier automobile traffic on the newly built freeways through the cities, and declining patronage and high fares contributed to transit insolvencies. Before 1960, there was little or no federal or state promotion of urban transit systems. Urban and traffic congestion, pollution, energy matters, deficient mass transit and reduced ridership were familar problems to most urban residents.

Although experimental projects were authorized in 1961, the major legislative effort was made in 1964 through passage of the Urban Mass Transportation Act. The purpose was to assist in the development of improved transit facilities, equipment, techniques and methods and to encourage planning and establishment of private and public companies. An appropriation of $375 million was authorized for state and local communities to finance up to two-thirds of the net project costs—that part of total costs unable to be covered by local revenues. Fare revenues could not be used as local matching funds, only for reduction of gross project costs. Federal funds could be used for a variety of capital expenditures such as right-of-way, structures and equipment but not for operating expenses. Eligibility required the design of an urban transit system coordinated with highway development and embracing an overall plan for the urban region or area. The objective was to plan mass transit programs to complement rather than compete one with the other. Under certain critical emergency conditions where communities faced a loss of service, federal aid would be supplied on a 50-50 matching basis. Low interest loans were also available. Administration of the program was placed in the Federal Housing and Home Finance Agency, later in the new Department of Housing and Urban Development, and finally in the the Urban Mass Transit Administration of the Department of Transportation.

An Urban Department was established by the Iowa Highway Commission in 1959, and during its first year 22 projects totaling 17 miles of improvements on primary extensions in cities and towns were completed. Between 1961 and 1969, approximately $135.2 million was spent on urban improvements and urban interstate highways. Under the Federal Aid Act of 1962, the state had to prepare a comprehensive plan for metropolitan cities of more than 50,000 population. Plans and supplemental studies were made for Des Moines, Cedar Rapids, Sioux City, Waterloo, Davenport, Council Bluffs and Dubuque.

The Federal Department of Transportation

In 1966, the Department of Transportation was created by Congress to be headed by a Secretary of Transportation with Cabinet rank. It exercised no regulatory authority over the various modes except for matters of safety, where it had extensive powers. Rather, the legislation brought under one administrative unit the many governmental activities relating to transportation, formerly the responsibility of other agencies and departments. Exceptions were the Federal Maritime Administration, which under strong opposition from maritime interests, remained in the Department of Commerce, and the Army Corps of Engineers. The department was expected to function in areas of transportation policy, encouragement of transportation coordination, and development of criteria for investment of public funds in transport facilities, although in the latter instance their responsibilities were limited under provisions of the act. In the Airport and Airway Act of 1970, the Secretary was given a specific mandate in the field of planning and coordination. He was required to formulate and present to Congress for approval "a national transportation policy." Two statements on policy issues and recommendations were submitted in 1971 and 1975. Intervention by the Secretary in cases before regulatory commissions was authorized when questions of policy were involved. When the Secretary did so he had the same standing as any other parties to the proceeding.

Social and Environmental Concerns

Although sociological and environmental issues concerned all phases of our national existence, this discussion pertains primarily to highway progress but recognizes that any policies directed toward highway transportation would also have an impact on other transportation and non-transportation developments. The early environmental problem for the traveler was mud in rainy weather and dust in dry periods, especially in the rural areas. Urban transportation was geared to horse-drawn vehicles, and city streets were the depository of manure and dead animals which were blamed as the chief offenders for the outbreak and spread of epidemics of cholera, smallpox, yellow fever and typhoid. The motor vehicle gradually reduced the sanitation problems but did not solve dust pollution in the late 19th and early 20th centuries. "The dust raised by an automobile, when running at a rate of less than twenty miles an hour, is not worse than that raised by many wagons, but when this limit is exceeded, the automobile becomes a dust nuisance."[6]

Crude oil or absorbent salts were used to control dust, and when these methods were considered too expensive, water was recommended. As new types of road surfaces became available, health factors were minimally included in the criteria for selection. Roadside beautification or scenic betterment was periodically suggested by 1915, and tree planting and billboard control were advocated in 1930. In 1938, the Federal Aid Act included approval for the use of construction funds to cover costs of roadside and landscape development, but it was not until the Highway Beautification Act of 1965 that states really took advantage of this permissive legislation. An awareness of hazards caused by vehicular emissions and poor air quality developed in the 1960s. Smog in large numbers of urban areas warned of future dangers and brought about a heightened environmental consciousness to people who increased demands for corrective action. Public hearings on environmental issues relating to bypass, freeway construction and interstate projects were required in the Acts of 1950 and 1958. Legislation in 1968 specified that social and environmental effects of such projects be considered and be consistent with the goals and objectives of urban planning.

The Federal Environmental Act of 1969 required impact statements to be prepared for all federal-aid projects affecting the quality of human life. In 1970, the Department of Transportation was requested to prepare and issue guidelines to assure that possible social, economic and environmental effects of proposed highway projects were fully considered and that the final decisions were made in the public interest. Results known as "Process Guidelines" aimed at influencing the methods by which highway projects were developed were issued in 1972. Each state highway agency was to prepare an Action Plan detailing the organizational arrangement, assignment of responsibilities and procedures followed in developing projects to conform to Congressional intent. By 1975, 52 of a possible 53 Action Plans were completed and approved for 50 states, Puerto Rico and the District of Columbia. Noise abatement and Air Quality Guidelines were also issued in the early 1970s. Public concern of social values in highway development occurred in 1962 through federal assistance to states and business firms for reimbursement of those displaced by highway construction. This federal assistance was broadened and extended in 1968. Another Act provided that federal aid would not be approved for urban area projects unless they were based upon a continuing comprehensive planning process carried on cooperatively by states and local communities. In 1966, a national safety program was initiated by which matching funds were authorized for estblishment of safety standards for motor vehicles. Thus, an awareness of environmental and sociological factors in road building was a gradual evolutionary process, for the original motivating force was in building highways to enable rapid movement from point to point. In earlier years these factors were either ignored or treated only when they became hazardous.

Highway Progress and Interstate Programs in Iowa

Transitional Trends

The 1960s were a period of transition in both State and Highway Commission Administration. Four Democratic and Republican Governors alternated in the Executive Office, beginning with Herschel C. Loveless and followed by Norman A. Erbe, Harold E. Hughes and Robert D. Ray. Governor Hughes had been a member of the Iowa Commerce Commission, and he and the others were vitally concerned and supportive of highway progress. At the Highway Commission, John Butter retired in 1960 and was replaced by L. M. Clauson as Chief Engineer. Under a staff reorganization, 21 departments and sections operated under three Divisions and six Operating Districts in 1960—a move designed to coordinate the activities of the departments into functional working groups. A steadily accelerating highway program prompted an addition to the main headquarters building in 1961, adding 60,000 square feet of working space to the original building. In the interim period of 37 years, the headquarters staff had increased from 100 to 800 employees and the Primary Road Fund had increased from under $13 million in 1924 to $95 million in 1961.

[6] Quoted in *America's Highways* from "What New York State is Doing," *Good Roads Magazine* (February 1908): p. 50.

Further administrative changes came on December 1, 1966, when Joseph R. Coupal Jr. was appointed the first Director of Highways. Among his responsibilities was the coordination of the work of the professional engineering staff with the Support Divisions and the six Operating Districts. Howard Gunnerson, the Chief Engineer and Deputy Director, was responsible for all professional engineering functions in development and operations. Staff reorganizations in 1968 increased the number of departments from 21 to 24, and further reorganization in 1969 increased the number to 26 (Fig. 10-4, 10-5).

These changes were considered necessary to meet the rapidly expanding traffic requirements of the state. Total annual daily traffic per mile of rural primary roads rose from 1,587 vehicles in 1960 to 2,113 in 1969, representing a gain of 33 percent, or 76 percent when compared to the year 1950. Legislation passed by the General Assembly in 1958 required the commission to plan and publish a series of five-year primary road construction programs, the first of which covered the years 1960-1964. The commission was also given the privilege of reviewing the progress each year and adding one year's work annually to the programs. Four additional plans projected estimated funds available and expenditures through 1970. Sufficiency ratings were used as guides in programming road projects, providing a means of numerically evaluating tangible items affecting the adequacy of an existing section of highway or bridge. Points were assigned to existing features on a highway system and related to standards desired. An example is given in Table 10-6 for 1960-1961.

Anson Marston
Iowa State Highway Commission,
1904-1927

Thomas H. MacDonald
Chief Engineer, 1913-1919

Fred R. White
Chief Engineer, 1919-1952

Edward F. Koch
Chief Engineer, 1952-1954

John G. Butter
Chief Engineer, 1954-1960

L. M. Clauson
Chief Engineer, 1960-1966

Joseph R. Coupal Jr.
Director of Highway Division,
1966-1974

Howard E. Gunnerson
Director of Highway Division,
1975-1977

Table 10-6
Sufficiency Ratings for Primary Roads and Bridges, 1960-1961

Classification	Sufficency Rating	Rural Primary (miles)	Municipal Primary Extensions (miles)	Bridges (No.)
Critical	0 - 49	3,322	258	394
Poor to Fair	50 - 79	2,168	478	1,716
Good	80 - 89	830	205	537
Excellent	90 - 100	2,267	113	725
Totals		8,587	1,054	3,372

(*Source:* Iowa Highway Commission, *Annual Report*, 1961.)
[1] Figures rounded to the nearest unit.

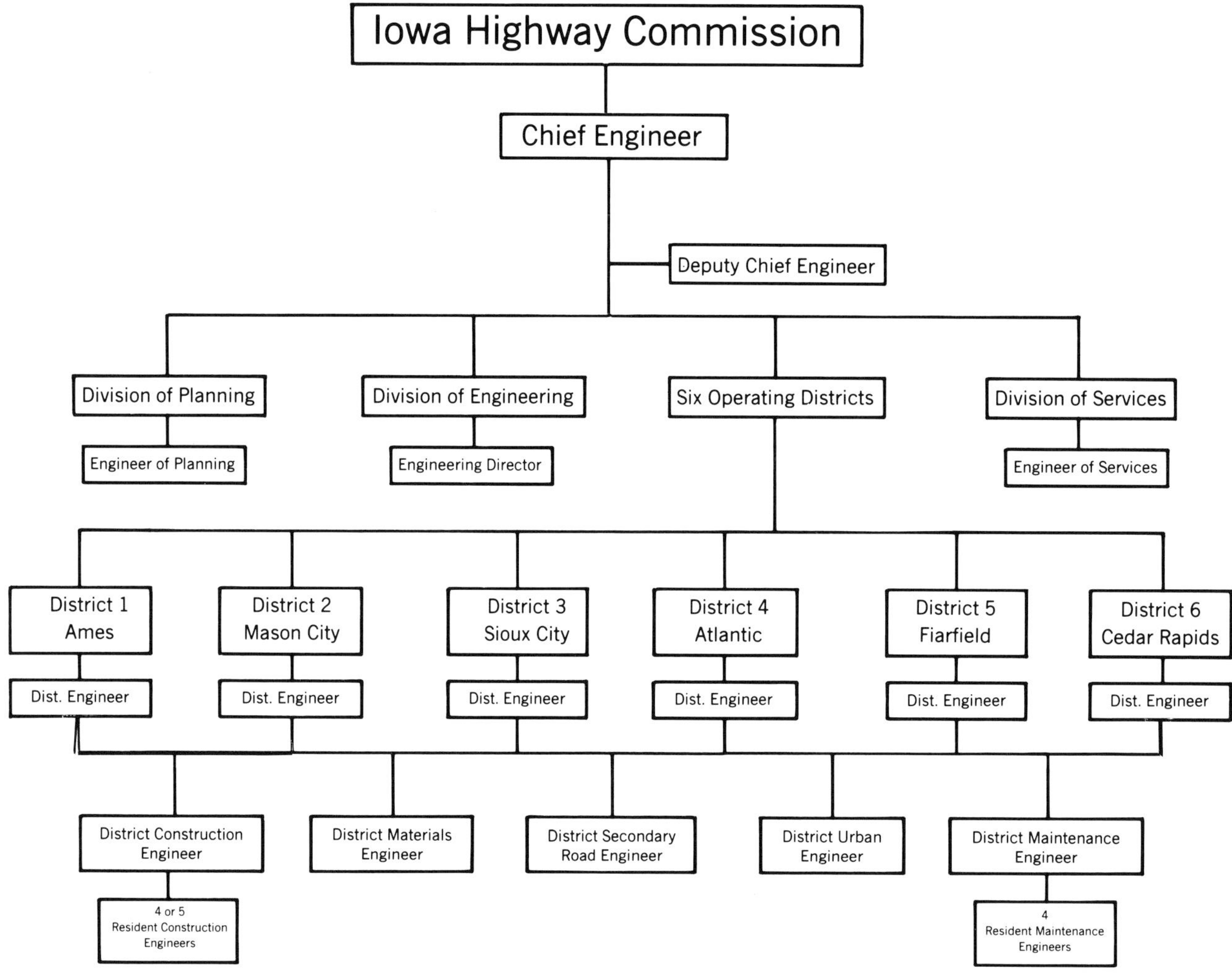

Figure 10-4
Highway Commission organizational chart prior to 1966.
(Courtesy: Iowa State Highway Commission)

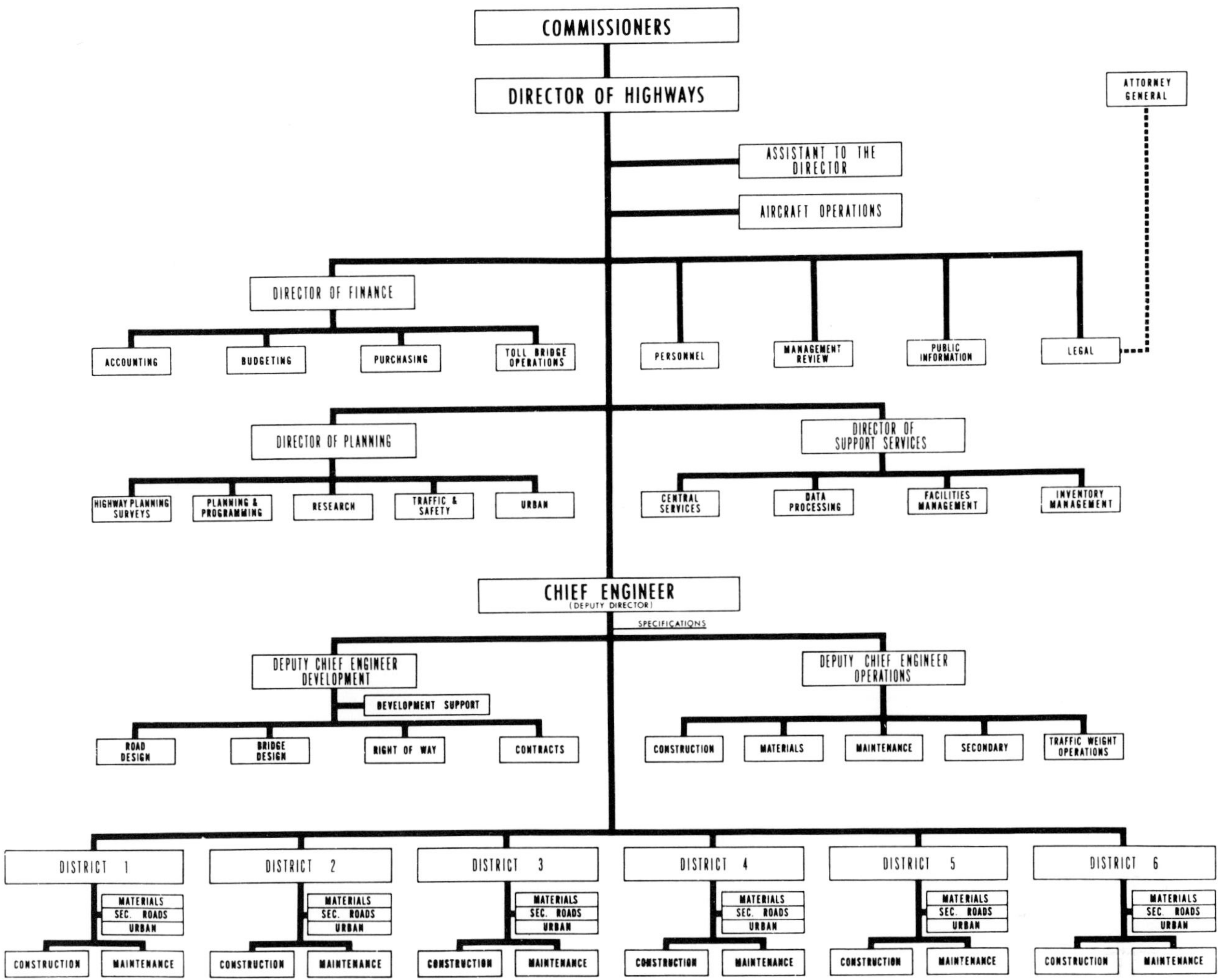

Figure 10-5
Highway Commission organization chart, 1969.
(Courtesy: Iowa State Highway Commission)

Interstate Highway Construction

From 1956, the commission allotted a major share of resources to the construction of the interstate roads in Iowa. With no four-lane highways or toll roads that could be incorporated, the state started from zero to design, acquire right-of-way and build a 710-mile ultra-safe highway system. Closing the gap between Grinnell and Iowa City in 1964 was probably the most spectacular effort that Iowa has seen in 50 years of road building, and it completed the work on Interstate 80 between Des Moines and Davenport. The 158-mile four-lane divided highway reduced driving time by one and one-fourth hours.

At Des Moines, Interstate 80 connected with Interstate 35, and fifty-four miles were built to Osceola, making 212 miles of continuous interstate open to traffic in 1964. To the north, 25 miles of Interstate 35 was under construction to Ames; in the west, 61 miles had been completed between Dexter and Atlantic. On Interstate 29, the road had been built between Onawa and Sioux City, and between Missouri Valley and State 480 (Fig. 10-6). Also under construction was the Des Moines Freeway (Interstate 235), a city connector and important link in the national system. Traffic needs in metropolitan areas required new highways to serve the central city as well

Interstate 235 in Des Moines.
(Courtesy: Iowa State Highway Commission)

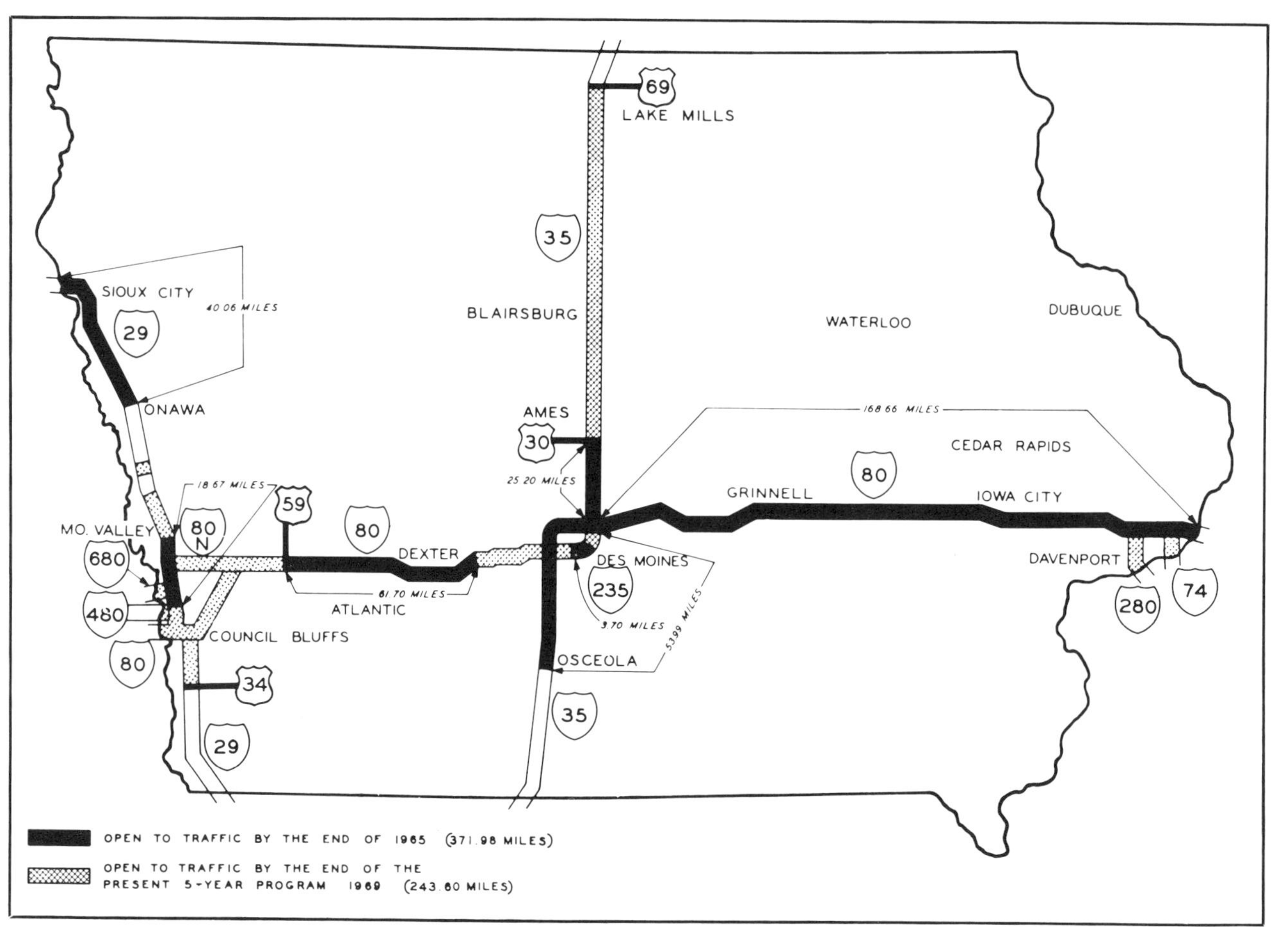

Figure 10-6
The Iowa four-lane interstate system in 1965.
(Courtesy: Iowa State Highway Commission)

as the peripheral sectors bypassing the cities. For these reasons, the national program provided for through-city freeways as well as circuitous roads.

By the close of 1968, Interstate 80 west to Council Bluffs, Interstate 29 north from Council Bluffs to Sioux City, and Interstate 35 north from Des Moines to Blairsburg were open to traffic, and the remaining segments were planned for completion in 1971 (Fig. 10-7). Iowa's share of the 1,500 miles added by Congress in 1969 to the national system would mean an estimated $125 million in additional federal funds over the following five years. The funds would be used to construct a four-lane controlled access road from Iowa City to Waterloo and for a new interstate bridge over the Missouri River at Sioux City.[7]

Interchange of Interstate 380, U.S. 20 and U.S. 218 at southeast corner of Waterloo. (Courtesy: Iowa Department of Transportation)

[7] Iowa State Highway Commission, *1964 Annual Report; 1968 Annual Report; 1969 Annual Report,* Ames: Iowa State Highway Commission. One of the major concerns of the Highway Commission was snow and ice removal. The average annual snowfall in Iowa is 30 inches. This amount would cover a 160-acre farm to a depth of 938 feet and if loaded into railroad box cars with a capacity of 50 cubic yards each, the train would be 45,833 miles long and would extend twice around the world. Snow fences were erected on certain sections of the primary system. Salting, initiated in 1954 and spread on the roads at 500 pounds to the mile, covered 3,800 miles of primary and interstate highways in 1963, with 1,700 miles to be added in 1964.

Interstate Progress In Iowa

(Total Miles In System—710)

TIMETABLE
To Open
Late 1968—10
Late 1969—66
Late 1970—59.5
Late 1971—76.5
212.0 miles

1956—Estimated Construction Cost	$428,007,000
Jan. 1967—Construction Cost to Date	$432,834,199
Estimated Cost to Complete	$271,000,000

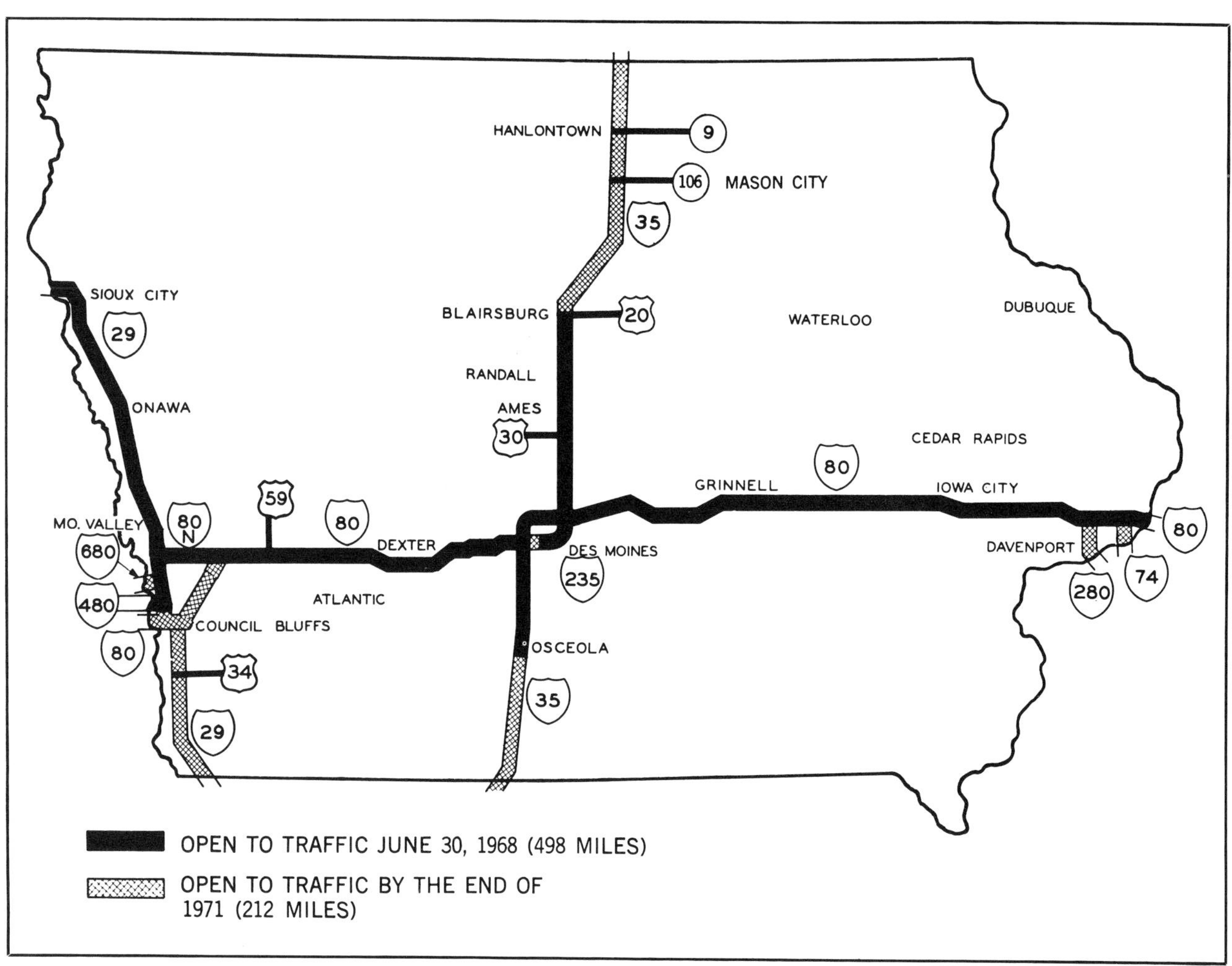

Figure 10-7
Interstate progress in Iowa.
(Courtesy: Iowa State Highway Commission)

An inadequate primary road bridge typical of the bridge problem that existed in the early 1960s. (Courtesy: Iowa State Highway Commission)

Primary and Secondary Roads

Emphasis on interstate construction by no means diminished the pace of modernization and improvement of the state's primary and secondary road systems and expansion of support services. Primary road activity involved relocation of both federal-aid and state numbered roads.[8] Primary extensions through urban areas embodied replacement of narrow brick or other surfaces with paved multi-lane roadways with curbs. Additional mileages on farm-to-market roads were graded and paved, and a more efficient system was adopted for marking highways. Of the almost 10,000 miles of primary roads, 907 miles were still 18 feet wide, and 206 miles were graded but not paved. In 1965 the General Assembly added one cent to the fuel tax, expected to increase highway revenues by $10 million, with one-half of the new funds earmarked for expansion of the program for widening roads and bridges then 20 feet or less in width.

In 1968, a Freeway-Expressway System was approved by the commission to serve traffic needs in the years following completion of the interstate program. The 833-mile Freeway System was designed for four-lane divided highways with access via interchange only, estimated to cost $901 million. The 1,139-mile Expressway System was also designed for four-lane divided highways with access via interchange and selected public road connections at grade. The estimated cost of construction was $889 million (Fig. 10-8).

[8] Iowa State Highway Commission, *1964-1965 Annual Report,* Ames: Iowa State Highway Commission, 1965, p. 15. The reconstruction of Iowa 150 between Fayette and West Union was interrupted by the discovery of three graves on the new right-of-way. It was alleged that a man, woman and child died at the Half Way House, four miles north of Fayette or were murdered in the 1860's and buried 1,000 feet from the Inn. None of these stories were verified. The graves were moved in April, 1965, under the supervision of the Commission Resident Engineer to Grandview Cemetery in Fayette. A simple bronze plaque placed on the headstone reads: "Three members Pioneer Family Died Enroute, 1868, Reburied 1965 by Order of the Court."

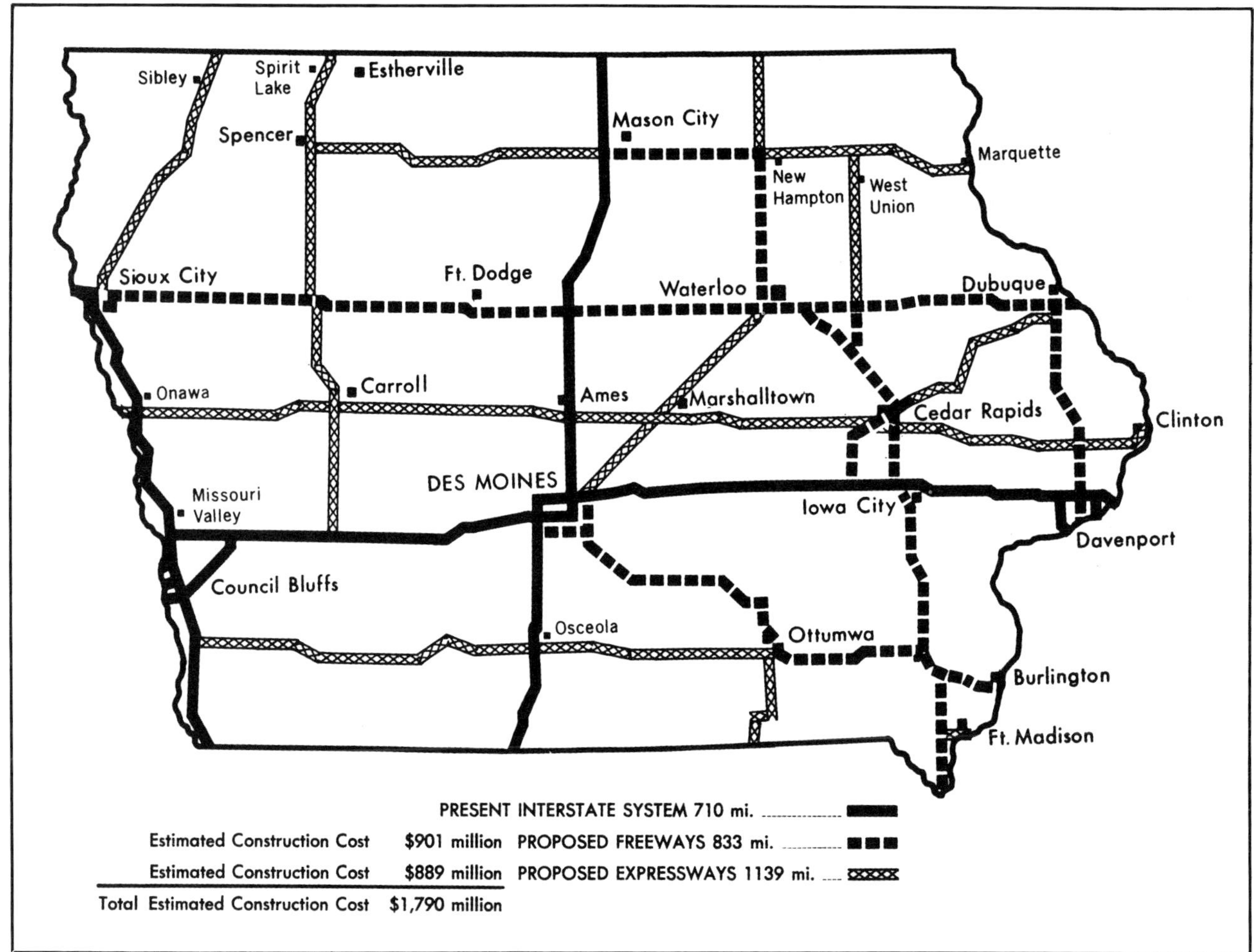

Figure 10-8
Iowa's proposed network of freeways and expressways.
(Courtesy: Iowa State Highway Commission)

Highway Improvements

Progress in highway improvements during the 1960s may be measured by comparisons of mileages by type of surface and a summary of highway contracts approved between 1960 and 1969. These are found in Tables 10-7 and 10-8.

The total expenditures of $910.8 million were considerably higher than the $700.2 million spent on highways from 1946 to 1960 and reflected the construction of interstates and modernization and urban extension programs.

A report on "Highway Needs and Finances, 1968-1988" was released in 1969, prepared by the commission staff under a new system designed for maintaining up-to-date needs and finances. All of the state's roads and streets and their structures were compared to desirable design standards to determine present or anticipated deficiencies for correction. Construction dollar requirements based upon 1968 prices were applied to improvement, maintenance and administrative costs for the 20-year period. Projected dollar needs amounted to approximately $10.6 billion while anticipated revenues were only $8.5 billion, leaving a deficit of $2.1 billion. Considering all factors in the study, a redistribution of road use tax funds was proposed. The Primary System would receive 63 percent; county roads, 20.9 percent; and municipal streets, 16.1 percent.

Table 10-7
Total Highway Miles by Type of Surface, Jan. 1, 1961 and Dec. 31, 1969

Type of Surface	1961 (mileage)	1969 (mileage)
Portland Cement Pavement	9,254	9,648
Asphaltic Concrete Pavement	6,599	15,521
Bituminous Treated	4,874	5,246
Gravel or Stone	80,091	74,215
Not Surfaced	10,852	7,664
Totals	111,670	112,294

(*Source:* Iowa Highway Commission, *Annual Reports.*)

Table 10-8
Highway Contracts Approved Between 1960 and 1969

Fiscal Year	Primary Roads (in millions)	Farm-to-Market Roads (in millions)	Total
1960	$ 48.7	$ 21.9	$ 70.6
1961	51.1	21.4	72.5
1962	42.3	19.8	62.1
1963	52.8	24.4	77.2
1964	79.3	22.7	102.0
1965	56.4	21.7	78.1
1966	97.0	23.7	120.7
1967	100.0	26.4	126.4
1968	66.2	25.7	91.9
1969	82.0	27.3	109.3
Totals	$675.8	$235.0	$910.8

(*Source:* Iowa Highway Commission, *Annual Reports.*)
[1] Expenditures include interstate, state park and institutional roads.
[2] Figures rounded to the nearest unit.

Trends in Air Transportation

Changing transportation conditions usually require a reevaluation of policies. Such was the nature of a two-volume report by Baxter, McDonald and Company, published in 1968. The study was contracted by the State Office of Planning and Programming for the purpose of analyzing state transportation policy. It discussed policy issues and recommended changes which are presented briefly in a later section. Excerpts from the report on airport planning, construction and improvement, air transportation and functions of the Iowa Aeronautical Commission are incorporated into this section.

In 1965 the Aeronautics Commission celebrated its 20th anniversary. During the period, the primary concern was meeting the needs of general aviation (non-commercial) through assistance in development of small airports and registration of pilots and aircraft, aircraft dealers, air schools and ground instructors. The commission functioned in four major programs: (1) airport development and improvement; (2) air age education; (3) aviation safety; and (4) administration and enforcement of Iowa aviation law. Decisions on planning and financing airports or improving old ones were shared by the federal government and municipalities with the commission representing the interests of the state, acting as liaison between the principal parties. The commission was not equipped by statutory powers or structure to conduct comprehensive airport planning. However, they actively participated by providing technical assistance and advice. They also supplemented federal navigation and safety measures by installing runway lights and rotating beacons, marking routes, and providing two-way radio communication systems and weather instruments. Scheduling of regular commercial service into and out of major airports was left to the initiative of individual cities and towns.

Nearly all of the revenues of the commission came from registration fees of pilots, small aircraft and the unfunded portion of the state aviation gasoline taxes. Within relatively modest budgets and under legal restraints they were obliged to favor general aviation, and in this context they were considered to have performed their function effectively. Yet the role of the state in aviation was seriously limited by interpretations of the commission as to its functions, and thus the "role of the state in airport planning and in expansion and improvement of air transportation service was viewed basically as a passive one."[9] There was no formal airport plan in Iowa at this time.

By the mid-1960s, Iowa had more than kept pace with national growth in aviation. The state had 31.2 aircraft per 1,000 square miles compared to a national average of 23.8, and 6.3 aircraft per 10,000 population contrasted to 4.6 nationally. In 1964, Iowa ranked 14th in the nation in the number of airports, 15th in the number of civil aircraft, fifth in the number of lighted airports and 15th in the number of airports with paved runways. Airport construction, improvements and air service, 1945 compared to 1965, are shown in Table 10-9.

The number of municipal airports represented nearly half of the 225 airports in the state. The remainder were owned and operated by private interests but were available for public use. There were also a large number of privately owned smaller airports and airstrips not available for public use and not under active supervision by the commission. For the first time since safety records had been kept, there were no aviation fatalities during the 1965 fiscal year. What made the record more noteworthy was the considerable increase in general aviation activity. Using the Des Moines airport as an example, civil itinerant aircraft movement rose about 22 percent over 1964, from 52,682 to 72,787. This was an average of 100 transient aircraft per day using the airport, and the figure did not include air carriers, military or local flights. One of the major problems facing Iowa was the introduction of jumbo jets in 1969, and no airport in the state had runways long enough to accommodate them.

Table 10-9
Airport Construction, Improvements and Air Transportation Service in Iowa, 1945 and 1965

Classification	1945	1965
Municipal Airports	43	101
Lighted Airports	7	101
Airports with Paved Surfaces	7	59
Airports with Two-Way Radio	6	64
Cities with Airline Service	2	15

(Source: Iowa Aeronautical Commission, *Annual Report,* 1965.)

There were two classifications of air service in Iowa in 1966. One was "general aviation"—aircraft owned by individuals and business firms. The other was scheduled commercial service into 15 cities with two communities receiving service through airports in contiguous states. Nine cities: Sioux City, Mason City, Fort Dodge, Ottumwa, Waterloo, Iowa City, Dubuque, Clinton and Burlington were served by Ozark Airlines, operating both local service and

[9] Baxter, McDonald and Company, Consultants, *Transportation in Iowa—A Review of Key Policy Issues* (two volumes), prepared for the Office for Planning and Programming, State of Iowa, Berkeley, Calif.: Baxter, McDonald and Company, September, 1968.

flights to Omaha, Des Moines and Chicago for connections to other destinations. North Central also served Sioux City with routes to Minnesota and the Dakotas. Four cities: Des Moines, Cedar Rapids, Council Bluffs (using the Omaha airport) and Davenport (using the Moline airport) had flights to major cities or metropolitan areas that did not involve interchanges. United and Ozark served all four airports. Braniff Airways operated from Des Moines and Omaha, the latter city also served by North Central and Frontier airlines. Two cities, Ames and Marshalltown, had air taxi or commuter service into Chicago (Fig. 10-9, 10-10).

The importance of federal grants to the annual funding of airport projects and improvements during the 1960s is shown in Table 10-10.

For the fiscal years 1965 to 1969, the National Airport Plan listed 88 Iowa airports for development and improvement. Thirteen new airports were projected for initial development, 44 airports were to acquire additional land, more lighting facilities were to be installed at 55 airports, and 23 would receive runway or taxiway extensions. In the first 11 months of 1967, the Des Moines airport reported 606,000 passenger movements (arrivals and departures), a gain of 112,000 over the same period in 1966, and over double the number of 300,000 in 1959. Estimates of over one million passengers through the airport by 1971 proved quite accurate. For airports statewide in 1966, the number of passenger departures alone totaled 577,000 for 11 airports reporting, not including the Iowa passengers embarking from the Moline and Omaha airports.

Table 10-10
Annual State and Federal Aid for Airport Projects and Airport Improvements, 1960-1970

Fiscal Year	Annual State Expenditures (in thousands)	Year	Annual Federal Expenditures (Iowa) (in thousands)
1960-1961	$ 48.4	1960	$ 243.1
1961-1962	38.6	1961	1,586.8
1962-1963	137.2	1962	476.2
1963-1964	93.2	1963	527.9
1964-1965	59.7	1964	861.1
1965-1966	125.5	1965	898.0
1966-1967	102.7	1966	1,481.5
1967-1968	189.4	1967	769.1
1968-1969	223.1	1968	2,186.0
1969-1970	218.4	1969	1,390.7
Totals	$1,236.2		$10,420.4

(*Source: Iowa Airport System Plan,* Vol. 1, Tables 4 and 5. Summary Report prepared for the Iowa Aeronautics Commission by the Engineering Research Institute, Iowa State University, Ames, November, 1972.)

[1] Figures rounded to the nearest unit.

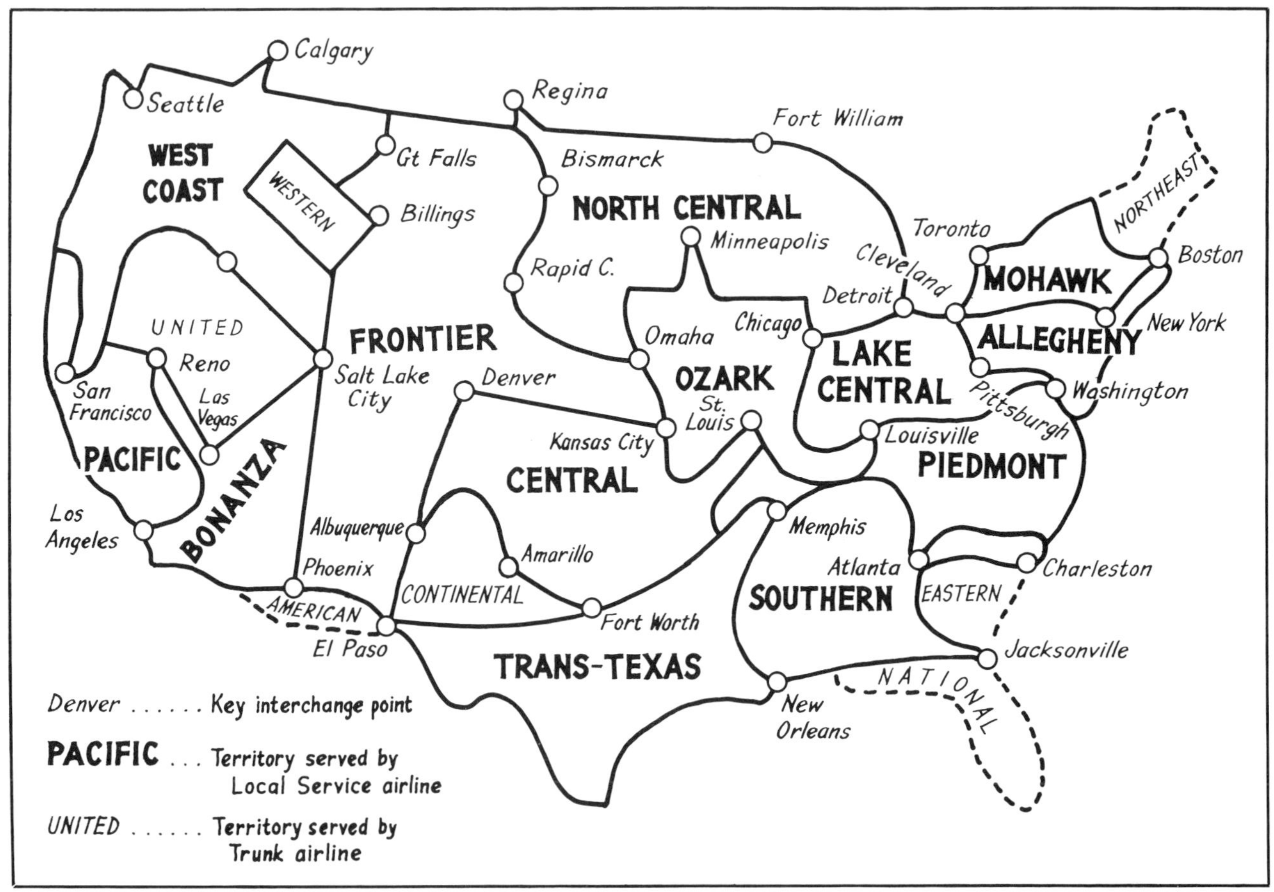

Figure 10-9
Territories served by local service airlines in the early 1960s.
(Courtesy: R.E.G. Davies Collection)

Waterborne Commerce—The Alter Company

Unique among those identified with Upper Mississippi River commerce was the Alter Company, organized in Davenport in 1916 by Frank R. Alter. The firm was engaged in processing and shipping scrap metal from the Quad Cities for more than a half century, starting with railroads and later by water when the nine-foot channel was completed. In May 1960, Alter moved into the towing business with four open hopper barges and a single towboat named after the owner. Gordon L. Jones was hired as executive of the newly formed Marine Division and later promoted to vice president. Under his leadership, the operation expanded to five towboats and 148 barges by 1972. Terminals were built at St. Paul and La Crosse in addition to the main base at Davenport. A terminal in the New Orleans harbor provided cleaning, repair and fleeting facilities for the company's barges.

Except for the Diamond Joe line of past fame, the Alter Company was the only barge line located in Iowa. It concentrated its efforts on service in the "Middle Upper Mississippi," the area between Cassville, Wisconsin, on the north and Hannibal, Missouri, on the south. Grains moved downstream and phosphate rock and coal upstream. The firm's outstanding features included the variety and frequency of services it offered shippers. It also provided somewhat unusual terminal operations by combining terminal and transfer facilities using railroad, truck and water to facilitate complete transportation services. The success of the Alter Company in offering low cost, reliable service to Upper Mississippi firms is a tribute to Iowa's contribution to inland waterway development.

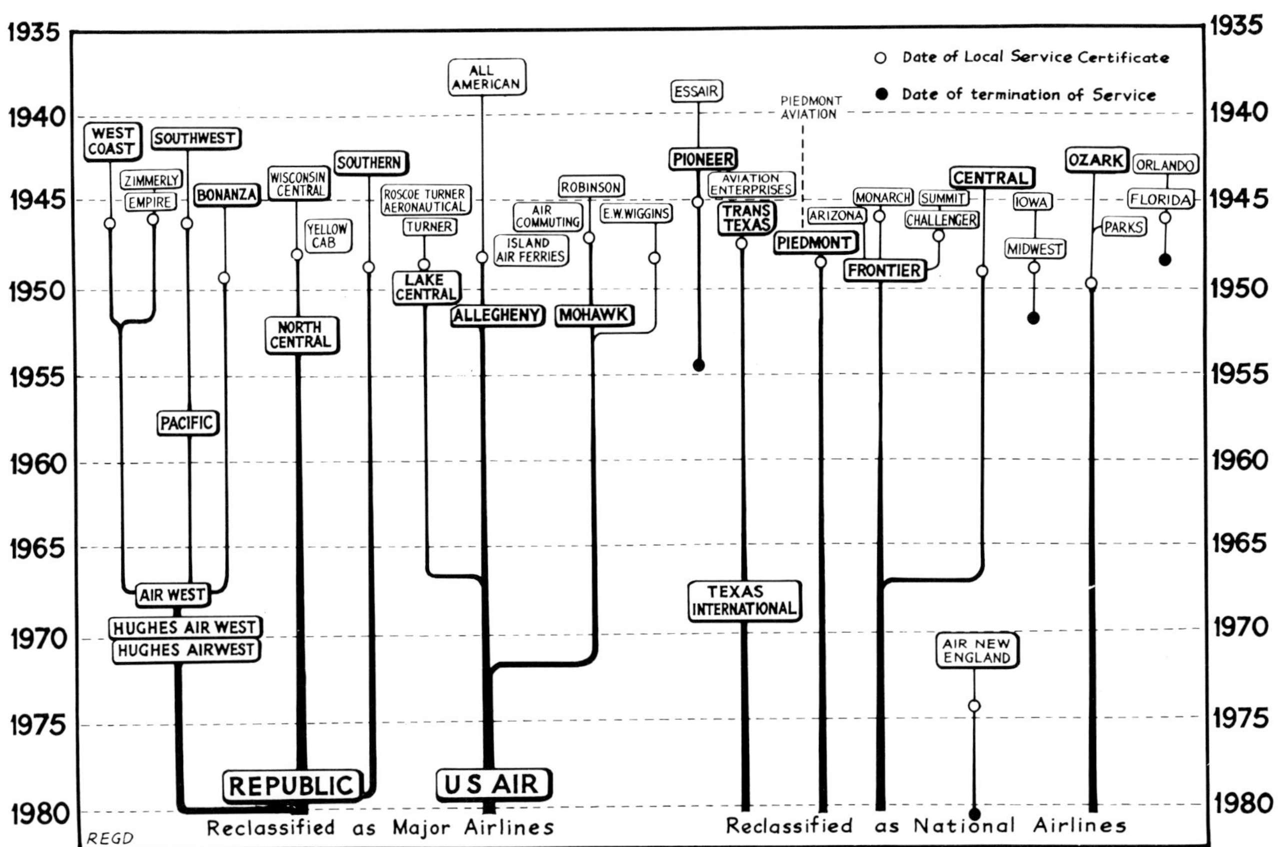

Figure 10-10
Genealogy of local service airlines.
(Courtesy: R.E.G. Davies Collection)

Transportation Policy Issues and Conflicts in the 1960s

Policy issues were presented and recommendations made in the Baxter Report. These are outlined briefly in the discussion which follows:

Regulation and Fragmentation of State Authority

The Commerce Commission was admonished for being too passive on proposals by shippers and carriers concerning rate and route changes, acquiesing in most cases to their requests. Where the interests of the state were argued before federal agencies, courts or congressional committees, there was a multiplicity of representation in some instances, in others, none. For consistency, the Governor's office was suggested as a clearing house for approval or disapproval of advocacy positions taken by state agencies in transportation matters.

Service to Small Towns

Small towns experienced increased isolation from reductions in both quantity and quality of public transportation and would be expected to suffer additional losses through the threat of "modal deregulation." Declines in passenger services, abandonment of freight agency service and/or removal of depots had been a progressive strategy of railroads during the postwar years. Branch lines, consisting of approximately 46 percent of Class I railroad mileages, were particularly vulnerable for further abandonment, and regulated motor carriers sought relief from operating requirements to serve low volume shippers. The issues were whether or not the social goal of low cost service to small communities could be reconciled with the economic objectives of the carriers in choosing the traffic which would result in higher returns on investment. On the assumption that preservation of small towns and family farms was a widely held political and social goal for Iowa, it was suggested that wherever necessary, subsidies be considered for needed transportation services. However, no suggestions were made as to the sources for such subsidies.

Airport Planning

Airport planning policies have been included in the previous section. It was recommended that immediate formulation of a statewide regional plan be implemented and studies made with neighboring states on the feasibility of constructing a mid-continent airport designed to relieve the congestion at O'Hare airport in Chicago and to function as an east-west interchange point.

Highway Financing

Division of responsibility between users and non-users in financing future highways was a basic policy issue in highway financing. Projections from 1967-1987 indicated user deficits in primary roads and municipal streets and surpluses in the county road system under the current user fund distribution program. The state primary system was financed entirely through user revenues while most of the municipal streets were financed by non-user revenues. Both supported traffic loads in excess of their share of user revenues. A change in the distribution formula was recommended.

Conflicts between Social and Economic Goals

Conflicts were a factor in secondary road policies and urban transportation corridors. In 1968 the state's highway system showed 81 percent of the total mileage classified as secondary roads, eight percent in primary roads, and 11 percent in primary and secondary extensions and city streets. Vehicle miles on primary roads accounted for 45 percent of the traffic, on city streets for 36 percent, and on secondary roads only 19 percent. The large rural population in earlier years made extensive use of secondary roads, but as population declined, the roads carried a smaller proportion. The public cost of providing for low density high-cost highways per vehicle mile was disproportionately high relative to the other systems. However, economic modification or abandonment had to be balanced against the possible loss of mobility into and out of rural areas. A similar balance was necessary in constructing city freeways as between the expansion of the economic base of the city against the social disruption of business firms, housing and residents. Therefore, the system planning would need to be broadened beyond the singular goal of physical considerations to include a combination of environmental, economic and social concerns—a difficult and challenging assignment in an ever-changing political atmosphere.

Creation of a State Department of Transportation

A separate section of the report developed the rationale for a State Department of Transportation. All functions of the state agencies would be combined except for the rate and regulatory duties of the Commerce Commission. The Department would have the powers and responsibilities for developing and implementing a state comprehensive transportation plan. Its establishment would provide the potential for solution of much of Iowa's policy problems, but the potential would not be automatically realized by simply combining the agencies under one administration. The merits of the reorganization lay in the new opportunities for integration of operations of the various modes and for the use of state and federal programs capable of providing the state with a more effective and efficent transportation system.

Summary

National trends in modal relationships and changing transportation markets were followed to a limited extent in Iowa. The merger movement of the railroads serving the state was a microcosm of national patterns designed to adjust to increased competition of surface and air carriers. Flexibility of motor carriers was enhanced by construction of interstate highways and improvements in state road systems. Inland water carriers gained through expansion of bulk commodity traffic. Intermodalism, particularly in rail-truck combinations, began a slow but steady evolvement to take advantage of the low-cost features of each mode. General aviation activity and commercial air transportation of passengers and mail showed substantial growth, putting emphasis on further development of airports, safety and navigational aids. More variety and frequency of waterway service was offered by the newly organized Marine Division of the Alter Company in Davenport. Traditional trends in markets and modal relationships brought transportation issues and conflicts between social and economic goals into public consciousness. This stimulated proposals for a State Department of Transportation as an agency with potential for a comprehensive analysis and study of the state's major transportation problems.

Selected References

American Association of Railroads. *Railroad Merger Movement Down to One*. Washington, D.C.: American Association of Railroads, February 10, 1972.

American Trucking Association. *Mergers in the Trucking Industry*. Washington, D.C.: American Trucking Association, October, 1968.

Barriger, John W. "The Effects of Mergers on Competition." *Transportation Journal* (Spring 1968): pp. 5-16.

Baumel, C.P., W.H. Thompson, and R.D. Hickman. *Impact of Transportation Equipment Shortages and Substandard Transportation Service on Iowa-Country Elevators*. Special Report No. 68. Ames: Iowa State University Agricultural Experiment Station, December, 1971.

Conant, Michael. *Railroad Mergers and Abandonments*. Berkeley: University of California Press, 1964.

Fair, Marvin L., and Ernest W. Williams, Jr. *Economics of Transportation*. rev. ed. New York: Harper & Bros., 1959.

Farris, Martin T. "Railroad Mergers: New Interest in an Old Approach." *Transportation Journal* (Summer 1962): pp. 30-38.

Federal Aviation Administration. *Airport Activity Statistics of Certified Route Air Carriers—1966*. Washington, D.C.: U.S. Government Printing Office, June, 1967.

Gallamore, Robert E. "Measurement of Cost Savings of Recent Mergers." presented at the Transportation Research Forum, Kansas City, September 4-6, 1968.

Harper, Donald V. *Transportation in America: Users, Carriers, Government*. 2nd ed. Englewood Cliffs, N.J.: Prentice-Hall, 1982.

Healy, Kent T. *The Effects of Scale in the Railroad Industry*. Monograph. New Haven: Yale University Press, 1961.

Hilton, George W. "Public Policy Toward Extinction of the Railroads." *Transportation Journal.* (Winter, 1963): pp. 17-25.

Interstate Commerce Commission Bureau of Economics and Statistics. *Piggyback Characteristics*. Statement No. 66-1. Washington, D.C.: U. S. Government Printing Office, December, 1966.

Iowa Aeronautics Commission. *Ninteenth Annual Report of the Iowa Aeronautics Commission Ending June 30, 1964*. Des Moines: State of Iowa, 1964.

Iowa Development Commission. *1970 Statistical Profile of Iowa*. Des Moines: State of Iowa.

______. *1979 Statistical Profile of Iowa*. Des Moines: State of Iowa.

Iowa Department of Transportation. *River Transportation in Iowa*. Ames: Iowa Department of Transportation, May, 1978.

Iowa Department of Transportation. *1980 Iowa Railroad Analysis, Update*. Ames: Iowa Department of Transportation, December, 1980.

Jorgenson, Roy, and Associates. *Iowa's Needs and Finances, 1967-1987. January, 1967.*

LemMon, Jean, ed. *50th Anniversary of the Des Moines Municipal Airport*. Des Moines: City of Des Moines and the Greater Des Moines Chamber of Commerce Federation, 1980.

McFarland, Walter R. "Unification of Carriers under the Interstate Commerce Act." *Practioners Journal* (1942): p. 325.

McGrath, John E. "Piggyback: Transportation of Trailers on Flat Cars." Ph.D. diss., Indiana University, Bloomington, 1956.

Owen, Wilfred. "Transportation and the City." *Transportation Journal* (Winter 1966): pp. 24-33.

Pegrum, Dudley F. "The Chicago and North Western—Chicago, Milwaukee, St. Paul and Pacific Merger. A Case Study in Transport Economics." *Transportation Journal* (Winter 1969): pp. 43-61.

Petersen, William J. "Upper Mississippi Towboating." *Palimpsest 53* No. 9 (September 1972): pp. 415-421.

Schlatter, H.W. *The Pennsylvania Railroad Company*. Philadelphia: Allen, Lane and Short, 1927.

Smerk, George M. "The Development of Public Transportation and the City." *Public Transportation: Planning, Operations and Management.* ed. by George E. Gray and Lester A. Hoel. Englewood Cliffs, New Jersey: Prentice-Hall Inc., 1979.

______. "The Urban Mass Transportation Act of 1964: New Hope for American Cities." *Transportation Journal* (Winter 1965): pp. 37-38.

Thompson, W. H. *Transportation of Grain and Mixed Feeds from Iowa.* Special Report No. 50. Ames: Iowa State University Agricultural Experiment Station, February, 1967.

______. *Transportation of Livestock and Meats from Iowa.* Special Report No. 60. Ames: Iowa State University Agricultural Experiment Station, April, 1969.

______. *Transportation of Poultry and Poultry Products from Iowa.* Ames: Iowa State University, November, 1970.

Transportation Association of America. *Transportation Facts and Trends.* Washington, D.C.: Transportation Association of America, July, 1978.

U. S. Department of Transportation. *The Railroad Situation, a Perspective on the Present, Past, and Future of the Railroad Industry.* Report No. FRA-OPPD 79-7. Washington, D.C.: U. S. Government Printing Office, March, 1979.

U. S. Department of Transportation Federal Highway Administration. *America's Highways 1776-1976.* Washington, D.C.: U.S. Government Printing Office, 1976.

U. S. Department of Transportation Secretary of Transportation. *A Statement of National Transportation Policy, 1971.* Washington, D.C.: U.S. Government Printing Office, September 17, 1975.

Chapter Eleven

Change, Confusion and Crisis— The 1970s and 1980s

Introduction

The period of 1970-1984 witnessed revolutionary changes in transportation philosophies and attitudes, structural organization, carrier operating strategies and coordinated federal-state policies. State Departments of Transportation were created to promote more orderly and effective planning and funding programs for balanced systems unique to a state's needs. In the early and mid-1970s, federal legislation was directed toward relief of the perennial financial problems of the railroads. Major roads in the East as well as two roads serving Iowa filed for bankruptcy, resulting in state involvement to replace parts of the route structures. The near completion of the interstate highway system and reconstruction and improvement in other highway programs brought demands for longer and heavier trucks, often requiring solutions through legal action. Environmental issues, the energy crisis, and the expected character of service were instrumental in establishing new standards for railroads and highways. Public transit became a prominent issue as rural areas faced losses of air service and railroad branch lines and as urban communities sought solutions to rising private and commercial traffic congestion. Mississippi River problems centered on the controversy over Lock and Dam No. 26 at Alton, Illinois, and user taxes were assessed against commercial water carriers. State airport and aviation system plans were developed in air transportation.

The State Department of Transportation

Until the 1960s, transportation planning and project implementation were the responsibilities of individual modal agencies with little coordination among them. The demand for more efficiency in developing balanced transportation systems led to the creation of the U.S. Department of Transportation, a consolidation of the modal agencies. The same trends occurred on the state level. Action plans on environmental issues, integrated transportation planning, and studies of the impact of highway improvements on other modes were called for in federal legislation. At the same time, independent of federal incentives, states were reorganizing government structures, and the creation of Departments of Transportation was one end result. By 1977, 38 states had organized such agencies, 21 of which preceded Iowa, and a number of these were dominated by one or two modal agencies, usually the highway division. In fact, of those created by 1979, five still had the word "highway" in their titles.

At the request of Governor Ray in 1970, the Office of Planning and Programming prepared a report which analyzed the requirements for an Iowa Department of Transportation, developing an understanding of the organization and its operations, and identifying issues to be addressed in its organization and implementation. The report was advisory in nature and recommended "a first generation" departmental structure (Fig. 11-1). The 65th General Assembly created the department, effective July 1, 1974, "to be responsible for the planning, development, regulation and improvement of transportation in the state as provided by law."[1] A state Transportation Commission consisting of seven members, no more than four from the same political party, was appointed to four-year terms by the Governor, subject to Senate confirmation. Their responsibility was to periodically review programs of the department and make all major policy decisions. Victor Preisser was selected as the first director and brought a wide and diversified experience in modal and general transportation to the task of organizing the department. He viewed Iowa as a "Transportation Laboratory"—a display state where transportation problems could be anticipated, studied and analyzed before national and state laws were passed.

From the Highway Commission, which ended its 62 year existence in 1975, to the new Transportation Commission, came Robert Rigler, New Hampton; Stephen Garst, Coon Rapids; and Donald K. Gardner, Cedar Rapids. Ann Pellegreno, Story City, was appointed from the Aeronautics Commission, which was terminated after 30 years of existence. Others appointed were William F. McGrath, Melrose; Allen Thoms, Dubuque; and L. Stanley Schoelerman of Spencer. In 1984, of the original membership, only

[1] 1974 Laws of Iowa, Chapter 307. See also James Bennett Jr. and William J. Dewitt, "The Development of State Departments of Transportation—A Recent Organizational Phenomenon," *Transportation Journal* (Fall 1982): p. 515.

Robert Rigler remained until his retirement in 1986. The organizational structure of the Department of Transportation in 1984 is shown in Fig. 11-2.

The Transportation Commission in 1986 consisted of Austin B. Turner, Corning, chairperson; C. Roger Fair, Davenport, vice chairperson; David Clemens, Dubuque; Del Van Horn, Jefferson; Robert Meir, Ottumwa; Molly Scott, Spencer; and Douglas Shull, Indianola. Barbara Dunn, Des Moines; Dennis Voy, Maquoketa; Darrel Rensink, Sioux Center; and Jules Busker, Sioux City, had also served terms on the Transportation Commission. Preisser was appointed state Social Services Director in 1977 and was succeeded by Raymond L. Kassel. Kassel retired in 1982, and Warren B. Dunham came from the Illinois Department of Transportation to replace him. When Dunham took a position in industry early in 1988, he was succeeded by Deputy Director Darrel Rensink.

Senate File 1141 (1974) mandated the commission to develop and coordinate a comprehensive transportation policy for the state. Following input by public, private and citizen groups, combined with staff expertise and contact with other state departments, a draft proposal was prepared for public hearing on November 24, 1974. The final policy statement was approved by the commission in December and adopted by the General Assembly in June, 1975. The initial policy and plan was published in *Trans Plan '76* and updated in *Trans Plan '79;* publications of the Department. The current policy statement is found in Chapter 12.

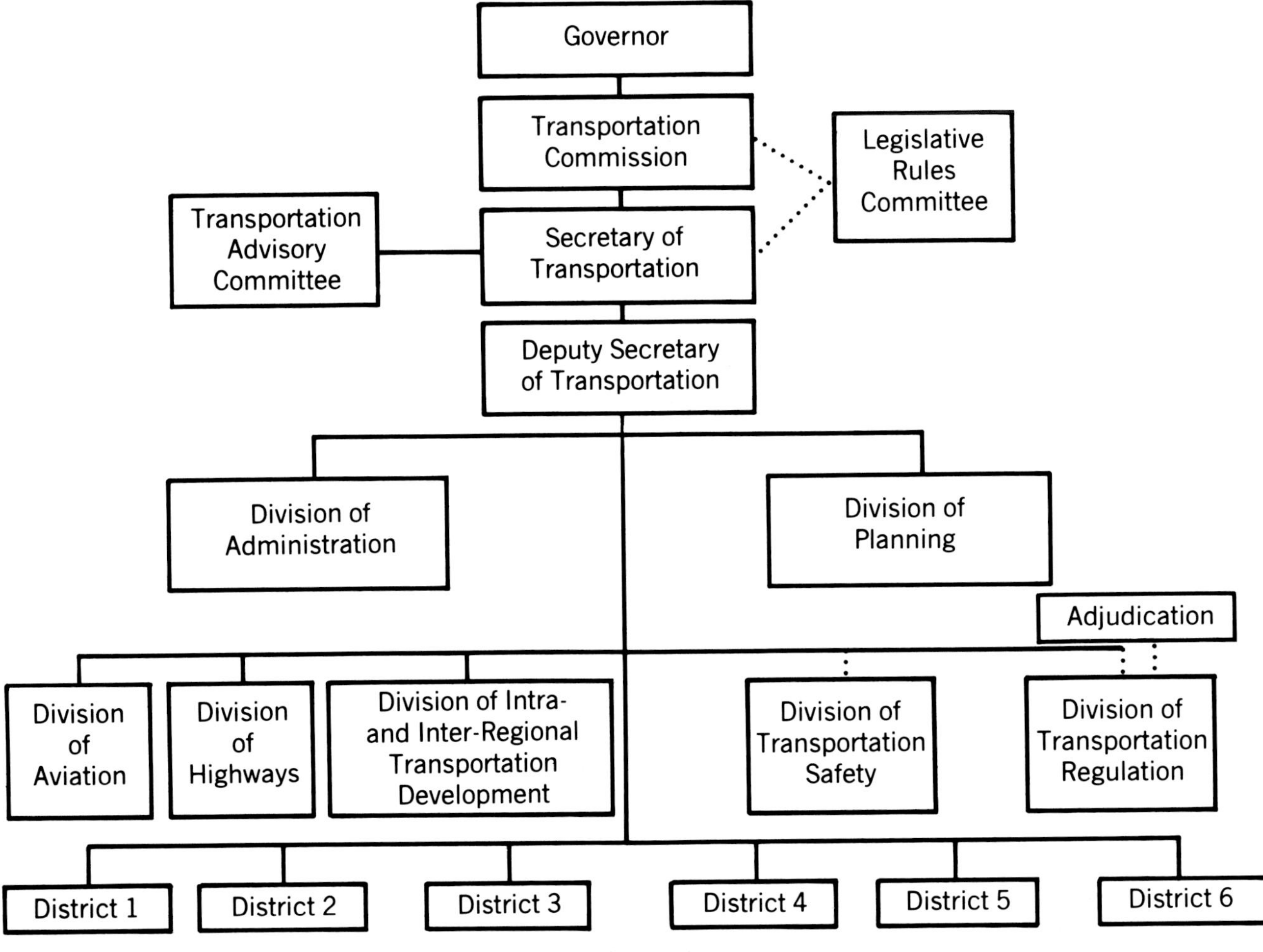

Figure 11-1
Proposed organizational chart for Iowa Department of Transportation.
(Courtesy: Iowa Office of Planning and Programming Report of November 1, 1971)

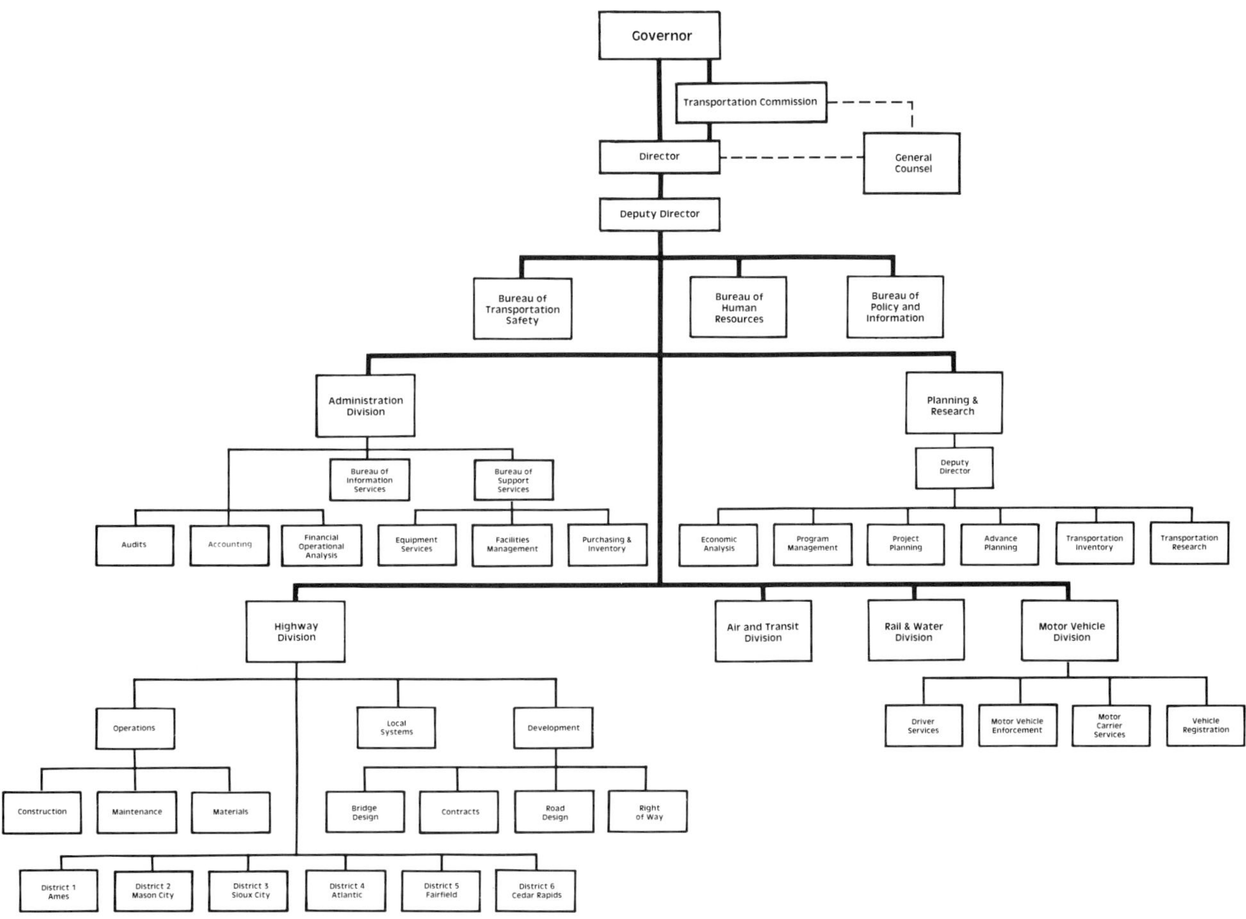

Figure 11-2
Department of Transportation organizational structure in 1984.
(Courtesy: Iowa Department of Transportation)

Victor Preisser
Director, 1974-1977

Raymond L. Kassel
Director, 1978-1982

Warren B. Dunham
Director, 1982-1988

Darrel Rensink
Director, 1988-

The National Transportation Dilemma

The need for a uniform national transportation policy was never more apparent than in the 1970s when the "transportation problem" hit the nation and dominated most of the domestic issues. Uneven regulation, unbalanced public expenditures for separate modal promotion and development, postwar environmental concerns, the OPEC oil embargo and energy crisis, inflationary trends, and economic and social structural changes combined to focus national attention on transportation matters. These interacting influences, some of long duration, were predicting trouble in the 1960s, but their potential collective impact was not recognized or was ignored. For a decade, hundreds of books, articles, newpaper reports and special studies diagnosed the "transportation problem" and prescribed for it. Forums of learned academic scholars and industrial and government specialists regularly assembled to argue the merits of proposals to deal with it. Periodically, congressional committees published volumes discussing and defining it, and Congress itself solemly debated measures to solve it.

If volumes moved and money spent were criteria for success, the American transportation system should have been the envy of the world. The Transportation Association of America (TAA) reported a total of 5.3 billion tons of intercity freight carried in 1976, and the Census of Transportation in 1977 covered $1.34 trillion worth of manufactured goods, weighing in excess of 3.3 billion tons and representing 759 billion ton-miles. The nation's estimated transportation bill for private and for-hire passenger and freight vehicles between 1964 and 1976 totaled $3.0 billion; for 1976 alone it was $358.7 million.

Private automobile and air expenditures accounted for 87.1 percent of the nation's passenger dollar, and private and for-hire highway carriers, 78.1 percent of the freight dollar. Between 1952 and 1976, almost one-half trillion dollars were spent on transportation facilities by federal, state and local governments. Eighty-seven percent was allocated to improved highways and streets, eight percent to airways and airports and four percent to waterways. The remaining one percent was for cash subsidies to domestic airlines. Up to 1975, loans and grants for railroad rehabilitation amounted to approximately $2.5 billion. Yet in 1970, Fortune's fifty largest transportation companies lost money.

Rescuing the Railroads

By 1977 a major effort of the federal government in the transportation sector was concentrated upon shoring up the precarious financial condition of the railroads. Although well known during the previous years, nothing of significance was done to relieve the problems until the Penn-Central bankruptcy in 1970, two years after the merger of the two giants. This petition, together with others in the Northeast, brought to public attention the lack of coordination and the weaknesses of regulatory policy and public assistance programs of past years. The bankruptcy threatened users with the loss of service in half of the railroad mileage in the Eastern District, and to a degree, the situation reflected the serious financial condition of the nation's railroads. Within a few years, the CRI&P and CMStP&P followed the same path. To restore vitality to railroad operations, three major pieces of legislation were passed by Congress: The National Railroad Passenger Act of 1970; The Regional Rail Reorganization Act of 1973 (3R Act); and The Railroad Revitalization and Reform Act of 1974 (4R Act).

The National Railroad Passenger Act

Measured by billions of passenger-miles, railroad service had declined from 2.8 percent of all private and public transportation in 1960 to 1.1 percent in 1970, during the same period when total passenger-miles of all modes had substantially increased. Alarmed by the trends, Congress, fearing that the service would soon cease to exist, passed the legislation to assure viable service between major population centers. The act was to be administered through the National Passenger Corporation, incorporated as a non-profit corporation, originally known as "Railpax," but later changed to "AMTRAK," a contraction of "American Travel by Track."

AMTRAK was created to operate rail passenger service over a basic intercity network selected by the Secretary of Transportation with operations to commence in 1971. Equipment was owned by AMTRAK, but operating personnel and facilities initially were utilized under contract with the railroads. However, since the early days, dining, parlor car and reservations employees became AMTRAK personnel. The familiar logo adopted was a headless arrow painted in red, white and blue colors.

Joining the system was voluntary. If the railroads did, they were relieved of their obligation to provide service either within or outside the system. Those who did not were required to maintain existing service until at least January, 1975. Most roads joined, becoming stockholders in the National Passenger Corporation through payments of cash, equipment or future services for which they received common stock in return. The cost was related to deficits in their passenger service as of 1969, the amount computed by one of three formulas, whichever was most favorable to the railroad.[2]

Railroads paid their subscriptions by releasing equipment to AMTRAK. Nine roads transferred 1,200 cars, some relatively new, especially those received from the AT&SF and the UP. They became the nucleus of a fairly modern fleet for mainline service. Under the terms of the Act of 1970 (as amended through 1981), states could request new routes to supplement the basic national system. As specified in Section 403 (b) of the Act, as amended, both capital costs and annual operating deficits on new state-sponsored routes would be shared by the states and AMTRAK. In 1981, a new phase-in period was set for sharing route-related deficits. States would pay 45 percent of operating deficits in the first year and 65 percent each year thereafter. A state was still required to pay 50 percent of capital improvements necessary to establish and maintain all Section 403 (b) routes sponsored.

From 1972, the annual deficit of $147.5 million rose to highs of $800 million in 1981-1982, making the service the most heavily subsidized of American transportation as measured by public funding relative to user expenditures. Proposed reductions in federal budgets included cuts in or elimination of AMTRAK subsidies which could affect low patronage lines.

Iowa's Segment of the AMTRAK System

The final AMTRAK system plan was announced in 1971. Twenty-nine city pairs or end points were designated as "essential service" routes. Among these was the Chicago-San Francisco route for which a number of possibilities were suggested through Iowa. Between Chicago and Omaha, the choices were the CRI&P, CMStP&P and the BN, the latter selected to operate the *San Francisco Zephyr*. The choice was not universally popular since the carrier operated across the thinly populated southern counties where approximately 10 percent of the state's population resided. The condition of the roadbed and track were the major criteria, not railroad passenger markets, when routes were selected.

A second carrier, the *Southwest Chief,* provided service between Chicago and the West Coast. It followed the AT&SF line through Fort Madison, Kansas City, and Albuquerque to Los Angeles. A third route, the *Black Hawk* of the IC, offered service between Chicago and Dubuque until September, 1981. It was discontinued due to low ridership and termination of an AMTRAK operating subsidy from the state of Illinois (Fig. 11-3).

The total number of passengers embarking and disembarking all regularly scheduled Amtrak trains in Iowa declined from 87,669 in fiscal year 1979 to 57,529 in fiscal year 1982, but increased to 62,596 in fiscal year 1984. Preliminary 1985 estimates of passenger counts indicated a reduction of 13 percent from the 1984 level. Probable reasons for the lower demand are strong competition from discount airline fares and the state's poor economy.

The 3R and 4R Legislation

The 1973 3R Act created the United States Railway Association (USRA), a non-profit government agency, to plan the restructuring of the Northeastern network covering 17 states and to guarantee up to $1.5 billion in loans. Grants totaling $550 million were given to the roads for operations while restructuring occurred. Another organization, the Consolidated Railroad Corporation (Conrail), was formed as a semi-public, for-profit operating road. USRA was to determine the viable routes for the restructured lines, abandoning unprofitable segments, and Conrail was to purchase the assets of the bankrupt carriers for cash and securities. The 4R Act provided the funding for Conrail ($2.1 billion) authorized in 1973, $1.6 billion in loans and loan guarantees for all railroads, and $1.75 billion for AMTRAK improvements and operations over five

[2] D. Phillip Locklin, *Economics of Transportation,* 7th edition, Homewood, Ill.:Richard D. Irwin, Inc., 1972, p. 276. The formulas for determining the price to be paid for joining were: (1) 50 percent of the "fully distributed" passenger deficit for 1969; (2) 100 percent of the "avoidable loss" on such operations; or (3) 200 percent of the "avoidable loss" on the intercity passenger services the railroad operated over routes within the basic system.

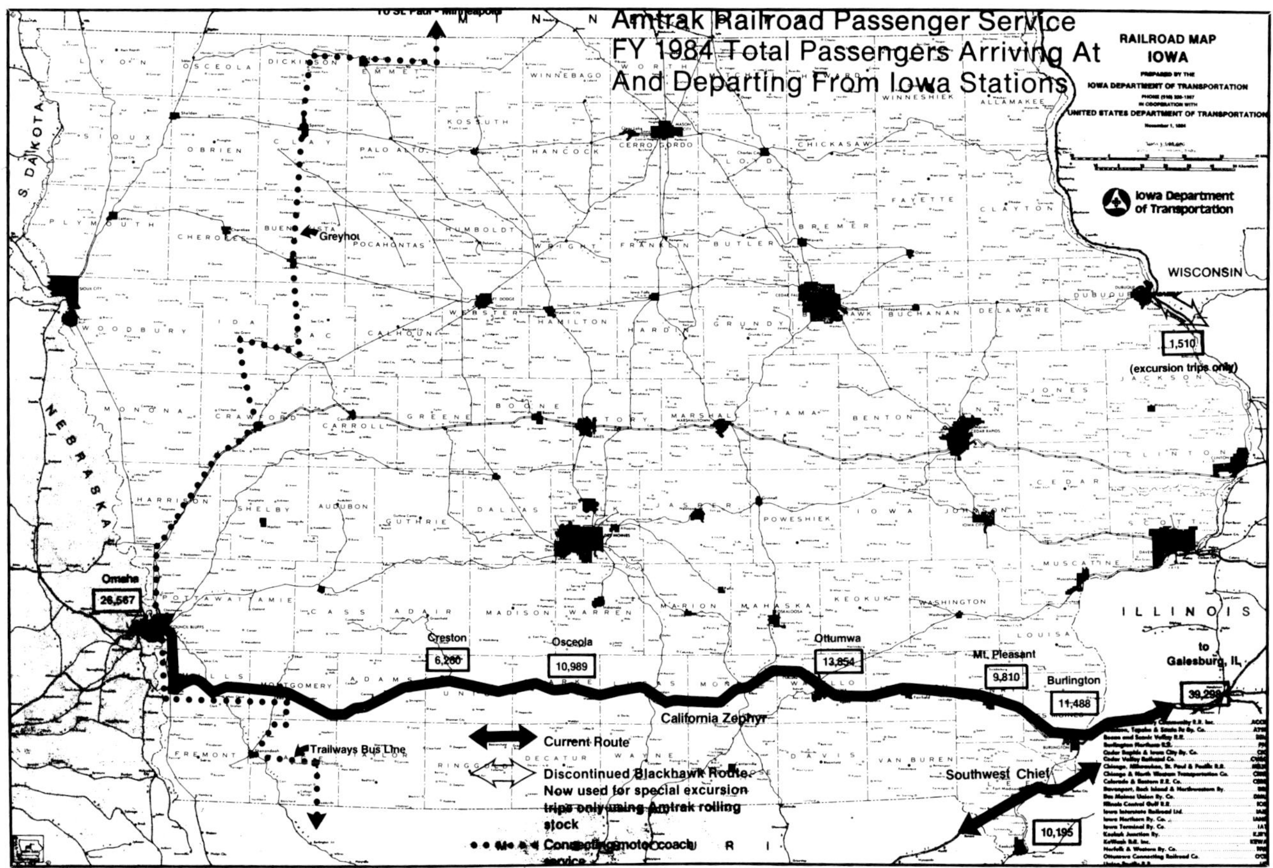

Figure 11-3
AMTRAK railroad passenger service in Iowa—FY 1984.
(Courtesy: Iowa Department of Transportation)

years in the Boston-Washington corridor. Section 15a was amended to provide new guidelines for the ICC to determine rate reasonableness, and new terms such as "Market Dominance" and "Yo-Yo" clauses sparked controversy as to intent and interpretation. All ICC rail merger evidentiary proceedings had to be concluded within two years and the decision made within 180 days thereafter.[3]

[3] "Market Dominance" was defined as the absence of effective competition by other rail or modal carriers. The "yo-yo" provisions stated that the ICC could not suspend a railroad rate which was less than a seven percent change from the existing rate proposal for two years after February 5, 1976, except for certain specified conditions. Donald V. Harper, *Transportation in America: Users, Carriers, Government,* Englewood Cliffs, N.J.: Prentice-Hall, 1982, pp. 563-564; Donald F. Wood and James C. Johnson, *Contemporary Transportation,* Tulsa, Okla.: PennWell Publishing Co., 1983, pp. 108-109; William C. Johnson, "Railroad Revitalization and Regulatory Reform Act," ICC *Practitioner's Journal* (November-December 1977): pp. 27-49; Stanley J. Hille, "Transportation Legislation—A Year of Action," *Adelphian* (May 1976): pp. 8-11; G.J. Rooney, "The RRRR Act—Some Implications for Rate Bureaus," *Transportation Journal* (Winter 1977): pp. 17-31.

AMTRAK passenger train.
(Courtesy: Ward B. McCarney III, photographer; 1982 edition of Rail Ventures.)

The Railroad Situation in Iowa

Eight Class I railroads operated 8,249 roadway miles in 1971, but were reduced to 4,144 miles by 1985 (Table 11-1). The 1970s were not prosperous years for a number of major Iowa roads. In approving the BN-Frisco merger in April 1980, the ICC commented on the financial condition of railroads affected. The CNW reported a net income in only one year since 1970, and lost more than $17.2 million in 1979. The Illinois Central-Gulf (ICG) lost $27 million in the same year, and both roads were heavily in debt to the federal government for loans to repair track and rehabilitate and purchase equipment. The CRI&P and CMStP&P sought bankruptcy protection.

The Chicago and North Western

On June 1, 1972, the CNW was sold by Northwestern Industries, a holding company, to a new organization formed by the employees and headed by Larry S. Provo. By 1974, the road had abandoned 1,500 system miles and had another 1,020 miles before the ICC for approval. The total system of 10,200 route miles in 1980 was slimmed down to 7,400 miles by 1984. The reorganization process had a significant impact upon Iowa. Nearly 325 miles of road were abandoned from 1975 through 1980 and an additional 694 miles through July 1985. Iowa mileage owned and operated by the CNW fell 18 percent since 1975, including 594 miles acquired from the CRI&P and the CMStP&P during the latter time period. Total tonnage originated or terminated in the state increased over 60 percent despite this loss of mileage. In terms of mileage operated, tonnage hauled and revenues earned in Iowa, the CNW was the dominant carrier. Almost half of the roadway miles of the state are under its jurisdiction. Reorganization also resulted in substantial financial gains, and in 1981 the railroad earned a record profit of $54.3 million.

The Final Days of the Rock Island

The demise of the CRI&P, the second largest railroad in the state, was a tragic story in the history of Iowa. In 1974 the railroad was technically solvent and hoped for a favorable decision on the 11-year UP merger proposal. In the intervening period, little or no investment had been made in track or equipment, and when grain exports boomed, the road was in no physical condition to handle increased traffic. A loan of $100 million had been requested from the USRA. In February 1975, the agency agreed to provide $9.1 million for working capital which never materialized. Ironically, in the same month a $19 million loan was approved for the Missouri-Kansas-Texas (KATY) lines. On March 17, 1975, the day that the daily cash forecast sheet predicted a negative balance, the CRI&P declared bankruptcy and petitioned for reorganization.

A drastic reduction in operating costs was initiated in 1974-1975. Forty percent of management personnel and about one-third of operating employees lost their jobs. Private funds were obtained for acquisition and rehabilitation of equipment but could not be used for upgrading track. Iowa alone financed approximately half as many track improvements as the Federal Railroad Administration did over the 13-state system. The CRI&P lost $45 million between January and June, 1979, and $145 million during the 1975-1979 period. Net railway operating income was negative from 1968 to 1978.

Experiments with fewer employees, jurisdictional labor disputes and new operating techniques brought threats of strikes when labor contracts expired in 1977. Labor-management negotiations over several months were unsuccessful and President Carter, in the sixth week of the strike in 1979, requested a directed service order from the ICC which was served without public hearings. The Kansas City Terminal Company was selected to operate the road for eight months under a guaranteed profit which cost the federal government about one-half million dollars per day. Serious questions were raised as to why this expenditure offered a more effective performance prospect than equivalent financial assistance to CRI&P management, certainly more familiar with operations than outside interests.

On May 17, 1980, the ICC recommended that the CRI&P "be allowed to die," abandon 6,960 miles of track and discontinue service over 763 miles of trackage rights. The road was to keep in place all track proposed for sale, decreed by Judge Frank McGarr of the U.S. District Court in Chicago on June 2. The ruling also stated that the railroad would not be responsible for protecting employees affected. The final chapters in the CRI&P saga were written in 1982 and 1983, when the CNW won a bidding war against the Soo Line Railroad for certain properties in Iowa. The 730-mile "spineline" from Minneapolis to Kansas City, 235 miles of branch lines in northern and central counties, and 10 miles of east-west track in Des Moines were purchased for $93 million. The largest remaining segment, between Council Bluffs and Davenport, was operated by the Iowa Railroad in 1982 under lease, pending approval of a permanent operating organization. On June 1, 1984, the CRI&P ceased to exist after years of reorganization efforts. Within Iowa, about 1,102 miles (64 percent) of the 1,733 miles operated in 1975 have been acquired and are operated by other carriers. Over 520 miles have been acquired by seven Class III or short lines operating in the state.

The Bankruptcy of the Chicago and Milwaukee

The CMStP&P filed for bankruptcy on December 19, 1977, and in 1979 a reorganization plan calling for a reduction of 4,500 miles from its 10,000 mile system was submitted to the court. Nearly half of the 1,341 miles of roadway in Iowa was excluded. The plan was rejected by the ICC on March 19, 1980. Another plan filed in September 1981 suggested a core of 2,900 miles—a streamlined railroad in Iowa to provide service along the northern route from Sheldon to Marquette, south along the Mississippi River to Davenport and southwest from Muscatine to Washington, Ottumwa and other points on the Kansas City route.

Three railroads were bidding for the railroad in 1983: the Soo Line, Grand Trunk Corporation and the CNW. The Grand Trunk dropped its proposal and the other two took turns in raising the bids throughout 1984 to a level of $786 million by the CNW and $571 million offered by the Soo Line. In February 1985, the final decision was handed down by U. S. District Judge Thomas R. McMillen who favored the Soo Line, stating that "the higher bid is not a controlling factor in which railroad should prevail in this particular contest. The major factor was determination of what was best for the public interest."[4]

Burlington Northern

In terms of miles of road and freight tonnage, the BN is Iowa's second largest railroad. Nearly 23 percent of Class I tonnage originated or terminated in the state is handled by the railroad. Included are nearly 53 percent of the coal delivered to Iowa and 12 percent of the grain handled by Class I roads in 1984.

Illinois Central Gulf

On August 10, 1972, the Illinois Central and Gulf, Mobile and Ohio railroads merged to form the Illinois Central Gulf Railroad Company. The railroad is a wholly owned subsidiary of the IC Industries, a consumer and manufacturing goods conglomerate headquartered in Chicago. In April 1985, the railroad agreed to sell 674 miles of track between Chicago and Omaha for $75 million to John Haley, who renamed the segment the Chicago, Central and Pacific Railroad. Within Iowa, major commodities moved are grains, grain milled products, fertilizer and Illinois coal into the eastern counties. The railroad accounted for 12 percent of originating and seven percent of terminating Class I tonnage in the state in 1984.

[4] U.S. District Court, Northern District of Illinois, Eastern Division, *In the Matter of Chicago, Milwaukee, St. Paul and Pacific Railroad Company, Debtor,* February 8, 1985, p. 14.

Table 11-1
Iowa Rail Mileage Operated as of July 1, 1985

Operating Carriers	Iowa Roadway Miles			
	Main	Branch	Trackage Rights*	Total
Class I Railroads				
Chicago & North Western Transportation Co.	789	1,204	85	2,078
Burlington Northern Railroad Co.	436	260	65	761
The Milwaukee Road Inc.	192	430	36	658
Illinois Central Gulf Railroad Co.	459	55	0	514
Norfolk & Western Ry. Co.	0	66	42	108
Atchison, Topeka & Santa Fe Ry. Co.	20	0	1	21
Union Pacific Railroad Co.	2	0	0	2
Missouri-Kansas-Texas Railroad Co.	0	0	2	2
Class I Subtotal	1,898	2,015	231	4,144
Class III Railroads				
Iowa Interstate Railroad Ltd.		359	14	373
Iowa Northern Railway Co.		142	0	142
Cedar Valley Railroad Co.		84	0	84
American Short Lines Inc.		66	0	66
Cedar Rapids & Iowa City Railway Co.		56	0	56
Davenport, Rock Island & North Western Railway Co.		35	1	36
Iowa Terminal Railroad Co.		25	0	25
Des Moines Union Railway Co.		19	0	19
KeWash Railroad Inc.		15	0	15
Appanoose County Community Railroad Co.		10	0	10
Ottumwa Connecting Railroad Co.		3	0	3
D&I Railroad Co.		0	41	41
Burlington Junction Railway Co.	Switching company only—no roadway miles reported.			
Waterloo Railroad Co.		**	**	**
Keokuk Junction Railway	Switching company only—no roadway miles reported.			
Class III Subtotal		814	56	872
Iowa Total	1,898	2,829	287	5,014

* Right obtained by one carrier to operate its trains over the tracks of another carrier, therefore, this mileage is counted twice in the statewide total.
**Six miles of road reported by ICG Railroad.

(*Source:* R-1 Report of State Statistics to the Interstate Commerce Commission and Annual Report of Class III Railroads to the Iowa DOT.)

Other Class I Railroads

The NW, AT&SF, UP and KATY railroads operated a combined total of 233 roadway miles in Iowa in 1984. In October 1964, the NW began operating in the state under lease arrangements with the Wabash. It was consolidated with the Southern Railway in July 1980, under a holding company known as the Norfolk Southern (NS). In June 1984, the road offered to purchase the federal government's 85 percent interest in Conrail to expand its system service and increase its competitive position with respect to its principal competitor—the CSX Corporation. Despite the selection of the NS by the Secretary of Transportation, Congress rejected the offer. Farm and food products were the principal tonnage hauled over its 107 roadway miles in 1984. The AT&SF operates only 21 miles of road in Iowa, serving the cities of Fort Madison and Keokuk. The UP and KATY lines operate two miles each in and around Council Bluffs.

In 1984 Iowa's Class I railroads transported over 24.4 million tons of freight that had originated within the state. The CNW alone carried more than 50 percent of this total. Together, the CNW, CMStP&P, BN, and ICG originated over 90 percent and terminated over 95 percent of the total Class I tonnage in Iowa. Coal accounted for about 63 percent of 1982 traffic entering the state, and farm products comprised about 48 percent of rail freight from Iowa. Predictions for the 1990 traffic flow call for substantial increases in Class I railroad traffic. From and to Iowa, grain, coal, nonmetallic minerals, grain mill products, pulp and paper products, chemicals and transportation equipment are expected to be the major commodities carried. The 1985 railroad map of Iowa is found in Fig. 11-4, whereas the trends in roadway railroad mileage between 1850 and 1985 are presented in Fig. 11-5. Class I railroad system financial indicators for 1984 reveal the positions of each of the carriers relative to the industry averages in the eight catagories listed in Table 11-2. The operating ratio was lowest for the BN and highest for the CMStP&P. Rate of return on net transportation investment showed similar positions. However, the percentage of revenues earned in Iowa indicated the importance of the CNW to the state, by far the leader in this category.

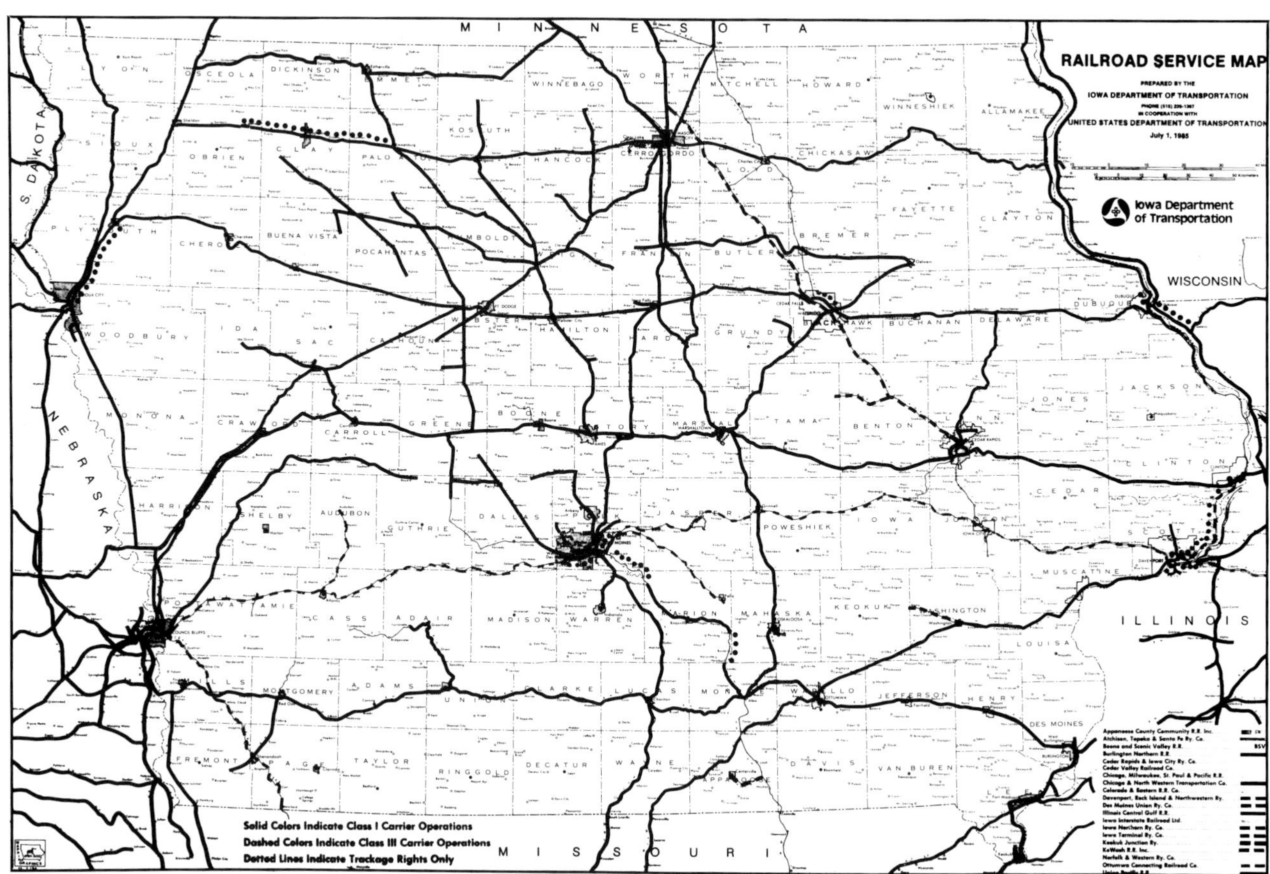

Figure 11-4
1985 railroad map of Iowa.
(Courtesy: Iowa Department of Transportation.)

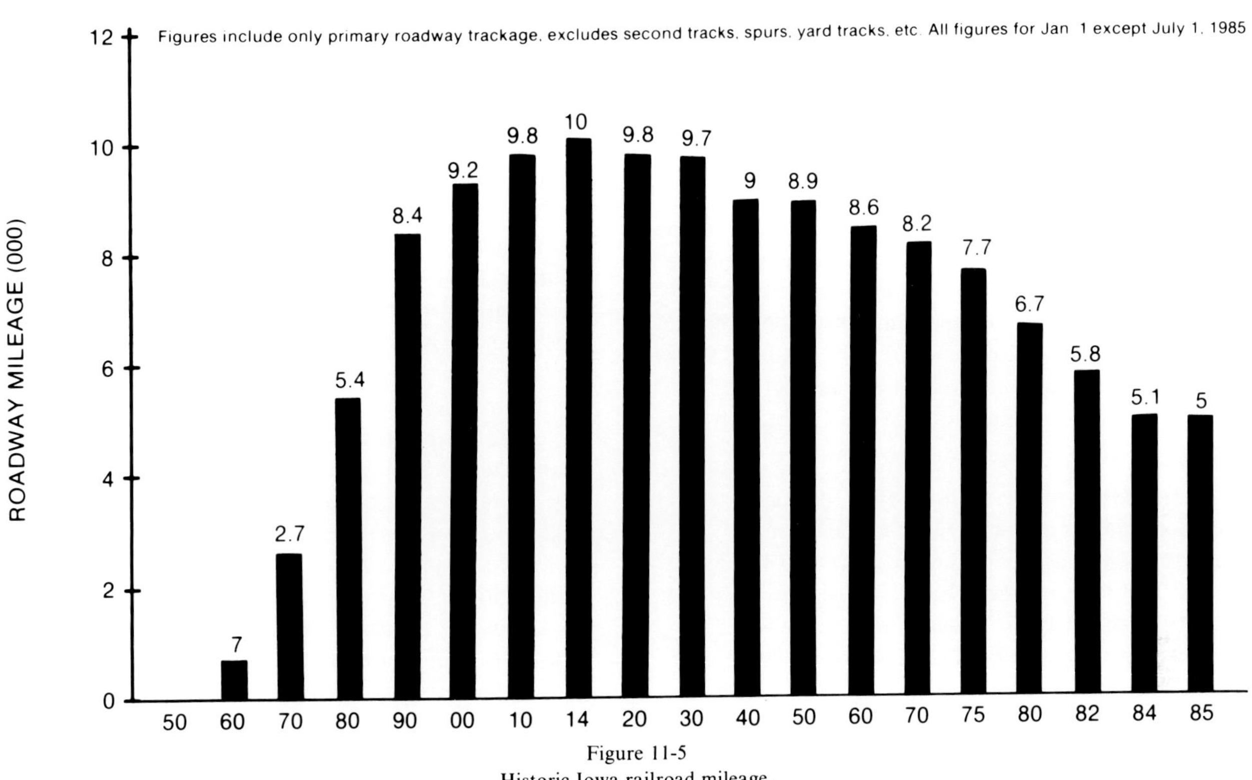

Figure 11-5
Historic Iowa railroad mileage.
(Courtesy: *Poor's Manual of Railroads, 1890 for 1800-1880;* Interstate Commerce Commission and Iowa DOT for 1890 to present.)

Table 11-2

System Financial Indicators, 1984

	Burlington Northern	Chicago & North Western	Milwaukee Road	Illinois Central Gulf	Norfolk & Western	Santa Fe	Union Pacific	Industry Average
Operating Revenues ($ Millions)	4,440	876	417	955	1,715	2,305	1,921	1,178
Percentage of Revenues Earned Within Iowa	2.7	33.4	NA	4.4	0.3	0.4	0.1	NA
Operating Expenses ($ Millions)	3,493	816	414	892	1,386	2,083	1,726	1,032
Operating Ratio	0.79	0.93	0.99	0.93	0.81	0.90	0.90	0.88
Net Railway Operating Income ($ Millions)	547.1	46.7	2.8	53.8	167.8	148.8	134.1	101.5
Rate of Return on Net Transportation Investment (percent)	9.9	5.7	0.4	3.1	6.3	4.5	4.2	5.7
Current Ratio	1.31	1.00	0.78	1.05	2.34	1.22	1.25	1.23
Debt-to-Total Capitalization Ratio	0.53	0.65	0.74	0.40	0.41	0.48	0.52	NA

NA = Not Available

Better Than Industry Average
Worse Than Industry Average

(Source: Interstate Commerce Commission)

Class III Rail Carriers

Iowa shippers are also served by 15 line haul, terminal and switching companies, designated by the ICC as Class III carriers (Fig. 11-6). These railroads, with an income of less than $17.5 million annually, are often referred to as short-line or feeder-line carriers. A rapid increase in the number of these roads during the decade 1974-1984, was the result of abandonments of Class I branch lines, wage rate and work rule differentials and the need for continuous local service. In Iowa, the motivation for short lines has been the extensive abandonments created by the CRI&P liquidation and reorganization of the CMStP&P and Conrail systems.

The importance of these railroads in the state's transportation system is evident in the dramatic increase in their operations during the 1980-1985 period. In 1980, five short-line railroads operated 101 miles of road. In 1985, 15 carriers owned and operated approximately 814 miles. About 89 percent of this mileage was operated by six Class I railroads in 1975. The short-line operations range from two-mile systems to one that exceeds 370 miles; the average is about 60 miles.

Twelve of the 15 carriers started and continue to operate with no financial assistance from either federal or state sources. Three railroads have received such assistance: Iowa Northern, Iowa Interstate, and Appanoose County Railroad. The two largest financial assistance projects for short-lines have involved the Iowa Railway Finance Authority. The first was a $2 million low-interest loan combined with a federal loan of $3.4 million to acquire 142 miles of former CRI&P track in northeast Iowa. The second loan was for $15 million to Heartland Rail Corporation for the purchase of the former CRI&P east-west line across Iowa plus three Iowa branch lines, one Illinois branch line and track into Chicago. The loan was combined with a $16 million package of commercial loans and stockholders equity to attain the $31 million purchase price. The track is operated by the Iowa Interstate Railroad. On September 30, 1985, Heartland obtained a $6.2 million federal track rehabilitation loan to upgrade east-west track to 40 mph standards.

The Iowa Railroad Finance Authority

For several years, Iowa financed branch line rehabilitation before the national program of local rail service assistance was enacted in the 4R Act. Between 1974 and 1982, over 1,100 miles of branch lines were improved at a cost of $78 million, funded by $26 million from shippers, $17 million from the state, $19 million from railroads and $16 million from the federal government.

Continued financial distress and the realization that AMTRAK and Conrail types of financing were not fɒrthcoming forced the state to examine internal solutions. In 1980, the 68th General Assembly created the Iowa Railroad Finance Authority (IRFA) as an automomous board of five members appointed by the Governor to staggered terms of six years. Its purpose was to finance the acquisition and improvement but not operations of railroad facilities in the state. Authorization was granted to issue bonds, notes or other revenue type obligations to a maximum of $100 million to overcome the shortage of private capital needed to maintain adequate service. In 1981 the authorization was increased to $200 million to be funded by a diesel fuel tax on railroads, a loaded mileage tax (after 1983), delinquent railroad property taxes, lease or sale of property owned by the IRFA, repayment of loans, and loans, guarantees, grants and contributions from any source. "The IRFA is to play the role of catalyst, banker and partner to the private enterprise sector in the transition of the lines from a non-operating status to operating status under private ownership."[5]

The most controversial source of funding was the railroad fuel tax of three cents per gallon between October 1, 1981 and June 30, 1982, after which it would increase to eight cents. Class I railroads filed suit in November 1981 in the Polk District Court, attacking the proposal on constitutional and other grounds, but lost on a decision by Judge Anthony Critelli. On September 21, 1983, a 5-4 decision of the Iowa Supreme Court reversed the lower court, stating that the tax violated the 4R Act which prohibited state tax policies from discriminating against railroads. The decision was appealed to the U.S. Supreme Court, which declined to hear the case on February 27, 1984. The General Assembly also

[5] Allen Vellinga and Bruce Ferrin, "A Review and Analysis of the Iowa Railway Finance Legislation: An Example of Defederalization of Transport Policy," *Transportation Research Forum Proceedings 23* (1982): p. 325.

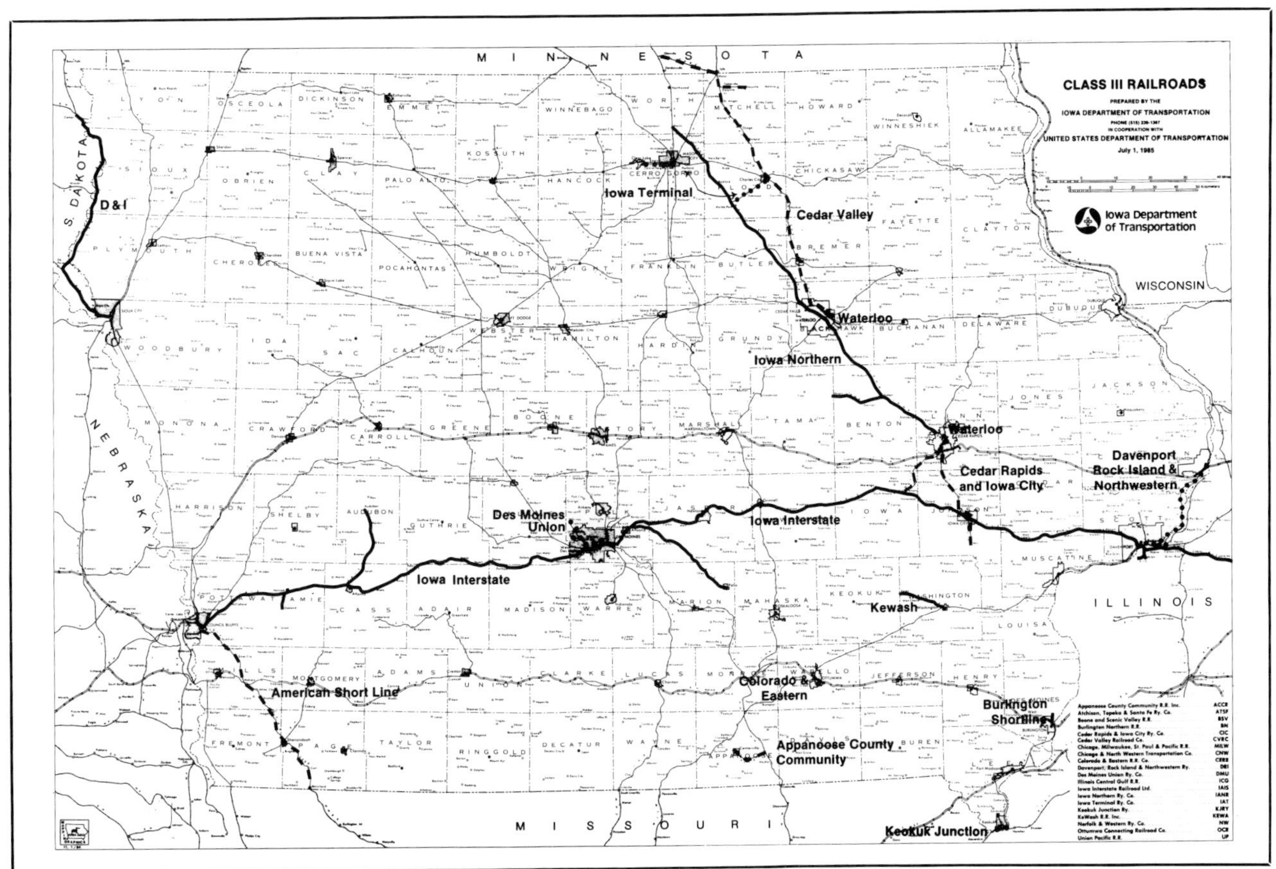

Figure 11-6
Class III railroads.
(Courtesy: Iowa Department of Transportation.)

authorized a diversion of $7.5 million per year for two years from the state road fund as a loan to assist them in the purchase of the east-west CRI&P lines.

Membership on the IRFA in 1986 was as follows: George Davison, Des Moines, chairperson; Fred McKim, West Bend, vice chairperson; O.R. Woods, Palo; J. H. Harper, Blue Grass; and Richard P. Flagg, Cedar Rapids.

The Heartland and Iowa Interstate Railroad Venture

Iowa shippers on the main line between Davenport and Council Bluffs had been served by the Iowa Railroad and CMStP&P since the CRI&P failed. The Iowa Railroad lacked the funds to buy the properties, and the CMStP&P wanted only to purchase the Iowa City to Davenport segment. Concerned that the line would be sold for scrap, Iowa business leaders, including the Maytag Company of Newton and Rolscreen Company of Pella, formed the Heartland Railroad Corporation to buy the road. The final roadblocks against the operation were removed when the Polk County Court and the ICC agreed that the two railroads no longer had authority to handle freight on the line.

For one year from June 1983, Heartland sought funding and negotiated for the purchase. In July 1984, a down payment of $500,000 was made to complete the sale. In October, the IRFA approved the $15 million loan as part of the package for the purchase. The CNW and CMStP&P opposed the loan, claiming that Iowa taxpayers would not be properly protected if the railroad defaulted. However, the state loan was secured by a lien on Heartland tracks between Iowa City and Council Bluffs, estimated to have a salvage value of $17.4 million.

The corporate offices of the Iowa Interstate Railroad were in Evanston, Illinois, but it operated out of Iowa City and served communities on the line between Council Bluffs and Bureau, Illinois, with trackage rights over other roads into Chicago. The railroad started with 80 employees, many of whom were former CRI&P workers, given preference under federal law. Equipment consisted of 14 diesel locomotives and 400 cars with possibilities of adding to the fleet through short-term leases. About 150 shippers were expected to provide traffic, of which the leading commodities were considered to be steel and scrap, grains and products, and lumber.

Confusion in Transportation Policy versus Export Trends

The attitude of the federal administration in the early 1980s suggested that midwestern grain-oriented railroads should be allowed to restructure themselves to lower operating levels. This came during a period when the federal government depended upon grain exports to balance international trade deficits. Important segments of the railroad system were on the verge of collapse, highways were crumbling faster than they could be repaired, and bridges were disintegrating, threatening the movement of exports—particularly grains and products—into export markets at reasonable costs.

In the 1960s, farm exports accounted for 15 percent of farm income, compared to 28 percent in 1980. The annual sale of 125 million tons of grain for $38 billion was one of the bright spots in the nation's international trade, and Iowa was contributing an average of two to three billion dollars or more each year to the total.

The importance of exports to the Iowa economy cannot be overemphasized. Between 1970 and 1980, the value of agricultural exports expanded from $551 million to $3.0 billion; that of manufacturers (a large percentage in agriculture-related industries) from $590 million in 1972 to $2.7 billion in 1982. In 1982 Iowa was the second leading state in agricultural exports, and in addition, more than 800 manufacturers were also in the export markets, contributing an approximate value of $2,211 per person, the third highest per capita value in the nation. Exports contributed substantially to the gross state product which rose from $12.3 billion to $34.0 billion during the 1970-1982 period. In constant 1972 dollars, the increase was from $13.4 billion to $16.4 billion. The fact that exports have declined in the recent past in no way detracts from the importance of transportation in the international logistical structure of grain and grain products movements.

Export trends give a clue to the reliance of the state upon transportation and concerns over developments which might interrrupt the movement to markets. Corn and soybeans were becoming important commodities in world trade, and export demand stimulated growth of motor and water carriage which challenged the traditional railroad share of the traffic. The competition was difficult for the railroads to overcome as they struggled to retain or expand agricultural business. To compete, they required new operating techiques and equipment, including the use of jumbo hopper cars and multi-car rates. These problems and possibilities were explored in a study by C. P. Baumel and associates at Iowa State University. They analyzed alternative grain transportation systems to Gulf ports from a six and one-half county area around Fort Dodge. The research was an in-depth analysis of one intensive grain production area with the objective of determining which system would yield the highest net revenue to the region under stated assumptions. Another study analyzed grain transportation throughout the United States by comparing 10 different sets of transport costs, rail systems and export demands.

Highways, Bridges, and the 65-Foot Double Bottom Controversy

Motor Vehicle Traffic and Highways

In 1980, 6,900 motor carriers provided intrastate service, and 13,500 moved on interstate routes connecting virtually every community in Iowa. Operating over a 112,300-mile highway system, their freight ton-miles since 1973 had increased over 50 percent. Freight carried by trucks in Iowa on the interstate system accounted for 45 percent of the primary system ton-miles and 36 percent of the total highway system ton-miles. Over two billion dollars had been spent on highway construction between 1970 and 1982, half of which was allocated to the primary system.

The Iowa DOT became one of the nation's leaders in completion of the four-lane interstate highways with the opening of the 50-mile segment on I-35 between U.S. 20 near Williams and Iowa 106 near Clear Lake on November 7, 1976, some six months ahead of schedule. The opening marked completion of the original 710 miles of the system which included I-35, I-80, I-29 and I-74. From Iowa City to Waterloo, I-380 was completed in two stages; the first stage in August, 1976, when the section from I-80 to Third Street in Cedar Rapids was opened, and the remaining mileage opened during the fall of 1985.

The new interstate highways, construction, reconstruction or resurfacing of primary highways and improved secondary highways resulted in substantial increases in vehicular traffic. Automobile registrations climbed from 1.48 to 1.68 million in the 1970-1980 period, and motor truck registrations almost doubled, from 378,000 to 608,000.

Bridges

Integral units in a highway system are bridges, spanning everything from small gullies to swamps and rivers. The large number in the state and their critical position as links between otherwise isolated areas commands attention in highway analysis. In recent years, bridges have become an important target in highway planning because of their deteriorating and dangerous conditions. A U.S. DOT study in 1981 reported that half of the substandard bridges in the nation were located in 10 states. Iowa ranked third in the number of deficient bridges, after Texas and Missouri (Table 11-3).

A structurally deficient bridge is one which has been restricted to light vehicles only, is closed to traffic, or must be rehabilitated to remain open. A functionally obsolete bridge is one whose narrow lanes, load-carrying capacity, clearance, or approach roadway alignment can no longer safely serve its current traffic load. The cost to replace or rehabilitate all of the bridges in the nation was estimated at $41.1 billion, of which $20.6 billion would be required for bridges on the federal-aid system. Federal allocation of funds in the Surface Transportation Act of 1978 ranged from $900 million in 1979 to $1.3 billion in 1980 and 1981, then dropped back to $900 million for 1982. Matching fund requirements from participating states were set at 20 percent, a reduction of five percent from the original bridge replacement program.

The bridge problem in Iowa was particularly vexatious. Half of the bridges were fragile, antiquated or crumbling, unable to support the heavy pounding of large trucks. On the heaviest traveled roads, 250 embargoes or load restrictions were placed on bridges in 1980-1981. More than 1,100 structures 40 years of age or older were built to carry 15 tons or less and had a life expectancy of 50 years. Currently, they carry loads of 40 or more tons. A similar situation existed on half of the county bridges, resulting in roundabout routing of vehicles on secondary roads.

Table 11-3
Top 10 States in Total Number of Deficient Bridges
(as of December 31, 1980, inventory)
Highway System

State	Total No. Inventory	Off Federal-aid	Deficient Federal-aid	Total	Percent Deficient
Texas	41,454	3,683	11,514	15,197	36.7
Missouri	20,911	3,400	10,413	13,813	66.1
Iowa	25,423	2,231	10,452	12,683	49.9
N. Carolina	14,960	2,630	8,689	11,319	75.7
Nebraska	16,767	1,726	9,439	11,165	66.6
Indiana	17,474	2,549	8,476	11,025	63.1
Mississippi	16,358	4,103	6,802	10,905	66.7
New York	17,189	3,411	6,620	10,031	58.4
Illinois	24,736	2,207	6,937	9,144	37.0
Kansas	22,424	2,442	6,579	9,021	40.2
Total	217,696	28,382	85,921	114,303	52.5

(*Source:* Wilbur Smith & Associates, *Bridge Deficiences in the United States: An Overview of the Problem.* Prepared for the United States Steel Corporation. The ATA Foundation, Washington, D.C., May, 1982. Tables 1, 2: 5-8.)

The 65-Foot Twin-Trailer Issue

Before the national interstate system was half completed, the use of twin-trailer trucks with an overall length of 65 feet became a controversial issue. In 1964 the Bureau of Public Roads, now the Federal Highway Administration (FHWA), recommended that these combinations be allowed on the interstate system. At hearings on the 1971 Highway Act, FHWA Administrator Norbert Tieman and James Lauth of the U. S. Department of Agriculture made similar recommendations as a means of increasing productivity and saving energy. Energy considerations, reduction of environmental pollution, greater cubic capacity, loading characteristics, maneuverability relative to the 55-foot tractor semi-trailers, and flexibility were the major pro arguments. Countering these alleged advantages was the question of highway safety. By 1978, 31 states permitted the 65-foot twins on designated highways. Iowa allowed 60-foot twins; four states, 55-foot doubles; and in 14 states, twin trailers were not permitted.

The Iowa Department of Transportation published a report on the 65-foot twins in 1975. It estimated a net annual nationwide saving of seven million gallons of fuel through legalization of the twins in Iowa; that one-half of one percent of additional wear on highways would result from increased numbers of the combinations on interstates, but that traffic would be reduced somewhat on primary roads. Over a 20-year period, net benefits in the amount of $145 million could accrue to the state, and net benefits to out-of-state firms would total $214 million. There was also the speculation that permitting the 65-foot twins would promote industrial growth in the state.

For some years, Wisconsin had issued annual permits for the operation of the 65-foot twins used in transporting Wisconsin manufactured products to markets. Raymond Motor Transport applied for permits to move interstate commerce over interstate highways in Wisconsin but was refused on grounds of safety. Raymond filed suit, claiming that the denial resulted in a burden on and was discriminatory against interstate commerce. The case was eventually decided by the U. S. Supreme Court in favor of the motor carrier.

Unlike other states in the West and Midwest, Iowa generally prohibited the 65-foot doubles within its borders. Most combinations were restricted to 55 feet in length except for some twins, mobile homes, trucks carrying vehicles such as tractors and farm equipment, and singles handling livestock which were permitted to be as long as 70 feet. By local ordinance, cities abutting the state line could adopt length limitations of adjoining states. Other exemptions allowed Iowa truck manufacturers to obtain a permit to transport trucks as long as 70 feet and to move oversized mobile homes, provided that the units were moved from a point within Iowa or delivered for an Iowa resident.

In 1974 the General Assembly passed House File 671 which allowed 65-foot twins within Iowa borders, but the bill was vetoed by Governor Ray. The Transportation Commission, pursuant to its authority conferred in Section 307.10(5), Code or Iowa, subsequently adopted regulations which would have legalized the twins provided that the legislature enacted a ban on studded snow tires. The Iowa Supreme Court declared the regulations void because they were impermanently tied to legislative action. The issue was decided when Consolidated Freightways, a participant in the Wisconsin case, brought suit against the state in district court for permission to use doubles on the interstate system and on feeder roads within five miles of these highways. The court followed the Wisconsin ruling and concluded that the law impermissibly burdened interstate commerce. The Court of Appeals of the Eighth Circuit Court affirmed and was upheld by the U. S. Supreme Court on March 24, 1981, by a vote of 6-3.

Energy considerations were of major interest to the nation even though they may have played a minor role in the 65-foot twin trailer controversy. The Arab oil embargo in 1973 resulted in a 55 mph national maximum speed limit law as a temporary conservation measure. It was made permanent in 1975 since it had ostensibly reduced highway accidents, injuries and deaths. For many years prior to 1973, highway speeds had been rising by about one-half mph per year to an average of 65 mph on the interstate highways. Highway fatalities reached an all-time high in 1972 and 1973, but the new speed limits were estimated to have saved the lives of 9,100 people in 1974. While gradually rising over the interim period, the average speed in 1983 was 59.1 mph, reflecting an 80 percent retention of the 1974 slowdown. From time to time, increases in the speed limits on interstate highways have been advocated by state legislators and other groups, but a 19-member National Research Council committee concluded that "the 55 mph limit is one of the most effective safety policies ever adopted" and recommended to Congress that it should be retained as national policy. The committee, however, did not make a judgment on whether or not individual states should be permitted some flexibility to raise the 55 mph limit on rural interstate highways.

Having lost the long truck battle, Iowa faced changes in truck sizes and weights as enacted in the Surface Transportation Act of 1982. The act mandated the previously permissive maximum weight limits of 80,000 pounds, gross; 20,000 pounds, single axle; and 34,000 pounds, tandem axle, on any segment of the interstate system and designated federal-aid primary roads, including reasonable access to terminals. Widths were increased from 96 to 102 inches, and all states were to allow the twin-trailer combinations. The same act increased federal fuel taxes from four to nine cents per gallon, with one cent allocated to public transit for capital projects and four cents to highway repair, rehabilitation or improvement. Iowa increased gasoline taxes from 10 to 13 cents per gallon, diesel fuel from 11.5 cents to 13.5 cents, and gasohol from five to six cents.

65-Foot Twin-Trailer (Double Bottom) Truck

102-inch wide truck permitted under Surface Transportation Act of 1982. (Courtesy: Dean Rappleye Trucking and the Spring Research Institute.)

Functional Classifications— Railroads and Highways

Railroads

In accordance with Section 503(b) of the 4R Act, the U.S. DOT in 1976 set preliminary standards, classifications and designations for Class I railroads in the United States. Four major standards were used: (1) density as measured by gross tons moved on a line; (2) service to major markets; (3) appropriate levels of capacity; and (4) defense essentiality. Two additional standards were the economic viability of the owning carrier and the probable economic vitality of connecting carriers. The following categories were established: (1) A Mainlines; (2) Potential A Mainlines; (3) B Mainlines; (4) A Branch Lines; (5) B Branch Lines; and (6) Defense Essential Branch Lines.

Railroads operating in Iowa were classified in every category except "A Mainlines," which required 20 million or more gross tons moved per year in the state. However, by 1980, the CNW had reached this level. To meet the Iowa DOT's interim requirement for identification of railroad needs, a preliminary assessment was prepared in 1980, at a time when the railroad system consisted of 7,008 roadway miles, from which 4,779 miles were determined as the minimum needed to adequately serve the state. Following public hearings for comments, suggestions and criticisms, railroad mileages were placed into five classifications: (1) lines of national interest, 840 miles; (2) lines of multi-state interest, 990 miles; (3) lines of regional interest with substantial traffic needs, 1,200 miles; (4) light-density branch lines with significant local traffic needs, 1,050 miles; and (5) low traffic needs, 1,120 miles.

Highways

Functional classification of highways began with the establishment of County Classification Boards in 1969 and was a requirement of the 65th General Assembly. Functional classification was defined as the grouping of roads and streets into systems according to the character of service expected and assignment of jurisdiction over each class to the government unit having primary interest in each type of service. As defined by the legislation, the classifications were summarized as follows:

A. Primary Road System

   1. The Freeway-Expressway System (3,000 miles)

      a. The National System of Interstate

and Defense Highways in Iowa

b. All roads connecting and serving major urban and regional areas of the state with high-volume, long-distance traffic movements and generally connecting with like roads of adjacent states

2. The Arterial System (3,500 miles)

3. The Arterial Connector System

B. Secondary Road System

1. The Trunk System (15,000 miles)
2. The Trunk Collector System (20,000 miles) Both would constitute the Farm-to-Market System
3. Area Service System—all other rural roads not otherwise classified

C. Municipal Street System

1. Arterial System
2. Collector System (limited to 20 percent of entire street mileage under jurisdiction of the municipality except in those municipalities under 2,000 population, in which cases the mileage may be exceeded)
3. Service System

D. Other Road and Street Systems

1. State Park, State Institutions, and other state land road systems wholly within the boundaries of state lands
2. County Conservation Parkway Systems, wholly within the boundaries of county lands operated as parks, forests or other public access areas.

Interstate 80 in Iowa.
(Courtesy: Iowa Department of Transportation.)

Rural Transportation

Concerns over the future status of commercial transportation to rural communities were consistently expressed during the 1970s and early 1980s. One stemmed from the continued abandonment of railroad branch lines which accelerated between 1976 and 1982 (Table 11-4).

Another concern related to the potential impact of motor carrier regulatory reform on service to rural areas, discussed in Chapter Twelve. As railroad branch line abandonments increased, the Iowa DOT was faced with selection of branch line upgrading projects to be funded by the Assistance Program—branch lines which had the greatest potential net benefit to the communities and state relative to the costs incurred. An Iowa State University study published in 1976 provided some insight into the problem through analysis of 71 low-volume rural branch lines on a benefit/cost basis. On only eight lines were the benefit/cost ratios favorable—ratios greater than 1.00—for upgrading track. Thirteen lines had ratios of 0.75 or greater under one of six alternatives used and 56 percent had ratios of less than 0.25. Two reasons were given for the low number of lines with favorable ratios; (1) the large number of branch lines in the state, and (2) their poor physical condition. It was estimated that almost $19 million annually would be required to upgrade and maintain the 71 branch lines studied.

The research focused upon agricultural movements and explored various alternatives available to grain shippers. These included the use of different grain elevators by farmers, shipment by truck and rail with or without multi-car rail rates and supplemental elevators, shipment by truck and barge, or in the case of elevators which would continue to receive rail service by rail and barge and direct shipments by trucks to nearby grain terminals. In terms of net benefits to shippers, all of these alternatives could be used with the actual one chosen dependent upon distance from a river, time of year, railroad rate structure and grain prices in different markets.

A program of selective upgrading of light density lines combined with abandonment of other lines was estimated to result in a net saving of $20 million annually in operations, maintenance and capital costs for Iowa railroads. By encouraging volume shipments the program could increase net revenue to grain producers and shippers by more than $14 million annually, assuming no change in the current rate structure; and by as much as $24 million annually if

Table 11-4
Iowa Rail Abandonment

	Rail Still in Place		Rail Removed		
Time Period	Miles	% of Total Miles Abandoned During Designated Time Period	Miles	% of Total Miles Abandoned During Designated Time Period	Total Length
Pre-1950	0	0%	1,278.66	100%	1,278.66
1950-1959	5.97	1%	451.46	99%	457.43
1960-1975	20.40	2%	883.90	98%	904.30
1976-1982	523.58	29%	1,264.26	71%	1,787.64
Total	549.95	12%	3,878.28	88%	4,428.23

(*Source:* Iowa Department of Transportation.)

rates permitting the use of 85-car unit trains were adopted. The study also analyzed the consequences of abandonment and found relatively little effect upon local communities. Comparisons of similar-sized towns with railroad service to those without showed only slight differences in such indicators as population, retail sales, bank deposits and bank earnings. These findings supported conclusions of an earlier study made at the Massachusetts Institute of Technology.

Public Transit

For those interested in the development of public transportation in cities, historical trends are discussed in detail by George W. Smerk, covering the variety of passenger services and vehicle types available to people. He described the evolution of the horse-drawn omnibus of 1662 in Paris to the modern double-decker bus in London, and the relatively slow development of transit systems in the United States.

The history of public transit (street cars) in Iowa was discussed in Chapter Six. Following World War II, availability of automobiles, gasoline and tires and continued improvement in highways provided an attractive alternative to public transit. Ridership declined and financial conditions of private transit companies became critical, leading to service discontinuance. However, local government units and citizen groups in the cities and regions decided that public transportation should be continued, and in the late 1960s public takeover of private systems began with assistance from the federal government.

Federal Transit Policy

George Smerk suggested that "the catalytic event that set in motion the activities leading to the urban transportation policy of the federal government was actually the Transportation Act of 1958, a piece of legislation that on the surface, had nothing to do with urban transportation."[6] The removal of passenger trains was a key factor in this legislation, and some of the first considered for elimination were those used in commuter operations in the large cities. Prodded by mayors of these cities who had no desire to lose this service, Congress moved toward mass transit aid. The Housing Act of 1961, the Highway Act of 1962, and the Urban Mass Transportation Act of 1964, discussed in Chapter Ten, marked the beginning of federal transit policy. Capital grants were provided for acquisition of new equipment and facilities. Funds were also provided for planning, management training, research and development.

In 1970 Congress made $3.1 billion available for capital improvements, portions of which could be obligated in advance to the year 1975. In the Highway Act of 1973, highway funds could be used for rural transit demonstrations. Formula grants to urban areas and possible funding for operations were included in the Urban Mass Transit Assistance Act of

[6] George W. Smerk, "Ten Years of Federal Policy in Urban Transit," *Transportation Journal* (Winter 1971): p. 46.

1974. In 1978, Title III of the Surface Transportation Act expanded funding and extended formula assistance to non-urbanized areas. Four-year funding was authorized at $13.58 billion, with yearly totals rising from $2.36 billion in fiscal year 1978 to $3.67 billion in fiscal year 1982. As the 1970s ended, efforts for additional funds by the transit community ran into an atmosphere of uncertainty as to the future of the federal programs. The Reagan administration proposed that transit operating aid be phased out in stages by 1985. Capital and other funding would be stablized at the 1981 level with no escalator for inflation. Further proposals for reductions in federal funding came in 1985 when preliminary budget conferences discussed the gradual elimination of almost $900 million in operating subsidies to states by 1990 and reduction of capital grants by about $2 billion by 1988.

Public Transit in Iowa

Under the Highway Commission, prior to 1975, the Urban Department had been active in planning and implementing urban improvements in the larger cities. A research study recommending a public transit division and a statewide transit policy was conducted by the Engineering Research Institute of Iowa State University and submitted to the Department in 1975. Included were inventories of transit operations in the state and examination of policies of other states regarding transit structures, responsibilities of a transit division, revenue sources and financial assistance. Four transit plans were presented, calling for state appropriations ranging from $3.1 to $6.25 million, dependent upon the program level selected. A second project analyzed Iowa intercity passenger carriers, with recommendations for specific changes in service and proposals for the state role in their implementation. These reports laid the background for the formation of the Public Transit Division in the DOT and furnished research data useful for the *Iowa Transit Plan '78* and the *1981 Transit Plan.* Earlier research studied intercity transportation and its relationship to socio-economic characteristics in rural regions, with the objective of relating intercity systems of small urban communities to their ability to attract and absorb growth.

In 1975, 14 transit operations in metropolitan and small urban areas served a population of over one million people and carried 13.5 million revenue passengers (Table 11-5). Twelve Class I passenger carriers provided scheduled intercity bus service in the state, but no service was available for 18 cities which were either county seats or had populations over 2,500 in 1970. Sixteen operations served rural regions in 37 counties, and 77 taxicab companies operated in 60 cities. By 1980, there were 17 urban systems, 16 multi-county operations, 25 intercity charter companies, 12 commuter companies, and 77 taxicab operations. Bus and taxi travel accounted for 1.2 percent of 18.7 billion passenger-miles in rural areas, and one percent of 12.1 billion passenger-miles in urban areas. Automobiles, trucks and motorcycles were utlized for 88 percent of total rural travel and 99 percent of urban transportation. The remaining 11 percent of rural travel was divided into rail, regular bus and aviation. Sources of transit financial assistance for operations between 1975 and 1980 are shown in Table 11-6; estimates of Iowa passenger transportation expenditures in Table 11-7; and operating statistics for transit properties in Iowa in 1984, in Table 11-8.

From $350,000 appropriated by the state for rural elderly demonstration projects in 1976, funding increased to $2 million annually in 1977 and remained at that level in later years. Most of the 1977 funds were used for operations that reached a level of 92 percent of the appropriation in 1981. The Transportation Commission recommended $5.56 million for 1982 and 1983 but the total remained at $1.9 million, ranking Iowa 24th of the 36 states that funded public transit systems. The 1981 Iowa Transit Plan listed 33 public systems including 16 regional systems based on the state's planning regions, seven large urban systems in cities with populations of 50,000 or more, and 10 small urban systems in cities with populations between 20,000 and 50,000. The number was increased to 34 public transit systems in 1985 (Fig. 11-7).

Between 1981 and 1984, a 28 percent increase occurred in transit expenditures in Iowa, rising from $30.3 to $38.2 million. Federal funding increased only slightly, from $12.2 to $12.6 million, and state aid declined from $2 to $1.8 million. The lack of funds necessitated reliance of transit systems more on local taxes, fare box revenues and contracts. In these categories, spending rose from $16.1 to $28.3 million between 1981 and 1984. The state's depressed economy throughout these years hurt transit operations, with some systems in better financial condition than others depending upon the location and the levels of economic activity. Ridership declined in the larger cities, and revenues and funding were unable to meet the rising costs of operation. The alternative was to reduce services both on city routes and on the regional systems, a trend which could continue unless new sources of funding are found.

Intercity Bus Service

Bus service in Iowa grew rapidly between 1940 and the mid-1950s but afterward reversed the trend in ridership to 1980. The decline in demand reached a point where many of the carriers could not afford to recapitalize fleets and physical facilities or upgrade operating capabilities, thus reducing the network and the communities served. In 1942, service was provided to 492 points throughout the state, dropping to 301 locations in 1981. Sixteen intercity bus carriers operated regular routes in 1942, compared with six carriers in 1983. Three of these, Greyhound, Trailways and Jefferson Lines, controlled nearly 75 percent of the total route service on a daily basis. Most of the service points were lost in communities of 2,500 population or less, and the areas that suffered severely were the southern two tiers of counties, eastern Iowa along the Mississippi River north of Davenport, and western Iowa, particularly from Des Moines to Sioux City. Intercity buses in the early 1980s carried more passengers annually in Iowa than competing rail or air carriers but were surpassed by publicly-funded regional transit systems.

Table 11-5

Summary of Urban Transit Operations in Iowa
April 1, 1975

City	Transit operator	Type ownership	Date of public ownership	Number of buses (active)	Number of routes	Base fare $
Metropolitan Areas						
Cedar Rapids	Regional Transit Corporation, Inc.	Municipal	1966	12	11	0.30
Council Bluffs	Metro Area Transit (Omaha)	Municipal	1972	16	7	0.40
Davenport	City Transit Authority	Municipal	1974	18	7	0.30
Des Moines	Des Moines Metropolitan Transit Authority	Regional	1973	72	15	0.50
Dubuque	Key Line	Municipal	1973	27	11	0.40
Sioux City	Sioux City Transit	Municipal	1963	21	11	0.25
Waterloo	Metropolitan Transit Authority of Black Hawk County, Inc.	Regional	1972	12	9	0.25
Small Urban Areas						
Ames	Midwest Transportation, Inc.	Private	--	3	3	0.30
Burlington	Burlington Urban Service	Municipal	1975	7	7	0.25
Clinton	Clinton Municipal Transit Authority	Municipal	1973	7	5	0.25
Iowa City	Iowa City Transit	Municipal	1971	15	10	0.15
Marshalltown	Marshall Motor Coach, Inc.	Private	--	2	3	0.25
Mason City	Public Transit Company	Private	--	3	3	0.40
Ottumwa	Ottumwa Transit Lines, Inc.	Private*	--	7	7	0.30

*Private contractor with Ottumwa Transit Authority.

(Source: Iowa State University Transit Assistance Program Report for Iowa.)

Table 11-6
Sources of Transit Financial Assistance for Operations, 1975-1980.
(Excludes Farebox Revenue)

Calendar Year	Federal Government (Percent)	State Government (Percent)	Local Governments (Percent)
1975	21.4	28.9	49.7
1976	25.7	22.3	52.0
1977	30.7	25.1	44.2
1978	30.9	25.3	42.8
1979	30.4	21.4	48.1
1980	30.2	22.7	47.1

(*Source:* Public Transit Workshop No.2, Transportation Commission Meeting, March 2, 1982.)

Note: In terms of total operating revenue in 1980, federal operating assistance accounted for 17.8 percent, state operating assistance for 13.0 percent and local operating assistance, 27.0 percent. Almost all transit capital revenue was received from government agencies. In 1980, the federal government contributed $2.8 billion toward the purchase of transit capital equipment. Based on a ratio of 80 percent federal contributions and 20 percent local contributions, state and local governments contributed an additional $0.7 billion toward capital purchases by transit systems.

Table 11-7
Estimated Iowa Passenger Transportation Expenditures
(Millions of 1980 Dollars)

	User Costs	Non-User Costs	Total Costs	% Paid By User
Automobiles, Light Trucks and Motorcycles	$3,373.5	$166.4 (a)	$3,539.9	95.3
Certified Air Carriers and General Aviation	476.5	30.7 (b)	507.2	91.9
Local Public Transit	8.8	25.1 (c)	33.9	26.0
Intercity Bus	14.5	1.0 (d)	15.5	93.9
Taxicabs	29.5	1.6 (d)	31.1	94.9
AMTRAK	1.3	2.9 (c)	3.3	39.4
Water Modes	---	---	---	---

(*Source:* Public Transit Workshop No. 1. Transportation Commission Meeting, February 16, 1982.)

Grand Total: Passenger Transportation	$4,130.9 M (11% of State GNP)
Total Iowa Passenger Bill:	$8,700.0 M (23% of State GNP)
Passenger Transportation Percentage:	47%

(a) Non-User charge: highway construction and maintenance.

(b) FAA and CAB programs net of user charges. General aviation portion of this subsidy would be large relative to its 3.2 percentage share of user-borne costs.

(c) Operating and capital subsidies: all non-farebox and contract-covered expenses plus non-user borne highway costs.

(d) Non-user borne highway costs.

Note: Accounts do not include some transportation costs: i.e., costs of congestion and noise, air pollution, visual intrusion, traffic congestion and litter opportunity costs on right-of-way (except for AMTRAK), or subsidized costs on capital facilities.

Table 11-8

Operating statistics for transit properties in Iowa, 1984

System Name	Passengers	Revenue Miles	Operating Revenue, $	Operating Expenses, $	Operating Deficit, $
Regional Systems					
Region 1	154,452	578,797	228,165	389,000	181,260
Region 2	157,170	334,331	133,027	210,684	114,944
Region 3	188,808	554,713	313,661	411,565	87,947
Region 4	97,650	367,089	144,860	245,741	128,706
Region 5	190,486	295,140	83,768	199,596	150,286
Region 6	48,447	233,236	8,321	127,329	128,071
Region 7	159,956	1,044,610	348,570	469,535	181,899
Region 8	34,581	139,997	37,923	103,223	61,290
Region 9	55,313	225,065	192,980	233,733	51,767
Region 10	337,922	823,273	410,581	716,230	251,389
Region 11	285,785	711,615	348,317	642,178	286,853
Region 12	184,867	382,854	137,640	212,264	74,166
Region 13	84,017	300,955	83,029	237,744	141,269
Region 14	88,815	211,454	128,258	231,057	84,880
Region 15	178,865	584,160	406,525	457,588	111,894
Region 16	119,034	252,072	151,696	226,402	53,692
Total	2,366,168	7,039,361	3,157,320	5,113,869	2,090,312
Small Urban Systems					
Ames	2,000,129	689,355	831,314	1,386,961	414,692
Burlington	353,699	289,110	108,866	577,343	331,079
Clinton	396,079	255,623	113,001	452,296	347,103
Marshalltown	62,311	87,168	25,372	173,354	147,780
Mason City	165,987	237,743	45,485	201,734	189,599
Muscatine	121,904	182,803	51,196	286,613	234,799
Ottumwa	240,575	149,546	89,469	311,286	227,691
Subtotal	3,340,684	1,891,348	1,264,704	3,389,588	1,892,744
Metropolitan Systems					
Bettendorf	141,367	239,985	40,018	297,546	275,001
Cedar Rapids	1,845,067	1,013,637	583,408	2,097,614	1,915,201
Coralville	550,351	237,380	218,954	476,262	252,872
Council Bluffs	560,793	395,721	253,249	889,712	635,948
Davenport	1,307,110	939,750	403,748	2,166,133	1,750,637
Des Moines	5,164,084	3,096,517	3,326,935	7,098,475	3,533,643
Dubuque	1,035,359	535,102	293,228	1,315,683	1,056,695
Iowa City	2,453,786	808,819	800,664	1,879,226	1,085,527
Sioux City	1,634,502	484,480	419,215	1,376,823	922,359
Waterloo	851,256	763,186	276,439	1,620,648	1,240,816
Subtotal	15,543,675	8,514,577	6,615,857	19,218,122	12,668,699
Total	21,250,527	17,445,286	11,037,881	27,721,578	16,651,755

(*Source:* Iowa Department of Transportation.)

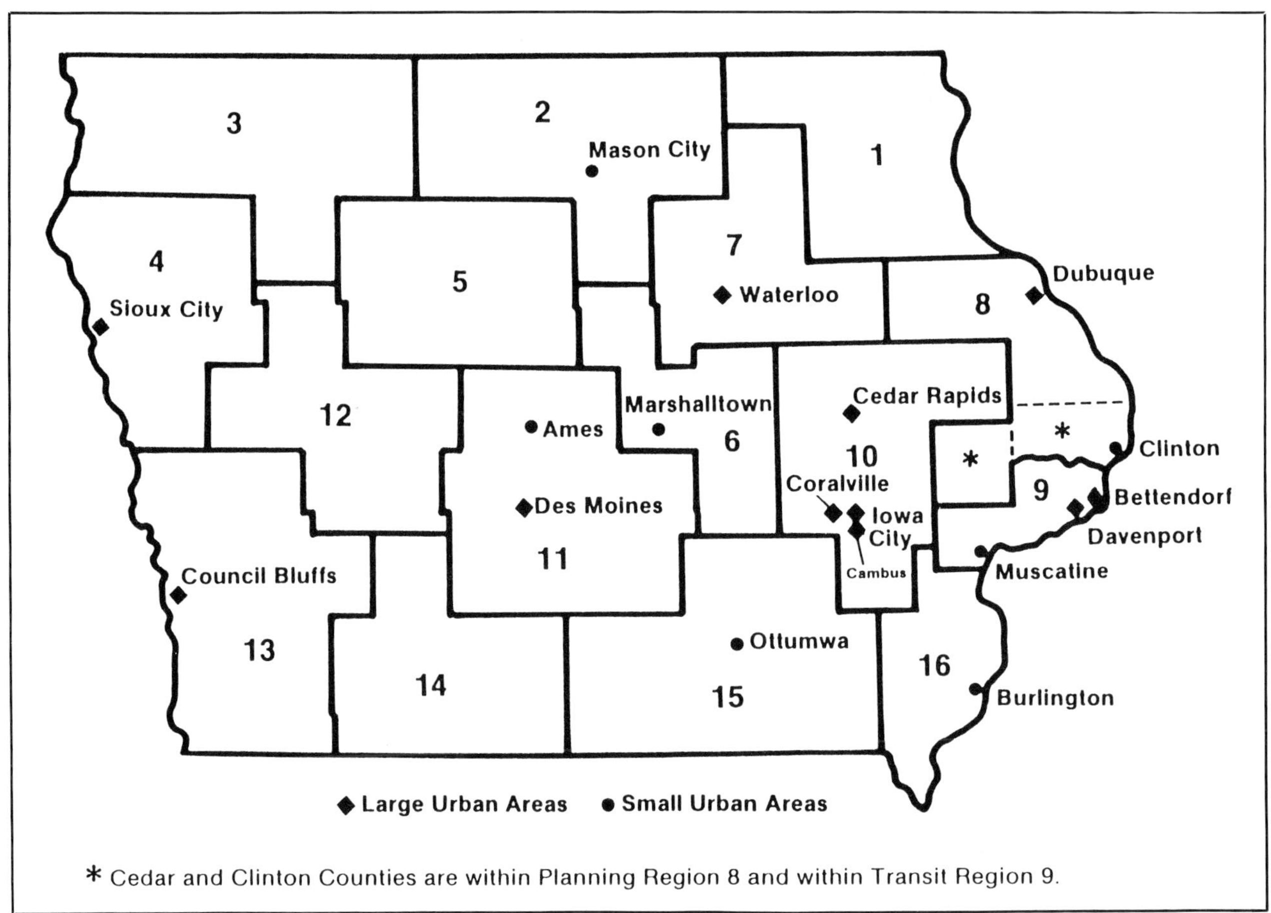

Figure 11-7
34 Public transit systems in Iowa.
(Courtesy: Iowa Department of Transportation.)

River Conditions

User Charges

Seven Presidents of the United States, beginning with Franklin D. Roosevelt, plus leaders of both political parties with liberal or conservative views, pledged to provide revenues to recover a portion of the public expenditures on inland waterways. Despite broad support, waterway charge proponents failed to gain congressional approval, and meanwhile, federal, state and local government expenditures continued to mount, reaching an estimated $21.2 billion by 1976. This amount covered funds for inland and intercoastal waterways; the Great Lakes and coastal harbors; construction, maintenance and operation of channels and harbors, locks and dams; alteration of bridges over navigable rivers; engineering and design and other costs associated with navigation. Not included were costs ascribed to non-navigation elements of the projects or the expenditures of the Tennessee Valley Authority and the U.S. portion of the construction of the St. Lawrence Seaway. Public Law 91-469, approved October 21, 1970, amended the Act creating the Seaway Corporation by terminating the payment of interest on the obligations of the corporation. Toll revenues on the Seaway failed by a large margin to cover total annual costs.

The overriding problem in assessing waterway user charges concerned the multi-purpose features of waterway projects. The concept of user charges is based upon benefits received on publicly-financed transportation routes. The difficult question to resolve lay in the method of isolating benefits to commercial users as against benefits accruing to the general public—the so-called "public interest principle." Flood control, water supply to communities and industries, wildlife and recreation enhancement and energy generation are waterway projects whose cost should be borne by the general public. On the other hand, commercial interests also benefited and had been freed from user taxes since waterway development began, successfully arguing that navigation was a by-product of these projects.

In 1976, the Iowa DOT staff reviewed accounting records of the Corps of Engineers to determine operating and maintenance costs on the 300-mile section of the Mississippi River from Guttenburg, Iowa, to Hannibal, Missouri. The area was considered typical of federal maintenance standards on the entire river. Following an examination of channel and local maintenance cost components, the staff used 43 percent as a basis for proposed user charges against barge companies—a figure comparable to the basis for taxes on trucks using public highways. Use of the base percentage translated into a proposal for a fuel tax of three cents per gallon and a $32 locking fee. It was estimated that grain rates from Davenport to New Orleans would increase by one-half cent per bushel and that the tax would generate $75-$100 million annually if applied nationwide. Costs, other than navigation, were not included. In May 1977, the Transportation Commission voted to make the staff proposal a DOT recommendation.

Mississippi River Lock and Dam No. 19 at Keokuk, Iowa.
(Courtesy: U.S. Corps of Engineers, Rock Island District.)

Locking a tow through Lock No. 19 at Keokuk, Iowa.
(Courtesy: Rail and Water Division, Iowa Department of Transportation.)

The Lock and Dam 26 Problem

Sixty-four terminals along the Mississippi and ten along the Missouri River provided facilities for handling nearly 13 million tons of commodities annually. Included were seven million tons of grain, two million tons of coal, one million tons of petroleum and three million tons of other commodities. Where speed of movement was not a major factor, productivity and the economic advantage of barges was tied to their ability to handle far larger volumes of traffic in single units or tows than was possible by railroads and trucks on competing routes. But economic operations require continuous movement, and interruptions for any reason tend to negate the comparative advantages of water carriers.

In April 1976, Lock and Dam No. 26 at Alton, Illinois, was partially closed, dramatically pointing to the importance of water transportation to users on the upper Mississippi River, including those in Iowa. The facility was in poor condition after approximately 40 years of service and had a history of excessive maintenance problems and costs. It was a vital link in the waterway system, accounting for 54 million tons of traffic valued at four billion dollars locked through in 1975—a volume eight million tons over its practical design capacity and four million tons over the total movement through the Panama Canal during that year.

The Iowa DOT supported replacement rather than rehabilitation of the existing locks and dam, favoring relocation some two miles downstream with one lock 1,200 x 110 feet at time of construction and the option of adding another lock in the future. Congress authorized construction in 1978 of one lock, but lawsuits in opposition by the railroads and environmental protection groups delayed the project until October 1979, when a Federal District Court ruling provided for the construction of the new lock and dam, to cost $861 million at the two-mile downstream location. The same legislation directed the Upper Mississippi River Basin Commission to conduct a master plan study of the entire upper Mississippi River system. An important part of this study, completed in 1982, was the recommendation concerning the economic need for a second lock. The legislation also provided for a waterway user tax of four cents per gallon of fuel effective October 1, 1980, to rise to 10 cents in 1985. The U.S. Transportation and Commerce Departments considered that the tax would have a short-term impact on barge operations and would probably be more lasting on grain interests, but overall would not be a major factor during the next decade. The Reagan Administration supported the user fees.

It was questionable whether the new lock would be adequate for current traffic plus projected increases and it was further suggested that a second lock would be necessary for emergency use. In 1985, the Corps of Engineers decided to utilize funds available for planning purposes to proceed with engineering and design of the second lock, action taken as an interim measure until congressional authorization for the new lock could be obtained. The second lock was included in the omnibus waterway legislation debated during the 1984 session of Congress (Fig. 11-8).

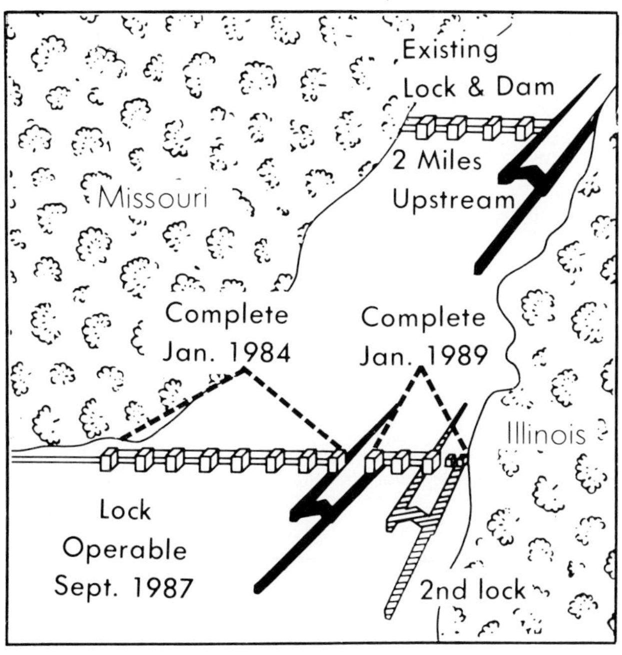

Figure 11-8
Lock and Dam 26.
(Courtesy: Iowa Department of Transportation.)

The Iowa Rail-Barge Tariff

Intermodalism in the form of rail/truck combinations (piggyback) had been commonplace in Iowa for many years and was a popular and effective system for moving selected classes of commodities. In 1976, the Iowa DOT brought together the CMStP&P and the Alter Barge Line for the purpose of discussing rail/barge combinations on grain movements to the Mississippi River under one tariff. Previously, shippers used one rate from inland origins to river terminals, another charge for transfer and a separate barge rate to destinations, under two bills of lading. The single tariff meant that shippers dealt only with one mode—the railroad—to arrange for shipments under one bill of lading. Uncertainty over barge rates, which fluctuated almost daily, was eliminated through stabilization by the barge line over three time periods: March-June, July-September and October-December. Barge availability was guaranteed by payment of rail car demurrage if the rail cars arrived at a terminal when barges were not ready for loading.

The tariff called for six consecutive 15-car movements to the river. To enable small elevators to participate, the railroad established 11 zones (Fig. 11-10). It was possible for up to three elevators within a zone to divide the 15 cars among themselves, or each of the six movements could originate from one to three elevators in that zone. Rates under the single tariff were lower than the sum of the individual charges and were competitive with 25, 50 and 75 railroad multi-car rates to the Gulf (Fig. 11-9). The advantages to the Iowa shipper were convenience, alternative routes, less documentation, increased competition and lower costs. By the close of 1978, three and one-half million bushels of grain had moved on the tariff, with a net saving of three to five cents per bushel to the Iowa farmer. Unfortunately, the plan collapsed when the CMStP&P filed for bankruptcy and restructured the system, and increasing barge rates were unattractive to the Alter Barge Line.

State Aviation System Evaluation

Before the Iowa DOT was organized, the Aeronautics Commission was the only state agency concerned with aviation goals. Its objective was to establish a public airport providing round-the-clock operation with an all-weather surface in each of the 99 counties. In 1973, through the efforts of the commission, local sponsors and the FAA, a network had been developed which consisted of 123 municipal and 111 private airports. Ten of these were in communities served by commercial air carriers: one medium hub (Des Moines); three small hubs (Cedar Rapids, Waterloo and Sioux City); and six non-hubs (Burlington, Clinton, Dubuque, Fort Dodge, Mason City and Ottumwa). Five sites (Des Moines, Ottumwa, Davenport, Fort Madison and Spencer) were also utilized by third level air carriers. Iowa was 25th in population, but eighth in the nation in the number of airports having paved and lighted runways, 21st in the number of active pilots (8,824), 18th in the number of aircraft (2,652) and 14th in the number of public use airports (234).

Airport development programs historically have been constrained by the lack of adequate funding, and since little construction occurred without state or federal aid, it was imperative that allocation of funds be made in the most judicious manner. In June 1971, at the request of Governor Ray, a detailed and comprehensive planning project was initiated by the Engineering Research Institute, Iowa State University, and submitted to the Aeronautics Commission in November, 1972. It made recommendations for improving and/or developing 117 airports with suggestions for implementation. The plan called for an expenditure of $126 million to be shared by the three levels of government and was approved by the FAA for inclusion in the National Airport System Plan, which became part of the National Transportation Plan.

The 1972 State Airport Plan was updated by the Iowa DOT in 1978, 1982, and 1985. The 1982 plan recognized the need for a total aviation system plan, one which emphasized the importance of aviation services as well as aviation facilities and covered a 20-year period in three phases: (1) a short-range period from 1982 to 1986, (2) an intermediate period, from 1987 to 1991, and (3) a long-range period from 1991 to 2001. It evaluated 114 existing publicly-owned airports and identified 80 airports eligible for state development, planning and safety project funds, and 41 local service airports eligible for state planning and safety projects but not developmental funding. Developmental costs were estimated at $291 million over the 20-year period.

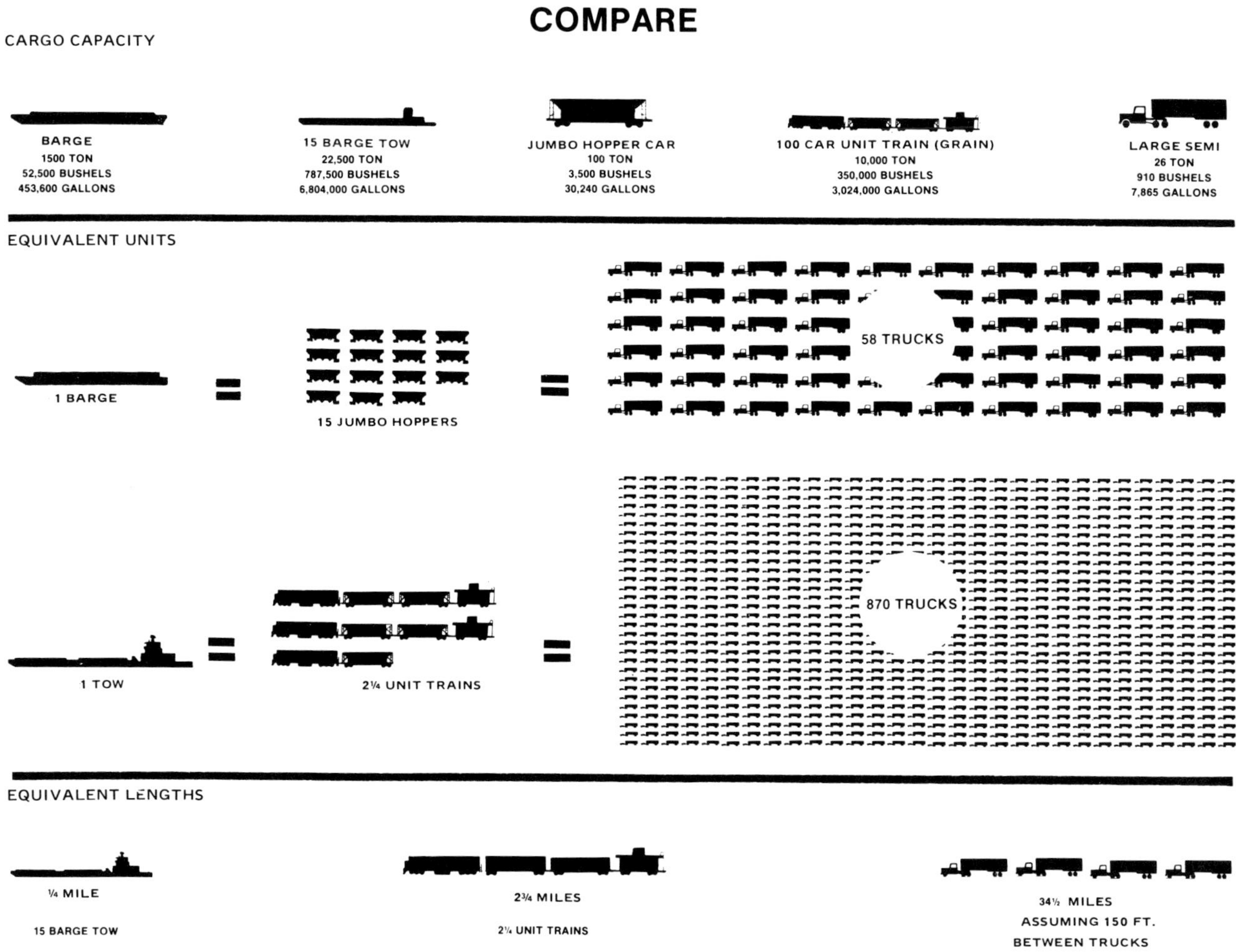

Figure 11-9
Comparison of tonnages carried by barge, rail and truck.
(Courtesy: Iowa Department of Transportation.)

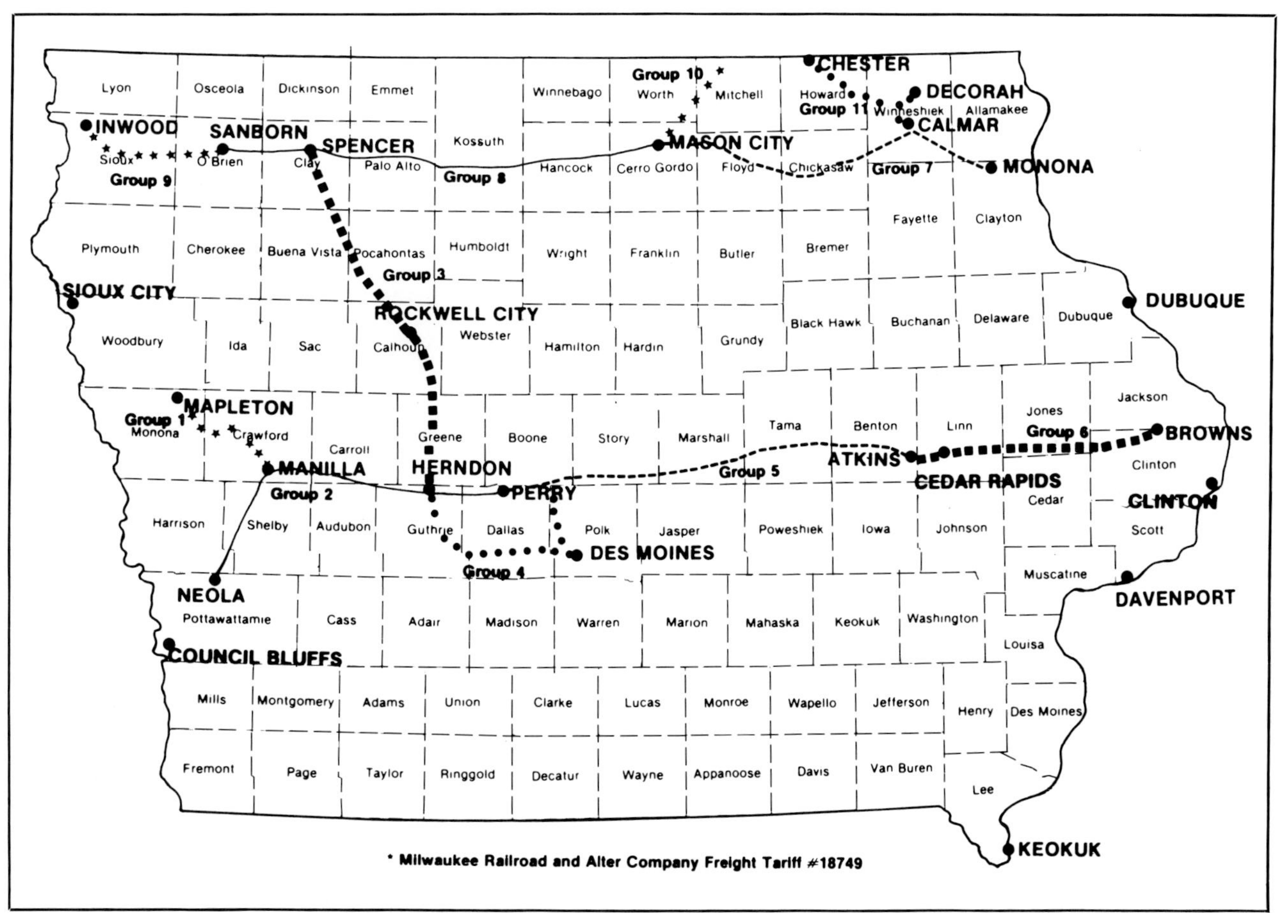

Figure 11-10
Rail/barge tariff shipping zones.
(Courtesy: Iowa Department of Transportation.)

In 1985 the state had 112 publicly-owned airports which provided access to the national system through direct commercial flights and air taxi services. They also provided access to communities by business interests and other users. There were 101 general aviation airports which provided service by aircraft ranging from single-engine airplanes to large corporate jets. Eleven commercial airports handled flights by major national airlines and/or commuter airlines as well as general aviation aircraft. All publicly-owned airports were included in the aviation system which provided service to all areas of the state (Fig. 11-11).

The number of registered aircraft increased in each year from 1970 to the peak year of 1979, when 3,530 were registered. In 1984, 3,079 aircraft were registered, a decline of 13 percent. Estimates for 1985 showed a further decrease of about 100 aircraft. In 1984, 2,935 aircraft or 95.9 percent of all aircraft registered were based at publicly-owned airports. These are aircraft that are regularly hangared or stored at a facility.

In 1980, Iowa had 12,101 registered pilots. The number fell to just over 10,000 in 1982 and to about 9,000 in 1984, representing a decline of 3,000 in four years. Projections of the number of future registered pilots show a growth rate of approximately 2 percent each year from 1985 to 2005, or a total of 13,400 pilots in the latter year.

Air passenger enplanements were expected to increase throughout the 20-year planning period. Enplanements on certificated air carriers declined between 1980 and 1982 but were beginning to increase from the 1982 low. Estimates based upon FAA forecasts showed just under one million enplanements for 1985, with an 8 to 9 percent increase each year through 2005. Enplanements on commuter airlines increased sharply—by 1985 they were estimated at four times the number in 1980. The increases can be traced to two developments: the Airline Deregulation Act of 1978 and an expansion in the number of commuter lines. Projections from 1985 to 2005 indicate that enplanements will rise from 106,000 in 1985 to 300,000 in 2005. Iowa has four airports served by certificated air carriers: Cedar Rapids, Des Moines, Sioux City and Waterloo. Commuter service is provided at these airports as well as at Spencer, Mason City, Dubuque, Clinton, Burlington, Fort Dodge and Ottumwa. However, the recent mergers involving Republic and Ozark Airlines and the bankruptcy of Frontier Airlines may significantly alter the air passenger service in Iowa (Fig. 11-12).

Des Moines Airport, 1970.
(Courtesy: Des Moines Municipal Airport)

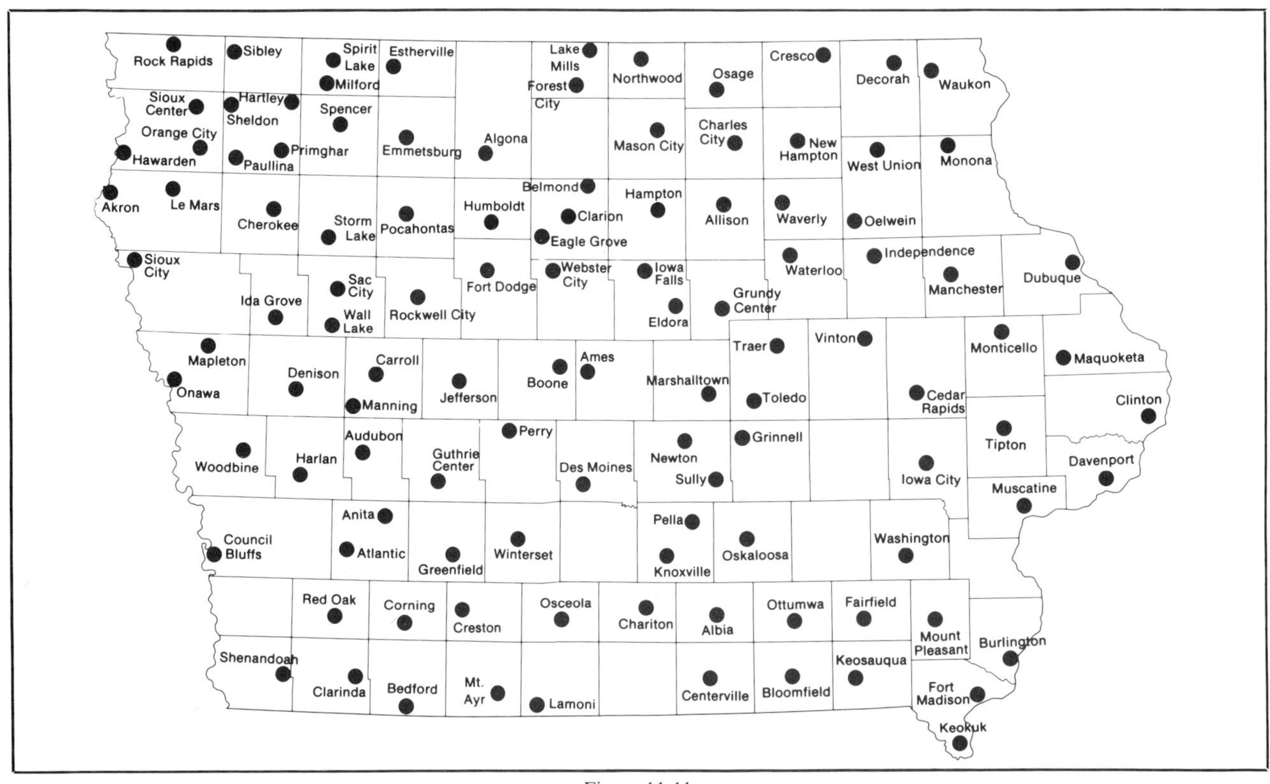

Figure 11-11
1985 Iowa aviation system plan.
(Courtesy: Iowa Department of Transportation.)

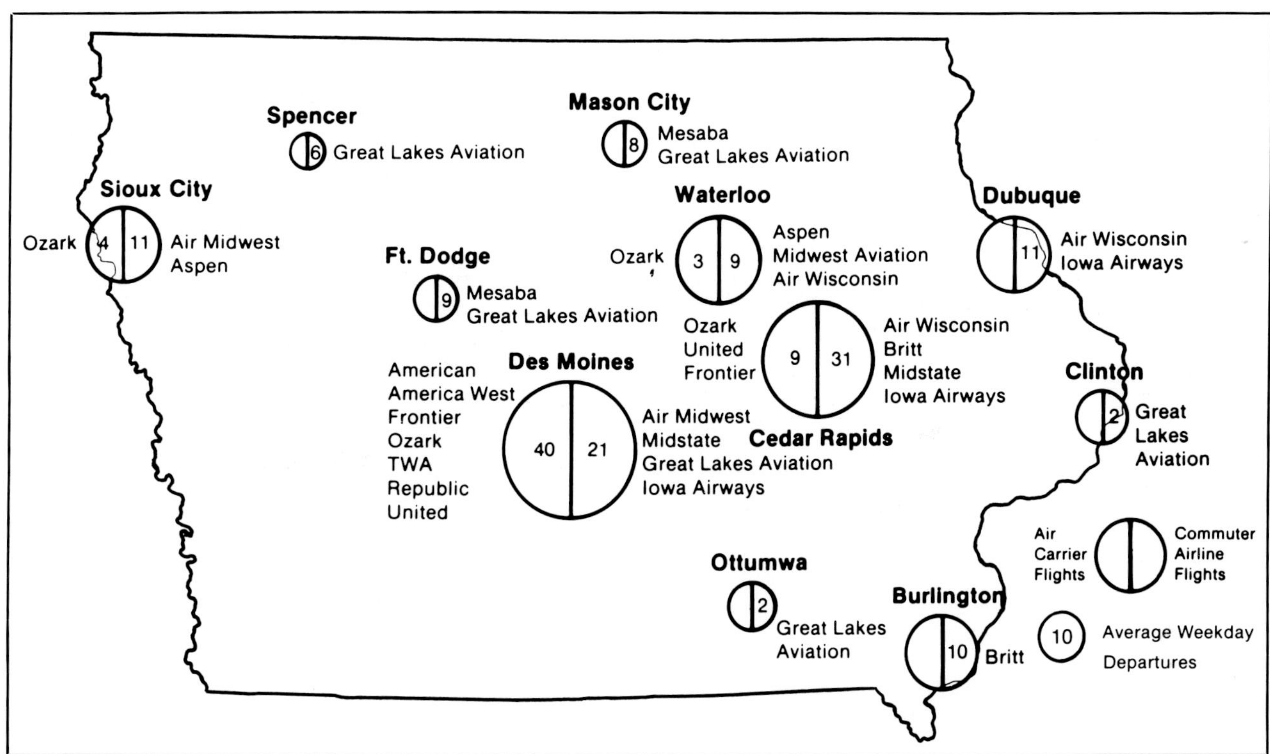

Figure 11-12
Air passenger service in Iowa, October 1985.
(Courtesy: Iowa Department of Transportation.)

Summary

The newly created Iowa Department of Transportation faced the problems of a distressed railroad industry which was hard-pressed to handle the rapid increase in agricultural and manufactured traffic, and to implement federal legislation passed in an effort to relieve railroad distress in passenger and freight movements. Bankruptcies and branch line abandonments reduced railroad mileage throughout the state during the 1970-1985 period. To counter the threat of reduced or completely eliminated service, the newly created Iowa Railroad Finance Authority was authorized to finance acquisition and improvement of railroad facilities.

Motor carrier traffic increased substantially during these years, partially because of the completion of interstate highways and the improvement of primary and secondary roads. However, the condition of bridges on all highways was a critical problem. The expansion in trucking brought controversy over the use of 65-foot twin trailers, fought by the state, only to lose the legal battle in the courts. Not only were the 65-foot twins mandated, but Iowa faced changes in truck sizes through federal legislation. Highway user taxes were raised at both state and federal levels.

Public transit became a salient issue in the nation and state as the demand for service increased faster than resources to meet that demand. Federal and state funding allowed the organization of regional and urban systems which had to weather the difficulties of an economic recession in the early 1980s. User charges were assessed against commercial waterway operators on the rivers bordering the state and the deterioration of Lock and Dam No. 26 at Alton, Illinois, pointed to the importance of water transportation to Iowa shippers. Aviation development was programed through state airport and system plans in 1972, 1978, 1982 and 1985.

The decade of 1970-1980 was one in which federal legislative reform measures freed carriers from long-standing rules and regulations. There were changes in the character of modal services and in the organization and reorganization of carrier management and operations. Environmental concerns and energy problems played an important role in the adjustment of the state to these developments. Nationwide economic recession in the early 1980s and its impact upon Iowa placed additional burdens on the transportation sector to meet the challenge of adequate service at reasonable costs.

Selected References

Allen, Benjamin J., and David B. Vellinga. "Public Financing of Railroads under the New Federalism: The Progress and Problems of Selected State Programs." *Transportation Journal* (Winter 1983): pp. 14-18.

American Association of Railroads. *Government and Private Expenditures for Highway, Waterway, Railroad and Air Rights-of-Way.* Washington, D.C.: U.S. Government Printing Office, September 1976.

______. *Statistics of the Railroads of Class I in the United States.* Washington, D.C.: U. S. Government Printing Office, September 1978.

American Trucking Association. *The Case for Twin Trailers.* Washington, D.C.: American Trucking Association, December 1978.

______. "The Urgent Need for Twin Trailers." *Distribution Worldwide* (March 1974): pp. 36-39.

Anthan, George, and Larry Fruling. "Transportation Woes Threaten Farmers." *Des Moines Register,* July 6, 1980.

Atchison, Topeka, and Santa Fe Railway Company v. Gerald Bair. 338 N.W. 2nd 338 (Iowa 1983).

Barnum, John W. "Railroads in Crisis." *Handling and Shipping* (August 1978): pp. 60-63.

Baumel, C. Phillip, Thomas P. Drinka, Dennis K. Leffert, and John J. Miller. *An Economic Analysis of Alternative Grain Transportation Systems: A Case Study.* Prepared for the U.S. DOT. Ames: Iowa State University, November 1973.

Baumel, C. Phillip, John J. Miller, and Thomas P. Drinka. *An Economic Analysis of Upgrading Branch Railroad Lines: A Study of 71 Lines in Iowa.* Prepared for the U.S. DOT, February 1976.

"Breaking a Bottleneck in Long Haul Trucking." *Business Week* (March 6, 1978): pp. 96-99.

Carstens, R. L. Project Director. *Integrated Analysis of Small Cities Intercity-Transportation to Facilitate the Achievement of Regional Urban Goals.* U. S. Department of Transportation Report No. DOT-TST-75-13, Washington, D.C.: U. S. Government Printing Office, June 1974.

______. *Transit Assistance Program for Iowa.* Prepared for the Iowa Department of Transportation. Ames: Iowa State University Engineering Research Institute, June 1975.

Carstens, R. L., K. A. Brewer, S. L. Ring and J. D. Grove. *Intercity Passenger Improvement Study.* Prepared for the Iowa Department of Transportation. Ames: Iowa State University, August 1977.

Evans, Randy. "Northwestern Wins War to Buy Rock Island Track." *Des Moines Register,* March 19, 1983.

______. "Northwestern Gets Rock Island Track for $93 Million." *Des Moines Register,* June 30, 1983.

Fruling, Larry, and George Anthan. "New Federal View: Let the Grain Belt Roads Shrink." *Des Moines Register,* July 8, 1980.

Graham, Dean. "Gas Tax Boost, Rail Plan Voted as Session Ends." *Des Moines Register,* August 15, 1981.

Harbeson, Robert W. "Some Policy Implications of Northeastern Railroad Problems." *Transportation Journal* (Fall 1974): pp. 5-13.

Hawthorne, D. Vance. "Iowa Bridges on Road to Collapse." *Des Moines Register,* July 26, 1981.

Heady, Earl O., and Won W. Koo. *An Interregional Analysis of U.S. Domestic Grain Transportation.* Ames: Center for Agricultural and Rural Development, Iowa State University, February 1975.

Hillman, Jordon J. "The Making of Conrail." *ICC Practitioners Journal* (November-December 1977): pp. 18-26.

Ingram, John I. "Government and the Midwest Railroads: Notes on the Demise of the Chicago, Rock Island and Pacific Railroad." *Transportation Journal* (Spring 1980): pp. 29-38.

Iowa Aeronautics Commission. *28th Annual Report of the Iowa Aeronautics Commission Ending June 30, 1973.* Des Moines: State of Iowa, 1973.

"Iowa—A Transportation Laboratory." Interview with Victor Preisser. *Des Moines Register,* November 16, 1975.

Iowa Department of Transportation. *1978 Update State Airport System Plan.* Ames: Iowa Department of Transportation, May 1978.

______. *1981 Iowa River Report.* Ames: Iowa Department of Transportation, October 1981.

______. *1982 Iowa Aviation System Plan.* Ames: Iowa Department of Transportation.

______. *1983 Intercity Bus Plan.* Ames: Iowa Department of Transportation, September 1983.

______. *1982 Iowa Rail Analysis Update.* Ames: Iowa Department of Transportation.

______. *1985 Iowa Aviation System Plan and Technical Supplement.* Ames: Iowa Department of Transportation.

______. *1985 Iowa Railroad Analysis Update.* Ames: Iowa Department of Transportation.

______. Office of Policy Analysis. *Receipts and Distribution of Road Use Tax Revenue Since Implementation of Iowa's First Motor Fuel Tax.* Ames: Iowa Department of Transportation, August 1, 1981.

______. River Transport Division. *Waterway User Charge Proposal.* Ames: Iowa Department of Transportation, September 22, 1976.

______. *Sixty-Five Foot Trailers on Iowa Highways: Perspective.* Ames: Iowa Department of Transportation, April 1965.

Iowa Highway Commission. *Iowa Road and Streets Functional Classification Manual.* Des Moines: State of Iowa, January 1975.

Iowa State University. *State Airport System Plan.* Vol. 1, Summary Report.Vol. 2, Technical Supplement. Prepared for the Iowa Aeronautics Commission. Ames: Iowa State University, November 1972.

Interstate Commerce Commission Bureau of Economics. *The Intercity Bus Industry: A Preliminary Study.* Washington, D.C.: U. S. Government Printing Office, May 1978.

Kannel, E. J., K. A. Brewer, and R. L. Carstens. *Intercity-Bus Route Evaluation for Statewide Planning.* Prepared for the Iowa Department of Transportation. Ames: Iowa State University, May 1981.

National Railroad Passenger Corporation. *Annual Report 1972.*

National Transportation Policy Commission. *National Transportation Policies Through the Year 2000.* Washington, D.C.: U. S. Government Printing Office, June 1979.

National Waterways Foundation. *U. S. Waterways Productivity: A Private and Public Partnership.* Huntsville, Ala.: The Slade Publishers, 1983.

Nupp, Byron. "Railroads and the Transportation Problems: Some Thoughts on Strategy of Political Roles." *Transportation Journal* (Winter 1973): pp. 34-37.

Petroski, William. "Fledgling Heartland Rail Sets Out to Prove its Critics Wrong." *Des Moines Register,* November 4, 1984.

______. "Iowa's Rural Transit Systems Face Rocky Road of Federal Budget Cuts." *Des Moines Register,* April 7, 1985.

Pickere, Luther, and Jerry Fruen, eds. *Rural Freight Transportation: New Policy Initiatives.* Minneapolis: Engineering Extensions Service, University of Minnesota, Special Report 86, 1980.

Pillar, Dan. "Rock Island Lines Gone but Will Always be a Part of Iowa." *Des Moines Register,* June 2, 1980.

"Reagan Would Move Funding Programs to States." *Traffic World,* Feb. 1, 1982.

"The Rock Island Domino Impact." *Business Week* (March 31, 1975): pp. 17-18.

"Rock Island Gets Nod to Abandon System Except Saleable Lines." *Traffic World,* June 9, 1980, p. 23.

Sloss, James, Thomas J. Humphrey, and Forrest N. Krutter. *An Analysis and Evaluation of Past Experience in Rationalizing Railroad Networks.* Prepared for the U. S. DOT, 1974.

Smerk, George W. "The Development of Public Transportation and the City." *Public Transportation: Planning, Operations, and Management.* Edited by George C. Gray and Lester H. Hoel. Englewood Cliffs, N.J.: Prentice-Hall, Inc., 1979.

______. "Federal Mass Transit Policy, 1981-1982: A Fall from Grace." *Transportation Journal* (Fall 1983): pp. 38-86.

Smith, Wilbur, and Associates. *Bridge Deficiencies in the United States: An Overview of the Problem,* Prepared for the United States Steel Corporation and the ATA Foundation. May 1982.

Thompson, W. H. "A Review of Grain Transportation in Iowa and the Midwest." *Proceedings of the Grain Transportation Symposium.* Ames: Iowa State University, February 24, 1970.

Transportation Association of America. *Transportation Facts and Trends.* 14th ed. Washington, D.C.: Transportation Association of America, July 1978.

"Transportation's Troubled Abundance." *Fortune* (July 1971): p. 59.

U.S. Department of Agriculture and U.S. Department of Transportation. *Agricultural Transportation Services, Needs, Problems, Opportunities.* Final Report of Rural Tranpsortation Advisory Task Force, Washington, D.C.: U.S. Government Printing Office, January 1980.

U.S. Department of Transportation. *Railroad Abandonments and Alternatives.* Washington, D.C.: U.S. Government Printing Office, December 1976.

______. *Preliminary Standards, Classifications and Designations of Lines of Class I Railroads in the United States.* Vol. I. Washington, D.C.: U. S. Government Printing Office, August 1976.

______. UMTA. *Urban Mass Transportation Act of 1964, As Amended Through 1983 and Amended Laws.* Washington, D.C.: U.S. Government Printing Office, 1983.

U.S. District Court, Northern District of Illinois, Eastern Division. In the Matter of Chicago, Milwaukee, St. Paul and Pacific Railroad Company, Debtor. February 8, 1985.

U.S. General Accounting Office. *The Surface Transportation Assistance Act of 1982: Comparative Economic Effects on the Trucking Industry.* Washington, D.C.: U.S. Government Printing Office, April 6, 1984.

USRA. *Final System Plan for Restructuring the Railroads in the Northeast and Midwest Pursuant to the Regional Reorganization Act of 1973.* Washington, D.C.: U.S. Government Printing Office, March 18, 1974.

Chapter Twelve
Deregulation and Transportation Policy Issues

Introduction

The vast complex of federal regulatory rules and regulations on the nation's for-hire transportation industry was seriously challenged during the 1970s. These controls over entry, exit, rates, routes and quality of service had become more extensive over the years, yet provided for exemptions and special privileges and treatment of particular modes. Too often the consequences of economic regulation appeared to be more costly than the abuses they were designed to correct. The rules were reasonable at the time of inception but were inappropriate as the economic and competitive environment changed.

From the beginning, economic regulation was controversial and became more so when applied to air and motor carriers as the new competition to the railroads developed. Periodically since then, the topic spawned proposals ranging from strengthening regulation or eliminating it together with the regulatory agencies, introducing reforms or reducing the increasingly frustrating bureaucratic processes to which carriers and shippers were subjected. These conflicting attitudes reached a climax in the late 1970s when the reform movement was addressed by the Congress.

Two fundamental public policy issues formed the basis of the debates that raged over regulation-deregulation, modified regulation, regulatory reform, reregulation, etc. One involved the philosophical question of the relative roles of government contrasted to the private sector of the economy in transportation matters. The other centered on the pragmatic question of continued effectiveness of government intervention vis-a-vis the free and open market mechanism in furthering the development and maintenance of transportation systems accessible to all and capable of providing the necessary services.

Supporters of regulation argued that "deregulation" would not yield the needed services at reasonable rates without a return to unjust and undue discriminations. Further, they argued that without some economic controls, private ownership and operation would place a premium on the profit motive to the exclusion of service and neglect of safety. Proponents based their arguments on competitiveness of the individual modes, resulting in advantages to users; the carriers were fully capable of providing the required services without regulatory supervision. From their point of view, any changes in regulatory policy would allow operations to be vastly superior under free market conditions than could be expected through decisions by the regulatory agencies.

The political climate of the nation contributed to the movement for economic liberalization. Proposals for nationalization of transportation as an alternative to the confusion emanating from the debates were cast aside as national conservative trends formed slowly during the last years of the Carter administration and reached full flower in the national elections of 1980. The most popular political philosophy designed to "get the government off the backs of the people" was reduction or elimination of federal rules and regulations, and the transportation industry was a prime candidate. Thus, the contentions of the supporters and opponents of regulation were to be tested by reform legislation which in three years, 1977-1980, reversed the 90 years of traditional federal regulatory policy.

Attempts to define and implement transportation policies often caused more confusion than clarity as issues became increasingly mixed with broad concepts of goals, objectives, programs, conflicts and perspectives. Policies are guidelines for choices and ideally are established within a framework of goals and objectives or in response to recurring or new problems. When the choices are simple, few disagreements occur; when complicated or difficult, controversy rages as various interest groups perceive a danger to their jealously guarded positions.

Federal Transportation Reform Legislation

The Airline Industry

The first attempt at regulatory reform was led by Alfred Kahn, chairman of the Civil Aeronautics Board, and supported by Congress in 1977. Nearly all of the statutes controlling rates, routes and competitive practices in the air cargo segment were repealed. Despite initial opposition of the carriers, similar legislation followed in air passenger operations. Airlines were permitted to expand immediately as to "dormant" routes once certified by the CAB but abandoned by the original carriers. One new market could be served and one route protected each year, meaning that no other carrier could compete on that route. CAB route authority expired in 1981.

Until 1983, carriers could increase fares to compensate for inflation plus five percent or reduce fares up to 50 percent each year, not subject to CAB supervision unless the adjustments were discriminatory. Abandonments were allowed in non-compensatory markets, with small markets protected by subsidy provisions to guarantee "essential service" for 10 years into previously served points. The federal government also assumed responsibility up to six years for employees who lost employment when carriers reduced their work force by more than 7.5 percent in any year through deregulation.

The CAB was to self-destruct on January 1, 1985, and did with a Marine bugler playing "Evening Colors," the first federal regulatory agency ever to go out of business. As one of its final major decisions, the agency decided that airline tickets could be sold anywhere instead of restricting sales to travel agencies and airline representatives. Consumer protection functions—overbooking flights, searching for lost baggage, enforcing charter provisions and no-smoking rules were transferred to the U.S. DOT.

The Motor Carrier Industry

Although diverse opinions were expressed by truckers, unions and shippers, regulatory reform for motor carriers followed on July 1, 1980. Its purpose was "to provide for more effective regulation of motor carriers of property and for other purposes."[1] Whereas airline legislation was directed toward passenger benefits, the Motor Carrier Act appeared to be aimed at correcting operational inefficiencies. "Statutes governing Federal regulation are outdated and must be revised to reflect transportation needs and realities in the 1980s: that historically the existing regulatory structure has tended in certain circumstances to inhibit market entry, carrier growth, maximum utilization of equipment and energy resources. . . that protective regulation has resulted in some operating inefficiencies and some anti-competitive pricing." One of the new features was the provision for congressional oversight to ensure that the act was implemented according to congressional intent and purpose. Among other major provisions were the easing of entry requirements, rate freedoms, removal of operating restrictions (gateways and circuitous route limitations on common carriers of property), expanded agricultural exemptions, new rules on intercorporate hauling, through and joint motor/water rates and mergers. Its major objective was use of the market mechanism; users were given only a passing reference.

The immediate reaction to the passage of the act involved the question of elimination or retention of the common carrier obligation to serve all comers without favor or discrimination as a result of lowering the barriers to common carrier entry. The ICC proposed to allow carriers to decide on the services offered and would place the burden of proof on shippers as to injury or discrimination. If implemented, the effect would be to terminate the common carrier obligation. The agency almost unanimously approved proposed rate reductions; tariff examinations were superficial or ignored; and strict rules for rate bureaus were adopted.

The Railroad Industry

Less than three months later, on October 14, 1980, the Staggers Railroad Act was passed "to reform the economic regulation of the railroads and for other purposes."[2] The clearly stated goal was financial support. "The purpose of this act was to provide for the restoration, maintenance and improvement of the physical facilities and financial stability of the railroads of the United States." Deregulation of rates was the method selected to achieve the goals except where "market dominance" prevailed. No rates were allowed below variable costs, and a zone of rate flexibility of six percent per year was established for a four-year period ending October 1, 1984, subject to a cumulative total of 18 percent. Any portion of the six percent increase not used could be carried forward, but no one yearly increase could exceed 12 percent. After 1984, the zone of flexibility could increase by four percent per year with no carry-over provisions. Future rate adjustments would be tied to the inflation index.

Martin T. Farris pointed out the similarities and differences in the three reform acts. All stressed the desirability of more competition through market emphasis. Rate flexibility was allowed and jurisdiction over rates liberalized in rail and air transportation.

[1] Public Law 96-296 (1980); "Truckers, Shippers Give Varied Views on Truck Deregulation Legislation," *Traffic World* (November 23, 1979): pp. 17, 19; Donald V. Harper, "The Federal Motor Carrier Act of 1980: Review and Analysis," *Transportation Journal* (Winter 1980): pp. 5-34.

[2] Public Law 96-448 (1980).

Entry restrictions were removed in air and motor carriage. Conference rate-making was modified in rail and motor operations. Ultimately, complete elimination of all economic regulation in air transportation was contemplated with modifications in rail and motor operations. The differences related to the goals and objectives of each act. In air transportation legislation, the user was to be the major beneficiary; inefficiencies were emphasized in the Motor Carrier Act; and financial support was stressed in the Staggers Act. The final deregulation act at this writing was the Bus Regulatory Act of 1982, signed into law on September 20 of that year. It covered the familiar issues of market entry, exit, operating restrictions, rates, insurance and safety.

The Impact of Regulatory Reform

General Observations

Perhaps in five or ten years it will be possible to more precisely judge the impact of reform legislation on the carriers, users and general public. Such analysis cannot be made with any degree of confidence in the relatively short period of 1978-1985. It is probably more accurate to predict that controversy will continue as the drama unfolds. Reactions to the regulatory policy changes came with the onset of an economic recession, and the immediate or preliminary results were difficult to isolate whether caused by one or the other or both. The discussion that follows briefly presents the pros and cons of the impact of the legislation and recognizes in its brevity the inevitability of further studies, public policy changes and industry and user responses to the newly created "free market" atmosphere.

It would be well to remember history, however. Transportation as an industry has come full circle from its unrestrained laissez-faire era through almost a century of government regulation to return to a relatively unencumbered free market. Will the mergers of giant carriers materialize as some predict, creating oligopoly-type structures generating anti-monopoly pressures? How long will the euphoria over the new economic freedoms last if discriminatory rate or service abuses flourish as between large and small shippers, regions or communities? Is there a correlation between regulation and safety? Will giving up government controls require the public to submit to the evils which historically the people decided to prevent? Finally, can the nation economically or socially afford a complete disregard for commercial transportation by total deregulation of the industry in the light of conservative political policies? These are but a few of the basic questions to be considered—questions which create more issues and bring no clear answers.

Airlines

The adjustment to "deregulation" by the airlines was traumatic. Route structures were altered, pricing strategies modified, and operating policies changed. Route expansion was vigorously promoted by some carriers while others consolidated existing routes by adding flights. Expansion proved costly to Braniff International, Air Florida and Continental, considered to have been a major factor in reorganizations or bankruptcies. A variety of pricing alternatives were available to passengers who could choose from a wide selection of services on heavily traveled routes between major hubs. Discount fares were common, used by approximately 80 percent of large city passengers as price competition outweighed service competition. However, on short and intermediate routes under limited competition, fares rose sharply. Warren Rose commented: "The results were predictable. Greater inconveniences and more depersonalization of travelers occurred. The traditional high standards of excellence were seen more in the breech than in the observance. Promotional efforts by the airlines were directed at pricing inducements with only occasional references to the quality of service."[3]

Small and mid-sized cities suffered. Between April 1980 and April 1981, the Civil Aeronautics Board reported that 40 airports serving 41 cities across the nation lost all scheduled airline service. From July 1978 to July 1981, 279 cities lost one airline; 38 lost two airlines; and nine lost three airlines. In some cases commuter carriers stepped in to provide replacement service, using smaller plans which many travelers might have found unattractive in terms of comfort and safety. It seems reasonable to conclude that deregulation did not benefit all consumers of air service equally—those who benefitted did so at the expense of others. On the other hand, it seems fair to

[3] Warren Rose, "Three Years After Airline Passenger Deregulation in the United States: A Report Card On Trunkline Carriers," *Transportation Journal* (Winter 1981): pp. 51-59.

point out that regulation often compelled consumers to pay for services that would not otherwise be provided. Mass marketing of airline services appeared to be the new operating strategy.

As the deregulation process ran its early course, airlines broke all records for financial losses. In 1981, 12 of the largest carriers lost $641 million and in 1982, airline revenues represented the first year-to-year decline in the nation's history. Only three of seven selected trunkline carriers reported modest profits, and losses from 1980 to 1982 amounted to over $1 billion. The strike of air traffic controllers in 1981 temporarily aided the industry when the FAA ordered a 25 percent reduction in flight schedules. However, despite financial problems and subsequent "reregulation" proposals by critics, airlines rejected any return to the regulatory environment of the past. They expected that reduced labor costs, stable fuel prices, recovery from the recession and higher patronage would bring prosperity to the industry by 1984. Airline economists predicted operating profits of approximately $2 billion and net income ranging between $600 and $800 million for the industry in 1985.

While the number of airlines nearly quadrupled during the six-year period following deregulation in 1978, approximately 161 trunk and commuter lines terminated service. In 1986, Frontier Airlines filed for bankruptcy when it could not be sold to United by People Express, which was also in financial difficulty and eventually merged with Texas Air. Delta merged with Western, Republic with Northwest, Ozark with TWA and Eastern with Texas Air. Airlines carried 90 percent of all non-automobile intercity transportation in 1985, and 80 percent of that figure was carried by five companies: United, American, Delta, Texas Air and Northwest, including their merger partners. It would seem that the question of oligopoly in the airline industry, previously raised, has been partially answered.

Commercial Motor Carriers

The large numbers of commercial motor carriers on the nation's highways with their inherent advantage of flexibility of operations and fast door-to-door delivery offered shippers a variety of services. Regulatory economic reform for for-hire trucking began in 1977, when the ICC allowed a more liberal approach to operating authority, favoring greater competition and freedom for the carriers. The act of 1980 substantially endorsed the ICC's pro-competitive policies and brought them into the legislative structure of motor carrier economic regulation.

Deregulation initially hit the industry with a harsh impact. Coupled with the 1981-1982 recession, economic indicators showed that industry earnings had progressively worsened. For example, for the top 10 motor carriers in the period 1976-1981, return on equity fell from 18.70 to 8.95 percent, and the operating ratio rose from 91.63 to 95.97 percent. In 1982, the operating ratio for the industry was 98.29 percent and return on equity, 2.90 percent, the worst year in the history of ICC regulated carriers. According to the American Trucking Association, a measure of profitability returned in 1983. For more than 2,000 trucking companies, earnings rose from $225 million in 1982 to $736 million in 1983, with the 100 largest carriers accounting for 57.5 percent of the total.

There appears to be no accurate estimate of the number of motor carriers who have declared bankruptcy or ceased operations without formal petition for reorganization. Sources place the figure at 350 to 400, affecting thousands of workers and millions of lost annual revenues. However, the 1980 legislation appeared to reward efficient carriers providing quality service with higher revenues and expanded markets. More attention was given to marketing and pricing plans and a vastly increased use of contracts. Rail/truck links made services, not possible in the past, available to additional users. A new sense of economic realism emerged in labor-management negotiations as new non-union firms entered the industry. A deceleration in the growth of union wages occurred, probably more than can be explained by falling inflation, and there was also evidence of the willingness of labor to consider work rules changes to enhance productivity. Shippers generally seemed to approve deregulation, although rates had not declined on an industry-wide basis. Increased competition benefitted those shipping full loads; less-than-truckload shippers had difficulty in getting rate discounts.

Railroads

Of the major carrier industries subjected to regulatory reform, railroads, when carrying large shipments of bulk commodities and serving certain geographical regions, come close to the "natural monopoly" concept. Air and motor carriers more easily entered new markets and expanded service territories, but deregulation in this respect had no effect upon railroads. "Regulatory freedom for railroads meant freedom to merge, freedom to abandon trackage and freedom to charge (usually higher) rates."[4] Mergers during the 1970s and early 1980s consolidated carriers into seven major systems in the nation. Even this number may be reduced as the single system in the Northeast (Conrail) was the object of a bidding war by the two Southern regional systems, CSX and Norfolk Southern. In the West, four major systems have emerged: the Burlington Northern, Inc. (BN, Frisco); Tri Pac or Rail Pac (UP, WP, MP); SP and AT&SF.

Railroad fortunes changed markedly under the Staggers Act. The industry came through the economic recession without additional bankruptcies and with earnings sufficiently high enough to make increases in capital expenditures. Innovative arrangements, improved services and rate flexibility recaptured traffic lost to motor carriers, reversing a 30-year trend. Whereas a major reduction in regulation appeared to have positive results for carriers and shippers, some areas of concern surfaced.

The railroads have been agressive in implementing their new freedoms, assisted by liberal ICC interpretations of the act. Increased rate competition developed and changes were made in joint rates, routes, gateways and reciprocal switching arrangements. These affected many "captive" shippers who experienced substantial rate increases. Rail services to many communities were abandoned, leading to substitution of more costly truck transportation.

Opposition to railroad practices and ICC interpretations of the act came in the form of coalitions of shippers who depended solely upon railroad transportation. Electric utilities, agribusiness firms, commodity groups, coal, farm and manufacturing companies complained that the Reagan administration and the ICC allowed railroads with monopoly power to charge excessive rates. These groups contended that the ICC had emphasized the creation of economically healthy and often wealthy roads while ignoring the problems of shippers so affected. The growing impressions of unfairness attracted the attention of members of Congress, who indicated a willingness to study the effects of the Staggers Act and raised the possibility of legislative changes unless corrective actions were taken. In response, the ICC announced that it would undertake a consolidated review of post-Staggers regulations in a single proceeding. Further clarification and interpretations will be required before railroads and shippers can operate with confidence and security. Issues such as market dominance determinations, maximum rates, box car exemptions, joint rate, route and switching cancellations and merger policies will need to be explored. How these matters are resolved will determine the extent to which the railroad industry becomes fully deregulated or reregulated. At the present time, it seems that regulatory reform efforts have produced both positive and negative results—that the Staggers Act presents major problems of interpretation and administration. Both carriers and shippers have an opportunity to benefit under it. However, it appears likely that the act is an intermediate stage in the regulatory revisionary process, and congressional action will be sought following the testing of its provisions in the courts and by the commission.

The Small Community Impact

Motor Carriers: The Pre-Deregulatory Period

The quantity, quality and cost of service to small towns and rural communities was a major concern of Congress and state agencies as regulatory reforms were being argued. While the debates were national in scope, they also applied to state regulatory rules and procedures. One of the deficiencies was the absence of empirical evidence to support the pro or con regulatory positions. Since railroads were abandoning branch and primary mileage, leaving small communities solely dependent upon truck transportation for freight movements, the potential impact initiated national and regional research studies between 1976 and 1980.

It was feared that Iowa would be greatly affected by the regulatory changes, having approximately 920 of 960 communities under 10,000 population, widely dispersed and potentially vulnerable to reform. When the Iowa DOT attempted to assess possible impacts, it found virtually no information available on the level of motor carrier service in these communities. Therefore, a research study was authorized in 1979 and published in 1980.

[4] Paul S. Dempsey, *Transportation Deregulation—On A Collision Course.* Presented before the Iowa Transportation Commission, December 20, 1983, p. 12.

Two levels of motor carrier operations were regulated under Iowa laws: Certificated Carriers who operated under a certificate of convenience and necessity; and Motor Vehicle Operators, running on an irregular basis. Researchers were interested in the service effectiveness of each class and their relative importance to the shipper/receivers. The study was conducted through 500 personal interviews with manufacturers, processors, retailers and civic bodies in 28 percent of cities and towns under 25,000 population, representing statistically every area of the state. The results showed that nearly nine of every 10 shipments to and from these communities moved by truck; that private carriers, parcel carriers (UPS), contract carriers and truck operators handled up to two-thirds of the total tonnage as alternatives to regulated carriers in the smaller towns.

There was evidence that a service network of regional (intercounty) carriers was emerging to meet the needs of small businesses. Users were more interested in availability of timely, reliable service than rates—service which gave them access to carriers who could haul their commodities with a minimum of loss and damage. There was no clear concensus on the possible impact of deregulation, mirroring the confusion on the national level, but some shippers/receivers expressed the opinion that little effects would result. Further investigations to support or refute these expressions were studied by the Iowa DOT (May 1986 Report) and presented to the Transportation Commission on July 15, 1986. There were few substantive changes from the earlier report.

The Post-Deregulatory Period

Section 28 of the Motor Carrier Act mandated a study by the ICC on the impact on small communities. No such requirements were found in the Airline or Staggers Railroad Acts. A randomly selected national sample of 1,200 shippers were requested to provide information in six-month intervals over an 18-month period beginning January, 1981. The response rate ranged from 67.3 percent to 77.1 percent of those contacted. Comparisons were made on services into communities of 5,000 or less with those of over 5,000 populations.

The results were remarkably consistent. No dramatic changes in rates or services occurred, and what changes were made were generally considered favorable. A majority of shippers reported practically no differences in the quality of service as measured by on-time performance, availability, and loss and damage claims. Where changes occurred, service improvement was reported more than service deterioration. Service complaints declined significantly during the period investigated. Rates for small communities increased less rapidly than the rates for the larger communities.

Richard Beilock and James Freeman analyzed a number of state studies examining the effects of the act on non-urban communities. "No matter how the study has been conducted, no matter what its funding source, no matter how it defines small or rural and no matter what its jurisdiction, the results are approximately the same. Deregulation has at most a neutral effect on non-urban shippers/receivers and is likely to exert a favorable influence on rates, service options and competitiveness of transportation in this areas. All shipper groups, small, large, urban or rural in the deregulated areas greatly prefer deregulation and the differences between the groups are for the most part statistically insignificant."[5]

Airline Service

According to witnesses testifying before a subcommittee of the House Public Works and Transportation Committee in 1983, the five-year history of airline deregulation had been a record of disaster, a partial success needing some adjustments, or a complete success. The objectives of Congress had not been achieved in many small cities and isolated areas as traffic declined and fares increased. Passenger service had been in a state of confusion and uncertainty through additions and suspensions of hundreds of flights, and under the law, small cities did not have a chance to build traffic to a level which was self-supporting. The Airline Act did not require the Civil Aeronautics Board to consider freight requirements when "essential air service" was established.

The president of the Association of Flight Attendants (AFA) stated that the level of safety had been reduced through cost-cutting programs. Allegations were made that the number of hours had declined in first-aid training at the same time that employees worked

[5] Richard Bielock and James Freeman, "Deregulated Motor Carrier Service to Small Communities," *Transportation Journal* (Summer 1984): p. 80.

longer hours, leading to fatigue and loss of effectiveness in emergencies. Competitive schedules to meet on-time departures made take-offs necessary before complete safety checks of the equipment were possible. Flight attendants flew an average of 10,000 hours on AFA carriers compared to an average of 3,000 hours on the new carriers entering the industry, offering less safety value to the traveling public.

In 1981, the Reagan administration proposed an end to subsidies for airline service to small and medium-sized cities effective on October 1, the beginning of the new fiscal year. The proposal would mean a restructuring of Iowa's air routes. More than $7.4 million annually was provided by the federal government to subsidize airline service at Sioux City, Burlington, Dubuque, Mason City and Fort Dodge airports. The loss would mean that Iowans would fly in smaller planes operated by smaller airlines with fewer ammenities. However, these planes may be flown more frequently and at more reasonable hours than the previous service. Following the end of the subsidy, "essential air service" would be guaranteed to certain airports, already in effect in some areas, including Clinton and Ottumwa. About $500,000 was paid in 1980 to Mississippi Valley Airlines, a commuter line flying into the two cities, but the service was discontinued at these airports as well as at Waterloo.

The big loser in subsidy terminations would be Ozark Airlines, paid about $6.7 million for service to Sioux City, Burlington, Dubuque, Mason City and Fort Dodge. Republic received about $750,000 for service into Sioux City. Ozark's financial condition improved during 1980, and it subsequently withdrew from all cities except Des Moines, Cedar Rapids, Waterloo and Sioux City, serving without subsidies.

Until deregulation took effect, 16 of the 19 Iowa and border airports were served by trunk air carriers using turboprop or turbojet planes seating 60-100 passengers (such as Ozark, Republic and United). Prior to deregulation, regulations provided for cross-subsidies—losses suffered in small markets with short-haul service balanced against profits in more lucrative large markets or by subsidies from the federal government for local service. The premise of "cross-subsidization" was abandoned in the deregulation process and emphasis placed upon individual route profitability with some exceptions. The situation opened markets for commuter airlines using piston or turboprop planes seating eight to 60 passsengers.

On an average day in the early 1980s, about 3,000 passengers boarded air carriers or commuter flights at 12 Iowa airports. Another 4,000 boarded from seven airports in states adjacent to Iowa. Omaha and Des Moines accounted for over half of these totals, and the 10 least busy Iowa airports handled only about four percent of the 7,000 daily enplanements. It was predicted that these patterns would not change for a decade. At the close of 1984, only four cities continued to be served by trunk airlines: Des Moines, Cedar Rapids, Waterloo and Sioux City. Commuter lines operated at Mason City, Fort Dodge, Dubuque, Clinton, Ottumwa, Burlington and Spencer. American Central served eight airports until it ran into trouble and was grounded by the FAA in December, 1984. Of the major airports, seven received "essential service" determinations. Commuter and other airlines enplaned enough passengers to cover costs at three, and four—Mason City, Fort Dodge, Ottumwa and Clinton—received the federal subsidies originally planned to be phased out in 1988. However, new federal budget proposals recommended that the subsidies be discontinued before that date, raising a major policy issue for the state in determining its role in insuring minimum service levels at these airports.

Scheduled airline service at Iowa airports gradually improved after the recession of 1981-1982. Passenger traffic at the Des Moines International Airport was 17 percent higher in 1985 (August) than in 1984, partly due to the addition of two new trunk carriers, American Airlines and America West Airlines. The airport recorded 60 daily flights in early 1985, up from 40 two years earlier. In addition to the trunk line carriers, the gain also was attributed to commuter airlines and the use of small jet planes by trunk carriers. At the bottom of the list were Ottumwa and Clinton with an average of 2,200 boardings.

Bus Service

Motorized intercity passenger transportation began during the first decade of this century and reached its record peak in 1946, when 27 million Iowa-originated passengers rode buses. Since 1942 approximately 30 regular route carriers provided service in the state, but only six operated continuously during the 40-year period: Greyhound, Jefferson, Missouri Transit, River Trails, Scenic Stage and Trailways. A seventh, Arrow Stage Lines, operated from the west into Sioux City, and three: Midwest Coaches, Iowa Coaches and Scenic Hawkeye Stages provided service since 1962. The latter two were based in Iowa while the remaining carriers were from outside the state. Almost two-thirds of all regular route passengers were served by Greyhound buses over routes which traverse much of the state. Since 1958, regular route service has been declining, both nationally and in Iowa. Between 1958 and 1970, state passenger traffic dropped by almost 47 percent to a low of 900,000 riders. The energy crisis of the early 1970s caused a resurrgence to 1.4 million route passengers during 1975, but ridership leveled off to an average of about 1.1 million annually. Iowa officials stated in 1984 that the bus companies had dropped 62 Iowa communities from their schedules, leaving more than 80,000 persons without convenient access to intercity buses. Hardest hit were the elderly and students, the most frequent bus riders who have no other affordable method of transport from city to city.

Through a federal grant of $100,000, the Iowa DOT established seven experimental feeder routes to allow residents in areas without scheduled bus service to reach the nearest bus terminals. Five of Iowa's 16 regional transit systems already serving multi-county sections of the state would provide feeder service. For example, daily routes from Forest City and Garner were established to meet the Jefferson Lines schedules at Mason City; from Clarion and Webster City to the Jefferson stop at Boondocks USA truck stop at Interstate 35; from Eldora to Jefferson's terminal at Iowa Falls and from Centerville to the Ottumwa Trailway station at Albia. Rural residents of Cerro Gordo, Story and Warren counties would be transported to Mason City, Ames and Indianola. The federal grant covered operating losses incurred by the five regional systems for the first six months of the experiment. The project was not successful and DOT plans for other feeder routes were dropped.

The End of the Regulatory Era?

According to Transport Policy Associates, a research group, 1984 was the first in almost 80 years that the major share of freight moving in the nation was exempt from government rate regulation. About 77 percent of rail freight and only 38 percent of truck traffic was regulated by the ICC. Regulation applied to 2.6 percent of domestic coastwise water traffic and six percent on the inland waterways. Airlines were virtually free from economic regulation while at the other extreme, 90 percent of the petroleum pipeline industry was still regulated. If rail and motor contracts were included, government-regulated traffic might be close to 40 percent.

What economic regulation remained was primarily on the national level. Federal deregulation legislation preempted state economic regulation in airlines, railroads and motor carriers of passengers. A section titled "Federal Preemption" was introduced in the Airline Deregulation Act which amended the Federal Aviation Act. It provided that federal law would preempt state regulation as soon as an intrastate airline received any interstate authority no matter how limited these interstate activities may be. State jurisdiction over those intrastate carriers, whose sole operations were of an intrastate nature, would not be changed. Implementation by the Civil Aeronautics Board exempted any federally certified carrier, including air taxis registered with the Civil Aeronautics Board, from any state economic regulation which covered certification, tariffs, flight frequency rules, liability, insurance, bonding and capitalization.

Federal-state regulatory conflicts in rail transportation began as intrastate operations became increasingly important. They started with the Minnesota and Shreveport cases in 1914 and continued through the 1920 and 1958 Transportation Acts as ICC authority over intrastate rates expanded. The Staggers Act provided that only those states who received certification from the ICC on standards and procedures could exercise jurisdiction over intrastate rates and the absence of such certification would prevent state rate regulation. Standards and procedure requirements were published by the ICC in 1980. Since then, conflicts over interpretation between states, railroads and the ICC brought the issues into the courts. Traditional federal-state rivalry over railroad regulation has not abated through federal preemption and has not furthered cooperation between the parties.

State sovereignty over motor carriers of property dating back to the Motor Carrier Act of 1935 resulted in a status quo situation and was not changed substantially by the 1980 legislation. A considerable portion of the motor carrier freight industry is local in structure and operation and there seemed to be no reason for federal preemption. The major concerns centered on the lack of uniformity of state laws relating to registrations, certification, permits and taxes. Where conflicts surfaced, they were between motor carriers of passengers and the states. The interstate bus industry argued that state regulation was a structure of inefficient, cumbersome rules and practices resulting in lower rates or fares for intrastate carriers than received by interstate carriers for the same or similar services, and service regulation was not consistent with federal regulation. These contentions were challenged by the states. The influence of the opposing groups made the Bus Deregulatory Act a mixture of preemption provisions of the Airline and Railroad regulatory reform legislation.

In projecting the future of state regulation, Keven H. Horn stated that economic regulation of airlines had been completely preempted; in railroad regulation, states were limited to exercising present and future ICC standards and procedures, and state rate regulation in the absence of market dominance was completely preempted. Few pressures existed for preemption of state regulation on motor carriers of property, but federal preemption of motor carriers of passengers was considered consistent with precendents established for exclusive federal regulation of railroad passenger service.

"The particular pattern of preemption reflects the scope of state regulation. Total preemption of state air regulation was relatively easy because of the small number of states affected. Preemption of rail and interstate motor bus operators has been less dramatic and effective. Federal efforts to certify or oversee state regulation essentially signifies the end of state regulation . . . While the formality of state regulation may persist, the substance has been preempted. Truly, independent state economic regulation no longer exists."[6]

Transportation Policy Issues

"Statements of policy," whether within or external to formal legislation, have not succeeded in the development of a workable national transportation policy, perhaps a seemingly impossible task in a dynamic society. Instead, the emphasis has been on modal programs administered by modal agencies using modal policies to promote modal goals. The results have been somewhat less than the often stated goals of efficiency, adequacy, reasonableness and fairness in transportation matters. Coordination of modal agencies into single administrative units and regulatory reform may offer opportunities for the unified goals and objectives relating to the overall development of the transportation functions. However, critical issues remain to test the wisdom and courage of transportation leaders. These issues are examined briefly through analysis of the National Transportation Policy Study Commission's (NTPSC) 527-page report published in 1979, and a series of reports by the Transportation Research Board (TRB) of the National Academy of Science, the latest published in 1984.

The NTPSC Study

With an appropriation of $5 million, the National Transportation Policy Study Commission study was mandated by Congress in 1976 to make "a full and complete investigation and study of the transportation needs and of the resources, requirements and policies of the United States to meet such expected needs."[7] Needs and requirements to the year 2000 were to be developed, and no aspect of transportation was to be excluded from the analysis.

The commission found 64 federal agencies administering approximately 1,000 programs and policies and 30 congressional committees with jurisdiction which affected the supply and demand for transportation services. The proliferation of authority and responsibility apparently was not disturbed by the creation of the Federal Department of Transportation, and fragmentation of jurisdiction among Congress and committees was a particularly troublesome problem. The report noted that federal policy-making was ad hoc. Numerous inconsistencies existed, and conflicts and jurisdictional duplications were frequent. The impact of non-transportation policies on the transportation sector was often not considered.

Three levels of growth; high, medium and low, were used for baseline forecasts of future transportation activities. On the medium level, which more nearly represented growth during the postwar years, it was predicted that transportation volumes of people and commodities would increase more rapidly than growth in population and the labor force. Fuel consumption would grow by 28 percent with no perceptible improvement in transport air pollution after 1985. Projected intercity ton-miles by all modes

[6] Kevin H. Horn, "Federal Preemption of State Transportation Economic Regulation: Conflicts Versus Coordination," *Transportation Journal* (Winter 1983): pp. 32-33, 42-43.

[7] Public Law 94-280 (1976).

would grow by a factor of 2.65 between 1975-2000, ranging from 1.14 for gas pipelines to 3.35 for water transport. Remarkably consistent in the range of 2.50 to 2.95 were railroads, motor carriers, oil pipelines and air freight. It was assumed that the nation would continue to be automobile-oriented during the period.

Although the study included all modes and markets, two dominant policy themes emerged. "The first is the importance of pricing mechanisms to allocate scarce resources in the context of transportation markets to determine the levels of transport required. . . There appears to be no mechanism superior to market-determined prices to decide which modes should provide services and which services should be provided. . . The second theme is for government to avoid distorting transportation markets and to maintain the role of private enterprise when transportation is made a tool for achieving non-transportation goals."[8]

Six major themes formed the basis of the policy section of the report:

1. **National Transportation Policy Should Be Uniform.**

   Most policies or programs are individually directed at particular problems. . . In particular, the important question of intermodal transportation has received little emphasis.

2. **There Should Be An Overall Reduction In Federal Involvement.**

   The private transportation sector should be permitted and encouraged to meet changing economic and other requirements without being unduly restrained by federal rules and laws that do not apply to other business sectors.

3. **Economic Analysis Of Intended Federal Actions Should Be Made**

   A careful analysis of benefits and costs might often serve to focus federal involvement on those issues where government could maximize its contribution.

4. **When A Transportation System Is Used To Pursue Non-Transportation Goals, Do So In A Cost-Effective Manner.**

   Where transportation policies are established to achieve other national goals such as safety, environmental protection, energy conservation, regional development, export expansion and national defense, such non-transportation goals should be pursued with minimum impediments to free transportation markets.

5. **Federal Involvement In Transportation Safety and Research Is Required.**

   Involvement, including financing to insure safety and research of national importance, can be beneficial if carefully structured.

6. **Users And Those Who Benefit From Federal Actions Should Pay.**

   Where assignable, direct charges should cover costs of government-supplied facilites. Where benefits are widespread, a general tax should be assessed to cover federal costs.[9]

The lengthy and detailed recommendations for policy changes were divided into five functional areas: (1) Regulation and Regulatory Reform; (2) Ownership and Operation of Federal Transportation Facilities; (3) Financing, Pricing and Taxation; (4) Planning and Information; and (5) Government Organization. The protracted discussion inhibits any attempt at analysis.

Ernest Williams, in a review of the report, noted that: "The broad themes are clear: place maximum reliance

[8] National Transportation Policy Study Commission (NTPSC), National Transportation Policies Through the Year 2000. Final Report, Washington, D.C.: June, 1979; Alan E. Pisarski and Rolf R. Schmitt "Critical Issues in Transportation," TRB *Transport Research News* No. 115 (November-December 1984): pp. 23-28. Two additional studies not analyzed are: U. S. General Accounting Office, *Evolving Transportation Issues for Analysis,* Washington, D. C.: U. S. Government Printing Office, January, 1982; and AASHTO, *A New Focus for America's Highways,* Washington, D.C.: April 30, 1985.

[9] Ernest W. Williams, Jr., "The National Transportation Policy Study Commission and its Final Report: A Review," *Transportation Journal* (Spring 1980): p. 11. Williams observed that these proposals have appeared in all studies since the railroads faced market competition in the late 1920's. Both the Federal Coordinator of Transportation in 1933 and the Board of Investigation in 1940 mandated studies of user charge poplicy. Competition in transportation was strongly supported by James C. Nelson in *Transportation and National Policy* published by National Resources Planning Board, Washington, D.C.: 1942. Freedom of transportation markets from government control and government promotional policy neutralized among modes have been topics of increasing interest especially in the post-World War II years.

on the market, utilize private enterprise to the maximum degree, avoid governmental policy which is prejudicial to market performance, subject policy to economic analysis, and move public investment decision-making as far as possible toward the local level. It is difficult to take issue with these propositions when thus broadly stated. Trouble appears when they are translated into specifics. . . Nor is their applicability fully demonstrated. Is competition indeed fully workable in the rail and pipeline industries? Is local decision-making likely to be superior to federal even when standards of analysis and processes of review are imposed? Will increasing shifting of highway financing to the levels below improve or worsen the prospects that effective user-charge policies will come into place? The report seems to proceed with much more assurance in dealing with regulatory policies than it does in confronting impacts of promotional policy."[10]

The 1984 TRB Report

In 1976, 1978 and 1981, the TRB developed lists of critical national issues. The purpose was to stimulate discussion, encourage research, and create a public awareness of problems considered crucial to transportation and non-transportation activities. The 1984 list included many of the previously selected issues such as safety, financing, energy, regulation and environment. Six are emphasized here as having been increasingly emerging on both national and state levels in the area of transportation planning and policy decisions. Accentuated in the report was the need for research to resolve some of the issues:

1. **Improved Management of Public Capital Expenditures**

   The infrastructure crisis in recent years has captured public attention and raised fundamental questions about the methods of making investments in public transportation. Are revenues adequate? Are they directed at the proper modes and locations? Are they efficient in their design and maintenance requirements? Are they financed by use of a proper mix of funds from users and various levels of government?

2. **Improved Transportation Productivity**

   Interstate highways, jet aircraft, unit trains, and containerization, among other innovations, have led to safer, less expensive, faster and more effective transportation which has changed the economic structure of the nation and enhanced mobility of the people. Cooperative federal-state research efforts on promising major projects which offer potential for further productivity breakthroughs should be seriously considered.

3. **Transportation and Economic Development**

   Although efficient transportation systems have historically been recognized as essential to commerce, transportation investments have been made with little knowledge or to what degree they influence the economic development of the nation, regions, states or industries.

4. **Decommission of Existing Infrastructure**

   Railroad branch lines, primary highways superceded by the interstate system, and transit routes with low ridership may have outlived their usefulnesss, and continued support diverts resources from more pressing problems. Decommissioning is a difficult process with probable perverse impacts upon industries and people who have located around the targeted facilities. Restriction or removal of low priority highways presents a difficult political problem even though research could clearly identify economic justification for such actions.

5. **Changing Character of Urban Services**

   The strain of financing existing urban transit has reached the breaking point in many communities. The public continues to voice support at the same time it refuses to approve funds for equipment and services, and it requests more services not matched by increased patronage. The changing character of urban transit, expected to operate like a private enterprise but constrained by law and custom, will probably remain a critical issue for many years.

[10] Ernest W. Williams, Jr., "The National Transportation Policy Study Commission and its Final Report: A Review," *Transportation Journal* (Spring 1980: pp. 18.19.

6. **Highway Goods Transportation**

   Truck traffic profoundly influences highway design, financing, productivity and safety. "User fees" continues to be a hotly contested topic. Public awareness of an involvement in highway transportation is increasing as communities become more and more dependent upon motor carriers for all of their supplies. Achieving a balance between truck needs and the consequences of their use is an arduous task, but the cost of neglecting issues relating thereto could be immense. Deregulation further compounds truck policy.[11]

State Transportation Policies

Policy statements have been issued periodically by the Iowa Department of Transportation and the Iowa Railroad Finance Authority. Their published statements are found in Figures 12-1 and 12-2. At the request of Governor Ray, a task force of 27 Iowans was organized on July 1, 1982, to study the state's transportation system and make recommendations for improvement over the next decade. The chairpersons were Robert K. Beck and Donald Gardner, and their report was published in December, 1982. Sixty recommendations involved policy modifications for consideration by the General Assembly, the Transportation Commission, Department of Transportation, counties, cities and public and private organizations. These are summarized in three major classifications:

A. **Shifting Emphasis on Transportation Programs**

   1. Revise the transportation goal to provide and **preserve** adequate, safe and efficient transportation services **based upon use and/or benefits that accrue** to the public. (Revisions are boldfaced).
   2. Top priority for maintenance in all programs was strongly recommended.
   3. No major expansions should be undertaken but need for selected improvements was recognized. Particular attention in this respect would apply to highways and airports; reducing the number of airports eligible for state project assistance and encouragement of the development of multi-jurisdictional district airports.
   4. Railway bonding and branch line assistance programs should be continued.
   5. Federal funding for operating costs of transit systems was expected to be reduced or eliminated. Shifting this responsibility to local communities could be met through local option taxes and selected fare increases with concessions to those unable to afford the increased fares. State funding should be indexed to cost increases.
   6. Iowa should continue to support waterway user taxes.

B. **Cost-Saving Measures**

   1. Legislation should be developed to reduce the number or vacate "low priority" roads. Only adjacent landowners would have usage privileges.
   2. Greater reliance should be given to the free market mechanism through relaxation of motor carrier regulation.
   3. Realign highway system responsibilities into state jurisdication of all federal-aid systems (25,000 miles); counties over the remaining roads including those in unincorporated areas (76,000 miles); and the jurisdiction of cities would cover all streets in incorporated areas not on the federal-aid system (11,000 miles). Consistency in design, construction and maintenance should be required as between state and county governments.
   4. A feasibility study of joint school bus/public transit operations should be undertaken by the state to explore improved operational efficiencies. Amend Chapter 601J of the Iowa Code to encourage coordination of school transportation programs with other public transit to achieve cost reduction.

[11] National Academy of Science Transportation Research Board, 1984 Report.

5. Eliminate one of two highway maintenance programs—state or counties—and include cities in a newly coordinated maintenance program.

C. **System Financing Measures**

1. Economies through implementation of the Task Force recommendations would adjust but not totally eliminate transportation system needs. Changes should reduce funding required but would not offset future inflation and subsequent reduced purchasing power of the transportation dollar.

2. The impact of demand elasticities should be carefully considered before changes or increases in transportation taxes are made by the legislature.

3. The 1976 appropriation of $2 million annually for transit should be continued with increments necessary for inflation to bring the total amount to approximately $3.5 million.

4. For rail branch line assistance, a $3 million annual appropriation should be considered. The Iowa DOT should monitor the program to insure the return of rollover funds to the state where needs of economically viable branch lines have been met.

5. Legislation is needed to fund airports through local option taxes. If additional revenues are needed, they should be provided by elimination of the aviation fuel tax refunds and assessment of a 13 cent per gallon fuel tax on general aviation with exemption for common carriers.

6. New motor fuel taxes should be delayed until the impact of the federal increase of five cents per gallon is known and until cost reduction proposals of the Task Force have been given an opportunity to be implemented. Iowa fuel taxes should be indexed to costs of reconstruction and maintenance of highways and revenue bonding may be necessary under certain circumstances and conditions.

7. The legislature should change the existing formula for distribution of Road User Tax Revenues if achievement of the recommendations relative to jurisdictional responsibilities are adopted.[12]

There was no significant opposition from the state or counties on the committee's recommendations. Most were supported, and where neutral positions were taken, it was usually because proposed legislation had died in House or Senate Committees or that specific recommendations were under study and investigation by the DOT staff. As of October 1, 1984, policy changes had been approved. Independent studies were underway on highway maintenance consolidations, jurisdictional responsibilities, consistency in standards on state and county roads and vacation of "low priority" roads. Project emphasis on maintenance over construction was included in the 1983-1984 highway program. Bus coordination rules were developed effective May 1, 1985, and six pilot programs on possibilities of coordination of school bus transportation with other transportation were identified and implemented at Nashua, Dubuque, Ottumwa, Sioux City, Burlington and in Dickinson County.

Legislation was still needed on local option taxes for airport and public transit funding. Proposals to raise transit fares to cover higher system costs were under DOT staff review. Reduction of fares for those unable to pay was the subject of investigation in 12-month pilot programs at Carroll and Denison. The legislative appropriation for railroad branch line assistance was $1 million annually for 1984 and 1985.

On May 30, 1985, a bill increasing state motor fuel taxes was signed by Governor Branstad. Gasoline taxes would increase from 13 to 15 cents per gallon on July 1, 1985, and to 16 cents on January 1, 1986. Gasohol would be taxed 14 cents and 15 cents respectively, and diesel fuel taxes would jump from

[12] Report of the Governor's Blue Ribbon Task Force, December, 1982. The appointment of the Task Force was recommended by the Transportation Committee at the Governors Conference, November 9-10, 1981. Responses to Key Transportation Issues Provided by the Transportation Committee, the Governors Conference, Institute of Urban and Public and Regional Research, Special Report No. 16, Iowa City:University of Iowa, November 10, 1981.

15.5 to 17.5 on January 1, 1986, and 18.5 cents on January 1, 1987. The increases were expected to raise $48 million when fully implemented; approximately two-thirds to be allocated to RISE (Revitalize Iowa's Sound Economy), a program for improvements on city streets, county roads and state highways to stimulate industrial development and economic growth. Part of the additional fuel tax would be used for other transportation programs including increased state aid for transit. Road use tax revenues for FY 1983 were distributed as follows: Primary Road Road Fund, 45 percent; Farm-to-Market, 9 percent; Secondary Roads, 28 percent and City Streets, 18 percent.

GOAL The transportation goal for Iowa is to provide and preserve adequate, safe, and efficient transportation services based on the use and/or benefits that accrue to the public.

POLICY The Iowa Department of Transportation will:

A. General

1. Promote a transportation system to satisfy user needs and maximize economic and social benefits for Iowa citizens.
2. Provide for a participatory planning process which: (a) involves public, private, and citizen interests, (b) encourages complementary transportation and land development patterns, and (c) gives consideration to the effects of transportation on the state's natural, cultural and human resources.
3. Encourage and support programs to provide commodity movement and mobility for all citizens.
4. Develop, promote, administer and enforce just and equitable policies and procedures for the registration, regulation and operation of motor vehicles and common carriers of passengers and freight.
5. Promote financing of the transportation system through user and non-user sources in an equitable manner.
6. Administer the lands and resources under its jurisdiction in a manner that both protects the rights of individuals and gives consideration to the effects of its activities on the environment.

B. Plan

1. Develop a total transportation system plan, subject to annual review, which;
   - considers all transportation modes as interacting elements;
   - considers facilities and services necessary for person and commodity movement from origin to destination;
   - contributes to the development and implementation of a comprehensive state plan;
   - exerts a positive influence on social, economic, and aesthetic values;
   - provides safe, convenient travel opportunities;
   - minimizes economic, energy and environmental costs;
   - coordinates available federal, state, and local resources;
   - recommends appropriate investment and funding procedures;
   - makes the best use of land resources for permanent transportation use;
   - encourages more efficient use of energy resources;
   - fosters usage of technological advancements in transportation facilities; and
   - evaluates progress toward achievement of the goal contained in this policy.
2. Encourage and assist in the development of general aviation, airport facilities, and air-carrier services.
3. Encourage and assist in the general development, preservation and efficient use of highway transportation through programs to equalize functional adequacy of roads and streets throughout Iowa.
4. Encourage and assist in the development, maintenance and improvement of public transit systems and services.
5. Encourage and assist in the development and maintenance of a viable railroad system which is responsive to the needs of Iowa and the United States.
6. Encourage and assist in the development of programs which promote efficient use of river transportation.
7. Develop and participate in programs to improve the safety of all transportation modes.
8. Encourage and support development of transportation education programs.

C. Program

1. Prepare a current and long-range program of capital investment, services, and regulatory practice--each year.
2. Propose and promote legislative programs to facilitate an integrated transportation system.

Figure 12-1
Iowa Transportation Policy.

The transportation goal for Iowa is to provide and preserve adequate, safe, and efficient transportation services based on the use and/or benefits that accrue to the public.

GOAL **The goal for the Iowa Railway Finance Authority is to preserve and improve necessary railway transportation facilities and services for public use in full cooperation with the Iowa Department of Transportation.**

POLICY **The Iowa Railway Finance Authority will:**

A. General

1. **Promote an economically viable railway transportation network to satisfy user needs and maximize economic, energy, and social benefits for Iowa citizens.**

2. **Encourage ownership and control of railway facilities by the private sector to the maximum extent practicable.**

B. Directions

1. **Assess the economic, financial, and social viability and desirability of all proposed railway transportation improvement programs. to determine if they are worthy of Authority support.**

2. **Assist in the construction, acquisition, rehabilitation, and repair of essential railway facilities.**

3. **Encourage the investment of private capital in the maintenance and improvement of railway services and facilities.**

4. **Assist the private sector in securing public or private funding for financing essential railway facility and service improvements.**

5. **Conduct its activities consistent with the policy, plans, and responsibilities of the Iowa Department of Transportation.**

Figure 12-2
Iowa Railway Finance Authority Policy.

Summary

Although the popular conception of the regulatory reform movement was sometimes interpreted as complete economic freedom for the carriers, the legislation did not discard all of the regulatory rules. The Airline Act of 1978 came close to regulatory freedom for the industry, but even it provided for a phase-in period to allow more use of the market mechanism. In the other industries, the legislation changed the application of the rules and eliminated parts of the regulations.

Objectives and meanings of deregulation differed in each of the legislative actions. Dissimilarities were evident in the targets of the reforms, ranging from wider airline passenger choices to correction of inefficiencies in the motor carrier industry and financial support for railroads. Similarities emphasized more reliance on the market function and less on social factors supported by government.

The operational structure and strategies of the transportation industries changed rather markedly through the deregulation process, but its impact upon the carriers was blurred by the onset of the economic recession of the early 1980s. The combination resulted in huge financial losses initially by the airlines and motor carriers, forcing bankruptcies, with only modest effects on railroads. The situation continued until adjustments were made to the new freedoms, and financial health improved as a result of economic recovery. Carriers, shippers and communities did not benefit equally by deregulation. Additional airline competition, expanded schedules and fare discounts favored the high volume markets; small shippers and communities faced the loss of services offered previously by scheduled carriers and were subjected to higher rates and fares. Captive shippers on railroads objected to the ICC's interpretation of the new rules and enlisted the aid of Congress for relief. Overall, the preliminary judgment indicated that the deregulation process in the short-run period had both positive and negative impacts, but generally the carriers and shippers found the market emphasis attractive for the future. Practically all state regulation of interstate carriers was preempted by the deregulation legislation.

Despite the movement toward regulatory reform, critical transportation issues were identified and recommendations made for policy changes on national and state levels. Some reflected broad policy themes, others addressed particular problems. Iowa joined in this exercise in 1982, when 60 policy issues were studied and recommendations for changes presented to the state, political subdivisions, public and private groups for consideration. Implementation was directed toward possible solutions as of 1985.

Selected References

"Airlines Will Net $1.50 for each $100 in Sales in 1985, Economists Predict." *Traffic World,* January 28, 1985, pp. 35, 56.

Alex, Tom. "Des Moines Airport Takes Off." *Des Moines Register,* August 8, 1985.

American Association of State Highway and Transportation Officials. *Deregulation of the Transport Industry.* Denver, Colo.: American Association of State Highway and Transportation Officials, October, 1983.

"An Ill Wind Blows Airlines Some Good." *U. S. News and World Report* (September 28, 1981): pp. 62-63.

Askari, Emilia. "Deregulation May Cost Cities Their Air Service." *Des Moines Register,* July 13, 1982.

Auerbach, Stuart. "The CAB Flies Off Into the Sunset." *Washington Post National Weekly Edition,* January 14, 1985.

Banks, R. L., and Associates. *Economic Analysis and Regulatory Implications of Motor Carrier Service to Predominantly Small Communities.* Report to the U.S. DOT. Washington, D.C.: U. S. Government Printing Office, June, 1976.

Barrett, Colin. "End of the Common Carrier Obligation?" *Distribution* (March 1981): p. 20.

"Battered Airlines Start to Take Off Again." *U. S. News and World Report* (March 12, 1984): pp. 51-52.

Chapman, Stan. "Staggers Returns to Center Stage." *Distribution* (January 1985): pp. 50-51.

Dempsey, Paul S. "Transportation Deregulation—On A Collision Course." Presented before the Iowa Transportation Commission, December 20, 1983.

"DOT Publishes Rules Detailing Assumption of CAB's Function." *Traffic World,* November 26, 1984.

"DOT's View of Airline Deregulation Challenged by Small Cities, Labor." *Traffic World,* June 20, 1983, p. 16.

Evans, Randy. "DOT Plans Bus Service for Rural Iowans." *Des Moines Register,* August 1, 1984. Farris, Martin T. "The Multiple Meanings and Goals of Deregulation—A Commentary." *Transportation Journal* (Winter 1981): pp. 45-46.

______. and Norman E. Daniel. "Bus Regulatory Act of 1982." *Transportation Journal* (Fall 1983): pp. 4-16.

Feaver, Douglas. "Civil Aviation Agency to be Grounded Today." *Des Moines Register,* December 31, 1984.

"Fewer Airlines are Flying High." *U. S. News and World Report* (September 22, 1986): pp.

Hawkins, Chuck. "Commuters Pick Up Air Service Slack but Bus Routes Decline." *Des Moines Register,* January 27, 1985.

"How Deregulation Puts Competition Back in Business." *U. S. News and World Report,* November 26, 1984, p. 54.

Hyde, John. "How Proposed Cuts in Airline Schedules Would Alter Iowa Air Service." *Des Moines Register,* June 14, 1981.

Interstate Commerce Commission, Office of Transportation Analysis. *Small Community Service Study.* Washington, D.C.: U.S. Government Printing Office, September, 1982.

Iowa Department of Transportation. *1982 Iowa Railroad Analysis Update.* Ames: Iowa Department of Transportation, July, 1982.

Keyes, Lucille Sheppard. *Regulatory Reform in Air Cargo Transportation.* Washington, D.C.: American Enterprise Institute for Public Policy Research, 1980.

Knudsen, Dewey. "Governor Signs Law Increasing Motor Fuel Tax." *Des Moines Register,* May 31, 1985.

Petroski, William. "Iowa's Rural Transit Systems Face Rocky Road of Federal Budget Cuts." *Des Moines Register,* April 7, 1985.

______. "Iowa DOT Lays Groundwork for Road Building Program." *Des Moines Register,* June 5, 1985.

"The Progress of Airline Deregulation—An Update." *ATA Research Review* (August 14, 1981).

Thayer, Frederick. "Strike Means Friendly Skies for Airlines." *Atlantic Monthly* (December 1981): pp. 14-16.

Thompson, W. H., R. D. Voorhees, and K. B. Boberg. *Motor Carrier Service to Small Communities in Iowa.* Prepared for the Iowa DOT, Ames: Iowa State University, May, 1980.

______. "Iowa, A Baseline Laboratory of Motor Carrier Service to Small Communities." *ICC Practioners Journal* (May-June 1981): pp. 431-443.

U. S. Department of Agriculture. Effects of the Staggers Rail Act on Grain-Marketing. Washington, D. C.: U. S. Government Printing Office, July, 1984.

Voytko, James. "How Shippers Have Fared Under Deregulation." *The Private Carrier* (February, 1985): pp. 8-11.

Williamson, Kenneth C., Mark Singer and Roger A. Peterson. "The Impact of Regulatory Reform on U. S. For-Hire Freight Transportation: The Users Perspective." *Transportation Journal* (Summer 1983): pp. 27-55.

Epilogue

The story of transportation in Iowa has not ended. What has been written here covers only a relatively short interval in the passage of time—a pause that reflects the indispensibility of effective transportation upon economic and social progress. The physical conquest of the state was underscored in terms of successive improvements in the means of transportation: flatboats, steamboats, stagecoaches, railroads, highways and motor vehicles; pipelines, airplanes and public transit. Each, in its unique way, contributed to the well-being of the people; each brought individual challenges and problems to be met, studied and integrated into state and local planning.

But technological advancements are but one phase in the development of a state or nation. Equally or more important is the genius, initiative, maturity and wisdom of those responsible for the legislation, administration and implementation of the transportation programs designed to accommodate the economic needs, social concerns and protection of the safety of the public. In this respect, Iowa has been historically and is presently in good hands.

The federal government has played the major role in transportation development in the United States. To a lesser degree was the role of the states as they shared financial support and political leadership in the improvement of waterways, the building of railroads, highways and aviation facilities to serve a growing and mobile population. Regulation became the primary policy instrument after 1877, promoted to a considerable extent by the local demand to curb railroad abuses. Iowa, among other Midwestern states, was a leader in this movement. Federal-state cooperation benefited the states, especially through the techological revolution during the 1920-1950 period. But as other modes were developed, new policies proliferated and often the states found themselves in adversarial relationships with the federal government as they tried to implement the new rules and regulations.

Intervention by government into the operation of transportation services, usually rendered by private enterprise, raised serious questions concerning the continuation of this practice when the service was no longer profitable, for what length of time and to what end. Demands for a national consensus of goals for transportation services was subordinated to the day-by-day implementation of individual modal development, and despite the formation of the U.S. Department of Transportation, the nation still lacks a single national transportation policy and a uniform plan for implementation. The absence of such a policy makes planning, funding and programming difficult on state and local levels.

The post-World War II period brought substantial changes in economic and social circumstances and conditions, in turn reflecting upon transportation developments. The relative roles of the modes were altered as public choices in one sense became limited; in another where services became more competitive and accessible. To attempt to bring some order out of economic regulatory chaos in the transportation sector, carriers were freed from some of the burdensome bureaucratic rules and regulations that had hampered their activities for years. Competition was to rule but the nature of "competition" was not addressed. Currently, the nation and the states are at a crossroad during this transition period, uncertain as to the direction of "market place" policies—whether or not they can or will provide the necessary incentives for improvement in services to the public.

Relaxation of the policy of economic regulation may result in other types of regulation. Limiting or eliminating past modal political protection may require an increase in other standards or regulations. Coordinated service may be required to facilitate intermodal arrangements. Mergers, some of which have already occurred, together with joint use of physical facilities should be monitored closely. Abandonments will probably accelerate as carriers seek to eliminate unprofitable business, in some instances to be succeeded by new entrepreneurs. Safety has become a high priority policy in highway and airline travel. Environmental programs will be under constant scrutiny by federal and state agencies. Individually and collectively, these forms of regulation may be more important than freedom of the carriers from rate control, entry, exit or collective rate-making. And as they multiply, it is essential that each be evaluated on the basis of net benefits to society relative to the costs to commerce and mobility.

The transportation drama will continue. It will involve conflicting interests and struggles for power, security and survival among promoters, owners, investors and users—between federal and state administrations and cities, towns and industries. The cast will include merchants, farmers, consumers, managers and employees, investors and financiers, commissioners and defendants, politicians and lobbyists. And as the various interests debate the impact of changing goals, policies and programs, the central question as evident from the beginning, should be: "Where does the public interest lie?" It seems evident that transportation services in the future will be rendered in a different and more difficult environment than in the past. This will require political decisions and public choices to determine where the transportation function is going to avoid being carried to unknown destinations. For as the Cheshire Cat said to Alice, "If you don't know where you are going, it makes no difference what route you take."

INDEX